The Power of Selling
Version 1.1

Kimberly K. Richmond

9781453385135

The Power of Selling
Version 1.1

Kimberly K. Richmond

Published by:

FlatWorld
175 Portland Street
Boston, MA 02114

Brief Contents

Contents

Chapter 10   The Presentation: The Power of Solving Problems   323

Chapter 11   Handling Objections: The Power of Learning from Opportunities   377

Chapter 12   Closing the Sale: The Power of Negotiating to Win   405

About the Author

Kimberly K. Richmond

Kimberly K. Richmond is an executive, author, speaker, and professor in the sales and marketing arena. She is a senior marketing executive with over twenty-five years of sales, marketing, and branding experience. She has held senior marketing positions at several major companies, including executive vice president of marketing at FAO Schwarz and other senior marketing roles at Kraft Foods, Sears, Zany Brainy, The Right Start, and Charming Shoppes.

She has been responsible for the integration and communication of a new corporate identity to the national sales force of 1,500 at Kraft Foodservice when the $5 billion division was sold. The sale of the company required a new name to be completely implemented within months of the transaction. In addition, Ms. Richmond developed seven new proprietary brands that were the focus of a massive internal training and communication campaign, which incorporated the company's Pro-Customer selling process. The campaign to launch the new brands was successful beyond expectations when the new brands accounted for over 11 percent of the company's revenues in less than eighteen months and generated a gross margin over six points higher than the rest of the brand portfolio.

Her leadership roles have included training and communication to the national consumer selling organization of over 10,000 salespeople at Sears in the Home Appliance Group. In addition, she was a member of the senior management team at FAO Schwarz that relaunched the brand and, in the process, completely transformed the brand, including the hiring process for store sales associates. The new process required candidates to "audition" for all sales positions (including sales managers) at a theater near the stores. The initial "open casting call" was so successful that the process became the standard for the company. It is a true example of why selling yourself as a brand is so important.

Ms. Richmond is currently a principal at Richmond Marketing + Communications, the marketing consultancy she founded. Her firm specializes in multichannel sales, marketing, and branding including traditional and online marketing and social networking strategies. She also consults with sales organizations to help them realize the true potential of their marketing and selling efforts.

She is the author of *Brand You*, a guide to building and marketing your personal brand that was published by Pearson Prentice Hall in November 2008. She is also an adjunct professor at the Haub School of Business at Saint Joseph's University (Philadelphia) and Rutgers University in New Jersey. She is a member of the Thought Leaders Panel for the Center for Consumer Research and the Advisory Board of the Department of Marketing at Saint Joseph's University. Ms. Richmond frequently speaks at industry and academic events. She also serves on the Board of Governors of the Philly Ad Club.

Ms. Richmond earned a Bachelor of Arts in Journalism from Northern Illinois University and a Master of Business Administration from Loyola University in Chicago.

Connect with Kim Richmond on LinkedIn:

http://www.linkedin.com/in/kimrichmond

Acknowledgments

The power to teach and inspire comes only from people who are willing to share and collaborate. I am fortunate to have worked with extremely talented people on this book who were very generous with their time. Without them, this book would not have been published.

First, many thanks to Jeff Shelstad, who encouraged me to share my enthusiasm and passion for sales, marketing, and teaching. It was Jeff who challenged me to develop the concept that selling is about getting what you want in life. He is an inspirational and supportive leader. His impact on the entire Flat World Knowledge organization is evident in the world-class people on his team. Thanks to Jenn Yee, the ultimate project manager. She is the person who kept this book on track, on target, and on schedule, with a perpetual smile on her face (and in her e-mails!). Thanks also to Sharon Koch, who took the book and made it come alive for the sales team and professors, and ultimately students, across the country. She is a delight to work with. My heartfelt thanks to the entire Flat World Knowledge team who dotted every "i" and crossed every "t" and made this book a reality online and in print. With over 150 links to videos, Web sites, articles, and podcasts, they had their work cut out for them.

My sincere thanks to the sales and marketing executives who shared their experiences and insights with me. Each of them helped provide additional dimension into the complex world of selling and what it takes to truly connect with customers. A special thanks to each of the selling executives featured in the video ride-alongs at the start of each of the chapters. They took the time out of their busy schedules to candidly share their knowledge and personal experiences on video for the benefit of the students. Their individual commitment to helping young people find their path is evident in the video clips that are used throughout the book and in the video learning segments that are included as an instructor supplement to this textbook.

- Paul Blake, Vice President of Sales, Greater Media Philadelphia
- David Fox, Founder and CEO, Brave Spirits
- Rachel Gordon, Account Manager, WMGK
- Priya Masih, Sales Representative, Lupin Pharmaceuticals
- Tonya Murphy, General Sales Manager, WBEN-FM
- Lisa Peskin, Sales Trainer, Business Development University
- Andrew Sykes, Pharmaceutical Sales Specialist, AstraZeneca

I also want to extend my gratitude to my colleagues at Saint Joseph's University who supported me every step of the way. My special thanks to Mike Solomon for teaching me the thrills (and challenges) of being an author. Thanks to Mike for taking the time out of his writing, teaching, speaking, and traveling schedule to record some videos for *The Power of Selling*. It's an honor to have exclusive video interviews with this renowned author and authority on consumer behavior included in this book. My appreciation to Carolyn Choh for taking the time to consult with me and connect me to pharmaceutical selling professionals.

All this effort would be irrelevant if not for the feedback from the faculty who reviewed the manuscript. Their comments truly helped shape the final product and made it immeasurably better. I appreciate the fact that each reviewer spent hours to review each chapter and provide concise and insightful feedback. I'm especially thankful for the suggestions about additional resources, which inspired the creation of the Power Tools feature in the Instructor Manual.

- Leon Chickering, South Puget Sound Community College
- Datha Damron-Martinez, Truman State University
- Dawn Edmiston, Saint Vincent College

- Robert Erffmeyer, University of Wisconsin–Eau Claire
- Douglas Friedman, Penn State Harrisburg
- Travis Hayes, Chattanooga State Community College
- Marvin Lovett, University of Texas–Brownsville
- Paul Myer, University of Maine Business School
- David Nemi, Niagara County Community College
- Mary Ellen Rosetti, Hudson Valley Community College
- Gary Schirr, Radford University
- John Weiss, Colorado State University
- Amy Wojciechowski, West Shore Community College

Finally, my thanks to students everywhere for being the true inspiration for this book. Their intellectual curiosity and quest to define their personal brand and role in the world is what motivates me to teach and write.

Welcome to *The Power of Selling*

Meet the Author, Kim Richmond

Video:

Hear Kim share her vision for your learning experience using *The Power of Selling*.

View the video online at: http://www.youtube.com/embed/knAgJtNBYqs

You're about to go on a journey that will take you to places you can't even imagine. Think about being able to get what you want in life. While that may sound far-fetched, it's not. You really can get what you want, if you learn to use the right skills. That's what this book is about.

Selling is a skill that everyone uses every day, no matter what they do for a living. Want to be successful? Learn how to sell. "You can have everything in life you want, if you will just help enough other people get what they want," according to famous sales expert, Zig Ziglar. That means listening and connecting with people, understanding their needs, what they want, what motivates them, and then capturing their imagination with a reason to buy...from *you* (Ziglar).

This book is different from other textbooks about selling. While it uses the traditional selling tenets as its foundation, it adapts the concepts to the rapidly changing world of business in today's environment, including the use of Twitter, LinkedIn, Facebook, blogs, wikis, and other interactive ways of connecting with customers. In addition, this book is filled with many unique approaches to traditional topics. For example, Chapter 10 covers how to create an elevator pitch for your product as well as for your personal brand; Chapter 13 explains Net Promoter Score, a nontraditional method of measuring of customer satisfaction; and Chapter 15 addresses how selling can help you realize your dream of being an entrepreneur and starting your own company.

There are four special features that make this book interesting and interactive:

1. **Links to videos, Web sites, articles, and podcasts**. The focus on real-world experience and sales professionals is carried throughout the book. This book takes full advantage of the Flat World Knowledge platform, including over 150 links to videos, Web sites, articles, podcasts, and interactive resources from YouTube, Blinkx, Selling Power, and many other Web sites that

demonstrate the concepts and make them interesting and fun to learn. Not only will you learn from real examples, but you'll also learn from current events.

2. **Video ride-alongs**. The best way to learn selling is to experience it. And just about every salesperson starts out in sales by going on ride-alongs with an experienced salesperson or manager to learn how selling is done firsthand. In order to provide the experience of a ride-along, each chapter starts with a short video featuring a sales professional who shares personal insights and practical tips about how he uses the key concepts that are covered in the chapter. These videos, which were made exclusively for *The Power of Selling*, highlight sales professionals who are personally interested in helping you learn and succeed. In fact, you can contact any of these selling professionals directly using the contact information at the end of this preface.

3. ***The Power of Selling* LinkedIn group**. Selling professionals from across the country are part of a LinkedIn group created expressly for the students and faculty who use *The Power of Selling*. Simply go to LinkedIn and join *The Power of Selling* group to network, connect, join or start discussions, or ask questions to the group. The people in the group are looking forward to connecting with you. The sales professionals featured in the video ride-alongs are also members of this group. Feel free to contact them individually or add them to your network. Visit http://www.linkedin.com and create a profile (see Chapter 3 for details), then search "Groups" for "The Power of Selling" and join the group. If you already have a LinkedIn profile, click on the following link and join *The Power of Selling* group.

http://www.linkedin.com/groups?gid=2566050&trk=anetsrch_name&goback=%2Egdr_1263094780871_1

4. ***Selling U***. The last section of each chapter is called *Selling U*, which applies the key concepts to selling yourself as a brand to get the job you want. *Selling U* teaches you how to think about yourself as a brand through every step of your career search. These sections throughout the book include details on key career searching tips such as how to create a cover letter and résumé that sells, how to target prospective employers, how to craft your personal elevator pitch, how to ace interviews, how to follow up, how to negotiate and accept the right job offer, and what to do to prepare for your first day of your new job. Links to videos, Web sites, articles, and other interactive resources make *Selling U* an excellent complement to the selling material and the ultimate resource for how to build your personal brand in this very competitive twenty-first century.

There are four features that are used throughout the book that reinforce key concepts:

1. **Power Selling: Lessons in Selling from Successful Brands**. These short vignettes highlight examples of how successful companies implemented one of the concepts covered in the chapter.

> ### Power Selling: Lessons in Selling from Successful Brands
>
> #### Handling Objections: All in a Day's Work
>
> At iCore Networks, a leading VoIP (voice over Internet protocol) provider, handling objections is an everyday learning experience. Sales reps gather at 8:00 a.m. sharp every day to discuss successes and failures from the previous day and role-play overcoming objections and then put what they learn to work in the field all day. The commitment to coaching and being in front of customers works for the company and its sales force: the average compensation for a first-year sales rep is $92,000.[14]

2. **Power Player: Lessons in Selling from Successful Salespeople**. Real-life advice from sales professionals about how to be successful in sales is showcased in these short accounts.

> ### Power Player: Lessons in Selling from Successful Salespeople
>
> #### Sign of Trust
>
> Imagine not even bringing in product samples or literature with you on your first sales call with a customer. That's what Susan Marcus Beohm, a sales manager for a handheld dental instrument manufacturer suggests. "I don't go in as a salesperson—I go in looking to see how I can help them. Not bringing my goods and wares with me says, 'I'm here to find out what you need,' and it makes an impact." When salespeople are too eager to start talking about features and benefits before they listen to the customer, they make it more difficult to establish trust.[26]

3. **Power Point: Lessons in Selling from the Customer's Point of View**. Feedback from customers about sales techniques and what they look for in a salesperson and a brand are brought to life in these short features.

> ### Power Point: Lessons in Selling from the Customer's Point of View
>
> #### The Making of a Fan—Yahoo!-Style
>
> Blogger Michael Eisenberg went from a detractor to a promoter of Yahoo! with one e-mail. Eisenberg made a "not-so-flattering post" about the functionality of what was then the new MyYahoo! in March 2007. Within twenty-four hours he received an e-mail from the manager of Yahoo!'s Front Doors Group that said, "I would love to find out what you would like to see and which features you are most concerned about losing. We want to be sure that our heavy users remain satisfied. If you have a few minutes to e-mail me, I'd very much appreciate it." Eisenberg promptly posted the response from the Yahoo! manager on his blog along with his fanatic endorsement of the company that can be summed up in one word: "Kudos!"

4. **You've Got the Power: Tips for Your Job Search**. Helpful tips highlighted in the *Selling U* section of each chapter are emphasized in these sidebars.

> ### You've Got the Power: Tips for Your Job Search
>
> #### When Do I Ask about Salary?
>
> Finally, even if you have questions about salary and benefits, *don't* ask them now. Always delay a conversation about salary as long as possible. In a sales presentation, you wouldn't pull out a pricing schedule before your customer had expressed a strong interest in buying the product; keep the same idea in mind going into a job interview. It's best to let your interviewer bring up salary—and that might not be until after the second or third interview. Be patient; the longer your prospective employer has to get to know you, the more opportunities you have to point out why you would be a good addition to the company. If you sell yourself well throughout the interview process, you might even receive a higher offer.

It's a powerful lineup designed to give you insight and experience into the profession of selling and teach you how to get what you want in life. Over the course of this semester, you'll learn how to sell products, services, concepts, and ideas. More important, you'll learn how to sell the most important product...yourself.

Selling is a journey. Your journey starts here.

Meet the Sales Professionals Featured in the Video Ride-Alongs

Sales professionals featured in video ride-alongs (left to right): Lisa Peskin, Paul Blake, Tonya Murphy, Andrew Sykes, Rachel Gordon, Priya Masih, David Fox.

Lisa Peskin, Sales Trainer at Business Development University

Lisa thought she wanted to be a doctor and declared her major as premed at Pennsylvania State University. It was only after she completed all the prerequisite courses, except one, that she decided she didn't like science. She graduated with a Bachelor of Arts in Psychology. After she completed her Master of Business Administration at Temple University, her plan was to pursue a career in marketing and decided to take a job in sales to learn the business. Once she started selling, she never looked back. Lisa now has over twenty years of sales and sales training experience in payroll and human resources services, financial services, and other business-to-business (B2B) industries. She started her selling career in 1989 at Automated Data Processing (ADP) and rose to become the vice president of sales where she was responsible for four district managers and forty salespeople. Then she decided to put her successful selling skills to work as a sales trainer at Bayview Financial and Interbay Funding. Today she is a principal, sales trainer, and coach at Business Development University, a company that conducts sales training with a focus in B2B selling.

Connect with Lisa Peskin on LinkedIn:

https://www.linkedin.com/in/lisapeskin/

Paul Blake, Vice President of Sales at Greater Media Philadelphia

Paul was born to sell. He started his career in sales in 1989 when he graduated from Bloomsburg University of Pennsylvania. He quickly rose to a leadership role as the director of sales at Global

Television Sports, then sales manager at Clear Channel Radio, WJJZ-FM, and WMMR-FM. In 2006, Paul was promoted to vice president of sales at Greater Media Philadelphia, responsible for the advertising sales for five radio stations in Philadelphia and managing over forty salespeople.

Connect with Paul Blake on LinkedIn:

https://www.linkedin.com/in/pauljblake/

Tonya Murphy, General Sales Manager at WBEN-FM

Tonya thought she wanted to be the next Barbara Walters, but soon learned that the newsroom was not the place for her. Thanks to internships at two television stations and a sales-savvy mentor, she found that her that her passion was sales. Tonya graduated from Cabrini College in 1989 with a Bachelor of Arts in English/Communications. She has been in sales for seventeen years and has held sales roles in media including at Greater Media Philadelphia. Last year, Tonya was promoted to general sales manager at WBEN-FM, one of the radio stations owned by Greater Media Philadelphia.

Connect with Tonya Murphy on LinkedIn:

https://www.linkedin.com/in/tonyamurphy/

Andrew Sykes, Pharmaceutical Sales Specialist at AstraZeneca

Andrew has always had a focus on selling and the pharmaceutical industry. He graduated from Saint Joseph's University with a Bachelor of Science in Pharmaceutical Marketing in 2005. After graduation Andrew landed his dream job at AstraZeneca, a major pharmaceutical company, and today he is a pharmaceutical sales specialist on the cardiovascular account team. Andrew's customers are doctors who prescribe the drugs he represents.

Connect with Andrew Sykes on LinkedIn:

https://www.linkedin.com/in/andrew-sykes-09752b7/

Rachel Gordon, Account Manager at WMGK-FM

When she graduated from Cornell University in 2003 with a Bachelor of Science in Fashion, Business Management, and Human Development, Rachel was certain she wanted to pursue a career in fashion merchandising. But she found she didn't enjoy it as much as she thought she would. She made a switch to the media industry with a job as the national director of marketing at Westwood One. It was there that she discovered her passion for sales. She is currently an account manager at WMGK, the classic rock station in Philadelphia, and happy that she made the decision to change the direction of her career.

Connect with Rachel Gordon on LinkedIn:

https://www.linkedin.com/in/rachelbgordon/

Priya Masih, Sales Representative at Lupin Pharmaceuticals

Since graduating from Saint Joseph's University in 2004 with a Master of Science in International Marketing and a Bachelor of Science in Business Administration, Priya has proven herself to be an outstanding sales achiever at The Hartford Customer Services Group, Creative Channel Services, and GlaxoSmithKline with recognition such as The Winner's Circle and the Top Sales Rep Award. She is currently a sales representative at Lupin Pharmaceuticals.

Connect with Priya Masih on LinkedIn:

https://www.linkedin.com/in/priyamasih/

David Fox, Founder and CEO at Brave Spirits

David gave up the corporate life to start Brave Spirits. His background in marketing, new product development, and sales includes work on major brands from Procter & Gamble, General Mills, and Mars; spirits brands from Diageo; and wine brands from Brown-Foreman. In 2005 he and his business partner conceived the concept for Brave Spirits and launched the company in 2007. Brave Spirits distributes premium vodka, gin, rum, and whiskey and donates $2.00 of every bottle sold to charities that support the men and women of America's military, police, fire, and emergency medical services (EMS). It is David's way of creating a toast to the brave.

Connect with David Fox on LinkedIn:

https://www.linkedin.com/in/david-francis-fox-4950b91/

References

Zig Ziglar, "Zig Ziglar's Little PDF of Big Quotes," Ziglar.com, http://www.ziglar.com/_cms/assets/Downloads/TheLittle BookofBigQuotes.pdf (accessed January 9, 2010).

CHAPTER 1
The Power to Get What You Want in Life

Welcome to *The Power of Selling* Video Ride-Alongs

Do you want to be successful in sales and in life? You'll have a chance to meet the pros, the people who have achieved success in their careers in sales. At the beginning of each chapter you'll have the opportunity to go on a **video ride-along**, a chance to hear from sales professionals and learn firsthand what it's like to be in sales. You'll go on video **ride-alongs** with some of the best in the business and hear about their personal selling experiences and tips of the trade.

Meet Lisa Peskin, sales trainer at Business Development University. Lisa has spent over twenty years in sales with sales and sales management positions at companies such as Automated Data Processing (ADP), Bayview Financial, and Interbay Funding. She is currently a sales trainer at Business Development University and works with sales forces across the country to become more effective. Lisa is an experienced and passionate seller who will share her insights and tips for success with you throughout the book.

Ride along with Lisa as she shares her thoughts on the power of selling in everyday life.

View the video online at: http://www.youtube.com/embed/9TLHt4PYGBc

---

1.1 Get What You Want Every Day

Learning Objective

1. Understand the role of selling in everyday life.

What does success look like to you?

For most people, to achieve personal success entails more than just making a lot of money. Many would claim that to be successful in a career means to have fulfilled an ongoing goal—one that has been carefully planned according to their interests and passions. Is it your vision to run your own business? Or would you rather pursue a profession in a service organization? Do you want to excel in the technology field or, perhaps, work in the arts? Can you see yourself as a senior executive? Imagine yourself in the role that defines success for you. Undoubtedly, to assume this role requires more than just an initial desire; those who are most successful take many necessary steps over time to become sufficiently qualified for the job presented to them. Think about your goal: what it will take to get there?

FIGURE 1.1
Selling can help you realize your dreams.

© 2010 Jupiterimages Corporation

personal selling

Communication between a customer and a salesperson with the intention of providing information for the customer to make a buying decision.

With a good plan and the right information, you can achieve whatever you set out to do. It may seem like a distant dream at the moment, but it can be a reality sooner than you think. Think about successful people who do what you want to do. What do they all have in common? Of course, they have all worked hard to get to their current position, and they all have a passion for their job. There is, additionally, a subtler key ingredient for success that they all share; all successful people effectively engage in **personal selling**, the process of interacting one-on-one with someone to provide information that will influence a purchase or action.[1]

Congratulations, You're in Sales!

If you think personal selling is only for salespeople, think again. Everyone in every walk of life uses personal selling (some more effectively than others!). Selling is what makes people successful. We all have to sell our ideas, our points of view, and ourselves every day to all sorts of people—and not just those related to our jobs. For example, when you work on a team project, you have to sell your ideas about how your team should approach the project (or, sometimes more delicately, you will have to persuade others as to what you should do about a lazy team member). When you are with your friends, you have to sell your point of view about which movie you want to see or where you want to go to eat. When you pitch in for a friend's gift, you have to sell your ideas about what gift to give. You are selling every day whether you realize it or not.

Think about the products and services that you buy (and concepts and causes that you believe in) and how selling plays a role in your purchase decision. If you rented an apartment or bought a car, someone sold you on the one you chose. If you read a product review for a new computer online then went into the store to buy it, someone reinforced your decision and sold you the brand and model you bought. If you ran in a 5K race to raise money for a charity, someone sold you on why you should invest your time and your money in that particular cause. A professor, an advisor, or another student may have even sold you on taking this course!

This video highlights how your life depends on selling.

Video Clip

View the video online at: http://www.youtube.com/embed/5v0kfEpdbJw

"I Sell Stories"

Selling is vital in all aspects of business, just as it is in daily life. Consider Ike Richman, the vice president of public relations for Comcast-Spectacor, who is responsible for the public relations for all NBA and NHL games and hundreds of concerts and events held at the company's Wachovia Center in Philadelphia. When you ask Ike to describe his job, he replies, "I sell stories." What he means is that he has to "pitch"—or advertise—his stories (about the games or concerts) to convince the press to cover the events that he is promoting. So, even though he is not in the sales department, his job involves selling. Gary Kopervas, similarly, is the chief creative strategist at Backe Digital Brand Communications. He works in the creative department in an advertising agency, yet he describes his job as "selling ideas," not creating ads. Connie Pearson-Bernard, the president and founder of Seamless Events, Inc., an event planning company, says she sells experiences. For many of her clients, she also sells time because she and her team execute all the required details to create the perfect event. As you notice, all these people are engaged in selling, even though "sales" may not be included in their respective job descriptions. Clearly, whether you pursue a career in sales or in another discipline, selling is an important component of every job...and everyday life.

Power Player: Lessons in Selling from Successful Salespeople

Who Wants to Be a Millionaire?

Imagine being a nineteen-year-old college dropout with a child on the way.

That described Tom Hopkins in 1976. He worked in construction to pay the bills. He realized there had to be a better way to make a living, so he took a job in real estate sales, but had no success. In fact, after his first six months, he had only sold one house and made an average of just $42 a month to support his family.

One day, he met someone who suggested that he go to a sales training seminar. Tom was inspired by the concepts in the seminar and put them to work. Before he was thirty, Tom was a millionaire selling real estate. Tom is now a legend in the selling arena with his "Training for Champions" and "Sales Boot Camp" programs. He is a successful author, speaker, columnist, and sales coach at Tom Hopkins International, which provides sales training for companies such as Best Buy, State Farm Insurance, Aflac, U.S. Army Recruiters, and more.[2]

Experience the power of Tom Hopkins in action.

http://www.tomhopkins.com/video_demo.html

Source: Tomhopkins.com

The New World of Selling

There are some people who might think of selling as a high-pressure encounter between a sales-person and a customer. Years ago, that may have been the case in some situations. But in today's world, successful selling is not something you do "to" a customer, it is something you do "with" a customer. The customer has a voice and is involved in most selling situations. In fact, Internet-based tools such as forums, social networks like Facebook, MySpace, and Twitter, along with Web sites, live chat, and other interactive features allow customers to participate in the process no matter what they are buying. Listen to consumer behavior expert and author Dr. Michael Solomon discuss the process of selling in today's world.

Video Clip

Dr. Michael Solomon Interview
The partnership of selling.

View the video online at: http://www.youtube.com/embed/7Rh1_t52R6g

Brand + Selling = Success

brand

A product, service, or concept that is unique, consistent, and relevant and has an emotional connection with its customers.

What do Ikea, Red Bull, Mini Cooper, and Apple have in common? All four are strong and highly identifiable **brands**. You might wonder what role a brand name plays in selling strategy. Perhaps it is not always noticeable, but when you buy a Red Bull at the corner store for some extra energy, at that very moment, a specific, chosen brand has become an extremely powerful selling tool, and it has significantly influenced your inclination to purchase *that* particular drink. Selling can only be successful when that thing that you sell has *perceived* value applied to it by the consumer—why Red Bull rather than another caffeine drink? Red Bull must be more effective if a person chooses it rather than the other brand nearby. A brand is a tool to establish value in the eyes of the customer because it indicates something unique. On the surface, a brand is identified by a name, logo, or symbol so that it is consistently recognized.[3] But a brand is more than that.

A great brand has four key characteristics:

1. It is **unique**. (Ikea furniture has exclusive, on-trend styling at unbelievable prices.)

2. It is **consistent**. (Red Bull looks and tastes the same no matter where you buy it.)

3. It is **relevant**. (Mini Cooper looks cool and doesn't use much gas, and you can design your own online.)

4. It has an **emotional connection** with its customers. (An iPod, with hundreds of personalized qualities, becomes a loved companion.)

A brand is important in selling because it inherently offers something special that the customer values. In addition, people trust brands because they know what they can expect; brands, over time, establish a reputation for their specific and consistent product. If this changes, there could be negative repercussions—for example, what would happen if thousands of Mini Coopers started to break down? Customers expect a reliable car and would not purchase a Mini if they could not expect performance. Brand names emerge in all different sects of the consumer market—they can represent products, like PowerBar, or services, like FedEx. Brands can also be places, like Macy's, Amazon.com, or even Las Vegas (everyone knows that what happens in Vegas stays in Vegas![4]). Brands can be concepts or causes like MTV's Rock the Vote or the Susan G. Komen Race for the Cure. Brands can also be people, like Lady Gaga, Jay-Z, Martha Stewart, or Barack Obama.

When products, services, concepts, ideas, and people demonstrate the characteristics of a brand, they are much easier to sell. For example, if you go to McDonald's for lunch, you know you can always get a Big Mac and fries, and you always know it will taste the same whether you go to the McDonald's near campus or one closer to your home. Or if you go to Abercrombie & Fitch, you can expect the store to look and feel the same and carry the same kind of merchandise whether you go to a store in Baltimore, Maryland, or Seattle, Washington.

The same concept applies to people. Think about your classmates: is there one that is always prepared? He or she is the one who always does well on the tests, participates in class, is a good team player, and gets good grades on assignments. This person has created a brand. Everyone knows that they can count on this person; everyone knows what to expect. Conversely, the same is true for a person who is often times late and sometimes arrives unprepared. You probably wouldn't want to work with that person because you're not sure if that person will hold up his or her end of the project. Which one would you choose as a teammate? Which one would you trust to work with on a class project? Which person is your brand of choice?

The Power of an Emotional Connection

Uniqueness (no other fries taste like McDonald's), consistency (a Coke tastes like Coke no matter where you buy it), and relevance (your college bookstore is only relevant on a college campus, not in your local mall) are clear as characteristics of a brand, but the most important characteristic is also the most abstract—the emotional connection it creates with its customers. Some brands create such a strong emotional connection that its customers become brand fans or advocates and actually take on the role of selling the brand by way of referrals, online reviews, user-generated content, and word-of-mouth advertising.

Harley-Davidson measures their customer loyalty by the number of customers who have the company's logo tattooed on their body.[5] These customers are emotionally connected with the brand, which offers unique selling opportunities for Harley-Davidson dealerships. Another example of emotional connection to a brand can be found by examining consumer relationships to sports teams. Fans willingly advertise their favorite team by wearing T-shirts, hats, and even putting decals and bumper stickers on their cars. They attend games (some of which require hours of standing in line) or watch them religiously on television. For popular events, in fact, many times customers are willing to pay more than the face value of tickets to attend; some will spend hundreds of dollars to see the NCAA Final Four, the World Series, or the Super Bowl. These consumers are emotionally connected to their teams, and they want to be there to support

unique

A product or service that is not available from any other competitor.

consistent

A product or service that is reliable or the same every time.

relevant

A product or service that is pertinent and important to specific customers.

emotional connection

A bond or relationship with a brand.

FIGURE 1.2

Harley-Davidson sells by using an emotional connection between the brand and its customers.

© 2010 Jupiterimages Corporation

them. A loud, sold-out stadium certainly illustrates why it's easer to sell brands when customers are emotionally connected.

Power Selling: Lessons in Selling from Successful Brands

Emotion Sells

Did you ever consider why the salespeople at Starbucks are called baristas instead of employees?

Howard Schultz, the chief executive officer of Starbucks, has built the brand in his vision since the company began in 1982. He believes strongly that the brand stands for more than beans. During an interview, he said, "By making a deeper emotional connection with your customers, your brand will stand out from the hundreds, if not thousands, of vendors, entrepreneurs, and business owners selling similar services and products."[6] Schultz is especially passionate about the role salespeople have in creating the "Starbucks" experience.

The brand recently launched a new marketing campaign called "It's not just coffee. It's Starbucks." Listen to what baristas have to say about the latest Starbucks marketing campaign.[7]

Starbucks baristas talk about their emotional connection to the brand.

Video Clip

Maisa Grant

View the video online at: http://www.youtube.com/embed/hkNp4xfk6xg?rel=0

The concept of emotional connection is not limited to the brand, it is also an especially critical component in the actual practice of selling. Customers are much more readily persuaded to make a purchase if they develop an emotional connection with the salesperson. If you go to Best Buy to look at a new home theater system, a helpful (or unhelpful) salesperson can make all the difference in whether you buy a particular system from that particular Best Buy or not. If the salesperson asks questions to understand your needs and develops a good relationship (or emotional connection) with you, it will greatly increase your chances of purchasing the home theater system from him. Rock star Gene Simmons, front man for the legendary rock band KISS and wildly successful entrepreneur, summed it up best: "I have to have an emotional connection to what I am ultimately selling because it is emotion, whether you are selling religion, politics, even a breath mint."[8]

Clearly, brands are fundamental building blocks in the selling process. The bottom line is, great brands = great sales.

Key Takeaways

- **Personal selling** is a powerful part of everyday life. The selling process can help you get what you want both personally and professionally.
- You are always selling your ideas, your point of view, and yourself in virtually every situation, from class participation to going out with friends.
- In order to understand the selling process, you have to understand **brands**. A brand can be a product, service, concept, cause, location, or even a person. A brand consistently offers value to a customer with something that is unique, consistent, and relevant and creates an emotional connection.
- **Brands** are important in selling because customers trust brands. The brand doesn't end with the product, service, or concept; the salesperson is also a brand.

Exercises

1. Identify a situation in which you were the customer in a personal selling situation. Discuss your impressions of the salesperson and the selling process.
2. Think about this class. In what ways do you sell yourself to the professor during each class?
3. Think about your school as a brand. Discuss what makes it unique, consistent, and relevant and have an emotional connection with its customers. How would you use these characteristics if you were trying to sell or convince someone to attend the school?
4. Think about the following brands: Xbox, Victoria's Secret, and BMW. Discuss how each brand forms an emotional connection with its customers. Why is it important in selling?

1.2 Selling: Heartbeat of the Economy and the Company

Learning Objectives

1. Discuss the role of selling in the economy.
2. Explain the role of selling in an organization.

Look around. Your computer, your car, your jewelry, your eyeglasses, and your cell phone—many of the things you own—were probably sold to you by someone. Now, think about things you *can't* see, like your cell phone service, your Internet service, and your car insurance. Chances are, those services were probably sold to you by someone as well. Now that you think about it, you can see that selling is involved in life in so many ways. But did you ever think about the impact that selling has on the economy?

In the United States alone, almost 16 million people were employed in jobs in sales in 2008. This number includes retail salespeople and cashiers, insurance sales agents, real estate brokers and sales agents, and manufacturing sales reps just to name a few. According to the Bureau of Labor Statistics, that number will increase to almost 17 million people employed in sales and sales-related occupations by 2018, which represents a 6.2 percent increase from 2008. That translates to one in every ten people in the United States having a job in sales.[9] Other estimates, such as the *Selling Power Magazine's* annual report of America's Top 500 Sales Forces in 2008, puts the total number of salespeople at the top 500 companies at over twenty million for the first time.[10]

multinational corporations (MNCs)

Large companies that have operations, including selling, in multiple countries.

But the bigger story is the fact that many companies sell their products and services globally. **Multinational corporations (MNCs)**, large companies that have operations, including selling, in several countries,[11] such as Procter & Gamble, Dell, Reebok, and Kraft Foods, employed 32 million workers in 2007.[12] Although not all these employees are engaged in selling, the number helps provide some sense of relativity as to the proportional impact of international business. Most large MNCs have offices (including sales offices) in many foreign countries. This provides the company with the opportunity to become integrated into the culture, customs, and business practices of each country in which it has operations.

A large number of MNCs generate a significant portion of their sales from countries outside the United States. If you've traveled outside the United States, think about the products you saw. Companies such as Coca-Cola, eBay, Gillette, KFC, and Starbucks have a significant presence in foreign countries. Many companies expand selling to international markets for several reasons, including slow population growth in their domestic country, increased competition, opportunity for growth and profit, and sometimes, out of sheer necessity due to the fact that globalization is rapidly changing the economic landscape.[13]

In the past, expansion to foreign markets was limited to those corporations that could make the investment required to locate offices and operations abroad. The Internet, however, has provided that same opportunity to small- and medium-sized companies, so that they may sell products and services internationally. Why would small companies want to do this? With only a one-to-five proportion of Internet users living in the United States, almost 80 percent of Internet users live in places abroad; thus, there is a much larger market to be found by way of the Internet. Before you take your lemonade stand global, however, remember that selling internationally is not as simple as just setting up a Web site. Language, shipping, currency exchange, and taxes are just some of the costs and considerations necessary for selling products and services internationally via the Internet. To help companies overcome these barriers of doing business internationally, organizations such as e-commerce service provider FiftyOne offer technology solutions that manage these important components of international selling.[14]

Think about the possibilities. When companies such as Overstock.com want to sell globally, companies like FiftyOne have a selling opportunity.[15] In other words, selling products and services can generate more opportunities for selling other products and services in the future. When companies (FiftyOne is a perfect example) and salespeople think creatively and see the environment through the customer's eyes, they can identify selling opportunities that might not otherwise exist. This is a basic tenet of selling, both domestically and internationally.

The Internet: Power to the People

The Internet has been a game changer for selling in many ways. Just like the Internet expands the reach of a company to virtually anywhere in the world, it also provides customers with access to information, products, and services that they never had before. In some industries, the Internet has virtually eliminated the need for a salesperson. Travel agents are no longer the exclusive providers of reservations and travel plans. Music stores are almost extinct. Newspaper want ads have almost vanished. In other industries, the relationship of the salesperson and customer has changed dramatically. The power has shifted from the seller to the buyer. Take, for example, the auto industry. It used to be that when you wanted to buy a car, you went to a car dealership. The salesperson would show you the cars, take you out on a test drive, and then negotiate the selling price when you were ready to buy, holding the dealer invoice close to the vest. Today, customers may e-mail a car dealership to set up an appointment to drive a specific car after they have researched different models of cars including features, benefits, competitive models, editor and customer reviews, competitive pricing, and dealer invoice pricing. In some cases, the customer may know more than the salesperson.[16]

Sales organizations are embracing a movement called **Sales 2.0**. You may have heard of Web 2.0, the second generation of the Internet, which includes interactivity, community, and on-demand information. Sales 2.0 is a term that appropriately describes a new way of thinking about the role of the Internet in the selling process as it encompasses the impact of constantly changing technology and multiple electronic devices, "mash-ups" of different sources of information, and user-generated content on sites like Facebook, LinkedIn, YouTube, and Twitter. According to Tim Sullivan, director of intellectual property and information for Sales Performance International, these Internet-based changes pose new implications for sales. Educating customers is no longer the primary function of the salesperson. Customers are actively involved in engagement, interaction, and collaboration to seek information. Salespeople need to understand the power of collaboration both inside their organization and with their customers, so that they may participate in the online conversation, enabling them to better deliver value. Just as customers use blogs, wikis, and social networking as tools to learn about a product, companies can use these tools to learn about customers (and what they want and need). It's a new mind-set and new technology tools are constantly changing the landscape—salespeople must be prepared to adjust their reactions accordingly.[17] The shift of power to the customer is underscored by Gerhard Gschwandtner, founder and CEO of Selling Power, Inc. According to him, "Sales 2.0 gives the customer a 360-degree view of the company and provides sales organizations with a variety of tools that help manage that two-way communication process."[18] Sales 2.0 takes the selling process to the next generation.

> **Sales 2.0**
>
> A term used to describe the role of the next generation of the Internet in the selling process including social networking, "mash-ups," communities, and collaboration.

Video Link

Whiteboard Session with David Thompson, CEO of Genius.com
Sales 2.0 and how it works.
http://www.bnet.com/2422-13731_23-187203.html

Source: BNET

Sales Is Not a Department, It's a State of Mind

Sold.

It's a deal.

Let's shake on it.

Sign on the dotted line.

You've got the job.

sale

The activity of selling a company's products and services.

touch point

Any point in which the customer comes in contact with a company, such as in person, by phone, by e-mail, Web site, invoice, advertising, and more.

customer-centric organization

All employees are focused on anticipating and meeting the needs of the customer.

Those are the words that signal success in selling. They seem simple, but according to Gerry Tabio, bringing a **sale**[19] to fruition is "not just about celebrating the sale; it's about celebrating the growth of the customer."[20] The most successful companies work to build and sustain relationships with the customer at every **touch point**, any way in which the company comes in contact with the customer, and consider selling the job of everyone in the organization. In other words, although there are specific functional departments such as sales, marketing, operations, human resources, finance, and others, everyone in the organization is focused on the customer. This is called a **customer-centric organization.**[21]

FIGURE 1.3

Customer touch points include any point at which the customer comes in contact with or "touches" the brand. Customer-centric companies ensure that every customer touch point provides a positive experience for the customer.

© 2010 Jupiterimages Corporation

You might wonder why all companies aren't considered customer-centric. After all, if they were in business to sell products and services to customers, it would make sense that they would be customer-centric. However, you have probably encountered companies that aren't really focused on the customer. How many times have you heard this message while you were on hold to talk to a salesperson or customer service representative, "Your call is important to us. Please stay on the line for the next available representative"? Being on hold and hearing a recorded message hardly makes you feel as if you are important to the company.

It's All about the Customer

support (or staff) function

A department that provides services that support those that are on the front lines with customers, such as human resources, finance, and marketing. This department is also called a staff function.

line function

A department that is part of the daily operations of a company such as sales and customer service.

Being customer-centric means insisting on accountability. Although everyone is focused on the customer, every employee is part of a department or function. Each department has goals and accountabilities. In a true customer-centric organization, the departments work together to satisfy the needs of the customer and achieve the financial objectives of the company. Most companies have core functions or departments such as sales, customer service (sometimes it is included as part of the sales department), marketing, operations, finance, human resources, product development, procurement, and supply chain management (also called logistics). Departments such as finance and human resources are called **support (or staff) functions** since they provide support for those that are on the front lines such as sales and customer service (these departments are also called **line functions** as they are part of a company's daily operations).[22] In a customer-centric organization, the focus on the customer helps prevent organizational "silos" (i.e., when departments work independently of each other and focus only on their individual goals).

The sales department is the heartbeat of every company. According to *Selling Power Magazine*, the manufacturing and service companies listed on its "Power Selling 500 Report" generate $6.7 trillion dollars in sales annually. Each salesperson supports an average of 12.9 other jobs within the company.[23] This means that the level of sales that is generated by each salesperson actually pays for the roles in human resources, marketing, operations, and other departments. It makes sense that the salespeople fund the operations of the company. After all, it is a salesperson with whom you interact when you buy a Nissan Cube, lip gloss at Sephora, or an interview suit at Macy's. The people in the sales department "ring the cash register" (whether the business has a cash register or not). They are responsible and accountable to deliver sales to generate revenue and profit, which are required to operate and to invest in the company. In fact, the sales department is considered so important that even in this difficult economy, companies should continue to fill open sales positions even if they are not hiring in other departments, according to Dennis J. Ceru, a professor of entrepreneurship at Babson College and the president of Strategic Management Associates, a consulting firm in Wellesley Hills, Massachusetts.[24] Without a healthy and strong sales department, companies can wither and die.

FIGURE 1.4
Each salesperson generates enough revenue and profit to support 12.9 jobs in the average company.

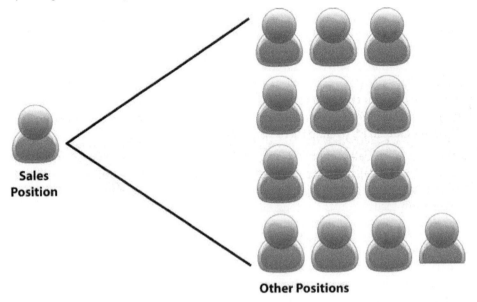

Sales Position

Other Positions

Power Point: Lessons in Selling from the Customer's Point of View

Role Reversal

How would you feel if you wanted to buy a new car, but every sales rep you called was in a meeting?

Brad Lathrop, a sales professional, learned the hard way about how a customer feels in this situation. When he was in the market for a new car, he called several dealerships. Every receptionist told him that all the salespeople were in meetings. The receptionist at the last dealership he called said the same thing, but added that if Brad would hold for a minute, she would get a salesperson out of a meeting. It's no surprise that was the dealership where Brad eventually bought the car and learned a powerful lesson about selling.

Is It Sales, or Is It Marketing?

So you might be wondering, if the sales department interacts with customers, what exactly does the marketing department do? That's a great question. Some people use the terms in tandem—sales and marketing—to refer to sales. Some people use the terms interchangeably and refer to marketing as sales. It's no wonder that it confuses so many.

According to the American Marketing Association, "**marketing** is the activity, set of institutions, and processes for creating, communicating, delivering, and exchanging offerings that have value for customers, clients, partners, and society at large."[25] In other words, it is the role of the marketing department to use the four Ps of the marketing mix (product, place, promotion, and price) to determine the brand message, which is ultimately communicated to customers.[26] Then, the marketing department uses the elements of the promotional mix of advertising, sales promotion, public relations, direct marketing, interactive marketing, and personal selling to get the word out to customers.[27] Marketers seek to motivate prospective customers to purchase by driving them

marketing

The activity of creating communicating and delivering brand messages to customers.

to a Web site, store, phone, event, or another related, desired action. Essentially, marketing builds relationships between customers and the brand. When you see an online ad for Best Buy, get a text message about the new release of *Terminator 2: Judgment Day* on Blu-ray, call the 800 number to check on your Rewards Zone point balance, post a comment on the Best Buy Facebook page, respond to a tweet from Best Buy on Twitter, see a newspaper insert or an ad on television, or read about the opening of a new store near year you, these are all examples of marketing. They are designed to encourage you to engage with the brand and encourage you to take an action—visit the store, go to the Web site, call the 800 number, or tell your friends about the brand.

When you go into the store or visit the Web site, it's the sales department that takes over. A salesperson will speak with you (either in person in the store, online with live chat, or by phone) to determine what you need and to help you make the best decision by communicating product information (*this printer is wireless*), service information (*we can deliver that tomorrow*), warranty information (*it has a 90-day manufacturer warranty*), and other pertinent facts. The salesperson extends the relationship that was established with the marketing contacts and makes a personal connection with you. If you have a good experience, your relationship with Best Buy gets even better, and you are more likely to shop there again and tell your friends.

At times, however, sales and marketing don't play well together. When organizations are not customer-centric, the departments may appear to have separate or conflicting goals. Marketing may feel that sales doesn't follow up on prospective customers, or perhaps sales feels that the marketing efforts are focused on the wrong customers. To understand more about the relationship between sales and marketing, watch Chip Terry, vice president and general manager of sales intelligence at Zoom Info, talk about how the two functions are aligned (and sometimes how they may not be aligned):

Video Link

Chip Terry Interview

How sales and marketing work together.

http://www.bnet.com/2422-13723_23-222675.html

Source: BNET

FIGURE 1.5 Marketing and Sales: How They Work Together

Marketing	Sales
• Uses the four Ps (product, place, promotion, and price) to determine the brand message.	• Identifies which customers to engage.
• Uses the promotional mix (advertising, sales promotion, public relations, direct marketing, interactive marketing, and personal selling) to communicate the brand message to customers.	• Interacts one-on-one with customers to identify needs and present solutions or opportunities.
• Motivates customers to take an action, such as going to a store or Web site or calling a phone number.	• Converts interested customers into purchasers.
• Builds ongoing relationships between the brand and customers.	• Builds ongoing personal relationship between the brand and the customer.
• Interacts with and gets feedback from sales.	• Is the brand in the eyes of the customer.
• Focuses on customer needs.	• Interacts with and gives feedback to marketing.
	• Focuses on customer needs.

In addition to closing the sale (when the customer purchases the product or service), the salesperson has a very important role in the marketing process. Because the salesperson (in the store, online, or on the phone) is a primary touch point and a personal interaction with the customer, the salesperson *is* the brand in the eyes of the customer. According to Dr. David A. Shore of Harvard University, "The sales force is the most visible manifestation of the brand. Salespeople need to say with a singular voice, 'This is who we are, and, by extension, this is who we are not.' The critical element that power brands have is trust, and a sales force needs to become the trusted advisor to the customer."[28]

So now you can see that marketing and sales work hand-in-hand: one develops the brand and the other assumes the image of the brand. Neither works without the other, and the relationship between the functions must be transparent to the customer. There's only *one brand* in the eyes of the customer, not two departments. When marketing and sales work well together, the customer experience is seamless.

Key Takeaways

- **Sales** is a career opportunity for you to consider; one in ten people in the United States has a job in sales or a sales-related occupation.
- In this global economy, many companies sell products in multiple countries around the world. Many **multinational corporations** have sales offices in foreign countries, and large and small companies sell globally by using the Internet.
- **Sales 2.0** is a term that is used to refer to the ever-changing technology, such as social networking, that is changing the relationship salespeople have with customers. It's important to understand how technology can support your communication and collaboration with customers.

- A **customer-centric** organization has the customer as the focal point. You work as a team with all functions in the company to provide products and services that meet customers' needs.
- **Sales** and **marketing** are two distinct but closely related functions. **Sales** converts the customer to a purchaser with one-on-one interaction. **Marketing** determines the brand message and uses the elements of the promotion mix to motivate the customer to take an action. Both work together to build ongoing relationships with customers.

Exercises

1. Visit http://www.sellingpower.com and review the "Selling Power 500." Discuss the top ten companies listed in one of the six categories of businesses (office and computer equipment, insurance, consumables, communications, medical products, or financial services). Did you realize these companies employed so many salespeople? Have you come in contact with salespeople from any of these companies? To whom do these salespeople sell?
2. Identify a company that you think is customer-centric and one that is not. Identify at least three touch points for each company. Based on this, discuss why you think each company is customer-centric or not.
3. Discuss the difference between sales and marketing. Choose one of your favorite retail brands and discuss one example of sales and one example of marketing.

1.3 *Selling U*: The Power of Your Personal Brand

Learning Objective

1. Understand how the selling process can help you get the job you want.

Ultimately, this book is about the power of YOU.

To help you realize that power and get the job you want, this textbook includes a section called *Selling U*. It is the final section in every chapter, and it is filled with proven methods, information, examples, and resources to help you apply the selling concepts you learned in the chapter so that you may sell yourself to get the job you want.

In the *Selling U* sections throughout this book you'll learn skills, such as how to create a cover letter and résumé that help you stand out, how to communicate with prospective employers, how to go on successful interviews, how to follow up, and how to negotiate and accept the right job offer. The complete table of contents is shown here.

Selling U Table of Contents

Getting Started

Some people know exactly what they want to do in life. Madonna, Venus and Serena Williams, Steve Jobs, and countless others have been preparing for their chosen careers since they were young. Dylan Lauren, daughter of designer Ralph Lauren and chief executive of Dylan's Candy Bar, could see her path even when she was young. With a father who was a fashion designer and her mother a photographer, she said, "I always knew I wanted to be a leader and do something creative as a career."[29] Katy Thorbahn, senior vice president and general manager at Razorfish, one of the largest interactive marketing and advertising agencies in the world, always knew she wanted to be in advertising. Her father was in advertising, her uncle was in advertising, and she had an internship at an advertising agency, so it was no surprise that she pursued a career in advertising. You probably know some people like this. They know exactly the direction they want to take and how they want to get there.

It's not that way for everyone, however. In fact, most people don't really know what they want to do for a career or even what types of jobs are available. Whether you are currently working at a job or you are just beginning to determine your career direction, it's never too early or too late to learn about what career might be a good fit for you. It's a good idea to use the three steps outlined below to help you begin your career search. These steps can be most effective if you complete them even before you put together your résumé (you'll get the tools to create your résumé and cover letter in *Selling U* in Chapter 2).

Step 1: Explore the Possibilities

Whether you know your direction or are trying to figure out what you want to do "when you grow up," there are some excellent tools available to you. The best place to start is at your campus career center. (If your school does not have a career center, visit the library.) The people who work there are trained professionals with working knowledge of the challenges to overcome, as well as the resources needed to conduct a career search. People find that visiting the career center in person to meet the staff is a great way to learn firsthand about what is available. Also, most campus career centers have a Web site that includes valuable information and job postings.

career assessment survey

A tool to determine which jobs might be the best fit for your skills, strengths, and experience.

skills inventory

A survey or questionnaire that helps identify your level of skills, strengths, and weaknesses to help determine what job or industry you might consider pursuing.

aptitude test

A test to determine your interest, skills, and abilities.

At this stage in your career search, you might consider taking a **career assessment survey**, **skills inventory**, and/or **aptitude test**. If you're unsure about your direction, these tools can help you discover exactly what you like (and don't like) to do and which industries and positions might be best for you. In addition, there are many resources that provide information about industries, position descriptions, required training and education, job prospects, and more. These are especially helpful in learning about position descriptions and job opportunities within a specific industry.

Here are some resources that you may find to be a good place to begin a search. Most of the Web sites listed provide surveys exercises and information at no charge.

TABLE 1.1 Resources for Your Job Search

Resource	Description
Career One Stop http://www.careeronestop.org/SKILLS/SkillCenterHome.asp	Information, job profiles, skills assessment, and more information available at no charge. The Skill Center is especially helpful. The site also includes salary and benefits information as well as other job search information.
Job Hunter's Bible http://www.jobhuntersbible.com/counseling/index.php	Links to job assessment tests, personality tests, and more. This is the companion Web site to the popular best seller *What Color Is Your Parachute?*
Queendom, the land of tests http://www.queendom.com/tests/testscontrol.htm?s=71	Free tests for leadership, aptitudes, personality traits, and more.
Riley Guide http://rileyguide.com/assess.html#tools http://rileyguide.com/careers.html	A robust Web site with free information and links to help with your career search. The assessment section and career and occupational guides are especially helpful. (Some charges may apply on some linked sites).
Lifeworktransitions.com http://www.lifeworktransitions.com/exercises/exercs.html	Articles and exercises to help you determine your strengths, passions, and direction available at no charge.
United States Department of Labor Occupational Outlook Handbook http://www.bls.gov/oco	Free detailed information about occupations by industry, training and education needed, earnings, expected job prospects, what workers do on the job, and more.

Step 2: Create Your Personal Mission Statement

personal mission statement

A brief but broad statement of who you are and what you want to accomplish.

You might be thinking that you just want to get a simple job; you don't need an elaborate **personal mission statement**. Although you may not be asked about your personal mission statement during an interview, it is nonetheless important, because it provides you with a concrete sense of direction and purpose, summarized in relatable words. Great brands have clear, concise mission statements to help the company chart its path. For example, Google's mission statement is "To organize the world's information and make it universally accessible and useful."[30] The mission statement for Starbucks is "To inspire and nurture the human spirit—one person, one cup, and one neighborhood at a time."[31]

It's worth your time to write a personal mission statement. You might be surprised to discover that people who have a personal mission statement find it easier to get an enjoyable job. This is precisely because a personal mission statement helps provide framework for what's important to you and what you want to do and accomplish.

A mission statement is a concise statement about what you want to achieve—the more direct, the better. It should be short (so don't worry about wordsmithing) and easy to recall (you should always know what your mission statement is and how to measure your activities against it). A mission statement should be broad in nature. In other words, it doesn't specifically state a job you want. Instead, it describes who you are, what you stand for, what you want to do, and the direction you want to take.[32]

Links

Learn more about how to write your personal mission statement.

Quintessential Careers

http://www.quintcareers.com/mission_statements.html

http://www.quintcareers.com/creating_personal_mission_statements.html

Time Thoughts

http://www.timethoughts.com/goalsetting/mission-statements.htm

Once you write your mission statement, you should put it somewhere where you can see it daily—perhaps on your computer wallpaper, on your desk, or on the back of your business card. It should remind you every day of your personal goals.[33]

Step 3: Define Your Personal Brand

Choosing a career direction and writing a personal mission statement are not things that can be done in one day. They require research, evaluation, consideration, and a lot of soul searching. The same is true for defining your **personal brand**.

personal brand

The characteristics that define you and what you have to offer to a prospective employer.

You've learned about the power of a brand in the selling process and that a brand can be a product, service, concept, cause, or even a person. Truly, the most important product, brand, or idea you will ever sell is yourself.[34] You're not just a person, you're a brand. When you begin your job search, you will need to sell yourself to prospective employers. When you sell yourself effectively, you will be able to sell your ideas, your value, your experience, and your skills to get the job you want.

It's easy to talk about brands. It's harder to define one, especially when the brand is *you*. Many people feel uncomfortable talking about themselves. Others feel as if they are bragging if they are forced to put themselves in a positive light. The fact of the matter is, to be successful and stand apart from the competition, you have to know yourself and carefully craft your brand story.[35] For the purposes of finding a career, it is important to carefully consider what you believe defines you—what makes you unique, consistent, and relevant—and how to tell your brand story to create an emotional connection with prospective employers.

Here's a strategy to help you think about defining your personal brand. If you were on a job interview and the interviewer asked you, "Tell me three things about yourself that make you unique and would bring value to my company," what would you say? Would you be able to quickly identify three points that define you and then demonstrate what you mean?

Many students might answer this question by saying, "I'm hardworking, I'm determined, and I'm good with people." Although those are good characteristics, they are too generic and don't really define you as a brand. The best way to tell your brand story is to use the characteristics of a brand covered earlier in this chapter—unique, consistent, and relevant and creating an emotional connection with its customers.

brand points

Specific characteristics that define your personal brand. They are platforms that you can use to demonstrate your skills and experience.

If you identify three "**brand points**" you can tell a much more powerful brand story. Brand points are like platforms that you can use to demonstrate your skills and experience. Here are some examples of powerful brand points:

- **Leadership skills.** This provides a platform to describe your roles in leadership positions at school, work, professional, or volunteer or community service organizations.
- **Academic achievement.** This provides a platform to highlight your scholarships, awards, honors (e.g., dean's list), and more. A prospective employer wants to hire the best and the brightest (if academic achievement isn't your strong suit, don't use this as one of your brand points).
- **Sales (or other) experience.** This provides a platform to underscore your contributions and accomplishments in your current and past positions. Past achievements are the best predictor of future success for a prospective employer so you can focus on results that you have delivered.

You can you see how specific brand points can make a big difference in how you might answer the question above; they help define your brand as being unique (no one else has this combination of education, skills, and experience), consistent (each one demonstrates that you are constantly striving to achieve more), and relevant (prospective employers want people who have these characteristics). Finally, the ability to communicate your brand story in a cover letter, a résumé, and an interview will help you establish an emotional connection with your prospective employer because he or she will be able to identify with components of your personality.

You've Got the Power: Tips for Your Job Search

You Have More to Offer Than You Think
If you're putting off thinking about your career because you don't have any experience and you don't know what you want to do, don't worry. Take a deep breath, and focus on how to define your personal brand. You have more to offer than you think.

- Have you worked in a restaurant, hotel, retail store, bank, camp, or other customer service environment? You have multitasking skills, customer service skills, and the ability to work under pressure and deliver results.
- Have you worked for a landscaping company, technology company, or other service provider? You have experience interacting with clients to understand their needs. (Also, don't forget to mention the fact that you increased the company's sales if you made any sales).
- Have you worked as a cashier in a bank or in an accounting department? You have had the responsibility of handling money and accurately accounting for it.
- Have you earned money on your own with a small business such as babysitting or lawn care? You have entrepreneurial experience. Include how you landed your clients, advertised for new ones, and managed your costs and time. Every company wants people who can demonstrate drive and independence.

Creating your brand points can effectively make the difference between being an ordinary applicant and being the person who lands the job. Indeed, your brand points are the skeletal framework for the way you sell yourself to get the job you want. You'll learn how to use your brand points as the core of your résumé, cover letter, and interviews in Chapter 2 and Chapter 10.

For now, just take the time to really think about what are the three brand points that define you. Your education, skills, and experience will probably be different from the example, but your brand points can be just as powerful. Use the box below as a starting point to identify your three brand points.

Suggestions for Brand Points

These are thought starters. You should define your brand based on what you have to offer.

- Sales experience (or experience in marketing, retail, finance, etc.)
- Project management experience
- Leadership experience
- Management experience
- Negotiating experience
- Work ethic and commitment (e.g., working while going to school)
- Entrepreneurial experience (e.g., eBay or other small business experience)
- Customer service experience (e.g., working in a restaurant, retail store, bank)
- Academic achievement
- Subject matter expert (e.g., author of a blog)
- International study
- Community service

Key Takeaways

- *Selling U* is the final section in each chapter that provides information, resources, and guidance about how to sell yourself to get the job you want.
- Getting started for your job search includes three steps:

  1. Explore the possibilities. Learn about yourself through **career assessment surveys**, **skills inventory questionnaires**, and **personality tests**. Investigate industries in which you may want to work by using the resources provided. Don't forget to visit your campus career center.

  2. Write a personal mission statement. State your purpose briefly and concisely. It will help you plot your course.

  3. Define your personal brand. Identify three **brand points** that define your personal brand and become platforms on which to showcase your skills and experience. These three **brand points** will be the basis of your résumé, cover letter, and interviews.

Exercises

1. Visit at least two of the Web sites listed in Table 1.1 for a career assessment, skills inventory, or personality test. Complete at least one of the free tests or surveys. Discuss one thing you learned (or the test confirmed) about yourself.

2. Write your personal mission statement. Discuss what you learned about yourself by creating it.

3. Discuss how the characteristics of a brand can relate to a person (e.g., unique, consistent, and relevant and has an emotional connection with its customers).

1.4 Review and Practice

Power Wrap-Up

Now that you have read this chapter, you should be able to understand the role of selling in everyday life, in the economy, and in companies.

- You can **identify** examples of selling in your everyday life.
- You can **describe** the characteristics of a brand.
- You can **compare and contrast** the difference between sales and marketing.
- You can **understand** how to define your personal brand.

Test Your Power Knowledge (answers are below)

1. Name three situations in your life in which you use selling.
2. Name the four key characteristics of a brand.
3. Describe what this sentence means: "Each salesperson supports an average of 12.9 other jobs within the company."
4. Is sales considered a line or a support function? Why?
5. What is the impact of Sales 2.0 on the selling function?
6. Which of the four characteristics of a brand is most important when you are selling your personal brand?
7. What is a customer-centric organization?

Power (Role) Play

Now it's time to put what you've learned into practice. The following are two roles that are involved in the same selling situation—one role is the customer, and the other is the salesperson. This will give you the opportunity to think about this selling situation from the point of view of both the customer and the salesperson.

Read each role carefully along with the discussion questions. Then, be prepared to play either of the roles in class using the concepts covered in this chapter. You may be asked to discuss the roles and do a role-play in groups or individually.

College Admissions: Who Is Selling Whom?
Role: College admissions director

You are the director of admissions at your school. You want to choose only the best candidates for admission for next year's class. The focus of the school is to attract and accept students that demonstrate diversity, academic achievement, life experience, community service, passion for learning, and potential to grow.

You personally meet with each one of the final candidates to determine how they will fit into the culture of the school and help the school meet its objectives. It's something you enjoy doing because it's a chance to put a name with a face and see exactly what makes each student special. You and the other management at the school consider it to be a customer-centric organization.

You are about to meet with a prospective student. You are under some pressure to increase enrollment (after all, the admissions department is really like the sales department in a lot of organizations). You are not sure he's a perfect fit for the school, but you are one of the school's customer contact points so you want to make him feel at ease while you are learning more about him.

- How will you greet this prospective student to make him feel welcome?
- What questions will you ask to learn about his personal brand and determine if he will be a good fit for the school?
- If he is not exactly the right fit for the school, will you admit him anyway because you want to increase admissions? Why or why not?

Role: Prospective student

You are a prospective student at your school. Your grades are good (not outstanding), but you have been involved in the drama club and Spanish club in high school. You don't know what you want to do in life, but you know you want to go to college and get a good job. You are nervous about your interview with the director of admissions because it's your first interview and you don't really know what to expect.

- How will you "sell" yourself to the director of admissions?
- How will you make an emotional connection with the director of admissions?
- What are your three brand positioning points, and how will you use them in this situation?

Put Your Power to Work: *Selling U* Activities

1. Visit your campus career center in person. (If you don't have a campus career center, visit your library and meet with a librarian.) Meet with one of the staff members to learn about activities, resources, and people that are available to help you with your career search. Learn about the campus career Web site and how to view job postings. Sign up for one of the upcoming workshops on career searching.
2. Write your personal mission statement. Meet with a professor or advisor to review it and get feedback.
3. Identify your three brand points. Write them down and determine at least two examples of experience that demonstrates each point. (Hint: This will become the basis for your résumé and cover letter in the *Selling U* section in Chapter 2.)

Test Your Power Knowledge Answers

1. Getting into the school of your choice, convincing your parents of something, getting the job you want (as well as other situations you may name).
2. The four characteristics of a brand are the fact that it is unique, consistent, and relevant and has an emotional connection with its customers.
3. "Each salesperson supports an average of 12.9 other jobs within the company" means that the level of sales that is generated by each salesperson is enough to fund the salaries and benefits of almost thirteen people in the organization in departments such as human resources, marketing, operations, finance, and others. Without the sales, the company would not be able to pay for the other jobs.
4. Sales is considered a line function because salespeople are part of the daily operations of the company.
5. Sales 2.0 is a term that applies to the ever-changing world of technology, communication, and relationships in selling. The evolution of the Internet has led to a change in the balance of power in the selling process. Now, customers may have more information than a salesperson due to the research they are able to do on Web sites, through communities, and user-generated content. (In other words, both good and bad news travel fast.) Salespeople have to focus on collaboration inside their companies and with their customers to deliver the best solution to meet their customers' needs.

6. All of the characteristics are important when you are selling your personal brand. It's important to define your brand by developing the three most important brand points that best describe you.

7. The organizational chart in a customer-centric organization has the customer at the center so that all functions focus on meeting the needs of the customer rather than working in silos.

Endnotes

1. Michael Levens, *Marketing: Defined, Explained, Applied* (Upper Saddle River, NJ: Pearson Prentice Hall, 2010), 181.

2. Tom Hopkins International, "Tom Hopkins Bio," http://www.tomhopkins.com/tomhopkins_bio.html (accessed June 7, 2009).

3. Michael R. Solomon, Greg W. Marshall, and Elnora W. Stuart, *Marketing: Real People, Real Choices* (Upper Saddle River, NJ: Pearson Prentice Hall, 2008), 286.

4. Michael McCarthy, "Vegas Goes Back to Naughty Roots," *USA Today*, April 11, 2005, http://www.usatoday.com/money/advertising/adtrack/2005-04-11-track-vegas_x.htm (accessed June 4, 2009).

5. Fred Reichheld, "The Ultimate Question: How to Measure and Build Customer Loyalty in the Support Center," presented via Webinar on May 14, 2009.

6. Carmine Gallo, "How to Sell More Than a Product," *BusinessWeek*, May 19, 2009, http://www.businessweek.com/smallbiz/content/may2009/sb20090519_058809.htm (accessed June 7, 2009).

7. Eleftheria Parpis, "Starbucks Claims 'It's Not Just Coffee,'" *Brandweek*, May 1, 2009, http://www.brandweek.com/bw/content_display/news-and-features/retail-restaurants/e3i88d85d6ede4fd0afae2e6d752751e2a3 (accessed June 7, 2009).

8. "Gene Simmons: Rock 'n' Roll Entrepreneur," *BusinessWeek*, September 5, 2008, http://www.businessweek.com/smallbiz/content/sep2008/sb2008095_987221.htm (accessed June 7, 2009).

9. United States Department of Labor, Bureau of Labor Statistics, "Employment by Major Occupational Group, 2008 and Projected 2018," Economic News Release Table 5, 2009, http://www.bls.gov/news.release/ecopro.t05.htm (accessed May 6, 2010).

10. "Selling Power 500: America's 500 Largest Sales Forces," *Selling Power*, October 2008, 52.

11. Karen Collins, *Exploring Business* (Nyack, NY: Flat World Knowledge, 2009).

12. Bureau of Economic Analysis, International Economic Accounts, "Summary Estimates for Multinational Companies: Employment, Sales, and Capital Expenditures for 2007," April 17, 2009, http://www.bea.gov/newsreleases/international/mnc/2009/mnc2007.htm (accessed June 5, 2009).

13. George E. Belch and Michael A. Belch, *Advertising and Promotion: An Integrated Marketing and Communications Perspective*, 8th ed. (New York: McGraw-Hill Irwin, 2008), 653–54.

14. FiftyOne, http://www.fiftyone.com/solution (accessed June 5, 2009).

15. Caroline McCarthy, "Overstock.com Will Extend Reach to Canada, Europe," CNET News Blog, http://news.cnet.com/8301-10784_3-9933344-7.html (accessed June 5, 2009).

16. Robert McGarvey and Babs S. Harrison, "The Human Element: How the Web Brings People Together in an Integrated Selling System," *Selling Power* 20, no. 8, http://www.sellingpower.com/content/article.php?a=5566 (accessed March 16, 2010).

17. Heather Baldwin, "What Does Sales 2.0 Mean for You?" Selling Power Sales Management eNewsletter, March 3, 2008, http://www.sellingpower.com/content/newsletter/issue.php?pc=801 (accessed March 16, 2010).

18. Selling Power, Sales 2.0 Newsletter, September 18, 2008, http://www.sellingpower.com/content/newsletter/issue.php?pc=868 (accessed June 21, 2010).

19. BNET Business Dictionary, "Sales," BNET, http://dictionary.bnet.com/definition/Sales.html?tag=col1;rbDictionary (accessed June 5, 2009).

20. Gerry Tabio, "How to Create Ideas That Sell," presentation at Greater Media Philadelphia Sales Meeting, Philadelphia, PA, May 15, 2009.

21. Barry Welford, "7 Habits of a Truly Customer-Centric Selling Organization," SMM Internet Marketing Consultants Newsletter 13, http://www.smmbc.ca/newsletter-13.htm (accessed June 5, 2009).

22. BusinessDictionary.com, "Staff Function," http://www.businessdictionary.com/definition/staff-function.html (accessed June 8, 2009).

23. "Selling Power 500: America's 500 Largest Sales Forces," *Selling Power*, October 2008, 53.

24. Elaine Pofeldt, "Empty Desk Syndrome: How to Handle a Hiring Freeze," *Inc.*, May 1, 2008, http://www.inc.com/magazine/20080501/empty-desk-syndrome.html (accessed June 7, 2009).

25. American Marketing Association, "About AMA," October 2007, http://www.marketingpower.com/AboutAMA/Pages/DefinitionofMarketing.aspx?sq=definition+of+marketing (accessed June 6, 2009).

26. Michael R. Solomon, Greg W. Marshall, and Elnora W. Stuart, *Marketing: Real People, Real Choices* (Upper Saddle River, NJ: Pearson Prentice Hall, 2008), 380.

27. George E. Belch and Michael A. Belch, *Advertising and Promotion*, 8th ed. (New York: McGraw-Hill Irwin, 2008), 10.

28. Gerhard Gschwandtner, "How Power Brands Sell More," *Selling Power* 21, no. 3, http://www.sellingpower.com/content/article.php?a=5705 (accessed March 16, 2010).

29. Patricia R. Olsen, "Sweets Tester in Chief," *New York Times*, June 7, 2009, business section, 9.

30. Google, "Corporate Information, Company Overview," http://www.google.com/intl/en/corporate/ (accessed June 6, 2009).

31. Starbucks, "Our Starbucks Mission," http://www.starbucks.com/mission/default.asp (accessed June 6, 2009).

32. Kim Richmond, *Brand You*, 3rd ed. (Upper Saddle River, NJ: Pearson Prentice Hall, 2008), 18.

33. Kim Richmond, *Brand You*, 3rd ed. (Upper Saddle River, NJ: Pearson Prentice Hall, 2008), 20.

34. Kim Richmond, *Brand You*, 3rd ed. (Upper Saddle River, NJ: Pearson Prentice Hall, 2008), 1.

35. Peggy Klaus, *Brag: How to Toot Your Own Horn without Blowing It* (New York: Warner Books, Inc., 2003), 3.

CHAPTER 2
The Power to Choose Your Path: Careers in Sales

Video Ride-Along with Paul Blake, Vice President of Sales at Greater Media Philadelphia

Meet Paul Blake, a senior sales executive. Paul has been in sales for twenty years with roles at various companies including sales rep, sales manager, and now vice president of sales. He is responsible for over forty salespeople and millions of dollars of revenue. He and his sales team sell media solutions, including radio spots, Internet streaming ads, text message campaigns, and more to help businesses build brand awareness and get more customers.

Ride along with Paul and find out what it takes to be a great salesperson and what he looks for when he's hiring new salespeople.

View the video online at: http://www.youtube.com/embed/1Btp351qros

2.1 What Does It Take to Be in Sales?

Learning Objectives

1. Discuss the characteristics required to be successful in a career in sales.
2. Understand what you can expect from a career in sales.

When Steve Jobs, the CEO of Apple, delivered the commencement address at Stanford University in 2005, he told the story of how he and Steve Wozniak started the now $32 billion company in a garage in 1976. Jobs said, "I was lucky—I found out what I wanted to do early in life."[1] But life at Apple wasn't always so perfect. When he was thirty, just one year after the launch of the Macintosh, he was fired from the company he founded. Although he was publicly humiliated and frustrated and didn't know what to do next, he realized that he indeed loved what he did. From there he went on to start Pixar, the company that created *Toy Story*, the world's first full-length computer-animated feature film.

He left the Stanford graduates with some personal words of wisdom to think about as they prepared themselves for their careers: "Your work is going to fill a large part of your life, and the only way to be truly satisfied is to do what you believe is great work. And the only way to do great work is to love what you do. If you haven't found it yet, keep looking. Don't settle. As with all matters of the heart, you'll know when you find it."[2]

To be successful in sales, and in life, you must love what you do. If you aren't passionate about your profession, you will never be the best. You will always fall short because the people who love it will naturally excel. It seems simple enough: do what you love. But what if you love many things or don't know if you've found your niche? Don't worry—there are questions you can ask yourself to help you determine whether a career in sales will excite you and make you want to leap out of bed every morning.

Are You Born to Sell?

How do you know if sales is your passion, the career of your dreams? The first step is taking this course. You'll have an opportunity to learn about sales and actually put your knowledge to work in real-life situations by role-playing with your classmates. After reading this chapter, you will better understand the profession of selling and what it has to offer. This chapter includes insights about which personal characteristics and talents are best suited to sales, which industries you might work in, and how you can be successful in the profession.

Just like being a teacher requires traits such as a love of learning, an ability to communicate, and the talent to make concepts come alive for people, selling calls for certain personal characteristics as well. Some people think that successful salespeople are those who have the "gift of gab," but that's not really what makes salespeople effective. Although communication and relationship building are valuable skills, just being able to talk to people is not enough to be successful in sales. Consider the following points that make a salesperson successful and see if these are a good match to you and your skills.

Character and the Ability to Build Trust

It never goes without saying that character—the combination of your beliefs, tendencies, and actions that you take—is the single defining trait for a salesperson (or any business person, for that matter).[3] Your character defines how you will conduct yourself, and it is the yardstick by which customers measure you. After all, your customers are spending their money based on what you say you will deliver; they have to trust you. If you ever break the trust for any reason, you will likely lose not only the sale, but you will most likely lose your reputation, and, ultimately, your livelihood. According to a survey by Forrester Research, trust and believability are so important in the buying and selling processes that 71 percent of buyers based their decisions on these traits.[4] See why Jake Nickell, founder, and Jeffrey Kalmikoff, chief creative officer, of Threadless.com think that being trusted by the customer makes a great salesperson.

Link

The Founders of Threadless.com on the Importance of Trust in Selling

http://www.inc.com/ss/what-makes-great-salesperson#4

The Ability to Connect

The most successful salespeople know how to engage their customers in a way that helps the customers identify for themselves the way the product or service offered can deliver value. The Xerox

Company, after conducting a survey to identify the characteristics of their peak-performing sales-people, says it best: "Your prospect will never buy because you present a pitch. She instead buys from what she convinces herself of. This means that if you are selling a watch, telling your prospect you will cure his ignorance of time will not be enough. Your prospect will literally talk to himself to discover that this watch will indeed keep him from running late. He will not listen to you; he will only listen to himself."[5]

A good salesperson will use his personal skills to connect with a customer, so that their conversation prompts and echoes the customer's own internal thought process. It is ultimately this ability to connect that allows the salesperson to build relationships and trust. This video highlights how a motorcycle trip, passion, and connecting led to a sale with Harley-Davidson.

FIGURE 2.1

A good salesperson uses his personal skills to connect with a customer.

© 2010 Jupiterimages Corporation

Video Link

Interview with Jim Cathcart, President, Cathcart Institute

Learn how a motorcycle trip led to a sale.

http://www.sellingpower.com/content/video/?date=8/12/2009

Listening Skills

Contrary to popular belief, speaking is not the most important aspect of selling—listening is, because "salespeople are communicators, not manipulators."[6] It's interesting to note that many of the salespeople who are constantly talking are actually not successful. It is those salespeople who have a genuine interest in listening who learn precisely what the customers' needs, priorities, and opportunities are. Listening skills are the fundamental basis for forming a connection. "Listening builds relationships," according to Marjorie Brody, author of *Help! Was That a Career-Limiting Move?* She suggests a "silent solution" to many problems in the form of listening.[7] The challenge for many people is that listening with undivided attention is hard to do. According to Barry J. Elms, CEO of Strategic Negotiations International, psychologists say that we listen using only 25 percent of our brain.[8] That means that the other 75 percent is thinking about a response or thinking about something else. Salespeople who take notes, refer to written material, and are intently aware of their nonverbal cues can be extremely successful because they see and hear things that people who are talking just can't absorb.[9] See why Andy Taylor, CEO of Enterprise Rent-A-Car, thinks great listening skills make a great salesperson.

Link

Andy Taylor, CEO of Enterprise Rent-A-Car, on Listening Skills

http://www.inc.com/ss/what-makes-great-salesperson#1

The Ability to Ask the Right Questions

It was Einstein who said, "If I had an hour to solve a problem and my life depended on it, I would use the first fifty-five minutes to formulate the right question because as soon as I had identified the right question, I knew I could solve the problem in less than five minutes."[10] This demonstrates the power of asking the *right* questions. Those questions can only be asked when you listen and have the ability to connect. Paul Blake, whom you met at the beginning of this chapter, believes that asking the right questions is vital to the success of his sales force. That's why he leads by example and always asks one key question when he is interviewing candidates for sales positions: "Do you believe you have the right to change someone's opinion?" That single question tells him all he needs to know about the candidate and how she would perform on his sales team.[11]

The Willingness to Learn

You might think that just because you are in school, you are learning everything you need to know for your career. Although you are building a strong foundation, you will continue to learn new things every day when you are working. Salespeople must not only have product knowledge and understand the buying and selling process; they must also learn skills that will make them more effective and efficient as salespeople. For example, in one study on salespeople, executives mentioned that salespeople must be willing to learn more than what appears to be required. Financial skills, negotiating skills, and even speed-reading courses were mentioned as additional training needs.[12] It's important to note that besides constantly learning new skills, salespeople have to be students of the business. Skills and abilities are developed and fine-tuned over time, and experience plays a role in the learning process. So it stands to reason that salespeople are not "made" simply because they have the title. Just as it takes seven years to become a doctor, three years to become a lawyer, and a thousand hours to become a barber, a great salesperson develops over time.[13] If you're thinking about pursuing a career in sales, keep in mind that like other professions it takes time, training, and experience to be successful.

The Drive to Succeed

You can't be successful if you don't set goals. Great salespeople set goals for themselves, achieve them, and celebrate those achievements. They visualize what they want, then put together a plan to get it.[14] The drive to succeed is important not only in sales, but also in life. Consider Olympic swimmer Michael Phelps. He set out to do something that no one else had ever done: win eight Olympic gold medals. It's instructive to look at his drive to succeed and what he did to prepare for and achieve his goals. While Phelps has had some recent public relations (PR) challenges about his behavior out of the pool, it doesn't diminish his hard work, drive to succeed, and accomplishments.

Which Generation Is Best at Selling?

There are now three generations in the work force: baby boomers (born 1946–1964); Gen X (1965–1980); and Gen Y, also known as millennials (born after 1980). According to a recent survey by the consulting firm Generational DNA, 42 percent of Gen X sales reps exceeded their sales goals while 37 percent of Gen Y and only 32 percent of baby boomers exceeded their goals. But everything is relative as the survey also revealed that boomers are more likely to have more ambitious goals, which is a reflection of their experience level.[15]

Resilience and a Positive Attitude

It's important to remember that you will hear "no" more frequently than you hear "Yes, I'll take it." That challenge, however, is offset by the thrill of victory when the sale is made and a relationship with the customer based on trust is built. You can only succeed when you go the extra mile, by investigating one more lead, going back for the second sales call even when the first hasn't been successful, and trial closing even if you are not sure you can really get the sale.[16] It's the eternal optimism that pushes you, even when others might think there is no reason to pursue the sale. If you think you can make it happen, you should definitely be in sales.

The Willingness to Take Risks

Has anyone ever told you, "You won't know until you try"? That statement is especially true in sales. You can set yourself apart by taking smart business risks. Think about how you consider taking risks in everyday life and how they pay off. For example, let's say you are from a small town and you chose to go to a college in a big city because you wanted to experience something new. That was a risk; it took you outside your comfort zone. But if you hadn't taken the risk, you would have never known what life in a big city was like. Great salespeople go beyond the norm to explore and test the waters. For example, making phone calls to senior executives that you have never met, networking with people you don't know, or making a presentation to a room full of customers all involve some level of risk. But getting out of your comfort zone and taking risks is how great opportunities are found.[17]

Taking risks in life and in selling is best summed up by Lisa McCullough, a high-profile stuntwoman: "Don't focus on your fears, focus on what you want."[18]

Video Link

Taking Risks

Lisa McCullough shares her thoughts on taking risks in this video.

http://www.sellingpower.com/content/video/?date=3/23/2007

The Secret to Success: Failure

"No risk, no reward" is a familiar saying. But best-selling author Jeffrey Gitomer says, "No risk, no nothing." He believes the only way to succeed is to take risks and sometimes fail. It's the failures that can lead to success.[19] He talks about the importance of taking risks and failing in this video.

Why Taking Risks Is Important to Success

Find out why salespeople need to take risks.

View the video online at: http://www.youtube.com/embed/UBHBk-A4a5M

The Ability to Ask for an Order

It may sound intuitive that successful salespeople shouldn't be afraid to ask for a customer's order, but you would be surprised at how often it happens. Most customers *want* you to ask for their order. "Would you like fries with your hamburger?" "What can I get you for dessert?" and "Would you like to pay with credit or debit?" are all examples of salespeople asking for the order.

A large percentage of the time these salespeople are successful and meet their customers' needs at the same time. You reduce your chances of being successful if you don't ask for the order.[20] In other words, if *you* don't ask for the order, someone else *will*. See why Fred Franzia, founder of Bronco Wine Company and creator of "Two Buck Chuck" wine, thinks that asking for the order makes a great salesperson.

FIGURE 2.2

Successful salespeople are never afraid to ask for the order.

© 2010 Jupiterimages Corporation

Link

Fred Franzia, Founder of Bronco Wine Company, on Asking for the Order

http://www.inc.com/ss/what-makes-great-salesperson#5

Independence and Discipline

Most sales positions require independence, self-motivation, and discipline. Although these traits may seem contradictory, they are actually complementary. Independence is especially important if you are calling on customers in person. It usually requires travel, either locally by car or by plane, which means that you have to be able to manage your time without being told what to do. In fact, it means that you set your schedule and do what you need to do to meet your sales goals. But having this kind of independence requires discipline. As Michael Janusz, an account manager at ACL Laboratories put it, "I went into sales because of the dynamic environment, competitive aspect, and income potential. I do think there is a shortage of good salespeople. I think this is because it takes a unique blend of skills and a disciplined person. There are many people who can talk well, manage a territory well, or work hard. However, not many can put it all together."[21] Besides having an independent streak, salespeople must be focused and hardworking in the long term, or they will not enjoy consistent success over time.

Flexibility

Along with the need for independence comes the importance of flexibility. Just as you are able to set your own schedule, you have to be flexible based on your customers' needs. Most sales positions are not nine-to-five jobs. That means you might be working nights or weekends, or you might be traveling out of town during the week or even long periods of time, especially if you are selling internationally. You have to be available when your customers want to buy. Before you cringe at the prospect of grueling hours and long flights, remember that this kind of schedule may also work to your advantage. You may have some weekdays off, which allow you to enjoy family, sports, or other outings that you might not otherwise have an opportunity to enjoy.

Passion

If you're not passionate about what you're selling, how do you expect your customers to believe in you and your product? You have to love what you do, believe in it, and feel passionately about it. Passion encompasses all the traits mentioned above; it's how they all come together. Passion is the element that sets you apart from other salespeople and makes your prospects and customers believe in you and your product or service. See why Selena Cuff, head of Heritage Link Brands, thinks passion is what makes a great salesperson.

Link

Selena Cuff, Heritage Link Brands on Passion

http://www.inc.com/ss/what-makes-great-salesperson#0

Bringing It All Together

If this seems like a lot of traits, think about the list of traits that might be required to be a doctor, lawyer, or college professor. Every profession requires a lot of those who pursue it. To make it easier, you may want to think about how these traits come together. Mahan Khalsa, founder of Franklin-Covey Sales Performance Group and author of *Let's Get Real or Let's Not Play: The Demise of Dysfunctional Selling and the Advent of Helping Clients Succeed*, sums up the traits of a successful salesperson this way: "There are three traits that define a successful salesperson: business intelligence (IQ or intelligence quotient), the ability to create rapport and build trust (EQ or emotional intelligence), and a good way to approach and to follow up sales (XQ or executional intelligence; the ability to execute the sale)."[22]

Want to know what employers look for when hiring a salesperson? This video features Mary Delany, chief sales officer at CareerBuilder.com, discussing what she looks for in candidates for sales positions.

Video Link

Interview with Mary Delany, Chief Sales Officer at CareerBuilder.com

Learn about the characteristics of a great salesperson.

http://www.sellingpower.com/content/video/?date=1/5/2007

Power Player: Lessons in Selling from Successful Salespeople

It's All about *Their* Stuff

Mark Bozzini, CEO of Infinite Spirits, learned a powerful selling lesson early in his career. His job was to sell more bottles of wine than were sold the previous year, which seemed easy enough. But when he called on a wine and spirits retailer, the storeowner told him that his products didn't sell and he would rather not have them on his shelves. So much for selling more bottles of wine. An average salesperson might become pushy, or even leave and seek a sale elsewhere. But Bozzini, an intuitive and passionate salesman, was determined to make the sale. He spent an hour rearranging the store display and asked the storeowner to give it a chance to see if the product sold better. The new display worked, and the storeowner became one of Bozzini's best customers. The moral of the story: always remember that "the customer doesn't care about your stuff. They care about *their* stuff."[23]

Creating Value Is the Name of the Game

The role of a salesperson can be summed up in one sentence: "Salespeople are value creators."[24] To further describe what this means, think about a recent visit to the Apple Store. If you go to the store at virtually any hour, it is filled with customers. The salespeople are not just those that are pushing a product, hoping that you buy so that they make their sales quota. They are experts who know everything about the products in the store whether they be MacBooks, iPods, or iPhones. The salespeople engage you in dialogue, listen, and learn about what you are looking for. They ask questions like, "What do you do with the photos you take? Do you like to make videos? Do you want to easily access the Web from your phone?" No techno-talk, no slick sales pitches. They just want to know what's important to you so that they can let you try the product that not only fits your basic computing needs, but blows you away.

Apple and its sales team know that computers are complicated and can baffle even savvy users. To build trust and confidence with their customers, they developed the "Genius Bar" so that Apple users know that they can always to talk to an individual and find help with any problem or question they may have. In fact, Apple dedicates a section of their Web site to the Genius Bar and invites customers to make an appointment online to come to a store to talk to one of the "resident Geniuses." Talk about creating value. As a result, Apple is able to charge a premium for its product and generate such demand that in some cases people are lined up to buy their products, as was the case for the launch of the iPhone 3GS in June 2009.[25]

WII-FM

WII-FM

The acronym for What's In It For Me.

While a job in sales can be demanding, it can also be very rewarding in many ways. Even in these days of iPods and Pandora, **WII-FM** (**W**hat's **I**n **I**t **F**or **M**e) is a radio station that everyone listens to. It's not a bad thing to think about what's in it for you. After all, if you are considering investing your career in the selling profession, you should know what's in it for you.

What Will You Be Doing?

The life of a salesperson is never dull. You could be working with a single customer or with multiple customers. You might work in a corporate office, or you might work from your home. You might talk to customers via phone, live chat, instant message, and text, or you might meet with them in their office in your neighborhood, your region, or anywhere around the world. You might be working on research to identify new customers, preparing a presentation for a new or existing customer, meeting with customers face-to-face, following up to get contracts signed, or communicating inside your organization to be sure all goes well to deliver the product or service to the customer on time and on budget. On any given day you might be working on any number of activities to support an existing customer or to approach, present, or close a new customer.

What Can You Achieve?

A job in selling can be a gateway to wherever you want to go. Stanley Marcus, the ninety-three-year-old chairman emeritus of Neiman Marcus, started as a messenger boy, then as a junior salesperson in his father's store before working his way to the top. Michael Dell started by selling computers from his dorm room.[26] Selling could eventually give you fame and fortune, but more immediately it can also give you the satisfaction of providing solutions to people, financial opportunity, and even financial independence. Even in today's challenging economy, these goals are possible.

Sales drive every company's growth. When you are in sales, you are responsible for the future of the company. That's why many sales positions offer unlimited income potential. Sales is considered a **pay-for-performance** profession.[27] That means that you are paid based on your performance, which in this case is sales. Your income is commensurate with the amount of sales you generate; simply put, you can make as much money as you want. This is a major difference between sales and most other disciplines. In most sales positions, you earn a salary and perhaps some other elements of compensation, such as a bonus. In sales, you can determine your income because it is usually not limited to a specific number; it is based on the amount you sell. Although this topic is covered in detail in Chapter 14, it's worth noting here that you have the power to determine how much you want to earn when you have a successful career in sales.

If you want to check out base salaries for sales positions in your area or the area in which you would like to work, go to Salary.com and use the Salary Wizard. You'll be able to see the average salary, bonuses, benefits, and more.

FIGURE 2.3
Everyone listens to the same radio station—WII-FM.

© 2010 Jupiterimages Corporation

pay-for-performance

A compensation method in which earnings are determined based on the results that are delivered.

Link

Salary Information
This is a resource to research salary and other compensation elements for different positions in areas across the country.

http://salary.com

Key Takeaways

- To be successful in sales and in life, you have to enjoy what you do for a living.
- A good salesperson does more than sell; he builds a relationship and trust with the customer and offers solutions.
- A successful salesperson is a good listener. It's important to listen and understand the challenges that the customer is facing in order to present solutions that will work.

- Asking the right questions is critical to being successful in sales. It is the right questions that provide an opportunity for customers to share their challenges. Successful salespeople are always learning new things from selling techniques to technology in order to bring the best ideas to customers.

- Selling requires independence and discipline. There is no typical day in selling so salespeople have to be able to manage their own time.

- One of the biggest challenges of being in sales is the number of times you hear "no." Successful salespeople are resilient, have a positive attitude, and are willing to take risks.

- Passion is one of the most important characteristics of a successful salesperson. If a salesperson isn't passionate about what he sells, it's unlikely that his customers will be motivated to buy.

- The primary role of a salesperson is to create value for the customer and the company.

- A job in sales can be very rewarding on both a personal and a financial level, and it can lead to just about any career path you choose.

Exercises

1. Think about someone you trust such as a parent, professor, friend, classmate, or colleague. Describe why you trust him or her. Now, think about that person again. Would she say that she trusts you? How would she describe why she trusts you?

2. Ask a classmate to describe his background and then describe yours for five minutes each. Write a summary of his background based on what he or she said and ask your classmate to do the same. How accurate was each of your summaries? How many details did each include in the summaries? What did you learn about listening skills?

3. Discuss the sentence, "Salespeople are communicators, not manipulators." What does it mean? Why is it important to know the difference in sales?

4. Describe at least three characteristics of a good salesperson. Do you have any or all of these characteristics? What is appealing to you about a profession in selling? What is not appealing to you about a profession in selling?

5. Invite a salesperson to visit your class (in person or via Skype) to discuss his career in sales, what he thinks is most rewarding, and what he finds most challenging.

2.2 Sales Channels and Environments: Where You Can Put Your Selling Skills to Work

Learning Objective

1. Understand the different types of selling channels and selling environments.

If you had an accident and broke your leg, you would go to an orthopedic surgeon to have a cast put on it. However, if you had a skin rash you would go to a dermatologist to get relief and clear up the rash. Several doctors may have a role in helping you manage your health, so it makes sense that not all doctors conduct the same procedures. Some perform surgery and others diagnose, monitor, and recommend tests or further steps. Just as doctors play different roles in the health care field, the same is true for salespeople in the business arena. Different people perform different functions in the selling process.

Is It B2B or B2C?

There are two major **distribution channels**, or organizations or group of organizations involved in the process of making products and services available to customers in which personal selling is conducted.[28] Personal selling involves communication between a customer and a salesperson with the intention of providing information for the customer to make a buying decision. **Business-to-business** (also referred to as B2B) is when businesses sell products or services to other businesses for consumption by the ultimate consumer. For example, Whirlpool sells washers and dryers to Sears and makes them to the specifications determined by Sears for the Kenmore name before they are sold in Sears and K-Mart stores. Other examples of B2B selling include parts or ingredients, such as when Intel sells computer chips to Toshiba to manufacture laptop computers or when a fabric company sells cotton fabric to Gap to make their T-shirts.

Many B2B companies, such as Intel, have branded their products so that these products are quickly identified by consumers even though the products are only sold to businesses. These companies believe so strongly in the power of branding (which you learned about in Chapter 1) that they are willing to invest in building the awareness and perception of their brand name despite the fact that you can't go to a Web site or store and buy their product; you can only buy their product because it is a part of another product.

On the other hand, the transactions in which you as a consumer participate are **business-to-consumer** (also called B2C), which means that a company is selling a product or service directly to you as the ultimate consumer. In the example above, when Sears and K-Mart sell the Kenmore washers and dryers to consumers, it is B2C personal selling. Other examples of B2C selling include a waiter taking your order at a restaurant, a salesperson helping you find jeans in your size at American Eagle Outfitters, or a real estate agent showing you a house.

Some companies engage in both B2B and B2C selling, such as Staples, FedEx, Microsoft, and Geek Squad, since they serve business customers as well as the ultimate consumer. Many manufacturers such as Dove, Coke, and Oscar Meyer don't actually participate in B2C personal selling, but these brands use B2C marketing to make consumers aware of their brands. Meanwhile, their B2B personal selling organizations focus on selling these products to retailers such as Safeway, CVS, and Sam's Club (i.e., their customers), which in turn, sell their products in B2C channels to consumers like you.

There are some important differences between B2B and B2C selling. B2B selling engages with fewer customers (which makes sense because there are fewer businesses than there are consumers). At the same time, however, B2B selling involves much larger purchases. Companies purchase parts, ingredients, or supplies to service many consumers, while consumers only purchase a product or service for their own consumption or that of their family and friends. Since B2B purchases are larger in value than consumer purchases, the selling process is usually longer. This is as a result of the size of the purchase, and in many companies, there are multiple people involved in the purchasing decision, as you will learn about in Chapter 6.

distribution channels

An organization or group of organizations involved in the process of making product or services available to customers.

business-to-business (B2B)

Businesses selling products or services to other businesses.

business-to-consumer (B2C)

Businesses selling products or services directly to the ultimate consumer.

FIGURE 2.4
Business-to-consumer selling is when businesses such as retail stores sell products or services directly to the ultimate consumer.

© 2010 Jupiterimages Corporation

FIGURE 2.5 Business-to-Business versus Business-to-Consumer Selling Characteristics

Business-to-Business (B2B)	Business-to-Consumer (B2C)
Relatively few potential customers	Many customers
Larger purchases (purchasing for production and/or sale to many ultimate consumers)	Relatively small purchases (for personal use or for family or friends)
Longer selling cycle	Relatively short selling cycle
Multiple influencers and decision makers	Fewer influencers and decision makers
More difficult to identify influencers and decision makers	Easier to identify influencers and decision makers

Types of B2B and B2C Selling

When you go to McDonald's and a salesperson asks you if you want fries with your order, there is not much involved on the part of the salesperson. In fact, you may not have even considered the person who took your order to be a salesperson. This is a selling situation that matches the needs of the buyer efficiently with the operation, but it doesn't require a personal relationship or detailed product information to consummate the sale.[29] The product or service is of low dollar value and no additional contact is required for the sale. This is called **transactional selling**, and it occurs in B2C situations like this one, as well as B2B situations.[30]

On the other hand, **consultative selling**, also called relationship selling, takes place when there is a long-term or ongoing relationship between the customer and the seller, and the salesperson takes on the task of truly understanding the customers' needs and providing solutions to meet those needs. In this type of selling situation, **adaptive selling** takes place. This occurs when a salesperson changes selling behavior during a customer call to improve the exchange or outcome.[31] Consultative selling takes place in both B2B and B2C environments. For example, if you were working with a financial advisor to develop a retirement plan, the advisor would be consulting you on the best ways to save and how to best invest your money. She would adapt to your needs based on your feedback. If you told her, "I don't want to be in such high-risk investments," this would prompt her to adapt her selling behavior to better match your needs.

In some cases, the selling relationship goes beyond consultative selling and establishes a true method for mutual benefit; this is called a **strategic alliance**. In this situation, sellers and buyers work together to develop opportunities and points of difference that wouldn't exist without the relationship.[32] This type of relationship is usually found in B2B environments because a strategic alliance typically involves two companies that have something to gain by each taking an appropriate risk.

For example, before introducing the iPhone, Apple contracted AT&T to be the exclusive service provider. Each company had something to contribute to the relationship, and each one had something to gain. In this case, AT&T pays Apple for each new customer it receives. Apple increases its revenues, and AT&T gains new customers. Both companies had to invest in research and development to make the relationship happen. Both companies "had skin in the game," so both worked hard to ensure success through public relations, advertising, personal selling, and follow-up customer service. As a result, the relationship has been extremely successful for both parties, as a strategic alliance should be.[33] It's important to note that not all strategic alliances are exclusive

transactional selling

Efficiently matches the customer's needs in an operational manner, and no personal relationship is formed.

consultative selling

Type of selling in which there is a long-term or ongoing relationship between the seller and the buyer and the salesperson provides ideas or solutions to the customer based on customer needs. Also called relationship selling.

adaptive selling

Situation in which the salesperson adapts or customizes her selling style based on the behavior of the customer.

strategic alliance

A business partnership in which all parties have something at risk and have something to gain.

deals like the iPhone with AT&T. Although the deal between the two companies includes exclusivity until 2010, it's not definite that exclusivity will expand beyond that.[34]

> ## Power Point: Lessons in Selling from the Customer's Point of View
>
> ### But Do the Customers Like It?
> Satisfied customers are the true measure of success in selling. The University of Michigan publishes the American Customer Satisfaction Index every quarter, which measures customer satisfaction in a number of industries. It's no surprise that in the fast food category, smaller chains led the pack in actual satisfaction scores with Domino's as the highest-rated larger chain restaurant in the May 2009 survey. McDonald's, Wendy's, and Taco Bell also got the thumbs-up from customers.[35]

Is It Inside or Outside Sales?

What is the difference between the salesperson with whom you live-chat on BestBuy.com and the person you talk to in the store? Although both are salespeople for Best Buy, the person with whom you conducted live chat is considered an inside salesperson; the salesperson you spoke with in the store is considered an outside salesperson. Inside salespeople rarely, if ever, meet face-to-face with customers, whereas outside salespeople communicate with customers in a variety of ways, including in-person meetings.[36]

FIGURE 2.6

Inside sales reps usually work inside the office and may interact with customers by phone, e-mail, text, social networking, or other method of communication, while outside sales reps meet with customers in person.

© 2010 Jupiterimages Corporation

For many B2B and B2C companies, the **outside salespeople** are generally the primary drivers of sales and costs of sales, since the outside salespeople travel to meet in person with customers to learn more about their needs, build relationships, and provide consultation and solutions. Inside salespeople usually perform more tactical selling functions such as providing product information (as in the Best Buy example above), following up on details, and keeping the customer informed of basic information.

outside salesperson

A salesperson who meets face-to-face with customers and performs a variety of sales functions. An outside salesperson may work with an inside salesperson to serve a customer.

inside salesperson

A salesperson who performs selling functions such as providing information, taking orders, and following up using communication methods such as telephone, e-mail, text, or fax but does not actually meet with the customer face-to-face. An inside salesperson may work with an outside salesperon to serve a customer.

Companies have traditionally used **inside salespeople** because they are part of a strategy that helps keep selling costs low. Today, many companies are converting outside salespeople to inside salespeople to further reduce selling costs. Advances in technology are blurring the lines between inside and outside salespeople by providing platforms for inside salespeople to be more collaborative and consultative with tools such as video conferences, Webinars, wikis, and more. Traditional thinking is changing, as evidenced in a recent study conducted by the International Data Corporation (IDC), a sales consulting firm, which found that currently 30 percent of revenues are influenced by inside salespeople.[37] As more companies leverage technology and think differently about customer relationships, the concept of inside and outside salespeople will evolve around the most mutually efficient and beneficial customer relationships, rather than the physical location of the salespeople.

Video Link

Bad Day

Selling is a challenging profession, especially when you say the wrong thing. If you think you are having a bad day, watch this video to hear about some actual selling blunders. It will make you feel as if your day isn't so bad after all!

A bad day in sales.

http://www.sellingpower.com/content/video/?date=11/3/2006

Source: SellingPower.com

What Kind of Job Can I Get in Sales?

You have the power to choose your career. Do you want to travel across the country or around the world to meet with customers and understand their needs and develop new business opportunities for your company? Or would you rather be a technical specialist, or a subject matter expert, and talk to customers about exactly how your product or service works? No matter what you want to do, chances are there's a sales role that you will enjoy. Table 2.1 shows a snapshot of several different types of B2B and B2C sales positions that you might want to pursue and the industries in which you might find them.

TABLE 2.1 Types of B2B and B2C Sales Positions

Title	Description	Industries
Sales representative, account executive, account manager, marketing representative, sales consultant, sales associate	• Responsible for a group of customers with primary responsibility to develop and maintain close relationships with existing customers by understanding their needs and providing solutions • Identifies and develops new customers • Meets revenue and profit goals	• **B2B**: Technology, IT services manufacturing, hospitality, pharmaceutical, telecommunications, media, packaged goods, real estate, professional services • **B2C**: Real estate, high-value retail, financial services
Territory manager	• Same as above, but customers are all in the same geographic area, or territory	• **B2B**: Technology, manufacturing, hospitality, pharmaceutical, telecommunications, media, packaged goods • **B2C**: Not widely used in B2C
Business development manager	• Responsible for identifying, prospecting, and developing new customers • After the customer signs the contract (or buys the product or service), the account manager takes over the day-to-day contact with the customer • Meets revenue, profit, and new customer acquisition goals	• **B2B**: Technology, IT services, manufacturing, hospitality, pharmaceutical, telecommunications, media, packaged goods, business services, professional services, transportation • **B2C**: Not widely used in B2C
Customer relationship manager	• Responsible for the overall satisfaction of the customer • Usually a part of selling organizations that provide long-term professional services	• **B2B**: Technology, IT services, manufacturing, hospitality, pharmaceutical, telecommunications, media, professional services, transportation • **B2C**: Not widely used in B2C
Product specialist, technical specialist	• Expert in a specific product or service area • Participates in sales calls after the customer shows an interest to demonstrate or describe use and applications of the product or service	• **B2B**: Technology, IT services, manufacturing, hospitality, pharmaceutical, telecommunications, media, professional services • **B2C**: High-value retail, financial services

Title	Description	Industries
Customer service representative	• Takes orders, provides product information, processes orders internally, and follows up as necessary with the customer • May also provide outbound calls to customers to follow up	• **B2B**: Technology, IT services, manufacturing, hospitality, pharmaceutical, telecommunications, packaged goods, professional services, health care • **B2C**: Retail (including online selling), packaged goods
Telesales representative	• Makes outbound or inbound contact with customers over the phone • Activities include identifying prospective customers, providing information, completing a sale, and performing any necessary follow-up	• **B2B**: Technology, IT services, telecommunications, media, professional services • **B2C**: Retail, insurance, financial services, publishing, political parties, causes

order-takers

Salespeople who consummate sales by taking orders from customers.

order-getters

Salespeople who develop sales through relationship selling and repeat sales.

missionary selling

Salesperson who contacts key influencers and discusses product or service benefits.

Just from the summary in Table 2.1, you can see that there are a variety of different types of sales positions in many industries. You might find it helpful to think about the overall roles and functions that each performs. For example, customer service reps and telesales reps are considered **order-takers** because they interact with customers to consummate a sale, but their role does not require planning or consultative selling. On the other hand, positions such as account manager, territory manager, customer relationship manager, and business development manager are **order-getters** because they actually work to develop a relationship and solve customers' problems on an ongoing basis.[38] Sometimes, account managers, account executives, territory managers, and other similar roles perform **missionary selling**, which means that they call on customers who are not the ultimate purchaser. For instance, if you were a professor and an account manager from a textbook company called on you and brought you a copy of a new book on sales management for next semester's class, that would be considered missionary selling because the sales rep would be telling you about the textbook, but you are not the ultimate purchaser. In this case, the sales rep is calling on you so that you adopt the textbook, put it on your syllabus, and as a result, your students purchase the textbook.

Power Selling: Lessons in Selling from Successful Brands

What's in a Name?

Nike no longer uses the title "sales rep" for people in their sales force; their titles are now "account executive" and "account manager." The change in titles is a reflection of their recent change in selling strategy. Nike realized that simply bringing new samples to retailers isn't enough in this competitive marketplace. They consider planning to be a major part of the selling process, and the sales team plays a key role in planning in two ways: helping customers, such as retailers, plan their business and providing feedback and insights back to Nike to help plan the next generation of products. At Nike, your title says it all.[39]

If you are considering a career in sales, the *Selling Power* magazine "50 Best Companies to Sell For Now" is an excellent resource to identify prospective employers.

Link

Selling Power Magazine

"50 Best Companies to Sell For Now"

http://www.sellingpower.com/2016/50-best-companies-to-sell-for/

You can also learn more about specific descriptions of sales positions by reviewing some job postings on Monster.com, Yahoo! HotJobs, or CareerBuilder.com using sales in the keyword search.

Direct Selling

You may have been invited to a "party" at a friend's or relative's house to see the new line of Nutrilite Ocean Essentials vitamins and supplements. You have heard good things about the products from your friend. You didn't realize that Nutrilite also made sports drinks and energy bars. You have a great time trying the products and talking to everyone at the party, so you decide to try the Nutrilite ROC 20 Antioxidant Enhanced Drink Mix, and you order it in three flavors.

You just experienced the **direct selling** process, "the sale of a consumer product or service away from a fixed retail location."[40] Some of the most well-known direct selling companies are Amway, Mary Kay Cosmetics, Avon, and Pampered Chef. There are over 15 million people in the United States who sell products or services via direct selling, which is almost four times more than twenty years ago. In 2007, the industry generated $30.8 billion in sales in the United States.[41]

What makes direct selling so appealing is the fact that you can run your own business using the power of an established brand name and without the costs of manufacturing or providing the product or service. More important, you are your own boss. Although direct selling usually requires an initial purchase of products or services, called starting inventory, many direct sellers have been able to supplement their incomes and in some cases make it their full-time job, earning more than six figures a year. Given the opportunities, you probably aren't surprised to learn that direct selling is growing as a result of the uncertain job market. Recent grads, retirees, and everyone in between are turning to direct selling as a way to safeguard them during the recession. It's attractive because those who sell or distribute the products (also called **independent business owners [IBOs]**) make a percentage on the products they sell.

> **direct selling**
>
> The sale of a consumer product or service away from a fixed retail location.

> **independent business owner (IBO)**
>
> A direct salesperson who distributes a company's products or services and earns income based on her sales.

Link

Popular Career

Learn about the current trends in direct selling.

http://amfix.blogs.cnn.com/2009/06/17/avon-mary-kay-making-comeback/

But direct selling isn't lucrative for everyone. Not all IBOs maintain their focus and develop their network. It's hard work running your own business. It takes time, discipline, effort, focus, and passion. In fact, only 10 percent of IBOs work full-time or at least thirty hours a week.[42]

Many direct selling companies engage in network marketing, also called **multilevel marketing (MLM)**, which allows IBOs to invite other people to sell the products and earn money based on the sales of those they recruited. If you think about the concept of social networking on Web sites such as Facebook, it's easy to understand MLM. You can expand your network of contacts simply by tapping into the network of your friends; MLM operates on the same principle. If you sell to your friends and they sell to their friends, your opportunity to earn money expands significantly with every contact. So if you were an IBO for The Body Shop and you recruited your friend Jessica to be an IBO, and she recruited her friend Lashanda to be an IBO, you would not only make commission

> **multilevel marketing (MLM)**
>
> A selling system in which independent business owners recruit people to become IBOs and earn incentives based on the sales of the new IBOs.

on your product sales, but also on the product sales of Jessica and Lashanda. You can see how being a part of an MLM company can offer significant earning potential.[43]

Unfortunately, there have been some unscrupulous people involved in the MLM business, and some have created **pyramid schemes** in which many people have lost money. As a result, most states have laws against "pyramiding," a practice that offers incentives simply for recruiting new members of the network or IBOs. The laws require incentives to be paid only when sales are generated.[44]

You might want to check out the top multilevel marketing companies worldwide at the Web site noted here.

pyramid scheme

A selling process that involves the exchange of money for recruiting people to participate in a multilevel marketing company without producing sales. This business practice is not sustainable and is illegal in many states.

Link

Top Multilevel Marketing Companies

http://www.mlmrankings.com

Other Selling Environments

You've now seen how B2B, B2C, and direct selling work. Still, there are some other selling environments that you may also want to explore.

Entrepreneurial Selling

Martha Stewart (Martha Stewart Living Omnimedia), Mark Zuckerberg (Facebook), and Jeff Bezos (Amazon) each had a unique idea for a product or service. And while good ideas are key to building a business, what ultimately made each of these people successful was their ability to sell their idea to their customers and to their investors.

If you have the passion and vision to start your own business, you will need selling skills no matter what business you decide to create. Being an entrepreneur can be exhilarating, invigorating, and exciting. But it can also be challenging, time-consuming, and frustrating. That's why successful entrepreneurs, like successful salespeople, plan, do their homework, listen to customers, and make ideas and solutions come alive. It's no surprise that the traits of a successful salesperson discussed earlier in this chapter are the same traits that are required of an entrepreneur. Just like the different types of sales positions covered previously, there are virtually unlimited types of businesses that can be started by entrepreneurs. Consider the fact that the Internet levels the playing field because it provides business opportunities to all businesses regardless of size. Many of these entrepreneurial business opportunities were not available even a few years ago (and will undoubtedly provide new opportunities that don't even exist yet). So whether you are a Power Seller on eBay or a dog-walker in your neighborhood, you have the power to start the business of your dreams. This course will give you the invaluable skills and the insights necessary to do so. In fact, Chapter 15 is devoted entirely to entrepreneurial selling.

Domestic versus Global Selling

Does technology eliminate the need for salespeople, or does it create opportunities to connect the dots between the company and the customer? Are salespeople more important domestically or globally? Is there a different expectation for global selling? Although these are complex questions that could take an entire course to address, you might find it helpful to know that the outlook for personal selling both in the United States and internationally is very strong. According to a study of executives from the United States, France, and Mexico, "Personal selling is not going to go away and the future looks bright." Furthermore, the study found that with the use of technology, and in many cases because of it, it's even more important that salespeople not only know the product and the customer, but also the industry and the environment. The diversification of product lines and customers' needs for ancillary products such as service agreements, maintenance contracts, and multilingual options, make a skilled salesperson even more important in the transaction.[45]

Companies expand internationally for several reasons, one of which is that business in the United States is extremely competitive, so companies need more opportunities to increase sales and profits. In some cases, the only opportunity for growth is to expand internationally. But international selling presents an additional level of challenges, including cultural, political, legal, demographic, and economic issues. Nonetheless, countries such as Brazil, Russia, India, and China, often referred to as the BRIC nations, are quickly transforming the global economy. China and India account for one-third of the world's population, and so they represent a huge opportunity for global companies.[46] It's likely that a company for which you sell will be doing business internationally, and if it's not now, it will be some time soon. Some global companies include a one- to three-year sales assignment based in a foreign country.

Nonprofit Selling

Nonprofit organizations are those that use their proceeds to reinvest in the cause and are granted "tax-exempt" status from federal and other taxes.[47] Religious organizations, charitable organizations, trade unions, and other specifically defined organizations may qualify as nonprofit.[48] In fact, your school may be a nonprofit organization.

You might be wondering what selling has to do with nonprofit organizations. The fact is that fund-raising and the development of endowments are actually the lifeblood of nonprofit organizations. Your school may have a director of alumni relations and development. This is the person who secures donations for the continued development of the school and facilities; for example, if your school needs a new athletic facility or classroom building, much of the funding would likely come through the alumni office. Just like for-profit businesses, selling is the engine of nonprofit organizations as well. If you have a passion for a particular cause, such as the green movement, breast cancer, literacy, or education, among others, and want to focus on making a contribution by choosing a career in the nonprofit sector, you can find selling opportunities at many organizations. Although you may want to volunteer for some organizations before you make a career choice, there are paying career fund-raising and development positions in the nonprofit sector. Check out these Web sites to see jobs and job descriptions in the nonprofit sector.

Links

Learn more about nonprofit job opportunities and job descriptions.

Idealist

http://www.idealist.org/

Key Takeaways

- Companies sell to customers in **business-to-business (B2B)** or **business-to-consumer (B2C)** channels. The type of channel is based on the type of consumer who is buying.
- **B2B** selling differs from **B2C** selling because there are relatively few customers, larger purchases, and longer selling cycle.
- When you are engaged in **consultative selling**, you build a relationship and tailor solutions according to your customers' needs. When you are engaged in **transactional selling**, you are focused on a single sale or transaction.

- There are many different types of selling positions that may vary by industry. You may be involved in **outside sales**, which includes meeting face-to-face with your customers or you may be involved in **inside sales**, which includes contact by phone, e-mail, text, instant messaging (IM), or fax, as well as sales support activities.
- Other selling environments include **direct selling** (independent sales agents), entrepreneurial selling (a business started by an individual), global selling (selling in countries outside the United States), and nonprofit selling (also called fund-raising or development).

Exercises

1. Identify two companies that sell in both business-to-business and business-to-consumer channels. Discuss at least two ways in which they sell differently to businesses as opposed to consumers.
2. Identify a company that uses both transactional selling and consultative selling. Discuss the difference in the types of products that are sold in each example. Discuss the difference in the customer experience in each example.
3. Discuss the different types of sales positions you learned about in this section. Which type is attractive to you as a possible career? Why?
4. Discuss the reasons why someone might want to pursue a career in sales. Discuss the reasons someone might not want to pursue a career in sales.
5. Research companies and identify which offer some of the sales positions described in this chapter.
6. Contact a salesperson at a company in your area. Ask him to describe his role in the company, what type of customers he sells to, and what it takes to be successful in sales.
7. Visit the Web site of one of the multilevel marketing companies such as Pampered Chef (http://www.pamperedchef.com), Amway (http://www.amway.com/en), or Silpada Designs (http://www.silpada.com/public/). Discuss the pros and cons of being an independent business owner (IBO). Discuss the type of selling used by the IBO; is it transactional or consultative?

2.3 *Selling U*: Résumé and Cover Letter Essentials

Learning Objective

1. Learn how to position your education and experience to create a résumé and cover letter to get the job you want.

Think about how you first learned about the new Palm Pre smartphone or that Gatorade had changed its name to simply "G." How did you know that Pre had even more capabilities than the iPhone or that Gatorade was "moving to the next level"? Chances are it was some kind of advertising or public relations that made you aware of these products before you even tried them.

Now think about your personal brand. How will employers know about you and what you have to offer? A résumé and cover letter serve as your "advertising" campaign to prospective employers. Just like there are lots of ads about products and services, there are an overwhelming number of **résumés** and **cover letters** that employers have to review before inviting someone in for an interview. How do you make yours stand out? How do you increase your chances of being one of the people who are interviewed? How do you use your cover letter and your résumé to get the job you want?

There are a few important steps to follow to create the résumé and cover letter that will make you different and compelling to a prospective employer. You will use both of these to apply for jobs online and to send to people with whom you are networking, and you will even send them directly to companies for whom you would like to work. You only have an instant (think nanosecond) to make a lasting impression. If you think you only need a résumé to get a job, you should think again. Your cover letter can play an even more important role than your résumé. Here are some steps to help you create a cover letter that gets read and a résumé that gets you the interview. If you already have a résumé and cover letter, it's worth reviewing this section because you will learn some important tips to improve them.

Five Steps for a Résumé That Stands Out

Looking for the right job to start your career is a process that includes preparing your résumé and cover letter, getting your cover letter and résumé to the right people, going on interviews, and negotiating and accepting the right offer. You are at the beginning of the process; you'll learn about the rest of the process throughout the *Selling U* sections in this book. This section focuses entirely on creating your résumé and cover letter. Keep in mind that the only purpose for a résumé and cover letter is to get an interview. So your résumé and cover letter need to be crafted in a way that tells what your personal brand has to offer, or your **brand story**, in a concise and compelling way.

Step 1: Define Your Three Brand Points That Make You Unique and Provide Value to a Prospective Employer

If this sounds familiar, it should be. This was covered in detail in Chapter 1, but it is such an essential concept that it deserves repetition here. If you haven't identified your three brand points, you should go back and review the section. Your brand points are actually the foundation of your résumé and cover letter; it is in their summary that you compose your brand story.

You might think of creating a résumé that is a chronological summary of your background. This is good, but it is not compelling enough to differentiate yourself amid the sea of résumés. There are two important things to remember when creating your résumé:

1. Tell your brand story with your brand points.
2. Your brand points should be clear at a glance (literally).

Let's say your three brand points are leadership experience, academic excellence, and community service. Those three brand points make up your brand story, the story that you want to tell about yourself, so your résumé headings should highlight these areas.

To see what this means, review the two versions of the same résumé for Julianna Lanely in Figure 2.7 and Figure 2.8. The first one was written using a standard résumé approach; the second one was built by incorporating her brand points of marketing and event planning experience, academic excellence, and creative mind-set. Can you see the difference? Which résumé do you think is more compelling? Before you create (or refine) your résumé, identify your three brand points.

FIGURE 2.7 Standard Résumé

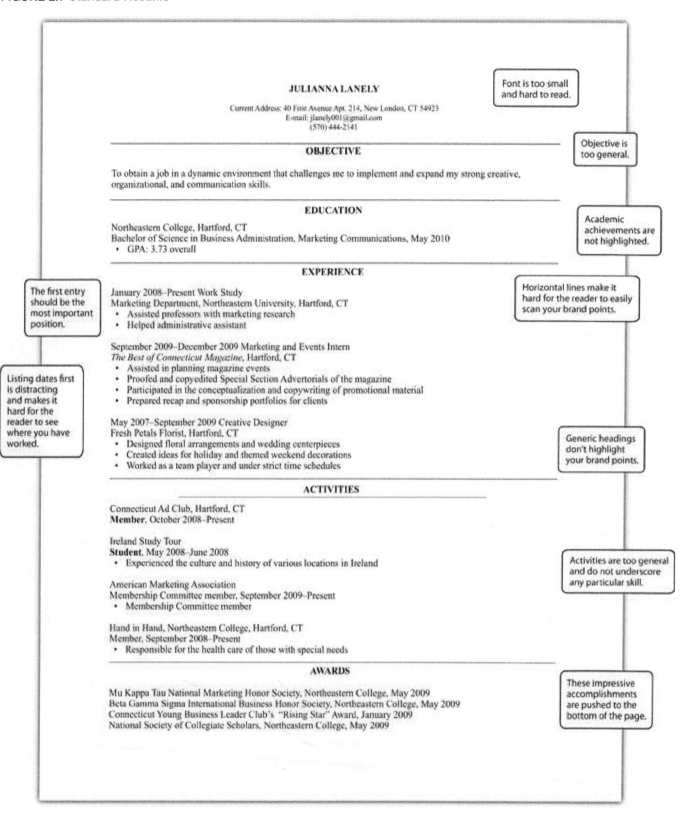

JULIANNA LANELY

Current Address: 40 First Avenue Apt. 214, New London, CT 54923
E-mail: jlanely001@gmail.com
(570) 444-2141

Font is too small and hard to read.

OBJECTIVE

To obtain a job in a dynamic environment that challenges me to implement and expand my strong creative, organizational, and communication skills.

Objective is too general.

EDUCATION

Northeastern College, Hartford, CT
Bachelor of Science in Business Administration, Marketing Communications, May 2010
- GPA: 3.73 overall

Academic achievements are not highlighted.

EXPERIENCE

January 2008–Present Work Study
Marketing Department, Northeastern University, Hartford, CT
- Assisted professors with marketing research
- Helped administrative assistant

September 2009–December 2009 Marketing and Events Intern
The Best of Connecticut Magazine, Hartford, CT
- Assisted in planning magazine events
- Proofed and copyedited Special Section Advertorials of the magazine
- Participated in the conceptualization and copywriting of promotional material
- Prepared recap and sponsorship portfolios for clients

May 2007–September 2009 Creative Designer
Fresh Petals Florist, Hartford, CT
- Designed floral arrangements and wedding centerpieces
- Created ideas for holiday and themed weekend decorations
- Worked as a team player and under strict time schedules

The first entry should be the most important position.

Listing dates first is distracting and makes it hard for the reader to see where you have worked.

Horizontal lines make it hard for the reader to easily scan your brand points.

Generic headings don't highlight your brand points.

ACTIVITIES

Connecticut Ad Club, Hartford, CT
Member, October 2008–Present

Ireland Study Tour
Student, May 2008–June 2008
- Experienced the culture and history of various locations in Ireland

American Marketing Association
Membership Committee member, September 2009–Present
- Membership Committee member

Hand in Hand, Northeastern College, Hartford, CT
Member, September 2008–Present
- Responsible for the health care of those with special needs

Activities are too general and do not underscore any particular skill.

AWARDS

Mu Kappa Tau National Marketing Honor Society, Northeastern College, May 2009
Beta Gamma Sigma International Business Honor Society, Northeastern College, May 2009
Connecticut Young Business Leader Club's "Rising Star" Award, January 2009
National Society of Collegiate Scholars, Northeastern College, May 2009

These impressive accomplishments are pushed to the bottom of the page.

FIGURE 2.8 Standard Résumé Incorporating Brand Points

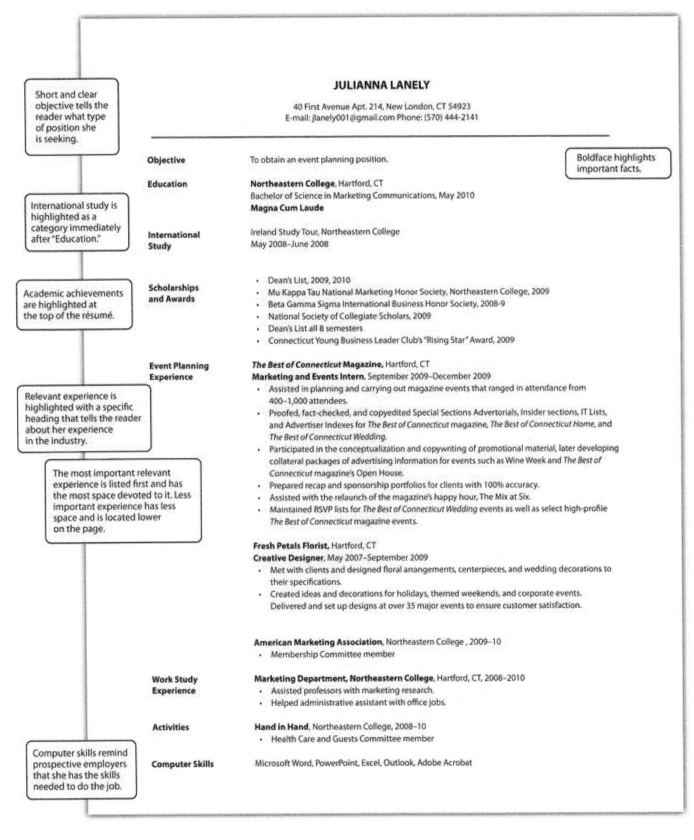

Short and clear objective tells the reader what type of position she is seeking.

International study is highlighted as a category immediately after "Education."

Academic achievements are highlighted at the top of the résumé.

Relevant experience is highlighted with a specific heading that tells the reader about her experience in the industry.

The most important relevant experience is listed first and has the most space devoted to it. Less important experience has less space and is located lower on the page.

Computer skills remind prospective employers that she has the skills needed to do the job.

Boldface highlights important facts.

JULIANNA LANELY

40 First Avenue Apt. 214, New London, CT 54923
E-mail: jlanely001@gmail.com Phone: (570) 444-2141

Objective — To obtain an event planning position.

Education — **Northeastern College**, Hartford, CT
Bachelor of Science in Marketing Communications, May 2010
Magna Cum Laude

International Study — Ireland Study Tour, Northeastern College
May 2008–June 2008

Scholarships and Awards
- Dean's List, 2009, 2010
- Mu Kappa Tau National Marketing Honor Society, Northeastern College, 2009
- Beta Gamma Sigma International Business Honor Society, 2008-9
- National Society of Collegiate Scholars, 2009
- Dean's List all 8 semesters
- Connecticut Young Business Leader Club's "Rising Star" Award, 2009

Event Planning Experience
The Best of Connecticut **Magazine,** Hartford, CT
Marketing and Events Intern, September 2009–December 2009
- Assisted in planning and carrying out magazine events that ranged in attendance from 400–1,000 attendees.
- Proofed, fact-checked, and copyedited Special Sections Advertorials, Insider sections, IT Lists, and Advertiser Indexes for *The Best of Connecticut* magazine, *The Best of Connecticut Home*, and *The Best of Connecticut Wedding*.
- Participated in the conceptualization and copywriting of promotional material, later developing collateral packages of advertising information for events such as Wine Week and *The Best of Connecticut* magazine's Open House.
- Prepared recap and sponsorship portfolios for clients with 100% accuracy.
- Assisted with the relaunch of the magazine's happy hour, The Mix at Six.
- Maintained RSVP lists for *The Best of Connecticut Wedding* events as well as select high-profile *The Best of Connecticut* magazine events.

Fresh Petals Florist, Hartford, CT
Creative Designer, May 2007–September 2009
- Met with clients and designed floral arrangements, centerpieces, and wedding decorations to their specifications.
- Created ideas and decorations for holidays, themed weekends, and corporate events. Delivered and set up designs at over 35 major events to ensure customer satisfaction.

American Marketing Association, Northeastern College , 2009–10
- Membership Committee member

Work Study Experience
Marketing Department, Northeastern College, Hartford, CT, 2008–2010
- Assisted professors with marketing research.
- Helped administrative assistant with office jobs.

Activities
Hand in Hand, Northeastern College, 2008–10
- Health Care and Guests Committee member

Computer Skills — Microsoft Word, PowerPoint, Excel, Outlook, Adobe Acrobat

Step 2: Choose Your Résumé Format and Font

Now that you have the foundation of your résumé message (or your three brand points), it's time to choose a résumé format. Executives in all industries encourage students and young professionals (those who have been working for five years or less) not to exceed one page for your résumé. In some cases, it may be difficult to keep all of your experience and accomplishments to one page, so choose those that best tell your brand story. As one executive said, "It better be worth my while to turn to page two."[49]

There are several appropriate résumé templates available at your campus career center or in Microsoft Word. The downside to some templates is that they are difficult to adjust or adapt. The most important thing to consider when you are choosing your résumé format is to be sure it is easy for the reader to skim. Some formats with horizontal lines separating the categories, or those with dates that precede company and position information, are harder to skim because the reader has to work too hard to see the brand story. See the comments in Figure 2.7 to recognize some things to avoid in your résumé.

It's easy to create a résumé that looks like Julianna Lanely's revised résumé shown in Figure 2.8. Simply watch this short video and see how you can format it.

Video Clip

Résumé Formatting
See how easy it is to format your résumé using a table in Word.

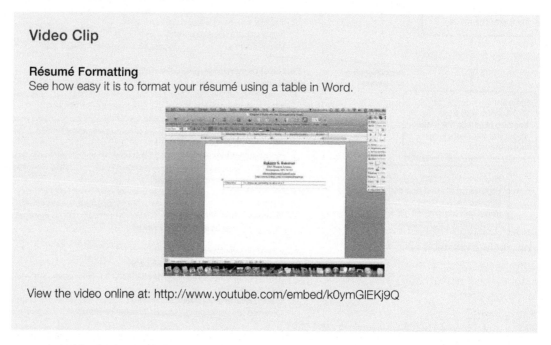

View the video online at: http://www.youtube.com/embed/k0ymGlEKj9Q

Once you choose the format you want to use, you should choose a font that you will use for your résumé and cover letter. The font should be easy to read like Arial or Times New Roman (Arial is a bit more contemporary; Times New Roman is more traditional). It's best to use twelve-point type (or eleven-point at the smallest) for ease of readability. If you need a little more space on your résumé, consider adjusting the margins slightly, keeping at least 0.7 for each margin. You don't want your résumé to feel crowded or that it is an effort to read.

Step 3: Choose Your Headings and Put the Most Important Ones First

Now that you've done your groundwork, it's time to actually create your résumé. Think about your brand points and then determine the headings you want to use. Use headings that help you tell your brand story at a glance. Don't focus yet on what you will write in each heading; that will be covered in Step 4.

There are some headings that are standard to include such as "Objective," "Education," and "Experience," but other headings should be used to support your brand story. For example, instead of having a heading for "Work Experience," be more specific and use "Sales Experience" to highlight that if it is one of your brand points.

One of the most critical things to remember is to put the most important things first. Start with a heading for "Objective," then "Education." As you gain more experience in your career, your education will move to the bottom. But at this point, it is a key selling point for your brand.

Now, it's time to put your brand points to work by choosing headings that tell your story. For example, if academic excellence is one of your brand points, you might consider adding a heading after "Education" called "Scholarships and Awards" or "Honors" to highlight honors and awards that demonstrate your academic excellence. This is the ideal place for things like dean's list, National Honor Society, or any other awards, honors, or scholarships that you have received.

It's a good idea for your next heading to reflect one of your brand points such as "Leadership Skills" or "Sales Experience" (or any other specific type of experience). If leadership skills are one of your brand points, it's better to *not* make the reader go all the way to the bottom of the page to read about your leadership skills under a generic heading called "Activities." If it's important to your brand story, bring your skills into focus in the first part of your résumé with a strong heading like "Leadership Skills." This section could include athletic, school or professional organization, or any other type of leadership position. If you don't have leadership skills, don't worry—you still have a lot to offer. Follow your brand points to tell your story.

Next, include your work experience. This is where you can really make your brand story come alive. Don't be restricted to a traditional chronological order of your jobs. If you have had an internship in marketing, sales, or other area that supports your brand points, make a separate heading for it, such as "Marketing Experience" or "Sales Experience." If you have had other jobs, you can simply add another heading after it called "Work Experience" below it. Or if your work experience has a common theme, you might want to name your heading "Retail Experience," "Customer Service Experience," or "Hospitality Experience." This approach tells the reader at a glance that you have valuable experience in the area you want to pursue. You should know that employers look for people who have worked in retail and in restaurants because they know that they can sell and work with customers. Use this type of experience to sell yourself.

If you have participated in projects or activities to support the community, you may want to include a heading for "Community Service." If you have additional activities that are worth noting, you might consider a heading for "Activities." It's best to avoid a long list of generic activities at the end of your résumé, so think about how they tell your brand story. It's best to include your most recent activities. Although you may include some key activities from high school, it's better if you can replace those with your more recent activities. It's not necessary to include the dates of your involvement.

It's a good idea to have a final heading for "Skills" at the end of your résumé. This should include computer software in which you are proficient such as Microsoft Word, PowerPoint, Excel, Access, Adobe Acrobat, and others. It's a good reminder to your prospective employer that you are skilled for any position. Although it may seem second nature to you to use these software products, there are employers who didn't learn them in school so they may not be aware that you are proficient in them.

A few things that should *not* be included on your résumé are "References available upon request," "Hobbies and Activities," or a photo. Prospective employers expect to check your references, you should have more substantial things to put on your résumé than hobbies and activities, and many companies cannot consider résumés with photos as it would be considered discrimination.

See Rakeem Bateman's résumé shown in Figure 2.9 to see how headings are used effectively to highlight his brand points of leadership skills, sales experience, and a committed work ethic.

FIGURE 2.9 Standard Résumé Incorporating Effective Headings

Rakeem S. Bateman
3901 Western Avenue, Minneapolis, MN 54321
Phone: 702-555-1234
rakeemsbateman@gmail.com
http://www.linkedin.com/in/rakeemsbateman

Objective	To obtain an internship in sales at a foodservice company.
Education	**Tri-State Community College**, Minneapolis, MN Associate's Degree, Business Administration, Expected 2010
Leadership Skills	**Green For Life**, Minneapolis, MN **President, Student Organization** • Provided leadership to 30-member student club that focuses on green initiatives in the community • Raised $2,300 to support sustainability efforts with a community service campaign called "Go Green Now"
Sales Experience	**Recovery Systems, Inc.**, Minneapolis, MN **Account Management Intern**, Summer 2009 • Conducted industry and client research for new business pitches for the $300 million systems disaster recovery provider • Assisted with new business presentation preparation including PowerPoint slides, video, and scripting • Developed social media strategy to develop a community for existing customers and attract new customers, including a blog, LinkedIn profile, and Twitter account; strategy generated over 30 new leads in 4 weeks • Provided weekly updates to 3 clients, including timelines and conference reports; created a new reporting dashboard that became the standard in the company for all client updates • Maintained budget and created reporting including graphs to easily communicate actual expenses compared to plan
Work Experience	**Olive Garden Restaurant**, Minneapolis, MN **Wait Staff**, June 2007–Present • Provided customer service to over 100 customers during each shift • Generated guest check average 8% higher than the restaurant average • Winner of "The Sweet Taste of Success" Sales Contest **Seymour and Jones Attorneys at Law**, Land of Lakes, MN **Administrative Assistant**, Summers 2005–6 • Maintained schedules and expenses for office to support 5 lawyers
Computer Skills	Proficient in Microsoft Suite (Word, Excel, PowerPoint), Outlook, Camtasia and iMovie video editing

Step 4: Write Your Bullet Points

Once you have determined your headings, it's time to make your brand points come alive with bullet points under each heading. Bullet points are better than a narrative format because they are easier for the reader to skim. But, since the reader is skimming, each bullet point is that much more important. Keep your bullet points concise, but specific, so that each delivers powerful information.

Start with your objective and write a short, specific goal. One sentence is perfect; you don't have to be flowery or profound. Something that helps the reader understand what you are looking for is best. For example, if you want to get a job in pharmaceutical sales, your objective might be, "To obtain a sales position at a pharmaceutical company." Or you might want to get a job in an advertising agency so your objective might be, "To obtain a full-time position in account management at an advertising agency." Short, sweet, to the point, and effective.

For your education, include the formal name of your college or university, city and state, formal degree (e.g., Bachelor of Arts, Communication Studies), and year or expected year of graduation. It's not necessary to include the range of years you attended school. Now that you are in college, it's best to remove your high school education. See Figure 2.9 for an example of how to list your education. You may be interested to know that your grade point average is not a requirement on a résumé. Generally, if your GPA is 3.5 or above, you may want to include it.[50] The fact is most business people don't recognize the significance of a GPA unless it's 4.0. So, if academic achievement is one of your brand points, you should consider adding a heading for "Scholarship and Awards" to demonstrate your accomplishments and make them come alive for the reader. If academics aren't your strong suit, don't include your GPA; just list your education.[51] If you have studied internationally, you might consider a heading or subheading named "International Study." Include the program name, school, and countries visited, as well as the dates of the travel.

Awards or honors can be listed as bullet points under the "Scholarship and Awards" heading. For experience headings such as "Leadership Experience," "Sales Experience," or "Customer Service Experience," list the name of the company, city and state, your title, and dates of employment. If you use boldface for the company name, it stands out and helps the reader see at a glance where you have worked. The bullet points in these sections are critical to setting yourself apart; they should be concise and specific, but descriptive, and they should focus on accomplishments and contributions, not a listing of activities or tasks. This will most likely take some time to write these bullet points, but it will be time well spent. Consider the difference between these two bullet points to describe a position at a restaurant:

- *Took orders over the phone and in person*

This statement can be more powerful when restated with quantitative details:

- *Provided customer service to over 100 patrons during every shift, including taking orders by phone and at table-side; named Associate of the Month in August 2009*

Consider the difference between these two bullet points to describe administrative responsibilities at an office:

- *Filled in for receptionist, answered phones, processed invoices*

This line can be more powerful when restated in the following manner:

- *Provided administrative support for the 30-person office; created new work flow for processing invoices that reduced turnaround time by 2 days*

Consider the difference between these two bullet points to describe responsibilities as a bank teller:

- *Processed customer transactions*

This statement can be more powerful when restated as the following:

- *Processed over 80 customer transactions daily with 100% accuracy.*

Your bullet points should help reinforce your brand points with details of how you delivered on those points. It might be helpful to write down all the things you did at each job and then identify the stories you can tell for each job. This is how you demonstrate traits such as ability to multitask, organizational skills, teamwork, and other skills.

Step 5: Review, Check Spelling, Proofread, and Repeat

It's true that some résumés are never even considered because of a typo or grammar error. After you finish your résumé, take a break, and then review it objectively. Does it clearly tell your brand story? Are your brand points the most important topics? If someone read your résumé, what would that person think you have to offer? Make any necessary adjustments. Then spell-check and proofread it carefully. It's a good idea to ask some people you trust—perhaps at your campus career center, a parent, professor, or mentor—to review and proofread your résumé. You can't be too cautious.

When you are satisfied that your résumé is perfect, print it on twenty-four-pound paper (you can buy it at your campus bookstore or any office supply store or Web site).

You've Got the Power: Tips for Your Job Search

How to Save It
It's best to save your résumé and cover letter in several formats. A Word document is standard for sending résumés and cover letters. However, online job posting boards remove formatting, so it's best to also save your documents as .txt files in Microsoft Word (File, Save As, for file type choose "Plain Text (*.txt)." Click OK when the dialogue box appears. Check your document to be sure elements are still in place; adjust accordingly, then save). It's also helpful to save your documents in PDF format by going to Acrobat.com.[52] It's a good idea to use a file name such as "John Jones Résumé" because it lets the reader know exactly what file he or she is opening and doesn't give away your working name.[53] Avoid file names such as "Official Résumé," or "Résumé January 2010" as they don't include your name and are not professional.

Three Steps for a Cover Letter That Gets Noticed

If you haven't prepared a cover letter to send with your résumé, you should consider writing one. According to a recent article in the *New York Times*, "Cover letters are still necessary, and in a competitive market they can give you a serious edge if they are written and presented effectively."[54] A cover letter is key if you need to set yourself apart, whether you are seeking an internship or a full-time position.

Step 1: Start with Your Three Brand Points

Maybe you are dreading the thought of writing a cover letter. It's easier than you think, since you have already identified your brand points. Write a summary statement for each of your three brand points. In other words, if you only had one minute to talk about your three brand points, what would you say about each one? Write two concise sentences for each point. It might be rough right now, but it will become the core of your cover letter.

Step 2: Understand the Elements of a Cover Letter

Now you just need to know how to structure your brand story to make it come alive for the reader. A cover letter has three major sections:

1. **First paragraph**. Introduction and purpose for your letter.[55]
2. **Second paragraph**. Reasons why you will bring value to the company (this is where you include your brand points).[56]
3. **Third paragraph**. Closing and follow-up.[57]

Since business people skim cover letters and résumés, it's a good idea to use boldface to highlight your brand points.[58] Take a look at the cover letter in Figure 2.10 to see how your brand points become the focus of your cover letter. It's important to *repeat* the highlights of your résumé in your cover letter so the reader can see at a glance how you can bring value as a prospective employee. Since you only have a few seconds to "sell" the reader on the fact that you are the right person for the job, you want to introduce the highlights in the cover letter and then provide the details in your résumé. Your cover letter and résumé work together to tell your brand story.

FIGURE 2.10 Effective Cover Letter

Julianna Lanely
40 First Avenue, Apartment 214
New London, CT 54923

June 26, 2010

Ms. Lynmarie Prosky
Vice President of Sales
Miller + Shane Event Group
9241 Old Town Road, Suite 401
Darien, CT 54992

Dear Ms. Prosky,

I attended an event planning career panel last year at Northeastern College where I heard you speak about Miller + Shane Event Group. Something you mentioned has stuck with me—to be successful, you must have passion for what you do. I believe I have the passion it takes to pursue a career in event planning. I am writing to express interest in an event planning position at Miller + Shane Event Group. I graduated from Northeastern College in May with a degree in marketing communications. As a recent graduate I believe I can bring new ideas, personal energy, and a fresh perspective to your company. Some highlights of my background include the following:

- **Event Planning Experience**—As a marketing and events intern at *The Best of Connecticut* magazine I assisted in planning and running events with attendance ranging from 400 to 1,000 people. I also helped conceptualize and create promotional material for all events, as well as prepared recap and sponsorship portfolios for clients with 100% accuracy.

- **Academic Excellence**—I graduated magna cum laude from Northeastern College and was named to the Dean's List in 2009–10. I have also been named to the National Society of Collegiate Scholars, Beta Gamma Sigma International Business Honor Society, and Mu Kappa Tau Marketing Honor Society. In addition, I was selected as one of the Connecticut Young Business Leader Club's "Rising Stars" and was featured in the January/February issue of Leadership Today magazine.

- **Creative Mind-Set**—I have worked as a creative designer at a hotel flower shop for for two years. I met with clients and developed ideas and created floral arrangements for over 35 major events.

I would appreciate opportunity to show you some samples of my work and discuss any open positions. I will contact you next week so we can set up a meeting time that is convenient for you. You can reach me at 570-444-2124 or jlanely001@gmail.com. I look forward to discussing your opportunities.

Sincerely,

Julianna Lanely

Julianna Lanely

Attachment

Besides the three core paragraphs of your cover letter, you will also want to know about the appropriate way to format a cover letter. Your cover letter should be limited to a single page and should include the same font that you used for your résumé. See Figure 2.11 for all the elements of a formal cover letter.

FIGURE 2.11 Elements of a Cover Letter

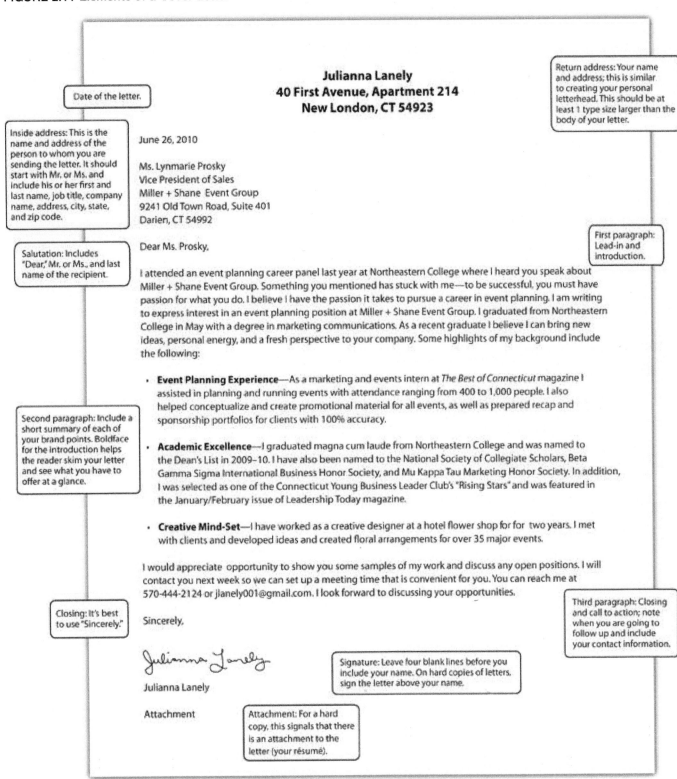

Step 3: Write Your Cover Letter

With your brand points in mind and the structure of a cover letter clearly defined, now you can get to writing. This is the place where you are able to demonstrate you personality and your selling skills. You can make your cover letter a powerful lead-in to your résumé and sell your prospective employer on the reasons why you should come in for an interview. As with your résumé, be sure to spell-check and proofread your cover letter carefully. Review your cover letter and résumé together to be sure your brand story is clear and powerful. Look at Rakeem Bateman's cover letter and résumé together in Figure 2.12 to see how the two documents can work together and really set you apart just at a glance.

FIGURE 2.12 Sample Cover Letter and Sample Résumé

Rakeem S. Bateman
3901 Western Avenue
Minneapolis, MN 54321

January 22, 2010

Mr. Jonathan Sikes
Director of Sales
Sorillos Foodservice Distribution
One Corporate Drive
Saint Paul, MN 54321

Dear Mr. Sikes,

I have an idea that will help you increase your sales. Does that sound like something that would be of interest to you?

I have a passion for creating solutions for customers and driving results for my customers and my company. I would like the opportunity to bring my skills to Sorillos Foodservice Distribution as an intern in your sales department. I have selling experience in addition to working toward my associate's degree in business administration at Tri-State Community College. Some of the highlights of my background include the following:

- **Sales Experience**—As an account management intern in the sales department at Recovery Systems, Inc., I participated in business development by doing research, generating and qualifying leads, and preparing PowerPoint and other presentation materials. I led the social networking efforts for the company and generated 30 new leads in 4 weeks by setting up and managing LinkedIn and Twitter accounts.

- **Leadership Skills**—As the president of the Green For Life student organization on campus, I provided leadership on community projects focused on sustainability. Our group raised $2,300 to support local recycling efforts as a result of our "Go Green Now" campaign.

- **Work Ethic and Commitment**—I am focused and determined to succeed. I have held a full-time job while attending school. In addition, I have participated in community service efforts.

I would like the opportunity to meet with you in person and talk about how I can help you and Sorillos Foodservice Distribution achieve your goals. I will contact you next week so we can set up a meeting time that is convenient for you. You can reach me at 702-555-1234 or rakeemsbateman@gmail.com. I look forward to discussing how I can bring value to Sorillos Foodservice Distribution.

Sincerely,

Rakeem S. Bateman

Rakeem S. Bateman

Attachment

Rakeem S. Bateman
3901 Western Avenue, Minneapolis, MN 54321
Phone: 702-555-1234
rakeemsbateman@gmail.com
http://www.linkedin.com/in/rakeemsbateman

Objective	To obtain an internship in sales at a foodservice company.
Education	**Tri-State Community College**, Minneapolis, MN Associate's Degree, Business Administration, Expected 2010
Leadership Skills	**Green For Life**, Minneapolis, MN **President, Student Organization** • Provided leadership to 30-member student club that focuses on green initiatives in the community • Raised $2,300 to support sustainability efforts with a community service campaign called "Go Green Now"
Sales Experience	**Recovery Systems, Inc.**, Minneapolis, MN **Account Management Intern**, Summer 2009 • Conducted industry and client research for new business pitches for the $300 million systems disaster recovery provider • Assisted with new business presentation preparation including PowerPoint slides, video, and scripting • Developed social media strategy to develop a community for existing customers and attract new customers, including a blog, LinkedIn profile, and Twitter account; strategy generated over 30 new leads • Provided weekly updates to 3 clients, including timelines and conference reports; created a new reporting dashboard that became the standard in the company for all client updates • Maintained budget and created reporting including graphs to easily communicate actual expenses compared to plan **Olive Garden Restaurant**, Minneapolis, MN **Wait Staff**, June 2007–Present • Provided customer service to over 100 customers during each shift • Generated guest check average 8% higher than the restaurant average • Winner of "The Sweet Taste of Success" Sales Contest
Work Experience	**Seymour and Jones Attorneys at Law**, Land of Lakes, MN **Administrative Assistant**, Summers 2005–6 • Maintained schedules and expenses for office to support 5 lawyers
Computer Skills	Proficient in Microsoft Suite (Word, Excel, PowerPoint), Outlook, Camtasia and iMovie video editing

This cover letter can be the basis of the letter you use for most situations. Now that you have your cover letter, you should adapt it and personalize it for every situation. For example, if you are applying for a job that is posted online, adapt the letter to show how your brand points address the needs of the position. You may even want to create one or two new brand points that also define your brand that you can change based on the job posting.

It's best to use your cover letter whenever you send your résumé to someone, whether you are responding to a job posting, networking, or sending out letters to your target companies. The *Selling U* section in Chapter 8 includes several ways to get your cover letter and résumé out to prospective employers.

Key Takeaways

- Your **résumé** and **cover letter** are your "advertising" tools for your personal brand.
- There are five steps that help you write a résumé that stands out from the crowd.
    1. Your brand points are the basis of your résumé because they define your brand and the value you can bring to a prospective employer.
    2. You can choose a résumé format that is easy for the reader to skim and see your brand points.
    3. The headings on your résumé help provide a framework to tell your brand story.
    4. The bullet points under each entry on your résumé should focus on your accomplishments and achievements, not just a listing of job tasks.
    5. Always spell-check and proofread your résumé carefully. In fact, it's a good idea to have several people review your résumé for accuracy before you send it to prospective employers.
- Your résumé should always be sent with your cover letter. Your cover letter highlights your brand points, which are further reinforced in your résumé.
- A cover letter contains three major parts: the first paragraph that acts as an introduction, the second paragraph that highlights the value you can bring to the company, and the third paragraph that is the closing.

Exercises

1. Visit your campus career center and learn about different formats for your résumé. Which ones do you like? Why? Which one will you use? Is it easy for the reader to skim and see your brand story?
2. Visit your campus career center and learn about the format for a cover letter. What elements are included in a formal cover letter, which are not included in a casual e-mail?

2.4 Review and Practice

Power Wrap-Up

Now that you have read this chapter, you should be able to understand the following opportunities that are available for a career in selling.

- You can **understand** what traits it takes to be a successful salesperson.

- You can **describe** the difference between business-to-business and business-to-consumer selling.
- You can **discuss** other selling environments such as direct, entrepreneurial, global, and nonprofit selling.
- You can **create** your résumé and cover letter so they quickly tell your brand story and focus on the value you can bring to a prospective employer.

Test Your Power Knowledge (answers are below)

1. Name at least four of the traits of successful salespeople that are discussed in the chapter.
2. What is WII-FM, and what role does it have in a career in selling?
3. What does pay-for-performance mean in selling?
4. Which is better, a job that pays more or a job that you enjoy?
5. Identify whether each of the following is a B2B or a B2C selling channel:

   a. ____ Selling a fence to a dog-training company.

   b. ____ Selling business cards to a small business owner.

   c. ____ Selling food to a school for the cafeteria.

   d. ____ Selling energy drinks to spectators at a race.

6. Are there selling opportunities in a nonprofit organization?
7. What are the foundation of your résumé and cover letter?

Power (Role) Play

Now it's time to put what you've learned into practice. The following are two roles that are involved in the same selling situation—one role is the customer, and the other is the salesperson. This will give you the opportunity to think about this selling situation from the point of view of both the customer and the salesperson.

Read each role carefully along with the discussion questions. Then, be prepared to play either of the roles in class using the concepts covered in this chapter. You may be asked to discuss the roles and do a role-play in groups or individually.

Trust Me?

Role: Seller of a home

You are the owner of a four-bedroom home in a very nice part of town. The home has a spectacular view and impeccable landscaping. It is decorated so well that everyone who comes over wishes his or her house could look like yours. You and your spouse have decided that you want to sell your home even though the market is soft. You think you have found the real estate agent with whom you want to list the house. You want to get top dollar for your home.

- What characteristics will you look for when you choose a real estate agent?
- What role do you have to help ensure a successful sale of your home?
- Is this a B2B or B2C sale?

Role: Real estate agent

You are a seasoned real estate agent with a loyal clientele in this part of town. You have a track record of selling very expensive homes and reaping the benefits. You have done very well because of your referral business. But lately, the soft economy has taken its toll on your sales. You believe that keeping the prices as low as possible will attract new buyers.

- Is this a B2B or B2C sale?

- If you are the real estate agent, how would you approach the sellers to get the listing at the price you want?
- What characteristics does the real estate agent need to be successful?
- What characteristics do the sellers need to be successful?

Put Your Power to Work: *Selling U* Activities

1. Follow the five steps in the chapter to create your résumé. Review your résumé with someone at the campus career center, a professor, a parent, or a mentor and get feedback as to how you might refine and improve it.

2. Follow the three steps in the chapter to write your cover letter. Review your cover letter and résumé with someone at the campus career center, a professor, or a mentor and get feedback as to how well they tell your brand story.

3. Use your cover letter and résumé to apply for an internship or job you want online. Adjust the cover letter to personalize your cover letter for the requirements of the position.

Test Your Power Knowledge Answers

1. Character and ability to build trust, ability to connect, listening skills, ability to ask the right questions, willingness to learn, drive to succeed, resilience and positive attitude, risk taking, ability to ask for the order, independence and discipline, flexibility, and passion.

2. WII-FM is the radio station that everyone listens to: *What's In It For Me*. It's always important to think about what you want out of life, and a career in selling has a lot of advantages for you, including financial opportunity, chance for advancement, and personal satisfaction.

3. Pay-for-performance is a term that describes the fact that you make more money based on selling more. Many sales positions include a pay-for-performance compensation structure, which means that the more you sell, the more money you make. Conversely, if you don't meet your objectives, your paycheck will be smaller.

4. Although compensation is important, it's not the only measure of a good job. Choosing a job that you enjoy with opportunities to achieve what you want and working in the environment that you like with people you like are important elements in evaluating a position.

5. a. B2B; b. B2B; c. B2B; d. B2C

6. Yes, fund-raising and development (as in creating and building endowments) are some of the selling opportunities available in the nonprofit sector.

7. Your brand points are the foundation of your résumé and cover letter.

Endnotes

1. Steve Jobs, "You've Got to Find What You Love," commencement address at Stanford University, Palo Alto, CA, June 12, 2005, in *Stanford Report*, June 14, 2005, http://news.stanford.edu/news/2005/june15/jobs-061505.html (accessed June 16, 2009).

2. Steve Jobs, "You've Got to Find What You Love," commencement address at Stanford University, Palo Alto, CA, June 12, 2005, in *Stanford Report*, June 14, 2005, http://news.stanford.edu/news/2005/june15/jobs-061505.html (accessed June 16, 2009).

3. Dave Kahle, "The Four Characteristics of Successful Salespeople," *Industrial Distribution* 97, no. 4 (April 2008): 54.

4. Robert W. Bly, "Everyone Loves a Story," *Target Marketing* 32, no. 6 (June 2009): 23.

5. Kerry Johnson, "Five Characteristics of Peak Sales Performers," Event Solution International, http://www.eventsolution.com/education/businessarticles.html (accessed June 16, 2009).

6. Monroe Porter, "Six Common Characteristics of Successful Salespeople," *Pro* 20, no. 6 (May 2008): 33.

7. Pamela J. Holland and Marjorie Brody, *Help! Was That a Career-Limiting Move?* (Jenkintown, PA: Career Skills Press, 2005).

8. Steve Atlas, "Listening for Buying Signals: Missing Your Prospects' Buying Signals," *Selling Power* 20, no. 2, http://www.sellingpower.com/content/article.php?a=5350 (accessed March 16, 2010).

9. Steve Atlas, "Listening for Buying Signals: Missing Your Prospects' Buying Signals," *Selling Power* 20, no. 2, http://www.sellingpower.com/content/article.php?a=5350 (accessed March 16, 2010).

10. Kim Michael, "The Most Powerful Tool in the Sales Arsenal—Part 1," *American Salesman* 54, no. 6 (June 2009): 3.

11. Paul Blake, interview with the author, Greater Media Philadelphia, Philadelphia, PA, December 11, 2009.

12. John F. Tanner, Jr., Christophe Fournier, Jorge A. Wise, Sandrine Hollet, and Juliet Poujol, "Executives' Perspectives of the Changing Role of the Sales Profession: View from France, the United States, and Mexico," *Journal of Business and Industrial Marketing* 23, no. 3 (2008): 193.

13. Margaret Norton, "Is the Successful Salesperson Made or Born?" EzineArticles, http://ezinearticles.com/?Is-the-Successful-Sales-Person-Made-Or-Born?&id=1020044 (accessed June 16, 2009).

14. Kelley Robertson, "10 Characteristics of Successful Salespeople," Business Know-How, http://www.businessknowhow.com/marketing/successful-salesperson.htm (accessed June 16, 2009).

15. Geoffrey James, "Which Generation Is Best at Selling?" BNET, July 29, 2009, http://blogs.bnet.com/salesmachine/?p=4424&page=2 (accessed July 27, 2009).

16. Dave Kahle, "The Four Characteristics of Successful Salespeople," *Industrial Distribution* 97, no. 4 (April 2008): 54.

17. Dave Kahle, "Characteristics of a Successful Professional—A Propensity to Take Risks," *Agency Sales* 36, no. 6 (June 2006): 40.

18. Lisa McCullough, "Lessons from a Stunt Woman," video, *Selling Power*, http://www.sellingpower.com/content/video/?date=3/23/2007 (accessed March 16, 2010).

19. Jeffrey Gitomer, "No Risk No Reward," video, May 17, 2008, http://www.youtube.com/watch?v=UBHBk-A4a5M (accessed August 28, 2009).

20. Monroe Porter, "Six Common Characteristics of Successful Salespeople," *Pro* 20, no. 6 (May 2008): 33.

21. "What Do Salespeople Want?" *BizTimes*, March 30, 2007, http://www.biztimes.com/news/2007/3/30/what-do-salespeople-want (accessed June 19, 2009).

22. Mike McCue, "Lessons from the Master," *Sales and Marketing Management*, March 1, 2008, 22–24.

23. Anna Muoio, "Sales School," *Fast Company*, December 18, 2007, http://www.fastcompany.com/magazine/19/one.html?page=0%2C2 (accessed June 23, 2009).

24. John F. Tanner, Jr., Christophe Fournier, Jorge A. Wise, Sandrine Hollet, and Juliet Poujol, "Executives' Perspectives of the Changing Role of the Sales Profession: View from France, the United States, and Mexico," *Journal of Business and Industrial Marketing* 23, no. 3 (2008): 193.

25. Brandon Griggs, "iPhone 3GS Launch Has App Developers Seeing Gold," *CNN.com*, June 19, 2009, http://www.cnn.com/2009/TECH/06/19/iphone.3gs.launch (accessed June 26, 2009).

26. Anna Muoio, "Sales School," *Fast Company*, December 18, 2007, http://www.fastcompany.com/magazine/19/one.html?page=0%2C3 (accessed June 23, 2009).

27. Michael Levens, *Marketing: Defined, Explained, Applied* (Upper Saddle River, NJ: Pearson Prentice Hall, 2010), 186.

28. Barton A. Weitz, Stephen B. Castleberry, and John F. Tanner, Jr., *Selling: Building Partnerships*, 7th ed. (New York: McGraw-Hill Irwin), 10.

29. Gerald L. Manning, Barry L. Reece, and Michael Ahearne, *Selling Today: Creating Customer Value*, 11th ed. (Upper Saddle River, NJ: Pearson Prentice Hall), 10.

30. Charles M. Futrell, *Fundamentals of Selling: Customers for Life through Service*, 10th ed. (New York: McGraw-Hill Irwin, 2008), 55.

31. Gerald L. Manning, Barry L. Reece, and Michael Ahearne, *Selling Today: Creating Customer Value*, 11th ed. (Upper Saddle River, NJ: Pearson Prentice Hall), 12.

32. Barton A. Weitz, Stephen B. Castleberry, and John F. Tanner, Jr., *Selling: Building Partnerships*, 7th ed. (New York: McGraw-Hill Irwin), 36.

33. Leslie Cauley, "AT&T: We're All About Wireless," *USA Today*, July 31, 2008, http://www.usatoday.com/tech/wireless/phones/2008-07-31-att-iphone-stephenson-apple_N.htm?csp=34 (accessed June 25, 2009).

34. Justin Sorkin, "AT&T Urging Apple to Extend Its iPhone Exclusive Agreement until 2011," *TopNews.com*, April 15, 2009, http://topnews.us/content/24841-att-urging-apple-extend-its-iphone-exclusive-agreement-till-2011 (accessed June 25, 2009).

35. American Customer Service Index, "Rise in Consumer Satisfaction Continues—Now Followed by Other Economic Indicators," First Quarter 2009, https://www.hotelnewsresource.com/article38884.html (accessed June 23, 2009).

36. Michael Levens, *Marketing: Defined, Explained, Applied* (Upper Saddle River, NJ: Pearson Prentice Hall, 2010), 184.

37. Heather Baldwin, "What Does Sales 2.0 Mean for You?" Selling Power Sales Management eNewsletter, March 3, 2008, http://www.sellingpower.com/content/newsletter/issue.php?pc=801 (accessed March 16, 2010).

38. Charles M. Futrell, *Fundamentals of Selling: Customers for Life through Service*, 10th ed. (New York: McGraw-Hill Irwin, 2008), 11.

39. Anna Muoio, "Sales School," *Fast Company*, December 18, 2007, http://www.fastcompany.com/magazine/19/one.html?page=0%2C3 (accessed June 23, 2009).

40. Direct Selling Association, "About Direct Selling," http://www.dsa.org/aboutselling/what (accessed June 21, 2009).

41. Alina Cho, "Avon, Mary Kay Making Comeback," *CNN American Morning*, June 17, 2009, http://amfix.blogs.cnn.com/2009/06/17/avon-mary-kay-making-comeback (accessed June 21, 2009).

42. Charisse Jones, "Want a Recession-proof Job? Think Direct Sales," *USA Today*, May 14, 2009, 1B.

43. "Multilevel Marketing," *Inc.*, http://www.inc.com/encyclopedia/multilevel-marketing.html (accessed June 21, 2009).

44. Federal Trade Commission, "The Bottom Line about Multilevel Marketing Plans and Pyramid Schemes," http://www.ftc.gov/bcp/edu/pubs/consumer/invest/inv08.shtm (accessed June 21, 2009).

45. John F. Tanner, Jr., Christophe Fournier, Jorge A. Wise, Sandrine Hollet, and Juliet Poujol, "Executives' Perspectives of the Changing Role of the Sales Profession: Views from France, the United States, and Mexico," *Journal of Business and Industrial Marketing* 23, no. 3 (2008): 193.

46. George E. Belch and Michael A. Belch, *Advertising and Promotion: An Integrated Marketing Communications Perspective*, 8th ed. (New York: McGraw-Hill Irwin, 2008), 653–57.

47. Carter McNamara, "Starting a Nonprofit Organization," Free Management Library, http://managementhelp.org/strt_org/strt_np/strt_np.htm#anchor516676 (accessed June 23, 2009).

48. Internal Revenue Service, "Tax Information for Charities & Other Non-Profits," http://www.irs.gov/charities/index.html (accessed June 23, 2009).

49. Connie Pearson-Bernard, "Careers in Communications Night," presentation at West Chester University, West Chester, PA, March 23, 2009.

50. Kim Richmond, *Brand You*, 3rd ed. (Upper Saddle River, NJ: Pearson Prentice Hall, 2008), 156.

51. Kim Richmond, *Brand You*, 3rd ed. (Upper Saddle River, NJ: Pearson Prentice Hall, 2008), 156.

52. Kim Richmond, *Brand You*, 3rd ed. (Upper Saddle River, NJ: Pearson Prentice Hall, 2008), 224.

53. Kim Richmond, *Brand You*, 3rd ed. (Upper Saddle River, NJ: Pearson Prentice Hall, 2008), 226.

54. Phyllis Korkki, "A Cover Letter Is Not Expendable," *New York Times*, February 15, 2009, business section, 10.

55. Kim Richmond, *Brand You*, 3rd ed. (Upper Saddle River, NJ: Pearson Prentice Hall, 2008), 162.

56. Kim Richmond, *Brand You*, 3rd ed. (Upper Saddle River, NJ: Pearson Prentice Hall, 2008), 162.

57. Kim Richmond, *Brand You*, 3rd ed. (Upper Saddle River, NJ: Pearson Prentice Hall, 2008), 162.

58. Kim Richmond, *Brand You*, 3rd ed. (Upper Saddle River, NJ: Pearson Prentice Hall, 2008), 162.

CHAPTER 3
The Power of Building Relationships: Putting Adaptive Selling to Work

Video Ride-Along with Tonya Murphy, General Sales Manager at Radio Station WBEN-FM

Meet Tonya Murphy. Tonya has been in sales for seventeen years and has developed long-term relationships with her customers. She is a general sales manager and responsible for the salespeople that sell advertising for WBEN-FM. Customers include national advertisers such as Toyota, AT&T, and Comcast as well as local businesses that want to build awareness and drive traffic to their stores. Tonya believes that building trust is key to building relationships and ultimately building sales. Listen to Tonya share her insights about why she believes relationships are so important in selling and her tips for building successful relationships.

Ride along with Tonya and hear her insights about the power of relationships in selling.

View the video online at: http://www.youtube.com/embed/vQTTyjev9uY

3.1 The Power of Relationship Selling

Learning Objectives

1. Understand why relationships are so important in selling.
2. Explain how relationships bring value through consultative selling.
3. Identify who wins in the win-win-win relationship model.
4. Explain how networking builds relationships and businesses.

It was 4:00 p.m. on Christmas Eve and Ray Rizzo's father, in town for the annual family get-together, had forgotten to bring his suit. What made the situation even more challenging was that

Ray's father is rather portly with a forty-eight-inch waist and even broader shoulders, a build that requires a fifty-three-short jacket. Ray and his father rushed to Mitchells, a local clothing store in Connecticut, and asked Jack Mitchell, the owner, for his help. It was hard to imagine that Ray's father would possibly be able to get a suit or even a sport jacket tailored to fit in time for the family gathering. After all, it was Christmas Eve, and the store would be closing in an hour. Jack didn't hesitate and immediately enlisted Domenic, the head tailor, and before 6 o'clock that evening, the largest pair of pants and jacket in the store were tailored to fit Ray's father perfectly. Needless to say, Ray is a customer for life.[1]

This situation is what Jack Mitchell calls a hug. If you go shopping for clothes at Mitchells or Richards in Connecticut, you will get hugged. Maybe not literally, but you will most definitely get "hugged" figuratively. Jack Mitchell, the CEO of Mitchells/Richards and author of *Hug Your Customers: The Proven Way to Personalize Sales and Achieve Astounding Results*, says, "Hugging is a way of thinking about customers. To us, hugging is a softer word for passion and relationships. It's a way of getting close to your customers and truly understanding them."[2]

From Personal to Problem Solving

Think about your best friend. You know her so well that you can just about finish each other's sentences. You know her favorite flavor and brand of ice cream, and you can sense when she is having a bad day. You text and talk to her all the time; you even go out of your way to surprise her sometimes with a gift that you know she will like. You have a great relationship with her.

Now think about the last time you went into your favorite restaurant. Was it the same kind of experience? Did the host greet you by name and seat you at your favorite table? Did the waitperson remember that you like to drink raspberry-flavored iced tea? Was your fish served with the sauce on the side, just the way you like it? Were you delighted with a new flavor of cappuccino after dinner? When these things happen, the people at the restaurant make you feel special; after all, you are the reason they are there. When you have a relationship like this with the people at the restaurant, you are more inclined to return to the restaurant again and again. If these things don't happen, it is easier for you to choose a different restaurant the next time you go out.

The bottom line is that to be successful in selling, any kind of selling, you have to make selling personal. People do business with people, not with companies. Even in the business-to-business (B2B) selling channel, it is people who are making decisions on behalf of the company for which they work. Every sale starts with a relationship. If your relationship is strong, there is a higher likelihood of a sale and a loyal repeat customer. That means you have to get to know your customer on a one-to-one basis to understand what he wants, what he needs, and what resources he has. This concept is called relationship selling (or consultative selling).[3] It is defined by working personally with your customer to understand his needs, put his needs first, and provide consultation to help him make the best decision for himself or his business.

You might be thinking that selling is about the product or service, not about relationships. But that's not true. You may have heard someone say, "He's just a pushy salesman," or you may have experienced someone trying to give you the "hard sell." The fact is that selling has evolved dramatically over the past thirty years. Business is more competitive. The use of technology and the expanded number of product and service offerings have developed a need for consultative selling in more industries than ever before. It used to be that salespeople wanted to simply make a sale, which meant that the sale began and ended with the transaction. But now, it's not enough to just make the sale. In today's competitive world, it's how you think about the customer that matters.[4] It's the difference between giving the customer what she needs rather than what you want to sell her.[5] The fact is that the sale is just one small part of the relationship. The real essence of selling is in the relationship.[6]

The salesperson has a new role in most companies. The days of the salesperson as "product pusher" are just about gone. Customers in B2B and business-to-consumer (B2C) environments want and demand more. Consider the evolution of some major industries. Many of the leading hotel chains keep your preferences in a database so that their front desk sales team can recognize you personally at check-in and provide the queen-sized bed in a nonsmoking room on the quiet side of the property that you prefer. Restaurants work hard to learn, remember, and greet you by your name, maintain your favorite table, wine, and entrée, and prepare to anticipate your every need. Airlines have tools to recognize you and the fact that you like an aisle seat as far forward as possible in the plane.[7] All these tactics are steeped in the theory that customers make choices on the relationship they have with brands. In each one of these situations, the salesperson is the difference that sets a brand apart at the **moment of truth**, the moment the customer comes in contact with the brand.[8] Some brands understand how important each moment of truth is when creating relationships with customers. For example, Southwest Airlines makes their Web site easy to use, has humans answer the phone, and has flight and ground attendants that make it a pleasure to travel with them.

FIGURE 3.1
Selling depends on developing relationships with customers.

moment of truth
Any time the customer comes in contact with a brand.

Power Selling: Lessons in Selling from Successful Brands

Boot Camp

Johnson Controls, manufacturer of heating and air conditioning systems, thinks that consultative selling is so important that it holds a Basic Boot Camp for the company's territory managers at its headquarters in Norman, Oklahoma, that focuses on leveraging relationships in selling. The classroom-style "boot camp" includes interactive exercises, product training, and business support training. The company's commitment to consultative selling doesn't end there. Participants who score at least an 85 percent on their final grade for the Basic Boot Camp and spend six months out in the field can qualify to attend the elite Special Operations Training, which is by invitation only.[9]

Relationships are so important in selling that one study surveyed one hundred top B2B salespeople and found that they attribute 79 percent of their success to their relationships with customers.[10] It is the relationship with a customer that allows you to bridge the gap between a customer's problem and the solution. The relationship is the framework for consultative selling; it's what allows you to have an open, honest dialogue, ask the right questions, understand your customer's needs, and go beyond advising to helping your customer make the decision that's right for her.[11]

Common Ground

Selling relationships start as personal relationships. Making a personal connection is vital in the two to ten minutes of a customer encounter or meeting.[12] Think about the last time you bought a new cell phone. Chances are, if the person didn't establish rapport with you from the start, you probably walked away and bought the phone from a different salesperson, maybe even at a different store. The relationship includes a sincere bond that goes beyond business and includes common interests and goals.[13] If you are selling medical imaging equipment to hospitals, you want to build relationships with the administrators, doctors, and nurses who will be using your equipment in each hospital. When you build a relationship starting with what's important to each person individually, it's easier to expand that relationship to sharing information and problem solving from a business perspective. As Bob Fitta, a manufacturer's rep for several tool companies said about Paul Robichaud, owner of Robi Tools, "I got to know him as a business person and a real person, and that relationship has endured."[14]

But consultative selling is more than simply building rapport. In fact, consultative selling goes beyond the product or service you are selling; it even goes beyond the selling process. It is the "X factor," the intangible element that makes a customer choose your product or service even when the competition is priced lower. Consultative selling is about *your* personal involvement and sincere focus on problem solving that goes beyond selling to true partnership with the customer.

lifetime value

The worth of the transactions that are done with a customer over the life of a relationship with a company.

Consultative selling doesn't start and stop at specific times during the relationship. In fact, it defines the relationship before the sale, during the sale, and after the sale.[15] You will learn about the seven steps of the selling process in Chapter 7 through Chapter 13 and how building long-term relationships and consultative selling are the basis of each step. The concept of building professional relationships is apparent in this example: If you are selling insurance, consider the fact that your customer may eventually buy a home, have a family, or purchase a second property. So the relationship you develop when you sell him car insurance as a young single man could and should be nurtured and developed over time to provide solutions that answer his needs as his lifestyle changes. Having this long-term view of customer relationships is called focusing on **lifetime value**. It means that you consider not just one transaction with a customer, but also the help and insight you can provide throughout the entire time frame during which you do business with him. So, although you may only provide him with basic car insurance now, over the course of more than twenty-five years that you do business with him, you may ultimately sell him thousands of dollars of insurance and investment products that meet his changing needs. But that won't happen if you don't continue your relationship and keep in touch, focusing on topics and events that are important to him. If you focus only on the immediate sale, you will miss a lot of business, not to mention future referrals.

There are several elements that can be included in the calculation of the lifetime value of a customer. However, a simple formula is

$$\text{dollar value of purchase} \times \text{gross profit percent} \times \text{number of purchases.}$$

For example, if a customer shopped at a retailer and spent $75 on one purchase that had a gross profit of 30 percent, the lifetime value of that customer would be $22.50, calculated as

$$\$75 \times 30\% \times 1 = \$22.50.$$

If the customer made five purchases for $75 each over the course of the time she shopped with the retailer (let's say five years), at a gross profit of 30 percent, the lifetime value of the customer would be $112.50, calculated as

$$\$75 \times 30\% \times 5 = \$112.50.^{[16]}$$

So you can see that the concept of retaining a customer for more than one purchase can provide financial benefits. In addition, working with the same customer over the course of time provides an opportunity to learn more about the customer's needs and provide solutions that better meet those needs.

CRM Tools Help You Manage Relationships

With so many demands on your time as a salesperson, sometimes it's easy to lose track of some customers and not follow up, which means that you may only be developing short-term relationships.

Or you might unintentionally let your relationship with a customer "lapse into laziness," which means that you let the relationship run on autopilot, relying on your established relationship to keep the business going. In this case, there's usually no pressing reason to change; you might think that as long as the customer is happy, everything is OK. But it's best to avoid complacency because the world is constantly changing. While you are enjoying a comfortable, easy relationship, there are probably new business challenges that you should be learning about from your customer. Or worse, you may open the door to a competitor because you weren't bringing new and relevant ideas to your customer and he began to think of you more as a nice guy than a resource for advice and new ideas.[17]

Many companies use **customer relationship management (CRM)** tools, which are technology solutions that organize all of a customer's interactions with a company in one place. In other words, CRM is a customer database that holds all the information regarding a transaction (e.g., date; products purchased; salesperson who sold the products; and name, address, and contact information of the customer). In addition, it captures all communication the customer has had with the company, including calls made to the company call center, posts and reviews made to the company Web site, and the details of each sales call made by a salesperson. Some CRM tools are extremely sophisticated and help the salesperson and the company to manage relationships with prospects and customers. Other CRM tools are simpler and are focused on helping the salesperson manage her relationship with prospects and customers.[18]

A CRM tool works in a variety of ways. Here are a few examples. A construction contractor calls a toll-free number for a plumbing supply company after seeing an ad in a trade journal. The prospect inquiry is sent via e-mail to the appropriate salesperson. The salesperson reviews the CRM system to see if there have been any previous contacts with the customer and if there is any information about the customer and his business. Then he returns the prospect's phone call and sets up a date to meet him to learn more about his business needs. The salesperson makes a note in the CRM system about the phone call and the date of the meeting and sets a follow-up reminder for himself for the meeting and for three days after the meeting. When the salesperson meets with the prospect, he learns that the prospect has five developments that he manages. The salesperson makes a note in the CRM system so everyone from the company who comes in contact with the prospect, such as other salespeople or customer service, know this information about the prospect.

CRM tools can be extremely helpful in managing customer relationships, especially where there are multiple people in the company who come in contact with prospects and customers. CRM tools also make it easier to understand the lifetime value of a customer since all purchases, inquiries, and other contacts are included in the system. It is the information that is gathered in a CRM system that helps a salesperson better understand customer behavior, communication patterns, and short- as well as long-term needs. For example, many companies offer loyalty programs as a tactic to increase sales but also to gather information about customer preferences to offer more relevant messages and offers. CRM tools are used to manage loyalty programs, such as Best Buy Rewards Zone, Southwest Airlines Rapid Rewards, and the Safeway card for their different local grocery chains. This information is then used for marketing and selling purposes. Best Buy can identify all the recent purchasers of Hewlett-Packard (HP) printers and send them an e-mail for HP ink cartridges. CRM tools are used to manage customer relationships in other ways. For example, Starbucks uses Salesforce.com, a widely used CRM tool, to power their MyStarbucksIdea Web site. The Web site is a collaboration and feedback tool that engages customers in providing ideas to the company. To manage the relationships with customers online, Starbucks uses a CRM tool. This allows Starbucks to provide personal feedback to each customer on all the ideas they submit. Visit MyStarbucksIdea.com to see this interactive suggestion box.

customer relationship management (CRM)

The process a company uses to organize and track their current and potential customer information.

Link

MyStarbucksIdea
http://mystarbucksidea.force.com

Face Time

FIGURE 3.2

Business entertaining is a good way to build relationships and get to know your customer outside the office.

© 2010 Jupiterimages Corporation

So you might think that customer relationships are easy to maintain with text messaging, e-mail, and other technology-based methods of communication. After all, that's how you communicate with your friends. But while technology can enhance an established relationship because it allows you to provide information and insight at a moment's notice, the fact is that most significant customer relationships, especially in B2B selling, require face-to-face communication.[19]

In this world of high-tech instant communication, some relationships can easily become "low-touch," or missing the human element. Meeting with and entertaining customers is an important part of the selling process. It helps you get to know customers in an environment outside the office, in a casual or social place such as a restaurant, sporting event, or concert. These can be excellent opportunities for you and your customer to "let your hair down," relax, and enjoy each other's company. Many sales positions include an entertainment budget for this reason. Taking someone out to eat is not the only part of a selling relationship, but it's an important part of building and developing a connection. One sales manager said that he can tell when one of his salespeople is struggling simply by reviewing his expense reports. He looks for activities that take place outside business hours because those are the activities that build relationships. In fact, according to one study, 71 percent of top-achieving salespeople use entertainment as a way to get closer to their customers.[20]

Fore Relationships

What makes golf a good way to build a business relationship? During eighteen holes of golf, the typical golfer actually hits the ball for only two and a half minutes during a four-plus hour round of golf.[21]

Speaker and author Suzanne Woo describes the secrets of using golf to build business relationships.

http://www.bnet.com/2422-13722_23-323018.html

Source: BNET

R-commerce

r-commerce

The act of establishing and building relationships with customers.

You've probably heard of e-commerce, selling products and services on the Internet, and m-commerce, selling products and services via mobile devices such as cell phones and smart phones. But you probably haven't heard of **r-commerce**, a term that refers to relationship marketing, which establishes and builds mutually beneficial relationships.

Terry L. Brock, an international marketing coach and syndicated columnist, says salespeople have the opportunity to make the difference in their relationships with the little things. Sending a thank-you note after a meeting, forwarding an article or video on a topic you discussed, remembering the names of your customer's children, even providing a personal suggestion for a vacation spot are all examples of little things that can set you apart from every other salesperson. You might think that these "little things" aren't important when you get into the big world of business. But Harvey Mackay, renowned author, speaker, and business owner, says it best: "Little things mean a lot? Not true. Little things mean everything."[22] Developing your own r-commerce strategy can help set you apart in sales. It's expected that you will make phone calls and follow up; it's the extra personal touch that makes your customer feel special and helps establish a strong relationship.

It's the Little Things

Here's an idea for a small activity that can turn into big opportunity along the way: every day take fifteen minutes at the beginning of the day to write three notes or e-mails—one to a customer, one to a prospect, and one to a friend just to say hi, follow up, or send an article of interest. At the end of the week, you will have made 15 contacts and 750 by the end of the year. What a great way to build relationships by doing the little things that make you stand out.[23]

Trust Me

"The check is in the mail." "The doctor will see you in ten minutes." "I'll call you tomorrow." How many times have you heard these promises, or ones like them? When people make promises that they don't keep, you lose trust in them. It's unlikely that you will trust a person who doesn't deliver on what he or she says.

Trust is a critical element in every relationship. Think again about your best friend. Is she someone you can trust? If you tell her something in confidence, does she keep it to herself? If you need her for any reason, will she be there for you? Chances are, you answered "yes," which is why she is your best friend. You believe that she will do what she says she will do, and probably more.

You can see why trust is so important in selling. If your customer doesn't believe that you will actually do what you say you are going to do, you do not have a future in selling. Trust is built on open and honest communication. Trust is about building partnerships. Salespeople build trust by following up on their promises. They are accessible (many times 24/7), and they work to help their customers succeed. Customers trust you when they believe you have *their* best interest at heart, not your personal motivation. According to Tom Reilly, author of the book *Value Added Selling*, "Consultative selling is less about technique and more about trust." Trust is what gives a relationship value. It is the cornerstone of selling. Trust creates value. In fact, one B2B customer described his salesperson by saying he was like an employee of the company. Another described her salesperson in terms of problem ownership by saying, "When we have a problem, he has a problem."[24] Trust is equally important in B2C selling. For example, at Zen Lifestyle, a salon in Edinburgh, United Kingdom, the approach to customers is described as soft sell with a focus on educating customers and providing information. Customers are encouraged to try products in the smallest size to determine whether they like the product. It is only after they have liked it that larger and more economical sizes are suggested. "This helps develop a relationship between customers and therapist built on trust, which in turn will generate future sales from recommendations," according to salon owner Fiona Macarthur.[25] In every business, these are all powerful testaments to great salespeople.

Power Player: Lessons in Selling from Successful Salespeople

Sign of Trust

Imagine not even bringing in product samples or literature with you on your first sales call with a customer. That's what Susan Marcus Beohm, a sales manager for a handheld dental instrument manufacturer suggests. "I don't go in as a salesperson—I go in looking to see how I can help them. Not bringing my goods and wares with me says, 'I'm here to find out what you need,' and it makes an impact." When salespeople are too eager to start talking about features and benefits before they listen to the customer, they make it more difficult to establish trust.[26]

People buy from people they trust. Consider the fact that customers put their trust in salespeople with their money and, in the case of business-to-business selling, with their business and ultimately their reputation. Customers actually become dependent on you, and their buying decisions are actually based on the fact that they trust you and believe what you say. Thus, the relationship can be even more important than the product.[27] It is said that you can give a customer the option to buy a product from a salesperson she knows or buy the same product for 10 percent less from someone she doesn't know, and in almost every case she will buy from the salesperson she knows.[28]

Trust is such an important topic that sales guru Jeffrey Gitomer has written a book dedicated to the topic of gaining and giving trust titled *Jeffrey Gitomer's Little Teal Book of Trust: How to Earn It, Grow It, and Keep It to Become a Trusted Advisor in Sales, Business, and Life.* The following video provides the highlights.

Video Clip

Jeffrey Gitomer on Trust
Learn the two important questions that can give you insight on trust.

View the video online at: http://www.youtube.com/embed/JsBNNIjiiAU

Underpromise and Overdeliver

One of the tenets of selling is establishing trust and setting expectations. The best salespeople underpromise and overdeliver. In other words, they say they will do something by a certain day, and then not only do they do it, but they deliver it one day early. Here's a way to think about the power of this approach: if you order a new pair of jeans online and the estimated date of delivery is Tuesday, but you receive them on Monday, you are delighted. You are pleased that they came early. However, if the jeans were promised for Tuesday delivery, but they arrived on Wednesday, you would be disappointed and probably would not trust that Web site for timely delivery in the future. You can imagine how this strategy builds trust with customers—not only can you rely on the salesperson to do what she said, but she never lets you down and even delivers earlier than promised sometimes. That's how trust is built between salesperson and customer, and the relationship goes to the next level: partnership.

When Times Are Tough

No one likes to deliver bad news. But it's not always good news that you will have to tell a customer. The best antidote for bad news is a good relationship. If you have nurtured your relationship with the customer and built trust, it is much easier to deliver bad news. When it's time to deliver bad news, like a delayed delivery, a cost increase, or a discontinued product line, don't put it off. Use the same practices that you use to build your relationships: open, honest, and timely communication.

As soon as you learn about information that may be bad news for your customer, contact her by phone to discuss the situation: "I realize we set Thursday as the installation date for phase one, but there have been some delays in development. Can we reschedule it for next Tuesday? I'm confident that everything will be complete by then. I apologize for any inconvenience. Let's talk about any challenges this may cause on your end. I have some ideas about how we might work around them." The sincerity in your voice and the dialogue you have with the customer can help avoid turning bad news into a serious problem. Because you have always made a point of underpromising and overdelivering, there is a high likelihood that your customer will respond positively to your ownership of the problem and solution-based conversation. It's always best to include a realistic solution to the problem and, if you don't have a solution, let the customer know exactly when you will get back to her with an update.

Video Clip

The Good News about Bad News
Here are tips for five ways to deliver bad news the right way.

View the video online at: http://www.youtube.com/embed/dvlMmiZNbyU

Win-Win-Win: The Ultimate Relationship

If you do volunteer work for an organization such as Autism Speaks, you get involved because you believe in raising awareness of autism to increase funds for research for the cure. Those who have autism and their families benefit from your involvement. This is win #1. You also benefit because you gain the satisfaction of helping people. This is win #2. You help build the strength of the organization, in this case, Autism Speaks. The more people that are involved, the more people they can reach with their message, and the more money they can raise to reach their goal of curing autism. This is win #3.

The above example is an illustration of the **win-win-win** concept in relationships. In other words, in the ultimate relationship, all parties have something to give and something to gain. This same win-win-win occurs in successful selling relationships. Your customer wins because he gets your advice and expertise to help him find a product or service that meets his needs. You win because you have enhanced your relationship and made a sale; and your company wins because the relationship, the sale, and the repeat sales help it achieve its goals.

Although the win-win-win may sound like a simple concept, it is a critical one to keep in mind in any business position, especially in selling. This art of collaboration actually results in more business with your existing customers because you have become a partner in solving their problems, and it brings you new business in the form of referrals. The win-win-win also plays a significant role in the negotiating process (covered in Chapter 12). The best business relationships and negotiations are based on the win-win-win model, not the win-lose model in which one party loses so that the other can win.[29]

win-win-win

All parties in a relationship win—your customer, you, and your company or organization.

A Seat at the Table

The seat at the table is given to those salespeople who deliver value, not sell products or services. They develop the relationship to assist customers in implementing their business strategies.[30] Customers want value in the form of strategic thinking around issues that are important to them and their company goals. As a result, your goal as a salesperson should be to help your customers create demand, secure a competitive advantage, and identify a new niche. When you deliver this kind of value, your customers will no longer see you as a salesperson; they will see you as a "business person who sells." It's this kind of thinking and value creation that earn you a seat at the table. The seat at the table also helps you expand your business because you will be integrated into your customer's business. That allows you to deliver your core products or services and be a part of developing the new opportunities. It helps cement the relationship and establishes a partnership that delivers value for all involved.[31]

Every salesperson wants "a seat at the table"; she wants to be a part of the decision-making process. That is the epitome of consultative selling: you are included in the process from the beginning. You want to be included as a valued partner with your business-to-business customers to discuss their company's strategic questions like "How will we grow our business in the next three years while technology is driving down the average selling price of our product?" "How can we extend our relationship with our customers beyond our contract period?" or "How can we expand to new markets and minimize our risk?" These are not traditional sales questions; they are strategic issues that companies wrestle with. When you are a true partner with your customers, you will be given a seat at the table when direction-setting issues are discussed. This allows you to participate fully as a trusted advisor and asset to the customer and to help shape the strategy of the company. It changes your relationship with the contact and the company from salesperson to partner. Although it may seem like a lofty goal, consider this: If you want to have a seat at the table, not only will you need to solve your customer's problems and anticipate her needs, but according to Tim Conner, sales trainer and author, you will also need to be a creative problem creator. That means that you will be in constant pursuit of identifying problems that your customer didn't even know she had. In other words, it means that you have to think *ahead* of your customer, not just along with her.[32]

Video Clip

How Do You Bring Value?
This video features Jeffrey Gitomer discussing the value of providing value to customers.

View the video online at: http://www.youtube.com/embed/vl6695w8Q08

Networking: Relationships That Work for You

You probably use Facebook frequently to keep in touch with your friends. If you want to know who took a particular course with a particular professor, you can ask your friends on Facebook. If none of your friends took the course, one of their friends may have taken it and could give you some insight about the course and the professor. Whether you realize it or not, you are networking.

Networking is the art of building alliances or mutually beneficial relationships.[33] In fact, networking is all about relationships and exchange. In the example above, while you are looking for feedback on a class from someone you know, someone else may be considering seeing a movie and wants to know if you've seen it and if you thought it was good. This is a value exchange. Although networking isn't exactly quid pro quo (something for something), it does include the element of exchange: if someone is looking for something, someone else can provide the information. What makes the network function is the fact that people in the network at some point have a need and at some point may be able to help someone else with his need. Said another way, networking is based on mutual generosity.[34]

Networking is an important part of the business world and an even more vital part of sales. It's no longer a question of "if" you should network; it's a requirement to stay competitive because it's virtually impossible to do your job alone. Just as in social networking, professional networking allows you to leverage the people you know to expand your relationship to people you don't know. Building strong relationships with customers is an excellent way to build your network. Satisfied customers will refer you to other people who might become potential customers.

It's best to always be networking rather than networking only when you want something. It makes it easier to network and expand your relationships when you're not asking for something. It also gives you the opportunity to help someone else first, which can go a long way when you need help in the future.

Networking Tips of the Trade

Today, networking can be done in person as well as online. Don't limit yourself to just one method. Networking is best done both in person and online to be truly effective. Here are a few tips for networking *in person*.

Start with People You Know

Make a list of all the people you know, starting with your current customers, family, friends, friends' family, and others. Include people such as your hair stylist, car mechanic, and others. Get to know everyone in your extended network as each can be a lead for a potential sale or even a job.[35]

Join and Get Involved in Professional Organizations

If you want to meet people who are in the same business or profession as you, professional organizations such as Sales & Marketing Executives International, Advertising Club of New York, Home Builder's Association, and so on are the best places to be. Joining is good, but getting involved in one of the committees is even better. It helps demonstrate your skills and knowledge to the other people in the organization. Since most professional organizations are made up of volunteers, it's usually easy to be invited to participate on a committee.[36]

networking

The art of building mutually beneficial relationships.

Attend Industry Events

Make an effort to attend industry or other professional events. Arrive early and work the room. If you come with someone, be sure to branch out to meet and mingle with other people. Set a time and a place to meet the person with whom you came so you can both maximize your networking. According to Peter Handel, the chairman and CEO of Dale Carnegie & Associates, a smile can be your greatest asset when networking in person. He suggests always asking questions of the people you meet; it helps keep conversation going and gives you more insight into their background and how you might work together in the future. But the other side of asking questions is listening; that's how you will learn. And always have your business cards handy. Give out your business card to those you talk to, and don't forget to get their business cards, too.[37]

Keep in Touch

Many people think that networking is just about collecting business cards. Networking is so much more than that. Networking is about creating mutually beneficial relationships. It's best to use one of the basic practices for building relationships when networking: keeping in touch. That means dropping an e-mail to someone with whom you have networked just to find out how their big project is going, how their twins' birthday celebration went, or even just to say hi. Go beyond the e-mail by inviting someone to lunch. It's the perfect way to build a relationship, share common ground, and learn more about the person.[38] Many people are gung ho about networking and meeting people, but rarely keep in touch. It almost defeats the purpose of networking if you don't keep in touch.

Online Professional Social Networking

online professional social networking

Online communities that focus on business members and provide a platform for members to communicate and share with each other.

Online professional social networking can be an equally powerful tool to build your contacts. But just like networking in person, you can't be passive and expect to expand your network. Consider a situation that Austin Hill, Internet entrepreneur and founder of the angel investment firm Brudder Ventures, encountered when his firm was trying to get access to someone in a specific department at a vendor. It was a large company, and he kept getting the runaround. But after going onto LinkedIn and getting introductions to the right people, within two days they were able to start doing business with the company.[39]

Create a Profile on the Major Professional Social Networks

LinkedIn, Ryze, ZoomInfo, and Plaxo are all online professional social networks that have a substantial number of members. You can also use Facebook MySpace, and Twitter to create profiles, peruse job boards, and join the conversation.

Join *The Power of Selling* Group on LinkedIn

You can join the conversation about careers in sales created for this course on LinkedIn. Visit http://www.linkedin.com and go to http://www.linkedin.com/groups?gid=2566050&trk=myg_ugrp_ovr. Or go to "Search Groups," search for "The Power of Selling," select it from the groups that are displayed, and click on "Join Group." Once you've joined the group, you can connect with sales professionals and other students across the country. You will be able to listen to the conversation, ask questions, and start or join discussions. This group is an excellent way to network and find people who work at companies that you may want to work at.

Start your professional networking now and network with sales professionals that want to help you.

LinkedIn

http://www.linkedin.com/home

The Power of Selling Group

http://www.linkedin.com/groups?gid=2566050&trk=myg_ugrp_ovr

Connect to People You Know, Then Network Personally

The number of connections you have is not a badge of honor. Take the time to connect to all the people you know, and network within their networks. If you only add people for the sake of having a lot of connections, you won't know who can really help you in your network. When you do make a connection, make it personal; don't just send a group invitation to join your network. It's always best to keep in mind that the foundation of your network is relationships.[40]

Be Proactive

Ask for introductions to people with whom you want to network and ask your boss, colleagues, and customers to write recommendations for you. It's a good idea to use the features included on the professional social networking sites such as groups, discussions, and "Answers" on LinkedIn, which allows you to ask questions of your network.[41]

Mind Your Manners

Just a word of caution about professional social networking: Be professional in all of your communications. You are participating in a professional forum so be aware that everything you "say" and do reflects on you and your company.

Key Takeaways

- **Consultative selling** is the process by which you get to know a customer personally, understand her needs, and put her needs first in the relationship.
- Relationships are vital to success in most selling situations. When you understand what the customer wants and needs, you can provide solutions to help your customer meet his goals.
- **Lifetime value** is a term that refers to the amount of business that you do with a single customer over the course of the relationship. When you have a long-term view of your relationships with customers, you have an opportunity to realize even greater success.
- **R-commerce**, or establishing and developing relationships with customers, focuses on the "little things" you can do to take advantage of opportunities and set yourself apart.
- Trust is the cornerstone of every relationship. If you don't have trust, you don't have a relationship.
- A solid relationship is essential, especially when delivering bad news. Always be honest and timely with customers when you have to communicate news that might not be what they want to hear. They will respect you and trust you for it.
- The **win-win-win** is when all parties in a relationship win: your customer, you, and your company or organization.
- **Networking**, the art of building mutually beneficial relationships, is an indispensable business tool.

Exercises

1. Identify a situation in which a salesperson has developed a relationship with you. Do you trust her more since you know her better? Identify at least one way she puts your needs first in the relationship.
2. Name a situation in which a salesperson provided you with information to make your purchasing decision. Did you trust him to provide this information? Why did you trust him?
3. Think about a situation in which a salesperson underpromised and overdelivered. How did your perception of the salesperson and the company change because of your experience?
4. Go to http://www.linkedin.com and create your profile. Then use the search box to search groups and search for "The Power of Selling." Click on the "Members" tab and search for members that you want to connect with and add them to your professional network. Click on the "Discussions" tab to begin or join into a discussion.
5. Research professional organizations that might be of interest to you that have a chapter on campus or in your local community. What is the mission of each organization? What events are scheduled soon? How can you become a student member of the organization?

3.2 Putting Adaptive Selling to Work

Learning Objectives

1. Explain the concept of adaptive selling and how to use it.
2. Understand how the social style matrix can help you be more effective in sales.

adaptive selling

Situation in which the salesperson adapts or customizes her selling style based on the behavior of the customer.

canned presentation

A selling presentation that is exactly the same for every customer.

Adaptive selling occurs when a salesperson adapts, changes, and customizes her selling style based on the situation and the behavior of the customer.[42] Adaptive selling allows you to truly listen, understand the customer's needs, and then adapt your conversation and presentation accordingly. On the other hand, if you were giving a **canned presentation**, you wouldn't be able to learn what the customer thinks is important. For example, if you were selling landscaping to a customer, you wouldn't know if the customer wanted the landscaping to provide privacy or create a view. The only way you would find out is by listening, asking questions, and adapting your recommendations and presentation accordingly. Adaptive selling is much easier to do when you establish a relationship with the customer.

Adaptive selling takes place in many situations in business and in life. It is the selling skill that allows you to adapt your communications to a person or situation. Chances are you already use adaptive selling in your everyday life, but you may not realize it. Do you approach your parents differently than your friends? Do you speak to a professor differently than you do to your roommate? These are examples of adaptive selling.

It's also likely that you interact with each of your friends differently. Do you have a friend that needs tons of information to make a decision, while another friend makes a decision in an instant? Do you know people who want to talk about their decisions before and after they make them and those who just decide and don't say a word? Understanding diversity, or the different ways people behave, is the cornerstone of adaptive selling.

The Social Style Matrix

What makes people so different in their style, perceptions, and approaches to things is defined in the **social style matrix**. It is an established method that helps you understand how people behave so you can adapt your selling style accordingly. The social style matrix is based on patterns of communication behavior identified by David Merril and Roger Reid.[43] It plots social behavior based on two dimensions: assertiveness and responsiveness. In the matrix below, the *x* axis is assertiveness, which indicates the degree to which a person wants to dominate or control the thoughts of others. The *y* axis represents responsiveness, which is the degree to which a person outwardly displays emotions or feelings in a relationship.[44] In Figure 3.4, you can see the four quadrants; each quadrant represents one of four social styles: **analytical**, **driver**, **amiable**, and **expressive**. Each of these styles describes a different type of behavior.[45]

FIGURE 3.4 Social Style Matrix[46]

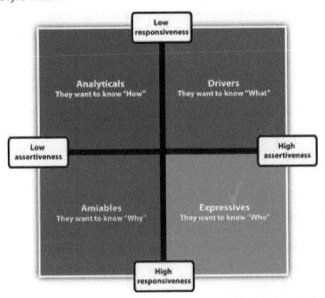

Each of the social styles has specific characteristics that are important to keep in mind as you prepare and present your sales presentation. Adapting to someone's social style demonstrates the law of psychological reciprocity, which says that when you adapt to someone's style, that person will move toward your style. In short, you are inspiring trust by acting according to the old adage of the golden rule.[47] So, whether you are asking to borrow your mother's car or asking someone on a date, understanding the social style matrix is important to get the result you want.

Analyticals: They Want to Know "How"

Do you know someone who only wants the facts to make a decision? Perhaps it's your father or mother or a professor. *Analyticals* are all about the facts. They are defined by low responsiveness and low assertiveness. In other words, they like to hear about the pros and cons and all the details before they decide. They are likely to have a financial or technical background, and they pride themselves on being an expert in their field. They want to hear about the tangible results, timelines, and details before they make a decision. In fact, they are the ones who will actually read the directions before they put together a new grill or set up a wireless home network. They are so focused on facts that they prefer to disregard personal opinions in their decision making. They like to understand all the facts before they decide so they know exactly how the product, service, or contract arrangement will work.[48]

social style matrix

An established method of identifying patterns of communication and behavior.

analytical

A social style that describes people who focus on facts, details, and analysis to make decisions.

driver

A social style that describes people who like to have all the facts and make decisions quickly.

amiable

A social style that describes people who focus on personal relationships in their decision making.

expressive

A social style that describes people who rely on their feelings to make decisions.

You might have some visual cues that will help you identify an analytical. She probably dresses conservatively and has her achievement awards proudly displayed on her office wall. She is organized and focused on work activities.[49]

If you are selling to a customer who is an analytical, she will ask you very specific questions about all the details, and she will respond positively if you make her feel as if she is right. In other words, don't challenge her facts and point of view. Rather, provide history, data, financial details, and other facts in an organized, structured format. She will ask many questions so that she clearly understands the product or service. Since it's important for her to make the right decision, she will take the time to gather all the facts. Because she puts so much effort into making the right decision, she tends to be loyal to the people from whom she buys, believing she doesn't need to reevaluate the same facts.

Adapt your style to an analytical by focusing on the "how." Slow down your presentation and let her take it all in; don't make her feel rushed. Use facts, historical data, and details to be sure she has all the information she needs to make the decision. Use guarantees or warranties to reduce any perceived risk. Give her the time she needs to analyze, evaluate, and decide.[50]

Drivers: They Want to Know "What"

You've probably watched Super Bowl champion Peyton Manning, quarterback for the Indianapolis Colts play football on television or the Internet. One of the traits that makes him a champion is the fact that he is focused exclusively on winning each game. When he is on the field, everything else is in second place in his mind. Peyton Manning is a *driver*.

Drivers have some characteristics that are the same as analyticals in that they like to have all the facts to make their decision. However, drivers are different from analyticals because they make decisions quickly. On the social style matrix, they are in the low responsiveness, high assertiveness quadrant. These are the people who are "control freaks"; they are decisive and controlling. They work with people because they have to; they see other people only as a means to their end of achievement. They are smart, focused, independent, and competitive. They have little regard for the opinions of others; a driver is rarely described as a "people person." They are high achievers who are in a hurry to meet their goals.[51] They don't want facts just for the sake of having them; they want relevant information that will help them decide quickly.

Like the analyticals, drivers dress conservatively and display their achievement awards on the wall of their office. A calendar is usually prominent to keep focus on how long it will take to achieve something. Because they are not focused on the feelings or attitudes of other people, drivers usually do business across the desk rather than on the same side of the desk.[52]

The best way to adapt to a driver is to be professional and to the point. Don't spend too much time on small talk; get to the point quickly. Provide options so that he can feel as if he is in control. Include a timeline so he can see how quickly he can get results.

Amiables: They Want to Know "Why"

Actress Reese Witherspoon was recently named the Honorary Chairperson of the Avon Foundation for Women because of her ability to unite women around the cause of breast cancer.[53] She rallies people and brings them together by focusing on the greater good, but she doesn't assert herself. She is an *amiable*.

An amiable is most likely to be described as a "people person." Amiables are team players who focus on innovation and long-term problem solving. They value relationships and like to engage with people whom they feel they can trust. They are less controlling than drivers and more people oriented than analyticals because they are in the low assertiveness, high responsiveness quadrant of the matrix.

Amiables provide some visual clues because their offices are typically open and friendly. They often display pictures of family, and they prefer to work in an open environment rather than sitting across the desk from you. They tend to have a personal style in their dress, being casual or less conservative than analytics or drivers.[54]

When you are presenting to an amiable, establish a personal relationship. She will be more likely to discuss issues with you. When you demonstrate your personal commitment, she will be open to doing business with you.

Expressives: They Want to Know "Who"

An *expressive* is intuitive, charismatic, persuasive, nurturing, and engaging. Oprah Winfrey is an expressive; she has excellent rapport with people, even people she has never met. Relationships are important to her, but only to help her achieve her higher goal of giving her viewers inspiration and a better way to live their lives.

Expressives are creative and can see the big picture clearly; they have a vision and use their style to communicate it and inspire people. They don't get caught up in the day-to-day details. Expressives build relationships to gain power, so people like employees, viewers, or voters are very important to them. Status and recognition are also important to them.

Since expressives are not big on details, you might find their offices to be a bit disorganized, even cluttered and messy. Their offices are set up in an open format, as they would prefer to sit next to you rather than across the desk from you. They avoid conservative dress and are more casual with their personal style. They want to engage with you and talk about the next big idea.[55]

When you are selling to an expressive, take extra time to discuss everything. Give them recognition and approval. Appeal to their emotions by asking them how they feel about the product or service; focus on the big picture of what is possible as a result of buying your product or service. If you try to dazzle them with facts and figures, you won't get very far.

TABLE 3.1 Selling Style Summary

Social Style You're Selling to	How to Adapt
Analyticals	• Focus on "how" • Include facts • Communicate the pros and cons • Provide history, data, financial details • Don't challenge her facts • Demonstrate results • Mention guarantees and warranties • Give her time to decide
Drivers	• Focus on "what" • Get to the point quickly • Provide options • Use facts • Focus on results • Provide timelines • Make him feel as if he is in control
Amiables	• Focus on "why" • Establish a personal relationship • Demonstrate personal commitment • Work as a team
Expressives	• Focus on "who" • Take extra time to discuss everything • Give her recognition and approval • Ask her how she feels about the product or service • Focus on the big picture • Use facts and figures to demonstrate what is possible

Source: Todd Duncan, "Your Sales Style," Incentive, December 1, 1999, 64–66.

What Is Your Selling Style?

Before you think about the social styles of other people, you might find it helpful to think about your own social style. Are you very emotional when you express your opinions, or are you more reserved and formal? Are you the type of person who agrees with everyone, or are you extremely interested in the details? You might want to take a few minutes to take the Keirsey Temperament Sorter to understand your social style. But don't stop here; visit your campus career center as it most likely offers several assessment tools that can help you identify your social style.

Link

Take the Keirsey Temperament Sorter to Determine Your Social Style
http://www.keirsey.com/sorter/register.aspx

It would be easy to get stuck in your own style preference. But getting out of your comfort zone and adapting quickly to your customer's style preference can make the difference between a sale and a "no thanks." It's important to note that most people are a combination of styles, but when you understand the basic behaviors of each style and how to adapt, you can increase your chances for success.[56]

Key Takeaways

- **Adaptive selling** occurs when you adapt and customize your selling style based on the behavior of the customer.
- The **social style matrix** is based on patterns of communication that characterize communication behavior based on two dimensions: assertiveness and responsiveness.
- **Analyticals** focus on facts, details, and analysis to decide but are reserved in their interactions with people. They want to know the "how."
- **Drivers** are similar to *analyticals* in that they like facts, but only the ones that will quickly help them achieve their goals. They are people who are in a hurry and don't really care about personal relationships, except as a means to their goal. They want to know the "what."
- **Amiables** focus on personal relationships in their communication style. They like to agree with everyone and focus on team building. They want to know the "why."
- **Expressives** enjoy building relationships, but don't like focusing on day-to-day details; they like to paint a vision and inspire everyone to follow it. They like to focus on the "who."
- Most people use a combination of styles, depending on the situation.

Exercises

1. Think about your professor for this course. What social style would you use if you went to see her about your grade on the midterm exam? Discuss why you would choose this style.
2. Using the social matrix in this section, identify a situation in which you would use each style. Discuss why you would choose the style for each situation.
3. For each of the following situations, identify the social style of the buyer and suggest how you would adapt to appeal to the buyer:
   - You are a salesperson for a floral wholesaler. Your customer owns a flower shop. When you arrive to meet her you notice her office is a bit messy (in fact, you can't understand how she finds anything), but she is very cordial and takes the time to hear about your product.
   - You are a salesperson for a company that specializes in social networking software for retailers. Your customer is the chief information officer for a growing online retailer. He was very precise about the meeting time and agenda. You hope you can establish rapport with him quickly as he was a bit brusque on the phone.
   - You are a commercial real estate agent. Your customer is the founder and CEO of a start-up Web site development company. Her enthusiasm is contagious as she describes her vision for the company and her office needs for the next five years.

3.3 *Selling U*: Networking—The Hidden Job Market

Learning Objective

1. Understand the role of relationships and networking in your job search.

Did you know that 80 percent of jobs are filled through networking?[57] Networking is sometimes referred to as the "hidden job market" because many jobs are filled before they are ever posted. This is true now more than ever because of the challenging economy. Traffic at job boards like Monster.com, CareerBuilder.com, and Yahoo! HotJobs is up 37 percent over last year, which means that companies are deluged with résumés. Despite the influx in résumés, companies are using more networking—traditional and online—to fill their open jobs. In fact, about 50 percent of Facebook's new hires come from referrals from existing employees. According to Molly Graham, manager of Facebook Human Resources and Recruitment, "One of our main philosophies is to get smart and talented people. They tend to be connected."

Zappos, a billion-dollar online retailer of shoes and apparel that was recently purchased by Amazon, has taken employee referrals to the next level and has implemented software that lets employees use their LinkedIn and Twitter contacts. The software uses an algorithm to identify people who might have a skill set and experience match for open positions and then allows employees to invite the prospective candidate to apply.[58]

So now you can see why networking can be a very effective method to potentially learn about or land the job you want. But you might be wondering where you start and exactly how you network effectively. Like everything else in selling, you need to develop a plan.

Create a Networking Plan

Before you start, it's a good idea to review exactly what networking is and what it isn't. Just as in selling, networking is about building relationships that are mutually beneficial; it is about the exchange of value between people, usually over the course of time. Someone might help you now, and you might help that same person or someone else later. It requires a relationship and ongoing commitment. Networking isn't a quick, easy way to get a job. Although it can be instrumental in helping you get a job, it isn't easy, and it might not be quick. You should approach networking for the long term and realize that you will help some people and some people will help you. You have the power to help other people and to ask for help; that's how networking works. To help guide you, here are six power networking tips.

Power Networking Tip #1: Network with Confidence

Don't think of networking as begging for a job. Start building relationships with people—family, friends, professors, and executives—now. That will give you the opportunity to build relationships and potentially help someone even before you begin your job search. When you do begin networking to find a job, be yourself and get to know as many people as possible using the methods described earlier in the chapter (e.g., professional organizations, events). Keep in mind that you may have the opportunity one day to help the person with whom you are networking, so network with confidence.[59] You will be surprised at how many people are willing to help you because you ask. The fact is people *want* to help you; they want to see you succeed.

Power Networking Tip #2: Join Professional Organizations

There's no better place to meet people you want to work with than to go where they go. Professional organizations such as your local chapter of Sales & Marketing Executives International, American Marketing Association, Entrepreneurs Organization, Public Relations Society of America, and others provide the perfect environment to meet people in the industry in which you want to work. Start by exploring the professional organizations on campus. Many are local chapters of national organizations designed to encourage students to get involved. If you don't know which organization is best for you, ask a professor; she will be happy to provide some insight. Or go to a meeting and check it out; most organizations allow nonmembers to attend at least one meeting or event at no charge. A good number of professional organizations offer student membership rates that are designed for student budgets. Besides providing an excellent method to network, being a member of a professional organization also enhances your résumé.

But don't just join—get involved. You can impress people with your skills, drive, and work ethic by getting involved in a committee, planning an event, working on the organization's Web site, or other project. It's a great way to build your experience and your résumé and impress prospective employers. At the same time, you can be developing professional references to speak on your behalf.

Power Networking Tip #3: Create Your Networking List

Networking, like selling, is personal. So make a list of all the people you know with whom you can network. Don't disqualify anyone because you think they can't help. You never know who knows someone who might be the link to your next job. Follow the same strategy for your personal networking as you would use for networking for selling: write down the four Fs—friends, family, friends' family, and family's friends using a format like the example shown in Table 3.2.[60] But don't stop there; include your manicurist, insurance agent, hairstylist, and anyone else with whom you have a relationship. Don't forget to visit your school alumni office. It's always easier to start networking with people with whom you already have a relationship.

TABLE 3.2 Sample Networking List

Name	Relationship	E-Mail	Phone	Date of Contact	Follow-Up Date
Manny Romeo	Dad's friend at Crane, Inc.	mromeo@craneinc.com	616-787-9121	March 4	Need to touch base again at end of the month
Marie Jennings	Mom's friend	mmjennings@comcast.net	616-231-0098	March 6	Early April (April 6)
Jamal Isper	Dad's friend at Polk & Polk	jasper@polk.com	791-887-9091	March 10	March 17
Shalee Johnson	Hairstylist	Not available; will talk to her on my next appointment	616-765-0120	April 7	To be determined based on first contact
Rajesh Sumar	Director of Alumni Relations at school	Rajesh.sumar@university.edu	891-222-5555 ext. 2187	March 12	To be determined based on first contact
Annette Roberts	General Sales Manager, Castle Controls	Annette.roberts@castle.com	888-989-0000 ext. 908	March 12	To be determined based on first contact

Video Clip

Networking Made Easy
This video gives you the highlights of how to network.

View the video online at: http://www.youtube.com/embed/Y9VUqB7wQpY

Power Networking Tip #4: Know What to Say

Everyone tells you to do networking, but after you create your list, what do you say? You will be delivering your brand message to everyone with whom you are networking, so be specific about what you are looking for. Always take the opportunity to expand your network by asking for the names of other people whom you might contact. For example, assume you are networking with Vera, a friend of the family:

> **You**: *I really enjoy marketing and advertising. In fact, I'm looking for an internship at an advertising agency in account management. Do you know of anyone who might be looking for an intern for the summer?*
>
> **Vera**: *I don't really know anyone at an advertising agency.*
>
> **You**: *Thanks. I was wondering if you might know anyone who might know someone who works at an advertising agency.*

You will be surprised at how many people may be able to give you the name of someone you can contact. Not everyone will give you a name, but if you don't ask, most people won't think about whom they might know.

You might also network with someone who gives you the name of someone to contact. For example,

> **You**: *I'm going to graduate from State College in May with a degree in business administration. I really enjoy the idea of helping people increase their company's sales, so I'm looking for a job in selling. Do you know of anyone who might have an opportunity in sales?*
>
> **Jon**: *Have you talked to anyone at Universal Parts? They have a great training program, and the sales reps get a company car. You might want to touch base with Chris Reddy, who is one of the sales managers. I can give you his contact information.*
>
> **You**: *Jon, I really appreciate your help. Can I mention your name when I contact him?*
>
> **Jon**: *Sure. Chris is a great leader and is always looking for good people.*

When you contact Chris Reddy, it's best to make contact by phone, if possible. That way you have an opportunity to create a relationship (remember how important relationships are in selling, especially when you are selling yourself). A phone call might start like this:

> **You**: *Hello, Chris. My name is Rakeem Bateman. Jon Keller suggested I give you a call.*
>
> **Chris**: *Hello Rakeem. Jon and I have known each other for several years. How do you know Jon?*
>
> **You**: *I met him at a Sales & Marketing Executives International event last week. He was one of the speakers. I enjoyed hearing what he had to say so much that I stayed to talk to him after the event. I'm going to graduate from State College in May with a degree in business administration. I really enjoy the idea of helping people increase their company's sales, so I'm looking for a job in selling. Jon suggested that I touch base with you to find out if Universal Parts might be looking to expand their sales organization.*

If someone has referred you, always include that as part of your introduction. If your networking takes place via e-mail, you should do the same thing. When you send your résumé to someone with whom you are networking via e-mail, it's best to include your three bullet points from your cover letter as the body of the e-mail (review the *Selling U* section in Chapter 2). That allows the person to whom you are sending the letter to see at a glance that he wants to open your résumé. In most cases the person to whom you are sending your résumé is forwarding it to someone else. Writing a short, easy-to-skim note helps tell every recipient what you have to offer. For example, see Figure 3.5 for a sample e-mail to Chris Reddy.

FIGURE 3.5 Sample E-mail for Networking

> To: Chris Reddy
> From: Rakeem Bateman
>
> Dear Chris,
>
> Jon Keller suggested that I touch base with you. He mentioned that you are one of those unique sales professionals who is always looking for creative ways to grow your business and good salespeople to help you do it. I believe I am one of those people. Some highlights of my background include the following:
>
> - **Sales Experience:** As an Account Management Intern in the Sales Department at Recovery Systems, Inc., I headed up the social networking efforts for the company and generated 30 new leads in 4 weeks by setting up and managing LinkedIn and Twitter accounts.
> - **Leadership Skills:** As the president of the Green For Life student organization on campus, I provided leadership to our group that raised $2,300 to support local recycling efforts as a result of our "Go Green Now" campaign.
> - **Work Ethic and Commitment:** I am focused and determined to succeed. I have held a full-time job while attending school. In addition, I have participated in community service efforts.
>
> I would like the opportunity to meet with you to talk about what you look for in a new salesperson. I'll follow up with a phone call on Friday so we can set up a time that is convenient.
>
> Sincerely,
>
> Rakeem Bateman

You can see that when you are networking you want to focus on being specific about what you are looking for, asking for names of people with whom you might network, and creating a relationship with those people.

Power Networking Tip #5: Online Professional Social Networking

Social networking sites can be a more powerful job search tool than most people realize, and their power can go both ways: The sites can work in your favor, but they can also work against you. When you're preparing to apply for jobs, keep in mind that a growing number of employers search social networking sites like Facebook and MySpace to weed out applicants who might not fit with their company culture. In fact, 22 percent of employers claim to use social networking sites when considering potential hires, and of those employers, 34 percent said they chose not to hire a candidate based on the information they had dug up about that person online.[61] One human resources manager based in Seattle, says she has turned down an otherwise promising job candidate's application on a number of occasions after visiting the applicant's networking profile. "Sometimes there are compromising photos or videos posted out there where anyone can find them," she says. "When that happens, those applications go right in the trash."[62] You can find out all kinds of things about a person from his MySpace profile that you couldn't necessarily learn from his cover letter or résumé! As social networking expert Patrice-Anne Rutledge says, before you go on the job market, make sure you "get rid of your digital dirt." In particular, look through any videos or photographs you may have uploaded to your profile, any Web sites you may have linked to, and any personal information you reveal that may be controversial or reflect on you in a negative light.[63]

You've Got the Power: Tips for Your Job Search

Clean Up Your Pages

"Get rid of your digital dirt"[64] now, before you even start applying for jobs. Your Facebook or MySpace profile could negatively impact your chances of getting a job at your chosen company. Gauge the appropriateness of the videos, photographs, and comments on your pages and decide whether it would be a problem if a potential employer saw them. Many employers *will* search your social networking profiles to learn the things your résumé and cover letter don't reveal.

On the other hand, professional social networking sites are tools you can leverage to great advantage in your job search if you use them proactively. LinkedIn is the biggest and most frequently used networking site, but there are a number of others, including Jobster, Ryze, ZoomInfo, and Plaxo, that allow you to create a professional profile and find contacts in your target industry or at target companies.[65] Although it's easy to create an account on these sites, you won't get the full benefit unless you do two things: make the effort to keep your profile up-to-date and make the effort to grow your network. Here are a few social networking tips to keep in mind:

- **Make yourself stand out**. Think about the skills and qualities that make you unique. What sets you apart as your own distinctive brand? Your online networking profile should reflect this. Don't just reproduce your résumé; make your profile into your "elevator speech," highlighting your interests and using power words to describe your experience and talents. Your network profile is searchable on Google, so give some thought to the keywords you use to describe yourself.[66]

- **Publicize your profile**. LinkedIn allows you to search your e-mail address book for contacts that also have accounts, so you can easily grow your network. You should also be willing to ask people you know in your industry, including professors and mentors, to join your network. These people are well connected and want to see you succeed. In addition, you can start using your LinkedIn profile badge on outgoing e-mails, and, if you have one, on your Web site. When you publicize yourself this way, people will start linking to you.[67] Many companies and recruiters are accelerating their use of LinkedIn. "We could not believe the candidates we got" from LinkedIn, says Scott Morrison, director of global recruiting programs at software giant Salesforce.com.[68]

- **Ask for recommendations**. As you begin to build a professional network online, you can use it the same way you would use a regular social network. Ask people for recommendations of your work and for referrals to new contacts. Maybe a former professor knows the marketing manager at a company where you want to work; ask her to introduce you. Making a request like this can be terrifying at first, but have confidence. Keep in mind that your professors, mentors, and fellow professionals *want* to help you, and when they can help you, they *will*. But you won't get the help if you don't ask for it.

- **Join groups**. Start by joining *The Power of Selling* group on LinkedIn. Sites like LinkedIn have thousands of groups that are specific to interest, location, hobbies, and industry. Join your local professional group—the Chicago Sales and Marketing Executives group, for instance—and join your school's alumni association. Your alumni group is an extremely important connection to make because people are almost always eager to help their fellow alumni succeed. But don't stop there; search for other groups that are in the industry you want to pursue. You can just listen to the conversation and then jump in when you feel comfortable.

- **Create content**. Think about when you are considering making a major purchase. What do you do? You probably conduct research online to determine the pros and cons of each alternative. Employers do the same thing, so be sure your profile is compelling and up-to-date. In addition, use your social networking pages to create content to demonstrate your skills. For example, write a blog and link it to your Facebook page or post tweets on Twitter about a project on which you are working, a topic about which you are passionate, or even your job search. Get people to follow you and engage in the dialogue. Direct them to your personal Web site, samples of your work, or the content you have created. Social networking gives you the opportunity to show and sell with content that you create.
- **Search the social networking job boards**. More and more employers are using professional social networking sites to post jobs and seek out prospective employees.[69] It's worth your time to review the job postings using the appropriate keywords.

Video Clip

Learn How to Use LinkedIn

This short video series provides step-by-step instructions as to how to use LinkedIn for networking.

Video:

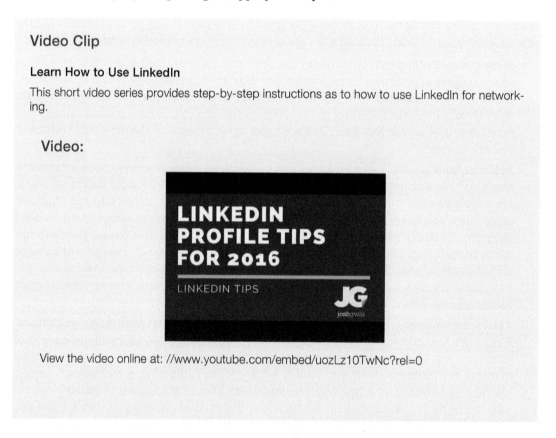

View the video online at: //www.youtube.com/embed/uozLz10TwNc?rel=0

Power Networking Tip #6: Follow-Up

It might seem like networking doesn't always work. It's good to keep in mind that networking is all about exchange of value. Sometimes, you may not find people who want the value you have to offer at the time you are offering it. Don't be discouraged. Follow-up is important in every part of your job search, so follow up with everyone with whom you network. Sometimes, people are simply distracted or overwhelmed at the time you first contacted them. Or sometimes their situation has changed, even in just a few days; you won't know this unless you follow up.

It's best to follow up by phone within one week of a contact. It may seem easier to follow up by e-mail, but you increase your likelihood of being successful and building a relationship when you follow up by phone. Don't simply leave a voice mail message as it is unlikely that someone will return your call. Continue to call until your contact answers the phone, or leave a voice mail and tell her when you will call back along with your e-mail address. Then, call back when you say you will. You will be pleasantly surprised at the results.

Keep in mind that networking is an ongoing process, whether you are looking for a job or not. When you establish a relationship with someone, keep in touch with her. You should touch base with people in your network at least once every four to six weeks. It's good to call to catch up, but an e-mail can be just as powerful. Send a link to an article or video that you think she will like. It's a perfect reason for keeping in touch and helps establish you as someone who delivers value, even when you are not looking for something.

Key Takeaways

- Creating a networking plan will help make your networking efforts more effective.
- **Networking** is about exchanging value, not collecting business cards. It's best to begin networking even before you are looking for a job so you can get to know people and provide value to them; it will help you when you begin your job search.
- Always network with confidence. You are not asking for a favor—you are simply tapping into a reciprocal business practice.
- It's a good idea to create a networking list including friends, family, family's friends, friends' family, and everyone else you know. Write down their names and contact information so you don't miss anyone.
- Practice what you want to say when you network with people. It's best to be specific about what you are looking for and always ask for another person with whom you can network.
- Online professional social networks such as LinkedIn, Plaxo, and other networking sites including Facebook and Twitter can help you expand your network and build relationships with many people who might be able to help put you in touch with the right people.
- Your social networking pages represent your personal brand. Be sure that all words, pictures, and videos are appropriate for prospective employers to view.
- Follow-up is the key to making networking work; don't assume that because you haven't heard back from someone that he doesn't want to talk to you. Take the time to follow up within one week of every contact.

Exercises

1. Choose one of your classmates. Review his social networking pages and do a search on major search engines to see what his personal brand communicates online. Is it appropriate for a prospective employer? What changes would you recommend?
2. Create your networking list. Identify at least fifteen people that you can contact about your internship or job search. How can you expand your network to include twenty-five people?
3. Assume you were at a campus networking event and met someone who works at a company where you would like to work. What would you say to her to try to learn about potential opportunities with the company? If she said nothing was available, what would you say to be able to contact her at a later time?
4. Review your LinkedIn profile and identify ways that you can stand out. Ask a professor or other professional to give you some feedback on your profile and other professionals you can add to your network.

3.4 Review and Practice

Power Wrap-Up

Now that you have read this chapter, you should be able to understand the importance of relationships in selling and how to develop effective relationships.

- You can **understand** why building relationships is important to selling.
- You can **describe** how consultative selling works.
- You can **identify** ways to develop long-term, effective relationships.
- You can **understand** how to build trust in a relationship.
- You can **list** the ways to network to build relationships.
- You can **recognize** how to use adaptive selling.
- You can **understand** how to integrate networking into your job search.

Test Your Power Knowledge (answers are below)

1. Describe consultative selling and why it is different from transactional selling.
2. Describe lifetime value and why it is important in consultative selling.
3. Explain how to communicate bad news to a customer.
4. Who wins in the win-win-win relationship?
5. What is networking, and why is it important in selling?
6. Describe adaptive selling and why it is important.
7. If your customer is a driver, what is the best way to adapt your selling style?
8. Name at least three ways you can use networking to get the job you want.

Power (Role) Play

Now it's time to put what you've learned into practice. The following are two roles that are involved in the same selling situation; one role is that of an interviewer and the other is that of the aspiring salesperson. This will give you the opportunity to think about this networking situation from the perspective of both the networker and the person with whom he is networking.

Read each role carefully along with the discussion questions. Then, be prepared to play either of the roles in class using the concepts covered in this chapter. You may be asked to discuss the roles and do a role-play in groups or individually.

Networking That Works

Role: Pharmaceutical sales manager

You are a sales manager at a major pharmaceutical company. You are always looking for extraordinary people—the ones who really stand out. You judge people by your first impression of them. Even if you are not hiring, you usually take the time to meet with people who impress you, or at the very least, you refer her to someone you think may be hiring. If you are not impressed, you are courteous to the person, but leave it at that.

- What would impress you if a potential candidate called to network with you?
- What information would you expect him to know about you?
- How would you respond to the networking phone call?

Role: College student

You are you. You are looking for a job in pharmaceutical sales, and you are networking to find any job opportunities in that area. You have been given the name and phone number of a sales manager at a major pharmaceutical company. You are not sure if the company is hiring right now, but the sales manager is well connected in the industry so he is a good person with whom to build a relationship and put your networking skills to work. You don't know much about him, but you learned on his LinkedIn profile that he went to the University of Florida and also volunteers for The Boys and Girls Clubs of America.

- What other research would you do before you called the sales manager?
- What is your objective for calling the sales manager?
- Assume you are calling the sales manager to network. How would you start the conversation?
- How would you wrap up the conversation?
- What would you do after the conversation?

Put Your Power to Work: *Selling U* Activities

1. Identify at least one professional organization on campus and one organization off campus that you can join to enhance your networking opportunities. Go to the campus student services office or career center. Also, talk to a professor and a librarian to conduct your research to identify the organizations.
2. Contact at least five people a week on your networking list. Ask for the names of additional people to contact and to build your network.
3. Set up a profile on LinkedIn (if you haven't already done so). Connect to at least fifteen people to start (use your networking list to build your LinkedIn connections). Ask for at least three introductions a week from people in your network. Contact each one personally and share what type of career you would like to pursue. Ask each one for additional names of people you can network with.
4. Using LinkedIn, ask at least three professional people to recommend you. Consider people such as previous supervisors, professors, and internship coordinators.
5. Create an account on Twitter. Follow at least twenty professional people in the industry in which you would like to get a job.

Test Your Power Knowledge Answers

1. Consultative selling occurs when you develop a one-to-one relationship with your customer and truly understand his needs, wants, and resources; it means putting the customer first. Consultative selling helps you develop short-term and long-term solutions for your customer. Transactional selling focuses on a single transaction with no input from or relationship with the customer.
2. Lifetime value means that you consider not just one transaction with a customer but also the help and insight you can provide throughout the entire period that you do business with him. A customer that has only limited needs right now may develop into a lucrative customer over the course of time based on your advice and guidance.
3. It's best to deliver bad news in person or over the phone when time permits. This tells your customer that you think this is important. You should always communicate in an open, honest, and timely manner and provide a realistic solution to the problem. If you don't have a solution, let the customer know when you will get back to her with an update.
4. The customer, you, and your company all win in a win-win-win relationship.
5. Networking is the art of building alliances or mutually beneficial relationships. Networking is built on the concept of exchange. In selling, you can expand the number of people you know, which can expand your business. When what you need provides value to someone else in

your network, networking works. The more you provide value to other people, the higher the likelihood that they will go out of their way to help you.

6. Adaptive selling occurs when a salesperson adapts and customizes her selling style based on the behavior of the customer. If you adapt to the customer's social style, you can increase the chances that he will be open to hearing your message.

7. Be professional; focus on facts and timelines that will allow your customer to see how quickly she can achieve her goal. Provide options that allow her to be in control.

8. Create a networking list, join professional organizations, use online professional social networks, publicize your profile, ask for recommendations, join groups, create content, and follow up.

Endnotes

1. Jack Mitchell, *Hug Your Customers: The Proven Way to Personalize Sales and Achieve Astounding Results* (New York: Hyperion, 2003), 22.

2. Jack Mitchell, *Hug Your Customers: The Proven Way to Personalize Sales and Achieve Astounding Results* (New York: Hyperion, 2003), 28.

3. Claire Sykes, "Relationship Selling," *Surface Fabrication* 12, no. 1 (January–February 2006): 58.

4. Jack Mitchell, *Hug Your Customers: The Proven Way to Personalize Sales and Achieve Astounding Results* (New York: Hyperion, 2003), 16.

5. Jack Mitchell, *Hug Your Customers: The Proven Way to Personalize Sales and Achieve Astounding Results* (New York: Hyperion, 2003), 20.

6. Jeffrey Gitomer, "The Difference between an Account and a Relationship," *Long Island Business News*, August 3, 2007, http://libn.com/blog/2007/08/03/the-difference-between-an-account-and-a-relationship/ (accessed June 29, 2009).

7. Jim Sullivan and Phil Roberts, *Service That Sells! The Art of Profitable Hospitality* (Denver: Pencom Press, 1991), 151.

8. Howard Lax, "Fun, Fun, Fun in a Customer Experience Way," *Banking Strategies* 84, no. 6 (November–December 2008): 64.

9. "Johnson Controls Runs Boot Camp," *Heating & Refrigeration News* 233, no. 6 (April 14, 2008).

10. Tom Reilly, "Relationship Selling at Its Best," *Industrial Distribution* 25, no. 9 (September 2006): 29.

11. Demmie Hicks, "The Power of Consultative Selling," *Rough Notes* 151, no. 7 (July 2008): 701.

12. Cathy Berch, "Consultative Selling: Ask, Don't Tell," *Community Banker* 18, no. 4 (April 2009): 261.

13. Tom Reilly, "Relationship Selling at Its Best," *Industrial Distribution* 25, no. 9 (September 2006): 29.

14. Brad Perriello, "Relationship—Selling at its Best," *Industrial Distribution* 97, no. 9 (September 2008): 34.

15. Cathy Berch, "Don't Wing It," *Community Banker* 18, no. 2 (February 2009): 18.

16. Michael Gray, "How Do You Determine Customer Lifetime Value?" Profit Advisors, May 20, 1999, http://www.profitadvisors.com/busfaq/lifetime.shtml (accessed November 30, 2009).

17. Claire Sykes, "Relationship Selling," *Surface Fabrication* 12, no. 1 (January–February 2006): 58.

18. SearchCRM.com, "CRM (Customer Relationship Management)," http://searchcrm.techtarget.com/definition/CRM (accessed November 30, 2009).

19. Susi Geiger and Darach Turley, "The Perceived Impact of Information Technology on Salespeople's Relational Competencies," *Journal of Marketing Management* 22, no. 7 (August 2006): 827.

20. Tom Reilly, "Relationship Selling at Its Best," *Industrial Distribution* 25, no. 9 (September 2006): 29.

21. "How to Use Golf as a Business Tool," video, BNET, http://www.bnet.com/2422-13722_23-323018.html (accessed July 27, 2009).

22. Terry L. Brock, "Relationship-Building Skills Pay Off for Your Bottom Line," *Philadelphia Business Journal*, June 12–18, 2009, 25.

23. Andrea Nierenberg, "Eight Ways to Say 'Thank You' to Customers," Manage Smarter, February 6, 2009, http://www.crystal-d.com/eight-key-ways-to-say-thank-you-to-customers (accessed July 3, 2009).

24. Tom Reilly, "Relationship Selling at Its Best," *Industrial Distribution* 25, no. 9 (September 2006): 29.

25. Annette Hanford, "Best Sellers Tell All," *Health & Beauty Salon* 25, no. 12 (December 2003): 50.

26. "A Foundation Built on Trust," Selling Power Sales Management eNewsletter, August 8, 2001, http://www.sellingpower.com/content/newsletter/issue.php?pc=146 (accessed March 16, 2010).

27. Brian Tracy, "Teaming Up with Your Customers," *Agency Sales* 34, no. 2 (February 2004): 59.

28. "Building Trust," Selling Power Presentations Newsletter, February 25, 2002, http://www.sellingpower.com/content/newsletter/issue.php?pc=186 (accessed March 16, 2010).

29. Stephen R. Covey, "Win-Win Strategies," *Training* 45, no. 1 (January 2008): 56.

30. J. D. Williams, Robert Everett, and Elizabeth Rogol, "Will the Human Factors of Relationship Selling Survive in the Twenty-First Century?" *International Journal of Commerce & Management* 19, no. 2 (2009): 158.

31. Marc Miller, "A Seat at the Table," *American Salesman* 54, no. 5 (May 2009): 9.

32. Tim Conner, "Sales Strategies of Six-Figure Salespeople," TimConnor.com, http://www.timconnor.com/articles_sales.html (accessed June 29, 2009).

33. "What Is Networking?" The Riley Guide, http://www.rileyguide.com/network.html#netprep (accessed July 3, 2009).

34. Meredith Levinson, "How to Network: 12 Tips for Shy People," *CIO*, December 11, 2007, http://www.cio.com/article/164300/How_to_Network_Tips_for_Shy_People?page=1 (accessed July 3, 2009).

35. Meredith Levinson, "How to Network: 12 Tips for Shy People," *CIO*, December 11, 2007, http://www.cio.com/article/164300/How_to_Network_Tips_for_Shy_People?page=1 (accessed July 3, 2009).

36. Kim Richmond, *Brand You*, 3rd ed. (Upper Saddle River, NJ: Pearson Prentice Hall, 2008), 176.

37. Meredith Levinson, "How to Network: 12 Tips for Shy People," *CIO*, December 11, 2007, http://www.cio.com/article/164300/How_to_Network_Tips_for_Shy_People?page=1 (accessed July 3, 2009).

38. Donna Rosato, "Networking for People Who Hate to Network," *CNNMoney.com*, April 3, 2009, http://money.cnn.com/2009/04/02/news/economy/networking_jobs.moneymag/index.htm (accessed July 3, 2009).

39. Lisa LaMotta, "How to Network Like a Pro Online," *Forbes*, August 9, 2007, http://www.forbes.com/2007/08/09/google-microsoft-walmart-ent-tech-cx_ll_0809networking.html (accessed July 3, 2009).

40. Clare Dight, "How to Network Online," *Times Online*, February 21, 2008, http://business.timesonline.co.uk/tol/business/career_and_jobs/graduate_management/article3402745.ece (accessed July 3, 2009).

41. Lisa LaMotta, "How to Network Like a Pro Online," *Forbes*, August 9, 2007, http://www.forbes.com/2007/08/09/google-microsoft-walmart-ent-tech-cx_ll_0809networking.html (accessed July 3, 2009).

42. Barton A. Weitz, Stephen B. Castleberry, and John F. Tanner, Jr., *Selling: Building Partnerships*, 7th ed. (New York: McGraw-Hill Irwin, 2009), 151.

43. Barton A. Weitz, Stephen B. Castleberry, and John F. Tanner, Jr., *Selling: Building Partnerships*, 7th ed. (New York: McGraw-Hill Irwin, 2009), 155.

44. Rick English, "Finding Your Selling Style," San Diego State University, Marketing 377 class notes, chapter 5, http://www-rohan.sdsu.edu/~renglish/377/notes/chapt05 (accessed July 7, 2009).

45. Barton A. Weitz, Stephen B. Castleberry, and John F. Tanner, Jr., *Selling: Building Partnerships*, 7th ed. (New York: McGraw-Hill Irwin, 2009), 151.

46. Todd Duncan, "Your Sales Style," *Incentive*, December 1, 1999, 64–66.

47. Ron Zemke, "Trust Inspires Trust," *Training* 10, January 1, 2002.

48. Barton A. Weitz, Stephen B. Castleberry, and John F. Tanner, Jr., *Selling: Building Partnerships*, 7th ed. (New York: McGraw-Hill Irwin, 2009), 158.

49. Barton A. Weitz, Stephen B. Castleberry, and John F. Tanner, Jr., *Selling: Building Partnerships*, 7th ed. (New York: McGraw-Hill Irwin, 2009), 159.

50. Sandra Bearden, "The Psychology of Sales: Savvy Selling Means Tailoring to Type," *UAB Magazine* 20, no. 2 (Fall 2000), http://main.uab.edu/show.asp?durki=41089 (accessed February 13, 2010).

51. Rick English, "Finding Your Selling Style," San Diego State University, Marketing 377 class notes, chapter 5, http://www-rohan.sdsu.edu/~renglish/377/notes/chapt05 (accessed July 7, 2009).

52. Barton A. Weitz, Stephen B. Castleberry, and John F. Tanner, Jr., *Selling: Building Partnerships*, 7th ed. (New York: McGraw-Hill Irwin, 2009), 158.

53. Avon Foundation for Women, "Reese Witherspoon Joins Avon Foundation for Women and San Francisco General Hospital to Celebrate 5th Anniversary of Avon Comprehensive Breast Center," press release, May 11, 2009, http://www.avoncompany.com/women/news/press20090511.html (accessed July 8, 2009).

54. Barton A. Weitz, Stephen B. Castleberry, and John F. Tanner, Jr., *Selling: Building Partnerships*, 7th ed. (New York: McGraw-Hill Irwin, 2009), 159.

55. Barton A. Weitz, Stephen B. Castleberry, and John F. Tanner, Jr., *Selling: Building Partnerships*, 7th ed. (New York: McGraw-Hill Irwin, 2009), 159.

56. Todd Duncan, "Your Sales Style," *Incentive*, December 1, 1999, 64–66.

57. Kim Richmond, *Brand You*, 3rd ed. (Upper Saddle River, NJ: Pearson Prentice Hall, 2008), 171.

58. Joseph De Avila, "Beyond Job Boards," *Wall Street Journal*, July 2, 2009, http://online.wsj.com/article/SB10001424052970203872404574260032327828514.html (accessed July 3, 2009).

59. Meredith Levinson, "How to Network: 12 Tips for Shy People," *CIO*, December 11, 2007, http://www.cio.com/article/164300/How_to_Network_Tips_for_Shy_People?page=1 (accessed July 3, 2009).

60. Howcast, "How to Network," video, http://www.youtube.com/watch?v=Y9VUqB7wQpY (accessed July 27, 2009).

61. Mike Hargis, "Social Networking Sites Dos and Don'ts," *CNN.com*, November 5, 2008, http://www.cnn.com/2008/LIVING/worklife/11/05/cb.social.networking/index.html (accessed May 16, 2010).

62. Elizabeth Lee, personal communication, June 26, 2009.

63. Mike Hargis, "Social Networking Sites Dos and Don'ts," *CNN.com*, November 5, 2008, http://www.cnn.com/2008/LIVING/worklife/11/05/cb.social.networking/index.html (accessed June 25, 2009).

64. Mike Hargis, "Social Networking Sites Dos and Don'ts," *CNN.com*, November 5, 2008, http://www.cnn.com/2008/LIVING/worklife/11/05/cb.social.networking/index.html (accessed June 25, 2009).

65. Kim Richmond, *Brand You*, 3rd ed. (Upper Saddle River, NJ: Pearson Prentice Hall, 2008), 134.

66. Diana Dietzschold Bourgeois, "Six Steps to Harnessing the Power of LinkedIn," Magic Marketing USA, January 7, 2009, http://magicmarketingusa.wordpress.com/2009/01/07/linkedin (accessed May 16, 2010).

67. Diana Dietzschold Bourgeois, "Six Steps to Harnessing the Power of LinkedIn," Magic Marketing USA, January 7, 2009, http://magicmarketingusa.wordpress.com/2009/01/07/linkedin (accessed May 16, 2010).

68. Matthew Boyle, "Enough to Make a Monster Tremble," BusinessWeek, June 25, 2009, http://www.businessweek.com/magazine/content/09_27/b4138043180664.htm (accessed June 25, 2009).

69. Matthew Boyle, "Enough to Make a Monster Tremble," BusinessWeek, June 25, 2009, http://www.businessweek.com/magazine/content/09_27/b4138043180664.htm (accessed June 25, 2009).

CHAPTER 4
Business Ethics: The Power of Doing the Right Thing

Video Ride-Along with Paul Blake, Vice President of Sales at Greater Media Philadelphia

You met Paul Blake in Chapter 2. With over twenty years of experience in selling, Paul has been in challenging situations when his ethics were at stake. He knows the importance of doing the right thing, even when it's not the easy thing to do. Because your ethics may be put to the test at any time by your co-workers, customers, or even your boss, Paul shares his thoughts on ethics in selling.

Ride along with Paul as he discusses doing the right thing.

View the video online at: http://www.youtube.com/embed/7Tb4K7uvkuk

4.1 Business Ethics: Guiding Principles in Selling and in Life

Learning Objectives

1. Understand ethics and what composes ethical behavior.
2. Discuss the role of values in ethics.
3. Understand how you define your personal code of ethics.

It seemed like a straightforward decision at the time—you could either pay ninety-nine cents per song on iTunes, or you could download for free from a peer-to-peer network or torrent service. After all, artists want people to enjoy their music, right? And besides, it's not like Kanye West needs any more money. So you pointed your browser to ThePirateBay.org.

Of course, that isn't the whole story. The MP3s you downloaded have value—that's why you wanted them, right? And when you take something of value without paying the price, well, that's theft. The fact that you're unlikely to get caught (and it isn't impossible; people are arrested, prosecuted, and ordered to pay massive judgments for providing or downloading music illegally) may make you feel safer, but if you are caught, you could pay from $750 to $150,000 per song.[1] Other variables can further complicate the situation. If you downloaded the MP3s at work, for example, you could lose your job. Acting unethically is wrong and can have enormous practical consequences for your life and your career.

What Is Ethics?

ethics

Moral principles that define what is right and wrong.

Ethics is moral principles—it is a system that defines right and wrong and provides a guiding philosophy for every decision you make. The Josephson Institute of Ethics describes ethical behavior well: "Ethics is about how we meet the challenge of doing the right thing when that will cost more than we want to pay. There are two aspects to ethics: The first involves the ability to discern right from wrong, good from evil, and propriety from impropriety. The second involves the commitment to do what is right, good, and proper. Ethics entails action; it is not just a topic to mull or debate."[2] Is it right? Is it fair? Is it equitable? Is it honest? Is it good for people? These are all questions of ethics.[3] Ethics is doing the right thing, even if it is difficult or is not to your advantage.[4] Carly Fiorina, former CEO of Hewlett-Packard, discusses the importance and impact of ethics on business.

Video Clip

Excerpt from Carly Fiorina's Speech on Ethics
Your success starts with personal ethics.

View the video online at: http://www.youtube.com/embed/WlH8uMu1_ng

Personal Ethics: Your Behavior Defines You

ethical dilemma

A situation in which options are presented which may be right or wrong.

Ethics comes into play in the decisions you make every day. Have you ever received too much money back when you paid for something in a store, didn't get charged for something you ordered at a restaurant, or called in sick to work when you just wanted a day off?[5] Each of these is an **ethical dilemma**. You make your decision about which path to take based on your personal ethics; your actions reflect your own moral beliefs and moral conduct.[6] Your ethics are developed as a result of your family, church, school, community, and other influences that help shape your personal beliefs—that which you believe to be right versus wrong.[7] A good starting point for your personal ethics is the golden rule: "Do unto others as you would have them do unto you." That is, treat people the way that you would like to be treated. You would like people to be honest with you, so be honest with others.

Your strong sense of personal ethics can help guide you in your decisions. You might be surprised to find yourself with an ethical dilemma about something that is second nature to you. For example, imagine that you're taking a class (required for your major) that has an assignment of a twenty-page paper and you've been so busy with your classes, internship, and volunteer work that you really haven't had the time to get started. You know you shouldn't have waited so long and you're really worried because the paper is due in only two days and you've never written a paper this long before. Now you have to decide what to do. You could knuckle down, go to the library, and visit the campus Writing Center, but you really don't have the time to do all that and still write the entire twenty pages. You've heard about some people who have successfully bought papers from this one Web site. You've never done it before, but you are really desperate and out of time. "If I only do it this one time," you think, "I'll never do it again."

But compromising your ethics even just once is a slippery slope. The idea is that one thing leads naturally to allowing another until you find yourself sliding rapidly downhill. Ethics is all about the art of navigating the slippery slope: you have to draw a line for yourself, decide what you will and won't do—and then stick to it. If you don't have a strong set of ethics, you have nothing to use as a guidepost when you are in a situation that challenges you morally. A highly developed set of personal ethics should guide your actions. The only way to develop a strong sense of ethics is to do what you believe in, to take actions consistent with your principles time and time again.

So if you buy the paper and get caught, you will not only fail the class, but you may also find yourself expelled from school. If you're tempted to consider buying a paper, take a minute to read your school's academic dishonesty policy, as it is most likely very clear about what is right and wrong in situations like this.

Link

Academic Dishonesty Policy at the University of Nevada, Reno

http://www.unr.edu/student-conduct/policies/university-policies-and-guidelines/academic-standards/academic-standards-policy-for-students

Even if you get away with using a paper that is not your own for now, it's always possible that you'll be found out and humiliated even decades after the fact. Southern Illinois University (SIU) had three high-ranking officials—a university president and two chancellors—revealed as plagiarists in a two-year period.[8] Even more embarrassing, the committee formed to investigate the charges of plagiarism against Chancellor Walter Wendler developed a new plagiarism policy whose parts were plagiarized—specifically, it copied its academic dishonesty policy from Indiana University without citing that source.[9] SIU was made a laughingstock, and its reputation has suffered considerably. Academic dishonesty is not a gamble worth taking; though many students are tempted at some point, those who give in usually regret it.

Do the Right Thing

If you rationalize your decisions by saying, "Everyone does it," you should reconsider. **Unethical behavior** is not only what you believe to be right and fair, it is a reflection of your personal brand and what people can expect from you personally and professionally. Even celebrities such as Wesley Snipes, Willie Nelson, and Darryl Strawberry have fallen from grace in the eyes of the public and learned the hard way that unethical—and in their cases, illegal—behavior such as tax evasion can result in a prison term.[10] The consequences of unethical behavior can range from embarrassment to suspension, loss of job, or even jail time, depending on the act.

Eliot Spitzer, the governor of New York, admitted that he violated his personal ethics and those of his office when he resigned in March 2008 because of alleged involvement in a sex ring. Ironically, he built his reputation as the "sheriff of Wall Street" due to his efforts to crack down on corporate misdeeds.[11] His disgrace was the topic of many conversations about ethics.

unethical behavior

Acting in a way that is not responsible or deemed to be the standard of what is right, good, and fair.

Video Clip

What Is Ethics?
This video includes interviews about ethics and perceptions of Eliot Spitzer and his actions.

View the video online at: http://www.youtube.com/embed/-amNlnSMFZI

You have no doubt heard the expression "Do the right thing." It is the essence of ethics: choosing to do the right thing when you have a choice of actions. Being ethical means you will do the right thing regardless of whether there are possible consequences—you treat other people well and behave morally for its own sake, not because you are afraid of the possible consequences. Simply put, people do the right thing because it is the right thing to do. Thomas Jefferson summed up ethics in a letter he wrote to Peter Carr in 1785: "Whenever you are to do a thing, though it can never be known but to yourself, ask yourself how you would act were all the world looking at you, and act accordingly."[12]

Ethical decisions are not always easy to make, depending on the situation. There are some gray areas depending on how you approach a certain situation. According to Sharon Keane, associate director of marketing at the University of Notre Dame, people have different approaches, so there may be multiple solutions to each ethical dilemma,[13] and every situation may have multiple options. For example, if one of your best friends told you in confidence that he stole the questions to the final exam would you say nothing, use them, or report him? Certainly, using the questions would not be ethical, but your ethical dilemma doesn't end there. Reporting him would be the right thing to do. But if you didn't report him, would it be unethical? You might not consider that unethical, but what if you just didn't say anything—is that still ethical? This is the gray area where your personal ethics come into play. Looking the other way doesn't help him or you. While you might be concerned about jeopardizing your friendship, it would be a small price to pay compared with jeopardizing your personal ethics.

Business Ethics: What Makes a Company Ethical?

business ethics

The application of ethical behavior by a business or in a business environment.

stakeholders

All parties that have a stake in an organization including employees, customers, investors, the community, and others.

Ethics apply to businesses as well personal behavior. **Business ethics** is the application of ethical behavior by a business or in a business environment. An ethical business not only abides by laws and appropriate regulations, it operates honestly, competes fairly, provides a reasonable environment for its employees, and creates partnerships with customers, vendors, and investors. In other words, it keeps the best interest of all **stakeholders** at the forefront of all decisions.[14]

An ethical organization operates honestly and with fairness. Some characteristics of an ethical company include the following:

- Respect and fair treatment of employees, customers, investors, vendors, community, and all who have a stake in and come in contact with the organization

- Honest communication to all stakeholders internally and externally

- Integrity in all dealings with all stakeholders
- High standards for personal accountability and ethical behavior
- Clear communication of internal and external policies to appropriate stakeholders[15]

High-Profile Unethical Behavior in Business

While ethical behavior may seem as if it is the normal course of business, it's unfortunate that some business people and some businesses do not operate ethically. Enron, WorldCom, Tyco, Health-South, and Lehman Brothers among other companies, have been highlighted in the news during the past several years due to unethical behavior that resulted in corporate scandals and, in some cases, the conviction of senior executives and collapse of some companies. While business has never been immune from unethical behavior, it was the fall of Enron in 2001 that brought unethical business behavior on the part of senior executives to the forefront. Enron began as a traditional energy company in 1985. But when energy markets were deregulated (prices were determined based on the competition rather than being set by the government) in 1996, Enron grew rapidly. The company began to expand to areas such as Internet services and borrowed money to fund the new businesses. The debt made the company look less profitable, so the senior management created partnerships in order to keep the debt off the books. In other words, they created "paper companies" that held the debt, and they showed a completely different set of financial statements to shareholders (owners of the company) and the government (U.S. Securities Exchange Commission [SEC]). This accounting made Enron look extremely profitable—it appeared to have tripled its profit in two years. As a result, more people bought stock in the company. This lack of disclosure is against the law, as publicly traded companies are required to disclose accurate financial statements to shareholders and the SEC. There began to be speculation about the accuracy of Enron's accounting, and on October 16, 2001, the company announced a loss of $638 million. On October 22 of that year, the SEC announced that Enron was under investigation. The stock price continued to fall, and the company was unable to repay its commitments to its shareholders. As a result of this unethical and illegal behavior on the part of senior management, the company filed for chapter 11 bankruptcy protection.[16] The unethical (and illegal) behavior of the senior management team caused a ripple effect that resulted in many innocent people losing their money and their jobs. As a result of the Enron scandal, a new law named the **Sarbanes-Oxley Act** (for Senator Paul Sarbanes from Maryland and Representative Michael Oxley from Ohio) was enacted in 2002 that requires tighter financial reporting controls for publicly traded companies.[17]

Sarbanes-Oxley Act of 2002

Regulation of corporate financial practices and protection for people who report violations.

The epitome of unethical (and illegal) behavior was Bernard Madoff, who was convicted of running a $65 billion fraud scheme on his investors. For years, he reported extremely high returns on his clients' investments, encouraging them to reinvest with even more money. All the time he was stealing from his clients and spending the money. He cheated many clients, including high-profile celebrities like actor Kevin Bacon and his wife Kyra Sedgewick and a charity of Steven Spielberg's.[18] He was arrested, tried, and sentenced to 150 years in jail, and his key employees were also sentenced to similar terms.[19],[20]

Ethical Dilemmas in Business

Not all behavior that is unethical is illegal. Companies frequently are faced with ethical dilemmas that are not necessarily illegal but are just as important to navigate. For example, if a travel company wants to attract a lot of new customers, it can honestly state the price of a trip to Disney World in its advertising and let customers decide if they want to purchase the trip. This would be ethical behavior. However, if the company advertises a free vacation in order to get customers to call, but the free vacation package includes a $500 booking fee, it is unethical. Or if an appliance store wants to get new customers by advertising a low-priced refrigerator, it is an ethical way to let customers know that the company has competitively priced appliances as well. However, if the store only has a higher-priced refrigerator in stock and tries to sell that one instead, it is unethical behavior.

FIGURE 4.1

Business cannot operate without ethical behavior on the part of all parties.

© 2010 Jupiterimages Corporation

---

corporate social responsibility (CSR)

Company actions that balance the interests of all stakeholders.

triple bottom line

Measurement of company performance along three dimensions—social, economic, and environmental.

Sometimes ethical behavior can be a matter of disclosure, as in the case of Enron, Bernie Madoff, or the examples above. Business ethics can also be challenged based on business practices. For example, in the 1990s Nike was accused of exploiting workers in third-world countries to manufacture their products. The low wages they were paying the workers made Nike's profits higher.[21] While this is not illegal behavior—they were paying the workers—it was considered unethical because they were paying the workers less than what is reasonable. Another example of unethical behavior is not disclosing information. For example, if a car salesperson knows that a used car he is selling has been in an accident but says that it has not been involved in an accident, that is unethical. Bribing an executive, saying or promising things that are knowingly untrue, or treating employees unfairly are all examples of unethical behavior in business.

Corporate Social Responsibility

You may choose to shop at companies because of their business practices. For example, you might like The Body Shop because of its commitment to selling products that do not use animals for testing. This is a case of ethical behavior that is socially responsible. In fact, **corporate social responsibility (CSR)** is when companies operate in a way that balances the interests of all stakeholders including employees, customers, investors, vendors, the community, society, and any other parties that have a stake in the company. While corporate social responsibility may seem easy, it's not always as easy as it looks. Keep in mind that in order to be socially responsible a company has to balance the social, economic, and environmental dimensions, which means generating a profit for investors while serving the best interest of all parties that have a stake in the operations of the company. When companies measure the impact of their performance along the three dimensions of social, economic, and environmental impact, it is called the **triple bottom line**. To learn more about McDonald's social responsibility, watch the following video.

Video Clip

McDonald's Commitment to Social Responsibility
See how the triple bottom line is part of the company culture.

View the video online at: http://www.youtube.com/embed/S_bgP3ASUM4

There are many companies that make a commitment to social responsibility and the triple bottom line.

Link

Most "Accountable" Companies for Socially Responsible Practices

http://money.cnn.com/popups/2006/fortune/g500_accountability/index.html

---

Good Ethics = Good Business

The impact of ethical behavior by companies cannot be underestimated. It's no surprise that companies that consistently demonstrate ethical behavior and social responsibility generate better results. In successful companies ethics is so integrated into the organization that it defines how every employee from CEO to the lowest-level employee behaves. Ethics is not a separate topic but is incorporated into company strategy. The company makes ethics part of every activity from strategic planning to operational execution.[22] For example, Target has been committed to the triple bottom line even before it was in vogue when the company's founder, George Draper Dayton, established a foundation to give back to the community. The company's commitment has grown, and since 1946 it has donated 5 percent of its income every year. Target's Corporate Responsibility Report is information that the company makes available to everyone on its Web site.[23]

Link

Target's Corporate Responsibility Report

Target's commitment to social responsibility is made public on the company's Web site.

https://corporate.target.com/corporate-responsibility

Target's commitment to ethics and social responsibility are especially impressive given the current economic challenges. It is times like these that can challenge many companies that do not have this kind of ethical commitment. With pressure on short-term results, many companies set unrealistic goals and employees feel extreme pressure to meet them or face the possibility of losing their jobs. Professor Neil Malhotra of the Stanford Graduate School of Business calls this an "overemphasis on instant gratification." In fact, he feels that is the root cause of the current economic crisis.[24] But business ethics, just like personal ethics, mean doing the right thing even when it is a difficult choice or doesn't appear to be advantageous.

But ethical behavior and integrity are clearly linked to profitability. In a study of seventy-six Holiday Inn franchises around the country conducted by Tony Simons, associate professor in organization management at Cornell University and author of the book *The Integrity Divided*, Simons found that the behavior of the hotel manager was the "single most powerful driver of profit."[25]

Ethical Behavior in Sales

One of the most visible positions in any organization in terms of ethics is *sales*. That's because it is the salesperson that comes in contact directly with the customer. What the salesperson says and does is a direct reflection of the organization and its ethics.

Consider this ethical dilemma if you were a real estate agent. You have just landed a fantastic listing: a home that in the hot neighborhood that will surely sell quickly and yield a nice commission for you. The seller tells you that the home inspector suspects there is insect damage to the siding of the house, but the seller says she has never had any problems. Also, the seller feels so strongly about not disclosing this information to prospective buyers that she said she would rather go with a different agent if you insist on disclosing the possible insect damage. What would you do?

In a situation like this, it's best to remember that doing the right thing can be a hard choice and might not be advantageous to you. Although you really don't want to lose this listing, the right thing to do is to disclose anything that affects the value or desirability of the home. Even if you think it might not be a major issue, it's always best to err on the side of honesty and disclose the information.[26] Either withholding or falsifying information is lying and therefore unethical.[27]

Imagine that you are a financial planner responsible for managing your clients assets. You make your income on commission, a percentage of the value of your clients' portfolios; the more you increase his portfolio, the more money you make. One of your clients is a very conservative investor; right now you are not making much money from his account. You have an opportunity to sell him a high-return investment, but the risk is far greater than you think he would normally take. You think you can sell him on it if you leave out just a few details during your conversation. The investment will actually be good for him because he will get a significant return on his investment, and besides, you're tired of spending your time on the phone with him and not making any money. This could be a win-win situation. Should you give him your pitch with a few factual omissions or just make the investment and tell him after the money starts rolling in? After all, he doesn't look at his account every day.[28] What should you do?

Even though the result of the investment could be a good one, it is your obligation to provide full disclosure of the risk and let the customer make the investment decision. You should never make assumptions and decisions on behalf of your customers without their consent. If you are frustrated about your lack of income on the account, you might not be the best financial planner for him. You should have an honest conversation with him and perhaps suggest a colleague or other planner that might be a better fit for his investment strategy. Sometimes it's better to part ways than to be tempted to behave unethically.

Just Say No

What if your employer asked you to do something that you are not comfortable doing? For example, if your employer asked you to complete the paperwork for a sale even if the sale hasn't been made, what should you do? It's best to say that you are not comfortable doing it; never compromise your personal ethics even for your employer. It's also a good idea to see someone in the human resources department if you have any questions about the best way to handle a specific situation.

What if you were a salesperson for a textbook company and you are only $1,000 away from your $1 million sales goal. If you make your goal, you'll earn a $10,000 bonus, money you've been counting on to put a down payment on your first house. But the deadline is only two days away, and none of your customers is ready to make a purchase. You really want the bonus, and you don't want to wait until next year to earn it. Then you remember talking to one of the administrators, and she mentioned the need for donations. What if you made a $1,000 donation to the school. It would help the school during this challenging financial crisis and it would be more inclined to make a purchase quickly. After the donation, you would still have $9,000. This could be a good move for everyone. Would you make the donation to "buy" your bonus?

When you are in sales, you are not only representing yourself, but you are also representing your company. Although it appears that all parties will benefit from the donation, it is not ethical for the school, you, or your company to make an exchange like that. Products such as textbooks should be purchased based on the organization's buying process. Donations should be made with no strings attached. You might miss the opportunity to earn your bonus this year, but you will learn valuable lessons to make next year an even better sales year.[29]

Imagine that you are a sales rep for a software company and you've just taken a customer to lunch. It was an expensive restaurant, and the two of you thoroughly enjoyed yourselves; you had steak, wine, and a chocolate dessert. Now you're filling out an expense report, and you need to fill in the amount of tip you left. In fact, you left a twenty-dollar bill—but forty dollars wouldn't have been an unreasonable amount to leave for outstanding service. You could fill in the higher amount and use the difference to take your girlfriend to the movies; you've been meaning to spend more time with her. After all, you make a lot of money for the company and have been working a lot of nights and weekends lately. You also didn't submit your expense account for the mileage you traveled last week, so this should make up for it. Is it OK to submit the additional tip money on this expense report?

It's no surprise that it's never acceptable to falsify information on an expense report (or any report for that matter). If you have legitimate expenses, they should be submitted according to the company policy. While it's hard to keep up with the paperwork, it's the right way to report and be reimbursed for company expenses. This can be another one of those slippery slope arguments; if you do it once, you might be tempted to do it again. Many people in many companies have been fired for providing false information on their expense reports.

Personal ethics and business ethics are a part of everyday selling. It's a good idea to remember the words of Peter Drucker, famous management consultant and author, "Start with what is right, rather than what is acceptable."[30]

Power Point: Lessons in Selling from the Customer's Point of View

Is the Customer Always Right?

The customer is always right, except when he asks you to do something unethical. What should you do to uphold your ethics and maintain your relationship? SellingPower.com suggests the following four steps:

1. Evaluate the situation with a clear head. Most unethical behavior is driven by emotions such as fear, greed, stress, and status. Identify what is causing the behavior but wait until you have some time to reflect.

2. Don't jump to conclusions; identify the circumstances. You might not know the entire story so determine what you know and what you don't know.

3. Identify the criteria you are using to make this judgment. Is the behavior against company policy? Is it against the law? Is it against your personal code of ethics?

4. Seek counsel. Always ask a trusted colleague, supervisor, or human resources representative for advice. Chances are, she has experienced the same situation and can provide insight from the company's perspective and policies.

Understanding Values

Ethics are defined by moral principles; they are actions that are viewed by society as "right," "just," or "responsible."[31] **Values** define what is important to you: they are your guiding principles and beliefs, they define how you live your life, and they inform your ethics. While certain values might be important to you, they may not be important to your best friends or even every member of your family. While family, friends, and your environment have a significant influence, you develop your own set of values. Consider the list below, which includes some examples of values:[32]

values

Guiding principles and beliefs that are important to you and define how you live your life.

- Honesty
- Open communication
- Teamwork
- Integrity
- Prestige
- Security
- Helping others
- Loyalty
- Social responsibility
- Impact on society
- Creativity
- Achievement
- Global focus
- Religion

Values provide your personal compass and your direction in life. When something is not in line with your values, you feel unhappy and dissatisfied.[33] Many people feel passionately about their values and want to have their environment align with their values. Examples of this are evident during political elections when people take sides on issues such as education, health care, and other social issues that reflect personal values.

You might be surprised to learn that your values are not set in stone. Your personal values will evolve and may even change drastically based on your experiences.[34] For example, Nikki Tsongas, wife of the late Senator Paul Tsongas from Massachusetts, got involved in public service after the death of her husband. She is now a congresswoman from the fifth district of Massachusetts.[35] She may have never considered serving in public office, but the death of her husband had a dramatic impact on her values.

You have a set of values that inform your ethics, which in turn inform your decision making. No one can tell you what your values are; that's something you'll have to decide for yourself. John C. Maxwell, in his book *There's No Such Thing as "Business" Ethics*, lists the values that he lives by, such as "put your family ahead of your work (having a strong and stable family creates a launching pad for many other successes during a career and provides a contented landing place at the end of it)"[36] and "take responsibility for your actions (if you desire to be trusted by others and you want to achieve much, you must take responsibility for your actions)."[37] If you are looking for a comprehensive list of values, check out HumanityQuest.com, which lists more than five hundred different values.

Link

Learn about What Values Are Important to You

http://highered.mheducation.com/sites/0073381225/student_view0/chapter2/self-assessment_2_2.html

Values of Organizations

Just like people, organizations have values, too. Values are "proven, enduring guidelines for human conduct" according to Stephen Covey in his book *Principles*.[38] Many companies choose their values and communicate them to employees, customers, and vendors on the company Web site and other company communications. For example, Whole Foods includes the following values, among others: "selling the highest quality natural and organic products available" and "caring about communities and their environment." You can see their entire values statement on their Web site.

Link

Whole Foods Market Values Statement

http://www.wholefoodsmarket.com/company/corevalues.php

Levi Strauss & Co. identifies four key values for their company: empathy, originality, integrity, and courage. Their values statement is also included on their Web site.

Link

Levi Strauss & Co. Values Statement

http://www.levistrauss.com/who-we-are/culture/

Microsoft includes integrity, honesty, personal excellence, passion for technology, and commitment to customers as part of their values statement on their Web site.

Link

Microsoft Values Statement

http://www.microsoft.com/about/default.mspx

Company values and personal values are important because your values motivate you to work.[39] You will enjoy and excel at your job if you choose a company whose values you share. For example, if the environment is one of your values, it's best to choose a company that includes a commitment to the environment as part of their values statement. Chances are you won't be happy working at a company that doesn't put a priority on the environment.

Mission Statements: Personal and Corporate Guidelines

Ethics and values are major concepts. If you have developed personal ethics and values, you might be wondering how they come together to help provide a roadmap for your life and your career. That's the purpose of your mission statement; it becomes your roadmap for your decisions, choices, and behavior. You learned about creating your personal mission statement in the *Selling U* section of Chapter 1. Mission statements such as "To gain experience in the public accounting field toward earning my CPA designation" and "To master the leading Web development tools and become a best-in-class Web developer" may sound simple, but each takes time, thought, and insight to create.[40] You may want to review the *Selling U* section in Chapter 1 if you haven't already created your personal mission statement.

Just as your personal mission statement is a blueprint for how you make decisions in life, companies also use a mission statement to define their direction, make operating decisions, and communicate to employees, vendors, shareholders, and other stakeholders. In fact, most companies have a formal, written mission that they include on their Web site. A mission statement is different than an advertising slogan or motto. It is based on the company's ethics and values and provides a broad direction as to what the company stands for. For example, Harley-Davidson's mission statement is below and can be found on their Web site.

Link

Harley-Davidson's mission statement

http://www.harley-davidson.com/content/h-d/en_US/company.html

FedEx expresses their mission statement a little differently as shown below and includes their mission statement along with their values on their Web site.

Link

FedEx Mission Statement and Goals

http://investors.fedex.com/company-overview/mission-and-goals/default.aspx

The mission statement of the insurance company Aflac is short and to the point as shown below. It can also be found on their Web site.

Link

Aflac Mission Statement
https://www.aflac.com/about-aflac/our-company/default.aspx

Many companies, like Google, put their mission statement or philosophy online—others use a printed manual. The mission statement is made available for the following reasons: employees can use it to aid them in ethical business decision making, investors can evaluate the company's ethics before making a decision about becoming involved with it, and customers can choose whom they will do business with based on their ethics and purpose. In addition to their mission statement (which you may remember from Chapter 1: "Google's mission is to organize the world's information and make it universally accessible and useful"[41]), Google's Web site gives their philosophy—ten guiding principles, ten "things Google has found to be true," which are values that reflect how the company conducts business:

1. Focus on the user and all else will follow.
2. It's best to do one thing really, really well.
3. Fast is better than slow.
4. Democracy on the Web works.
5. You don't need to be at your desk to need an answer.
6. You can make money without doing evil.
7. There's always more information out there.
8. The need for information crosses all borders.
9. You can be serious without a suit.
10. Great just isn't good enough.[42]

These ten things are the principles that Google uses to make decisions as a company; this list, with accompanying explanations, details why they do things the way that they do. It is both practical and concerned with ethics—the idea that "great just isn't good enough" is part of their values, a declaration that Google wants to do the best that it can in every endeavor—it means that they will not take shortcuts, but will constantly strive to be more ethical, efficient, and user-friendly.

Character and Its Influence on Selling

character

Features and beliefs that define a person.

As you have probably figured out, ethics, values, and missions are all very personal. Together they guide you in the way you behave at home, school, work, or out with your friends. Your **character** is what sets you apart; it includes the features and beliefs that define you. It's no surprise that the word has it origin in the Latin word *character*, which means mark or distinctive quality and from the Greek *charaktr*, which means to scratch.[43] The Josephson Institute defines character as being composed of six core ethical values:

1. Trustworthiness
2. Respect
3. Responsibility
4. Fairness
5. Caring
6. Citizenship[44]

This is a comprehensive description of character. Consider how you perceive other people; it's their character that defines who they are. Can you depend on him? Is she fair? Does he respect you? Just as these ethical pillars define other peoples' character, they also define your character to other people. Customers ask the same questions about you: Can I trust her? Will he give me fair pricing? Is she honest? Does he care about the best interest of my business?

The Power of Your Reputation

In November of 2008, *Tomb Raider: Underworld* was released for multiple gaming systems. Knowing how important a game's reputation can be for sales, public relations firm Barrington Harvey—in an attempt to massage the Metacritic score, a less-than-ethical move—asked reviewers to hold their scores until after the first weekend of the game's release. "That's right. We're trying to manage the review scores at the request of Eidos." When asked why, a spokesperson for Barrington Harvey explained, "Just that we're trying to get the Metacritic rating to be high, and the brand manager in the United States that's handling all of Tomb Raider has asked that we just manage the scores before the game is out, really, just to ensure that we don't put people off buying the game, basically."[45] Eidos, the company that published the game, tried to take an ethical shortcut—they wanted to be sure that the game's reputation *could not* precede it—but paid for that decision with a great deal of negative publicity that adversely impacted their reputation.

Your overall character as judged by other people is your **reputation**.[46] Consider some celebrities who have had unethical acts negatively impact their reputation: Tiger Woods, known as one of golf's greats has been reduced to tabloid fodder since the news of his extramarital affairs; Michael Phelps, the only person to ever win eight gold medals in a single Olympic Games, has become the poster boy for marijuana use. Both had stellar reputations and were considered role models. Now both are working to gain back the trust of the public. Reputation isn't limited to the wealthy or powerful. In high school, you knew that Sharon was a brain and Timothy was the sensitive, poetic type. You may never have had a conversation with either one of them, but you knew their reputations. Meanwhile, you avoided classes with Mrs. Avar because she had a reputation as a hard grader. Your reactions to many of the people in your day-to-day life are affected by their reputations.

reputation
Overall character as judged by other people.

Build Your Reputation: Be an Industry Expert

A great way to build your reputation in a specific industry is to become an industry expert: write a blog, tweet regularly about industry issues, be a guest speaker or panelist at industry conferences or events online or in person. Decision makers hear and see you take on a leadership role and seek you out to gain your expertise. You can build your reputation, which, in turn, will help you build your client list.[47]

When you work in sales, you are selling yourself; you will have greater success with customers if you are someone they want to "buy." When customers buy from you, they are investing in your reputation. George Ludwig, author of *Power Selling*, explains that "you've got to live out your identity consistently in every facet of your life and make sure prospective clients bump into that identity everywhere they turn."[48] In other words, every action you take affects your reputation. If you fail to follow up, forget details, or even if you are consistently late for meetings, you may become known as unreliable. On the other hand, if you consistently deliver what you promise, you will be known as reliable; if you always meet your deadlines, you will have a reputation for punctuality.

Power Player: Lessons in Selling from Successful Salespeople

Do the Right Thing

Robert L. Bailey, retired CEO, president, and chairman of the State Auto Insurance Companies, knows how important a salesperson's reputation can be and the value of consistent ethical behavior. "Back in my corporate days I regularly met with new employees. I would tell them,

'Regardless of the circumstances, regardless of what the contract says, we always want you to do the right thing. Do you know what it means to do the right thing?' I would ask." Bailey knows that any action taken by a salesperson can affect his or her reputation: "If your actions are described on the front page of our local newspaper or *USA Today*, will most people read the account and say, 'I think they did the right thing?" That's the kind of action we encourage and expect."[49] Your reputation speaks for you; make sure it's saying what you want customers to hear.

You're Only as Good as Your Word

Unfortunately, not everyone in sales is ethical or honest. David Chittock, president of Incentra, Inc., discusses one encounter in which a customer shared her view of salespeople: "The prospect's body language told me she wasn't just uncomfortable—she was downright hostile to me. Finally, she shared this sentiment out loud: 'I have to be honest with you. I think that all salespeople are liars, and I don't trust any of them, and I don't trust you.'" He goes on to explain that "many (if not all) of our prospects, view salespeople with suspicion, assuming that in attempting to make a sale, we will be self-serving, manipulative, and possibly even untruthful."[50] Chittock and his employees overcome that suspicion by making promises to their customers and then keeping them—sure, it sounds simple, but too many salespeople are willing to promise their customers the moon in order to close the deal.

Dr. Pat Lynch conducted a study that was published in the *Journal of Business Ethics* in which he asked more than seven hundred businesspeople and graduate business students to rank their values in the workplace; these included competency, work ethic, overcoming adversity, seniority, and promise keeping. Lynch found that keeping promises was that the bottom of people's lists, whatever their gender, supervisory experience, or religious background.[51] Honesty is a way to stand out and to build your reputation.

Video Clip

View the video online at: http://www.youtube.com/embed/MH21D2Fjv9M?rel=0

If you are committed to finding win-win-win solutions for your customers, you need to be honest with them and with yourself. Figure out what you can realistically guarantee, make the promise, and then keep it. Jack Welch, in his book *Winning*, declares that "too many people—too often—instinctively don't express themselves with frankness. They don't communicate straightforwardly or put forth ideas looking to stimulate real debate. But when you've got candor, everything just operates faster and better."[52] If circumstances change and you realize that you will be unable to keep your promise, immediately communicate with the customer; explain what has happened, offer a new solution, and apologize. While that can make for an awkward conversation, in the long run, that kind of honesty and openness will help you to build strong business relationships.

Where the Rubber Meets the Road: Facing Challenges

Imagine that you are the buyer for Chez Food, a popular pan-European restaurant on the West Coast. You have good relationships with your suppliers, especially your produce guy, a genial fellow who owns his own business. As the holidays approach, Ray, your produce guy, approaches you with a gift. He tells you that he really appreciates both your business and your friendship, and he hands you two tickets to a Caribbean cruise. The company policy is clear: you aren't supposed to accept gifts from suppliers, but, you argue to yourself, what could be the harm? After all, you were planning to keep buying from Ray before he offered you the tickets; it's not as though he's asking you for anything, anyway. What will you do? Your ethical obligation, of course, is to refuse the tickets—politely. Your relationship with Ray is important, but doing the right thing—and keeping your job—is important too.

At some point in your selling career—in fact, probably at many points—you will be faced with a situation that challenges your ethics. At these times, it is best to follow your code of ethics and the company's code of ethics; when in doubt, don't make an exception. If you're having trouble finding the motivation to refuse a gift or accurately detail your résumé, remember that you will very like be found out—and when you're found out, you will be very lucky not to lose your job. Is the case of wine from a supplier worth losing your job over? But more important, when you fail an ethical challenge, you trade in your integrity. If you are tempted to inflate your expense report by fifty dollars, ask yourself, "Is my integrity worth more than fifty dollars?" The answer, of course, is that your integrity is worth more than any amount of money—and once gone, it cannot be bought back. Ken Lay, former CEO of Enron, was a man with a great reputation and an oil portrait displayed at his alma mater; once his crimes were discovered, however, his name was forever associated with a willingness to break the law and exploit his own employees.[53]

Sir Michael Rake, chairman of KPMG International, says in *Leading by Example*, "Enron had an enormously laudable charter of values in corporate social responsibility, but actually it was almost a smokescreen for abuse…In investigations we've done into companies and individuals where things have gone wrong…have crossed from white, to gray, to black. Most of them have to operate in the gray a lot of the time…because of the aggressiveness with which the targets are set of the way in which their achievement of those targets is rewarded, intelligent, honest people suddenly think that this act is OK: because within that environment it seems to be OK. It isn't OK; they've actually done something which is illegal or amoral."[54]

Finding yourself in a corrupt corporate culture is not reason enough to violate your own code of ethics or break the law. If you find yourself in a situation where you feel pressured to do something unethical (or even illegal), talk to your supervisor about it. If you don't feel that you can talk to your supervisor—or your supervisor is part of the problem—talk to someone in the human resources department. Give the company a chance to resolve the situation; if they are not aware of it, they can't make it right.

If you're wondering about how the role of human resources works in a situation like this, it might be helpful to think about an analogy: When you were in high school and you went out with your friends, your mother, at some point or another (or perhaps every Friday night!), must have given you a talk that went something like this: "I want you to have a good time with your friends—but if anything happens, just call us and we'll come pick you up and we won't be mad. If there's drinking at the party, or if someone has drugs, just call us if you need to, OK?" While you probably won't be calling your mom when an ethical problem arises at work (much as you might secretly like to), you *can* call the human resources department. Human resources departments oversee hiring, promotions, and performance reviews, but they also deal with employee relations and can provide confidential counseling to workers. It is important for a company's success that employee goals align with corporate goals; when this is the case, the corporate culture is considered "successful."[55] If your supervisor is involved in the wrongdoing, the human resources department can be an excellent resource for you.

Key Takeaways

- **Ethics** is moral principles, a system that defines right and wrong.
- **Business ethics** is ethical behavior applied to a business situation.
- An **ethical dilemma** is a situation that is presented with options that may be right or wrong.
- **Values** define what is important to you: they are your guiding principles and beliefs, they define how you live your life, and they inform your ethics.
- A mission statement is a roadmap of where a person or company wants to go.
- Your **reputation** will affect how people see you throughout your life, which can have either a positive or a negative impact on your career.
- Every action you take defines you; bear that in mind when making decisions.
- If you find yourself in a situation that challenges your ethics, talk to your supervisor. If you don't feel that you can talk to your supervisor, talk to someone in the human resources department.
- A good rule of thumb is that if you would be ashamed to tell your boss about it, don't do it.

Exercises

1. Watch the following video about ethics and stop it after each scenario is shown. Discuss what you would do in each situation, then play the rest of the video and watch the suggested action.

   View the video online at: http://www.youtube.com/embed/sDPsSyaZNlw

2. Evaluate your values. Choose three values that are important to you and discuss how they may impact your decision making.

3. Think of someone you know only by reputation; what do you know about that person, and what assumptions do you make about him or her?

4. Discuss the reputation of the following people. What actions has each taken that reflect their reputation?

   - Britney Spears
   - Chris Brown
   - Simon Cowell
   - Angelina Jolie

5. Discuss what you would do in each of the following situations. Is it ethical behavior?

   - You are not really sick, but you want to take the day off. What do you say when you call your supervisor?

- You are on a job interview for a job you really want, and the interviewer mentions that the candidate she hires will need to be fluent in Excel. Although you are familiar with Excel, you are not especially good at it and don't really know all the features. What would you say when she asks you about your skill level with Excel?

- You went on a business trip for the company you work for and are preparing your expense report. You are able to include tips, mileage, and other categories without a receipt. Since you've been working a lot of overtime without pay, you consider adding in an additional $25 to cover your extra hours; no one will notice. What do you do as you are completing the expense report?

- Your boss takes the afternoon off but asks you to tell everyone at the staff meeting that he is in a meeting with a client. When you are in a staff meeting, a manager asks you why your boss isn't there. What would you say?

4.2 Policies, Practices, and Cultures

Learning Objective

1. Identify how company policies reflect business ethics.

You might be wondering how a company provides guidance to all employees about what behavior it expects from them. Imagine a global company like Wal-Mart, which has over two billion employees worldwide.[56] How do all the employees know what is considered ethical behavior by the company? Can they take as much time as they want for lunch? Are they able to take off as many days as they wish? What expenses qualify for reimbursement? All the policies of a company are included in its **employee handbook**.

> **employee handbook**
>
> Written policies of a company as they relate to the ethical actions of its employees.

Employee Handbooks: Your Practical, Professional How-To

Every company has a highly specific code of ethics governing the actions of its employees. This manual, the employee handbook (sometimes called the code of ethics or code of conduct or other similar name), outlines the company's policies concerning gift giving, nondisclosure of company information, and other areas of behavior. Starbucks' code of ethics, *Business Ethics and Compliance: Standards of Business Conduct*, for example, explains when employees may and may not accept gifts: "You may not encourage or solicit meals or entertainment from anyone with whom Starbucks does business or from anyone who desires to do business with Starbucks. Giving or accepting valuable gifts or entertainment might be construed as an improper attempt to influence the relationship."[57] An employee handbook will also include the company's sexual harassment and nondiscrimination policies, an explanation of procedures including breaks and scheduling principles, a list of benefits for part- and full-time employees, a breakdown of disciplinary policies and grounds for dismissal, as well as rules concerning phone, fax, mail, Internet use, and the permissible use of company vehicles. The handbook will additionally contain information like the history and goals of the company.

FIGURE 4.3

Starbucks communicates its expectations in terms of ethics in this handbook called *Business Ethics and Compliance: Standards of Business Conduct*.[58]

While all employee handbooks are slightly different, all include the guidelines and policies that define ethical behavior in that company or organization. You can review several different companies' policies at the Web sites below:

Company Policies

Gap Code of Business Conduct

http://www.gapinc.com/content/gapinc/html/investors/corporate_compliance/cobc.html

Source: The Gap, Inc.

McDonald's Standards of Business Conduct for Employees

https://www.mcdonalds.com/dam/AboutMcDonalds/Investors/9497_SBC_McD_US_interactive_final_112408.pdf

Source: McDonald's Corporation

United States Government—Code of Ethics

http://usgovinfo.about.com/blethics.htm

Source: United States House of Representatives Ethics Committee

What Company Policies Say and What They Mean

Whatever company you end up working for will have its own policies with which you will need to familiarize yourself. But most companies include the same basic issues that are frequently encountered in sales: conflicts of interest, bribes, and noncompete clauses. The specifics of these policies will vary from company to company, but this section will give you a good idea of what to expect, the meaning of key terms you will encounter, and some sample policies to study.

A Page from IBM's Employee Handbook

Most companies include a gift and entertainment policy in its employee handbook. IBM has a specific policy that covers these areas.

No IBM employee, or any member of his or her immediate family, can accept gratuities or gifts of money from a supplier, customer, or anyone in a business relationship. Nor can they accept a gift or consideration that could be perceived as having been offered because of the business relationship. "Perceived" simply means this: if you read about it in your local paper, would you wonder whether the gift just might have something to do with a business relationship? No IBM employee can give money or a gift of significant value to a supplier if it could reasonably be viewed as being done to gain a business advantage. If an employee is offered money or a gift of some value by a supplier or if one arrives at their home or office, a manager should be informed immediately. If the gift is perishable, the manager will arrange to donate it to a local charitable organization. Otherwise, it should be returned to the supplier. Whatever the circumstances, the employee or the manager should write the supplier a letter, explain IBM's guidelines on the subject of gifts and gratuities. Of course, it is an accepted practice to talk business over a meal. So it is perfectly all right to occasionally allow a supplier or customer to pick up the check. Similarly, it frequently is necessary for a supplier, including IBM, to provide education and executive briefings for customers. It's all right to accept or provide some services in connection with this kind of activity—services such as transportation, food, or lodging. For instance, transportation in IBM or supplier planes to and from company locations, and lodging and food at company facilities are all right. A violation of these policies may result in termination.[59]

A **conflict of interest** is "a situation in which a person, such as a public official, an employee, or a professional, has a private or personal interest sufficient to appear to influence the objective exercise of his or her official duties."[60] There are four types of conflicts of interest that you may encounter in your career: family interests, gifts, private use of employer property, and moonlighting.

Family interests create a conflict when a relative of yours is either someone from whom you might purchase goods or services for your employer or when you have influence over the potential hiring of a family member of yours. It's best to avoid these types of situations as it can be difficult to make an objective decision.

Gifts create a conflict of interest when they are given to you by someone with whom you do business. Gifts are frequently given at the holidays and may include something small like a case of wine or something more extravagant like a trip.

private use of employer property can be anything from stealing pens to using your work computer to work on editing your vacation pictures to driving the company car on a weekend getaway and then reporting the mileage on a corporate expense report.

conflict of interest

A situation in which a person in a position of power may benefit personally from his actions or influence.

family interests

A situation in which a relative has influence over the hiring of a family member.

gifts

Something received without compensation or exchange.

private use of employer property

Using an employer's property—cars, software, staplers, and so on—for nonbusiness purposes.

moonlighting

Holding a second job.

Moonlighting is holding down a second job. While that might not sound insidious at first, if you work two jobs in the same field, it is almost inevitable that you will run into ethical problems. Who gets your best ideas? Where does most of your energy go? And if you have inside knowledge of two different corporations, working not to let that information influence you will be terribly difficult.

bribe

Money or favor given or promised in order to influence the judgment or conduct of a person in a position of trust; something that serves to induce or influence.

A **bribe**, according to Merriam-Webster, is "money or favor given or promised in order to influence the judgment or conduct of a person in a position of trust; something that serves to induce or influence."[61] Soliciting, accepting, offering, or giving a bribe is illegal—even if your offer is refused, you are committing a crime. Bribery can take place in many different venues. Pharmaceutical companies attempt to persuade doctors to prescribe their products by buying them meals and giving them pens and other trinkets as well as trips to medical conventions. Business gifts are considered a form of bribery when they are given by someone who could benefit from having influence on a decision maker. For example, if you are the buyer of electronics at Wal-Mart, you are not able to accept any gifts from vendors or prospective vendors as it might appear to influence your buying decisions for the chain.

noncompete agreement

A contract that prevents you from taking a job with a competitor after you've quit or been fired.

A **noncompete agreement** (sometimes called a covenant not to compete, or CNC) prevents an employee from entering into competition with the employer once his job has ended—in other words, it prevents you from taking a job with a competitor after you've quit or been fired. A noncompete agreement may also prevent former employees from starting their own businesses in the same field. The reasoning behind the CNC is the fear that a former executive could take his insider knowledge and **trade secrets**—as well as his contacts—with him to a new position. No employer wants to expose its strategy to its competitors. Noncompete agreements are generally upheld by the courts as long as they contain reasonable limits as to the time period and geographical space—that is, for example, that you may not compete in the state for two years after your termination. Noncompete agreements are not legal in California, although there are still measures in place in that state to protect trade secrets.[62] Not every job will ask you to sign a noncompete agreement, and if you haven't signed one, then there are no restrictions on your future employment. This is one reason it's so important to read and understand anything you sign. However, even if you don't sign a noncompete agreement, you may be asked to sign a **nondisclosure agreement (or confidentiality agreement)** or your company may have a nondisclosure or confidentiality policy that requires you to protect your former employer's trade secrets; you may not exploit that information in future employment.[63] A trade secret is "any kind of information that allows you to make money because it is not known."[64] For example, Coca-Cola's signature formula is a trade secret, as is the recipe for Kentucky Fried Chicken. Information about the internal workings of a company that could only plausibly be gained by working for that company is usually a trade secret.

trade secret

Something (as a formula) which has economic value to a business because it is not generally known or easily discoverable by observation and for which efforts have been made to maintain secrecy.

nondisclosure agreement (or confidentiality agreement)

A contract that protects the secrecy of information that is exchanged.

If you find yourself between jobs and worry about the legality of finding another (having signed a noncompete agreement with your previous employer), bear in mind that noncompete agreements are most likely to be enforceable if your new job is strikingly similar to your old job. If you go from the sales department at Target to the advertising department of Kmart, you are probably (legally) in the clear.[65] Your new job is different enough that you are unlikely to be seen by the court as exploiting your knowledge of Target's sales practices. Remember that this is only a concern if you have signed a noncompete agreement previously; while noncompete clauses are common, they are not universal.

What Is Whistle-Blowing?

whistle-blowers

One who publicly exposes the misconduct of a company or organization.

Jeffrey Wigand, former head of research and development for Brown & Williamson Tobacco Corporation (the third-largest tobacco company in the United States), is one of the most famous **whistle-blowers** in America. He says of himself, "The word whistle-blower suggests that you're a tattletale or that you're somehow disloyal. But I wasn't disloyal in the least bit. People were dying. I was loyal to a higher order of ethical responsibility."[66] Wigand's testimony against the tobacco industry, his claims that executives at Brown & Williamson knew that cigarettes were addictive, lied about it under oath, and destroyed documents related to that fact, led directly to the lawsuit brought by forty state attorneys general against tobacco companies.

Whistle-blowing, the act of publicly exposing the misconduct of a company or organization, is a courageous act. Wigand's reputation was destroyed by a punitive smear campaign conducted by the industry he spoke out against, and the stress resulting from that and the trial destroyed his marriage. Brown & Williamson filed a lawsuit against him for revealing confidential company information (the suit was dismissed as a condition of the $368 billion settlement against the tobacco industry).[67] But Wigand blew the whistle in order to save thousands of lives. The true story was made into a blockbuster movie in 1999 called *The Insider*.

Video Clip

The Insider
The movie trailer includes highlights from the movie inspired by a true story.

View the video online at: http://www.youtube.com/embed/zaYNT9ZMqW4

Another famous whistle-blower is Erin Brockovich, whose story was also brought to life on the big screen in the movie of the same name.

Video Clip

Erin Brockovich
The video includes highlights from the 2000 movie.

View the video online at: http://www.youtube.com/embed/9TjEklyF7-E

Of course, whistle-blowing exists on a less grand scale. If you know which of your classmates stole the answer key to an exam and you tell the professor, you have blown the whistle. Whistle-blowing doesn't always involve risking your life, and it doesn't always involve bringing a corporation to its knees. At its heart, it is action taken to reveal wrongdoings in hopes of seeing justice done.

Only limited protection existed for whistle-blowers until recently; today, the best protection they have (unless they work for the federal government) is the Sarbanes-Oxley Act of 2002, mentioned earlier, which states that "whoever knowingly, with the intent to retaliate, takes any action harmful to any person, including interference with the lawful employment or livelihood of any person, for providing to a law enforcement officer any truthful information relating to the commission or possible commission of any federal offense, shall be fined under this title, imprisoned not more than ten years, or both."[68] It's important to bear in mind that you have no obligation to blow the whistle; you can simply refuse to take part in any unethical or illegal activity. If you know that crimes are being committed at your place of business, you have to decide for yourself what form that refusal will take: you may simply not commit any crimes yourself, you may try to persuade others to behave ethically, or you may feel that you must resign your position. It will depend on your situation and your personal code of ethics.

Ethics and the Law

The ever-changing landscape of technology has created new opportunities to test ethics; spammers, scam artists, and identity thieves have created the need to clearly define legal, and in some cases, ethical behavior online. An increasing number of cases of fraud committed via social networking sites have taken place. There have been cases of people who create Twitter profiles in the names of other, real people. News anchor Keith Olbermann and Tony La Russa, manager of the St. Louis Cardinals, have both been victims of such hoaxes.[69] If tempted to such behavior yourself, remember: you are what you tweet. Your reputation will be affected by all the things that you do—make sure that you're making yourself look good.

Tightening Legal Loopholes

One of the best examples of laws being enacted in response to unethical business practices is the Robinson-Patman Act. In 1914, the Clayton Act became the first federal statute to expressly prohibit price discrimination in several forms. Large chain grocery stores used their buying power to negotiate lower prices than smaller, independent grocery stores were offered. The Robinson-Patman Act was passed in 1936, during the Great Depression, as a direct response to that unfair business practice, closing the loophole.[70] Buyers for the big chain stores weren't breaking the law when they used their influence to get better prices than small stores could, but they were behaving unethically—and the law caught up with them in the end.

Another example of ways in which it can take the law some time to catch up to reality is the CAN-SPAM Act (**C**ontrolling the **A**ssault of **N**on-**S**olicited **P**ornography **A**nd **M**arketing Act) of 2003.[71] CAN-SPAM purports to take on spam—that is, unsolicited marketing e-mails, often with sexual or "STAY AT HOME, EARN $$$!!!"-type messages. Perhaps the most famous arrest of a spammer came in 2005, when Anthony Greco was arrested at Los Angeles International Airport and charged with violating CAN-SPAM by sending more than 1.5 million messages to users of the MySpace instant messaging service that advertised pornography and mortgage-refinancing services.[72]

Culture and Ethics

When you are working in a different country, or with professionals from other cultures, there may be different ideas as to what is appropriate and ethical. The Japanese, for example, have a culture of corporate gift giving; *kosai hi* (literally "expense for friendly relations")[73] refers to the Japanese business practice of maintaining large expense accounts used for entertaining clients and nurturing other professional relationships. This money is, for example, often used to buy golf club memberships as gifts for people with whom Japanese businessmen and women have valuable working relationships. When you come face-to-face with these different customs, it is important not to be insulting, but you also cannot ignore your company's policies. "When in Rome" will only carry you so far.

A good rule of thumb is this: if you wouldn't be comfortable telling your boss about it, or if you'd be embarrassed to tell your mom about it, don't do it. If you're working for a company that does business in more than one country, odds are they will have a liaison from each country that can help you to navigate the intricacies of cultural difference. In Middle Eastern countries, there is a custom of *baksheesh*, a word that encompasses everything from tipping to alms for a beggar to out-and-out bribery. If you are working in the Middle East, there may be an expectation that you will help to grease the wheels; your supervisor should be able to brief you on company policy in such situations.[74]

One excellent example of the ethical struggles unique to international business can be found in Michael Crichton's book *Rising Sun*, which deals with the clash of Japanese and American business practices. At one point, two police officers are discussing how often they are offered gifts by the Japanese: "Giving gifts to ensure that you will be seen favorably is something the Japanese do by instinct. And it's not so different from what we do, when we invite the boss over for dinner. Goodwill is goodwill. But we don't invite the boss over for dinner when we're up for a promotion. The proper thing to do is to invite the boss early in the relationship, when nothing is at stake. Then it's just goodwill. The same with the Japanese. They believe you should give the gift early, because then it is not a bribe. It is a gift. A way of making a relationship with you before there is any pressure on the relationship."[75] When you need to decline a gift yourself, apologize and explain that company guidelines prohibit your acceptance of the gift. You should then promptly report the gift to your supervisor.

Key Takeaways

- Your company will make available to you their policies on various ethical issues in the **employee handbook**; it is your responsibility to read the materials provided and remain familiar with their contents.
- There are four different types of **conflicts of interest: family interests, gifts, private use of employer property**, and **moonlighting**.
- **Bribery**, the use of gifts to influence someone, is both unethical and illegal.
- Many employers will require you to sign a **noncompete agreement**; be sure that you understand the details before you agree.
- A company's **trade secrets** should never be disclosed.
- **Whistle-blowing**, the exposure of a company's wrongdoing to the public, is never your ethical obligation—you are obligated only to refuse to participate. However, it can be a deeply noble act. You must analyze the situation yourself and decide what is called for.
- **Sarbanes-Oxley Act of 2002** regulates corporate financial practices and provides protection for whistle-blowers.
- While different cultures have different ideas about what is ethical, working in a different country or with a client from another culture does not excuse you from following company policies regarding gifts, and so on.

Exercises

1. Review the employee handbook of the company for which you work (or have worked). What are the company policies as they relate to travel expenses? How do you substantiate your travel expenses in order to get reimbursement? What are the company policies as they relate to confidentiality? What kind of information do you know that might be considered confidential?

2. Identify a situation in which you found yourself facing a conflict of interest: perhaps you had two after-school activities with equal claims on your time, or maybe you wanted to use your part-time job to give discounts to your friends. How did you resolve the conflict? Would you handle things differently if faced with the same situation again?

3. Research a whistle-blower not mentioned in this chapter. Who was he or she, and what did he or she expose? Do you agree with his or her decision to blow the whistle? Why or why not?

4. Find an example of someone who took part in bribery and was found out. Who was he or she, and what were the consequences of his or her illegal actions?

5. Describe what is meant by confidentiality. What does a company expect when a company policy states that employees are bound by confidentiality?

6. Describe the difference between unethical and illegal behavior. Is unethical behavior always illegal?

4.3 *Selling U*: Selling Your Personal Brand Ethically—Résumés and References

Learning Objectives

1. Learn about the ethics of your résumé.
2. Understand how to ask references to speak honestly on your behalf.

You've been asked to submit your résumé because your roommate knows someone in the marketing department at a major national food company. You really want this job, but you are concerned that you don't really have the qualifications yet. As you work on your résumé, you exercise your creativity: "cashier" becomes "marketing representative." You add to your skills "management of personnel"—of course, you don't have any management experience, but you just know you'll be good at it. By the time you've finished, you are surprised to realize that, looking at your résumé, you don't recognize yourself. Maybe this truth-stretching exercise wasn't such a good idea.

Behaving in an ethical fashion throughout the hiring process only strengthens your personal brand—and that's just good business.

Selling Yourself versus Stretching the Truth about Your Background and Experience

When you create your résumé, you are selling yourself to potential employers; where do you draw the line between putting your best foot forward and stretching the truth past the breaking point? The difference between "attended Pacific Coast Baptist College" and "received degrees in theology and psychology from Pacific Coast Baptist College" can be the difference between a successful tenure and an embarrassing resignation, as former RadioShack CEO David Edmondson discovered in 2006.[76] Edmondson, by claiming that he had earned degrees he had not (and, in one case, a degree not even offered by the college), set the stage for the embarrassing scandal that cost him his job. It can be tempting to gamble on the likelihood that an employer won't do a background check—but even if you get away with a fib once or twice, it's not something you should bet on for your entire career. Social networking will out you. The Internet has led to professional networks that are incredibly far reaching; your boss may have a connection on LinkedIn to a manager at the company you pretend to have interned for. And, of course, lying on your résumé is unethical; you should sell *yourself*, not an exaggerated version of yourself.

Your experiences as a waitress, cashier, retail store salesperson, babysitter, or any other part-time or summer job can be very valuable on your résumé. Being able to demonstrate that you can multitask under pressure, resolve problems quickly to customers' satisfaction, be responsible, or increase sales are the types of skills that prospective employers are looking for from entry-level employees. Use your experience to tell a story about what makes you different and delivers value to your prospective employer. For example, if you want to pursue a career in finance, your experience handling money and balancing the cash drawer at the end of the day is important to highlight on your résumé. It's also a good idea to put your most important and relevant internships or jobs first on your résumé rather than adhering to the traditional chronological order. Since you are just beginning your career, your most important jobs can be listed first. When you gain more experience, it's better to use the chronological format. The bottom line is that you have a brand story to tell on your résumé; no matter what your background, you don't need to stretch the truth.

Prospective employers want to see evidence that you are hardworking and have done things to distinguish yourself by holding part-time jobs, completing internships, participating in professional organizations, performing community service, and gaining other experiences. But one thing to remember about entry-level positions in virtually every industry is that none of the hiring companies expects you to come in and do the job from day one. The company will train you to do the job it wants done. That doesn't mean that you won't be asked to "jump in" and do things, because you will. But companies don't expect you to have skills and experience that you will have after a few years of working. So use your résumé to sell yourself in an honest but compelling way.

Asking References to Speak about Your Personal Brand

References, simply put, are people you can rely on to speak on your behalf; they come in two flavors, personal and professional. **Personal references** are people like aunts or family friends—**professional references** are by far the more important and are usually supervisors, professors, or managers. While some prospective employers may accept personal references, you should have at least three **professional references** available if a prospective employer asks for them.

You might be wondering what employers do when they receive your references. This video is helpful to understand exactly what an employer may ask one of your references.

references

People who will speak on your behalf about your experience, skills, and character.

personal references

Family or friends who will speak on your behalf about your character and work ethic.

professional references

Managers, supervisors, professors, mentors, and other professionals who can speak on your behalf about your character, experience, skills, quality of your work, and work ethic.

Video: Letters of Recommendation

View the video online at: http://www.youtube.com/embed/4NMXeuATQz0?rel=0

When choosing references, be sure that the people you have in mind have good things to say about you. It's a good idea to keep in touch with your former boss from your internship or summer job. People with whom you have had a good working relationship can be excellent references. It's always best to contact someone whom you would like to be a reference in person or on the phone. That way you will be able to let them know exactly how much you respect her, and it will give you an opportunity to cement your professional relationship. If she shows any kind of hesitation, you may not want to use her as a reference.

When you speak to a prospective reference, be professional and be specific. Here's an example of a conversation you might have with a professor whom you are asking to be a reference. If you are asking a professor, it's best to make an appointment or stop by his office.

You: *Dr. Feng, I wanted to stop by and give you an update on my job search.*

Dr. Feng: *Great. I would like to hear about what companies you are interested in.*

You: *Well, I've been trying to get a sales position at one of the pharmaceutical companies in the city. I think that's what I'd like to do since I enjoy sales and I am very interested in science and medicine. So I've sent my cover letter and résumé to all the pharmaceutical companies, and I have a second interview with Ainion Pharmaceuticals next Thursday. I was wondering if you would be a reference for me. They are looking for a sales assistant—someone who is organized, analytical, good with follow-up, and is a creative thinker. I thought that you might be able to speak about my work for the research practicum. I think it's a great example of my work ethic and drive as well as my attention to detail and ability to solve problems creativity.*

Dr. Feng: *I would be happy to speak on your behalf. It sounds like the position could be a good fit for your skills. I'll let you know when someone from the company contacts me.*

You: *Dr. Feng, thank you very much. I really appreciate all that you have done to help me start my career. I'll let you know how the interview goes on Thursday.*

Once you know whom you'd like for your references, *ask them*. This is not a situation in which you want to surprise people. Instead, talk with each person; you should personally speak with each person, preferably in person or by phone as opposed to by e-mail. (By all means, avoid the group e-mail requesting references.) Explain what the job is that you are applying for and ask for her permission to list her as a reference. Always personally thank each of your references, even if you don't get the job. Express your gratitude—preferably in a handwritten note, but you must at least send an e-mail and let them know how things turned out. Don't feel as if you let down your references if you didn't get the job. Each of your references was in your situation at one point in time, and she didn't get an offer from every job interview. Stay positive and keep in touch with your references. They will appreciate it, and you will keep your professional network strong.

If your potential employer wants references, he or she will ask for them; you should have them already prepared, but they should *not* be listed on your résumé.

You've Got the Power: Tips for Your Job Search

Reference Checks

When you are asked to provide references, you will need to provide for each reference: full name, mailing address, phone number, e-mail address, employer, job title, e-mail address, and relationship to you. Have the information collected in a professional document (see Figure 4.4). Remember to get someone's permission before listing him or her as a reference *every time*; the fact that your internship supervisor was willing to be a reference two years ago doesn't mean that you can take his assent for granted in the future. Your references are chosen to be advocates for you—in return for their generosity of spirit, do them the courtesy of asking whether they are still willing to speak well of you.

FIGURE 4.4 Sample References

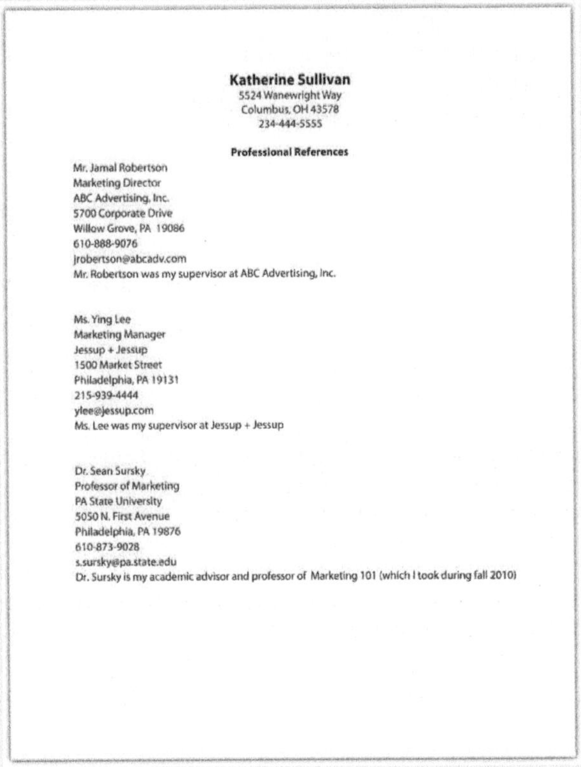

Katherine Sullivan
5524 Wanewright Way
Columbus, OH 43578
234-444-5555

Professional References

Mr. Jamal Robertson
Marketing Director
ABC Advertising, Inc.
5700 Corporate Drive
Willow Grove, PA 19086
610-888-9076
jrobertson@abcadv.com
Mr. Robertson was my supervisor at ABC Advertising, Inc.

Ms. Ying Lee
Marketing Manager
Jessup + Jessup
1500 Market Street
Philadelphia, PA 19131
215-939-4444
ylee@jessup.com
Ms. Lee was my supervisor at Jessup + Jessup

Dr. Sean Sursky
Professor of Marketing
PA State University
5050 N. First Avenue
Philadelphia, PA 19876
610-873-9028
s.sursky@pa.state.edu
Dr. Sursky is my academic advisor and professor of Marketing 101 (which I took during fall 2010)

Letters of Recommendation

letters of recommendation

Letter written by a professional (supervisor, manager, professor, or other professional) to testify to the skills and characteristics of a job candidate.

As you go through classes and internships, collect **letters of recommendation** for your portfolio; such letters demonstrate that people think highly of you. When you finish a class in which you did well, ask your professor for a letter of recommendation. When you finish an internship, ask your supervisor. Not only will these letters demonstrate your credibility, they will help to build your confidence. It's a good idea to ask each of your references to write a letter of recommendation for you. That way you can bring the letters to your interview to demonstrate the support you have from professionals. This video gives you more insight into using letter of recommendation in addition to your list of references.

Video Clip

Letters of Recommendation
Letters of recommendation can help sell your personal brand.

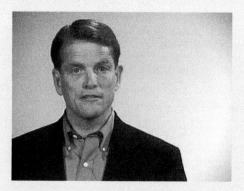

View the video online at: http://www.youtube.com/embed/pJ2w5O1PiUU

Don't hesitate to reread your letters after you've had a career setback. If you're going to effectively sell yourself, you need to believe in your personal brand. A reminder that Dr. Messimer thinks that you're awesome could be just the pick-me-up you need in order to dust yourself off and reenter the job market with aplomb.

Key Takeaways

- Lying on your résumé is not ethical and can have catastrophic consequences for your career.
- It is in your best interests to market yourself on your résumé—list your internships first, then your jobs, including any "nonprofessional" jobs that are important to the history of your personal brand.
- **Personal references** are family and friends; **professional references** are people whom you have worked with, and are vastly more important.
- Have at least three professional references available. Present your references only if asked for them; do not include them on your résumé.
- Speak to each of your references before you provide their name and contact information to a prospective employer. Get their permission, thank them, and let them know how things worked out.
- **Letters of recommendation** are important testaments to your character and abilities; when you finish an internship or a class, ask your supervisor or professor for a letter of recommendation. Letters of recommendation are excellent to present with your list of references.

Exercises

1. Identify three people you could potentially use as professional references. Create a references sheet using the information for these people.
2. Ask one of your former supervisors or a professor to write a letter of recommendation for you.

4.4 Review and Practice

Power Wrap-Up

Now that you have read this chapter, you should be able to understand ethical behavior in selling as well as how to determine what the ethical decision is in a given situation.

- You can **understand** why behaving ethically is important to selling.
- You can **describe** how ethical decision making works.
- You can **identify** different ethical pitfalls, including bribery and conflicts of interest.
- You can **understand** how to locate and implement company policies.
- You can **implement** ethical decision making in the workplace.
- You can **recognize** an ethical challenge and know how to respond.
- You can **analyze** a company's ethics based on their mission statement and philosophy.
- You can **organize** your work experience on a résumé in a way that is both honest and effective.
- You can **understand** how to integrate references into your job search.

Test Your Power Knowledge (answers are below)

1. What is ethical behavior?
2. What is an ethical dilemma?
3. What is an example of personal values?
4. What is an example of corporate values?
5. What is the purpose of a mission statement?
6. Why is your reputation important?
7. Explain how to determine a company's policies on issues such as gifts, conflicts of interest, and so on.
8. Define a "conflict of interest."
9. What is whistle-blowing?

Power (Role) Play

Now it's time to put what you've learned into practice. Following are two roles that are involved in the same selling situation—one role is the customer, and the other is the salesperson. This will give you the opportunity to think about this ethical dilemma from the point of view of both the customer and the salesperson.

Read each role carefully along with the discussion questions. Then, be prepared to play either of the roles in class using the concepts covered in this chapter. You may be asked to discuss the roles and do a role play in groups or individually.

Ethics that Work

Role: Sales rep for Rold Gold, a fine jewelry wholesaler

You are a sales rep for Rold Gold, a jewelry wholesaler that specializes in high-end gold jewelry. The holidays are coming, and one of your best customers, the owner of an independent jewelry store, has sent you an expensive gift in appreciation for all that you have done to help her increase her business over the past year. Your employee handbook makes it clear that you could be fired for accepting it, but you didn't actually accept it; it just turned up at your home, neatly wrapped, with a card attached. What will you do?

- Since no one will know that you received the gift, should you just keep it?
- If you decide to return the gift, what will you say to your customer?
- Will you write a thank-you note?
- If you decide to return the gift, what is the best way to do so?
- What, if anything, will you tell your sales manager?

Role: Owner, Jewels to the World jewelry store

You are the owner of a popular jewelry store. It has been a challenging year given the state of the economy. One of your sales reps has really gone above and beyond the call of duty to help you increase your business throughout the year with extra training, cost reductions, and promotional ideas. You want to let him know that you appreciate all he does to support your business, so you send him a very generous gift. You are not aware of any reason he wouldn't accept it. Nonetheless, you have it sent directly to his home to avoid any appearance of impropriety. You would be extremely disappointed if he didn't accept your gift.

- What will you say when the sales rep calls to thank you for your gift?
- If the sales rep decides not to accept the gift, will you insist that he keep it?
- If the sales rep doesn't accept your gift, will it have an impact on your relationship?
- Will you expect special pricing and other deals in return for your gift?

Put Your Power to Work: *Selling U* Activities

1. Identify at least one professor who might be willing to write you a letter of recommendation. Approach him or her and make the request—be prepared to talk about your career aspirations. Be sure to choose a professor in whose class you received a good grade and who likely remembers you.
2. What influences your values? Make a list of your values and try to determine their origin. Do they come from your parents, your church, or your own experiences?
3. Use the Internet to find a company whose mission statement and values statement reflects your mission and values. Write a cover letter to that company explaining why you would be a good hire.

Test Your Power Knowledge Answers

1. Ethical behavior is morality applied to specific situations; it is behavior that addresses your obligations.

2. An ethical dilemma is a situation in which options are presented that may be right or wrong.

3. Personal values include (but are not limited to) honesty, integrity, accountability, drive, determination, and sincerity.

4. Corporate values may be the same as personal values, which may also include teamwork, open and honest communication, and diversity.

5. The process and reason for creating a mission statement, whether it is for a person or a company, is the same: to develop a roadmap, a guide by which all future decisions will be made.

6. When you work in sales, you are selling yourself; you will have greater success with customers if you are someone they want to "buy." When a customer buys from you, they are investing in your reputation.

7. The employee handbook will outline the company's policies concerning gift giving, nondisclosure of company information, and other areas of behavior.

8. A conflict of interest is "a situation in which a person, such as a public official, an employee, or a professional, has a private or personal interest sufficient to appear to influence the objective exercise of his or her official duties."

9. Whistle-blowing is the act of publicly exposing the misconduct of a company or organization.

Endnotes

1. Elianne Friend, "Woman Fined to Tune of $1.9 Million for Illegal Downloads," *CNN.com*, June 18, 2009, http://www.cnn.com/2009/CRIME/06/18/minnesota.music.download.fine/index.html (accessed February 13, 2010).

2. John C. Maxwell, *There's No Such Thing As "Business" Ethics* (New York: Center Street, 2003), 23–24.

3. Manual Velasquez, Claire Andre, Thomas Shanks, and Michael J. Meyer, "What Is Ethics?" Santa Clara University, http://www.scu.edu/ethics/practicing/decision/whatisethics.html (accessed August 31, 2009).

4. Karen Collins, *Exploring Business* (Nyack, NY: Flat World Knowledge, 2008), 27.

5. College Confidential, http://talk.collegeconfidential.com/california-institute-technology/427749-ethical-dilemma-question.html (accessed August 31, 2009).

6. Manual Velasquez, Claire Andre, Thomas Shanks, and Michael J. Meyer, "What Is Ethics?" Santa Clara University, http://www.scu.edu/ethics/practicing/decision/whatisethics.html (accessed August 31, 2009).

7. Manual Velasquez, Claire Andre, Thomas Shanks, and Michael J. Meyer, "Ethics and Virtue," Santa Clara University, http://www.scu.edu/ethics/practicing/decision/ethicsandvirtue.html (accessed August 29, 2009).

8. Margaret Soltan, "Southern Illinois University an Official Laughingstock," *Inside Higher Ed*, August 30, 2007, http://www.insidehighered.com/blogs/university_diaries/southern_illinois_university_an_official_laughingstock (accessed February 18, 2010).

9. Wendy Weinhold, "SIU Accused of Copying Plagiarism Policy," *Daily Egyptian*, January 29, 2009, http://web2.collegepublisher.com/se/daily-egyptian/siu-accused-of-copying-plagiarism-policy-1.1318397 (accessed February 18, 2010).

10. Stefanie Fontenez, "Tax-Troubled Celebrities, Politicians, Outlaws," *CNN.com*, April 15, 2008, http://www.cnn.com/2008/LIVING/wayoflife/04/15/famous.tax/index.html (accessed August 29, 2009).

11. Danny Hakim, "Eliot Spitzer," *New York Times*, Times Topics, August 31, 2009, http://topics.nytimes.com/topics/reference/timestopics/people/s/eliot_l_spitzer/index.html (accessed August 31, 2009).

12. Gerhard Gschwandtner, "Lies and Deception in Selling: How to Tell When Customers or Prospects Are Lying to You," *Selling Power* 15, no. 9, http://www.sellingpower.com/content/article.php?a=4256 (accessed March 16, 2010).

13. "An Education in Ethics," Selling Power Sales Management eNewsletter, April 17, 2002, http://www.sellingpower.com/content/newsletter/issue.php?pc=197 (accessed March 16, 2010).

14. Karen Collins, *Exploring Business* (Nyack, NY: Flat World Knowledge), 27.

15. Karen Collins, *Exploring Business* (Nyack, NY: Flat World Knowledge), 27.

16. NewsHour Extra, "What Happened to Enron?" Paul Solman, PBS, January 22, 2002, http://www.pbs.org/newshour/extra/features/jan-june02/enron_past.html (accessed December 6, 2009).

17. SearchCIO, "Sarbanes-Oxley Act," http://searchcio.techtarget.com/sDefinition/0,,sid182_gci920030,00.html (accessed December 6, 2009).

18. "Bernie Madoff Ponzi Scheme: Victim List Grows," *Huffington Post*, December 15, 2008, http://www.huffingtonpost.com/2008/12/15/bernie-madoff-ponzi-schem_n_151018.html (accessed December 6, 2009).

19. Julie Creswell and Landon Thomas Jr., "The Talented Mr. Madoff," *New York Times*, January 24, 2009, http://www.nytimes.com/2009/01/25/business/25bernie.html (accessed August 31, 2009).

20. Jack Healy and Diana B. Henriques, "It Was All Fake: Madoff Aide Details Scheme," *New York Times*, August 12, 2009, http://dealbook.blogs.nytimes.com/2009/08/12/madoff-aide-reveals-details-of-ponzi-scheme/?scp=2&sq=madoff%20sentencing&st=cse (accessed August 31, 2009).

21. Aaron Bernstein, "Nike's New Game Plan for Sweatshops," *BusinessWeek*, September 20, 2004, http://www.businessweek.com/magazine/content/04_38/b3900011_mz001.htm (accessed December 6, 2009).

22. Jeremy Dann, "Business Ethics Integral to Corporate Strategy, Says Stanford's Malhotra," BNET, July 1, 2009, http://blogs.bnet.com/mba/?p=927&tag=content;col1 (accessed August 29, 2009).

23. Target, "Corporate Responsibility Report," http://investors.target.com/phoenix.zhtml?c=65828&p=irol-govResponsibility (accessed September 1, 2009).

24. Jeremy Dann, "Business Ethics integral to Corporate Strategy, Says Stanford's Malhotra," BNET, July 1, 2009, http://blogs.bnet.com/mba/?p=927&tag=content;col1 (accessed August 29, 2009).

25. Heather Baldwin, "There's a Price on Your Integrity," Selling Power Sales Management eNewsletter, September 16, 2008, http://www.sellingpower.com/content/newsletter/issue.php?pc=867 (accessed March 16, 2010).

26. Buck Wargo, "5 Everyday Ethical Dilemmas," Realtor, March 2007, http://www.realtor.org/archives/feat2200703?presentationtemplate=rmo-design/pt_articlepage_v1_print&presentationtemplateid=1b18c0004a12c9a4b7e1ffbdd1ec736f (accessed August 29, 2009).

27. Gerhard Gschwandtner, "Lies and Deception in Selling: How to Tell When Customers or Prospects Are Lying to You," Selling Power 15, no. 9, http://www.sellingpower.com/content/article.php?a=4256 (accessed March 16, 2010).

28. Mark P. Cussen, "Ethical Issues for Financial Advisors," Investopedia, http://investopedia.com/printable.asp?a=/articles/financialcareers/08/ethics-for-advisors.asp (accessed August 29, 2009).

29. Shel Horowitz, "Should Mary Buy Her Own Bonus?" Business Ethics, November 11, 2009, http://business-ethics.com/2009/11/11/should-mary-buy-her-bonus (accessed February 18, 2010).

30. Dr. Frank Crane, "The Truth in Business," Selling Power, http://www.sellingpower.com/html_newsletter/motivation/article.asp?id=2691&nDate=November+20%2C+2006&lid=SP69444 (accessed August 29, 2009).

31. BNET Editorial, "Understanding Your Values," BNET, http://www.bnet.com/2410-13070_23-55147.html?tag=content;col1 (accessed August 29, 2009

32. BNET Editorial, "Understanding Your Values," BNET, http://www.bnet.com/2410-13070_23-55147.html?tag=content;col1 (accessed August 29, 2009).

33. BNET Editorial, "Understanding Your Values," BNET, http://www.bnet.com/2410-13070_23-55147.html?tag=content;col1 (accessed August 29, 2009).

34. BNET Editorial, "Understanding Your Values," BNET, http://www.bnet.com/2410-13070_23-55147.html?tag=content;col1 (accessed August 29, 2009).

35. "Niki Tsongas: Long Bio," http://tsongas.house.gov/index.cfm?sectionid=54&sectiontree=2,54 (accessed September 1, 2009).

36. John C. Maxwell, There's No Such Thing as "Business" Ethics (New York: Center Street, 2003), 102–3.

37. John C. Maxwell, There's No Such Thing as "Business" Ethics (New York: Center Street, 2003), 93–94.

38. Thomas E. Ambler, "The Strategic Value of Values," Center for Simplified Strategic Planning, http://www.cssp.com/CD0402/ValuesAndStrategy/default.php (accessed August 29, 2009).

39. BNET Editorial "Understanding Your Values," BNET, http://www.bnet.com/2410-13070_23-55147.html?tag=content;col1 (accessed August 29, 2009).

40. "Develop Your Personal Career Mission Statement," CollegeGrad.com, http://www.collegegrad.com/book/Job-Search-Prep/Develop-a-Personal-Career-Mission-Statement (accessed September 1, 2009).

41. Google, "Corporate Information: Company Overview," http://www.google.com/corporate (accessed September 1, 2009).

42. Google, "Corporate Information: Our Philosophy," http://www.google.com/intl/en/corporate/tenthings.html (accessed September 1, 2009).

43. "Character," Merriam-Webster Online Dictionary, http://mw1.merriam-webster.com/dictionary/character (accessed September 1, 2009).

44. Josephson Institute, "The Six Pillars of Character," Josephson Institute, http://charactercounts.org/sixpillars.html (accessed September 1, 2009).

45. Mike Fahey, "Eidos Trying to Fix Tomb Raider: Underworld Metacritic Scores," Kotaku, November 21, 2008, http://kotaku.com/5095674/eidos-trying-to-fix-tomb-raider-underworld-metacritic-scores (accessed September 1, 2009).

46. "Reputation," Merriam-Webster Online Dictionary, http://www.merriam-webster.com/dictionary/reputation (accessed September 1, 2009).

47. Renee Houston Zemanski, "The Power of Your Reputation," Selling Power, http://www.sellingpower.com/article/display.asp?aid=SP1900197 (accessed August 29, 2009).

48. Renee Houston Zemanski, "The Power of Your Reputation," Selling Power, http://www.sellingpower.com/article/display.asp?aid=SP1900197 (accessed August 29, 2009).

49. Robert L. Bailey, "A Story of Two Salespeople," BNET, April 2008, http://findarticles.com/p/articles/mi_qa3615/is_200804/ai_n25420875/pg_2/?tag=content;col (accessed February 18, 2010).

50. David Chittock, "Outside the Box: A Question of Integrity," Manage Smarter, May 28, 2009, http://www.presentations.com/msg/search/article_display.jsp?vnu_content_id=1003977677 (accessed February 18, 2010).

51. John C. Maxwell, There's No Such Thing as "Business" Ethics (New York: Center Street, 2003), 121

52. John C. Maxwell, There's No Such Thing as "Business" Ethics (New York: Center Street, 2003).

53. "Ken Lay's Final Act," New York Times, July 6, 2006, http://www.nytimes.com/2006/07/06/opinion/06thurs4.html (accessed September 1, 2009).

54. Sir Michael Rake, "Setting the Right Tone at the Top," Leading by Example (Cambridge, MA: Harvard Business School Press, 2007), 9–11.

55. David Towers, "An Investigation into Whether Organisational Culture Is Directly Linked to Motivation and Performance through Looking at Google Inc.," extended essay, The University of Birmingham, The Birmingham Business School, 2005–6, http://www.towers.fr/essays/culture%20performance%20and%20motivation %20review%20and%20the%20google%20case%20study%20success.pdf (accessed September 1, 2009).

56. "Fortune Global 500," CNN.com, http://money.cnn.com/magazines/fortune/global500/2008/snapshots/2255.html (accessed September 1, 2009).

57. Starbucks, Business Ethics and Compliance: Standards of Business Conduct, http://assets.starbucks.com/assets/sobc-fy09-eng.pdf (accessed September 1, 2009).

58. Starbucks, Business Ethics and Compliance: Standards of Business Conduct, http://assets.starbucks.com/assets/sobc-fy09-eng.pdf (accessed September 1, 2009).

59. Milton Snoeyenbos, Robert Almeder, and James Humber, Business Ethics (Amherst, NY: Prometheus Books, 2001), 133.

60. Michael McDonald, "Ethics and Conflict of Interest," University of British Columbia Centre for Applied Ethics, http://web.archive.org/web/20071103060225/http://www.ethics.ubc.ca/people/mcdonald/conflict.htm (accessed September 1, 2009).

61. "Bribe," Merriam-Webster Online Dictionary, http://www.merriam-webster.com/dictionary/bribe (accessed September 1, 2009).

62. "California Non-compete Agreements," Lawzilla, http://lawzilla.com/content/noncompete.shtml (accessed September 2, 2009).

63. Gene Quinn, "What Is a Confidentiality Agreement?" IPWatchdog, http://www.ipwatchdog.com/2008/01/03/what-is-confidentiality-agreement/id=31 (accessed September 2, 2009).

64. "What Is a Trade Secret and How Is It Different from a Patent or Copyright?" HowStuffWorks, April 30, 2001, http://www.howstuffworks.com/question625.htm# (accessed February 14, 2010).

65. Russell Beck, "Noncompete Agreements That Don't Mean What They Say," Journal of New England Technology, September 5, 2008, http://www.masshightech.com/stories/2008/09/01/focus4-Noncompete-agreements-that-dont-mean-what-they-say.html (accessed February 14, 2010).

66. Chuck Salter, "Jeffrey Wigand: The Whistle-Blower," Fast Company, December 19, 2007, http://www.fastcompany.com/articles/2002/05/wigand.html (accessed February 14, 2010).

67. Jeffrey Wigand, "Biography," http://www.jeffreywigand.com/bio.php (accessed September 2, 2009).

68. Cornell University Law School, "Retaliating against a Witness, Victim, or Informant," http://www.law.cornell.edu/uscode/18/1513.html#e (accessed September 2, 2009).

69. Danielle Citron, "Twitter Fraud," Concurring Opinions, June 10, 2009, http://www.concurringopinions.com/archives/2009/06/twitter-fraud.html (accessed September 2, 2009).

70. Donald S. Clark, "The Robinson-Patman Act: General Principles, Commission Proceedings, and Selected Issues," Federal Trade Commission Web site, June 7, 1995, http://www.ftc.gov/speeches/other/patman.shtm (accessed September 2, 1010).

71. Federal Trade Commission, "The CAN-SPAM Act: A Compliance Guide for Business," September 2009, http://www.ftc.gov/bcp/edu/pubs/business/ecommerce/bus61.shtm (accessed February 14, 2010).

72. Paul Roberts, "Arrest, but No Relief from IM Spam," InfoWorld, February 22, 2005, http://www.infoworld.com/d/security-central/arrest-no-relief-im-spam-863 (accessed September 2, 2009).

73. Boye Lafayette de Mente, Japan's Cultural Code Words (North Clarendon, VT: Tuttle Publishing, 2004), 225.

74. S. E. Smith, "What Is Baksheesh?" wiseGEEK, http://www.wisegeek.com/what-is-baksheesh.htm (accessed February 14, 2010).

75. Michael Crichton, Rising Sun (New York: Ballantine Books, 1992), 136.

76. Associated Press, "RadioShack CEO Resigns amid Resume Questions," USA Today, February 20, 2006, http://www.usatoday.com/money/industries/retail/2006-02-20-radioshack-ceo_x.htm (accessed February 14, 2010).

CHAPTER 5
The Power of Effective Communication

Video Ride-Along with Andrew Sykes, Pharmaceutical Sales Specialist at AstraZeneca

Meet Andrew Sykes. He is a pharmaceutical sales specialist in the medical care division at AstraZeneca, one of the largest pharmaceutical companies in the world. He has been in sales for five years. Andrew calls on doctors and educates them about the products he represents. His success is measured by the number of prescriptions written by doctors for the drugs for which he is responsible.

Ride along with Andrew and get his perspective on how communication works (and doesn't work) in sales. Learn about Andrew's tips for effective communication. You might be surprised by what you hear.

View the video online at: http://www.youtube.com/embed/moQ4jgGk-84

5.1 Ready, Set, Communicate

Learning Objectives

1. Understand the elements of effective business communication.
2. Recognize the implications of different types of verbal and nonverbal communication.
3. Learn how your dress communicates in an interview and the workplace.
4. Discuss how technology tools can help a salesperson manage customer relationships.

A text message.

A voice mail.

A passing comment.

A Facebook post.

An unreturned phone call.

Have you ever had one of these communications be misinterpreted? You meant one thing, but your friend thought you meant something else? Sometimes, the miscommunication can result in the confusion of a meeting time or a place to get together. Or worse, it can be entirely misunderstood and may have a negative impact on your relationship.

communication

The exchange of information or ideas between sender and receiver.

soft skill

A term that relates to a person's communication skills, social graces, personality traits, language abilities, and the ability to work with others.

emotional intelligence

A person's ability to manage herself as well as her relationship with others so she can live her intentions.

hard skills

Technical knowledge required to perform a specific job.

Communication, the exchange of information or ideas between sender and receiver, is a challenging aspect in your personal life, at school, and especially in selling. Today, it's even more complex with business being conducted around the world and with varying communication methods. In this constant, high-speed business environment, communication blunders can cost you more than you might think. Did you ever hear the saying, "You only have one chance to make a good first impression"? It couldn't be truer when it comes to communication: The first two seconds of communication are so important that it takes another four minutes to add 50 percent more information to an impression—positive or negative—within that communication.[1] Communication has often been referred to as a **soft skill**, which includes other competencies such as social graces, personality traits, language abilities, and ability to work with other people. Soft skills also encompass **emotional intelligence**, which Adele B. Lynn, in her book *The EQ Interview: Finding Employees with High Emotional Intelligence*, defines as "a person's ability to manage herself as well as her relationship with others so she can live her intentions."[2] But in today's business world, communication has become part of the new "**hard skills**" category, a technical job requirement, because of the critical role that it plays in business.[3] According to Peter Post, great-grandson of the late Emily Post, "Your skills can get you in the door; your people skills are what can seal the deal."[4]

Misunderstood = Miscommunicated

In Chapter 3 you learned about the importance of relationships. In fact, it is almost impossible to be in sales without developing relationships inside your organization and with your customers. Your relationship skills build trust, allow you to be a true partner, and help solve your customer's problems; both internal trust and external communication are essential keys to your ability to deliver on your promises. How are these qualities intrinsically related? The way in which you communicate can determine the level of trust that your colleagues or customers have in you.[5]

Just like relationships are the cornerstone of trust, communication is the foundation of relationships. But it's difficult to establish and develop relationships; it takes work and a lot of clear communication. You might think that sounds simple, but consider this: Nearly 75 percent of communications that are received are interpreted incorrectly. At the same time, interestingly, many people consider themselves good communicators. The telling disconnect occurs because people tend to assume that they know what other people mean or people assume that others know what they mean. This is compounded by the fact that people tend to hear what they want to hear—that is, a person may interpret elements of a conversation in such a way that the taken meanings contribute to his already established beliefs. When you put these assumptions together, communication can easily become "miscommunication."[6]

The Communication Model

The standard model of communication has evolved based on two parties—the **sender** and the **receiver**—exchanging information or ideas. The model includes major processes and functions categorized as **encoding, decoding, response,** and **feedback**. In addition, the model accounts for **noise**, which symbolizes anything that might disrupt the sending or receiving of a message.[7] The communication model is shown in Figure 5.1.

FIGURE 5.1 Traditional Communication Process[8]

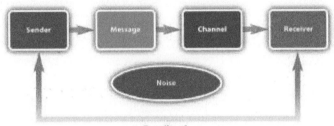

Feedback

The model helps describe exactly how communication takes place. For example, if you send a text message to your friend to ask him if he wants to go a movie, you are the source, or sender, of the message. You translated or encoded your message into text characters. A personal digital assistant (PDA) such as a BlackBerry, iPhone, or cell phone is the **channel**, or the method by which you communicated your message. Chances are, if your friend does not have his PDA or cell phone with him, your message will not reach him, and you might miss the movie. So in this example, the PDA or cell phone is the channel. When your friend, the receiver, reads the message, he decodes it or determines what you meant to communicate, and then he responds. If he was talking to another friend while he was reading your text message and didn't see the time the movie started, that conversation would be considered noise because it would be interfering with the communication of your message. Noise interferes with communication or causes distraction, whether it is heard or seen. When your friend responds to you by saying that he wants to go see the movie, he is providing feedback (or a response to your message). Figure 5.2 shows this example applied to the communication model.

The same thing can happen in a selling situation. For example, if you call a prospect to set up a meeting, you are the sender. The message is the meeting information (e.g., date, time, and place) that you encode into words. The channel is the telephone, and the receiver is the prospect. It sounds easy enough. Assume, however, that the prospect responds to you and agrees to the meeting. But because he was checking his e-mails while he was talking to you (which is noise), he puts the wrong time on his calendar. When you come for the appointment, he's out of the office, and your sales call doesn't take place. Now you have to start the communication process all over again. This is only an example of simply setting up a meeting. Now imagine the challenges if you started explaining the features and benefits of a complex product or negotiating a contract. You can see why understanding the communication process is so important in selling.

FIGURE 5.2 Communication Process Example

Feedback = Response to invitation

sender

Person who originates a message or communication.

receiver

Person who is the intended recipient of a message or communication.

encoding

The process of converting a message to be sent to a receiver into a symbolic form such as letters, pictures, or language.

decoding

The process of converting an encoded message into meaning on the part of the receiver.

response

An action taken by the receiver in response to a message.

feedback

The method of providing information back to the sender in response the message.

noise

Anything that can interfere with the communication of a message between sender and receiver.

channel

The method by which a message is communicated.

Did You Know...?

- Positive e-mail messages are likely to be interpreted as neutral.
- Neutral e-mail messages are likely to be perceived as negative.
- People who send e-mails overrate their ability to communicate feelings.
- There is a gap between how a sender *feels* when he writes the e-mail and the way the emotional content is communicated that can cause an error in decoding on the part of the receiver.
- One simple e-mail can lead to a communication debacle if the e-mail is not clearly written and well thought out from the recipient's point of view.[9]

Effective Communication

How do you avoid the pitfalls of poor communication and build productive business relationships? It's best to always communicate in a timely manner and in the method that your customer prefers. That may be easier said than done. Here are six tips that can help you increase your chances of making your communications effective.

Tip 1: Empathy Is Essential

One of the key elements of being a good communicator is having empathy. That means thinking about your communication from the receiver's point of view. It's focusing on what *she* wants to learn as a result of your communication, not what you want to tell her. Empathy is about demonstrating that you care about the other person's situation. Think about when you received your acceptance letter from your college; the letter probably mentioned what an exciting time it is in your life. The author of the letter demonstrated empathy because she focused on the situation from your perspective. A purely factual letter, without empathy, might have said that you were accepted and that now the school can make their budget since they met their enrollment goal. That would be quite a different letter and would make you feel very different (and probably not very welcome). Although it's always best to be candid, you should deliver information from the receiver's point of view and address her concerns.[10]

Empathy is an integral part of emotional connection, one of the elements of a brand that you learned about in Chapter 1. (Keep in mind that when you are in sales, you *are* the brand to the customer.) It is especially important to have an emotional connection and empathy when apologizing to customers. Chances are the customer is already angry, or at least disappointed, when you are not able to deliver as expected. You can express empathy in your communications by saying or writing, "You have every right to be upset. I understand how you must feel. I apologize for the late delivery. Let's work on a new process that will help prevent it from happening again."[11] Some of the best brands have disappointed their customers but showed empathy when they apologized. For example, the letter from then JetBlue CEO David Neeleman shown in Figure 5.3 is an example of a letter of apology that demonstrates empathy and emotional connection and also offers corrective action.

FIGURE 5.3 Letter of Apology from JetBlue[12]

An apology from David Neeleman

Dear JetBlue Customers,

We are sorry and embarrassed. But most of all, we are deeply sorry.

Last week was the worst operational week in JetBlue's seven year history. Many of you were either stranded, delayed or had flights cancelled following the severe winter ice storm in the Northeast. The storm disrupted the movement of aircraft, and, more importantly, disrupted the movement of JetBlue's pilot and inflight crewmembers who were depending on those planes to get them to the airports where they were scheduled to serve you. With the busy President's Day weekend upon us, rebooking opportunities were scarce and hold times at 1-800-JETBLUE were unusually long or not even available, further hindering our recovery efforts.

Words cannot express how truly sorry we are for the anxiety, frustration and inconvenience that you, your family, friends and colleagues experienced. This is especially saddening because JetBlue was founded on the promise of bringing humanity back to air travel, and making the experience of flying happier and easier for everyone who chooses to fly with us. We know we failed to deliver on this promise last week.

We are committed to you, our valued customers, and are taking immediate corrective steps to regain your confidence in us. We have begun putting a comprehensive plan in place to provide better and more timely information to you, more tools and resources for our crewmembers and improved procedures for handling operational difficulties. Most importantly, we have published the JetBlue Airways Customer Bill of Rights – our official commitment to you of how we will handle operational interruptions going forward – including details of compensation. We invite you to learn more at jetblue.com/promise.

You deserved better - a lot better - from us last week and we let you down. Nothing is more important than regaining your trust and all of us here hope you will give us the opportunity to once again welcome you onboard and provide you the positive JetBlue Experience you have come to expect from us.

Sincerely,

David Neeleman
Founder and CEO

Tip 2: Think Before You Communicate

Quick responses, whether verbal or via electronic methods, can be less effective than those that are considered and can even cause misunderstanding. Although a timely response is critical, it's worth a few minutes to think about exactly what you want to say before you say it (or type it).

Tip 3: Be Clear

It seems obvious, but not everyone is clear in his communications. Sometimes, people are trying to avoid "bad news" or trying to avoid taking a stand on a topic. It's always best to avoid confusion and clearly say what you mean by framing your message in a way that is easily understood by all receivers. It's also a good idea to avoid **buzz words (or jargon)**—those words, phrases, or acronyms that are used only in your company. If they can't be avoided, explain them in the same communication terms. You should also avoid jargon on your résumé and cover letter—help your reader see your brand story at a glance without needing a decoder ring.

> **buzz words (or jargon)**
>
> Words, phrases, or acronyms that are used only in a company.

Tip 4: Be Brief

Business communication should be short and to the point. Your customers are busy and need information—whether it's a proposal, report, or follow-up to a question—in a clear, concise way. It's best to avoid being verbose, especially in any business plans, proposals, or other significant documents.[13]

Tip 5: Be Specific

If you go to dinner at Cheesecake Factory and there is a wait to get a table, the hostess will hand you a portable pager and tell you that the wait will be twenty to twenty-five minutes. Perfect. You have just enough time to run a quick errand at a nearby store at the mall and be back in time to get your table. If, on the other hand, she told you that you will be seated shortly, you might have an expectation of being seated in five to ten minutes. Meanwhile, "shortly" might mean twenty to twenty-five minutes for her. You would probably forgo running your errand because you think you are going to be seated soon but end up waiting for twenty-five minutes and being frustrated. Being specific in your communication not only gives clarity to your message but also helps set your customer's expectations. In other words, your customer won't expect something you can't deliver if you are clear about what exactly you *can* deliver and when. The same is true for prices. For example, if you order from the menu at the Cheesecake Factory, you know precisely what you will get to eat and how much it will cost. However, if there is a menu special that you heard about tableside, but weren't told how much the dish was, you might be surprised (and disappointed) when you receive the check. Specificity avoids surprises and sets expectations. See some examples in Table 5.1 of general statements that can be communicated more effectively when made into specific statements.

TABLE 5.1 General versus Specific Statements

General Statement	Specific Statement
I'll get back to you shortly.	I'll get back to you by Tuesday.
It will only take a few minutes.	It will take less than 5 minutes.
It will cost about $5,000 plus installation.	The cost is $4,800 plus $200 for installation.
Everything is included.	It includes your choice of entrée, vegetable, dessert, and coffee.

Tip 6: Be Timely

Timing is everything in life and most certainly in selling. It's best to be proactive with communication, and if you owe someone a response, do it sooner rather than later. If you are slow to respond to questions and communication, it will be difficult to develop trust, as prolonged responses may seem to imply that you are taking action without informing the customer what it is you are doing. Timing is especially important when you are communicating a negative response or bad news. Don't put it off; do it as soon as possible and give your customer the benefit of complete information.

Rules of Engagement

At the beginning of each relationship, ask your customer how he prefers to communicate. Getting the answers to these simple questions will save time and confusion throughout your relationship and help ensure good communication.

- How do you prefer to receive regular communication (e-mail, text, phone, in person, hard copy)?
- What can I expect as a standard turnaround time for response to questions and issues?
- How do you prefer to receive urgent communication (e-mail, text, phone)?
- Who else (if anyone) in the organization would you like to also receive communication from me?
- When is the best time to touch base with you (early morning, midday, or later in the afternoon)?
- How frequently would you like a status update and in what format (e-mail, phone, in person)?

Listen Up

While you may think you are ready to communicate, it's a good idea to stop and listen first. Creating your message is only half of communication; listening is the other half. But it's difficult to listen because we listen faster than we speak—that is, based on what the other person is saying, we are already constructing responses in our minds before they have even finished. As a result, many people are guilty of "listening too fast."[14] Cicero once said that it is good thing that humans were given one mouth and two ears, in light of the way we use them.[15]

Listening, in fact, is so important that companies like Starbucks believe that it may directly improve profits. According to Alan Gulick, a Starbucks Corporation spokesperson, if every Starbucks employee misheard one $10 order each day, it would cost the company one billion dollars in a year.[16] That's why Starbucks has a process to teach their employees how to listen. Although listening may seem passive, it is actively linked to success: One study conducted in the insurance industry found that better listeners held higher positions and got promoted more than those who did not have developed listening skills.[17] So it's worth it to hone your listening skills *now* so that when you get into the business world you can be successful. Here are a few tips:

- **Use active listening**. Confirm that you heard the sender correctly by saying something like, "Just to be sure I understand, we are going to move forward with twelve cases for your initial order, then revisit your inventory in five days." Review the communication model above and take notice of the importance of decoding. If you decode a message from your customer incorrectly, the communication is ineffective and could even be costly. In the example above, the customer might have said in response, "I meant that the initial order should be five cases, and we'll revisit the inventory in twelve days." That's a big difference.

- **Ask questions**. Questions are a way to gather more information and learn about your customer and their business. They are also an excellent way to demonstrate that you are communicating by listening. You learned in Chapter 2 that asking the *right* questions is critical to being a successful salesperson. Focus on listening and asking the right questions, and you'll be rewarded with great information.

- **Focus**. Although multitasking has seemingly become a modern virtue, focus actually helps create more effective communication. Stop and focus on your customer when he is speaking. This is a sign of respect, and this concentration allows you to absorb more information. Take notes to remember exactly what you discussed. There's nothing more important than what your customer has to say.[18]

- **Take notes**. While it may seem like you will remember everything that is said at a meeting or during a conversation, taking notes signals that you are listening, and it provides you with an accurate record of what was said. "The palest ink is better than the best memory."[19]

Video Clip

Listen More, Talk Less
This video highlights some challenges and tips for listening in sales.

View the video online at: http://www.youtube.com/embed/iyHkkAzDTXk

Link

Are You a Good Listener?
Take this quiz to find out if you are a good listener.

https://www.mindtools.com/pages/article/listening-quiz.htm

There's More to Communication than Meets the Eye...or Ear

It's important to remember that you will be communicating with many different people about many different topics in selling. Sometimes, you will be communicating one-on-one and sometimes you will be communicating with a group. Just as people have varying social styles (as you've learned in Chapter 3), it's important to know that people also absorb information differently. Research conducted in the 1970s indicates that people comprehend information in four distinct ways:

- **Why**. They want to know the reasons for doing something.
- **What**. They want to know the facts about it.
- **How**. They want to know only the information they need to get it done.
- **What if**. They want to know the consequences of doing it.

This can be a helpful road map of the elements you will want to include in your communications, especially if you are communicating with a group, since you may not know everyone's best method of absorbing information. It's been proven that if people don't receive the type of communication they prefer, they tend to tune out or reject the information.

You've probably noticed that both people and brands communicate the same message multiple times and usually in multiple ways. Creative repetition is key to successful communication. Think about the advertising Pepsi ran when it launched its new logo in early 2009; you most likely saw the television commercial during the Super Bowl, noticed a billboard in a high-traffic area of a major city, received an e-mail, saw banner ads on the Internet, reviewed the commercial on YouTube, and saw the new logo on the packaging. Pepsi's ad campaign illustrates the "three-times convincer" concept, which claims that 80 percent of people need to be exposed a message three times to buy into it, 15 percent need to be exposed to it five times, and 5 percent need to be exposed to it up to twenty-five times.[20] You may have seen the message so many times that it's hard to remember what the old logo even looked like.

Types of Communication

It is important to use multiple types of communication so that repetition does not become boring like a broken record. There are three types of communication: **verbal**, which involves speaking to one or many people to convey a message; **nonverbal**, which includes body language and other observations about people; and **written**, which includes a message that is read in hard copy, e-mail, text message, instant message, Facebook, Twitter, blog, or other Internet-based written communication.[21] Varying the usage of these mediums can help ensure your customer's attention, but you must carefully develop each skill separately to communicate effectively.

Verbal Communication

An introduction, a presentation, a telephone conversation, a videoconference call: these are all examples of verbal communication because information is transmitted orally. Despite the ubiquitous use of technology in the business world, verbal communication is the most common method of exchanging information and ideas. Verbal communication is powerful, fast, and natural and includes voice inflections that help senders and receivers understand the message more clearly. The downside to verbal communication is that once it is spoken, the words are essentially gone; they are preserved only in the memory of those present, and sometimes the memories of the specific words spoken vary dramatically. The he-said-she-said argument is an example of this. No one really knows who said what unless the words are recorded. Recall is rarely exactly the same between two or more people.

Voice inflection, the verbal emphasis you put on certain words, can have a significant impact on the meaning of what you say. In fact, the same words can take on completely different meaning based on the inflection you use. For example, if you say the sentence in Figure 5.4 with an inflection on a different word each time, the sentence communicates something completely different each time.

verbal

Communication that involves speaking to one or many people.

nonverbal

Communication that includes body language and other observations about people.

written

Communication that is done by way of printed words on paper or a screen.

voice inflection

Verbal emphasis on certain words.

FIGURE 5.4 The Impact of Intonation

Sentence	Meaning
I borrowed your book.	I was the one who took your book.
I **borrowed** your book.	I didn't take your book; I only borrowed it.
I borrowed **your** book.	Your book was the one I borrowed.
I borrowed your **book**.	I borrowed your book, not your laptop.

Source: Based on ideas in Kiely, M. (October, 1993). When "no" means "yes." Marketing, 7–9.

videoconference

A meeting that takes place in at least two remote locations and includes technology support to see and hear people in all locations simultaneously.

podcast

An audio broadcast transmitted via an MP3 player.

Webinar

A meeting that takes place on the Internet that allows participants in remote locations to view what is on the screen and hear the speaker and ask questions.

Verbal communication may take place face-to-face, such as an in-person conversation or group meeting, speech, or presentation. It could also take place by phone in an individual conversation, a conference call, or even a voice mail. Other forms of verbal communication include **videoconferences**, **podcasts**, and **Webinars**, which are increasingly common in business. All these methods allow you to use inflection to communicate effectively. Face-to-face meetings also provide the opportunity to use and interpret other visual cues to increase the effectiveness of your communication.

Verbal communication is especially important throughout the steps of the selling process. Your choice of words can make the difference in someone's decision to first hear your sales presentation, and your presentation can determine whether that person will purchase your product or service. You will learn more specifically about how communication is used throughout the selling process covered in later chapters.

Nonverbal Communication

Imagine that you are in a retail store buying a suit for an interview. When the salesperson approaches you, she smiles, makes eye contact, and shakes your hand. You respond positively. You notice that she is dressed professionally, so she makes you feel as if you will receive good fashion advice from her. When you make your choice, the tailor comes over wearing a tape measure around his neck. You know he is a professional and you can trust him to alter your new suit properly. On the other hand, if the salesperson waits on you only after you interrupt her personal phone call, doesn't make eye contact or shake your hand, acts as if she is bored being at work, and is dressed in worn jeans and flip-flops, it's unlikely that you trust her to help you choose your suit.

You have, no doubt, used and noticed nonverbal communication in virtually every personal encounter you have had. Think about it: A gesture, a smile, a nod, eye contact, what you are wearing, the fact that you are frequently checking your cell phone for text messages, and how close you stand to someone are all examples of nonverbal communication.

Video Clip

Say versus Do
This video describes the difference between verbal and nonverbal communication.

View the video online at: http://www.youtube.com/embed/ihuGFUrzD30

Nonverbal communication is extremely powerful. In fact, some studies indicate that the influence from nonverbal communication such as tone and visuals can have a greater impact than the spoken words. Dr. Albert Mehrabian, a famed psychologist and professor emeritus of psychology at University of California, Los Angeles, is considered a pioneer in the area of body language and nonverbal communication. His research includes an equation, called the **Mehrabian formula**,[22] that is frequently used to define the relative impact of verbal and nonverbal messages based on experiments of communication of feelings and attitudes. Dr. Mehrabian developed the formula shown in Figure 5.5 to define how communication takes place.

FIGURE 5.5 The Mehrabian Formula

> **Total liking = 7% verbal liking + 38% vocal liking + 55% facial liking**

The Mehrabian formula is used to explain situations in which verbal communication and nonverbal communication do not match. In other words, when facial expressions contradict words, people tend to believe the facial expressions.[23]

Types of Nonverbal Communication

- Handshake
- Body language
- Gestures
- Nodding or shaking your head
- Eye contact (or lack of eye contact)
- Eye roll
- Facial expressions
- Touch
- Space or proximity
- Dress
- Multitasking (e.g., texting while listening to someone, earphones in ears while working)

Your Handshake Says It All

In some countries, you might bow when you meet someone; in others you might kiss; but when you meet someone for a business meeting in the United States, it's best to shake hands.[24] Although fist bumps and high fives may be trendy as friendly greetings, neither is appropriate in a business setting.

Mehrabian formula

Formula used to explain situations in which verbal communication and nonverbal communication do not match; in other words, when facial expressions contradict words, people tend to believe the facial expressions.

FIGURE 5.6
Your handshake says a lot about you.

© 2010 Jupiterimages Corporation

Be Memorable

Here's a networking tip: When you shake hands with people at a meeting, they are two times more likely to remember you than if you don't shake hands, according to a recent study conducted by the Incomm Center for Trade Show Research.[25]

The exact history of the handshake is unknown; however, at one time it was used as method to prove that you had no weapons in your hands.[26] A good handshake is essential in business; it is the first nonverbal cue that you give to the person with whom you are meeting. It's so important to have a good handshake that a recent study conducted at the University of Iowa showed that during mock interviews, those students who scored as having a better handshake were also considered more hirable by interviewers. According to Greg Stewart, a business professor who conducted the study said, "We found that the first impression begins with a handshake and sets the tone for the rest of the interview."[27]

Do you think you have a good handshake? Believe it or not, it's worth practicing your handshake. Here are five tips for a good handshake:

1. Extend your right hand when you are approximately three feet away from the person with whom you want to shake hands.[28]

2. Keep your wrist straight and lock hands connecting your hand with the same part of the other person's hand.[29] Apply appropriate pressure; don't crush the person's hand.

3. Shake up and down three or four times.[30]

4. Avoid the "wet fish" handshake.[31] This is where practice is really important. The more you shake hands, the less nervous you will be.

5. Smile and make eye contact.[32] This is your opportunity to use multiple types of nonverbal communication to get your meeting or interview off to a good start.

Link

Shake on It

What does your handshake say about you?

http://www.howcast.com/videos/105154-How-To-Shake-Hands

Body Language

body language

Nonverbal communication using body elements such as gestures, facial expressions, eye contact, and proximity.

Do you use your hands when you talk? If so, you are using body language to help make your point. But body language includes more than talking with your hands. **Body language** is what we say without words; nonverbal communication using your body includes elements such as gestures, facial expressions, eye contact, a head tilt, a nod, and even where and how you sit. Body language can indicate an unspoken emotion or sentiment that a person might be feeling either consciously or subconsciously. Body language can indicate if you are listening to someone and are engaged in what he is saying, disagreeing with him, or getting bored. (You might want to think twice about the body language you are using in class.) It's important that you are aware of what you communicate with *your* body language and to understand and respond to the cues you are getting from *someone else's* body language.

Do You Speak Body?

Here are some common examples of body language and what they mean.[33],[34]

- Crossed arms: discomfort
- Spreading fingers: territorial display
- Mirroring (i.e., mimicking your body position to another's): comfort
- Drumming or tapping fingers: frustration
- Hands on hips: there is an issue
- Hands behind the back: "leave me alone"
- Hands clasped, thumbs up: positive
- Thumbs down: don't like
- Hands clasped with fingers forming a steeple: confidence
- Touch neck: insecurity
- Crossed legs: comfort
- Glancing at watch: concerned about time or bored

Body language is not just an interesting topic to consider; it's a proven science that can help you improve your communication. If you would like to see how body language is used in everyday life, watch this video featuring Tonya Reiman, national television commentator and author of *The Power of Body Language.*

Video Clip

Tonya Reiman, Body Language Expert
Learn what your body language is communicating.

View the video online at: http://www.youtube.com/embed/7cg192cQYUA

Here are some tips to remember about your body language to be sure you are sending the right nonverbal message to your customer or interviewer.

- **Make eye contact** with the person to whom you are speaking. Eye contact avoidance can be distracting and can prevent you from establishing a relationship as shown in this video.

Video Clip

Eyes Have It
Eye avoidance can be damaging to your career.

View the video online at: http://www.youtube.com/embed/nwbUy3MHZGg

- **Smile** when you meet someone and throughout the conversation. A smile is a positive response to another person and has a significant impact on how people perceive you. A smile can break the ice and help you start a conversation.
- **Dress for success** at all times, which means always dressing appropriately for the situation. The *Selling U* section in this chapter covers how to dress for an interview. But it's best to keep in mind that even after you get the job you want, it's a good idea to dress a little better than the position. Even in very casual work environments, what you wear is a nonverbal communication about who you are. If you don't dress for the next promotion, chances are you won't be considered for it. Be aware of the company policy and dress code, and if in doubt, dress more conservatively. This podcast featuring Peter Post discusses how to handle casual dress in the workplace.

Written Communication

wiki

A collaborative Web site that allows multiple people to share information, documents, videos, and pictures.

Although verbal and nonverbal communications usually take place in real time, written communication has a longer consideration period. The sender must encode the message in words to be communicated on paper or a screen.[35] Business reports, proposals, memos, e-mails, text messages, Web sites, blogs, wikis, and more are all examples of written communication. Each of them is created over a period of time and can include collaboration from multiple people. Collaboration is especially important for communicating, planning, and creating documents so many people use tools such as **wikis** to share documents. To see how a wiki works, watch this video.

Video Link

Collaborate Online

A wiki can help any team share and collaborate...anywhere, anytime.

http://www.bnet.com/2422-13731_23-187449.html

Written communication is preferred to verbal communication when careful consideration is important or the information needs to be permanent, such as a company policy, sales presentation, or proposal. Written communication can also take place when verbal communication isn't an option, like when you need to respond to an e-mail or text message at 1:00 a.m.

Although verbal communication is faster and more natural than written communication, each has its pros and cons. Generally, written communication is better at conveying facts, while verbal communication is better at conveying feelings. Verbal communication has another significant drawback: consider the fact that humans listen much faster than they speak. For example, the average public speaker speaks at about 125 words per minute. Although this sounds natural, the average person can listen at 400 to 500 words per minute. That means that listeners' minds have time and space to wander, which can impact the effectiveness of verbal communication.[36] (You may have noticed your mind wandering during a class lecture—even if you found the topic interesting.)

Written communication requires a good command of the English language, including the rules of grammar and spelling. If you think that business exists solely on quick instant messages and text messages, you might be surprised to learn that they are only a portion of the communication within a company and between the company's vendors and other partners. Because the nature of written communication is such that it allows time for consideration and composition, the standards for writing are much higher than for a casual conversation. Customers and colleagues alike expect clear, concise written communications with proper grammar and spelling. And because written communication is long lasting—whether on paper or on the Internet—errors or misstatements exist for an irritatingly long time. So whether you are writing a proposal, a presentation, a report, a meeting recap, or a follow-up e-mail, it's best to take the time to think about your communication and craft it so that it is effective. Consider using the following tips:

- **Be short and sweet**. Shorter is always better when it comes to business correspondence. It's best to include all pertinent facts with concise information. If you write your communication with the receiver in mind, it will be easier to make it shorter and more effective.

- **Grammar, please**. Sentences should be structured correctly and use proper grammar, including a subject and a verb in each sentence. Business correspondence should always include uppercase and lowercase letters and correct punctuation.[37] If writing is not your strong suit, visit your campus student services office or learning center to provide information about upcoming writing clinics and access to other tools that can help improve your writing skills.

- **Check spelling**. Use the spell-check tool on your computer. There is no excuse for a misspelled word. Text abbreviations are not acceptable in business correspondence.

- **Read before you send**. Reread your document or electronic communication before it goes out. Is everything complete? Is it clear? Is it something you will be proud of days or weeks later? Take the extra time to review before you send. It's difficult to revise a communication as revisions cause confusion.

- **Just the facts**. Stick to the facts to maximize the impact of your written communications; leave the emotional topics for verbal dialogue. For example, send an e-mail to confirm meeting time, date, and location; use a verbal communication for the content of the meeting to be discussed, such as a negotiation.

You Are What You Write

You might not think twice about sending a text to your friend. But in the business world, everything you write in an e-mail, text message, letter, or memo is a direct reflection of your personal brand. This video highlights the power of written communication and how it can help you build your personal brand.

Video:

View the video online at: http://www.youtube.com/embed/JiUUQafcsqc?rel=0

Which Is Best?

Although verbal, nonverbal, and written communication all play a role in your communication with your customers, you might be wondering which one is best. It depends on your customer and on the situation. Some customers want to work day to day using all the latest technology tools, including text messaging, social networking, Web conferences, wikis, and more. Other customers prefer more traditional face-to-face meetings, phone calls, and some e-mail correspondence. Adapt to the method of communication that your customer prefers and not the other way around. In some situations, a face-to-face meeting is best—for instance, if you wish to discuss a complex issue, negotiate, or meet some additional members of the team. Sometimes, a face-to-face meeting isn't feasible, so other verbal communication methods such as a videoconference, phone call, or conference call can be efficient and effective if used properly.

Chances are you will use a combination of communication types with each customer tailored to his particular preferences and situation. Be guided by the fact that you want to keep your communication personal in meaning and professional in content. Think about it from the receiver's point of view, and deliver bad news verbally whenever possible.

Which Is Better: E-mail or Face-to-Face?

It might seem intuitive, but it's not always true that a face-to-face meeting is better than an e-mail. It depends on the type of relationship you have with the person. If you are competitive with her, it's best to use e-mail to communicate. According to a study conducted by Robert B. Cialdini and Rosanna Guadagno in 2002, if you have a more cooperative relationship, a face-to-face meeting is probably a better choice if it's physically possible.[38]

Key Takeaways

- **Communication** is vital in selling and is the foundation of relationships.
- The **communication model** describes exactly how communication is sent and received and provides clues as to how to improve the effectiveness of communication.
- Empathy is thinking about your communication from the receiver's point of view. Empathy helps build an emotional connection.
- Effective **communication** is clear, concise, brief, specific, and timely.
- Creating your message is only one half of **communication**; listening is the other half. Being a good listener improves your ability to be a good communicator.
- There are three types of **communication**: **verbal**, which involves speaking to one or many people to convey a message; **nonverbal**, which includes body language and other observations about people; and **written**, which includes a message that is read in hard copy, e-mail, text message, instant message, Facebook, Twitter, blog, or other Internet-based written communication.
- **Verbal communication** provides the opportunity to change communication with inflection, or the emphasis put on certain words in a conversation or presentation.
- **Nonverbal communication** provides additional insights into the sending and receiving of a message through gestures, eye contact, proximity, and other elements of **body language**.
- Your handshake can be one of the most powerful elements of nonverbal communication and sets the tone for the meeting or interview ahead.
- **Written communication** includes printed words designed to communicate a message on paper or a screen and is more permanent than **verbal** or **nonverbal communication**.
- **Written communication** is best used for factual information, whereas **verbal communication** is best used for emotional topics or those that require discussion.
- The best method of **communication** depends on your customer's preferences and on the situation.

Exercises

1. Choose an advertisement online or in a magazine. Apply the communication model by answering the following questions: Who is the source? What is the message? How is the message encoded? What is the channel with which it is communicated? How is the message decoded? Who is the receiver? What might be an example of potential noise that would interfere with the communication of the message? How can the sender receive feedback from the receiver?

2. Are you a good listener? Complete this online listening activity to see how well you listen. http://www.bbc.co.uk/skillswise/words/listening/listeningforspecificinformation/activity.shtml

3. Can you listen to directions accurately? Take this online listening exercise to see how well you listen. http://www.bbc.co.uk/skillswise/words/listening/typesoflistening/game.shtml

4. Test your listening skills. Do this exercise with a partner, one is the speaker and one is the listener. The speaker has three minutes to describe what he is looking for in a vacation des-

tination. The listener has to use active listening skills. Then, the listener has three minutes to "sell" a destination to the speaker, based on what the speaker said he wanted. The speaker has one minute to review how close the listener was to his destination. Reverse roles and repeat.

5. Name the three types of communication and give an example for each one. How might the communication be misinterpreted in each example? How might the communication be made more effective in each example?

6. Visit a local retailer that uses personal selling and ask a salesperson questions about purchasing a product or service. Identify three types of communication the salesperson uses. Were they effective? Why or why not?

7. Identify four examples of nonverbal communication you observe in class. What does each example communicate?

8. Visit your campus student services or learning center and learn about the resources that are available to help you develop your writing skills. What information, classes, or workshops are available? Which ones sound like they might be helpful? Why?

9. Consider this situation: You are a salesperson who has to tell your customers that the original shipping date will not be met and the new date is one week later. What are the four things that your customers would want to know?

10. Visit http://www.pbworks.com to set up a wiki for the class. Discuss a situation in which you could use a wiki for class projects, campus activities, or other personal projects. Discuss a situation in which a salesperson might use a wiki with a customer.

5.2 Your Best Behavior

Learning Objective

1. Understand the appropriate etiquette for business communication.

You probably learned about table manners, thank-you notes, and other forms of etiquette when you were younger. The way you conduct yourself says a lot about who you are in life and, by extension, in business. Although many companies have a casual dress code, don't be quick to assume that protocol and established practices aren't important. It would be easy to misinterpret lack of formality as lack of professionalism. Manners matter in selling, now more than ever.

Never Underestimate the Power of Good Etiquette

etiquette

Manners, customs, and protocols that are the norm in specific situation.

How do you make a positive impression when you meet someone? What's the best way to ask for her business card? When is it appropriate or expected to send a thank-you note? Who picks up the bill at a business lunch? It's hard to know the "rules of the road," especially in today's casual, fast-paced selling environment. **Etiquette** can make the difference in how your customer perceives you and your personal brand.

Etiquette Tips for Letters and Memos

Despite the use of electronic devices in business, formal written communication such as letters, memos, proposals, reports, and presentations are still major methods of communication in selling. These more official methods of communication reflect factual statements that you are making on behalf of the company. Here are some tips for writing business communications:

- Use company letterhead where appropriate. For example, letters are always written on letterhead, whether in hard copy or in an electronic format that can be sent via e-mail.

- Use the formal elements of a business letter shown in Figure 5.7.

- For a company memo, use the company format. Most companies have a set format for hard copy and electronic memos. See an example of a company memo in Figure 5.8.

- Spell-check and proofread your document carefully before you send it. Be sure it is complete and factually correct and does not include any grammar or spelling errors.

- Use CC to indicate the names of other people who should also receive a copy of the letter or memo. The term "CC" is short for "carbon copy," which dates back to the days of typewriters when carbon paper was used to make multiple copies of a document. It can also mean "courtesy copy": an additional copy provided to someone as a courtesy.[39]

- Use BCC (blind carbon copy) to send copies to other people without having the primary recipient see it.[40]

Video Clip

Tips for Writing a Business Letter
Etiquette makes all the difference in the quality of your communication.

View the video online at: http://www.youtube.com/embed/unggnlyr18M

FIGURE 5.7 Business Letter Format

Moore Manufacturing Group 575 Parkland Avenue Lake Forest, IL 60515

August 28, 2009

Ms. Janice Lee
Buyer
Universal Parts, Inc.
101 Corporate Drive
Deerfield, IL 60511

Dear Ms. Lee,

Productivity and cost savings are even more critical today than ever before. But you can't afford to give up customer service for reduced costs. You deserve impeccable service from a supplier who also keeps costs among the lowest in the industry.

Based on the research I have done on Universal Parts, it appears that switching to Moore Manufacturing could save you as much as 12% on your annual purchases. In addition, you would have a dedicated customer service expert available to you 24/7 for any questions or issues you may have.

I'd like the opportunity to meet with you and learn more about your priorities and business challenges. I will call you on Tuesday to set up a time that is convenient for you.

In the meantime, you might find it interesting to review the attached audit that was conducted on your current offering. It reflects where you can potentially realize savings.

Sincerely,

Rachel Grossman

Rachel Grossman
Account Manager

Attachment

FIGURE 5.8 Company Memo Example

Good to be Green.com
Internal Memo

TO: Jason Sedgewick
FROM: Abe Forte
RE: September 12 Sales Meeting

The quarterly sales meeting will be held on September 12 at the Radisson City Center.
You are cordially invited to participate in the interactive planning session at
10:00 a.m. Your insights will be extremely valuable as the sales team frames the plan
for next year.

Please confirm your attendance by Friday by calling me at x5432 or by e-mailing me
at aforte@goodtobegreen.com.

Thanks in advance for your participation.

CC: Alena Adamonis

BCC: Justin Jankowski

Etiquette Tips for Conversations, Meetings, and Presentations

Although common sense should prevail in all business communications, here are some tips that
will help make your conversations, meetings, and presentations more effective forms of communication:

- Be prepared; don't waste anyone's time or focus.
- Prepare a written agenda and hand it out at the start of the meeting to keep the group focused
  on the desired topics.
- Speak clearly and at a volume that is easy to hear, but not too loud so as to be distracting.
- Be professional and respectful; don't interrupt when others are speaking.
- Use eye contact.
- At the end, recap your key points and identify next steps.

  In sales, time is money so conducting effective and efficient meetings is critical to your success.

Link

Seven Tips to Make Your Meetings More Effective[41]
http://www.sellingpower.com/content/newsletter/issue.php?pc=972

Doodle to Save Time

If you are setting up a meeting that involves several people and it's difficult to agree on a meeting date and time, you can use Doodle.com to identify the best date and time to meet. You choose the options and e-mail a link to the participants; when people respond, you see the Doodle.com summary that indicates the best date and time for the meeting. Set up an account at http://doodle.com.

FIGURE 5.9 Sample Poll on Doodle.com[42]

	July 2009					
	Wed 15			Thu 16		
	9:00 AM	10:00 AM	12:00 PM	9:00 AM	10:00 AM	12:00 PM
Kim Richmond						
Laura Reed	OK			OK		
Alan Tempest	OK	OK		OK	OK	
Kimberly Neff	OK	OK	OK	OK	OK	OK
Jason Wisdom	OK	OK	OK	OK	OK	OK
Kim Richmond	☐	☐	☐	☐	☐	☐
Count	4	3	2	4	3	2

Etiquette for Requesting and Giving Business Cards

Business cards are a branding tool for your company and a way to stay in touch with your customers and other people in your network.[43] In fact, giving out and requesting a business card is considered good etiquette.[44] Here are some tips to exchange business cards in a professional manner:

- Carry your business cards in a case or protective holder; never give anyone a card that is worn, dirty, or out of date.[45]
- Always put a supply of business cards in your case when you attend a business event.[46]
- Present your card with the print facing up so the recipient can easily read it.[47]
- Never force anyone to take your card.[48]
- When receiving a business card, take a minute to review the information to make sure you remember who gave you the card. Make any notes or comments on it later.[49]

Video Clip

The Etiquette of Exchanging Business Cards
This is the right way to exchange cards.

View the video online at: http://www.youtube.com/embed/J8bG2Lb5fv8

Etiquette for Business Meals

The purpose of a business breakfast, lunch, or dinner is to get to know someone and build a relationship. As you learned in Chapter 3, to engage in business entertainment is considered part of the sales job description. Table manners are a form of nonverbal communication, and impolite etiquette can reverse all the effort you have put into a relationship. Business meals are so important that many companies use business lunches or dinners as part of the interview process. Whatever the situation, you want to be prepared with proper etiquette for the occasion.

- A meal is considered a business meeting, no matter where it is held.[50]
- To help you remember which dishes and utensils to use, think BMW: **B**read plate on your left, **M**eal in the center, **W**ater goblet on the right.[51] Use silverware starting at the outside and work your way in as the meal progresses.
- As a general rule of thumb, the person who invites pays. If you are invited to lunch for an interview, your host pays. If you take a customer out to lunch, you pay.[52]
- If you don't know what to order, ask your host what's good. Order a midpriced entrée rather than ordering the least expensive or most expensive item on the menu. If you are the host, make some suggestions so your customer feels comfortable with her choice.[53]
- Don't order anything messy; stick to food that is easy to eat.[54]
- Be courteous to the wait staff. Many people observe how you treat other people, even when you think no one is watching.

Etiquette for Thank-You Notes

There's nothing more personal than a thank-you note. For the most part, you and your customers are very busy, which is why a thank-you note is even more appreciated. Whether it's a handwritten note or an e-mail thank you, it will go a long way in building your relationship. It's a personal touch that sets you apart. It's never inappropriate to say thank you, but it may be inappropriate *not* to say thank you.

Video: When to Say Thank You

Sending a thank-you note is always appropriate in business.

View the video online at: http://www.youtube.com/embed/NzpIXSz0S6I?rel=0

Video: Why to Say Thank You

There are many reasons to send a business thank-you note; this video includes some ideas.

View the video online at: http://www.youtube.com/embed/qITRJTyQJSg?rel=0

Here are some tips for writing thank-you notes:

- Start with a clear introduction and let the reader know right away that the purpose of the note or e-mail is to thank him.
- Be specific about the situation, date, or other information surrounding the reason for the thank-you note.
- Make it personal and make it special by including your own sentiments. A generic message such as "thanks for a great job" really doesn't fill the bill. Think about exactly what moved you to write the note and be sure your reader knows what she did that was special.[55]

Video: How to Say Thank You

This video includes some guidelines about what to include in a business thank-you notes.

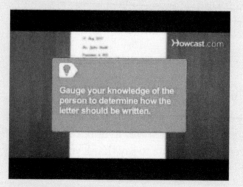

View the video online at: http://www.youtube.com/embed/qZ_Y6qw8wZM?rel=0

Power Selling: Lessons in Selling from Successful Brands

SimplySoles
Imagine getting a personalized handwritten thank-you note when you order a pair of shoes online. That's what SimplySoles.com does for each customer. Founder Kassie Rempel feels so strongly about thanking customers for their business that every customer who purchases a pair of shoes receives one; each note even mentions the name of the shoe that was purchased.[56]

High Tech, High Touch

The year was 1982, and the world was just beginning to realize the amazing potential of computer technology. John Naisbitt wrote a book called *Megatrends: Ten New Directions Transforming Our Lives*, where he coined the term "high tech, high touch," which he defined as the contradictory state in which people are driven by technology yet long for human interaction.[57] He wrote about how the United States has been transformed from being comfortable with technology to being intoxicated with technology, a state he calls the "Technologically Intoxicated Zone" in his 1999 book, *High Tech/High Touch*. You probably can't imagine living without your cell phone or personal digital assistant (PDA), iPod, computer, or other electronic devices. In fact, it's likely you can't even remember what communication was like before the Internet.

Technology, with all of its efficiency and benefits, cannot, however, become a substitute for old-fashioned human efforts. "Technology makes *tasks* easier, but it does not make our *lives* easier," according to July Shapiro in a recent article in *Advertising Age*.[58] Shapiro's observation is true, especially as it relates to business; sometimes, the crush of technology takes precedence over business etiquette. However, people have begun to rethink the lack of personal interaction and its corresponding etiquette in the workplace. Yes, "there's even an app for that"; a firm named Etiquette Avenue has recently launched an iPod app for business etiquette. The fact is, technology isn't personal and can't behave in the right way at the right time with your customer or on an interview; that's completely up to *you*.[59],[60]

Now, we're seeing a bit of a reverse movement: Technology is so pervasive in selling that salespeople are actually pushing back on their managers and asking them for more face time and less gadget time. One of the best opportunities for sales managers and their salespeople to discuss business problems and build relationships with one another has traditionally been during "windshield time," which is the time in the car driving between sales calls. "Sales reps report that the intrusion of technology has stolen this valuable time from reps and their principals [bosses]," according to a recent article in *Agency Sales*, because as soon as they get into the car to drive to the next call, the sales manager pulls out his BlackBerry. "If there's one thing I could tell my principals [bosses] when they come see me in the field is to ditch the electronic communications and pay attention to me and our customers," said one salesperson quoted in the article.[61] It's no surprise that there's a need for business etiquette, especially as it relates to technology.

Being Connected versus Being Addicted

In a recent pitch to a potential client, a marketing executive in Manhattan thought it was strange that his potential customer was so engaged with his iPhone that he hardly looked up from it during the meeting. After ninety minutes, someone peeked over the customer's shoulder and saw that he was playing a racing game on his iPhone. This was disappointing, but not shocking according to the marketing firm that was doing the presentation; they continued with their pitch because they wanted the business. Some are not as tolerant. Billionaire Tom Golisano, a power broker in New York politics, recently announced that he wants to have State Senate majority leader Malcolm A. Smith removed from office because Smith was focused on his BlackBerry during a budget meeting with him. Recently, in Dallas, Texas, a student lost his opportunity for an internship at a hedge fund when he checked his BlackBerry to check a fact during an interview and took an extra minute to check his text messages at the same time.[62] It's no surprise that BlackBerrys are also called "CrackBerrys." According to Maggie Jackson, author of *Distracted: The Erosion of Attention and the Coming Dark Age*, we are living in "an institutionalized culture of interruption, where our time and attention is being fragmented by a never-ending stream of phone calls, e-mails, instant messages, text messages, and tweets."[63]

The need to be connected should not overwhelm respect for colleagues and customers. Although texting has become a national pastime, especially among teenagers, it's important to know the appropriate etiquette for the use of handheld electronic devices when conducting a sales call.

FIGURE 5.10
Etiquette applies to the use of electronic devices.

© 2010 Jupiterimages
Corporation

First, it's best to turn off your electronic devices *before* you enter every meeting. If you think you can't live without checking your text messages, think about how you would feel if you went on a job interview and the person with whom you were meeting was checking his electronic device during your interview. Just because some people demonstrate bad behavior and check their electronic devices for messages during a meeting doesn't make it appropriate. In fact, it will help you stand out as a good listener, and you will make your customer feel even more important when you focus exclusively on her, as shown in this video.

Video Clip

To Text or Not to Text
Learn about appropriate business etiquette.

View the video online at: http://www.youtube.com/embed/FBnKwjDwQB8

Etiquette Tips for Telephone, Cell Phone, Voice Mail, and Conference Calls

Sometimes, however, the use of technology is entirely necessary to conduct business when personal interaction is impossible. It's important that verbal communication that is not face-to-face is effective and professional. Because you don't have the benefit of using or seeing the receiver's nonverbal communication, the challenges for effective and appropriate communication are even greater.

Here are some dos and don'ts of telephone etiquette:

- **Do** be aware of the volume of your voice when you are speaking on the phone in the office or on a cell phone.[64]

- **Do**, when using a speakerphone, conduct the call in an enclosed or isolated area such as a conference room or office to avoid disturbing others in the area.

- **Do**, when leaving a voice mail message, speak slowly, enunciate, spell your name, and leave your number (this makes it much easier for the recipient to hear your message the first time).[65]

- **Do**, when you leave a voice mail message, be specific about what you want: make it easier for the caller to get back to you and include what time you will be available for a callback to avoid playing telephone tag.[66]

- **Do** customize your voice mail message: create a different message for each of your customers or prospective customers so the message is personal and relevant.[67]

- **Do** speak with enthusiasm: it's best to convey a smile in your voice, especially if it is the first time you are calling or leaving a message for someone.[68]

- **Don't** take another phone call during a meeting.[69]

- **Don't** discuss confidential or personal issues during business calls.

- **Don't** discuss confidential issues in public areas—you never know who might overhear a conversation in the hallway, on a train, or in other public areas.[70]

- **Don't** leave a long, rambling voice mail message: be prepared with a message that is no longer than sixty seconds.[71]

- **Don't** multitask during a long phone call or conference call—give the other person or people the courtesy of your full attention.

FIGURE 5.11
When you communicate by phone, you don't have the benefit of nonverbal communication.

© 2010 Jupiterimages Corporation

Etiquette Tips for E-mails, Text Messages, Instant Messages, and Social Networks

Written communication has evolved to include multiple methods, all of which have appropriate places in selling. Notice the operative word here is *appropriate*. E-mail has become an accepted method of communication in most businesses, whereas text messages, instant messages, and social networks are commonplace for only some companies. That's why etiquette is especially important when using any of these methods of communication, and you should take time to choose your method carefully. Letters, memos, proposals, and other written communication are considered formal, whether they are sent on paper or transmitted via e-mail. However, text messages, instant messages, and social networking are considered informal methods of communication and should be used only to communicate less formal information, such as a meeting time when schedules have been adjusted during a factory tour. Text and instant messages should never be used to communicate company policies, proposals, pricing, or other information that is important to conduct business with customers. It's also worth noting that in all these methods your communication is permanent, so it's a good idea to know the dos and don'ts of electronic communication.

- **Do** use an e-mail subject line that clearly tells the recipient about the content of the e-mail.

- **Do** create a short, concise message that uses proper grammar and spelling—use spell-check to be sure all words are spelled correctly.[72]

- **Do**, in all electronic communications, use uppercase and lowercase letters as grammar dictates.[73]

- **Do** use e-mail, text messages, and instant messages when appropriate, according to your company's practices, and with your customers to communicate factual information such as to confirm meeting date, time, and location.[74]

- **Do** use social networking sites to join the conversation and add value—you can build your personal brand by creating a blog or joining a professional conversation on social networking sites such as Twitter or Facebook.[75]

- **Don't** use all capital letters in an e-mail; it appears that you are shouting or angry.[76]

- **Don't** use "Reply to All" unless it's absolutely necessary that all the recipients see your response—be selective to avoid mailbox overload.

- **Don't** send an e-mail, text message, or instant message when you are angry; take the time to think about what you send because you can't take it back after it's sent.[77]

- **Don't** use abbreviations like "ur," "2b," and others—this is not appropriate business communication.[78]

- **Don't** use company e-mail, text message, or instant message accounts to send personal correspondence, and don't check your personal accounts or pages during company time, as all communication that takes place on company hardware and servers is property of the company.

- **Don't** use electronic communication to transmit bad news: talk to the person first, and if follow-up is necessary, reiterate the information in written form.

- **Don't** use text messages, instant messages, or social networks to communicate information such as pricing, proposals, reports, service agreements, and other company information that should be sent using a more formal method.

Video Clip

Telephone and E-mail Etiquette at Work
Understand what makes a good impression on your customers.

View the video online at: http://www.youtube.com/embed/DmVd8MT9XyA

Power Point: Lessons in Selling from the Customer's Point of View

When the Customer Tweets
Social media give customers a voice like never before. When companies listen to customers, they can turn a bad situation into a good one; but if they don't respond, customers speak out. For example, a dissatisfied Virgin America passenger posted a tweet on Twitter during a flight to Boston, thanks to the Wi-Fi service onboard. Virgin America monitors Twitter so closely that by the time the plane landed, a ground team met the customer at the gate to be sure his needs were met, and he left the airline with the memory of extraordinary service.[79]

Music to Your Ears

When is an iPod or other MP3 player or a handheld gaming device appropriate at work? Only when it is used for business purposes. "You're isolating yourself," says Dale Chapman Webb, founder of The Protocol Centre in Coral Gables, Florida. "You are sending a message that my music is more important than the work at hand." If you feel the need to listen to your iPod or use handheld gaming devices at work, sales may not be the right profession for you.

Key Takeaways

- Proper **etiquette** is a necessity in selling. There are etiquette guidelines for virtually every form of communication, including conversations, meetings, business cards, business meals, thank-you notes, e-mails, text messages, and even social networking.
- **Written communication** should always include proper grammar and spelling. This applies to formal business communications such as letters and memos, as well as informal business communications such as e-mails and text messages.
- **Written communication** such as letters, reports, and memos are considered formal methods of business communication; many formal communications are transmitted via e-mail. Text messages, instant messages, blogs, and social networks are considered informal communications and should only be used for informal communications such as confirming a meeting place when noise is an issue, such as on a factory floor.
- It's best to remember that most **written communication** is permanent, so take the time to craft it carefully.
- Professionalism should prevail in all business meetings and communications, including meals. When you are at a restaurant, it's is good idea to remember BMW: **B**read to the left, **M**eal in the middle, **W**ater goblet to the right. Use silverware starting with the utensils on the outside and work your way in throughout the meal.
- You can add a personal touch to a business relationship by sending a thank-you note. Although it is acceptable to send a thank-you note via e-mail, it is recommended to send a personal handwritten note to reflect a sincere sentiment that really stands out.
- It is never appropriate to use an electronic device such as a cell phone, BlackBerry, or iPhone while you are talking with someone else. Turn off your devices before you enter a meeting.
- When talking on the phone, be courteous and use an appropriate volume in your voice. Never discuss confidential or personal topics on the phone when others might overhear.

Exercises

1. Assume you work for a textile manufacturer. Draft a letter to invite your customer to tour your company's factory next month. Choose a specific date, time, and location for your tour to be included in your letter. Who, if anyone, should be included as a CC? Why? Who, if anyone, should be included as a BCC? Why?

2. Create a voice mail message that you would leave on a customer's voice mail if you were calling to set up a meeting to follow up from your first sales call. What information is essential to be included in the voice mail? What information should *not* be covered in the voice mail?

3. You are scheduled to meet your customer for an off-site training meeting. You just realized you are at the wrong meeting location, and you need to contact your customer and let her know that you are on your way to the right location. What is the best method to communicate with your customer? What would your message be?

4. You just learned about a delayed shipment date for your customer's order. What is the best method to communicate this to your customer?

5. You are in a meeting with a customer, but you have a potential problem that is developing with a different customer. You are expecting a phone call about the second situation during

your meeting with the other customer. How would you communicate this to the customer with whom you are meeting?

6. You are at a business dinner with your boss and her husband in a very nice restaurant. Watch the following video and answer the following questions.

View the video online at: http://www.youtube.com/embed/vwPsKZZhbJE

- From which side of the chair do you sit down?
- How do you determine which bread plate is yours?
- When do you put your napkin on your lap?
- When someone asks you to pass the salt, what do you do?
- When you want to excuse yourself, what is the appropriate way to do it?

5.3 *Selling U*: The Power of Informational Interviews

Learning Objective

1. Learn about informational interviews and how they can help your career search.

informational interview

A meeting with a professional to learn more about pursuing a career in a specific industry, profession, or job.

"Find someone who does what you want to do, then go talk to them." That's the advice that Ike Richman, vice president of public relations at Comcast-Spectacor consistently tells students when he is a guest speaker. That is the essence of what an **informational interview** is: one-on-one communication that helps you learn about different industries and potential careers. You learned about the power of networking in the *Selling U* section of Chapter 3. And informational interviews are one of the best ways to network. They are the ultimate in business communication because you are "trying on jobs for size to see if they fit you," according to Richard Nelson Bolles, author of *What Color Is Your Parachute?* and the person who coined the term "informational interview."[80]

What Is an Informational Interview?

An informational interview is exactly what it sounds like; it's an opportunity to learn about a particular profession, industry, or job.[81] That means that if you are interested in sales, you might meet with an account manager for a software company and talk to her about what it's like to be in sales. Or, if you think you want to pursue a job in advertising, you could meet with someone who works at an advertising agency. This gives you the chance to learn the inside story about what it takes to start a career and work in your target industry.

You've probably learned about several different professions in your classes; you most likely heard from guest speakers. And through your networking activities, chances are you've met people who do what you think you want to do. But it's impossible to know exactly what career you want to pursue without getting some one-on-one information. What does the job entail? Will you be working with people out in the field or sitting at a desk? What kinds of opportunities are available for personal development? What kind of skills and experience do you need? Is this really a career you will enjoy? What's the best part of the job? What's the worst part of the job? All these are excellent questions to ask during an informational interview. Learn more about informational interviews by watching this video.

Video Clip

Informational Interviews
Learn how to maximize them.

View the video online at: http://www.youtube.com/embed/oWyQlPLTksc

Ask for Information, Not a Job

Informational interviews are an excellent source of information and insight. In fact, you can gain knowledge through informational interviews that you might not be able to gain in any other way. It's important to note that informational interviews are *not* the place to look for an internship or job.[82] A job or an internship could result from an informational interview because it is a time to make an impression on someone, demonstrate your skills, and network. However, it's best to keep in mind that when you ask for an informational interview, you are asking for someone to take the time to share insights and information with you. If you ask the interviewer for a job, you misled the interviewer about the purpose of the meeting.[83]

Informational Interviews Made Easy

Informational interviews are an excellent way to gather real-world information about your career direction. Here's a guide to everything you need to know to get the most out of informational interviews using the tenets of journalism. As a guide, remember the five *W*s and an *H*: who, what, when, where, why, and how.

Why Go on Informational Interviews

You might think that if you shouldn't ask for a job, why bother going on an informational interview? There are plenty of reasons to pursue informational interviews.

- You can learn about what it is like to work in a particular industry, company, or job.[84]
- You have the opportunity to get to know key people in the industry.[85]

- You can learn about jobs that you didn't realize exist—jobs that are open now or that might be open in the future.[86]
- You can learn about where you might fit in a specific organization.[87]
- You can ask for referrals for the names of other people in the industry or company with whom you can meet.[88]
- You can hone your interviewing skills in a low-pressure environment.
- You can get "insider" information that other job seekers might not get, because informational interviews are an underused approach.[89]

Who to Ask for an Informational Interview

Here's where your networking skills come into play. Identify people who do what you want to do or do something that you think is interesting. Make a list of people using the following resources:

- Think of people in professional organizations you may have heard speak or may have met at an event.
- Think of guest speakers you may have heard speak in class or at a campus event.
- Talk to friends and family to get ideas for people they may know in the profession you want to learn more about.
- Talk to your professors about people in the industry they may know.
- Visit the campus career center and alumni office to identify people with whom you can meet.
- Use online professional networking to find people whom you would like to talk with and learn from.
- Read local business journals and professional organization publications to identify people who have jobs that you want to learn more about. You can usually find these publications online or in person at your school library or public library.[90]

How to Ask for an Informational Interview

Informational interviews are usually twenty to thirty minutes long and can take place in person or by phone. Once you identify the people with whom you would like to have an informational interview, it's time to contact each person and ask for a meeting. It's always best to request an informational interview in person because you have the opportunity to communicate verbally as well as nonverbally. Although it's appropriate to send a letter or e-mail to request an informational interview, it's best to call each person to request the interview or talk to him or her in person. If you use your communication skills, a personal conversation will be much more persuasive than a passive e-mail or letter, which could easily go unanswered.

A telephone conversation should include an introduction along with the reason you are calling. Be clear that you are seeking information; don't frame your request as a veiled strategy for a job offer. If you are honest about learning about the industry, most people will take the time to help you. You might consider a telephone conversation like this:

You:	My name is Jorge Ebana, and I am a student at State University majoring in business administration. I was in Dr. Wolf's Creative Selling class on Thursday when you were a guest speaker. I really enjoyed your presentation. I especially enjoyed hearing about how you landed the XPress account.
Interviewer:	Jorge, thank you so much for calling. I'm really glad to hear that you found my presentation interesting. I enjoyed speaking to your class very much. Yes, the XPress account took a lot of work to land, but it's been a great relationship for all parties involved.
You:	As you were speaking, I realized that as you described the research, preparation, presentation, and follow-up, what you do daily is something that I would really enjoy, too. You made me realize that sales could be the career I might want to pursue.
Interviewer:	Jorge, that's so good to hear. I always like to share my experiences with young people so that they understand the rewards and the challenges involved in selling. Personally, I enjoy selling so much that I can't imagine doing anything else.
You:	I would really like to learn more about how you got into sales. It sounds like you had some very interesting positions at Intuit and CreditSys. I'd like to hear about what's it's like to sell for a major corporation compared to a start-up company, and their differing advantages. Would it be possible to get together for twenty minutes or so? I'd really like to learn more about your background in the field.
Interviewer:	Why don't you drop by on Thursday morning at 8 o'clock. We can touch base, and I can give you a quick tour of the office.
You:	That would be perfect. I really appreciate your taking the time to help me.
Interviewer:	It's my pleasure. I'll see you on Thursday morning.

If you use this type of approach when you are speaking with someone with whom you would like to meet, you increase your chances of getting a positive response. If you don't know the person or have a connection to him, it's still appropriate to call him directly to request an informational interview.

What to Wear, Bring, and Ask on an Informational Interview

Just like any sales call, business meeting, or job interview, you should always be prepared for an informational interview. Treat it as if it were a job interview and dress in a conservative, professional suit.[91] Men should wear a white or light shirt, conservative tie, and dark-colored suit. Women should wear a skirt or pants with a blazer in a dark color. Some things the interview "fashion police" would tell you to avoid: too much aftershave or cologne, low-cut blouse or short skirt, wrinkled anything, and athletic-looking shoes or sandals.

Video: What Employers Want

Learn about what employers expect when someone comes in for an informational interview or job interview.

View the video online at: http://www.youtube.com/embed/Fx312Y_CX7Q?rel=0

Come prepared as if it were a job interview, even if you already know the person with whom you are interviewing. That means doing research on the industry, company, and person before you arrive. Visit the company's Web site as well as those of competitors, research the industry on databases such as Hoovers.com, and do a search on Google to learn more about the person with whom you are interviewing. Also, look her up on LinkedIn, Plaxo.com, Ryze.com, or other professional social networking Web sites to learn more about her professional background before your meeting.

Bring extra copies of your résumé printed on twenty-four-pound paper (this is also called résumé paper; you can buy it at your campus bookstore or at any office supply store or Web site). It's best not to use regular copy paper as it is lightweight and doesn't provide strong nonverbal communication about your brand. You never know when the person with whom you are meeting will ask for an extra copy of your résumé. And, even if she already has a copy, she may not have it handy.[92]

This is a perfect opportunity to bring samples of your work. See the *Selling U* section in Chapter 6 for some tips about how to put together a portfolio that helps you show and sell yourself. If you have had an internship, bring clean samples of any projects you worked on; the same is true for any student organizations, volunteer work, or community service that you have done. You should also include a few key class projects to demonstrate your versatility.

Now prepare for the questions. Unlike a regular job interview, you have requested this meeting so you should be prepared to ask the questions. Keep the questions focused on learning about how your interviewer broke into the business and what he can share as a result of his experience. Here are some questions you might consider:

- How did you decide to go into this field?
- What was your first job?
- How did you get to your current position?
- What was your favorite job?
- What is the best thing about your current job?
- What is your least favorite part of your job?
- What is the single most important attribute someone needs to have to be successful in this industry?
- What is the typical salary range for an entry-level job in this industry?
- What advice would you give to someone starting out in the industry?
- What is the outlook for the industry?[93]

In addition to having your questions ready, also be ready to talk about your brand positioning points (review this concept in the *Selling U* section in Chapter 1). Use your communication skills to make your experience and interest come alive in the interview. It's a good idea to offer to show the samples of your work while you are talking about why you are interested in pursuing a career path in the industry.

Take the time to print out your questions so you are organized during the interview. Put your questions and spare copies of your résumé in a professional portfolio or folder. Don't be afraid to refer to your questions and take notes during the interview; it's an excellent nonverbal cue that you think what the interviewer has to say is important.

Wrap up your informational interview by asking for your interviewee's business card. Also, ask for the names of some other people that you might be able to learn from; for example, "I really enjoyed our conversation today, and I learned so much about the industry. You have helped me realize that I would like to pursue a career in sales. Can you give me the names of some other people I might be able to learn from?"

You've Got the Power: Tips for Your Job Search

Keep in Touch

What about after the informational interview? Keep in touch. People who take the time to help students also want to know what is going on with the young job-seeking population. Send an e-mail or touch base by phone at least every four to six weeks. It's a great way to develop a relationship and network, even after you land your internship or job. Part of networking is providing exchange, and keeping in touch is your part of the bargain. When you keep in touch, your interviewer might be able to help you in the future; or better yet, you might be able to help her and return the favor.

When to Ask for an Informational Interview

It's always a good time to meet and learn from experienced people in the industry in which you are interested. However, you should actively pursue informational interviews when you are prepared with your résumé and have compiled some samples of your work. Keep in mind that every contact you make is a selling opportunity for your personal brand so it's best to be ready as early as possible in your academic career. It's never too soon to prepare your résumé even as you are building your experience with internships and other jobs. Whenever you meet someone interesting, follow up and ask him for an informational interview so you can learn more about how he got into the business.

Where to Have an Informational Interview

Your interviewee will most likely suggest a location for your meeting; it might be in her office, or you might meet for breakfast or lunch. Some informational interviews might take place by phone. The objective is to connect, learn, and network.

Whatever the location, always prepare and dress for each informational interview as if it were a job interview. Also, always send a thank-you note to thank your interviewer for his time. You should send a thank-you e-mail and a handwritten thank-you note on the same day, so your interviewer will receive your e-mail followed by your handwritten note. That way, you leave a lasting impression and demonstrate your good etiquette.

Key Takeaways

- An **informational interview** is an underused career search method that includes a meeting with a professional to learn more about pursuing a career in a specific industry, profession, or job.

- You go on **informational interviews** to learn what it's like to work in a particular industry, company or job, connect and network with people in the industry, and hone your interviewing skills.

- One thing you should *never* do on an **informational interview** is ask for a job or internship. If the opportunity presents itself and your interviewer asks if you might be interested, it's appropriate to say yes. However, you should not be the one to initiate dialogue about the possibility of a position with the company.

- You should ask anyone who is in the industry or profession that you would like to pursue. It's a good idea to use your networking skills to identify people with whom you can have an informational interview. Professionals such as guest speakers in class, prominent executives, and those in local professional organizations are ideal people to ask for an informational interview.

- It's best to request an **informational interview** in person or by phone because you increase your chances for a positive response. You can also request an **informational interview** by letter or e-mail.

- Prepare for an **informational interview** as if it were a job interview, even if you already know the person. Research the company, bring extra copies of your résumé and samples of your work, and prepare questions that you would like to discuss.

Exercises

1. Identify three people with whom you would like to have an informational interview. Write down each person's name, company, title, and phone number. Write a phone script that you would use when you call to ask for the interivew. Discuss your approach.

2. Write down a list of six to eight questions that you would like to ask on each informational interview. Which questions would you ask on all informational interviews? Which questions would be specific to a particular interview? Why?

3. How would you answer the following question on an informational interview: "Why do you want to pursue a career in (name of industry)?"

4. Identify at least four samples of your work that you would include in a binder when you go on informational interviews. Why would each one be included? What would you tell an interviewee about each sample? How would each sample demonstrate one of your brand positioning points?

5. Write a thank-you e-mail and a handwritten thank-you note that you would send after an informational interview. Would you send both? Why or why not?

5.4 Review and Practice

Power Wrap-Up

Now that you have read this chapter, you should be able to understand how to communicate effectively and with proper etiquette in business.

- You can **discuss** the communication model and how it works.

- You can **compare and contrast** the different types of communication: verbal, nonverbal, and written.
- You can **recognize** the strengths and weaknesses of each type of communication and when each is appropriate to use.
- You can **understand** the role of listening in effective communication.
- You can **recognize** the impact of nonverbal communication.
- You can **practice** how to shake hands properly.
- You can **discuss** the appropriate etiquette for business situations, including the use of electronic devices.
- You can **understand** the role that informational interviews may play in your career search.

Test Your Power Knowledge (answers are below)

1. Describe the difference between soft skills and hard skills.
2. Discuss two ways to demonstrate active listening.
3. Name the three types of communication. Identify at least one pro and one con for each one.
4. Which type and method of communication would you use to tell your boss that your car broke down and you can't make it to the customer presentation?
5. If you invite a customer to lunch, who should pay? If your customer invites you to lunch, who should pay?
6. When is it appropriate to write a thank-you note in sales?
7. Identify three situations in which it would be appropriate to have your electronic device such as a cell phone turned on in a meeting.

Power (Role) Play

Now it's time to put what you've learned into practice. The following are two roles that are involved in the same selling situation—one role is the customer, and the other is the salesperson. This will give you the opportunity to think about this selling situation from the point of view of both the customer and the salesperson.

Read each role carefully along with the discussion questions. Then be prepared to play either of the roles in class using the concepts covered in this chapter. You may be asked to discuss the roles and do a role-play in groups or individually.

Safe and Secure

Role: Sales rep for Sun Security Systems for retail stores

You are meeting with a potential customer who is responsible for purchasing security systems for over two hundred retail stores. He is convinced that your company's security system is the one he wants to use, but he has to convince his boss. The key selling point in his mind, he mentions to you, is the fact that the system carries a money-back guarantee so that if anything happens, the company will be protected. You realize that he has misinterpreted the terms of the guarantee. It is a money-back guarantee only on the security system itself, not for any other loss. It appears that there was some miscommunication between all the meetings and follow-up e-mails.

- How would you tell this customer about the correct terms of the guarantee, even though it might be the sale at risk?
- Since you are meeting in person, what type of follow-up would you consider to ensure that the information is clearly understood? Why?

- What do you think caused this miscommunication?
- Using the communication model, describe what happened with the communication.

Role: Security manager at Argon Retail, Inc.

You have been looking at security systems for several months and reviewing the offering from different suppliers. Sun Security Systems appears to offer the best performance at the best value. The key selling feature is the money-back guarantee. It's a strong statement about how the company stands behind its products. This kind of low-risk investment is important to you and your company.

- Do you assume that what you heard or saw about the money-back guarantee is true? After all, it's up to the salesperson to be sure you're informed, right?
- If you probe the details with the salesperson, what questions will you ask to be sure you understand the terms of the guarantee?
- What type of communication will be best to learn about this information?

Put Your Power to Work: *Selling U* Activities

1. Invite someone on your informational interview list to come to class to speak about why he or she gives informational interviews.
2. Invite three people on your informational interview list and ask them to participate in a panel discussion in class about how to use informational interviews as an effective career search tool.

Test Your Power Knowledge Answers

1. Soft skills include communication, relationship building, emotional intelligence, and the ability to interact with people. Hard skills are the technical skills required to perform your job, such as analytical skills in the finance area.
2. The sender is Axe (Clix); Nick Lachey acts as the spokesperson in this commercial. The message is that Clix is such a great scent that it attracts lots of women. The message is encoded in video: a commercial. The receiver is the viewer of the commercial, and the target audience is young men. The decoding occurs when a young man sees that Clix is so good that it can attract more women than Nick Lachey. The sender (Clix) gets feedback in several ways: when people view the video, when people post comments about the video or the product, and when people buy the product.
3. Repeat the information that you heard by saying, "Let me be sure I understand what you're saying...," nodding your head, and taking notes.
4. Verbal communication is best for communicating emotions because you can use or hear intonation. It is also natural and fast and provides instant feedback. However, verbal communication is gone in an instant (unless it's recorded), and people remember what was said differently. Also, we speak at about 125 words per minute, but listen at about 400 to 500 words per minute, so people's minds wander during a good amount of verbal communication. Nonverbal communication includes body language and any other type of communication that can be observed. Nonverbal communication can underscore a message, such as hand gestures, or can send a different signal than the spoken words, such as crossed arms or physical proximity. But sometimes people don't realize the messages they are sending when they use nonverbal communication because it can be more difficult to interpret. Written communication is the most permanent of all communication types. It is usually considered and is used for formal business communication such as policies, pricing, and other information. Written communication lacks intonation and is best used for communicating factual information. Grammar and spelling are critical for written communication to be effective.

5. It would be best to call him to let her know. This would allow you the opportunity to demonstrate a high sense of urgency, explain the situation, and discuss possible options. It's always best to communicate bad news (especially to your boss) verbally, whether in person or by phone.

6. You should pay when you invite. Although it is appropriate to let your customer pay for a meal once in a while, it's usually expected that the salesperson's company will pick up the tab.

7. Whenever someone does something that is worth noting—referring you to a new prospect, hosting a productive meeting, being a great business partner, providing some information that was difficult to get, or any other situation that is worth a thank you—then note it. People rarely send thank-you notes, so it's an excellent way to set yourself apart. A thank-you e-mail is always appropriate, but a handwritten thank-you note is more personal.

8. The only time it is appropriate is if you are waiting for an *urgent* phone call. If that is the case, you should mention it before the meeting starts, put your cell phone on vibrate, and step out of the meeting to take the call. If you are waiting for a text, only check your device occasionally as to not send the message that the other matter is more important than the meeting you are in.

Endnotes

1. Dave Rothfield, "Communicating Simply, Directly Will Improve You, Your Business," *Orlando Business Journal*, May 15, 2009, http://orlando.bizjournals.com/orlando/stories/2009/05/18/smallb2.html?t=printable (accessed July 12, 2009).

2. "Interviewing for Emotional Intelligence," Selling Power Hiring & Recruiting eNewsletter, October 15, 2008, http://www.sellingpower.com/content/newsletter/issue.php?pc=878 (accessed March 16, 2010).

3. Patricia M. Buhler, "Managing in the New Millennium: Six Tips to More Effective Communication," *Supervision* 70, no. 7 (July 2009): 19.

4. The Emily Post Institute, http://www.emilypost.com/business/index.htm (accessed July 13, 2009).

5. Gail Fann Thomas, Roxanne Zoliln, and Jackie L. Harman, "The Central Role of Communication in Developing Trust and Its Effect on Employee Involvement," *Journal of Business Communication* 46, no. 3 (July 2009): 287.

6. Patricia M. Buhler, "Managing in the New Millennium: Six Tips to More Effective Communication," *Supervision* 70, no. 7 (July 2009): 19.

7. George E. Belch and Michael A. Belch, *Advertising and Promotion: An Integrated Marketing Communications Perspective*, 8th ed. (New York: McGraw-Hill Irwin, 2009), 146.

8. Source: Adapted from Michael R. Solomon, Greg W. Marshall, and Elnora W. Stewart, *Marketing: Real People, Real Choices*, 5th ed. (Upper Saddle River, NJ: Pearson Prentice Hall, 2008), 378.

9. Jeremy Dean, "Avoid Email Miscommunication," PsyBlog, http://www.spring.org.uk/2007/10/avoid-email-miscommunication.php (accessed July 15, 2009).

10. Steve Adubato, "Empathy Is Essential to Effective Communication," NJBiz, http://www.stand-deliver.com/njbiz/2008/020408.pdf (accessed July 14, 2009).

11. Mary Ellen Guffey, *Business Communication*, 6th ed. (Mason, OH: South-Western Publishing, 2008), 280.

12. JetBlue Airways, "An Apology from David Neeleman," http://www.jetblue.com/about/ourcompany/apology/index.html (accessed February 18, 2010).

13. Patricia M. Buhler, "Managing in the New Millennium: Six Tips to More Effective Communication," *Supervision* 70, no. 7 (July 2009): 19.

14. Jeffrey J. Denning, "How to Improve Your Listening Skills, Avoid Mix-ups," *Ophthalmology Times* 26, no. 10 (May 15, 2001): 28.

15. Patricia M. Buhler, "Managing in the New Millennium: Six Tips to More Effective Communication," *Supervision* 70, no. 7 (July 2009): 19.

16. Tayla Bauer and Berrin Erdogan, *Organizational Behavior* (Nyack, NY: Flat World Knowledge, 2009), 169.

17. Beverly Davenport Sypher, Robert N. Bostrom, and Joy Hart Seibert, "Listening, Communication Abilities and Success at Work," *Journal of Business Communication* 26, no. 4 (Fall 1989): 293.

18. Jeffrey J. Denning, "How to Improve Your Listening Skills, Avoid Mix-ups," *Ophthalmology Times* 26, no. 10 (May 15, 2001): 28.

19. "A Lesson on Listening,"Selling Power Pharmaceuticals eNewsletter, April 9, 2008, http://www.sellingpower.com/content/newsletter/issue.php?pc=814 (accessed March 16, 2010).

20. Natalie Zmuda, "Pepsi, Coke Try to Outdo Each Other with Rays of Sunshine," *Advertising Age*, January 19, 2009, http://adage.com/abstract.php?article_id=133859 (accessed July 14, 2009).

21. Tayla Bauer and Berrin Erdogan, *Organizational Behavior* (Nyack, NY: Flat World Knowledge, 2009), 169.

22. Albert Mehrabian, "Silent Messages," http://www.kaaj.com/psych/smorder.html (accessed July 15, 2009).

23. "Mehrabian's Communication Research," Businessballs.com, http://www.businessballs.com/mehrabiancommunications.htm (accessed July 15, 2009).

24. Terri Morrison, "Kiss, Bow, or Shake Hands," http://www.getcustoms.com/2004GTC/Articles/new011.html (accessed July 23, 2009).

25. Rachel Zupek, "The Worst Way to Shake Hands," *CNN.com*, http://www.cnn.com/2007/LIVING/worklife/11/05/cb.hand.shake/index.html (accessed July 13, 2009).

26. Rachel Zupek, "The Worst Way to Shake Hands," *CNN.com*, http://www.cnn.com/2007/LIVING/worklife/11/05/cb.hand.shake/index.html (accessed July 13, 2009).

27. "Good Handshake Key to Interview Success," BC Jobs, http://www.bcjobs.ca/re/career-advice/career-advice-articles/interview-advice/good-handshake-key-to-interview-success (accessed July 12, 2009).

28. Rachel Zupek, "The Worst Way to Shake Hands," *CNN.com*, http://www.cnn.com/2007/LIVING/worklife/11/05/cb.hand.shake/index.html (accessed July 13, 2009).

29. John Gates, "A Handshake Lesson from Goldilocks," Free-Resume-Help.com, http://www.free-resume-help.com/handshake-interview.html (accessed July 12, 2009).

30. "Good Handshake Key to Interview Success," BC Jobs, http://www.bcjobs.ca/re/career-advice/career-advice-articles/interview-advice/good-handshake-key-to-interview-success (accessed July 12, 2009).

31. "Good Handshake Key to Interview Success," BC Jobs, http://www.bcjobs.ca/re/career-advice/career-advice-articles/interview-advice/good-handshake-key-to-interview-success (accessed July 12, 2009).

32. "Good Handshake Key to Interview Success," BC Jobs, http://www.bcjobs.ca/re/career-advice/career-advice-articles/interview-advice/good-handshake-key-to-interview-success (accessed July 12, 2009).

33. Kathryn Tolbert, "What We Say without Words," *Washington Post*, http://www.washingtonpost.com/wp-dyn/content/gallery/2008/06/23/GA2008062301669.html (accessed July 15, 2009).

34. Neal Hendes, "How to Read Body Language: Ten Tips," EzineArticles, http://ezinearticles.com/?How-to-Read-Body-Language—Top-10-Tips&id=991635 (accessed July 15, 2009).

35. Tayla Bauer and Berrin Erdogan, *Organizational Behavior* (Nyack, NY: Flat World Knowledge, 2009), 171.

36. Tayla Bauer and Berrin Erdogan, *Organizational Behavior* (Nyack, NY: Flat World Knowledge, 2009), 172.

37. Patricia M. Buhler, "Managing in the New Millennium: Six Tips to More Effective Communication," *Supervision* 70, no. 7 (July 2009): 19.

38. "Communicating Persuasively: Email or Face-to-Face," PsyBlog, http://www.spring.org.uk/2007/03/communicating-persuasively-email-or.php (accessed July 15, 2009).

39. Mary Ellen Guffey, *Business Communication*, 6th ed. (Mason, OH: South-Western Publishing, 2008), 175.

40. Mary Ellen Guffey, *Business Communication*, 6th ed. (Mason, OH: South-Western Publishing, 2008), 175.

41. Renee Houston Zemanski, "Seven Ways to Make Your Meetings More Memorable," Selling Power Meetings eNewsletter, July 7, 2009, http://www.sellingpower.com/content/newsletter/issue.php?pc=972 (accessed March 16, 2010).

42. Kim Richmond, "Poll: Entrepreneurial Series," Doodle, http://doodle.com/participation.html?pollId=g9cp9d7bn96yy34y (accessed July 17, 2009).

43. Miss E, "The Art of Giving Business Cards," 123etiquette.com, http://www.123etiquette.com/business-etiquette/business-card-etiquette (accessed July 17, 2009).

44. Ben Preston, "Good Business Etiquette Includes Giving Out Business Cards," Businesstoolchest.com, http://www.businesstoolchest.com/articles/data/20060201225647.shtml (accessed July 17, 2009).

45. Barbara Bergstrom, "Business Card Tips," *Orlando Business Journal*, July 3, 2009, http://orlando.bizjournals.com/orlando/stories/2009/07/06/smallb3.html?t=printable (accessed July 12, 2009).

46. Barbara Bergstrom, "Business Card Tips," *Orlando Business Journal*, July 3, 2009, http://orlando.bizjournals.com/orlando/stories/2009/07/06/smallb3.html?t=printable (accessed July 12, 2009).

47. Barbara Bergstrom, "Business Card Tips," *Orlando Business Journal*, July 3, 2009, http://orlando.bizjournals.com/orlando/stories/2009/07/06/smallb3.html?t=printable (accessed July 12, 2009).

48. Barbara Bergstrom, "Business Card Tips," *Orlando Business Journal*, July 3, 2009, http://orlando.bizjournals.com/orlando/stories/2009/07/06/smallb3.html?t=printable (accessed July 12, 2009).

49. Barbara Bergstrom, "Business Card Tips," *Orlando Business Journal*, July 3, 2009, http://orlando.bizjournals.com/orlando/stories/2009/07/06/smallb3.html?t=printable (accessed July 12, 2009).

50. Louise Lee, "Meet and Eat," *BusinessWeek*, June 5, 2009, http://www.businessweek.com/magazine/content/09_66/s0906025664520.htm (accessed July 13, 2009).

51. Joe Morris, "Not Knowing Basics Is Simply Impolite," *Nashville Business Journal*, November 21, 2008, http://www.bizjournals.com/nashville/stories/2008/11/24/focus2.html?t=printable (accessed July 12, 2009).

52. Joanne McFadden, "Rules of Etiquette Are Important for the Business Lunch," *Milwaukee Business Journal*, October 24, 2008, http://www.bizjournals.com/milwaukee/stories/2008/10/27/focus4.html?t=printable (accessed July 12, 2009).

53. Joanne McFadden, "Rules of Etiquette Are Important for the Business Lunch," *Milwaukee Business Journal*, October 24, 2008, http://www.bizjournals.com/milwaukee/stories/2008/10/27/focus4.html?t=printable (accessed July 12, 2009).

54. Louise Lee, "Meet and Eat," *BusinessWeek*, June 5, 2009, http://www.businessweek.com/magazine/content/09_66/s0906025664520.htm (accessed July 13, 2009).

55. Terence P. Ward, "Expressing Gratitude in Writing Builds Business Networks," May 18, 2008, Suite101.com, http://business-writing.suite101.com/article.cfm/business_thankyou_notes (accessed July 17, 2009).

56. Justin Martin, "6 Companies Where Customers Come First," *CNNMoney.com*, http://money.cnn.com/galleries/2007/fsb/0709/gallery.where_customers_come_first.fsb/5.html (accessed July 23, 2009).

57. John Naisbitt, *Megatrends: Ten New Directions Transforming Our Lives* (New York: Grand Central Publishing, 1998).

58. July Shapiro, "A Digital Myth: Technology Doesn't Make Life Easier," *Advertising Age*, May 11, 2009, http://adage.com/digitalnext/post?article_id=136533 (accessed May 12, 2009).

59. CommercialsKid, "iPhone 3g Commercial 'There's an App for That,'" video, http://www.youtube.com/watch?v=szrsfeyLzyg (accessed July 16, 2009).

60. "Good Advice in Bad Times: New Etiquette Avenue iPhone App Puts Professional Protocol at Fingertips," *Business Wire*, June 29, 2009.

61. "Reestablishing the Inside Connection: Open Communication with Inside Sales Strengthens the Rep Bond," *Agency Sales* 39, no. 5: 38.

62. Alex Williams, "At Meetings, It's Mind Your Blackberry or Mind Your Manners," *New York Times*, June 22, 2009, A1.

63. Patrick Welsh, "Txting Away Ur Education," *USA Today*, June 23, 2009, A11.

64. Joanna L. Krotz, "Cell Phone Etiquette: 10 Dos and Don'ts," Microsoft, http://www.microsoft.com/smAllBusiness/resources/ArticleReader/website/default.aspx?Print=1&ArticleId=Cellphoneetiquettedosanddonts (accessed July 12, 2009).

65. John R. Quain, "Quain's Top Ten Voice Mail Tips," *Fast Company*, December 18, 2007, http://www.fastcompany.com/magazine/18/topten.html (accessed July 17, 2009).

66. John R. Quain, "Quain's Top Ten Voice Mail Tips," *Fast Company*, December 18, 2007, http://www.fastcompany.com/magazine/18/topten.html (accessed July 17, 2009).

67. Keith Rosen, "Eight Tips on Crafting Effective Voice Mail Messages," AllBusiness, http://www.AllBusiness.com/sales/selling-techniques-telesales/2975818-1.html (accessed July 17, 2009).

68. Keith Rosen, "Eight Tips on Crafting Effective Voice Mail Messages," AllBusiness, http://www.AllBusiness.com/sales/selling-techniques-telesales/2975818-1.html (accessed July 17, 2009).

69. Joanna L. Krotz, "Cell Phone Etiquette: 10 Dos and Don'ts," *Microsoft*, http://www.microsoft.com/smAllBusiness/resources/ArticleReader/website/default.aspx?Print=1&ArticleId=Cellphoneetiquettedosanddonts (accessed July 12, 2009).

70. Barbara Bergstrom, "Good Etiquette Is Recession-Proof," *Baltimore Business Journal*, April 17, 2009, http://www.bizjournals.com/baltimore/stories/2009/04/20/smallb3.html?t=printable (accessed July 12, 2009).

71. John R. Quain, "Quain's Top Ten Voice Mail Tips," *Fast Company*, December 18, 2007, http://www.fastcompany.com/magazine/18/topten.html (accessed July 17, 2009).

72. "Shouting and Other E-mail Faux Pas," *BusinessLine*, April 20, 2009.

73. "Shouting and Other E-mail Faux Pas," *BusinessLine*, April 20, 2009.

74. Patricia M. Buhler, "Managing in the New Millennium: Six Tips to More Effective Communication," *Supervision* 70, no. 7 (July 2009), 19.

75. Norman Birnbach, "10 Twitter Etiquette Rules," *Fast Company*, July 2, 2008, http://www.fastcompany.com/blog/norman-birnbach/pr-back-talk/10-twitter-etiquette-rules (accessed July 17, 2009).

76. "Shouting and Other E-mail Faux Pas," *BusinessLine*, April 20, 2009.

77. Paul Glover, "Why We Need E-mail Etiquette," *Fast Company*, December 30, 2008, http://www.fastcompany.com/blog/paul-glover/surviving-workquakec/why-we-need-e-mail-etiquette (accessed July 17, 2007).

78. Norman Birnbach, "10 Twitter Etiquette Rules," *Fast Company*, July 2, 2008, http://www.fastcompany.com/blog/norman-birnbach/pr-back-talk/10-twitter-etiquette-rules (accessed July 17, 2009).

79. Gerhard Gschwandtner, "Wow Your Customers with Twitter in Real Time," *Selling Power*, http://sellingpower.typepad.com/gg/2009/07/wow-your-customers-with-twitter-in-real-time-.html (accessed July 23, 2009).

80. "Informational Interviewing Tutorial: Background Information about Informational Interviews," Quintessential Careers, http://www.quintcareers.com/information_background.html (accessed July 12, 2009).

81. "Informational Interviewing Tutorial: Background Information about Informational Interviews," Quintessential Careers, http://www.quintcareers.com/information_background.html (accessed July 12, 2009).

82. "Informational Interviewing Tutorial: Never Ask for a Job," Quintessential Careers, http://www.quintcareers.com/information_job.html (accessed July 12, 2009).

83. "Informational Interviewing Tutorial: Never Ask for a Job," Quintessential Careers, http://www.quintcareers.com/information_job.html (accessed July 12, 2009).

84. "Informational Interviewing Tutorial: Potential Results of Informational Interviews," Quintessential Careers, http://www.quintcareers.com/information_results. html (accessed July 12, 1009).

85. "Informational Interviewing Tutorial: Potential Results of Informational Interviews," Quintessential Careers, http://www.quintcareers.com/information_results. html (accessed July 12, 1009).

86. "Informational Interviewing Tutorial: Potential Results of Informational Interviews," Quintessential Careers, http://www.quintcareers.com/information_results. html (accessed July 12, 1009).

87. "Informational Interviewing Tutorial: Potential Results of Informational Interviews," Quintessential Careers, http://www.quintcareers.com/information_results. html (accessed July 12, 1009).

88. "Informational Interview Questions," Career Choice Guide, http://www.careerchoiceguide.com/informational-interview-questions.html (accessed July 20, 2009).

89. Kate Lorenz, "How Does an Informational Interview Work?" CareerBuilder, http://www.careerbuilder.com/Article/CB-481-Getting-Ahead-How-Does-an-Informational-Interview-Work (accessed July 20, 2009).

90. "Informational Interview Tutorial: Identify People to Interview for Informational Interviews," Quintessential Careers, http://www.quintcareers.com/information_people.html (accessed July 12, 2009).

91. Katharine Hansen, "Informational Interviewing Do's and Don'ts," Quintessential Careers, http://www.quintcareers.com/informational_interviewing-dos-donts. html (accessed July 20, 2009).

92. Kate Lorenz, "How Does An Informational Interview Work?" CareerBuilder, http://www.careerbuilder.com/Article/CB-481-Getting-Ahead-How-Does-an-Informational-Interview-Work (accessed July 20, 2009).

93. "Informational Interview Questions," Career Choice Guide, http://www.careerchoiceguide.com/informational-interview-questions.html (accessed July 20, 2009).

CHAPTER 6
Why and How People Buy: The Power of Understanding the Customer

Video Ride-Along with Rachel Gordon, Account Manager at WMGK Radio

Meet Rachel Gordon. Rachel has been in sales for three years and has learned that selling is about understanding the customer's needs and wants. Rachel sells advertising and marketing programs to businesses such as casinos, restaurants, car dealerships, and local businesses. Rachel graduated from Cornell University with a degree in fashion merchandising. After two years in retail, she learned that selling is her passion.

Ride along with Rachel and learn how she identifies the decision maker versus the influencer in a sales call and why each is important to making the sale.

View the video online at: http://www.youtube.com/embed/lrQ7HHct4ZE

6.1 Buying 101

Learning Objectives

1. Describe the different types of customers and why this information is important in determining customers' needs.
2. Discuss the implications of Maslow's hierarchy of needs for selling.
3. Learn the types of buyers and buying situations in the business-to-business (B2B) environment.

You walk into an Abercrombie & Fitch store at the mall, and without thinking about it, you turn to the right and make your way through the denim, past the belts, and to the sweaters. You are so engaged in the experience that you didn't even realize that the huge mural at the entrance to the store serves a purpose other than to make you look twice at the hot model in the larger-than-life photo. Before you know it, one of the oh-so-gorgeous salespeople dressed in Abercrombie from head to toe approaches you with a smile. "These hoodies are awesome," she says as you pick up the pale blue one.

Shopping. It's the national pastime for some but a detested necessity for others. Whether you love shopping ("Oh, that is sooooooo cute!") or do everything to avoid it ("I'm not going to the mall, no matter what"), it is a major source of spending in the United States. In fact, the retail industry generated $4.475 trillion in sales in 2008, including everything from products and services in retail stores and e-commerce to food service and automotive.[1] That's a lot of selling—and a lot of buying. But what makes you stop and pick up one sweater but not another? What makes you buy a pair of jeans you weren't even looking for? What makes you walk out of the store spending more than you had planned?

FIGURE 6.1
Retailers recognize that displays can impact how customers buy.

© 2010 Jupiterimages Corporation

Inside Consumer Behavior

The science of consumer behavior describes and even defines how you shop and, more importantly, why you buy. Smart retailers study consumer behavior patterns and lay out their stores and merchandise accordingly. For example, did you know that 86 percent of women look at price tags when they shop, while only 72 percent of men do?[2] And did you know that the average shopper doesn't actually notice anything that's in the entrance of a store? According to Paco Underhill, famous marketer, CEO and founder of EnviroSell, and author of the book *Why We Buy: The Science of Shopping*, consumers don't actually begin shopping until a certain point after they enter the store. That's why smart retailers include a "transition zone" at the entry to their store; it allows customers to get their bearings and choose their shopping paths. In other words, products, signs, and displays that are in the very front of the store might not be seen if there is not a transition for the customers when they enter. In the case of Abercrombie & Fitch, the transition is the space just inside the entrance that includes the humongous photo of the Abercrombie model du jour. When you go into Hollister, it's the outside porch that serves the same purpose; it's a transition that allows you to get your focus and plot your course in the store, even if you don't consciously realize it.

Think about the last time you went into a grocery store or drug store; you might not have noticed anything until you were well inside the store, which means that the merchandise and signs that were displayed in the area before you got your bearings were virtually invisible to you.[3] Based on consumer research, there's a high likelihood that you turned right when you entered the store. Take note the next time you go shopping; chances are, you'll turn right after you walk in.[4]

Understanding how and why customers buy can make a significant difference in how you sell. Is the product a considered purchase, like a computer or car, or an impulse buy, like a sweater or music download? Is the product bought frequently, like an energy drink, or only once every few years or even once in a lifetime, like a car or a college education? For each of these products, the customer goes through a buying process. Understanding the customer and the buying process can make your selling efforts successful. This video featuring Martin Lindstrom, the author of *Buyology: Truths and Lies about Why We Buy*, highlights the science of consumer behavior in selling and marketing

Video Clip

Video Book Review
Buyology: Truths and Lies about Why We Buy

View the video online at: http://www.youtube.com/embed/M6UzQU5Ye3U

Do You Need It or Want It?

Think of something you need, like an annual medical checkup, a new apartment because your lease is up, or even food to survive. There are some products and services you purchase solely because you can't exist without them. Now think about something you want: a new pair of jeans, an iPhone, tickets to a concert. There is a significant difference in what motivates you to buy products and services you need, compared to those you want.

Needs versus Wants

Needs are essentials, those products and services you literally cannot live without. Food, shelter, clothing, transportation, and health care are all examples of needs. **Wants**, on the other hand, are products, services, and activities that can improve your quality of life; you don't need them to exist, but rather you desire to have them because you think they will make you happy.[5] Cell phones, vacations, sporting events, restaurants, amusement parks, cable television, and fashion are all examples of wants. People are motivated differently depending on if they are making a purchase for a need or a want.

Needs and wants have different motivations. Think about buying a car; you could focus on the functional attributes of the car such as miles per gallon, maintenance costs, and safety ratings. Those are considered **utilitarian needs**, or the objective, tangible aspects of a product or service.[6] So, if those were your only needs, you might choose a Smart Fortwo, Ford Focus, or Toyota Prius. But you might want to have something a bit sportier, maybe even hipper, to get around campus, and you might choose a Mini Cooper, a Scion, or even a Jeep. These cars would do more than simply provide transportation; they would meet your **hedonic needs**, which are subjective aspects of a product or service.[7] You might choose to buy a Mini Cooper because you can customize the design online. That would certainly meet a need other than providing basic transportation. Some people buy a BMW because they want the status that goes with owning that make of car, or perhaps they think that having a Mercedes-Benz means they have arrived.

When you understand the difference between needs and wants and between utility needs and hedonic needs, you are better able to tailor your selling communications. Listen to consumer behavior expert Dr. Michael R. Solomon discuss the difference between needs and wants and the impact it has on selling.

needs

Products or services that are essential in order to survive.

wants

Products, services, or activities that enhance the quality of life, but which are not essential for survival.

utilitarian needs

Functional needs that are served by objective, tangible attributes of products or services.

hedonic needs

Emotional needs that are served by products or services that bring pleasure.

Interview with Dr. Michael Solomon
Needs versus wants.

View the video online at: http://www.youtube.com/embed/NVIC8uQWZB8

Maslow's Hierarchy of Needs

When Hurricane Katrina hit the United States on August 28, 2005, the Gulf Coast was devastated. Thousands of people were stranded for days, some without food, water, or shelter due to overwhelming flooding. Almost two thousand people lost their lives in the natural disaster.[8] During those horrible days and in the aftermath, those who were affected by the catastrophe did not care what kind of car they drove, what anyone did for a living, or if they forgot to sign up for French or scuba lessons. They were focused on the basics: food, shelter, and clothing.

FIGURE 6.2 Hurricane Katrina Aftermath

© 2010 Jupiterimages Corporation

This tragedy is a demonstration of exactly how **Maslow's hierarchy of needs** works. Abraham Maslow is among the most renowned psychologists of the twentieth century. His theory explains human behavior in simple terms: A hierarchy of needs that begins with the most basic of **physiological needs** (e.g., food, water, shelter, and clothing) motivates people, and when the lowest-level needs are satisfied, they are no longer motivators.[9]

During the days after Hurricane Katrina hit, people were rescued and provided with water, food, and shelter. Many were relocated to temporary housing or even to housing outside the affected areas. It was not until after the physiological needs were met that people became concerned about the next level of needs on Maslow's hierarchy: **safety needs**. Looting of shops in some of the cities began to occur, and there was even concern that the police force in some cities was not taking an active role in arresting those who were breaking the law.[10] The people of the Gulf Coast were no longer motivated by simply getting water, food, or shelter; they had moved up Maslow's hierarchy and were concerned about their personal security and well-being.

FIGURE 6.3
Maslow's hierarchy of needs demonstrates that humans fill higher needs only after lower needs are met.

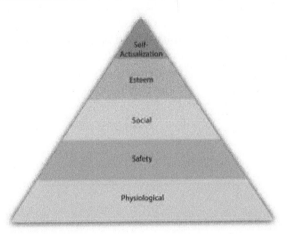

As the days and weeks passed after Hurricane Katrina hit, its victims wanted to get back to their normal lives. They searched for options to put their children back in school, ways to get jobs, and options to rebuild their lives. By Christmas 2005, people stopped to celebrate the holiday together. According to a story reported by CBS Evening News on December 25, 2005, about the Christmas gatherings in New Orleans, "The will to be home for the holidays outweighed everything else."[11] By this time, they were motivated by **social needs**, or the need to belong and have an attachment or bond to others.[12]

Slowly but surely, people began to rebuild their lives and their cities. People took on leadership roles and began to take recovery to the next level. Even people who were hundreds of miles away from the hurricane-ravaged area wanted to help. Volunteers from all over the country began to make the pilgrimage to the Gulf Coast to help in any way they could. In fact, volunteer vacations to help rebuild cities such as New Orleans became commonplace and are still going on today.[13] This is an example of **esteem needs**, or the need to feel respected and appreciated by one's peers. Although volunteers were motivated by social needs and the need to help their fellow human beings, they found that they were also greatly appreciated for their efforts.

Although recovery will be going on for years to come, many of the people affected by the destruction of Hurricane Katrina are striving for **self-actualization**, which focuses on learning new skills, taking on new challenges, and "being all you can be."[14] John and Starr Chapman are perfect examples of this; their restaurant, Chappy's Seafood Restaurant, was lost in the hurricane. The couple relocated to Nashville, Tennessee, and in 2006, opened Chappy's on Church Street. Although it was challenging and overwhelming at times, the husband-and-wife team is not only surviving but also thriving after this life-changing experience.[15]

Maslow's hierarchy of needs

The behavior theory that recognizes that people are motivated by their most basic needs first; only after those needs are met do they strive to meet higher-level needs.

physiological needs

The most basic elements required to survive such as food, shelter, and clothing.

safety needs

Concerns for personal security and well-being.

social needs

Bonds or attachments to other people and feelings of love and belonging.

esteem needs

Feelings of being respected and appreciated by one's peers.

self-actualization

Focus on learning new skills, taking on new challenges, and "being all you can be."

Power Point: Lessons in Selling from the Customer's Point of View

Self-Actualization Means Help for Others

Nikki Olyai, president and CEO of Innovision Technologies, recently made a significant investment for her company and purchased new software and hardware. Her buying philosophy? Nikki looks for a strong value system, trust, commitment, a proactive approach to helping her solve her business problems, and cost-effectiveness. But she expects more from a vendor and business partner; she gives extra consideration to vendors who have demonstrated a commitment to community service and development. Nikki believes that businesses and their vendors need to give back to the communities they serve.[16]

This all comes together at the point of sale, whether you are selling in business-to-consumer (B2C) or business-to-business (B2B) environments. When you understand the motivation of your customer, you can customize your solution and your message to meet their needs, emotions, and motivations. Consider the Hurricane Katrina example; would you attempt to sell fine jewelry, pitch the benefits of a landscaping service, or suggest a home theater system to someone in New Orleans on August 29, 2005? Probably not. People were focused on their most basic needs at that time, and none of these products or services would have been appropriate to sell. Although this may seem like an extreme example, it's a good way to remember to look at the world through your customer's eyes, as you'll see a completely different view. Now that you can see what motivates people to buy, it's time to learn who is buying. Although the buying process is similar for B2C and B2B, there are some distinct differences that can make a difference in the way you sell.

Business-to-Consumer (B2C) Buying

Think back to your visit to the Abercrombie & Fitch store. It's pretty obvious that you are the customer, or in marketing parlance, you are the **consumer**, the end user of the product or service. You might be shopping for yourself or buying a gift for a family member or a friend. Either way, you (or the person to whom you are giving the product) are the ultimate consumer, which is what defines B2C buying. So, whether you are buying a cell phone and service at a Verizon store, a music download from iTunes, or a burger and fries at Burger King, you are buying in the B2C arena. Even though you may behave differently than your brother or roommate in terms of your purchasing decisions, you are all described as B2C customers because you are the ultimate consumer of the products or services you buy.

consumer
The end user of a product or service.

Why People Buy: Virtual Purchases

Clothes for your avatar, "bling" for your online profile, or a virtual birthday cupcake are all reasons to make digital purchases virtually: paying real money for something that exists only online. Facebook, SecondLife.com, and Stardolls.com are just a few Web sites that give users the option to buy virtual goods. Why do people buy things that aren't even real? For some of the same reasons people buy the real thing: to be able to do more (i.e., increase functionality), build relationships, and establish identity.[17]

Business-to-Business (B2B) Buying

With B2B customers, sometimes referred to as **organizational (or institutional) markets**, there are several different types of situations that define needs and purchasing behavior. Some companies buy products to sell directly to consumers, whereas others purchase products as ingredients or components to produce their product. Still other companies lease products or services, while others serve the public, such as government or nonprofit organizations. Each of these different types of companies and organizations has different needs and requirements that impact the buying process.[18]

organizational (or institutional) markets
Another term for B2B buying or selling, which means selling products or services to another company rather than selling directly to the ultimate consumer.

Producers

Companies that buy products to make or build a product or service to sell for a profit are called **producers**. For example, in the case of Reebok, the company purchases components for its athletic shoes from a variety of vendors around the world. Reebok uses the components to manufacture the shoes and sell them to retailers such as Foot Locker, which in turn, sell the shoes to consumers like you. In this example, Reebok is engaged in B2B buying as a producer because the company purchases parts or materials to make shoes and then sells them to other companies.[19] Reebok is a B2B purchaser but not a B2C seller; the company markets its brand directly to B2C consumers to gain recognition and drive consumers to participate in B2C buying at retailers that carry its brand.

producers
A B2B company that purchases parts, products, or ingredients for the production of other goods or services to sell at a profit.

FIGURE 6.4 Types of B2B Buyers

Producer	**Reseller**	**Organization**
A B2B company that purchases parts, products, or ingredients for the production of other goods or services to sell to other companies or consumers	A B2B company that buys finished goods to sell, lease, or rent to other companies or consumers	A government (federal, local, municipal) agency or nonprofit group that puchases products or services to serve or sell to its constituents

Resellers

resellers

A company that buys finished goods, to sell, lease, or rent to other companies or consumers.

Resellers purchase finished goods to sell, lease, or rent to B2B or B2C purchasers. In the example above, Foot Locker is a reseller because the company buys finished products from manufacturers such as Reebok, Nike, New Balance, Ryka, and others. In other words, Foot Locker doesn't manufacture products but rather buys them from other companies to sell them. It's important to note that although Foot Locker buys in the B2B arena as a reseller, the company sells in the B2C arena because it sells its products to the ultimate consumer.[20] Besides retailers, other types of resellers are wholesalers, brokers, and agents.

Organizations

organizations

Federal, local, and municipal government bodies and nonprofit groups such as churches, schools, American Red Cross, Salvation Army, and others that purchase products or services to serve or sell to constituents.

organizations include government bodies (federal, local, and municipal, as well as the District of Columbia) and nonprofit groups (churches, hospitals, colleges, and cause-related groups like the American Red Cross). The government is a huge consumer, using over $1 trillion in goods and services annually.[21] In fact, according to the U.S. government budget in 2010, the government outlays are projected to be 24.4 percent of the U.S. gross national product.[22] This makes the U.S. government the single largest customer in the world. In fact, government purchases are so large that when the Obama administration decided to replace its fleet of government vehicles in 2009, it purchased 17,205 cars for a total of $287 million—that's just one government purchase![23] As a result of the government being such a huge customer, there are processes for prospective vendors to apply to provide products or services to the government. The Web site https://www.fbo.gov provides information about federal business opportunities.[24]

Nonprofit organizations such as the Salvation Army, the Susan G. Komen Foundation, the American Cancer Society, churches, schools, shelters, and others are also B2B purchasers of goods and services. Some may be producers, such as a soup kitchen that buys ingredients for soup and other meals, and some may be resellers, such as the yellow bands for LIVESTRONG, the Lance Armstrong Foundation.[25]

FIGURE 6.5

Nonprofit organizations such as the Lance Armstrong Foundation are purchasers of products and services.[26]

Big Differences

B2C and B2B purchasers are different for several reasons. The most important differentiator is that consumers purchase for their own consumption (or the consumption of their household or friends), whereas B2B customers purchase to produce or resell the product to a company or the ultimate consumer. There are also several other key differences between B2C and B2B buyers. Generally, B2C buying is based—for the most part—on impulse, low-risk decisions for products and services that are readily accessible. Whether you shop online, in a store, or at a direct selling party, your buying decisions impact only yourself and your family and do not put you at risk. Although you may make some significant buying decisions such as a house or a car, your options are easily accessible (go online, go to the mall or store), and your decisions don't put you in danger of losing anything—except, of course, if you spend money you don't have.

TABLE 6.1 Comparison of B2C and B2B Buying Decisions

B2C Buying Decision	B2B Buying Decision
Impulsive	Methodical
Simple	Complex
May or may not be budgeted	Budgeted
Low risk	High risk
Individual decision	Coordinated decision with buy-in and approval from many people
May or may not include some research	Analytical including cost-benefit analysis

Source: Data from Randy Shattuck, "Understand the B2B Buying Cycle," http://www.internetviz-newsletters.com/PSJ/e_article001037852.cfm (accessed August 1, 2009).

However, in a B2B buying decision, the buying decision is complex, and there is significant risk because a single decision can affect the quality of a product or service offered by a company to its customers, safety of consumers, or even profitability of the company. If a B2B buying decision is the wrong decision, the person or people who made the decision might suffer the consequences, including the loss of his job.[27]

Size of Purchases

Because B2C buyers are purchasing only for their consumption or for the consumption of a limited number of people, the size of the purchases is relatively small. By contrast, B2B purchases are significant because the companies are purchasing to sell to other companies or to many consumers. Consider this difference: you might buy ten pairs of jeans in a year, but Nordstrom buys hundreds of thousands of pairs of jeans to stock in their inventory.[28] The size of B2B purchases is always significantly larger than B2C purchases simply because a company is buying for more than one consumer.

Multiple Buyers

If you think it's difficult to keep everyone in your apartment happy with the food purchases you make at the supermarket, that's easy compared to the number of people involved in a B2B purchasing decision. In most B2B transactions, there are multiple decision makers involved in each purchase. Think about your trip to the supermarket from the B2B buyer's perspective. The decision about which products to stock on the shelves was ultimately made by someone who holds the title of "buyer" in the company. However, she could not decide unilaterally what to carry in the bottled water section. She has to understand which bottled water her customers want, consult with the general merchandise manager, who is responsible for the shelf space, and the vice president of merchandising, who oversees all product choices. She may even need to make a presentation to a buying committee before she makes the decision to carry another flavor of Vitaminwater. She will need to get approval for the money to invest in the inventory and shelf space. Depending on the organization and the size and impact of the decision, several people from several different departments may be involved in a B2B buying decision.

Number of Customers

There are over three hundred million people who live in the United States and approximately a hundred million households. However, there are less that half a million businesses and other organizations.[29] Because B2B buyers are making decisions that may ultimately impact the sale of a product or service to millions of consumers, there are naturally fewer businesses. Consider the fact that according to the United States Census Bureau, there are only 7,569 hospitals in the country, yet there are over 110 million visits to emergency rooms annually.[30]

Geographic Concentration

Since there are many fewer businesses and organizations compared to the number of ultimate consumers, it makes sense that there is a geographic concentration of B2B customers. For example, the fashion industry is primarily located in New York, filmmaking in Los Angeles, and technology in Silicon Valley. B2B buyers can determine where they want to be located based on resource or on access and can even choose where to build warehouses or call centers based on costs, transportation, and availability of labor.[31]

FIGURE 6.7 Comparison of B2C and B2B Buyers

B2C Buyers	B2B Buyers
Make buying decisions for individuals or households	Make buying decisions for companies that serve other companies or many consumers
Purchase size is small	Purchase can be in the millions or billions of dollars
One buyer, may include some influencers or other users	Many people, even departments involved in buying decision
300 million people in the United States; 100 million households	500,000 businesses and organizations in the United States
Located throughout the United States	Concentrated in areas based on cost, access, and availability of resources to produce products or services

Business-to-Business Means Person-to-Person

Although B2C buying behavior is very complicated, B2B buying behavior is even more complex. The fact is, although it's called business-to-business buying, the term actually describes *people* doing business with *people*. A *business* never makes a buying decision; the decision is made by *people* who work for the company. So B2B buying decisions are subject to the same behaviors as B2C buying decisions, but on a more challenging level because B2B buying decisions usually include multiple decision makers, an extensive evaluation process, extended analysis, and they represent a high risk on the part of the decision makers.[32]

buying center

Cross-functional team of people who make buying decisions on behalf of the company or organization.

While many B2B buying decisions are made by an individual decision maker, many are made by a group of people working together, usually from different departments. When this is the case, the group is called a **buying center**, all the people in a group who are involved in the buying decision.[33] For example, hospitals use buying centers to make decisions on new equipment, a retail company might use a buying center to determine which point-of-sale register system to purchase. The buying center usually includes people from the organization who have expertise in different areas, and each may play a different role in the buying decision. Following are some roles that may be included in the buying center.

Users

The people in the B2B buying process may include some or all of the following roles. **Users** are the people who are actually using the product or service. In the case of a company purchasing a telecommunications system, the users are all employees of the company because each uses the telephone, Internet, and other communications technologies. But in the case of a company purchasing a security system, only the employees in the security department would be users of the product; other employees would simply enjoy the benefits of the product without actually using it. Because the users' satisfaction is so important, many companies involve users at various points throughout the buying process, including gathering input, participating in product demonstrations, or even using the product as a test.

users

People in a company who use the product or service but may not be the decision maker in the buying process.

Initiators and Influencers

Initiators are those people in the company who start the purchasing process for a particular product or service.[34] For example, the e-commerce manager in the marketing department may begin the process of seeking a new technology provider for e-mail and social networking services on the company's Web site. However, he may not be the final decision maker. There may be several departments involved in the purchasing decision including marketing, IT, and customer service, just to name a few. The e-commerce manager will most likely be a user and will take part in the buying process. In fact, he may even be an **influencer** in the final buying decision because he can lend his expertise to the team of people who will be making the final decision. He may compare the offerings from competitive companies, do a competitive cost analysis, and even conduct a cost-benefit analysis to determine which product will provide the most benefit for the least amount of cost. He might have a preference of which vendor to choose as a result of this information and his knowledge of the different companies in the industry. His influence may be quite significant as to what choice the company makes for the purchase. There may be other people in the organization who are also influencers, such as the IT manager, customer service manager, and others.

initiators

Person who starts the buying process in a company but who may not be the decision maker in the buying process.

influencer

A person who has a role and perhaps some authority in the purchasing decision at a company but is not the sole decision maker.

Decision Makers

At the end of the day, it is the **decision maker** or decision makers who will make the final purchasing decision. Decision makers could be anyone who holds the responsibility or accountability for making buying decisions for the company. In the case of the e-mail and social networking technology purchase, depending on the company, the decision maker might be the CEO, the head of the marketing department, or even a committee of people from marketing, IT, and customer service. A smart decision maker involves the users and influencers in her decision-making process to make the best choice. An investment in technology will not only be expensive, but will last for years; once a company makes a commitment to integrate their systems with a technology company, it is not practical to make frequent changes. The decision making process in B2B can take days, weeks, months, or even years to make, depending on the company and the product or service being purchased.

decision maker

The person or people who are responsible for making the final purchasing decision at a company.

Finding the "Power Level"

When you are selling in a B2B environment, you may not always have access to the ultimate decision maker. But building a relationship with the initiator, influencers, and users can be just as important and effective as meeting with the decision maker. However, you should always be aware of the "**power level**," or exactly the level in the organization that is making the buying decision. Sometimes, salespeople don't get to the power level, but instead stop at one or two levels below that critical level where the purchasing decision is being made. If the vice president of human resources is making the decision as to which vendor to choose for the company's training programs, it's impor-

power level

The level in a company or organization at which the buying decision is made.

tant to build a relationship with her. Having a relationship with the director of training is critical, but a successful salesperson wouldn't stop there; he would work to secure a relationship at the power level, which is the vice president.

Types of B2B Buying Situations

There's still more you can learn about the B2B buying environment. Although companies are so different from each other (some are large multinational corporations while others are one-person operations) and the types of products and services being purchased are so different (everything from business cards to office buildings), it might seem difficult to know how to apply the concepts covered to every buying situation. One way is to understand the different types of buying situations that face a B2B buyer.

New-Task Buy

new-task buy

A purchase made by a company for the first time.

If a company is moving its headquarters to a new building that does not come equipped with office furniture, the company will need to acquire furniture for all of its employees. This is a new purchase for the company, which would classify it as a **new-task buy**.[35] When a customer is contemplating a new-task buy, it is an excellent opportunity to use your consultative selling skills to bring information to your customer to help her make the best possible decision.

Straight Rebuy

straight rebuy

A routine repurchase of a product or service.

What if your customer is already purchasing the product or service regularly? Although he may currently be purchasing the product from you, he already knows about the product or service, how to use it, and how much he is currently paying for it. This is called a **straight rebuy**,[36] a routine repurchase of a product or service. Usually, straight rebuys are consumable products or supplies such as office supplies, maintenance supplies, or parts. This is an opportunity for you to shine, whether the customer is currently purchasing from you or not. When purchases are on "auto pilot," sometimes the salesperson gets lazy, takes the business for granted, and doesn't go the extra mile to suggest something new or better. If a prospective customer is already buying from someone else, you have the opportunity to win her over by suggesting a better or more efficient product, a different pack size or method of replenishment, or other ideas that will help the customer save time or money or increase quality. For straight rebuys, it is often price that gets the customer's attention, but it is service (or lack of it) that makes the customer switch providers.

Modified Rebuy

modified rebuy

A product or service that is already being purchased, but the specifications are changed.

Sometimes, your customer may already be purchasing the product but wants to change the specifications; this is called a **modified rebuy**.[37] For example, when the magazine *Vanity Fair* did a split run of their magazine cover for their September 2009 issue, they printed half of the copies with Michael Jackson on the cover and half with Farrah Fawcett.[38] Although they print the magazine monthly, they modified the printing specifications for that issue. Therefore, the sales rep from the printer sold the September 2009 print run as a modified rebuy. Selling to a customer who is purchasing a modified rebuy is an excellent opportunity to demonstrate your flexibility and creativity. Many times, customers have an idea in mind for a modification, but if you can bring them ideas and insights that will help them increase their business profitably, you will have the upper hand in securing the buy.

Strategic Alliance

Although most B2B selling depends on relationships, some selling situations go above and beyond the traditional relationship between a salesperson and the customer. Some relationships go to the next level and actually create a partnership that puts both parties at risk and provides opportunities for all parties to gain; this is called a **strategic alliance**. The relationship between Yahoo! and Microsoft is an example of a strategic alliance. The two companies finally decided to join forces in July 2009 in an effort to leverage resources as a stronger competitor to industry leader Google. As part of the relationship, Microsoft will power Yahoo!'s search with its new engine called Bing; Yahoo! will receive 88 percent of the search-generated advertising revenues from Bing.[40] Both Microsoft and Yahoo! have "skin in the game," which means that each party has something at risk and much to gain. The strategic alliance represents a way for both companies to prosper in the Internet search business. Separately, each represents less than one-fifth of the searches done in the United States. Together, their market share is 28 percent, still a far cry from industry-leading Google at 65 percent.[41] Despite spending billions, neither company has been successful overtaking Google alone; the strategic alliance gives these companies a chance to compete.[42]

FIGURE 6.8
The September 2009 issue of *Vanity Fair* magazine is an example of a modified rebuy because the normal print order was adjusted to print two different covers.[39]

strategic alliance

A business partnership in which all parties have something at risk and have something to gain.

FIGURE 6.9
Bing, the search engine created by Microsoft, is now also the search engine used on Yahoo!

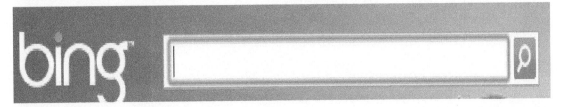

Who Makes the Buying Decision?

In many companies, there is a function called buyer, purchasing manager, materials manager, or procurement manager. These are the people who are responsible for making buying products, services, and supplies for the company or for the company's customers. In most cases, they are the decision makers for purchasing decisions.

Because most purchasing decisions in a company have a significant impact on the users and on the profitability of the company, some companies create cross-functional teams called a buying center. These people work together to make important buying decisions for the company or organization. For example, many colleges and universities have a buying center that makes decisions that impact all users in the school such as a new e-mail system, classroom, or dormitory supplies.[43]

Key Takeaways

- Customer behavior is a science, not an art, driven by specific needs that drive motivation.
- A **consumer** who purchases in a B2C environment is the end user of the product or service.
- A B2B purchaser, also called an **organizational** or **institutional** purchaser, buys a product or service to sell to another company or to the ultimate consumer.
- B2B purchasers may be **producers**, **resellers**, or **organizations**.
- B2B buys are characterized by being methodical, complex, budgeted, high risk, analytical, and coordinated across different parts of the company.
- B2B purchases are larger than B2C purchases, include multiple buyers, involve a smaller number of customers, and are geographically concentrated.

- **Maslow's hierarchy of needs** describes how people are motivated based on the level of needs that are being satisfied. Understanding a customer's motivation based on the hierarchy can provide valuable insights for selling.

- There can be several types of people involved in a B2B purchasing decision, including **users**, **initiators**, **influencers**, and **decision makers**.

- An individual such as a buyer, purchasing manager, or materials manager might make buying decisions. Some companies use a **buying center**, a cross-functional team that makes buying decisions on behalf of the company.

Exercises

1. Visit at least two different retailers. Determine whether each has a transition zone at the front of the store. Discuss the differences between the shopping experiences. Which one is more conducive to buying?

2. Identify one B2C seller and one B2B seller. Describe at least three differences between their buyers.

3. Identify one B2B company or organization that fits each of the following descriptions and describe why each belongs in the category:
   - Producer
   - Reseller
   - Government
   - Nonprofit organization

4. Consider each of the following products and services. Evaluate each one based on utilitarian need and hedonic need:
   - Trip to Las Vegas
   - Subscription to *Rolling Stone* magazine
   - Internet service
   - College education
   - iPod Touch

5. Jessica wants to celebrate her twenty-first birthday in style. She bought a new outfit, had her nails done, and went to the tanning salon. She is not only having a party for one hundred of her closest friends, but she is going to broadcast it live on Facebook and Twitter while the party is going on. Which need on Maslow's hierarchy is Jessica striving to satisfy?

6. Assume you are a salesperson for Chevrolet and you are among the first to sell the new electric-powered car called Volt. Which need on Maslow's hierarchy is the car designed to meet?

7. Imagine you work in the communications department of your school. Homecoming is just a few weeks away, and you are in charge of getting the banner for the parking lot, which will direct alumni where to park. This year, the directions to the parking are different than they were on the banner last year. Identify the type of purchase a new banner for the parking lot is and explain.

8. Assume you are selling printers and copiers to a group of clinics. The buying center includes people from purchasing, information technology, administrative assistants, doctors, and nurses. Discuss the role that each might take on as part of the buying center and the impact they may have on the final buying decision. How might you interact with each one?

6.2 How the Buying Process Works

Learning Objectives

1. List the steps in the buying process and describe how and why the process is evolving.
2. Understand the role of emotions in the buying decision.
3. Learn how to use FAB for effective selling.

For years, the buying process was considered to be linear; scholars and researchers who closely monitored buying behavior identified several steps that the B2B customer goes through before she makes a purchase. It's helpful to understand these steps to appreciate the changes that are taking place, even as you read this.

The Traditional View of the Seven Steps of the B2B Buying Process

You are probably familiar with buying as a consumer. But did you ever think about how Aéropostale decides what products will be in their stores for the spring season, how a restaurant determines which beverages it will offer, or how Hewlett-Packard (HP) identifies which parts it will use to manufacture its printers? The buying process outlines the steps that the B2B customer goes through when he is making a purchasing decision on behalf of the company. This process applies whether the buying decision is being made by an individual or by a buying center.

1. **Recognizing the need**. The buyer realizes there is a need for the product or service.[44] In the B2B environment, this might occur because of an internal need (e.g., the company needs more office space) or because of a customer need (e.g., green tea is becoming more popular, and so we want to offer it on our menu). This is the ideal opportunity for you to learn about your customers' needs, although it may be difficult to know exactly when a customer or prospective customer is beginning this step. That's why it's important to engage your customer in dialogue to understand their current and future needs. Sometimes, you can help your customer see an opportunity that he didn't realize.

2. **Defining the need**. This step usually involves users as well as initiators to put more definition around the type of product or service that will help meet the need.[45] For example, in the case of office space, the head of facilities would ask the head of human resources about the types of new positions that will be needed and the type of workspace each requires. He might also ask for insight from each hiring manager or department head in the company, such as the head of operations, marketing, finance, and other areas. This will help him more fully understand the general type of product or service that is needed. Salespeople can play a role in this step of the buying process by sharing information and insights from other customers, without divulging any confidential information.

3. **Developing the specifications**. This is the step at which the exact needs are outlined.[46] For example, if Target identified the need to create its own brand of DVD player, the appropriate people in the company would determine the exact specifications of the product: what functions it will have, how large it will be, what materials it will be made of, how many colors will be offered, and all other attributes of the product. When a salesperson has a good relationship with a customer, the buyer might ask the salesperson for insights and advice on different features, functionality, and production costs to finalize the product or service specifications.

4. **Searching for appropriate suppliers**. This step is focused on researching potential suppliers. This research can be conducted online by doing a Google search for suppliers of the desired product or service.[47] Trade associations are also an excellent source as many provide unbiased evaluations of suppliers; for example, Forrester Research publishes a report on Web site analytic tools.

And industry trade shows can be an excellent source of information about prospective suppliers. One of the best ways to identify suppliers is by referrals; use your business network, including LinkedIn, to get feedback about reliable suppliers that might be able to meet your needs.

request for proposal (RFP)

A formal request from possible suppliers to provide or create a specific product or service.

proposal

A written document that outlines a company's capabilities, delivery, and pricing in relation to a specific product or service.

5. **Requesting proposals**. This is when the buyer or buying center develops a formal **request for proposal**, often called an RFP, and she identifies several potential vendors that could produce the product or service.[48] For example, if Home Depot decided that it wanted to upgrade its bags, the buyer would have determined the specification, quantity, shipping points, usage, and other requirements (e.g., being environmentally friendly), and put the information into a formal document that is sent to several bag manufacturers along with questions about the history of the company, key customers, locations, manufacturing capacity, turnaround time, and other relevant information. Each manufacturer would have the opportunity to respond to the RFP with a formal **proposal**, which means that each company would provide information about their company, capabilities, delivery, and pricing to manufacture the bags. This is an opportunity for a salesperson to respond with a complete proposal that addresses the customer's needs and concerns. See the sample RFP template for a nonprofit organization below.

Link

RFP Template for a Nonprofit Organization
http://www.npguides.org/guide/grant1.htm

6. **Evaluating proposals**. After the proposals are submitted, the buyer or buying center reviews each one and determines whether the company would be a good fit for the project. At this point, the number of potential vendor choices is narrowed to a select few. Usually, salespeople from each of the chosen companies are invited to meet with the buyer or buying center to discuss the proposal, capabilities, and pricing. Negotiation for pricing, quality, timing, service, and other attributes may also take place during this step.[49] This is the step where a salesperson may need to overcome objections, or the reasons why the customer may not want to choose her as the company of choice.[50]

7. **Making the buying decision**. The buyer or buying center chooses one (or the necessary number) of companies to execute the project, finalizes details, negotiates all aspects of the arrangement, and signs a contract. This step requires perseverance and attention to detail on the part of the salesperson. Once the decision is made, the real business of selling begins: delivering the product or service as agreed upon and building the relationship.

8. **Postpurchase evaluation**. Throughout the buying process, the buyer is provided all the good news: how the new product or service will solve her company's problems, increase demand, reduce costs, or improve profitability. It is the postpurchase evaluation that tells the tale. Did the product or service perform as promised? Was the delivery and installation done correctly and on time? Are the business results in line with expectations? Is the relationship growing? Do the salesperson and his company really care about the performance of the buyer's company? Does the salesperson add value to the buyer's company? This is where the rubber meets the road; it presents an opportunity for the salesperson to communicate, anticipate, and solve any problems that may have arisen.[51]

The process makes sense and is a flow of systematic steps that leads a B2B buyer through a logical buying process. But there are two flaws in this thinking that significantly impact the buying process and, as a result, the selling process: (1) the Internet changes everything and (2) emotions dominate B2B buying.[52],[53]

The Internet Changes Everything

It used to be that B2B buyers relied on salespeople to get information, demonstrations, and cost about products and services. Salespeople sold, and buyers bought; the world was a simpler place.

Today, B2B buyers are doing the work of two or even three employees because there are fewer people working at companies due to cutbacks and restructuring. The fact is, buyers don't have the time to meet with salespeople like they used to. And the Internet has been a game changer. Buyers can not only research product and supplier options online, but they can also see product specifications, view demonstration videos, participate in online forums, get real-time recommendations and feedback from users on social networks, and basically be smarter than any salesperson before he even calls for an appointment.[54] The power has shifted from sellers to buyers. In fact, the Internet has had such a profound effect on how people make purchasing decisions that the *Wall Street Journal* has coined a new term: "new info shopper." These are people who can't buy anything without getting information online first. What's even more important to note is the fact that 92 percent of new info shoppers have more confidence in the information they get online than from an ad, salesperson, or other company source.[55]

So what's a salesperson to do? Stop, listen, and help your customer make the best decision for her business, even if it means that she doesn't buy your product. Despite the importance of the Internet in providing information throughout the buying process, B2B buyers still gather insight from a variety of sources that include salespeople. Successful salespeople are those that truly focus on the buyer's needs, which may mean giving up the sale and bringing valuable feedback to your company to change the product, service, or other options that are reasons why customers might not buy from you. The new world order requires everyone to rethink the conventional wisdom. *Selling* used to be something you "do to" a customer; now it's something you "do for" a customer.[56] The salespeople who win are the ones who listen in person, on the phone, and online, then make the recommendation that is in the customer's best interest.

Information is no longer the exclusive domain of the salesperson. But great salespeople bring value to their customers with ideas, insights, knowledge, and personal commitment that can't be duplicated on a Web site, online forum, or even on a social network. And the role of the Internet in B2B buying decisions is changing quickly.

Sales 2.0 has changed the way people seek, receive, and interact online. The Internet used to be only an information source, a place to search Web sites for information. But static Web sites have given way to not only information gathering, but to problem solving. **Crowdsourcing** occurs when a company takes a job that is traditionally done by an employee and issues an "open call," usually online, to people all over the world to solve the problem. This is a new way for businesses and individuals to leverage the Internet in an efficient and effective way.[57] Crowdsourcing uses the wisdom of the crowd in a virtual way to make information and solutions readily available to everyone. This video describes how crowdsourcing has changed the photography business forever.

crowdsourcing

Situation in which a company takes a job that is normally performed by an employee and puts out an "open call," usually on the Internet, for people all over the world to work on it.

Video Clip

Crowdsourcing
Learn how to make the crowd work for you.

View the video online at: http://www.youtube.com/embed/F0-UtNg3ots

Salespeople can embrace crowdsourcing and bring the power of the crowd to solve any customer problem. Facebook, iPhone apps, and YouTube are just three examples of crowdsourcing. Consider this example of the power of the crowd: Apple offered more than 65,000 apps for its iPhone in less than two years, and the number is projected to rise to 300,000 in 2010.[58],[59]

Power Selling: Lessons in Selling from Successful Brands

What's Next? Ask the Crowd
How do content companies know what people will want to read about in six months? How do retailers determine what color will be hot next season? How will car companies know what defines luxury next year?

Trendwatching.com, a global trend service, uses a team of global network of business and marketing-savvy "spotters" (a.k.a. the crowd) in 120 countries to gather data, observe consumers, and talk to the people who are innovators and trendsetters to identify what's next. Trendwatching.com offers a free version of its basic trend reports on its Web site (http://trendwatching.com), but also sells premium and customized trend information to all types of companies such a retailers, media companies, manufacturers, and others.[60]

---

digital natives

People who grew up with interactive technology.

digital immigrants

People who did not grow up with interactive technology but have adopted it.

The use of technology in B2B selling, especially social networking, will continue to explode as **digital natives** (people, probably like you, who are under the age of 27) move into the workplace and meet the **digital immigrants**, Generation X and baby boomers who accept technology, but developed their online habits during a different time. Processes, behaviors, communication, and decisions will occur differently in the future.

Emotions Dominate B2B Buying

Whether you look at the traditional buying process or the role the Internet plays in providing information, it appears that the B2B buying process is logical and rational, but appearances can be deceiving. Despite the implication and belief that companies make purchasing decisions based on facts, it's a good idea to remember one of the key tenets of B2B buying mentioned earlier: business-to-business means person-to-person. That means that although a B2B buyer is making a decision on behalf of her company, she still behaves like a consumer and is subject to emotions and feelings. "People rationalize buying decisions based on facts, but they make buying decisions based on feeling," according to Bryan Eisenberg from ClickZ.com.[61]

Fear and Trust

You learned in Chapter 3 how important trust is in a relationship. People won't buy from someone they don't trust, which is why some salespeople are more successful than others; they work to establish and develop trust with the customer. People buy when they feel comfortable with the product and the salesperson and when they believe it is the best decision they can make. They want to do business with someone who understands all their needs, not just the needs of the product or service. And because the B2B purchasing process usually includes multiple people, it means that the salesperson needs to develop a relationship and establish trust with as many people involved in the purchasing process as possible.

Although trust is a positive emotion that can influence a sale, an even stronger emotion in B2B buying is fear. B2B buyers have several fears, not the least of which is being taken for a fool. Many executives have had the experience of being told one thing by a salesperson only to learn the hard way that what he said just wasn't true. "People are afraid of being sold," according to Tom Hopkins, author of *How to Master the Art of Selling*.[62] The best way to overcome this fear is to demonstrate that you are trustworthy. That means something as simple as returning a phone call when you say you will, or following up with information as promised. Even the language that you use can signal trust. For example, "initial investment" is a better term than "down payment," "fee" is more customer-friendly than "commission," "agreement" says something different than "contract," and "can't" sounds more negative than "would you consider." Understand your customer's fear of buying and replace it with comfort, trust, and confidence—in you.[63]

Power Player: Lessons in Selling from Successful Salespeople

Fear as an Opportunity

Norm Brodsky is the owner of an archive-retrieval business called CitiStorage. He is a master salesperson because he is an astute listener and understands how to "listen between the lines" to pick up on customers' fears. One day he was showing a prospective customer through his facility when she saw all the boxes and said, "Gee, aren't you afraid of having a fire in this place?" Norm was not concerned at all because he already had backup coverage. But he realized that *she* was afraid of a fire so instead of simply saying that he was not concerned, he took the opportunity to address and respect her fear, not gloss over it. He responded by saying, "Yes, certainly, I've thought about the danger of a fire, and let me show you what we've done about it."[64] He used the opportunity to put her fear to rest, even before his sales presentation.

Some consumer products such as virus protection, security systems, or insurance, appeal to the emotion of fear; consumers balance the assurance of owning it with the pain of acquiring it. (Let's face it: It's more fun to buy a new PC than to buy virus protection.) However, in the B2B buying process, the buyer is not the person who experiences the benefits of the product or service she purchased.[65] The fact is if the product or service doesn't perform as expected or doesn't generate the desired results, the decision maker could put their job in jeopardy.[66] "B2B buying is all about minimizing fear by minimizing risk," according to a recent study by Marketo, a B2B marketing company.[67] There are actually two kinds of risk: **organizational risk** and **personal risk**. Most salespeople address the organizational risk by discussing the rational aspects of the product or service with information such as, "This server accommodates more than five times as much traffic as your current server." However, it is the personal risk, which is usually not articulated, that has a significant impact on the buying decision. This is especially true today given the focus on personal accountability, budgets, and performance. Imagine being the buyer at a fashion boutique that bought too many plaid skirts and has to request a budget for markdowns, or the decision maker who bought the computer system to power the United States' government car rebate program, Cash for Clunkers, which was delayed for over three weeks because the system crashed.[68] Some purchasing decisions at certain companies have been so bad that people have been fired as a result. Every B2B purchaser thinks about nightmares like this, so she is naturally risk-averse. The best approach in these instances is for the salesperson to reassure her that you realize how important it is for her to look good to her boss and throughout her organization as a result of the decision and show her exactly how you will help her do that.[69]

Fear is a strong motivator in a B2B buying decision, and it can't simply be addressed in one meeting or conversation. Successful salespeople are aware of it in each contact and use every opportunity to demonstrate trustworthiness. "It's how you handle the little things that show customers how you'll handle the big ones," says Tom Hopkins.[70] It's best to look at the situation from your customer's vantage point; you'll see more clearly how you can deliver value.[71]

The Evolving Buying and Selling Processes

The framework for the buying and selling processes has been in place for many years. The buying process changes literally every day and has dramatic impact on the selling process. As a result, the "new" processes are not yet clearly defined. One thing is for certain; the processes are no longer organized, controllable functions. "Linear is so twentieth century," according to Michael R. Solomon, author of *Consumerspace: Conquering Marketing Strategies for a Branded World.*[72] Cultural, social,

organizational risk

Potential exposure, hazard, or danger for a company.

personal risk

Potential exposure, hazard, or danger for a person, especially the potential of losing his job.

and technological changes will continue to drive companies for even better performance, faster, and with ideas as currency, which will continue to drive change in the buying process.

To understand the impact of the rapid changes occurring in the buying process, it's important to know the basic steps in the selling process. The next seven chapters review the selling process in detail and include insights into how the process is changing. A study by William Moncrief and Greg W. Marshall provides a roadmap for the evolution of the selling process in Table 6.2.

TABLE 6.2 The Evolution of the Seven Steps of Selling

Traditional Seven Steps of Selling	Transformative Factors	Evolved Selling Process
1. Prospecting	• Telemarketing • Internet selling • Organizational prospecting	Customer retention and deletion
2. Preapproach	• Laptop account data • Support staff	Database and knowledge management
3. Approach	• Build a foundation	Nurturing the relationship (relationship selling)
4. Presentation	• PowerPoint/multimedia • Listening • Team selling • Multiple calls • Value-added • Buying centers	Marketing the product
5. Overcoming Objections	• Predetermining needs	Problem solving
6. Close	• Identifying mutual goals	Adding value/satisfying needs
7. Follow-Up	• Increased effectiveness of communication through technology	Customer relationship maintenance

Source: Reprinted from Industrial Marketing Management, 34/1, William C. Montcrief and Greg W. Marshall, "The Evolution of the Seven Steps of Selling," 13–22, Copyright (2005), with permission from Elsevier.

Buying Process Meets FAB

No matter how the buying process evolves, customers continue to make purchase decisions driven by emotions. You learned how motivating trust and fear are for people who are making B2B buying decisions. Comfort, vanity, convenience, pleasure, desire to succeed, security, prevention of loss, and need to belong are all emotions that motivate purchases. A company may want to build a new building that carries its brand name downtown to signal its importance to the city and business community; that would be an example of vanity as a motivator. Or perhaps the company wants to move its headquarters to a better part of town to provide better security for its employees. Maybe a prominent figure in the community donates a large sum of money to your college motivated by the desire to give back. The same types of motivations apply to B2C purchases: a woman purchases makeup in the hopes of looking as beautiful as the model in the ads, a man buys a sports car in the hopes of turning heads, a student buys a microwave for the convenience of having food when she wants it.

Emotions are the driving force in so many B2C and B2B purchases that you might not even realize it. Consider this: would you buy the product in Figure 6.10?

FIGURE 6.10 Nutritional Information

FIGURE 6.11
The Doritos bag is more appealing than the nutritional information.

Source: http://fritolay.com/our-snacks/doritos-cool-ranch-chips.html

So how do you create the same type of emotional appeal with your customers? The answer is simple: FAB.

While you might not consider buying it based on only this factual information, you probably have bought this product based on the emotional appeal of the packaging, advertising, and other marketing messages that tell you that the product is the best late-night snack.

Consider this information that was on the home page of Amazon recently:

> *3G wireless means books in 60 seconds. No monthly fees, service plans or hunting for Wi-Fi hotspots. Over 300,000 of the most popular books, newspapers, magazines, and blogs available.*[73]

Amazon truly understands how to use **FAB**, a selling technique that focuses on **F**eatures, **A**dvantages, and **B**enefits, to sell its Kindle electronic reader. FAB is more than a way of selling; it's a way of thinking like your customers. Using the Kindle as an example, here are the details about how to use the FAB approach for effective selling.

- A **feature** is a "physical characteristic" of the product.[74] In the Kindle example above, the *feature* is the 3G wireless capability. Features are characteristics of the product; a feature comparison chart between the Kindle and the Kindle DX is shown below.

Nutrition Facts
Serving Size: 1 bag

Amount per Serving

Calories 140	Calories from Fat 60

	% Daily Value *
Total Fat 7g	11%
Saturated Fat 1g	5%
Trans Fat 0g	
Cholesterol 0mg	0%
Sodium 170mg	7%
Potassium 0mg	0%
Total Carbohydrate 18g	6%
Dietary Fiber 1g	4%
Sugars 1g	
Protein 2g	4%

Calcium	2%
Iron	2%
Vitamin E	4%
Thiamin (B1)	2%
Riboflavin (B2)	2%
Niacin (B3)	2%
Vitamin B6	4%
Magnesium	4%

Est. Percent of Calories from:
**Fat 45.0% Carbs 51.4%
Protein 5.7%**

Source: http://www.thedailyplate.com/nutrition-calories/food/doritos/cool-ranch-ind-bag

FAB

Selling technique that focuses on **F**eatures, **A**dvantages, and **B**enefits.

feature

A physical characteristic of a product.

FIGURE 6.12 Feature Comparison Chart between the Kindle and the Kindle DX

Source: http://www.amazon.com/dp/B0015T963C

advantage

The performance characteristic of a product that describes how it will help the buyer.

benefit

The result a buyer will realize because of the product advantage.

- A product **advantage** is the "performance characteristic" of the product, or what the feature does.[75] In the information about Kindle included at the start of this section, the advantages of the 3G service are that the user doesn't need to hunt for Wi-Fi hotspots and that over 300,000 of the most popular books, newspapers, magazines, and blogs are available in sixty seconds.

- The **benefit** is the "result" the buyer will realize from the product because of the product advantage, or in other words, what the feature does or the result it delivers.[76] The benefit of the Kindle is the fact that you can "rediscover reading anywhere, any time."[77]

Why does FAB work? Because customers want to know what a product or service will do for them—not just what it's made of. B2C and B2B customers seek information before making a buying decision but are also driven by emotions. FAB helps you appeal to a customer's rational and emotional buying behavior by providing the most compelling features and factual information and then showing how the features provide an advantage that delivers a benefit. This is how salespeople help customers establish an emotional connection with a product. You remember from Chapter 1 the power of an emotional connection between a customer and a brand.

You probably use FAB sometimes without even realizing it. "My new Lucky Brand jeans have a dirty wash, fit great, and make me look thin. The best part is they were on sale for only $89.00." The features are the dirty wash and the fact that they were on sale for $89.00; the advantage is that they fit well (no easy feat when it comes to jeans); the benefit is that they make you feel like you look thin and, as a result, make you feel good when you wear them. Your statement is much more powerful when you frame it with FAB than if you simply say, "I got some new jeans today for $89.00."

Or maybe you stopped into McDonald's and tried one of their new Angus Third Pounders. The product feature is that the burger is one-third of a pound and is available in three flavor options; the advantage is that it is thick and juicy; the benefit is that you will enjoy the taste and your hunger is satisfied. The FAB message is more compelling than simply saying that you had a hamburger that was one-third of a pound; that would be stopping at the feature and not offering an advantage or benefit.

If you want to be able to use FAB in conversation, simply think in terms of the following:

- **Feature**: what the product *has*
- **Advantage**: what the features *do*
- **Benefit**: what the features *mean*[78],[79]

Table 6.3 gives features, advantages, and benefits for some common products.

TABLE 6.3 FAB in Action

Product	Feature	Advantage	Benefit
HP Pavilion Computer	250-GB hard drive	Enough space to store music, pictures, documents, and more.	Do more from playing video games to downloading all of your favorite music and still have space for your homework projects.
Caribbean Vacation	4 all-inclusive nights with airfare for only $599 per person	Don't worry about how to budget for the cost of the vacation because everything is included in one low price.	Enjoy a spring break you will never forget on a beach in the Caribbean.
Honda Insight	40 mpg highway/43 mpg city	Lower your gas prices with a fuel-efficient Insight.	Be kind to the environment and travel in comfort for less with an Insight.

For example, if you were describing Netflix in terms of FAB, you might say something like the following:

For only $8.99 a month you can watch as many movies as you want and never be charged a late fee. You can order online and have a DVD delivered in about a day and exchange it as many times as you want without a late fee, or you can watch streaming video of your favorite movies online anytime. Now that's total personalized entertainment.[80]

Now look at this FAB statement with the features, advantages, and benefits in bold:

*For only **$8.99 a month** [feature] you can **watch as many movies as you want** and **never be charged a late fee** [advantage]. You can **order online** and **have a DVD delivered in about a day** [advantage] and **exchange it as many times as you want without a late fee** [advantage], or you **can watch streaming video of your favorite movies online anytime** [advantage]. It definitely **saves you time and money** [benefit] and gives you **total personalized entertainment** [benefit].*

It's easy to remember by using the FAB framework as your guide.

[Name feature] means you [name advantage] with the real benefit to you being [name benefit].[81]

Here's another example, based on research about the 2009 Nissan Cube:[82]

The Nissan Cube has funky, Japanese-like design and is friendly to the environment with a fuel-efficient 1.8-liter, 4-cylinder engine that gets over 30 miles per gallon. It's hip, cool, and fun to drive. At $15,585, it's a great value for the money.

How to Use FAB

Now that you know what FAB is, you probably want to know how to use it most effectively in selling. Here are three easy steps to put FAB to work for you:

1. **Know your customer.** Benefits speak emotionally to customers in a way that rational facts can't. But you need to know what is important to each customer. The health club that's open twenty-four hours might be attractive to a young professional because he can work out late in the evening after a long day, whereas the club's day care center might be appealing to a young mother. Similarly, in a B2B selling situation in which a buyer is evaluating warehouse space, one customer might be interested in the warehouse because of its state-of-the-art systems, while another might be focused on location. Know what motivates your customer, and then you can craft an effective FAB statement.[83]

2. **Think outside your box.** If you want your FAB to work for your customer, you will need to deliver value in the form of benefits that she can't get from anyone else. Think about your product or service in a different way; talk to people, watch the trends, see what else you can bring when you look at your product or service in a different way. Baking soda had traditionally been used as a leavening agent for baking. Arm & Hammer reinvented baking soda as a way to remove odors from refrigerators. Can you be as creative with the application for your product or service?[84]

3. **Get in touch with your customer's motivation.** Listen, learn, and craft an FAB message that will "have your customer at hello."[85] Although that might be an overly romantic notion of how selling works, your goal is to have your customer fall in love with your product or service so much that it's something he can't live without. Imagine living without iTunes, your cell phone, or your favorite pair of jeans. That's how your customer should feel about the product or service you are selling. If you understand his motivation, you can deliver features, advantages, and benefits that not only tell him why he should buy, but why he can't afford not to.

Key Takeaways

- The traditional B2B buying process has seven steps: need recognition, defining the need, developing the specifications, searching for appropriate suppliers, evaluating proposals, making the buying decision, and postpurchase evaluation.
- The Internet is a game-changer as it relates to the buying process because information is no longer the exclusive domain of the salesperson; the power has shifted from the seller to the buyer.
- **Crowdsourcing** occurs when a company takes a job that is traditionally done by an employee and issues an "open call," usually online, to people all over the world to solve the problem. Salespeople can use **crowdsourcing** to get the best solutions for their customers.
- Emotions such as comfort, security, convenience, pleasure, and vanity are major motivations for buying decisions.
- Trust and fear are especially important in B2B buying because the decision maker has to consider **organizational risk** and **personal risk** as part of his buying decision.
- The buying process continues to evolve, which changes the selling process; the traditional selling process provides a foundation and insight into the evolution.
- **FAB** (a.k.a. *features*, *advantages*, *benefits*) is the way to appeal to your customer's emotions with factual and emotional appeals.
  - A **feature** is what a product *has*.
  - An **advantage** is what the feature *does*.
  - A **benefit** is what the features *mean* to the customer.

Exercises

1. Identify a recent major purchase that you made recently. How did you recognize the need for the product or service? Where did you go to gather information about the options that were available to you? Did you use one method or a combination of methods?

2. Contact a buyer at the headquarters of a retailer such as Dick's Sporting Goods, GameStop, Costco, Urban Outfitters, or another company. Ask him about the process he uses to determine which products to put in the retail stores. Is his process similar to the process outlined in this chapter? How does it differ? How does his postpurchase evaluation impact his decision to buy the product again?

3. Describe a situation in which a salesperson might use crowdsourcing.

4. Assume you are a salesperson for a major telecommunications company and you are calling on a major construction company that is considering buying smart phones for the key people in the company. Describe at least one organizational risk and one personal risk that might be involved in the customer's decision.

5. Identify a feature, advantage, and benefit for each of the following products and services:

   - MTV
   - Kia Sportage
   - Palm Pre
   - Virgin Mobile phone

6.3 *Selling U*: Developing and Communicating Your Personal FAB

Learning Objectives

1. Understand how to develop your personal FAB message.
2. Learn how to make your FAB message memorable in an interview.

You can see that FAB is a powerful way to build an emotional connection with a customer. It is also an excellent way to stand out to a prospective employer in an interview. You'll learn more about the interviewing process in the *Selling U* section of Chapter 10, but now it's a good idea to do some advance preparation.

You've already done a lot of work that will serve you well as you network and interview—you've identified your brand positioning points in the *Selling U* section of Chapter 1, put them to work in your résumé and cover letter in Chapter 2, and developed your elevator pitch in Chapter 5. All these activities help you bring your personal FAB (feature, advantage, benefit) message into focus. Your FAB message will help you tell the details about your brand and will help you tell your "stories" about your experience and accomplishments during your interviews.

Stories Paint Pictures

If getting the job or internship you want were only about the facts, you would only need to present your résumé on a job interview. But prospective employers are looking for that "certain something," an emotional connection that helps them know that you are *the* one.[86] Every candidate comes into an interview trying to impress the interviewee and saying how much he wants the job. Why not stand out, show, and sell?

Think about your three brand positioning points you developed in Chapter 1. Now, think about the stories that demonstrate each one in terms of FAB. Table 6.4 shows you some examples.

TABLE 6.4 Personal FAB Example

Brand Positioning Point	Feature	Advantage	Benefit
Marketing Experience	Had an internship at an advertising agency	I worked on the Limited, Too account developing Twitter conversations with target customers.	I can help SpitFire engage its customers directly and learn about shopping preferences using social networking.
Customer Service Experience	Worked as a server at Olive Garden	I interacted with customers and provided excellent customer service under pressure.	I understand how to handle multiple tasks under pressure without losing my cool.
Leadership Experience	President of Young Entrepreneurs Club	I developed a forum for local investors to regularly hear pitches from student entrepreneurs, which led to the launch of three new products.	I understand the process it takes to turn ideas into profitable businesses, and I'm able to be the driving force behind bringing people, ideas, and money together.

Every Picture Tells a Story

portfolio

A collection of work samples from class projects, internship, volunteer projects, and any other work that demonstrates your skills.

Take your FAB one step up and create a **portfolio** that you can show during job interviews. When you *tell* someone about your experience and accomplishments, that's good, but *showing* them really helps you stand out in the crowd. If you are lucky enough to get an interview, capitalize on the opportunity to sell yourself. Keep in mind that most companies interview at least two or three people, and sometimes more, before they make their hiring decision.

A portfolio isn't just for creative or advertising people; everyone should have a portfolio. It is simply a collection of samples of your work from class projects, internships, volunteer projects, and any other work that demonstrates your skills.[87] Creating a portfolio is as simple as putting samples of your work in a three-ring binder. You might find it helpful to view this video about how to create a portfolio.

Video Clip

How to Create Your Portfolio

View the video online at: http://www.youtube.com/embed/hQhigdJ-xEk

You probably have more samples of your work than you think. And each sample is an excellent way to show *and* tell your FAB. Here are some ideas about what to put in your portfolio:

- **Class projects**. Choose those projects that demonstrate your skills, especially in your major. For example, if you did a sales presentation, include a video clip along with your selling aids. Or if you created a PR plan, include the plan along with the exhibits. Group projects are acceptable as long as the group names are included on the title page. A team project allows you to talk about how you provided leadership to the team or helped the team get focused.

- **Internship projects**. If you had an internship or multiple internships, include samples of the projects on which you worked. For example, include copies of Web pages, brochures, flyers, graphs, presentations, or other samples of your work.

- **Volunteer projects**. If you have been involved in a student group, community service, or other service organization, include samples of the projects on which you worked. For example, if your group did a fundraiser for breast cancer, include the flyer for the event along with photos and a summary of the contributions.

You've Got the Power: Tips for Your Job Search

Keep a Copy

Whenever you work on a class project, internship, volunteer project, or any other type of project that demonstrates your skills, keep a copy for your portfolio. The same is true when you begin working; keep copies of all your projects to continue to build your portfolio throughout your career. You never know when you will need to show samples of your work. It's best to avoid including any confidential or proprietary information from companies or organizations.

- **Other work samples**. If you enjoy photography, writing, design, selling on eBay, or other activity that has application to the position for which you are seeking, include that work. In other words, print the Web page for your eBay store along with the feedback you have received, include photographs or other projects on which you have worked to show your work. If you don't have samples of your work for your portfolio, consider starting a blog and print copies of your entries.

- **Letters of recommendation**. Ask for a letter of recommendation from former supervisors, colleagues, team leaders, professors, and other people who will be happy to write a letter about your skills.[88] If you have had a summer job or internship, ask your former boss and other people with whom you worked to write a letter of recommendation. Keep the copies of the letters in your portfolio and show them to prospective employers during your interview. Although these letters are different from references, they serve the purpose of *showing* your prospective employer how highly people regard you and your work. You will be asked for references after the interview process if you are one of the final candidates. See the *Selling U* section in Chapter 4 for more information about how to contact and submit references, including how letter of recommendation from references can help set you apart.

Tips to Make Your Portfolio Even More Powerful

After you gather all of your work samples, here are a few tips that will help you organize them for an effective visual story.

- **Choose a few work samples**. Select samples (no more than five or six) that reflect your brand positioning points. If leadership is important, be sure to include projects, results, pictures, and other visual elements that will demonstrate your leadership story.

- **Create a summary page for each work sample**. Include bullet points for the project name, objective, approach or strategy, and results. A sample is provided in Figure 6.13. This will help you quickly summarize the key points when you are showing your portfolio.

FIGURE 6.13 Sample Summary Page

Project Name:	Rold Gold Pretzels Integrated Marketing Communication Plan Semester Project for MKT 2335
Project Objective:	Create an integrated marketing communication plan that will reverse the negative sales and market share trends
Project Strategy:	Reposition Rold Gold pretzels as the cool, must-have treat for college students
Project Results:	The three-person agency team presented the plan and won the class competition as judged by four advertising executives

- **Use clean copies, in color where appropriate**. Avoid using papers that include comments or grades. Use fresh, clean copies of all samples. If you need to make a copy of an original document that was in color, splurge and pay for color copies; it's worth it.

- **Include extra copies of your résumé**. Your portfolio is a great place to keep at least three or four extra copies of your most current résumé printed on twenty-four-pound paper. Although your interviewer may have already received your résumé before the interview, he may not have it handy when you come in. Or you may be asked to meet with some people that were not on the original interview schedule. If this is the case, you can be the consummate professional and offer your interviewer a reference copy of your résumé. It's also the perfect time to mention your portfolio.

- **Use a professional binder or portfolio**. Visit a local or online art supply or office supply store and get a professional three-ring binder or portfolio. You can include your work samples in plastic sleeves, but it is not required. Many portfolios include plastic sleeves for your samples. Ask if the store offers a student discount.

Make It Memorable

As you develop your FAB and portfolio, think about the stories you want to tell about each one. Stories are much more powerful than facts. For example, "I can really appreciate what it takes to go the extra mile for a customer. When I worked at J&J Catering, they needed someone to mix the giant vats of cookie dough. Needless to say, I spent hours working with the dough, but I wanted to make it interesting, so I learned how ingredients work together, and I created a new recipe for lemon cookies that became the signature dessert of the company."

www.You.com

A portfolio is a must to bring on a job interview. You might be wondering if it's a good idea to also create an online portfolio. The answer is "yes." Creating your own professional Web site as a way to showcase your résumé, samples of your work, awards, and letter of recommendation is a perfect way to build your brand and demonstrate to your prospective employer that you have additional technology skills.

Your online portfolio, or Web site, should include all the elements that are included in your offline portfolio. Since space is not an issue, you may want to include even more samples of your work, especially if you have writing or design samples. This is also an ideal place to include a link to your blog.

A word of caution: Your professional Web site should be exactly that—professional. That means no personal photos, comments, or casual blog posts from friends. In other words, your Facebook page is not an appropriate place for your professional Web site. Use a business-like domain name (http://www.yourname.com); if you don't already have one, you can get one at Google or GoDaddy.com, for a minimal annual fee. The following article provides six steps to set up a domain name and your own Web site.

Video Link

The Ultimate Guide to Creating Your Personal Website

https://collegeinfogeek.com/personal-website/

Use your online portfolio as a way to sell yourself on your résumé: add your Web site address to your contact information and mention it in your cover letter.[89] See résumé and cover letter samples in the *Selling U* section in Chapter 2.

How to Use Your Portfolio in an Interview

It's always best to bring your portfolio to every interview, even if it's an informational interview. In most cases, the interviewer will not ask you about your portfolio so you will have to bring it up in the conversation. The following video provides some tips about how to introduce your portfolio during an interview.

Video Clip

Using a Portfolio in an Interview
Learn how to use your portfolio to make the sale and get the job you want.

00:00:54:27

View the video online at: http://www.youtube.com/embed/lBIQPcW_DN0

Be proud of showing your work samples. The *Financial Times*, in reference to Peggy Klaus' book *Brag: The Art of Tooting Your Own Horn Without Blowing It*, wrote, "Start bragging...if you don't speak up for yourself, who will?"[90] To ensure that you are getting all of your FAB points across, it's best to rehearse how you will review your portfolio in an interview. Keep in mind that time is short so it's best to be concise and underscore the FAB points you want your interviewer to remember. A portfolio is an excellent visual tool that makes your FAB message come alive for your prospective employer. The bottom line is, "If you walk into an interview empty-handed, you're missing an opportunity."[91]

Key Takeaways

- Develop your **FAB** message using your brand positioning points as a foundation. Develop one or more **FAB** messages for each point.
- Create a **portfolio** to bring on job interviews to visually tell your FAB messages. Include extra copies of your résumé, samples of your work from class projects, internships, volunteer work, and relevant hobbies in a professional three-ring binder. Be sure all samples are clean and are in color where appropriate.
- You can also create an online **portfolio** on a professional Web site that includes the same information as your physical **portfolio**. Also include your Web site address in the contact information on your résumé and mention it in your cover letter.
- Be ready to introduce and review your **portfolio** in an interview; you'll need to take the initiative as your prospective employer won't know you have work samples to show.
- Be proud of showing your work samples. Rehearse exactly what you will say about each sample and keep it concise.

Exercises

1. Write down your FAB using the chart below. What examples or stories can you tell about each one?

Brand Positioning Point	Feature	Advantage	Benefit

2. Identify at least four samples of your work that you can include in your portfolio. Discuss which FAB message each sample demonstrates. Create a summary sheet for each sample.
3. Shop online or in a local art supply or office supply store and identify a professional binder or portfolio for your samples.
4. Review your portfolio with a professor, supervisor, or other professional. Ask for feedback on your portfolio and presentation.

6.4 Review and Practice

Power Wrap-Up

Now that you have read this chapter, you should be able to understand why and how people buy in B2C and B2B situations.

- You can **describe** the types of customers and why this information is important in determining customers' needs.
- You can **discuss** the implications of Maslow's hierarchy of needs for selling.
- You can **learn the types of buyers and buying situations in a B2B environment**.
- You can **list** the steps in the buying process and describe how and why the process is evolving.
- You can **understand** the role of emotions in the buying decision.
- You can **learn** how to use FAB for effective selling.
- You can **understand** how to develop your personal FAB message.
- You can **learn** how to make your FAB message memorable in an interview.

Test Your Power Knowledge (answers are below)

1. Describe the three types of B2B customers and what makes them different.
2. Name at least three differences between a B2C and a B2B purchase.

3. Describe two products or services a B2B purchaser would buy to meet esteem needs.

4. True or false: B2B buying decisions are rational.

5. True or false: The initiator in a B2B buying situation is also the decision maker.

6. Describe the first step in the buying process.

7. What is an RFP, and at which stage in the buying process is it used?

8. Describe FAB and how it is used in the selling process.

Power (Role) Play

Now it's time to put what you've learned into practice. Following are two roles that are involved in the same selling situation—one role is the customer, and the other is the salesperson. This will give you the opportunity to think about this selling situation from the point of view of both the customer and the salesperson.

Read each role carefully along with the discussion questions. Then, be prepared to play either of the roles in class using the concepts covered in this chapter. You may be asked to discuss the roles and do a role-play in groups or individually.

The Best Way to Reach Boomers

Role: Director of marketing at Shooz Athletic Shoe Company

Sales have been far less than expected as a result of the economy. Shooz brand athletic shoes are targeted to baby boomers; they are flexible and comfortable, yet look cool. They are priced higher than the competition, and it seems to have been suffering at the hands of the promotional efforts of competitors. But the marketing strategy of Shooz is to continue to focus on its niche and be higher priced, despite the sinking economy.

You have a limited advertising budget that has been devoted primarily to television advertising. You are in the process of reviewing the numbers before your next meeting.

- Should you be open to new options and ways to increase your business?
- What role could a salesperson play in helping you think about different advertising options?

Role: Internet advertising salesperson

You are a salesperson for an advertising company named Online Marketing Concepts. You sell banner ads, e-mail, and social networking advertising for several online networks. Despite the growth of Internet advertising in the past several years, online advertising sales have been down due to the economy, which has had an impact on your paycheck. You would really like to get the Shooz account to buy some Internet advertising. You've done your homework, and you think that online advertising could really help the Shooz business. You haven't found any ads online for Shooz, and you have a great idea for an interactive advertising campaign targeted to baby boomers. Now, you're confident that if you get in front of the right person, you can see your idea and help Shooz grow its business.

- What step in the buying process is the director of marketing currently in?
- How might you prepare for this sales call based on what you know?
- How will emotions come into play in the purchase of advertising for Shooz?

Put Your Power to Work: *Selling U* Activities

1. Ask a professor, mentor, or other professional to share her portfolio with you. Ask her how she gathered examples of her work that she shows to prospective customers or employers. Ask for feedback on your portfolio.

2. Create an online portfolio including your résumé, samples of your work, letters of recommendation, awards, and other proof of your skills. Review Web sites such as http://sites.google.

com and http://www.myevent.com. Don't forget to include your URL on your résumé in the contact information area.

3. Create a blog to demonstrate your skills. Review Web sites such as https://www.blogger.com/start and http://wordpress.com as possible hosts for your blog. Choose a topic that you are passionate about (sports, music, movies, fashion, or whatever moves you). Follow the directions to personalize your blog and start writing. Remember to make regular and frequent posts; there's nothing less professional than an out-of-date blog. Keep it professional. Promote your blog on Facebook, Twitter, LinkedIn, and other professional networking Web sites.

Test Your Power Knowledge Answers

1. Producers are companies or organizations that buy parts or ingredients to make a product or service. Resellers are companies or organizations that buy finished products or services to sell them to other companies or consumers. Organizations are government or nonprofit groups that buy products or services for consumption or to be sold to companies or consumers.

2. Size of purchases, multiple buyers, number of customers, and geographic concentration.

3. A building that bears the company name; doing business with only those companies that have the best reputations, such as McKinsey & Company; hiring only people who have an Ivy League education.

4. False. B2B decisions are dominated by emotions, especially trust and fear.

5. False. Although the initiator may be the decision maker, that is not always the case, especially in complex B2B buying decisions.

6. Need recognition includes the realization that there is a need for the product or service. The need might be identified by a user or anyone else inside the organization or by a customer.

7. The request for proposal is part of step four: searching for appropriate suppliers.

8. Feature, advantage, benefit is used in B2B and B2C selling and is used to appeal to a customer's emotions as in "what will this product or service do for me?"

Endnotes

1. Barbara Farfan, "Retail Industry Information: Overview of Facts, Research, Data, and Trivia," About.com, http://retailindustry.about.com/od/statisticsresearch/p/retailindustry.htm (accessed August 3, 2009).
2. Paco Underhill, *Why We Buy: The Science of Shopping* (New York: Touchstone, 1999), 99.
3. Paco Underhill, *Why We Buy: The Science of Shopping* (New York: Touchstone, 1999), 46.
4. Paco Underhill, *Why We Buy: The Science of Shopping* (New York: Touchstone, 1999), 46.
5. Kristin Biekkola, "Needs versus Wants," slide show, Wisc-Online.com, http://www.wisc-online.com/objects/index_tj.asp?objID=ABM3302 (accessed August 2, 2009).
6. Michael R. Solomon, *Consumer Behavior: Buying, Having, and Being*, 8th ed. (Upper Saddle River, NJ: Pearson Prentice Hall, 2009), 133.
7. Michael R. Solomon, *Consumer Behavior: Buying, Having, and Being*, 8th ed. (Upper Saddle River, NJ: Pearson Prentice Hall, 2009), 133.
8. United States Department of Health and Human Services, http://www.hhs.gov/disasters/emergency/naturaldisasters/hurricanes/katrina/index.html (accessed August 2, 2009).
9. Talya Bauer and Berrin Erdogan, *Organizational Behavior* (Nyack, NY: Flat World Knowledge, 2009), 91.
10. Associated Press, "Looters Take Advantage of New Orleans Mess," *msnbc.com*, August 30, 2005, http://www.msnbc.msn.com/id/9131493 (accessed August 2, 2009).
11. Joel Roberts, "Christmas After Katrina," *CBS Evening News*, December 25, 2005, http://www.cbsnews.com/stories/2005/12/25/eveningnews/main1165360.shtml (accessed August 2, 2009).
12. Talya Bauer and Berrin Erdogan, *Organizational Behavior* (Nyack, NY: Flat World Knowledge, 2009), 92.
13. Sheryl Kane, "Volunteer Vacations: Rebuilding New Orleans," June 26, 2009, SingleMindedWomen, http://singlemindedwomen.com/2009/06/rebuilding-new-orleans (accessed August 2, 2009).
14. Talya Bauer and Berrin Erdogan, *Organizational Behavior* (Nyack, NY: Flat World Knowledge, 2009), 92.
15. Joy Messer, "Survivors of Hurricane Katrina Overcome Adversity and Open 'Chappy's on Church Street,'" July 23, 2008, Associated Content, http://www.associatedcontent.com/article/887343/survivors_of_hurricane_katrina_overcome.html?cat=22 (accessed August 2, 2009).
16. Mary Cantando, "How Savvy Women Entrepreneurs Make Buying Decisions," Women Entrepreneurs, Inc., January 1, 2005, http://www.perfectbusiness.com/articles/newsarticle.cfm?newsID=948&news=1 (accessed August 1, 2009).
17. Jeremy Liew, "Why Do People Buy Virtual Goods?" *Wall Street Journal*, February 9, 2009, http://online.wsj.com/article/SB123395867963658435.html (accessed August 1, 2009).
18. Michael R. Solomon, Greg W. Marshall, and Elnora W. Stuart, *Marketing: Real People, Real Choices*, 5th ed. (Upper Saddle River, NJ: Pearson Prentice Hall, 2008), 179.

19. Barton A. Weitz, Stephen B. Castleberry, and John F. Tanner, Jr., *Selling: Building Partnerships*, 7th ed. (New York: McGraw-Hill Irwin, 2009), 86.

20. Michael R. Solomon, Greg W. Marshall, and Elnora W. Stuart, *Marketing: Real People, Real Choices*, 5th ed. (Upper Saddle River, NJ: Pearson Prentice Hall, 2008), 180.

21. Barton A. Weitz, Stephen B. Castleberry, and John F. Tanner, Jr., *Selling: Building Partnerships*, 7th ed. (New York: McGraw-Hill Irwin, 2009), 88.

22. Office of Management and Budget, "Updated Summary Tables, May 2009: Budget of the U.S. Government, Fiscal Year 2010," http://www.usgovernmentspending.com/us_20th_century_chart.html (accessed August 2, 2009).

23. Jeremy Korzeniewski, "U.S. Government Buys 17,205 Cars for $287 Million, Ford Represents," Autoblog Green, http://www.autobloggreen.com/2009/06/11/u-s-government-buys-17-205-new-cars-for-287-million-ford-repr (accessed August 2, 2009).

24. Michael R. Solomon, Greg W. Marshall, and Elnora W. Stuart, *Marketing: Real People, Real Choices*, 5th ed. (Upper Saddle River, NJ: Pearson Prentice Hall, 2008), 181.

25. Lance Armstrong Foundation, http://www.livestrong.com (accessed August 2, 2009).

26. Lance Armstrong Foundation, http://www.store-laf.org (accessed August 2, 2009).

27. Randy Shattuck, "Understand the B2B Buying Cycle," http://www.internetviz-newsletters.com/PSJ/e_article001037852.cfm (accessed August 1, 2009).

28. Michael R. Solomon, Greg W. Marshall, and Elnora W. Stuart, *Marketing: Real People, Real Choices*, 5th ed. (Upper Saddle River, NJ: Pearson Prentice Hall, 2008), 177.

29. Michael R. Solomon, Greg W. Marshall, and Elnora W. Stuart, *Marketing: Real People, Real Choices*, 5th ed. (Upper Saddle River, NJ: Pearson Prentice Hall, 2008), 177.

30. United States Census Bureau, http://www.census.gov/Press-Release/www/releases/archives/facts_for_features_special_editions/004491.html (accessed August 2, 2009).

31. Michael R. Solomon, Greg W. Marshall, and Elnora W. Stuart, *Marketing: Real People, Real Choices*, 5th ed. (Upper Saddle River, NJ: Pearson Prentice Hall, 2008), 178.

32. Kae Groshong Wagner, "The B2B Buying Process," http://www.internetviz-newsletters.com/PSJ/e_article001037852.cfm (accessed August 2, 2009).

33. Michael R. Solomon, Greg W. Marshall, and Elnora W. Stuart, *Marketing: Real People, Real Choices*, 5th ed. (Upper Saddle River, NJ: Pearson Prentice Hall, 2008), 184.

34. Barton A. Weitz, Stephen B. Castleberry, and John F. Tanner, Jr., *Selling: Building Partnerships*, 7th ed. (New York: McGraw-Hill Irwin, 2009), 97.

35. Gerald L. Manning, Barry L. Reece, and Michael Ahearne, *Selling Today: Creating Customer Value*, 11th ed. (Upper Saddle River, NJ: Pearson Prentice Hall, 2010), 163.

36. Gerald L. Manning, Barry L. Reece, and Michael Ahearne, *Selling Today: Creating Customer Value*, 11th ed. (Upper Saddle River, NJ: Pearson Prentice Hall, 2010), 163.

37. Gerald L. Manning, Barry L. Reece, and Michael Ahearne, *Selling Today: Creating Customer Value*, 11th ed. (Upper Saddle River, NJ: Pearson Prentice Hall, 2010), 163.

38. Lorena Bias, "Fawcett, Jackson Get 'Fair' Magazine Play," *USA Today*, August 3, 2009, life 1.

39. "Vanity Fair's Two September 2009 Covers: Michael Jackson, Farrah Fawcett Split Cover," *Huffington Post*, August 3, 2009, http://www.huffingtonpost.com/2009/08/03/vanity-fairs-two-septembe_n_249809.html (accessed February 20, 2010).

40. "Yahoo-Microsoft Deal," *New York Times*, July 30, 2009, http://topics.nytimes.com/top/news/business/companies/yahoo_inc/yahoo-microsoft-deal/index.html (accessed August 3, 2009).

41. Patricia Resende, "Microsoft Keeps Watchful Eye on Yahoo's Earnings," *Yahoo! Tech*, July 20, 2009, http://tech.yahoo.com/news/nf/20090720/tc_nf/67859 (accessed August 3, 2009).

42. "Yahoo-Microsoft Deal," *New York Times*, July 30, 2009, http://topics.nytimes.com/top/news/business/companies/yahoo_inc/yahoo-microsoft-deal/index.html (accessed August 3, 2009).

43. Michael R. Solomon, *Consumer Behavior: Buying, Having, and Being*, 8th ed. (Upper Saddle River, NJ: Pearson Prentice Hall, 2009), 184.

44. Ron Brauner, "B2B Buying Process: 8 Stages of the Business Sales Funnel," http://www.ronbrauner.com/?p=68 (accessed August 1, 2009).

45. Ron Brauner, "B2B Buying Process: 8 Stages of the Business Sales Funnel," http://www.ronbrauner.com/?p=68 (accessed August 1, 2009).

46. Barton A. Weitz, Stephen B. Castleberry, and John F. Tanner, Jr., *Selling: Building Partnerships*, 7th ed. (New York: McGraw-Hill Irwin, 2009), 93.

47. Ron Brauner, "B2B Buying Process: 8 Stages of the Business Sales Funnel," http://www.ronbrauner.com/?p=68 (accessed August 1, 2009).

48. Ron Brauner, "B2B Buying Process: 8 Stages of the Business Sales Funnel," http://www.ronbrauner.com/?p=68 (accessed August 1, 2009).

49. Ron Brauner, "B2B Buying Process: 8 Stages of the Business Sales Funnel," http://www.ronbrauner.com/?p=68 (accessed August 1, 2009).

50. Ron Brauner, "B2B Buying Process: 8 Stages of the Business Sales Funnel," http://www.ronbrauner.com/?p=68 (accessed August 1, 2009).

51. Michael R. Solomon, Greg W. Marshall, and Elnora W. Stuart, *Marketing: Real People, Real Choices*, 5th ed. (Upper Saddle River, NJ: Pearson Prentice Hall, 2008), 190.

52. Geoffrey James, "Is Your Sales Process Obsolete?" BNET, March 30, 2007, http://blogs.bnet.com/salesmachine/?p=30 (accessed August 1, 2009).

53. Bryan Eisenberg, "Buying Is Not a Rational Decision," ClickZ, November 26, 2001, http://www.clickz.com/927221 (accessed August 1, 2009).

54. Geoffrey James, "Is Your Sales Process Obsolete?" BNET, March 30, 2007, http://blogs.bnet.com/salesmachine/?p=30 (accessed August 1, 2009).

55. Mark Penn, "New Info Shoppers," January 8, 2009, *Wall Street Journal*, http://online.wsj.com/article/SB123144483005365353.html?mod=dist_smartbrief# (accessed August 1, 2009).

56. Geoffrey James, "Is Your Sales Process Obsolete?" BNET, March 30, 2007, http://blogs.bnet.com/salesmachine/?p=30 (accessed August 1, 2009).

57. BrightSightGroup, "Jeff Howe: Crowdsourcing," video, July 6, 2008, http://www.youtube.com/watch?v=F0-UtNg3ots (accessed August 3, 2009).

58. Will Park, "Apple Bans Hundreds of Spammer's iPhone Apps," *Into Mobile*, August 3, 2009, http://www.intomobile.com/2009/08/03/apple-bans-hundreds-of-spammers-iphone-apps.html (accessed August 3, 2009).

59. Daniel Ionescu, "Android Market Hits 20,000 Apps Milestone," *PC World*, December 16, 2009, http://www.pcworld.com/article/184808/android_market_hits_20000_apps_milestone.html (accessed December 20, 2009).

60. Trendwatching.com, http://trendwatching.com (accessed August 9, 2009).

61. Bryan Eisenberg, "Buying Is Not a Rational Decision," ClickZ, November 26, 2001, http://www.clickz.com/927221 (accessed August 1, 2009).

62. "Fear of Buying," Selling Power Sales Management eNewsletter, August 18, 2003, http://www.sellingpower.com/content/newsletter/issue.php?pc=296 (accessed March 16, 2010).

63. "Fear of Buying," *Selling Power*, August 18, 2003, http://www.sellingpower.com/content/newsletter/issue.php?pc=296 (accessed June 21, 2010).

64. Norm Brodsky, "Listen and Earn," *Inc.*, March 1, 1997, http://www.inc.com/magazine/19980301/878.html (accessed August 9, 2009).

65. "Beyond the B2B Buying Funnel: Exciting New Research About How Companies Make Complex Purchases," Marketo, April 22, 2009, http://blog.marketo.com/blog/2009/04/beyond-the-b2b-buying-funnel-exciting-new-research-about-how-companies-make-complex-purchases.html (accessed August 1, 2009).

66. "Fear of Buying," *Selling Power*, August 18, 2003, http://www.sellingpower.com/content/newsletter/issue.php?pc=296 (accessed June 21, 2010).

67. "Beyond the B2B Buying Funnel: Exciting New Research About How Companies Make Complex Purchases," Marketo, April 22, 2009, http://blog.marketo.com/blog/2009/04/beyond-the-b2b-buying-funnel-exciting-new-research-about-how-companies-make-complex-purchases.html (accessed August 1, 2009).

68. "Cash for Clunkers Launch Postponed Due to Computer Crash," *U.S. News and World Report*, July 24, 2009, http://usnews.rankingsandreviews.com/cars-trucks/daily-news/090724-Breaking-News-Cash-for-Clunkers-Launch-Postponed-by-Computer-Crash (accessed August 4, 2009).

69. "Fear of Buying," *Selling Power*, August 18, 2003, http://www.sellingpower.com/content/newsletter/issue.php?pc=296 (accessed June 21, 2010).

70. "Fear of Buying," *Selling Power*, August 18, 2003, http://www.sellingpower.com/content/newsletter/issue.php?pc=296 (accessed June 21, 2010).

71. Bryan Eisenberg, "Buying Is Not a Rational Decision," ClickZ, November 26, 2001, http://www.clickz.com/927221 (accessed August 1, 2009).

72. Michael R. Solomon, *Conquering Consumerspace: Marketing Strategies for a Branded World* (New York: AMACOM, 2003), 11.

73. Amazon.com, http://www.amazon.com (accessed August 4, 2009).

74. Charles M. Futrell, *Fundamentals of Selling: Customers for Life through Service*, 10th ed. (New York: McGraw-Hill Irwin, 2008), 114.

75. Charles M. Futrell, *Fundamentals of Selling: Customers for Life through Service*, 10th ed. (New York: McGraw-Hill Irwin, 2008), 114.

76. Charles M. Futrell, *Fundamentals of Selling: Customers for Life through Service*, 10th ed. (New York: McGraw-Hill Irwin, 2008), 114.

77. Amazon.com, http://www.amazon.com (accessed August 4, 2009).

78. Laura Clampitt Douglas, "Marketing Features vs. Benefits," *Entrepreneur*, http://www.entrepreneur.com/magazine/homeofficemagcom/2000/december/34942.html (accessed August 4, 2009).

79. Bryan Eisenberg, "Want The to Buy? Sell Benefits," ClickZ.com, April 9, 2001, http://www.clickz.com/840121 (accessed August 4, 2009).

80. Netflix, http://www.netflix.com (accessed July 12, 2009).

81. Charles M. Futrell, *Fundamentals of Selling: Customers for Life through Service*, 10th ed. (New York: McGraw-Hill Irwin, 2008), 116.

82. Ben Stewart, "2009 Nissan Cube vs. Kia Soul vs. 2009 Scion xB: 300-Mile Fuel-Economy Test-Drive," *Popular Mechanics*, February 24, 2009, http://www.popularmechanics.com/blogs/automotive_news/4306145.html (accessed August 4, 2009).

83. Laura Clampitt Douglas, "Marketing Features vs. Benefits," *Entrepreneur*, http://www.entrepreneur.com/magazine/homeofficemagcom/2000/december/34942.html (accessed August 4, 2009).

84. Laura Clampitt Douglas, "Marketing Features vs. Benefits," *Entrepreneur*, http://www.entrepreneur.com/magazine/homeofficemagcom/2000/december/34942.html (accessed August 4, 2009).

85. IMDB, *Jerry McGuire*, written and directed by Cameron Crowe, released December 13, 1996, http://www.imdb.com/title/tt0116695 (accessed August 4, 2009).

86. Bryan Eisenberg, "Buying Is Not a Rational Decision," ClickZ, November 26, 2001, http://www.clickz.com/927221 (accessed August 1, 2009).

87. "Job Search: Back Up Your Resume with a Portfolio," WorkForce2.org, http://www.workforce2.org/resume-portfolio.htm (accessed August 5, 2009).

88. Maureen Crawford Hentz, "How to Obtain and Use References and Recommendation Letters," Quintessential Careers, http://www.quintcareers.com/references_recommendation_letters.html (accessed August 5, 2009)

89. Resumemic09, "What Is a Portfolio and How Can I Use One to Get a Job?" video, July 24, 2009, http://www.youtube.com/watch?v=PrHI0m0B1I4 (accessed August 5, 2009).

90. Peggy Klaus, *Brag: The Art of Tooting Your Own Horn Without Blowing It* (New York: Hachette Book Group, 2003), front cover.

91. "How to Create an Awesome Work Portfolio," ManifestYourPotential.com, http://www.manifestyourpotential.com/en/work/tensteps/4preparework/howto/jobsearch/portfolio.htm (accessed August 5, 2009).

CHAPTER 7
Prospecting and Qualifying: The Power to Identify Your Customers

Video Ride-Along with Lisa Peskin, Sales Trainer at Business Development University

You met Lisa Peskin in Chapter 1. She has over twenty years of experience in sales and sales training at companies such as Automatic Data Processing, Inc. (ADP), Commercial Direct, and Interbay Funding. Lisa is now a sales trainer and works with companies to help increase their sales. She understands the importance of always identifying potential new customers. Without new customers, businesses would ultimately die. Great salespeople are constantly looking for new prospective customers everywhere. By the way, listen closely to Lisa's advice, as the same methods that help generate new customers are the same ones that can help you find your prospective employer.

Ride along with Lisa and hear her tips for identifying new customers.

View the video online at: http://www.youtube.com/embed/kb7pjzqfmdc

---

7.1 It's a Process: Seven Steps to Successful Selling

Learning Objective

1. Explain the role of the seven steps of the selling process.

You may have been surprised if someone told you that movie scripts, regardless of the genre, all follow the same basic formula—the same sequence of events—almost down to the minute: after three minutes, the central question of the movie is introduced; after twenty-seven more minutes, the main character will set off on a new path; fifteen minutes more, and something symbolic will happen; and so on.[1] It's hard to believe that *The Fast and the Furious* would follow the same formula as *The Notebook*, but once you know what to look for, you'll see that the structure holds up. Clearly, Hollywood has come to learn that this particular structure is the secret to keeping the audience's attention, earning positive reviews, and selling movies.

In the same way, almost all selling—regardless of the product that's being sold—follows a particular sequence of steps. It's a simple but logical framework that has been the accepted model for almost a hundred years.[2] Salespeople have adapted the specifics of the process as culture and technology have changed, but the fact that they've followed the same basic model has for so long testifies to its effectiveness. The **selling process** is generally divided into seven steps that, once you understand them, will empower you to sell virtually anything you want and satisfy your customers:

1. Prospect and qualify
2. Preapproach
3. Approach
4. Presentation
5. Overcome objections
6. Close the sale
7. Follow-up

Each step of the seven-step process is covered thoroughly in this and the next six chapters so that you can learn the details of each step and how to apply them in various selling situations.

FIGURE 7.1 Seven-Step Selling Process[3]

When the Seven-Step Selling Process Is Used

As you learned in Chapter 3, the sales process is adaptive, which means that each situation may be different and salespeople have to adapt and understand what is important to each customer and where each is in the buying process. But in order for a salesperson to use adaptive selling, he or she

---

seven-step selling process

A sequence of steps that builds a framework for selling.

must thoroughly understand the steps in the selling process and how each works to can use them effectively.

The Evolving Role of Technology in the Selling Process

While the basics of the selling process have remained the same over the years, the methods of communication and the way people interact are quickly evolving with the use of the interactive capabilities on the Internet by customers and salespeople alike. Each step now includes much more collaboration between customers and salespeople (and even between customers) with the use of social networking, consumer reviews, wikis, and other community-based tools. This technology allows salespeople to learn more about their customers at each step, and therefore provide more relevant and powerful solutions to customers at each stage of the buying process (covered in Chapter 6).[4]

Business-to-Consumer (B2C) Sales

Let's say you want to buy a gym membership. Maybe you received a promotional offer in the mail, your friends on Facebook have had good things to say about a particular gym, or you picked this club because it's close to home. Whatever the reason, you wander in and ask to speak to the membership director who seems to know a lot about the club and what you might be looking for. After some small talk about the fact that you both live in the same apartment complex, he tells you about the gym's amenities and gives you a tour of the facility. Then, you sit down to discuss pricing options and payment plans. If you have any questions or concerns (i.e., "I noticed there are only three tennis courts. Is there usually a long wait to use one?" or "Why aren't there any kickboxing classes on your class schedule?"), the membership director will attempt to address those. Maybe he will tell you there is occasionally a wait to use the tennis courts at peak times, but you can reserve a spot up to a week in advance, in which case you can get right in. Or maybe he'll say that while they don't have kickboxing classes, they offer Zumba, which is a fun aerobic alternative.

If you're satisfied with his responses, and the price and product meet your needs, you will probably decide to sign a contract. Once you've signed, someone from the club will probably follow up with a call in a few weeks to see if you're satisfied with your experience at their gym, or you may get an e-mail from them with a membership satisfaction survey or a text message about an upcoming event.

The example above is an actual selling situation. Although you may not have realized it while you were reading it, the situation follows the seven-step selling process.

Whether you're buying a gym membership or a car, cell phone service or a new computer, the situation may be different, but the steps in the selling process will follow the same pattern.

Business-to-Business (B2B) Sales

The process isn't only limited to business-to-consumer sales; it's also the process that IBM will use to sell servers to a corporation, that Accenture will use to sell consulting services to a technology company, or that the Coffee Brewers Company will use to sell espresso machines to coffee shops. Imagine you run a chic new restaurant. You get a call from a salesperson who compliments you on the roasted chicken she had at your restaurant last weekend. After some conversation, she asks if you're satisfied with your commercial ovens. You have been having some problems with them and have been doing some casual research online. You know that her company is rated as one of the best oven manufacturers, so you tell her: the ovens are over ten years old, they take a long time to heat up, and they sometimes cook things unevenly.

"Many older ovens have this problem," she says. "Would you be interested in learning about the state-of-the-art commercial ovens our company sells?"

Since you need a solution for your current ovens, you agree to set up an appointment with the salesperson. When the she arrives, you are impressed that she knows so much about your business. She visited your restaurant, reviewed your menu, spoke with some of the wait staff, read reviews on the city magazine Web site, and even had some conversations with some of your patrons on Chef's Blog. She explains that the ovens she sells heat up quickly and use energy more efficiently. She gives you an estimate of your annual savings on energy costs if you switched over to her product line.

You're interested, but you're concerned that the ovens might not cook food evenly. Ovens are a big expense—what happens if you aren't satisfied with the product? The salesperson says you can lease an oven for a trial period at no obligation, and she shows you reviews from other customers on her company's Web site and on some restaurant industry blogs. You feel like this might help you solve your problem, so you agree to lease the machine for four months.

After two months, the salesperson calls to ask if you've been satisfied with the product so far, and she offers you a discount if you sign a contract to purchase two ovens in the next ten days. Since you have been happy with the leased oven and checked out the company's service record online from other current customers, you make the purchase.

As in the gym membership example above, this B2B selling situation follows the seven-step framework. Now, take a minute to review this selling situation in the box below to see exactly how the steps are implemented.

The Seven Steps of Selling

Compare the B2B and B2C examples you just read about. Do you notice a pattern? Although the products and customers were quite different, both salespeople adapted to the situation and the customer's needs, but followed the same seven steps to successfully complete their sales. In fact, you've probably used a version of these seven steps yourself before without even realizing it. Take a look at some real-world selling examples below and how of each of the steps is used.

Step 1: Prospecting and Qualifying

prospecting

Identifying potential buyers for a product or service.

lead

A potential buyer for a product or service that has not yet been qualified.

prospect

A potential buyer for a product or service; also referred to as a qualified lead.

Before planning a sale, a salesperson conducts research to identify the people or companies that might be interested in her product. In the B2B example, before the salesperson called the company, she had to find the company's information somewhere—probably in a local business directory. This step is called **prospecting**, and it's the foundational step for the rest of the sales process. A **lead** is a potential buyer. A **prospect** is a lead that is qualified or determined to be ready, willing, and able to buy. The prospecting and qualifying step relates to the needs awareness step in the buying process described in Chapter 6. In other words, in a perfect world, you are identifying customers who are in the process of or have already identified a need.

Undoubtedly, when the salesperson called the target customer to discuss his ovens (in the example, you were the customer), she asked some questions to **qualify** him as a prospect, or determine whether he has the desire and ability to buy the product or service. This is the other component to step one. What happens if the customer is not interested in the salesperson's product, or he's interested but his business is struggling financially and doesn't have the resources for a big purchase? Perhaps he is only an employee, not the manager, and he doesn't have the authority to make the purchasing decision. In this case, he is no longer a prospect, and the salesperson will move on to another lead. Salespeople qualify their prospects so they can focus their sales efforts on the people who are most likely to buy. After all, spending an hour discussing the capabilities of your company's ovens with a lead that is about to go out of business would be a waste of time. It's much more fruitful to invest your time with a **qualified prospect**, one who has the desire or ability to buy the product or service.

Step 2: Preapproach

The **preapproach** is the "doing your homework" part of the process. A good salesperson researches his prospect, familiarizing himself with the customer's needs and learning all the relevant background info he can about the individual or business.[5] Remember that in the B2B example, the salesperson knew important information about the restaurant beforehand. She came prepared with a specific idea as to how her service could help the prospect and gave a tailored presentation.

Step 3: Approach

First impressions (e.g., the first few minutes of a sales call) are crucial to building the client's trust.[6] If you've ever asked someone on a first date (yes, this is a selling situation), chances are you didn't call the person and start the conversation off with the question, "Hey, do you want to go out on Saturday night?" Such an abrupt method would turn most people away, and you probably would not score the date you were hoping for. Similarly, as a professional salesperson, you would almost never make a pitch right away; instead, you'd work to establish a rapport with the customer first. This usually involves introductions, making some small talk, asking a few warm-up questions, and generally explaining who you are and whom you represent.[7],[8] This is called the **approach**.

qualifying

Determining whether a lead has the desire and ability to buy your product or service.

qualified prospect

A prospect a salesperson has determined has the desire and ability to buy the product or service.

preapproach

The preparation and research a salesperson does before making the sales call.

approach

The first few minutes of a sales call, during which the salesperson explains her purpose for coming and establishes a rapport.

FIGURE 7.2
The approach may be on the phone, in person, or via e-mail or other online method such as a social network.

© 2010 Jupiterimages Corporation

Step 4: Presentation

There's a good deal of preparation involved before a salesperson ever makes her pitch or **presentation**, but the presentation is where the research pays off and her idea for the prospect comes alive. By the time she presents her product, she will understand her customer's needs well enough to be sure she's offering a solution the customer could use. If you're a real estate agent selling a house and your customers are an older, retired couple, you won't take them to see a house with many bedrooms, several flights of stairs to climb, and a huge yard to keep up—nor will you show them around a trendy loft in a busy part of town. The presentation should be tailored to the customer, explaining how the product meets that person or company's needs. It might involve a tour (as in this real estate example), a product demonstration, videos, PowerPoint presentations, or letting the customer actually look at or interact with the product. At this point, the customer is using the information that is being shared as part of his evaluation of possible solutions.

Step 5: Handling Objections

After you've made your sales presentation, it's natural for your customer to have some hesitations or concerns called **objections**. Good salespeople look at objections as *opportunities* to further understand and respond to customers' needs.[9] For instance, maybe you're trying to convince a friend to come camping with you.

"I'd like to go" your friend says, "but I've got a big project I need to finish at work, and I was planning to spend some time at the office this weekend."

"That's no problem," you tell him. "I'm free next weekend, too. Why don't we plan to go then, once your project's out of the way?"

Step 6: Closing the Sale

Eventually, if your customer is convinced your product will meet her needs, you **close** by agreeing on the terms of the sale and finishing up the transaction.[10] This is the point where the potential gym member signs her membership agreement, the restaurant owner decides to purchase the ovens, or your friend says, "Sure, let's go camping next weekend!" Sometimes a salesperson has to make several **trial closes** during a sales call, addressing further objections before the customer is ready to buy.[11] It may turn out, even at this stage in the process, that the product doesn't actually meet the customer's needs. The important—and sometimes challenging—part of closing is that the seller has to actually *ask* if the potential customer is willing to make the purchase.[12] When the close is successful, this step clearly aligns with the purchase step in the buying process.

Step 7: Following Up

OK, so you've completed a landscaping job for your customer or sold him a car or installed the software that meets his needs. While it might seem like you've accomplished your goal, the customer relationship has only begun. The **follow-up** is an important part of assuring customer satisfaction, retaining customers, and prospecting for new customers. This might mean sending a thank-you note, calling the customer to make sure a product was received in satisfactory condition, or checking in to make sure a service is meeting the customer's expectations. This is the follow-up e-mail you get from Netflix every time you return a movie by mail. It's Amazon's invitation to "rate your transaction" after you receive your Amazon order. Follow-up also includes logistical details like signing contracts, setting up delivery or installation dates, and drawing up a timeline. From the buyer's perspective, the follow-up is the implementation step in the buying process. Good follow-up helps ensure additional sales, customer referrals, and positive reviews[13] and actually leads you back to the first step in the selling process because it provides the opportunity to learn about new needs for this customer or new customers through referrals.

Key Takeaways

- The **seven-step selling process** refers to the sequence of steps salespeople follow each time they make a sale. The process gives you the power to successfully sell almost anything.
- The first step of the selling process, **prospecting** and **qualifying**, involves searching for potential customers and deciding whether they have the ability and desire to make a purchase. The people and organizations that meet these criteria are **qualified prospects**.
- Before making a sales call, it is important to "do your homework" by researching your customer and planning what you are going to say; this is the **preapproach**.
- The **approach** is your chance to make a first impression by introducing yourself, explaining the purpose of your call or visit, and establishing a rapport with your prospect.
- Your research and preparation pays off during the **presentation**, when you propose your sales solution to your prospect.
- Your prospect will naturally have **objections**, which you should look at as opportunities to better understand and respond to his or her needs.
- Once you overcome objections, you **close** the sale by agreeing on the terms and finalizing the transaction.
- The sales process doesn't end with the close; **follow-up** (i.e., ensuring customer satisfaction and working out the logistics of delivery, installation, and timelines) is essential to retaining existing customers and finding new ones.

Exercises

1. Think of a personal interaction in which you sold someone on an idea (e.g., a vacation, a choice of movies, or a date). Explain how the seven steps applied to this particular situation.
2. Consider the last major purchase you made. Did the salesperson use the seven steps? In what ways could he or she have done a better job? What eventually sold you on the product?
3. Imagine you are trying to sell season tickets to your local ballpark. After you present the product to your prospects, a middle-aged married couple, they tell you they are very interested but are concerned they might be out of town on some of the weekends when there are home games, and they don't want their tickets to go to waste. What solutions could you offer to overcome their objections?
4. Discuss the difference between a prospect and a customer.

7.2 Prospecting: A Vital Role in the Selling Process

Learning Objective

1. Understand the role prospecting plays in the selling process.

Imagine you decide to build a house from the ground up. After designing your ideal house, of course it would be nice if you could snap your fingers and get to the fun part: watching the finishing touches come together. But before the walls go up you have to make detailed plans and measurements, find your materials and negotiate with contractors, and lay the foundation. All these things require patience, time, and effort, but these steps are absolutely necessary for the project to move forward.

Planning and laying a foundation is a little like prospecting and qualifying. Finding leads (or people who *might* be prospects) is the most vital part of the selling process—you can't make a sale without identifying the people to whom you'll be selling.[14] In other words, without prospecting, nothing else can happen. Yet, unlike laying a foundation, prospecting doesn't happen just once; it's a constant process. Businesses lose some customers every year for a variety of reasons: customers may no longer need the product or service, have the financial means to purchase the product or service, or live or do business in the area, or the business may no longer be open. So if you haven't been building your prospect list, you won't have new customers to replace the ones you lose. More than this, finding new prospects is the only way you can increase your sales and expand your business.

The Value of a Lead

Think of the last time you went to the store to make a major purchase and you started by browsing the products. A salesperson probably approached you with the standard "Can I help you?" and you may have responded with the equally standard "No, thanks. I'm just looking." Chances are good that the salesperson left you alone after that, very likely assuming you weren't genuinely interested in making a purchase. Most people—salespeople and customers alike—are surprised to learn that over two-thirds of shoppers who give the "just looking" response end up purchasing the product within a week.[15] In other words, these customers are valuable leads, and all too often their business goes to a competitor.

Let's say you are planning to buy a new refrigerator. That's generally not the kind of purchase you make on the spot; you will probably go to a number of stores to compare products and prices first. If you tell the salesperson at the second store that you're just looking, you may then go to a third store and decide you're ready to buy. As a customer, if the vendors seem more or less equal, you will base your purchasing decision on price, product features, convenience, or a combination of these things. But imagine the salesperson at the second store who took the time to determine your specific needs, wrote down your contact information, and followed up with you. It's very likely she would make a sale. Her products might be quite similar to her competitors', but if she goes out of her way to provide you with a solution, you have a reason to buy from her over someone else.

Now let's change hats. What does knowing this information mean for you as a salesperson? Most importantly, it means that you should never write off a lead until you are *certain* he can't be qualified as a prospect. If you work in a showroom that sells only high-end cars like Lexus or BMW and a potential customer walks in wearing torn jeans and a T-shirt, you might be tempted to mentally disqualify him, assuming he won't have the money to buy such expensive cars. But appearances are often misleading, and you won't know whether or not your lead is *actually* qualified until you ask some specific, qualifying questions. When you realize that a lead is the only thing you can turn into a sale, you also realize just how valuable every lead is.

This is true for both B2C *and* B2B sales, wherein 30 percent to 50 percent of companies that see and respond to business-specific ads end up purchasing the product or service about which they've inquired within one or two years. This percentage is nothing to sneeze at. Yet, according to businesses, only about 1 percent to 5 percent of the ad-related inquiries they get from businesses translate into sales.[16] That's a big gap. In other words, a lot of valuable leads can slip through your fingers if you don't follow up and qualify them.

The Sales Funnel

If you talked to a guidance counselor when you were applying to colleges, he probably told you to consider several and then apply to a number of schools (more than just two or three) even though you would only end up choosing one school in the end. This is because not all the schools that you

FIGURE 7.3
Prospecting and qualifying are the foundation for a solid selling process.

© 2010 Jupiterimages Corporation

apply to end up being a good fit. Sometimes you aren't accepted, sometimes you are accepted but don't get an ideal financial package, and sometimes as you learn more about a school you decide it isn't the right one for you. Whatever the reason, you start out by considering many schools and generally end up deciding between a few.

The same can be said of the selling process. In fact, the process is often compared to a funnel. You start out with many leads, and after gathering more information, you come up with a smaller list of qualified prospects. As you communicate with these potential customers and work toward a solution, some will turn out to be more likely to buy than others. It's common sense to assume that you will have more leads than you have buyers since not all leads turn into customers. The concept of the **sales funnel** is a helpful way to visualize the process of finding and qualifying your customers and effectively illustrates the value of identifying a large pool of potential prospects. If you don't bother to find more than a handful of leads, you limit your chances of ever closing a sale no matter how much effort you put into your sales presentation. It's a common temptation that most people want the results without having to put in the foundational work of finding and contacting prospects.

> **sales funnel**
>
> An illustration of the way the sales process begins with a large pool of prospects and ends with a more focused number of buyers.

FIGURE 7.4 Traditional Sales Funnel

But wait a minute, you might think, "Isn't it hugely inefficient to spend time and effort communicating with so many prospects with the expectation that only a handful of those will turn out to be buyers?" This is also true, which is why qualifying and prioritizing your prospects is such an important part of the sales process. Technological tools like collaborative communities and other online resources can help you identify, qualify, and prioritize prospects. But you might wonder how do you decide which prospects you should invest your time in pursuing. To begin with, you should create a profile of your ideal buyer.[17]

Create a Profile of Your Ideal Buyer

- What particular qualities and characteristics will define this individual or company?
- What specific problems would this buyer have that your product could solve?
- In what ways should the buyer be compatible with you or your organization?

For instance, if your company sells expensive, high-quality kitchen utensils, the average college student *won't* fit your ideal profile. While a young adult living away from home for the first time might have something in common with your ideal customer, the college student likely won't have the budget or desire to go out and get the top-of-the-line products.

Your ideal customer profile will help you prioritize and target your efforts because it provides a model against which you can measure your leads to determine whether a potential customer is worth pursuing. If you focus your energy on prospecting and qualifying, which is learning more about your target prospects, you will save valuable time and resources, which you can then devote to giving your customers a more satisfying experience. Effective prospecting and qualifying empower you to invest in the opportunities that count.[18]

Video Link

Prioritizing Leads

Understand how to use the sales funnel to maximize leads.

http://www.sellingpower.com/content/video/?date=2/9/2007

Now that you understand the concept of prospecting and why it's important, you'll find the next sections helpful as they will provide you with tools to help you find prospects and qualify prospects.

Key Takeaways

- Prospecting is the most vital part of the selling process. Without prospects, you won't be able to make sales, and without constantly searching for new prospects, you won't be able to replace the customers you lose and grow your business.
- A **lead**, or **prospect**, is the only thing you can turn into a sale, so it's important to follow up with your leads. Don't write someone off without legitimately qualifying him.
- The concept of the **sales funnel** illustrates the value of generating a large pool of leads because many of your prospects won't qualify or will drop out during the selling process.
- You should begin searching for leads by building an ideal customer profile to help you target your search efforts.

Exercises

1. Describe the ideal customer for the following products or services:
   - iPod Touch
   - Ferrari sports car
   - GEICO car insurance
   - Flat World Knowledge textbooks
2. Discuss the sales funnel and why leads are important to the selling process.
3. Discuss the difference between a prospect and a customer.
4. If someone goes into a Best Buy store and looks at the home theater systems, is he a lead or a prospect? Why?
5. Visit a local jeweler and shop for a watch. What questions does the salesperson ask to qualify you as a prospect?

7.3 Go Fish: Resources to Help You Find Your Prospects

Learning Objective

1. Identify resources to use when prospecting.

In the last section, you read that prospecting can be compared to setting up the plans and laying the foundation for a building project. You could also say that prospecting is a little like going to class or making your bed—you've got to do it, and you know that it won't be long before you're doing it again (assuming you make your bed regularly!). Because prospecting is one of those jobs that's never truly finished, it's helpful to draw on a number of sources and be creative about the places where you find your leads.

Where to Find Prospects

Knowing your ideal customer and where he or she is likely to go for information will allow you to choose the best prospecting sources for your business. It helps to *be* your customer. Imagine yourself in your prospect's shoes and think about where you would go for information. For instance, if you are a photographer who specializes in professional yearbook and graduation pictures, you might want to set up a Facebook account so you can let students in local schools know about your services.[19] Meanwhile, if you're in B2B sales and your ideal prospects are car dealerships in northern California, you might build up your professional network by joining the local branch of the National Auto Dealers Association or by joining some community organizations in your city.

Prospecting takes knowledge and creativity, so start your prospecting and qualifying with the top ten power prospecting list below. No matter what business you're in, think of this section as your GPS for finding the leads that will fuel your business growth.

Top Ten Power Prospecting List

1. Existing customers
2. Referrals
3. Networking and social networking
4. Business directories in print
5. Online databases and directories
6. Newspapers, trade publications, and business journals
7. Trade shows and events
8. Advertising and direct mail
9. Cold calling
10. Being a subject matter expert

Power Prospecting Source #1: Existing Customers

It costs five times more to attract a new customer than to keep an existing customer.[20] So it stands to reason that your best new customers are your existing customers. Salespeople who make an effort to deliver excellent customer service during *and* after a sale know the secret that some of their best prospects are the customers they already have. To keep and develop your existing customers, love them, service them, be partners with them, live and breathe in their world, understand them, and anticipate their needs, and you will succeed in sales.

One of the keys to retaining your best customers is to keep in touch with your customers' needs and update your solutions as their needs change. Say you work for a marketing company that offers a variety of services to businesses. One of your customers, a record company, is using your printing services, but they're turning to another organization for their public relations needs. If you're aware of this, your existing customer is now a prospect for additional sales. You might tell the record company, "You know, your current PR people are setting up events and concerts to increase your publicity, and that seems to be working only moderately well. If we were running your PR, we would integrate your events with a variety of other media. For instance, we think a blog would be a hugely effective tool...." If the company is already a loyal customer and you let them know that you are aware of their needs and can offer a better solution, then you may very well make a new sale.

Power Prospecting Source #2: Referrals

There's nothing more powerful than getting information about a product or service from a friend or people you trust before you buy. Think about the last time you bought a printer. You probably checked out the customer reviews on Amazon, asked your friends, checked out some blogs, and maybe even got some insights on Twitter (in 140 characters or less). Before you bought the Hewlett-Packard (HP) OfficeJet 6310, you knew exactly what to expect from people who have bought and used the product, and you learned that if you buy it at Office Depot, you get free shipping and two free ink cartridges. Although you never shopped at Office Depot before, you were sold before you even clicked "buy now" on the Office Depot's Web site. Imagine that you didn't even come in contact with HP or Office Depot. You made your purchase based solely on the information from others. The power of the referral cannot be underestimated.

Referrals and word-of-mouth advertising have always been one of the most effective—and cost-efficient—ways to get new customers. It used to be that the circle of referrals was limited to people who used your product or service in a given geographic area. The Internet has amplified that network, especially with user-generated content such as communities, blogs, customer ratings and reviews, and social networking sites. So as a salesperson, you have to think creatively about all of resources you have to generate referrals.

Want to see how it works? When Naked Pizza, a small takeout and delivery operation in New Orleans, decided they wanted to compete with the city's chain pizza places, they turned to their existing customer base for sales prospects by putting their Twitter address on every pizza box that went out the door. As Jeff, Randy, and Brock, the company's founders put it, "Even your most core customers must be continually and softly nudged."[21] The prospecting effort has been a huge success with their existing customers posting tweets that have introduced the brand to new customers. The Twitter-enabled follow-ups allowed Naked Pizza to continue the conversation and ensure that a greater number of first-time buyers become repeat customers—and that *they* spread the word to more new customers. Talk about a megaphone!

Whether you sell pizza or insurance, if your existing customers are happy, they're usually happy to refer you to their friends, online or offline. Consider Flycaster & Company, a Florida-based branding and advertising agency for businesses. For a number of years now, almost 100 percent of the firm's new customers have been referred to them by friends and colleagues. According to John Spence, one of the company's managers, referrals are the "best possible" source of prospects for any B2B business.[22]

So let your customers speak for you. Their voices will be heard by people you could never reach.

Power Prospecting Source #3: Networking and Social Networking

Networking works.

The art of networking, developing mutually beneficial relationships, can be a valuable prospecting tool, not only for retaining old prospects, but also for connecting with new ones. The larger and more diverse your network becomes, the bigger your pool of potential prospects. Your networking connections often become sources of referrals for your business, just as you will become a referral source for theirs.

If you're a member of the American Chemical Society and you work for a chemical supply company, you might use your membership to get acquainted with chemists who work at a variety of labs. You could offer them your card and let them know that you provide supply discounts for fellow Chemical Society members. Now these prospects will be more likely to buy their chemical supplies from you than from a company or individual with whom they have no personal connection. If one of your customers needs a chemist with a particular specialty, you, in turn, will be able to refer him to someone in your network. Joining a professional trade association is one simple way to network with others in your field, or with prospects in your target industry.

If your business is location specific, joining community organizations can also be a valuable tool for connecting with local business leaders and prospects. Consider service organizations (like the Rotary Club), fraternity organizations, and other affinity groups that will allow you to build relationships with members of the community.

What about social networking? You're probably well acquainted with online social networking sites like Facebook or MySpace, but you may be less familiar with the ways people leverage these tools in a professional capacity. According to professional networking expert Clara Shih, online social networks can be an effective means of prospecting for sales with organizations. After all, the decision makers at any organization are *individuals* with whom you can build relationships (remember, you learned in Chapter 3 that even though it's called business-to-business, buying decisions are made person-to-person, so relationships matter).[23] By connecting socially with key individuals, not only can you open lines of communications with potential customers, but you can also build your knowledge of your prospect base.

Professional networking sites like LinkedIn are increasingly important as well. (In fact, the *Selling U* section of this chapter includes information about how you can use professional social networking sites to help you network to find a job.) And there are many industry-specific networking sites you can join, like Sermo for doctors or INmobile.org for people in the wireless industry.[24] Your profile on professional networking sites becomes a tool for selling yourself as a brand. These sites allow you to list your education, professional experience, and testimonials from satisfied customers, and as you add contacts, you become connected to their contacts, allowing your network to grow.[25]

Link

This article includes examples of how some major companies are using Twitter to drive sales.

http://www.sellingpower.com/content/newsletter/issue.php?pc=1007

Power Prospecting Source #4: Business Directories in Print

FIGURE 7.5

American City Business Journals publish the *Book of Lists* in cities across the country. The book includes lists of local companies by category including fastest-growing privately held companies, women-owned companies, nonprofit organizations, and more. The book is also available online at http://www.bizjournals.com.

Source: Philadelphia Business Journal, used with permission.

North American Industry Classification System (NAICS)

System that classifies businesses by sector and industry. NAICS and SIC codes are helpful ways to search directories for businesses that fit your ideal prospect profile.

Standard Industrial Classification (SIC)

System that classifies businesses by sector and industry. NAICS and SIC codes are helpful ways to search directories for businesses that fit your ideal prospect profile.

trade association

An organization whose members are individuals or businesses that operate in a specific industry.

Forget Google for a minute. It might surprise you to know that your local library can actually be a potential goldmine for finding prospects in B2B sales. If you spend even twenty minutes with a knowledgeable librarian, he can point you to business lists, journals, and business directories that will help you generate a pool of leads to contact. Your ideal customer profile is an important guiding tool here.

If you want customer information that's location specific, check out your local chamber of commerce listing. It's one of the best sources for finding local businesses. If the listing is not at the local library, chances are the librarian will have the contact information for the chamber office.

You can also review business lists and directories published by local newspapers and regional business journals. Local newspapers and their Web sites often provide listings of local businesses along with key information about the company. Also, the *Book of Lists* is published locally by the American City Business Journals in several cities—for example, the *Philadelphia Business Journal* publishes the *Book of Lists* for the Philadelphia, South Jersey, and Delaware area. It is a book that includes lists of companies organized by groupings. For instance, the fastest-growing companies, minority-owned businesses, and lists of companies by industry such as video production companies, health care companies, public relations agencies, law firms, and more are included with the contact information, profiles, and key facts for specific businesses in your state or city. You can generally find these books at your local library, and they're an excellent source for digging up prospects that most closely match your ideal profile. Business lists are also published by other business journals such as *Crain's* in some key cities or are available online (also see Power Prospecting Source #6: Trade Journals and Business Journals below).

If you want to search businesses by industry, ask a reference librarian to help you look up the **North American Industry Classification System (NAICS)** code and the **Standard Industrial Classification (SIC)** code that most closely matches your ideal prospect's business—or access the indexes online, and bring the codes with you to the library. NAICS and SIC codes are numbering systems that classify businesses by their particular industry, so they can be valuable search criteria to mine general business directories (e.g., *Ward's Business Directory of U.S. Private and Public Companies*) for specific kinds of companies. For example, you could use the SIC code 6371 to find all businesses that deal with pension, health, and welfare funds.[26] You can also search through *industry-specific* directories like the *Standard Directory of Advertisers*, and you can check out professional **trade associations** related to your prospect profile. These organizations, whose members all operate in a particular industry, are especially good places to look if your ideal prospect is a smaller business because smaller businesses and individuals are the most likely to join. Ask your librarian if she can access a copy of *Gale's Encyclopedia of Associations*, which lists more than 160,000 trade organizations. Finding a relevant association should be no problem, as you can find a professional organization for virtually any industry you can think of. Even the pecan shellers of America have a professional association![27]

Power Prospecting Source #5: Online Databases and Directories

Going to the library can be hugely helpful because it gives you access to people who are pros at finding information. Also, the *added* perk is that your library will probably give you free access to several online business directories and databases.[28] Of course you can search these directories from the comfort of your own home or office, but if you want the deluxe package—the most up-to-date directories that cover industries of all types nationwide—you'll have to pay a price. Online business directories, such as those listed in the table below, are searchable by industry and will give you access to company contact info, number of employees, financial standing, industry rankings, names of executives, and other company profile information. Most of these directories allow you to search businesses by SIC or NAICS codes.

So how do you know which business directory to use? For one thing, it helps to know whether your ideal prospect would be a private company or a public company or whether it could be either. Is your ideal prospect a large organization that attracts top executives? In this case, you'll mostly be searching for **public companies**—companies that sell stocks and bonds to the general public. Public companies are required to file financial information and other company reports with the U.S. government, so these organizations are easier to find in general business directories, and their directory listings usually provide more detailed company information.[29] However, not all large companies are publicly owned. State Farm Insurance and Cargill Foods, for example, are both private companies.[30] If you're only interested in smaller, local businesses, you will be dealing with **private companies**, or companies that aren't owned by the public. In this case, some directories and databases will be more helpful to you than others.

Another thing to consider is whether you want the option to refine your search to include a number of criteria closely matching your ideal prospect profile. Several online databases allow you to input multiple search terms like location, company size, and minimum and maximum sales volumes.

public company

A company that sells stocks and bonds to the general public.

TABLE 7.1 Online Databases and Directories for Prospecting

Database or Directory	Good source for private companies	Good source for public companies	Description
infoUSA http://home.infousa.com	X	X	• **For B2B prospecting**: Allows you to search for businesses by criteria such as industry, SIC, sales volume, and number of employees. Particularly useful for finding smaller companies. Their Web site offers a video with instructions on how to build a business list. • **For B2C**: Provides phone and e-mail contact lists for consumers by criteria like income, geography, and/or interest. See their instructional video for more detail.
Proquest http://www.proquest.com	X	X	• Allows researchers to perform advanced searches based on a number of criteria, such as company financial information, industry trends, and market research. • Option for subscription to automatic news alerts that will keep you up-to-date on your target industries and prospects.
Bizjournals http://www.bizjournals.com/bizjournals/sales_marketing/prospecting	X	X	• Offers several directories that are searchable by industry. • Allows you to subscribe to company-specific and industry-specific e-mail alerts. • Option to create a customized prospect list by specific search criteria. • Provides access to local Books of Lists for location-specific company profiles.
Hoovers http://www.hoovers.com	X	X	• **For B2B**: Contains directories that are searchable by industry, region, and other characteristics; also provides detailed information about companies including address, phone number, key decision makers, financial data, business strategy, competitive information, and more. • **For B2C**: Provides phone and e-mail contact lists for consumers by criteria like income, geography, and/or interest.
Standard & Poor's http://www.netadvantage.standardandpoors.com	X	X	• Directory that is searchable by a number of criteria, including NAICS code. • Has data on more than 85,000 private companies. • Includes biographies of corporate executives and directors.
D&B Prospector http://www.dnb.com/us/dbproducts/sales_marketing/find.html	X	X	• Option to search using over thirty-five search criteria to create an ideal prospect profile as a search tool.

Database or Directory	Good source for private companies	Good source for public companies	Description
Mergent Online http://www.mergentonline.com	X	X	• Directory that includes domestic and international annual reports from 1996 to the present.
Directory of Corporate Affiliations http://www.corporateaffiliations.com	X	X	• Directories searchable by location, revenue, industry, NAICS and SIC codes, and so on. • Especially good for finding out about key individuals in your target companies. • Search tool for finding out about company relationships and outside vendor relationships.

Power Prospecting Source #6: Trade Publications and Business Journals

FIGURE 7.6

Business journals such as the *Philadelphia Business Journal* can be an excellent source of leads. Business journals for various cities are available at http://www.bizjournals.com.

Source: Philadelphia Business Journal, used with permission.

Where could you go to learn that three bottled beverage companies have recently lightened their package designs, that a new biodegradable shrink film is now on the market, and that the Pharmaceutical Packaging Forum has chosen a location for its next event? These definitely aren't top headlines on Yahoo! But to people in the packaging and packing materials industry, this is important news, and many of them use Web sites like Packworld.com to stay updated. **Trade publications**, journals geared toward people who work in a certain industry, and **trade Web sites** are good sources for netting prospects. For instance, if you work for a company that designs food and beverage packaging, and your department specializes in bottle design, you might read an article on Packworld.com and find out that Pepsi has released a new, eco-friendly bottle design for its Aquafina product that uses 50 percent less plastic than the 2002 version.[31] You decide to make a call to some managers at competing companies like Fiji. You tell these prospects that you've read about

Trade publications

A publication (online or in print) targeted to professionals in a particular industry.

trade Web sites

Web sites with content that is focused on a specific industry.

their competitor's new bottle design and ask if they are interested in some packaging updates as well, which will help save on shipping costs and provide some good PR.

Many industry trade journals offer free e-mail newsletters or even free copies of the magazine. If you don't know the best trade journals to read in the industry in which you are interested, ask a professor. Your professor will be happy to show you copies of specific trade journals and the corresponding Web sites. It's a good idea to take the time to sign up for the free updates and check to see if the publication offers a free subscription to the magazine.

business journal

A publication offering business news and industry information that is usually specific to a certain region.

But what if your ideal prospects aren't limited to a particular industry but *are* specific to a certain location? In this case, **business journals**, which are often regionally published and offer business news and industry information for particular cities or states, will be helpful. Your local library will undoubtedly have a subscription to one, or even several, business journals for your region. Additionally, Bizjournals.com links you to the Web sites for forty regional business journals.

Power Prospecting Source #7: Trade Shows and Events

trade show

A gathering of resources for people in a particular industry or those who have a common interest in a topic.

If you've ever been to a **trade show** or expo, like a career fair or bridal show, you know they're a good place to find out about products and services about which you might not otherwise be aware (and to get some fun free giveaways while you're at it). While most people who stop by a given booth at an expo might *not* be seriously interested prospects, trade show displays and product demonstrations generate enough strong leads to make this activity a worthwhile prospecting endeavor. For one thing, trade shows are industry-specific events that have the advantage of bringing your target market to you. If you are a horse breeder and you know that an estimated ten thousand visitors will attend the Horse World Expo in Syracuse, New York, you might decide it's worthwhile to go.[32] You could look into giving a presentation about judging horse pedigrees, for instance, or maybe you will pay to set up a booth with videos and photos of the horses you breed and sell.

As a salesperson, you can use trade shows not only to present and demonstrate your products but also to identify and qualify prospects.[33] Asking a few specific questions can help you assess a prospect's needs and determine whether he has a genuine interest—as well as the resources—for buying. Trade show booths usually have a place for leads to enter their contact information so you can follow up with your prospects and save leads in your customer database. If you are a sales representative for a textbook company and you attend a faculty book fair at a large university, when professors stop by your booth, you might ask them which texts they are currently using and what they like or dislike about these books. This is a quick way to identify potential need. One professor might tell you she uses such-and-such a textbook, which is thorough, but her students don't find it very engaging. Aha! You have identified a need, and you now have a prospect. You might tell the professor about a textbook that covers similar information but uses a more conversational style and ask if she would like you to send her a complimentary copy. If she says yes, you now have an opportunity to take her contact information, and you have permission to follow up.

Power Prospecting Source #8: Advertising and Direct Marketing

When you think of "junk mail," you probably think about something you would normally throw in the trash. But have you ever received a direct-mail advertisement that you've actually considered, or even responded to? Maybe you're a member of the American Library Association, and someone has sent you an e-mail about an upcoming library conference in a nearby city because you opted in, or gave permission to receive information from the company. Or maybe a local real estate agent has sent out fliers to the residential areas in your zip code and you just happen to be thinking of selling your house.

direct marketing

Communication in the form of mail or e-mail that is sent directly to a lead.

As a sales professional, **direct marketing**, or communication in the form of direct mail or e-mail sent directly to your potential prospects, gives you the advantage of reaching a large pool of leads without having to invest the time to individually contact each one. Methods such as direct mail and e-mail allow your prospects to self-qualify since only the ones with genuine interest will follow up. On the flip side, direct mail yields a lower rate of return than most other methods: usually only about one to three percent.[34],[35] E-mail has similar response rates depending on the offer or communication. These methods can still be worth the investment, considering the relatively low inputs of time and money it takes to reach so many.

However, the time and money you *do* put into direct mailing or e-mail campaigns will be wasted if you send out your communications at random. There are three ways you can go about generating targeted mailing lists:

1. Every major city has organizations that specialize in mailing list research, allowing you to order up-to-date address lists organized by zip code, income, age, interests, or other characteristics that matter to you. For as little as $25, you can get lists of up to a thousand prospects.

2. Many of the business directories and databases you read about earlier in this section provide e-mail and postal mailing addresses for businesses and private households based on specific criteria.

3. Professional salespeople also develop personal directories for their mailing lists. When you meet prospects, trade business cards with them. If these prospects pass your initial stages of qualification, you can add them to your personal list of mail recipients.[36]

Power Prospecting Source #9: Cold Calling

In the last ten years, Pat Cavanaugh, CEO of a Pittsburgh-based promotional products company, has grown his business 2,000 percent—and he's done almost all of it through cold calling. **Cold calling**, or making an unsolicited phone call or visit to a prospective customer, can be quite effective for the salespeople who know the right approach, but it's also most salespeople's least favorite prospecting activity. For one thing, you never know whether the person on the other end of the line will be rude or hang up on you altogether. Additionally, most salespeople feel pressured to actually sell their product or make a pitch during a cold call, but according to Cavanaugh, cold calling isn't about making sales; it's about establishing a connection with the prospect.[37]

According to Cavanaugh, it's essential to get the prospect to like you in the first thirty seconds.[38] While this may *sound* like it's putting a lot of pressure on you as the caller, you can actually think of it as a way of taking the pressure off. Remember, you don't have to sell your product during the call; the goal is only to make a positive connection. You don't have to lay the schmooze on either. Instead, be direct and sincere, and be yourself. Your prospect, who is probably very busy, will appreciate directness and brevity.

Hanzo Ng, CEO of the Malaysian company Sales Ninja, agrees. Ng says the goal of the cold call should be to find out whether your prospective buyer's needs match your solutions. If you know you can't help your lead solve her problems, you shouldn't pursue the call further.[39] A cold call is a perfect way to find out at what stage the lead is in of his buying process. She might still be a lead for future sales, but at this time she isn't a qualified prospect. For that matter, if your lead seems unreceptive, you might also decide to end the call or to offer to try back at another time. Ultimately, it's important that your prospective buyer doesn't feel like she's being pressured in any way; people have come to expect pushy salesmen and saleswomen on the phone, and you want to set yourself apart from this perception.

If the lead *does* have a problem that you can address, you should go ahead and offer to make an appointment to meet in person. Again, there should be no pressure on either end; your prospect will accept an appointment if she is interested. If she doesn't agree to an appointment, don't try to press it. Sometimes, it may simply be a matter of timing: your prospect might ask you to call back in few months. In this case, get your calendar out and set up a *specific* time when you can try to call back. For instance, "Three months from now will be early March. Is it all right for me to try calling again then?" If she agrees, go a step further and ask something like this: "In the meantime, would it be OK if I sent you occasional updates by e-mail to let you know about new developments and promotions with our product?" This enables you to periodically follow up so that you maintain a connection with your lead.[40]

cold calling

Making an unsolicited phone call or visit to a sales lead.

Finally, it's important to research your prospect before making a call. You should know the size and scope of the company, key people, company culture, and anything about the company that has recently come up in the news. Doing your research allows you to personalize your introduction. After explaining who you are, you might say, "I recently read in *Crain's Chicago Business* that your company's number one priority in the coming year is doubling revenues by increasing your sales force...." Doing your research and keeping a few simple tips in mind should take the pressure off in cold calling and give you the confidence to establish crucial prospect connections.

Power Prospecting Source #10: Be a Subject Matter Expert

subject matter expert

Being an authority in a specific industry or topic.

Wouldn't it be great if, rather than going out to track down prospects, you could get your prospects to come to you? Presenting yourself as a **subject matter expert**, an authority in your field, is one secret for making this happen. CEO and consultant Keith Ferrazzi, started using this technique shortly after graduating from college. Even though he didn't have much experience under his belt as a new graduate, he picked an area and began researching until others in his industry came to know him as an expert and would go to him for consultation and advice. Set up a blog or write articles offering free advice. According to Ferrazzi, you should make a habit of writing and publishing articles in your industry.[41]

If you include your contact information and a brief bio on the page, then qualified prospects will often find you on their own. For instance, maybe you work for a company that sells résumé and cover letter consulting services for job seekers. You decide to write an article explaining "10 Things to Avoid When Dressing for a Job Interview," and you post the article on your blog and submit it to CollegeGrad, a Web site that publishes helpful blog posts like yours. You allow CollegeGrad to use your article for free in exchange for posting a link to your Web site in the margins of the Web page. Now when people perform a Google search on "dressing for a job interview," your article may come up, ensuring that a number of people who match your ideal prospect profile see the information about you and your product.

white paper

An informative report that offers practical solutions to a specific problem.

When generating B2B leads, you can often find prospects by offering Web-based seminars, or Webinars, with helpful advice on some aspect of marketing, or by publishing informative reports (**white papers**) that people can download for free. For instance, a marketing consulting firm might offer a white paper on "Increasing Your Open Rate on E-mails" that businesses can download for free as long as they register their information on the firm's Web page. Requiring users to register allows the firm to track contact information for new leads with whom they can then follow up by e-mail, cold call, or mail. Even better, if a lead finds that the free advice they downloaded is useful, they will quite likely contact the firm voluntarily to find out about the marketing services they provide.

Organizing Your Prospect Information

customer relationship management (CRM)

The process a company uses to organize and track their current and potential customer information.

If you've ever ordered shoes from Zappos, you might be aware that the company is known for its excellent customer service. But you might not know one of their secrets to achieving this: keeping detailed records of every interaction they have with a customer. These records are part of a **customer relationship management (CRM)** system, the tools a company uses to record and organize their contacts with current and prospective customers. If you ever shop at Amazon, you'll notice the product suggestions that pop up on your screen when you log on. That's also an example of how CRM is used.[42]

Choosing a System

CRM software allows you to maintain relationships in a systematic way, following up more consistently with your leads and continuing to meet the needs of your existing customers. If the individual with whom you've been doing business at a particular company leaves, you should update that in your database and begin prospecting for another lead at the company. If you've recently mailed information to some of your leads, CRM software will help you keep track of which customers the mailing went to and how recently it went out, so you know when to follow up with those prospects by phone. You have a huge range of CRM programs from which to choose, and while these applications were once large-business luxuries, more recently there are versions that are priced within the reach of smaller businesses as well.[43]

On the other hand, depending on the type of sales and prospecting your company does, you may only need to use a **contact management system (CMS)**, a system that keeps track of your customer calls and meetings, which is usually less expensive than CRM software. CMS programs are another means of tracking and organizing customer and prospect information, but unlike CRM, CMS programs don't track all information about every customer interaction. If you are the only person from your organization dealing with a particular prospect (e.g., if you're a stockbroker or a real estate agent), you usually only need CMS software. The CMS will allow you to keep current contact and company information on your prospects and to record detailed notes about your conversations with them. But if your company uses multiple methods and/or multiple salespeople to communicate with a prospect (think Zappos.com or Best Buy), then CRM will be a better tool so that each salesperson who interacts with the customer can record their interactions with that individual or company and so that your organization know how and when to follow up.[44]

> **contact management system (CMS)**
>
> A system for tracking and organizing customer and prospect information that is less complex than CRM and doesn't necessarily keep a record of every customer contact.

Gathering Intelligence

If you know your prospect is an eight-year-old online auction house with fifty-two employees operating out of Atlanta, that's information—statistics you regularly update in your customer databases. These are facts that your competitors can also easily access using a simple online directory search. But what about the last time you visited your prospect in person? While waiting to meet with your contact, you overheard the receptionist talking about the complaints the company had been getting recently because of their confusing Web page layout. If you represent a Web design firm, that's valuable information, and it's news your competitor can't access. In other words, it's not just information, it's *intelligence*. You can use this intelligence to your advantage when you put it together with other information. In this situation, assume you happen to know that one of the competing design firms in town just lost its best online retail specialist, while *your* company has two designers who have worked with similar online retailers in the past. So you know your company can address your prospect's need in a unique way. Now you're armed with *competitive intelligence*. Keeping your eyes and ears open for intelligence during every interaction is an important part of prospecting, and it's particularly important to track the intelligence you gather in your customer databases. You never know when it might prove useful.

It's also helpful to think about information that will help you make a personal connection to your prospect (remember from Chapter 1 how important the emotional connection is). Your observations and information gathering should carry over to personal details like your prospect's family, his birthday, or his hobbies. Include these insights as part of your organized records, too. It might seem strange at first to make a formal record of personal details, but keeping track of things like the name of your prospect's two children sends the message that you care about the person, not just his business, and this in turn builds customer loyalty. Upscale hotels like the Four Seasons do this kind of customer relationship management particularly well. Receptionists and concierges track personal details of repeat customers, learning to greet them by name and ask about specific details from previous visits: "Did your sister like the gift you bought her last time you were here?" or "How was your recent trip to Japan?"

Keep It Up-to-Date

Things can change quickly in business, particularly at large companies. The account manager you spoke with last month may have moved to another company yesterday, or the purchasing agent who seemed excited about your product last year may have had to deal with significant budget cuts this year that prevent him from buying again. That's why it's crucial to keep your prospect information current. If your competitor sees an opportunity before you do, you're likely to lose yourself a prospect. And if the individual with whom you've been doing business at a company is no longer working there, it's important to find another key person to contact soon if you want to keep your customer.

Several online business directories (like those mentioned earlier) let you subscribe to customized alerts that will notify you when one of your target companies appears in the news, when there's turnover of key personnel, or when companies in your industry merge or split off. Most of the directory services have a fee, but there are a number of ways to stay current, on industry news at least, without paying. RSS (Really Simple Syndication) readers (Microsoft Outlook has one, and so does Google) allow you to subscribe to specific news feeds, like *The Hollywood Reporter* or *Advertising Age*'s Web page, so that you can keep abreast of the news that affects your industry without having to go out and mine several Web pages every day. Google News Alerts (http://google.com/alerts) is a free service that sends you e-mail updates of the latest Google search results based on your choice of search criteria so you can keep current on your competitors and prospects.

Qualifying Your Prospects

After you've identified your prospects, it's important to understand that *all customers are not created equal*. Some customers are willing to form business partnerships and grow with you over time while others are just looking to do business with whoever offers the lowest price. Some prospects may never be able to help you or your company achieve your business goals, or their goals may not be strategically aligned with yours, even if you really like doing business with them. Choosing customers carefully will save you time and energy and help you meet you goals. You don't want to spend several hours writing up a proposal for one of your prospects only to find out they were never genuinely interested.[45]

Think back to the sales funnel and the idea that you start out with a large pool of leads and end with a much smaller number of customers. While it is important to cast your nets broadly when you're rounding up leads, you'll work most effectively if you weed out the likely from the unlikely early on. You can qualify your leads to determine whether they are legitimate prospects by discovering whether they have the *willingness* and the *ability* to make a purchase. Consider these five questions to help you meet your qualifying objectives:

- **Does your prospect have a need?** This is the most basic thing to figure out about your prospect. There is no use pursuing another individual in the company or delivering a persuasive presentation if there is nothing you can do for this person or organization. If you sell new cars, and your lead is satisfied with the car he bought three months ago, you don't have anything to offer him.

- **Does he or she have the authority to make the buying decision?** You can try to sell candy to a five-year-old, and he'll probably want to buy it, but unless you can convince his parents to make the purchase you don't have a sale. Similarly, your lead at a company may love your product and tell you it's exactly what her company needs. But if she isn't the person with the power to buy, she isn't a qualified prospect. This doesn't mean you should write the company off, but you'll have to figure out how to get in touch with the person who *can* make the buying decision.

- **Does he or she have the resources to purchase the product or service?** Sometimes knowing the answer to this question involves contacting the lead and asking some questions. Other times, you can figure this out by doing company research before ever getting in touch with the lead. You wouldn't have tried to make a major sale to Circuit City just before they went out of business because they wouldn't have had the resources to buy.

- **Does he or she have the willingness to purchase the product?** Even if your lead has the resources and authority to buy, he might not be interested in what you're selling. He might be dead set on a Caribbean cruise when you are selling packages to a ski resort.
- **Do you have access to the influencer or decision makers?** This is relatively straightforward in B2C sales, but in B2B, it can be hard. If you wanted to sell your clothing line to Macy's, you couldn't go downtown to your local branch and pitch your product. Large organizations have layers of personnel, and it's challenging to ferret out the people whose can influence the buying decision. Think about whether you *can* reasonably access these individuals.

Managing Your Prospect Base

So you've qualified your prospect and you have his or her information in your CRM system. It would be nice if that were all it took. But your CRM is only a way of tracking and organizing customer information; making an **action plan**, a specific plan of approach, for each customer is up to you. And you won't make any sales if you don't act.

After qualifying, you might have some prospects with a clear need, buying authority, and a fairly high level of interest, while others seem uncertain. If you classify your prospects as "hot," "warm," and "cold," you can prioritize by devoting the most initial energy to your top potential customers.[46] No two customers are alike. This means that even though you've qualified prospects A and B and determined that they *do* have needs you think you can meet, those needs will be different, possibly drastically so. It's a good idea to begin your action plan by conducting a careful needs analysis—that is, what specific problems is this prospect facing and how can my product help solve those problems?

Finally, think about the next steps in the sales process. Based on this customer's specific needs, how will you design your preapproach? What details should be in your presentation, when should you make your presentation, and how and when will you try to close? Develop a timeline and plot out the steps. If you can envision the sale, you are already halfway there.

> **action plan**
>
> A specific method of approach for each customer.

Key Takeaways

- Prospecting takes creativity and knowledge. You have to look for potential buyers in many places.
- Existing customers and referrals can be excellent sources of prospects because the customers are already familiar with your service and can speak on your behalf.
- Networking provides the opportunity to leverage your existing relationships to develop new leads.
- Business directories and databases (in print and online), trade publications, business journals, are all excellent sources to identify leads.
- **Trade shows** and events give you an opportunity to talk to prospects.
- Advertising and **direct marketing** provide a way to reach out to many prospects who may have an interest in your product or service.
- **Cold calling** is an opportunity to approach the prospect and learn more about how you can meet her needs.
- Being a **subject matter expert** can set you apart and help generate leads because of your expertise.
- Qualifying the lead includes identifying if the prospect is ready, willing, and able to make a purchasing decision about your product or service.

Exercises

1. Assume you are selling staffing services to banks and financial institutions. Identify three sources you would use to identify prospects.
2. Imagine that you sell real estate in your area. Discuss three ways referrals can find you.
3. Assume you are selling advertising. Identify three trade organizations that you might use as sources for leads.
4. Assume you are responsible for donations at a local nonprofit organization that provides services for battered women. You are looking for possible corporate sponsors for your shelter. Visit your campus library and review at least two of the databases or directories listed in this section and identify two leads from each one.
5. Assume you sell lumber to construction companies. How would you use a trade show to identify leads?
6. Identify the industry for each of the following NAICS codes. How would this information be helpful in prospecting?
   - 44
   - 62
   - 71
   - 54

7.4 *Selling U*: How to Use Prospecting Tools to Identify 25 Target Companies

Learning Objective

1. Understand how to identify prospective employers.

If you've ever applied for a job or an internship, you know how frustrating it can be. You might scour the local paper or Craigslist for new postings, only to find one or two promising leads. This is especially true if you're applying during peak times (e.g., the beginning of summer, when all the students are looking for work at once) when you know that tens, maybe hundreds of others, are sending in applications for the same positions. The good news is that now that you know about prospecting and qualifying, you are in control of your job search and have the power to set yourself apart from your competitors.

Three Steps to Prospecting for the Right Employer

cold-contact application

Employment prospecting in which the applicant submits a cover letter and résumé even though a position has not been advertised.

You don't have to limit yourself to a handful of job prospects. Once you know where to look, you'll be overwhelmed with the possibilities. There is no need to wait for your prospects to post job openings or to find your résumé somewhere and approach you; instead, *you* identify your "buyer" and approach them. Most job seekers look for advertised positions through Internet job sites, newspaper want ads, or employment agencies. This is a fair starting point, especially if some of your target companies have posted vacancies. But it's important to know that only about one-fifth of the jobs are actually advertised this way.[47] The other four out of five positions are never publicly announced; they might be filled internally, by networking (covered in Chapter 3), or through **cold-contact (or unsolicited) applications**. This means that prospecting and qualifying potential employers (whether or not they are advertising for a position) is likely to yield good results, provided you do your research first.

If this sounds far-fetched—*What? You can send an application when there's no job posting?*—think about J. Crew. When the company has new merchandise, they send out a catalog. You don't usually request the catalog, but when it comes, if you like J. Crew's products, you'll take a look, and you might just buy. Just because a company hasn't posted a position doesn't mean there isn't a need. Let them know what you have to offer.[48]

Step 1: Build Your Ideal Company Profile

If you could work for your dream company, what would it look like? Would it be a fast-paced, competitive environment with good opportunities for advancement? Would it be a creative organization where you could work collaboratively with like-minded individuals? Would it be a company that includes social responsibility as part of its mission statement? Would you work for a nonprofit, where you could see firsthand the difference you were making in the world? Just as you begin prospecting by building an ideal customer profile,[49] you should also prospect potential employers by visualizing your ideal work environment.

Consider not only the criteria that are most important to you (e.g., benefits, company values, advancement opportunities), but also location. Do you want to stay in a particular region of the country? Is it important that you live in or near a big city? Do you want to live somewhere with good outdoor recreation? Is there some other condition that matters to you? You're free to choose. FindYourSpot.com is a resource that can help you with your location decision. You can also look at lists like Relocate-America's Best Places to Live and then visit Salary.com (use the Cost of Living Wizard) to determine how much more or less it will cost you to live in your favorite location.

Finally, you should consider which employers will be interested in the skills you have to offer. But don't sell yourself short here, either. Just as in prospecting you should never write off a lead without investigating it, *you should also never write off a lead in your job search.* If you can see how your skills would benefit a company, that company is a potential employer.

Essentially, there are three things to consider when you build your prospective employer profile:

1. What are the most important characteristics of your ideal company?
2. In which location would you most like to live?
3. Which companies might be interested in the skills you have to offer in return?

You can use all these factors as guidelines to generate a list of target companies. Building the ideal company profile isn't about saying "wouldn't it be nice if...." Instead, it's about empowering you to go out and find the employer for whom you want to work.

Step 2: Make a List of 25 Target Companies

So how many companies should you consider? Definitely more than the four or five that have recently posted ads in your local paper. Think about the sales funnel model: cast your net broadly to begin, but after some qualifying research, you should have a list of at least twenty-five prospects you'd like to target. Don't define your targets too narrowly. For instance, if you're going into accounting, consider service providers (accounting firms), but also consider companies that have an accounting department and recruiting firms that are interested in people with your skills.[50]

Twenty-five prospects is a good rule of thumb for the top of your funnel because it doesn't leave you with so many that you will overwhelm yourself with research and applications, but it is enough to allow for the fact that some prospects will drop out along the way. After additional research and contact with your prospects, you will find that some don't meet your qualifications after all. Some companies in turn might not be willing to give you an interview; others might give you an interview, and even hang onto your résumé, but will tell you they don't have any openings at the moment. Others might give you an interview but decide your qualifications aren't what they are looking for. Even as the funnel narrows, an initial pool of twenty-five prospects should leave you with a number of companies that are interested in you and in whom you are also interested. Just as you learned earlier in this chapter, prospecting is never ending so you should always be adding new qualified prospects to your target company list.

Finally, it is critical that as you define your prospects and perform your research, you keep records. Think about the contact management systems businesses use to organize and track their prospects. While you don't need such a complex system for a job search, taking notes on Post-its or scraps of paper that you *might* or *might not* find later on, or trying to commit details to memory, will sabotage your hard work. You can use a simple spreadsheet in Excel to organize and track prospective employer information. Even if you don't consider yourself an organized person, if you use a simple tool like this one, you have the ability to keep your job search organized—and make your life much easier.

Step 3: Forget about "To Whom It May Concern"

If you ever get mail addressed to "Resident at (your address)," you know that these are the letters that end up straight in the trash. If someone can't be bothered to find out your name, you won't bother yourself to read their mail. The same is true with your job search: keep in mind that *people*, not organizations or departments, are ultimately responsible for hiring. So it's essential to find key individuals at each company, especially when you're sending out cold-contact cover letters and résumés. You want to make sure your letters actually get read, and if you open your letter with a general, impersonal address, it immediately sends the message that you don't care enough to learn about the company and its people—more likely than not, your letter will end up in the recycle bin.[51]

On the other hand, a little knowledge can go a long way. If a letter with the hiring manager's name on it comes across his desk, he isn't likely to ignore it. The best thing to do is begin with the company's general number listed on their Web site (or in a directory or phone book) and ask the receptionist for the name, contact info, and title for the hiring manager in your field. If the receptionist gives you the name of the human resources manager, be persistent until you get the name of either the hiring manager, the head of your targeted department, or the company president (if it is a smaller organization). Especially if a company hasn't announced that they are hiring, sending a letter to human resources means that your hiring manager—who might very well be interested in what you have to offer—will probably never receive your application. If calling the company's general number doesn't get you the contact information you need, the directory of Corporate Affiliations is an online source where you can find contact information for the key individuals in many companies.

You've Got the Power: Tips for Your Job Search

Every Company Should Get More than One
You might think that you should send only one letter to each company. Don't stop there! Increase your chances of getting a call by sending as many letters as possible to appropriate hiring managers at each company. For example, if you are applying to an advertising agency for a position in account management, send a letter to the agency president, vice president of account services, account directors, account supervisors, even account executives. Don't be afraid to send your letter to people like the president or vice president. Often times they will pass it along to the hiring manager and ask him to follow up with you.[52]

Sources for Prospecting: How to Identify Your Target Companies

So how do you go about finding prospective employers? The task may seem overwhelming, but there is a wealth of resources to help you once you've asked yourself some questions to help guide your search. You can start by choosing the specific area of your field you'd like to focus on.[53] For instance, an environmental designer might choose to specialize in sustainability issues, health care environments, or the design of retail spaces. Your prospects should be the companies who hire people with your skill set and particular focus.

A number of good online business databases can get you started here; many are the same directories and databases you would use to find prospective buyers for your products (see the previous section). Keep in mind that while many of these databases charge a fee for their services, your local or school library should have free subscriptions. Directories are good resources for finding industry-specific companies (e.g., accounting firms if you're an accountant). But since you want to keep your search open to several kinds of companies, try using a combination of prospecting sources.

Many sources you would use for prospecting potential customers are also good sources for finding employment prospects. You can try membership lists for professional organizations, such as the American Marketing Association or the American Institute of Architects. It's especially helpful to look for local chapters or organizations in the city in which you would like to work. For example, at the Philly Ad Club's Web site, you can find a list of over one hundred advertising agencies in the region. Trade publications and trade Web sites are good sources for industry and employment information as well—as are business journals and business journal Web sites. Just as you might subscribe to an RSS (Really Simple Syndication) feed or Google News Alerts to stay up-to-date on your leads and competitors in business prospecting, you can do the same when prospecting for employers by subscribing to feeds for trade Web sites or business journals. Again, don't underestimate the effectiveness of going to your local library. Ask your librarian to point you to some business lists, journals, and directories and take advantage of their free online subscriptions.

FIGURE 7.7

Local business journals, like the *Philadelphia Business Journal*, can be found online at http://www.bizjournals.com. Find the business journal for forty different cities by using the drop down menu at the top. Enter "book of lists" in the search box and find the link for the *Book of Lists* for all sixty-six markets.

Source: Philadelphia Business Journal, used with permission.

TABLE 7.2 Sources for Finding Your Target Companies

Business Directories and Databases	
Riley Guide http://rileyguide.com/careers.html	This Web site is loaded with information on job searching, and it provides a customized Google search to help you identify target employers. Best of all, it's free.
Hoovers http://www.hoovers.com	The site allows you to search by industry and geography. It also provides the name of the top companies in an industry segment.
Advertising Redbooks http://www.redbooks.com	The Web site contains information on over 20,000 advertising companies. This is an excellent source if you're considering work in advertising or marketing.
Business Lists	
Book of Lists	Published in most major cities by American City Business Journals, these have contact information, company profiles, and key facts for specific employers in your targeted region. Most libraries have a hard copy available at no charge.
Bizjournals http://www.bizjournals.com/bookoflists	The site links you to the *Book of Lists* for 40 U.S. cities (for a fee).
"Best of" and "Top" Lists	Top Entry Level Employers, and *Fortune* 100 Best Companies to Work For are some examples.
Professional Membership Organizations	
Local Professional Organizations	Location and industry specific: Use your local online resources to identify local organizations. For example, http://www.iloveseattle.org includes a listing of local professional organizations for multiple industries.
National Professional Organizations http://www.associationjobboards.org	The Web site includes a listing of many professional organizations. Also, check out the Web sites of national organizations; many include links to local chapters. For example, http://www.smei.org, the home page for Sales and Marketing Executives International includes a link to local chapters.
Trade Journals and Web Sites	These often have listings for the top companies in their industry.

Keep your ideal employer profile in mind as you generate leads. If you know the region or some specific cities in which you'd like to live, that can help refine your search because many directories are searchable by state or city. If you want to find a company with specific characteristics, business lists are good sources for prospects. For instance, if you want a workplace with young employees that offers good training and opportunities for advancement, you might search CollegeGrad.com's list of "Top Entry Level Employers." *Fortune* publishes an annual list of the top one hundred companies to work for overall (http://money.cnn.com/magazines/fortune/bestcompanies/2009), and they also provide top company lists by state, if you are considering a particular region of the country. Of course, the "Fastest-Growing Companies" list in national and local business publications is always a good reference with which to start.

Qualifying Prospective Employers: Four Things to Consider

After doing industry research, you might have a fairly large list of potential companies, but you can narrow it down to your twenty-five targets by doing more directed research on each of your prospects.

Company Web Sites

According to Amazon's Web site, the company defines itself as technologically innovative, customer-centric, and a global leader in e-commerce. If you were to browse the Safeco Insurance Web site, you would find a company that describes their core values as diversity and an inclusive work environment, community outreach and sponsorship, and service that reaches a broad customer base. Any company's Web site will give you insight into how the company presents itself: their mission and values, the benefits of the products and services they offer, and the culture they want to cultivate. The design of the Web site itself can tell you something about the company. Are they conservative or cutting edge and creative? Is the page well organized and well maintained, or is it convoluted and difficult to navigate? Additionally, even if you plan to cold-contact an employer, the company's career page will let you know if the organization has any advertised vacancies.

Insider Perspectives

The Web site lets you know what the *company* wants you to know about itself. But what about what other people are saying about a company? That's certainly something that you'll want to find out. Some Web sites, like Vault or WetFeet, offer honest, insider profiles of companies based on employee surveys about things like company culture, dress code, diversity, hours, vacation time, and opportunities for advancement. Does the company have a relaxed atmosphere? Do they expect employees to work long hours? These are things that the company Web site itself won't tell you.

Company News

It's also a good idea to check the news for the latest on what's happening in a company. While companies promote their own good news, the media picks up everything in between. For instance, when the MGM Mirage corporation was facing massive debt and the possible failure of its extravagant City Center construction project, the news hit major papers across the country. But if you had gone to the company's Web site or checked their press releases, you would have found announcements about "cost savings," followed by praise for the scope and incredible amenities of the Mirage's construction project—clearly a very different picture. To get company news, you can search national news sites for archived articles, or if you want to learn about a smaller, localized company, try searching local newspapers. It's also a good idea to set up Google News Alerts or subscribe to RSS feeds for your field of interest (see the more detailed explanation in the previous chapter goal) so that you are constantly updating your intelligence, just as you would for a prospective buyer.

Company Stats

Finally, when qualifying prospective companies, there are a handful of other things to consider. How does the company measure up against its competitors? How large is the company? Is it profitable? For *public companies* you can use databases like D&B and Hoovers to research stock prices, quarterly earnings, and senior management changes. You can access this information on multiple companies at a time by taking advantage of free database subscriptions at your local library, or you can go to individual company Web sites to gather stats. Publicly held companies usually post recordings of quarterly conference calls with analysts on their Web sites in the investor relations section.

While you won't be able to research stock prices or quarterly earnings on *private companies*, you can still find out about personnel turnover using most online databases. Ask yourself how this turnover might affect the way business is conducted and check the Better Business Bureau (BBB) to find out if any complaints have been lodged against the company. Finding an employer that closely matches your ideal profile is well within your power, if you consider yourself—your unique brand—as a solution that can meet a prospective employer's needs. The prospects are out there just waiting to be identified.

Key Takeaways

- To get the job you want you need to prospect to find prospective employers.
- It's best to create a list of twenty-five target companies for which you would like to work.
- Do your prospecting thoroughly to identify not only the companies but also multiple hiring managers at each company.
- You can use the same tools to identify your target companies that you use to identify sales prospects.
- Qualify your employment leads with additional research about the company from the company Web site, insider perspectives, company news, and company stats.

Exercises

1. Create your ideal prospective employer profile using the following points:
   - What are the most important characteristics of your ideal company?
   - In which location would you most like to live?
   - Which companies might be interested in the skills you have to offer in return?
2. Discuss how the sales funnel applies to your job search.
3. Visit your campus library and meet with the librarian to learn about the databases, directories, or business lists that are available for your job search. Use at least two different sources to identify target companies (hint: the *Book of Lists* is available in many cities and provides a list of top companies in several categories).
4. Using the list you created in Exercise 3, conduct further research about each company and identify at least three hiring managers to whom you can send your résumé and cover letter.

7.5 Review and Practice

Power Wrap-Up

Now that you have read this chapter, you should be able to understand the seven steps of the selling process and how to identify and qualify sales prospects.

- You can **list** the seven steps of the selling process and how they work.
- You can **understand** the vital role of prospecting in the selling process.
- You can **compare and contrast** the difference between a lead and a prospect.
- You can **discuss** the role of the sales funnel.
- You can **identify** ten prospecting sources.
- You can **understand** how to qualify leads to become prospects.
- You can **apply** the tools of prospecting to your job search.

Test Your Power Knowledge (answers are below)

1. List the seven steps of the selling process.
2. Why do salespeople qualify their leads before they call on them?
3. When a customer says, "It's too expensive," that's an example of which step in the selling process?
4. True or false: After the sale is made, the salesperson's job is done.
5. Why is prospecting considered the foundation of the selling process?
6. Describe the sales funnel.
7. Describe the difference between a lead and a prospect.
8. Identify at least three business directories or databases that you can use to identify prospects.
9. Identify three business journals that can be used for prospecting.
10. Why is cold calling effective for prospecting?
11. What is a subject matter expert? How can being a subject matter expert help you prospect for leads?

Power (Role) Play

Now it's time to put what you've learned into practice. Following are two roles that are involved in the same selling situation—one role is the customer, and the other is the salesperson. This will give you the opportunity to think about this selling situation from the point of view of both the customer and the salesperson.

Read each role carefully along with the discussion questions. Then, be prepared to play either of the roles in class using the concepts covered in this chapter. You may be asked to discuss the roles and do a role-play in groups or individually.

Count on Me

Role: Controller

You are the controller of a paper company. You currently have an internal accounting department, but since your company is growing so quickly, you are considering using an accounting services company to supplement the internal department. You met a sales rep from AccountSource at the last trade show, and their services sounded like what you need at your company.

- What do you expect the sales rep to know about you and your business when she calls you?
- What do you want to know about AccountSource and the sales rep when she calls?
- What will convince you to agree to meet with the sales rep?

Role: Sales rep for AccountSource

You are prospecting for new customers because your sales goals have increased and you need to expand into new areas. You met the controller from a paper company at the latest trade show, and you think this could be a good lead. You have some questions that you would like to ask the controller to see if this is a qualified lead.

- Will you conduct research before you call the lead or after?
- What research, if any, will you do?
- What questions will you ask the controller?
- How will you qualify this lead?

Put Your Power to Work: *Selling U* Activities

1. Visit your campus career center to learn about prospective target companies, especially those that interview on campus. Do research on the companies including the names of hiring managers in the department in which you may want to work.

2. Create your complete list of twenty-five target companies including at least three hiring managers at each company.

Test Your Power Knowledge Answers

1. Prospecting and qualifying, preapproach, approach, presentation, handling objections, closing the sale, and follow-up.

2. Qualifying helps save time so you don't waste time calling on people who don't have the time, money, or authority to purchase your product or service.

3. Handling objections.

4. False. The salesperson's job really begins when the sale is closed.

5. When prospecting is done correctly, the other steps in the selling process build upon it.

6. The sales funnel is a helpful way to visualize the process of finding and qualifying new prospects and ultimately converting them to customers. Not all leads become prospects, and not all prospects become customers.

7. A lead is a qualified prospect.

8. There are several databases and directories, including Directory of Corporate Affiliations, Hoovers, and D&B Million Dollar Database.

9. There are several business journals including *Wall Street Journal*, *Business Journals* (by city), *Crain* (by major city).

10. Cold calling gives you an opportunity to talk to the prospect and learn more about his goals and how you can add value.

11. Subject matter experts are people who are authorities in their field. Subject matter experts share their knowledge at trade shows, at industry events, on blogs, and in other online communities and social networks. Being a subject matter expert helps establish you as being a leader in a particular area. Prospects usually want to learn more from and do business with subject matter experts.

Endnotes

1. Viki King, *How to Write a Movie in 21 Days* (New York: Quill Harper Resource, 2001), 34–37.
2. William C. Moncreif and Greg W. Marshall, "The Evolution of the Seven Steps of Selling," *Industrial Market Management* 34, no. 1 (2005): 13–22.
3. Adapted from Michael R. Solomon, Greg W. Marshall, and Elnora W. Stuart, *Marketing: Real People, Real Choices*, 5th ed. (Upper Saddle River, NJ: Pearson Prentice Hall, 2008), 450.
4. Selling Power Sales 2.0 Newsletter, *Selling Power*, September 18, 2008, http://www.sellingpower.com/content/newsletter/issue.php?pc=868 (accessed June 21, 2010).
5. Geoffrey James, "6 Things to Know about Every Prospect," BNET, January 12, 2009, http://blogs.bnet.com/salesmachine/?p=705 (accessed June 9, 2009).
6. Michael T. Bosworth, *Solution Selling: Creating Buyers in Difficult Selling Markets* (New York: McGraw-Hill, 1995), 106.
7. Paul Cherry, *Questions That Sell: The Powerful Process of Discovering What Your Customer Really Wants* (New York: AMACOM, 2006), 21.
8. Neil Rackham, *The SPIN Selling Fieldbook* (New York: McGraw-Hill, 1996), 40.
9. William C. Moncreif and Greg W. Marshall, "The Evolution of the Seven Steps," *Industrial Marketing Management* 34, no. 1 (2005): 14, 15.
10. Thomas A. Freese, *Secrets of Question Based Selling* (Naperville, IL: Sourcebooks, Inc., 2003), 166.
11. Dave Dolak, "Sales and Personal Selling," http://www.davedolak.com/psell.htm (accessed June 10, 2009).
12. William C. Moncreif and Greg W. Marshall, "The Evolution of the Seven Steps," *Industrial Marketing Management* 34, no. 1 (2005): 14, 15.
13. Dave Dolak, "Sales and Personal Selling," http://www.davedolak.com/psell.htm (accessed June 10, 2009).
14. Charles M. Futrell, *The ABC's of Relationship Selling*, 9th ed. (New York: McGraw-Hill Irwin, 2005).
15. Channel Intelligence, "2004 Channel Intelligence Consumer Buying Intent Survey Reveals Online Shopping Trends," http://channelintelligence.vnewscenter.com/press.do?step=pkview&contentId=1184050872399&companyId=1123580114932 (accessed June 10, 2009).
16. John Coe, *The Fundamentals of Business-to-Business Sales* (New York: McGraw-Hill, 2003), 125.
17. Ron Hubsher, interview by Gerhard Gschwandtner, *Daily Report*, Sales Optimization Group, *Selling Power*, http://www.salesog.com/index.html (accessed June 9, 2009).

18. Ron Hubsher, "Turning the Sales Funnel Upside Down," interview by Michelle Nichols, Savvy Selling, podcast audio program, *BusinessWeek*, July 13, 2007, http://www.businessweek.com/mediacenter/podcasts/savvy_selling/savvy_selling_07_13_07.htm (accessed June 9, 2009).

19. Adam Stone, "Dennis Kelly Photography Took a Shot with Facebook," *Philadelphia Business Journal*, June 5–11, 2009, 10–11.

20. Jeff Bressler, "How Much to Spend to Acquire New Customers?" *CEO World Magazine*, May 13, 2009, http://ceoworld.biz/ceo/2009/05/13/hto-much-to-spend-to-acquire-new-customers (accessed June 10, 2009).

21. Jeff Leach, Randy Crochet, and Brock Fillinger, "How One Small Business Uses Twitter to Build Its Brand," *Advertising Age*, May 29, 2009, http://adage.com (accessed June 9, 2009).

22. John Spence, "Seven Steps to Successful B2B Marketing," John Spence Blog, comment posted October 31, 2007, http://johnspence.com/blog/?p=52 (accessed June 9, 2009).

23. Clara Shih, *The Facebook Era* (Upper Saddle River, NJ: Prentice Hall, 2009), 2.

24. Jessica E. Vascellaro, "Social Networking Goes Professional," *Wall Street Journal*, August 28, 2007, http://online.wsj.com/article/SB118825239984310205.html (accessed June 9, 2009).

25. Clara Shih, *The Facebook Era* (Upper Saddle River, NJ: Prentice Hall, 2009), 2.

26. Occupational Health and Safety Administration, "SIC Search," United States Department of Labor, http://www.osha.gov/pls/imis/sic_manual.display?id=56&tab=group (accessed June 9, 2009).

27. David Whitford, "Built by Association," *Inc.*, July 1994, http://www.inc.com/magazine/19940701/3005.html (accessed June 10, 2009).

28. Boston Public Library, "Directories on the Internet," http://www.bpl.org/research/kbb/websites/dirs.htm (accessed February 15, 2010).

29. Center for Business Research, "Public vs. Private Companies," Long Island University, http://www2.liu.edu/cwis/cwp/library/cbr/publicvprivate.htm (accessed June 10, 2009).

30. "About Hoovers Handbook of Private Companies 2009," Hoovers, http://images.hoovers.com/images/i/books/lookinside.pv2009.pdf (accessed June 10, 2009).

31. "Beverage Bottles Lighten Up," Packworld, May 1, 2009, http://www.packworld.com/news (accessed June 10, 2009).

32. Paige Palmateer, "Inaugural Horse World Expo Coming to Syracuse," *CNY Business Journal*, May 4, 2007, http://findarticles.com/p/articles/mi_qa3718/is_20070504/ai_n19304825/?tag=content;col1 (accessed June 10, 2009).

33. Barton A. Weitz, Sephen B. Castleberry, and John F. Tanner, Jr., *Selling: Building Partnerships* (New York: McGraw-Hill Irwin, 2003).

34. Tony Alessandra, "Direct Mail Prospecting," Speakers Roundtable, http://www.speakersroundtable.com/sales-training-tony11.html (accessed February 15, 2010).

35. Tony Alessandra, "Direct Mail Prospecting," Speakers Roundtable, http://www.speakersroundtable.com/sales-training-tony11.html (accessed February 15, 2010).

36. Tony Alessandra, "Prospecting, " Assessment Business Center, http://www.assessmentbusinesscenter.com/media/articles/article_prospecting.pdf (accessed February 15, 2010).

37. Susan Greco, "The Nonstop, 24-7 CEO Salesman," *Inc.*, August 2000, http://www.inc.com/magazine/20000801/19766.html (accessed June 11, 2009).

38. Susan Greco, "The Nonstop, 24-7 CEO Salesman," *Inc.*, August 2000, http://www.inc.com/magazine/20000801/19766.html (accessed June 11, 2009).

39. Hanzo Ng, "Prospecting, Cold Calling & Networking," *Malaysian Business*, October 1, 2008, http://findarticles.com/p/articles/mi_qn6207/is_20081001/ai_n30902653/?tag=content;col1 (accessed June 11, 2009).

40. Keith Rosen, "Keep the Lines of Communication with Your Prospects Open," AllBusiness, http://www.AllBusiness.com/sales/sales-management/4001387-1.html (accessed June 11, 2009).

41. Keith Ferrazzi, "To Be Known, or Unknown," *Inc.*, http://www.inc.com/resources/sales/articles/20061001/kferrazzi.html (accessed June 11, 2009).

42. "Making Customer Relationship Management Work," *Inc.*, 2001, http://www.inc.com/articles/2001/07/23102.html (accessed June 11, 2009).

43. Karen M. Kroll, "CRM: Software as a Customer Service," *Inc.*, 2007, http://technology.inc.com/software/articles/200706/CRM.html (accessed June 11, 2009).

44. Andrew Boyd and Alex Jeffries, "The Crucial Difference Between Contact Management and CRM," *E-commerce Times*, January 29, 2009, http://www.ecommercetimes.com/story/smb/65995.html?wlc=1244423929 (accessed June 11, 2009).

45. Paul Cherry, *Questions That Sell: The Powerful Process of Discovering What Your Customer Really Wants* (New York: AMACOM, 2006), 37.

46. Derek Brown, "Growing and Managing Your Prospect Pipeline," Coreconnex, February 2, 2009, http://www.coreconnex.com/2009/02/04/growing-and-managing-your-prospect-pipeline (accessed June 11, 2009).

47. Katherine Hansen and Randall Hansen, *Dynamic Cover Letters: How to Write the Letter That Gets You the Job* (Berkeley, CA: Ten Speed Press, 2001), 2.

48. Kim Richmond, *Brand You*, 3rd ed. (Upper Saddle River, NJ: Pearson Prentice Hall, 2008), 140.

49. Brian Carroll, "10 Lead Generating (Prospecting) Tips for Sales People," B2B Lead Generation Blog, May 21, 2007, http://blog.startwithalead.com/weblog/2007/05/10_lead_generat.html#ixzz0GAhpeddB&B (accessed June 11, 2009).

50. Kim Richmond, *Brand You*, 3rd ed. (Upper Saddle River, NJ: Pearson Prentice Hall, 2008), 140.

51. Katherine Hansen and Randall Hansen, *Dynamic Cover Letters: How to Write the Letter That Gets You the Job* (Berkeley, CA: Ten Speed Press, 2001), 4.

52. Kim Richmond, *Brand You*, 3rd ed. (Upper Saddle River, NJ: Pearson Prentice Hall, 2008), 140.

53. "Do the Research That Supports Your Job Search," The Riley Guide, May 2009, http://rileyguide.com/jsresearch.html#r201 (accessed June 11, 2009).

CHAPTER 8
The Preapproach: The Power of Preparation

Video Ride-Along with Tonya Murphy, General Sales Manager at Radio Station WBEN-FM

You met Tonya Murphy in Chapter 3 when she talked about the power of relationships. Part of building relationships that work is doing your homework. It's not enough to simply use the information you gathered when you were prospecting and qualifying.

Ride along with Tonya and learn how she researches and develops an "I know" statement as part of her preapproach before every sales call.

View the video online at: http://www.youtube.com/embed/KKAuEtNAlNo

8.1 Researching Your Prospect: Going Deeper

Learning Objective

1. Explain how to research a qualified prospect and list resources to conduct prospect research.

Spring break is just around the corner. You and your friends definitely want to go away somewhere great. You decide on Cancún, Mexico, as a destination. Since you want to get the best plane fare and hotel rate, you will have to book early. That means planning, coordinating, and even doing some research on the area. You want everything to be perfect—after all, this is spring break.

Just as preparation made your spring break trip come together perfectly, preparation also makes a sales call successful. By now you've identified and qualified your prospects, you've come up with an action plan, and you're probably eager to get down to business. However, you can't just call your prospect or show up at his door without doing your homework first. How big is his business? What are his business goals? What is his company culture? Is he already doing business with any of your competitors? In what ways do your products or services present a solution he could use? The preapproach, or the process of finding out the answers to these questions, is critical.[1] Doing your research and coming prepared gets your prospect's attention and shows him that you care. It gives you the power to sell adaptively and puts you ahead of your competitors.

Keep in mind that when someone ultimately decides to do business with you, he is trusting you with one of the things that's most important to him—his money. Furthermore, he is trusting in you above all other people and companies to help him with his challenges. Consider that your company is using personal selling because customers want additional information or customization of the product or service in order to make a decision. People only buy from people they trust.[2] You have to earn that trust every day. The first step starts here: how well are you prepared to earn his respect and trust?

Gather Information

By the time you're ready for the preapproach, you've already done some initial research as part of the qualifying process. With the preapproach, you take your research to the next level; you find out as much as you possibly can about the company or individual with whom you want to do business. As marketing and strategy expert Noel Capon says, a thorough understanding of your prospect's business processes and challenges gives you the crucial insights you'll need to offer specific, workable solutions your customers can use. Gathering this information demonstrates personal commitment and boosts your credibility with your prospects.[3]

target account

A new, qualified prospect.

key account

An existing customer that is (or has the potential to be) a significant source of sales for your company.

Your research will pay off whether you're preparing to contact a new prospect—a **target account**—or whether you're working with an existing customer. In Chapter 7, you read that some of your best prospects are the customers you already have. It's particularly important to identify your **key accounts**, your current customers who are—or have the potential to be—your most significant sources of sales. Maybe you sell insurance, and you've contracted with a large restaurant chain to provide their employee health and dental plan. This key account is one of the largest companies with whom you do business, so you make an extra effort to stay informed about developments that affect this company. You've recently received a news alert that due to an unstable economy the restaurant chain has decided to cut employee hours. As a result, many of the staff members are now working part-time and no longer qualify for full health benefits. Based on this information, you call your contact at the company and offer to provide a more flexible and less expensive partial employee benefits package for which their part-time workers could still qualify. You tell her that this solution will serve her company's need to cut costs and will allow them to retain employees who might otherwise become dissatisfied and leave.

precall planning worksheet

A document that details the goals you hope to achieve during a particular sales call.

Whether you're contacting new or existing customers, it's important to have your specific call objectives in mind and to clearly map out the information you've already gathered about the company so that you can refer to it during the call. You can keep this information organized using a **precall planning worksheet** that lists the key company statistics you've identified as part of your research and includes a checklist detailing the purpose of the call: the information you'd like to learn about the company, the solutions or key facts you plan to communicate, and any other goals you hope to achieve. The worksheet doesn't have to be complex; it can be as straightforward as the sample in Figure 8.1. Your customer relationship management (CRM) or contact management system (CMS) may also provide a place for you to do your precall planning work. A sample precall planning worksheet is shown in Figure 8.1.

FIGURE 8.1 Precall Planning Worksheet

Sample Precall Planning Worksheet	
Company:	
Contact:	
Phone:	
Location:	
Source of Lead:	
Key facts I already know about...	
The company:	
My contact/prospect there:	
Goals to achieve by end of call	
Information I plan to gather about the company:	
Information I plan to gather about my contact/prospect:	
Information the prospect should know about me/my company:	
Specific actions the prospect should agree to take:	
How the company should feel about working with me/us:	

Listing your goals in writing before you make a sales call gives you the power to measure the success of your call. Did you get the information you needed? Did you communicate the information you listed in your checklist? If not, how can you adapt your approach and set goals for your next sales call?

Going Deeper with the Fundamentals: What You'll Want to Know

The first sales call (or calls) is often an extension of the qualifying process. Even if the company passes initial qualification, as you learn more you might find out that they aren't your ideal customers after all. You might discover that your contact at the company is about to leave or change positions. Or you might realize that the company's current situation isn't one in which they're willing or able to buy. The following are some things you'll want to know as you research the company during your preapproach.

About the Company

- **Demographics**. Understanding the basics will help you ensure the company fits your ideal prospect profile and allow you to tailor your solution to fit the company's particular situation. What kind of business is it? How large is the business? How many locations do they have? How many people work for them? Where is the home office located? How many years have they been in business?

- **Company news**. Tracking company news is another way to discover opportunities for sales. Has the company put out any recent press releases? (You can generally find these on the company Web site in the investor relations, press release, or press room section.) Has the company recently appeared in the news? (Setting up Google News Alerts at http://www.google.com/alerts for your current and potential customers will keep you up-to-date on this.)

Don't just read the news; creatively think about what the news is telling you about selling opportunities with a prospect. For example, if you were selling paper goods (cups, lids, straws, bags, cup jackets, napkins, etc.) to coffee shops, you would have read a press release about the test marketing of McCafés several months before the national launch. Then you would have read about the announcement of the national launch a few months before it was planned to occur. These press releases are selling opportunities. You might think it would only be a selling opportunity if you were selling to McDonald's, but that's not true. The fact is McDonald's announced that it was about to expand the market for premium coffee. That's an opportunity to help your customers and prospects. For example, what if you suggested that your customers and prospects print an advertisement on their bags, napkins, cups, and cup jackets to announce a promotion called "Morning Joe Wake-up Call"? "Buy a cup of coffee every day for ten days and get a free cup of Joe!" This helps increase their sales, which ultimately increases your sales. You could bring this idea to your customer or prospect in advance of the McCafé launch and discuss how your idea can help him build his brand prior to the competitive effort. Now that's using company news to drive sales.[4]

- **Financial performance**. Keeping up-to-date on the company's financial performance will help you determine whether your prospect is currently able to buy, which might lead you to discover sales opportunities. All publicly held companies are required to post their quarterly earnings on their websites. Generally there will be a link for "investors" or "investor relations" on the company home page that will take you to financial data, including a recording of the company's quarterly earnings conference call. It's a good idea to listen to these conference calls to learn important information about the company's strategy and financial performance.

Link

Listen to the Most Current Quarterly Earnings Conference Call for Macy's
http://phx.corporate-ir.net/phoenix.zhtml?c=84477&p=irol-webcasts

About the Company's Customers

- **Customer demographics**. Are the company's products used by businesses or individual consumers? If consumers, what age, education, and income level? If businesses, what size and kind of businesses? Knowing the organization's customer demographics will help you tailor your solution to the company. For instance, if you're selling clothing designs to Old Navy, knowing that the company appeals to families and that it draws in value-conscious customers, you might send them samples from your more basic and reasonably priced clothing line, rather than your top-of-the-line products or your trendiest designs.

FIGURE 8.2
Understanding customer demographics can provide important insight for selling. For example, each of the customers shown above has different demographics and different needs.

© 2010 Jupiterimages Corporation

- **Size of customer base**. In B2B sales, it's important to know whether your prospect serves many customers or primarily works with a few large accounts. Microsoft, for example, sells its products to large corporations, but they also deal with individual consumers. Some companies, on the other hand, work with a few large accounts, so their success is very dependent on the success of their key customers. If your prospect is a sporting goods manufacturer that only sells its products to Dick's Sporting Goods, Dick's Sporting Goods' financial performance will affect the performance of your prospect's business.

- **What customers are saying about your prospect**. You can learn a lot about a company by paying attention to its reputation with customers. If the business has a lousy customer service record, they might not treat their vendors well either. This is why it's worthwhile to read customer reviews as part of your qualifying process. For instance, if you do business with airline companies, you might prefer to fly with Southwest (whose customer reviews say things like "This is an airline I'll use again and again!") than United Airlines (where one reviewer writes, "United Airlines hands down has the worst customer service of any company I have ever dealt with"). For large companies, doing a Google search will often bring up customer reviews on the organization, or you can try a Web site like Epinions. For local companies, try searching your regional Better Business Bureau (BBB) to see if any customer complaints have been filed against the company.

FIGURE 8.3
Customer reviews can tell you a lot about a company and help you identify your best prospects, as in the case of the customer reviews for Southwest Airlines compared to those for United Airlines.

© 2010 Jupiterimages Corporation

About the Current Buying Situation

- **Type of purchase**. In Chapter 6, you learned the different types of buys—straight rebuy, modified rebuy, or strategic alliance. Knowing that information is extremely valuable during your preapproach research. Is the customer making a first-time purchase of the product? (For instance, maybe you're selling disaster recovery services to a company that has previously lived with the risk of not having their data backed up.) Or will this purchase be a rebuy? Maybe the customer is an interior design firm. The firm already buys paint from a certain supplier but is thinking of making a modified rebuy: purchasing a more environmentally friendly line of paints, either from the same supplier or from someone else (hopefully you!). On the other hand, maybe the design firm is already buying from you and is perfectly happy with the paints and with you as a supplier, so it decides to make a straight rebuy of the same product. It's also possible that your prospect is considering a strategic alliance with your company in which your organizations would make an agreement to share resources. For example, Pepsi has a strategic alliance with Frontier Airlines in which Frontier agrees that all the soft drinks it serves on board the airline will be Pepsi brand.[5] Knowing the type of purchase will help you position your solution to best fit the situation.

- **Competitor/current provider**. If your prospect is already buying from another company, you'll want to know who your competitor is. What do you know about this company and their products? Most important, what are your competitor's strengths and weaknesses? Consider the interior design firm that is about to make a rebuy. If you've done your research, you might be able to tell the firm, "I know your current supplier offers a high-quality paint product in a wide range of color choices. Our company offers a wide range of color choices, too, and our product consistently gets high reviews. However, unlike your current provider, we also have a line of soy-based paints, which are better for the environment and for your customers' and employees' health than the regular latex variety. Using soy-based paints will increase your reputation as a progressive, socially responsible business." Knowing your prospect's current supplier gives you the power to favorably position your product by highlighting the things that set you apart from the competition.

- **Current pricing**. If the information is available, find out what your prospect's current supplier charges for their product or service. This information will give you the edge to competitively position your solution. If you charge less than your competitors, you can highlight your product as a cost-saving alternative. If your products cost more, you might consider offering a discount or other benefit to provide a better solution. On the other hand, if your products are more expensive because they're of a higher quality, you should emphasize that fact. For example, soy-based paint is generally more expensive than latex paint, but depending on your customer's needs, the extra cost might be worth the benefits of a healthier, "greener" product.

Video Clip

Preparation Is Essential
Listen to Priya Masih, sales representative at Lupin Pharmaceuticals, talk about how she prepares for a sales call.

View the video online at: http://www.youtube.com/embed/IY1ObVnOlzg

About the Contact Person

- **Title and role in the company**. This is basic and essential information to know. It will help you to personalize your communications and will give you a better sense of your business situation. What role does this person have in the buying decision? Are you dealing with an influencer in the organization? Does this contact person have the authority to make a buying decision, or is this person a gatekeeper, a person with whom you must talk in order to get to the decision maker?

- **Professional background**. How long has this person been at the company, and what positions has he held? What roles has he had at other companies? This information will help you to adapt your communications and solutions to the individual. You can find valuable information on professional social networks such as LinkedIn and Plaxo.com and use it as you prepare your approach and presentation. For instance, you might find out that someone in your network knows the person you are planning to approach and she can provide an entry for you. You might also learn that the person you plan on calling on was previously a buyer at two other companies and usually likes to bring in his previous vendors. If that's the case, you might adapt your approach to include benefits that you have brought to other buyers who switched to your company.

- **Personal information**. Everyone likes to do business with people they like. Learning what you can about your contact's family, hobbies, and interests demonstrates that you care about him as an individual and helps you build a relationship with your customer. This is useful information to keep on hand for the opening of the sales call when you want to put your prospect at ease and convince him of your goodwill. And it's good information to use as follow-up or just to keep in touch. ("I know you are a huge University of Florida fan so I thought you would enjoy this video of the team's summer training camp.")

- **Essential problem(s) your contact needs to solve**. Knowing this information takes you right to the heart of the issue. Maybe your prospect is the marketing manager at the company and has recently been given the task of finding a new breakthrough idea for a promotional product to give away at a major upcoming industry trade show. Or maybe your prospect owns a grocery chain and needs to increase her sales in the frozen food area with organic products. Learning the specific problems your contact faces in his role at the company is the only way you can adapt your solution to meet his needs. The best way to identify your prospect's problem (or opportunity) is to do extensive research on the company.

- **Motivation for buying**. If your contact is already buying from another supplier, what reasons might he have to start buying from you instead? For instance, is he dissatisfied with the quality of his current provider's service or the price of the product? If he is satisfied, what value can you bring that provides a reason for him to consider changing suppliers? On the other hand, if this is a first time purchase, what will drive his initial decision to buy?

About Your Existing Customers

Your current customers are your best prospects. While you might be excited about a new account, make sure you don't spend so much time and energy on new prospects that you neglect the ones with whom you've already established a relationship.

- **Opportunities to expand the relationship**. There's no better place to increase your sales than with your existing customers. They know you and your product or service, you know them and their needs and challenges. So start by leveraging the information you already know about your customer's business. This is the best way to expand your relationship. For instance, if you have sold fitness equipment to a regional chain of health clubs and you know that it is important for them to minimize maintenance costs and down time, you could target the buyer as a prospect for the new line of weight machines with hydraulics. You could also expand your research and determine how much money the club could save in a year based on the number of machines and include that as part of your presentation. This is establishing your **value proposition**, what you have to offer that your prospect or customer is willing to pay for.

If your customer is using some of your services in combination with your competitor's services, this is also a sales opportunity: find out how satisfied your customer is with the competitor's services and see if you can come up with a better solution. ("You're currently using our hydraulic weight machines, but I see that you're buying your exercise machines from this other company. Did you know that we offer treadmills, exercise bikes, and elliptical machines that come with free maintenance and product replacement guarantees?") If your customer has a contract with this competitor, finding out when the contract expires will help you time your sales call effectively.[6]

And what about *your* contracts with the customer? If you have a **service-level agreement (SLA)** with the customer, you can leverage this opportunity to strengthen the customer relationship. SLAs define the terms of the service you will provide, and they generally expire after a certain length of time (think about the contract you have with your cell phone provider). Establish open lines of communication to make sure your customer is consistently satisfied with your service. You might discuss expanded service options he can purchase, or you could offer a discount for renewing the contract early. Consider giving a short survey to gauge your customer's satisfaction level and find out whether there are additional services you might be able to offer her.

You can also consider moving into other departments of the organization: use your CRM system to track the organizational structure of the company and find the influencers in other departments. Of course, you can ask your current contacts at the company for referrals of other prospective buyers within the company.[7] Maybe you're formatting documents for the research branch of the company, but you know the company also has a communications department that puts out brochures, reports, and newsletters. You can scan your CRM database (or look on the company's Web site) for the names of managers in the communications department and ask your contact in the research department if he could give you a good referral.

- **Opportunities for synergy**. How can you partner with your customer in new ways that will benefit both companies? For instance, maybe there's an opportunity for a strategic alliance like the one between Pepsi and Frontier Airlines: Frontier buys exclusively from Pepsi, while Pepsi helps promote Frontier. Or are there additional services or products you offer that, used in combination with your customer's current purchases, would create an even stronger solution? For example, Linksys has its Linksys One program, which offers B2B customers high-speed wireless networks combined with an Internet telephone service and several software services. By combining one company's software and hardware products and services, customers are able to streamline their work, creating a simpler, more efficient system.[8] If you can demonstrate potential **synergy** with an existing customer—that is, collaboration that produces greater results than individual products, services, or parties could produce alone—you have an opportunity to expand your business with that customer.

Sources of Information

When you want to dig deeper with your research, you can often return to the same sources you used during the qualifying process and simply get more specific with the information you gather.

- **Online searches**. Search online databases and directories such as Hoovers and current news stories on Yahoo! Finance, Bloomberg, and other business Web sites (see Chapter 7 for a complete list of sources for company information) to find out about company demographics and key people in the organization. If you want to learn more detailed information about your contacts in the company, try online professional social networks like LinkedIn.

- **Business directories**. Remember the value of your local library where you can search business directories in print and access some online directories free of charge.

- **Publicly available contracts**. Real estate closings, government contracts, and other vital information that is part of public records can help provide pricing, terms, and other important data that can help you benchmark against the competition and better understand your prospect's current situation.

- **Trade journals**. Trade journals are a good source for learning more about people and companies in your target industry. Making a habit of reading these publications (or subscribing to RSS [Really Simple Syndication] feeds, as described in Chapter 7) helps keep you up-to-date on developments in these companies and in the industry.

- **Blogs, social networks, and online forums**. These online resources can provide insight about the prospect, the competition, and the environment. Many company employees and executives post regularly about their perceptions and feelings on many topics. These comments can provide valuable insight about the prospect.

- **Professional organizations**. Joining professional organizations (in person and online) can help you build relationships with contacts at your target companies. These organizations also serve as a source for competitive knowledge and for your connection to industry buzz.

In addition to these sources you've already used, consider another powerful resource: people. If you've already formed a relationship with key people in your target company, you can ask them for referrals to influencers in other departments of the organization. Your contacts at an organization have inside knowledge and will usually be able to tell you whom to talk to if you want to make something happen. If they're satisfied with the service you've been providing, these contacts are often happy to give you the names of others who might be able to use your solutions. Complementary salespeople can also be an excellent source of information about a prospect. For example, if you are selling computer hardware you might find nuggets of information from the person who sells office furniture. You can help each other by sharing insights and information.

It might surprise you to know that competitive salespeople can also be a resource. If you're a member of a professional organization, if you attend conferences or tradeshows, or if you're simply connected in your community, you'll probably know competitive salespeople. While your competitor isn't going to give you the inside scoop on a prospect he's currently pursuing, he might share some useful insights about companies or people he has worked with in the past. Maybe he used to do business with one of your current contacts and can tell you things to avoid or things that will impress her. ("She will eat you alive if you don't have all your information.") Maybe one of your target companies is an organization he has sold to in the past, and he has some useful advice about the way they work. Never underestimate the power of relationships and networking.

Key Takeaways

- The preapproach is a critical step that helps you earn your customer's trust and sell adaptively; this is true whether you are meeting with a new customer—a **target account**—or an existing customer—one of your **key accounts**.
- Before you make your sales call, you should know the objectives of the meeting. You should record these objectives, along with basic company information, on a **precall planning worksheet**.

- Preapproach research includes information like company demographics, company news, and financial performance to help you discover sales opportunities and go deeper in your qualifying process.
- Research the company's customers, the current buying situation, and your contact person at the company to help you tailor your sales approach.
- Research your existing customers to find opportunities for expanding the relationship and creating more sales.

Exercises

1. Assume you have identified Gap as a prospect for your product line called "Green" Jeans, blue jeans made with completely recycled materials. You are preparing for a sales call with the denim buyer in the Gap's home office. What demographic information would you gather about the company during the preapproach stage? What would recent company news tell you in preparation for your sales call? What do current customers think about Gap? What is your value proposition, and how does it fit Gap's need?

2. Imagine you work for a company that sells interior design services and acts as an art broker (finding and purchasing artwork to display) for large companies. One of your customers has used your broker services in the past, but you are hoping to expand the relationship. What additional information would you need to know to make a proposal?

3. Assume you are selling payroll services to small businesses. Identify three pieces of information you would learn about your prospect during your preapproach research and identify the sources where you would find the information.

4. Imagine that you sell life insurance. Describe how customer demographics can help you with your preapproach research.

5. Assume you are selling security systems and you have just qualified a prospect, Fine Dining, Inc., that owns a chain of fifteen restaurants in the area. Your contact is Lee Crowan, the operations manager. The corporate office is located in the Willowwood Corporate Center in Willowwood. You have learned that the chain is growing, with expansion to ten new restaurants planned in the next twelve months. You have also learned that security is a major issue since two of the existing restaurants have had break-ins during the past six months. Complete a precall planning worksheet for your upcoming call with Lee Crowan at Fine Dining, Inc.

6. Assume you are selling financial services to consumers. You have identified a couple in their forties as qualified prospects. They are interested in retirement planning. What are three questions you would ask them during your initial meeting with them?

8.2 Solving, Not Selling

Learning Objective

1. Understand how to identify needs and opportunities.

Imagine you wanted to sell a new digital camera to your teenage sister. How would you convince her to buy? You might start by thinking of the things that matter to teenagers—specifically your sister. Maybe you'd say, "It's small and lightweight so you can fit it in your purse and take it with you when you go out with your friends. It has a new sleek design, and you can customize it by ordering it in one of six different colors." You've considered things your sister might need (a camera she can take on a night out), and you've identified an opportunity that might appeal to a teenaged girl (a combination of appearance, style, and functionality).

Now what if you were selling the same product to your grandmother? She might be more concerned with reliability than appearance, and she might also be intimidated about using a digital camera if it's a technology she hasn't tried before. "This camera doesn't have a lot of bells and whistles," you could say. "It's straightforward and easy to use and makes an excellent choice for a first digital camera purchase. It's perfect for taking pictures of the grandkids. It has also been highly rated as a reliable and high-quality product." You've addressed her problem (intimidation about using a new technology), and you've helped her discover opportunities (taking photos of the grandkids).

Even though you're selling the same product to both people, you're using a very different approach. Ultimately, what you're selling is not a product but a *solution* based on your customer's specific needs. This is the heart of the preapproach. There are three simple steps you can follow to turn your products and services into customer-specific solutions.

Step 1: Complete a Needs and Opportunity Analysis

Great salespeople don't sell, they solve. As you research your prospect, you should be able to identify problems that are specific to that person or organization: Do they need to reduce costs? Do they need to increase sales? Do they need to drive traffic to a Web site or generate leads for their new service? Or maybe they need something that will set their brand apart from their competitors. In the case of individual consumers, the problem might be very different: Does she want to have the latest in fashion without couture prices? Does she want the latest technology "toys" as soon as they are available? Does she want a car that is a dependable form of transportation and friendly to the environment?

Sometimes people are forthcoming about their problems, but many times it's up to you to ask the *right* questions; the ones that will uncover what your prospect needs or where opportunities exist. (Remember from Chapter 1 that is one of the traits of a successful salesperson.) For instance, if your prospect is buying from a competitor, you might ask questions like "What were your expectations when you signed up for this service? What has your actual experience of the service been? What would you like to see happen differently?" The prospect might not fully realize what his problems are.[9] Often, especially in B2B sales, the goal of your first sales call will simply be to identify your prospect's specific areas of need. You won't make a pitch; you'll just ask questions and listen.[10]

Asking questions often opens up opportunities you might not otherwise discover. There will be occasions when your prospect doesn't have an immediate problem she can identify, but if you've done your research and know something about her goals and priorities and if you ask the right questions, you have the chance to uncover useful opportunities. What can help him achieve his goals even more efficiently? What kinds of results would he like to see?[11] What would he like to have if he only knew it was possible?

Think about the advent of the cell phone. Consumers had a problem: their lives were getting busier, and they wanted to be able to communicate on the go. They needed a phone they could use when they weren't at home or in the office. What do you do on a car trip if you get lost or your car breaks down? How do you find someone in a crowded place? How can people get in touch with you if you're almost never home? Cell phone providers figured out consumers' problems, and they solved them. Then along came the iPhone. Most cell phone users wouldn't have said they *needed* a device that could capture videos and photographs, play MP3s, store a day planner, surf the web, run hundreds of different applications—oh, and make phone calls too—using a single slick interface. But Apple saw an opportunity, and they helped consumers to see it too: over a million iPhones sold the first weekend the product came out in stores.[12]

Step 2: Brainstorm Solutions and Generate Ideas

Once you've identified your customer's problems, take the time—either with a team or on your own—to brainstorm solutions and opportunities that address your prospect's specific needs. Sometimes solving your prospect's problem is a straightforward task, but often with larger sales, particularly B2B sales, coming up with a solution that is tailored to your customer's needs requires time and thought. No two prospects are the same, so no two solutions will be exactly the same. When Joel Ronning, CEO of e-commerce company Digital River, wants to solve customer problems and generate ideas, he sits down with the senior employees of his company for a brainstorming session. The technique has boosted sales, earned the company hundreds of thousands of dollars, and led to a small business award for "best idea."[13] As a salesperson, your job is to solve customer problems, *not* push a product. In other words, you're offering solutions that include unique and different ideas, not selling products. For this reason, brainstorming—the process of generating ideas—is a crucial part of the selling process.

When you go into a brainstorming session, there are several techniques that will help you generate effective results.

- **Know your problem or opportunity**. If you've already completed your needs analysis, you're off to a good start. According to James Feldman, a Chicago-based idea-generation consultant, "Most people do not identify their problem correctly" going into the brainstorming session. Once you have a clear idea of the problem or opportunity, set it out in specific terms to guide your brainstorm. Just make sure you don't define the problem so narrowly that you'll limit your results. Start the session by stating the objective. What problem do you want to solve? It also helps to frame the question in positive terms. For example, rather than asking "How will this company's new computer system change the way they do business?" you could ask "How can this company get the most out of their new computer system?"[14]

- **Generate; don't evaluate**. Brainstorming isn't about coming up with the best, most carefully polished solutions. As Gary Kopervas, chief creative strategist at Backe Digital Brand Marketing, says, "When you're brainstorming, don't be perfect; be prolific." Get your ideas out there, on paper, without disrupting the flow. Once you've exhausted your resources, you can worry about sorting out the stronger ideas from the weaker ones. If you're too critical of your ideas to begin with, you'll never access that part of your brain where the creative ideas are generated. In fact, Kopervas has devised the Five Fs of Brainstorming to guide a more effective process. They are outlined in Figure 8.4.[15]

FIGURE 8.4 Five Fs of Brainstorming

Element	Description
Focus	Start with an objective; identify the problem you want to solve.
Flow	Invite a diverse group of people to participate to get a mix of ideas.
Freshness	Use critical customer insights to ignite idea generation.
Follow-through	Appoint a scribe for each brainstorming session to take notes, then prioritize and digitize.
Frequency	Incorporate brainstorming into as many activities as frequently as possible; the more often you brainstorm, the better you will get at it.

- **Push beyond the wall**. At some point during every brainstorming session, whether group brainstorming or individual, people tend to hit a wall. Ideas flow quickly, and then they seem to stop altogether. Cognitive psychologist Paul Paulus says this point in the session may seem like a wall, but in reality it's just "a space in [the] brain." Pushing past this space often leads to the best ideas.[16]

- **Seek strategic stimuli**. Sometimes you have to disrupt your normal routine to get the ideas flowing. Putting yourself in a new environment or doing something with your hands—molding clay, for instance—can often be a surprising way to unlock ideas in your subconscious that your rational mind might otherwise block off.

Brainstorming, as an idea-generation tool, is a proven and powerful part of creative development. However, keep in mind that some of the ideas you come up with in the brainstorming process will be stronger than others. A great idea has two important elements: it solves your customer's problems and, in B2B sales, it reinforces your customer's brand. Consider consultant Mike Rubin's solution to a problem faced by one of his customers, a Harley-Davidson dealer, who wanted to boost sales and appeal to a broader customer base. Mike's Famous Harley-Davidson Dealership was already drawing in the "hard-core" bikers, but the store's owner wanted to reach the more conservative, baby boomer demographic too. By turning the dealership into a destination, complete with a Harley museum and restaurant, Rubin hit on a solution that both addressed the customer's problem and remained true to the Harley brand image. The restaurant, designed to resemble a factory cafeteria, appealed to tough bikers and families alike, and the museum—also a family-friendly draw—was laid out in a warehouse style that reflected the company's brand image of independence, toughness, and the open road. The result? In three years, bike sales increased from 800 to over 1,700 annually.[17]

Power Selling: Lessons in Selling from Successful Brands

They Practice What They Preach
Ideo, a premier product development company, believes that innovation is the only path to success. Collaboration and idea generation are a way of life at the company that invented the Apple mouse, Polaroid I-Zone pocket camera, and Palm V. This article highlights how they support and encourage this creative culture.[18]

http://www.fastcompany.com/articles/2001/03/kelley.html

Source: Fast Company

If you are working out of your home and you don't have a group of people with which to brainstorm, it's not a problem. Get your colleagues in other areas involved by having a brainstorming conference call. Or have a virtual brainstorming session through your professional social network by using the discussion feature on LinkedIn, getting ideas from your followers on Twitter, or creating a **wiki** where people can share ideas at any time and see the ideas that others have created.

The bottom line is that selling is all about selling your brand (remember from Chapter 1 that a brand is unique, consistent, and relevant and has an emotional connection with its customers). When you really understand your customer and their needs and motivations, you can be extremely creative about the way you position and tell the story of your brand.

wiki

A collaborative Web site that allows multiple people to share information, documents, videos, and pictures.

Video Clip

How Ideas Are Born
Tim Brown, the CEO of the creative design firm Ideo, discusses how ideas are created.

View the video online at: http://www.youtube.com/embed/fzW8Y6F-mQ4

Step 3: Identify General and Specific Benefit Statements

Once you have brainstormed a customer-specific solution, you want to find a way to showcase your solution in the best light. How will you present this idea to your prospect so that he can immediately see its relevance to his situation? How will you establish the value proposition you have to offer? How will you position your idea as a benefit to your prospect, not a self-serving sales pitch? As part of your preapproach, you should identify both a general and a specific statement to highlight the benefits of your solution or opportunity. When you deliver value to your prospect, you earn the opportunity to be a business partner, not just someone who is trying to sell something.

Imagine you work for a dairy products distributor that sells wholesale to restaurants. You've researched one of your prospects, a downtown deli, and have identified one of its major problems: the company is losing business to the sandwich place across the street. Your prospect may not yet realize the source of the trouble, but you have an idea. It seems that the prospect's competitor has cheaper sandwiches, and you know for a fact that part of the problem lies in the cost of the ingredients. Your prospect currently pays 10 percent more for the cheese it gets from its current vendor than you would charge for the same product. If the deli started buying cheese from you, it would be able to lower the cost of its sandwiches to a more competitive price and draw some of the sales that are going to its competitor. You have also brainstormed how the deli can create a "signature sandwich": a unique combination of meat and cheeses that only it offers. The sandwich provides a point of difference for the deli and a reason for previous deli customers to come back. In other words, you are helping to build your prospect's brand and business with a great idea.

general benefit statement

An opening statement for a sales call that gives the big picture of how your solution meets your prospect's need.

This is a good solution, but you can't walk into the deli and tell your prospect, "I want to sell you some cheese." Your prospect doesn't need cheese; he needs to increase his sales, and he'll probably tell you to go away because he already has a dairy products vendor. It's your job to frame the solution in such a way that your customer can easily see its relevance to his problem; you want to answer the "What's in it for me?" question early on in the sales call.[19] Begin by drafting a **general benefit statement**, a statement that gives the big picture of how your solution will meet your prospect's need. For instance, you might say, "I have an idea for a way to increase your sandwich sales by 15 percent." Your statement showcases a solution rather than a product.

General benefit statements, as opposed to specific benefit statements, are broad enough that they would be important to most people.[20] They might address things like improving company visibility, expanding the business, increasing profits, or cutting costs. The **specific benefit statement**, on the other hand, comes once you've grabbed your prospect's attention. It identifies the particular way your solution applies to your prospect, and it demonstrates that you've done your research and understand the needs that are unique to his company or situation. For instance, you might say, "Your food cost is too high, and it's keeping you from competing with other businesses. I can help you cut your food costs so that you can afford to sell your breakfast burrito for under $2.99. Would that be something you would be interested in?" If you've done your research and brainstormed an effective solution, your benefits statements are the tools that will give you the power to convey that information clearly and effectively.

specific benefit statement

Identifies the way a solution addresses a prospect's particular situation and needs.

TABLE 8.1 Benefit Statement Examples

General Benefit Statement	Specific Benefit Statement
I have an idea that can help you lower your labor costs. Is that something you might be interested in?	If I can prove that I can help you reduce your labor costs by 10 percent, would you be willing to make a commitment?
I have some ideas about how to increase traffic to your Web site. Is that something that is of interest to you?	If I can show you how our social networking tool can drive 15 percent more traffic to your Web site during key seasonal periods, would you be willing to consider it?
I have some ideas about how to decrease your transaction time and take care of more customers every hour. Is that something you are interested in?	If I can show you how our product can decrease your transaction time for each customer by at least one minute, would you be interested in looking at the proposal?

Key Takeaways

- Good salespeople don't sell products; they sell *solutions* to their customers' problems or challenges.
- Your research, including the questions you ask your customer, should help you identify needs and opportunities.
- Once you have identified your customers' problems and goals, brainstorm solutions and opportunities that will meet their needs.
- Knowing the best solution for your customer will help you craft a **general benefits statement** and a **specific benefits statement** that will help the customer envision the way your solution or opportunity meets his needs.

Exercises

1. Think about a local bank that offers free checking accounts. How does free checking provide a solution for a business customer? How would this solution be different for an individual customer? How do you think the personal banker changes her sales pitch based on the customer?
2. Describe a time when you made a purchase, or modified a planned purchase, because a salesperson revealed an opportunity that you wouldn't have otherwise considered.
3. Think of the last major purchase you made where you bought from a salesperson (not online). Did the salesperson adapt his or her approach to address your specific needs and concerns? If so, how?
4. Imagine that you sell Hershey's chocolate products to grocery stores. One of your prospects said that he cannot carry the complete line of Hershey's Kisses because there isn't enough

shelf space in the store. Conduct a short brainstorming session to identify ten ideas that might solve this prospect's problem.

5. Assume you worked in the Apple Store. Identify one general benefit statement and one specific benefit statement for each of the following:

   - iPod
   - MacBook Pro
   - iTunes

6. Assume that due to the recession, donations to the Make-A-Wish Foundation are below expectations. The foundation's director of development has asked your class to identify ideas to increase donations in the next three months. Work in teams of two to conduct a brainstorming session using the guidelines covered in this section. Each team should present their ideas to the class.

8.3 Identify Precall Objectives: Getting Smart about Your Sales Call

Learning Objective

1. Learn how to set SMART precall objectives.

Identifying your prospect's need is only part of your preapproach research. There's still more research and planning for you to do before you meet with or speak to the customer.

Determine Your Objectives

precall objectives

Goals that are determined for the sales call before the call is made.

If you haven't determined what you hope to achieve before going into your sales call, it will be difficult to figure out what to say once you arrive or once you have your prospect on the phone. Setting **precall objectives** is a strategically important step. If you have clear goals, you will be more confident and appear more organized, and it's more likely that you will see results. Your customers are busy people, and you don't want to waste their time. They will appreciate your organization and will be more likely to trust your judgment if you come prepared. You also don't want to waste *your* time or your company's time. According to Hoovers, the average sales call costs a company nearly $400![21]

one-call close

A sales call that results in a sale after one call.

sales cycle

The length of time it takes to go from the first contact with the customer to closing the sale.

As you plan your meeting, ask yourself this question: "What will success look like for this call?"[22] That may seem like a question with a straightforward answer, but success doesn't always mean closing the sale. In some situations, you'll experience a **one-call close**, but with larger sales, particularly in B2B sales, the **sales cycle**, or the length of time it takes to go from the first contact with the customer to closing the sale, is generally longer—sometimes even taking up to a year or longer. Consider Telegraph Hill Robes, a San Francisco-based company that sells bathrobes to upscale hotels with spas. Buying enough bathrobes to stock a hotel spa is a large investment, one that most customers have to carefully consider. The sale has to clear with two contacts at every company: the general manager and the head of housekeeping. As a result, when Telegraph Hill first started selling its product in 1996, its average sales cycle was two years![23]

If you know that you are facing a longer sales cycle, the goal of your initial call might be gathering and conveying specific information to move forward in the sales process or further qualify your prospect. According to Gary Duncan, principal of the sales training organization Leadership Connections, "In more complex sales it's realistic to set a precall objective of establishing rapport and trust, making new contacts in the organization, qualifying your prospect's budget, or discovering what your prospect's decision-making process is. For instance, you might decide you want to find out who your prospect's current vendors are, any issues your prospect has with the services she is receiving, and what her goals are for future purchases."[24] You should also consider your prospect's objectives: what outcome is she hoping for from this call?

Sometimes, setting strategic, information-gathering objectives may actually help you shorten your overall sales cycle. Take Acumen, a company that sells high-capability accounting software to corporations. Originally, the company's sales cycle lasted around nine months. However, once the company became more strategic in its precall planning, designing a system of rigorous qualifying questions that its salespeople had to resolve before making a sales pitch, Acumen actually decreased its average sales cycle to somewhere between three and six months. Asking detailed questions during early sales calls allowed the company to cut back on the time it wasted brainstorming solutions and making sales pitches for underqualified leads.[25]

Make Your Objectives SMART

So it's early in the process of a complex sale, and you are setting your goals for your next meeting with your customer. You know it will primarily be an information-gathering session because you need to know more before you can propose a workable, specific solution. However, if you go into the meeting with a vague plan like "I want to find out more about my prospect's business," you won't accomplish much.[26] Instead, you might come up with a goal similar to the one mentioned earlier: "By the end of this meeting, I want to know who my prospect's current vendors are, what issues or challenges he faces with this vendor's services, and what three priorities he has for future purchases." This objective, like all effective precall objectives, is **SMART**. That is, the goal is **S**pecific, **M**easurable, **A**ctionable, **R**ealistic, and **T**ime-bound.[27]

- **Specific**. The goal should clearly define which actions you want your customer to take, what information you hope to convey, and/or what information you hope to learn from your sales call. In the example cited by Gary Duncan, the salesperson is setting out to gather three specific pieces of information.

- **Measurable**. You want to be able to measure the results of your efforts so that you'll know at the end of your sales call how close you came to achieving what you set out to do. This will help you strategize about which actions to take next. The first two parts of the example are measurable with a simple yes or no (Did I find out the names of the current vendors? Did I identify issues and challenges my customer has encountered?), and the last part of the goal is quantifiable (How many of my customer's priorities was I able to help him articulate?).

- **Actionable**. If a goal is actionable or attainable, it's something you can actually *do*. It might involve asking questions, explaining something, or suggesting something. Whatever the case, it should be something on which you have the ability to act. In some instances, the actionable goal might be as simple as closing the sale: "By the end of the meeting, I plan to convince my prospect to sign a contract."

- **Realistic**. If you set your goal too high or try to move your sales process along too quickly, you will only be setting yourself up for disappointment and failure. Ask yourself, "What can I reasonably hope to accomplish given the current situation with my prospect?" If you decide you want to get appointments with ten top people in the organization during your first contact with the company, or if you intend to close a major account by your first call, you will probably not be able to achieve what you set out to do.

- **Time-bound**. Not only should you know *what* you hope to achieve, but you should also know *when* you hope to have it accomplished. In the example objective, your time frame is "by the end of the sales call." Other times, you might set a specific date—for example, "Get the prospect to agree to schedule a face-to-face meeting by the 15th."

SMART

An acronym to identify the elements of a successful sales goal: **S**pecific, **M**easurable, **A**ctionable, **R**ealistic, and **T**ime-bound.

FIGURE 8.5 SMART Objectives

S = Specific

M = Measureable

A = Actionable

R = Realistic

T = Time-bound

SMART objectives give you the power to sell strategically by setting goals you can achieve. Another powerful tool is the simple act of putting your goals down in writing. Not only are you likely to make a stronger commitment to your goals when you have them on paper, but you will also be able to use your written goals for reference later on—even during the sales call if you need to.[28]

Video Clip

Setting SMART Objectives
Watch this short video about setting SMART objectives for your sales calls.

View the video online at: http://www.youtube.com/embed/1P6bU1efZbl

FIGURE 8.6 Examples of SMART Objectives

SMART Objectives	Objectives that are not SMART
• Complete at least 25 cold calls to qualified prospects by September 1, 2010.	• Conduct as many sales calls as possible as soon as possible.
• Increase sales of Waffle Wraps to chain grocery stores by 8% over last year by December 31, 2010.	• Sell as many Waffle Wraps as possible this year.
• Convert 33% of leads to customers within 30 days of initial contact.	• Convert some leads every day so that you always have new customers.
• Follow up with every prospect and customer within 48 hours of sales call.	• Follow up with every prospect and customer after a sales call.

Key Takeaways

- It's important to know exactly what you want to accomplish when you go into a sales meeting.
- The goals for your sales call should be specific, measurable, actionable, realistic, and time-bound: **SMART**.
- Setting **SMART** goals will help you direct your approach, take action, and measure the results of your sales call.

Exercises

1. Which of the following is a SMART goal for your first sales call on a prospect to sell car insurance? Rewrite each of the other goals to be SMART.
   - Identify current insurance carrier and conduct needs analysis by Friday.
   - Call the customer and ask some questions to learn about his current situation.
   - Conduct online research about the customer and understand why he chose his current insurance carrier.
   - Call at least six new prospects by the end of the day today.
2. Imagine you sell Web site consulting services and are going into a sales call with an existing customer. You want to expand the selling relationship in two ways: by extending your contract with the customer for another two years and by getting referrals for the network support department. Identify your SMART goal for this sales call.
3. Assume you are a financial advisor and you are meeting with a prospect for the first time. Identify a SMART objective that you would set prior to your first meeting.

4. Describe the difference in the sales cycles between selling jeans to a college student compared to selling a home to a newly married couple. What impact will that have on your SMART objectives?

5. You are a sales rep for medical supplies and just took on a new prospect, Springfield Nursing Homes, a regional chain of twenty-two nursing homes. You have a contact, but you are not clear if he is a decision maker. In the past, the company has allowed each nursing home to make its own purchasing decisions, but it is moving toward a more centralized approach. This is an excellent opportunity for you to present your comprehensive product line. You are preparing for your first call, and your sales manager has asked you to review your SMART objectives for the call with him. What are your SMART objectives for the call? How you will present them to your sales manager?

8.4 Prepare Your Presentation

Learning Objective

1. Discuss key elements of presentation preparation.

Once you've done your research, brainstormed your solution, and set your SMART objectives, you've got a good foundation to move forward. The only homework left to do is planning your sales presentation. Even if you have a stellar solution to offer, and even though your objectives may be clearly defined, you can't make your sales pitch hoping to just "wing it." A well-planned presentation can often be the thing that makes or breaks a sale. If your customer sees you as well prepared (i.e., if you have thoughtfully tailored your style, presentation materials, and agenda to match what you know about your contact and his company culture), you will go far in establishing a strong rapport with your customer and earning his trust and respect.

Four Ps of Presentation Preparation

Preparing your sales presentation can seem like an overwhelming task. How long should you speak, and how much time should you allow for questions? Should you use demonstrations or examples? How formal should you be? What points should you address first? Here are four general guidelines to keep in mind as you begin the planning process.

Prioritize Your Agenda

Your presentation should be well organized. Think about how you want to lead in, when you will introduce key information in your presentation, and when you will use product demonstrations. When Tom Szaky, CEO of the garden products company TerraCycle, gives a sales presentation, he prepares by drawing up an agenda that prioritizes the information he wants to convey and arranging it in a strategic order. For example, Szaky knows that if he presents his product near the beginning of the presentation, his customers will make their buying decision before they know what makes TerraCycle unique, so he starts off all of his presentations by talking about the features that set his company apart.[29] Not only will prioritizing your agenda give you a strategic edge, but it will also help your customer to see that you are organized. Bring copies of your agenda to distribute at the beginning of the meeting so that your customers can follow along with you as you give your presentation.

Personalize It

At this phase in the preapproach you should have some knowledge about your contacts in the company, and you should understand the company's particular culture and priorities. As you plan your presentation, you can use this knowledge to tailor your approach to your prospect. What tone will you set for the presentation? Is your prospect a "fun" company that would respond well to humor or interactive opportunities during the presentation? Are you presenting to a group of busy executives who would value an efficient, no-nonsense approach? Think about the level of formality your customers will expect. This will dictate how you dress, how you speak, and how you design your visual aids and demonstrations. When Tom Szaky gives a presentation to buyers from Wal-Mart (one of his biggest customers), he dresses casually, perhaps wearing a corduroy jacket, a John Deere cap, and frayed shoes.[30] Wal-Mart presents itself as a no-frills company, and this attitude carries over into its corporate culture. Understanding this aspect of the company and the contacts with whom he's working—representatives from the garden department—Szaky adapts his approach to match.

FIGURE 8.7
It's best to dress the way your customers dress for a sales call. If in doubt, always choose conservative business attire.

© 2010 Jupiterimages Corporation

Power Player: Lessons in Selling from Successful Salespeople

Do Your Homework...Even When You Know Your Customer
Cris Cavanaugh, now a CustomerCentric selling affiliate, learned the hard way that assuming in selling is not a good thing. He was asked by a customer to do a presentation at a conference. Cavanaugh accepted and gave a confident presentation. He failed miserably because the audience was not as well educated on the topic, so the audience was left confused. Cavanaugh now asks questions and gets input before every presentation because he realizes that every audience, just like every customer, is not the same.[31]

Prepare Illustrations

People respond best to things they can see and experience for themselves. Your sales presentation won't be complete without product demonstrations and visual aids to inspire your customers and help them see the value of your product firsthand. As you develop this aspect of your presentation, consider slides or handouts that will reinforce key points. Consider the things that will best help this particular customer visualize your solution as a winning one. For example, in one presentation to Wal-Mart buyers, Szaky displayed a binder full of newspaper clippings in which TerraCycle had helped Wal-Mart generate positive publicity. He also used a short video and brought in a live plant grown with his potting mix. In addition, because his contact at the company had asked to see what the product might look like on the sales floor, Szaky brought in a merchandising mockup to help his buyers visualize TerraCycle's potting mix in their stores.[32]

Practice

Finally, once you've created your presentation, practice it. Practice in front of a mirror, deliver the presentation to family members and colleagues (if you can get a willing audience!), and run over your agenda until you know it inside and out.[33] You want the presentation to come off smoothly, but you also want it to seem natural. Even experienced salespeople like Tom Szaky practice a presentation—perfecting their pacing and delivery and making sure they know their stuff—before going into a sales call.[34]

Key Takeaway

As you plan your sales presentation, keep four things in mind:

1. Prioritize and organize your agenda.
2. Personalize the presentation to match your customer's needs and preferences.
3. Prepare visual aids and product demonstrations to illustrate your point and engage your audience.
4. Practice your delivery.

Exercises

1. Think of ways you might personalize a sales presentation for the following situations:
   - You are a public relations manager pitching a story about your company's new chic waterproof boots to the editorial staff of a fashion magazine.
   - You are a commercial real estate agent making a presentation to top-level managers at an accounting firm for the new location of their downtown office.
   - You are a video game developer presenting your newest game concept to a small start-up company that makes video games.

2. Assume you are the director of development for Jessica's Haven, a nonprofit organization that provides support to children with terminal illnesses and their families. You have identified Gymboree as a prospective corporate donor. Develop an agenda for a sales call to learn about how Gymboree might support Jessica's Haven and share information with the company about who the nonprofit serves and how it operates.

3. If you were the salesperson for Red Bull and you were calling on a major grocery store chain, identify three potential illustrations that you could use during your presentation.

4. Describe how your preapproach would differ (in dress, tone, conversation) for each of these situations:
   - Selling pharmaceuticals to a doctor
   - Meeting with the dairy farmers of Wisconsin to sell cheese packaging
   - Calling on a professor to sell textbooks
   - Selling computer software to a start-up liquor manufacturer

8.5 *Selling U*: Six Power-Packed Tools to Let the Right People Know about Your Brand

Learning Objective

1. Learn about six different ways to get your cover letter and résumé to the right people.

Now that you understand how preparation can help you be successful in selling, let's go back to selling the most important brand of all—you! In the *Selling U* section in Chapter 7, you did your research, identified and qualified your twenty-five target companies, and obtained the contact information for at least two key people at each organization. Of course, there is still some homework to do before you see the payoff of securing an interview. As Andrew Sum, director of Northeastern University's Center for Labor Market Studies, says, "You're never going to find anything unless you apply."[35] However, you can think of this step in the process as the exciting part. Consider what happens when a company releases a new product. The company doesn't keep the news to themselves, discreetly shipping the product out to stores with the hopes that the right buyers will just happen to find it. Instead, it leverages every resource it has to get the word out. Think about the new Prius. Toyota took advantage of publicity surrounding the car's fuel efficiency to generate buzz with newspapers, radio, and television reporting on Prius-related press releases. Toyota leveraged Web resources (e.g., blogs, discussion forums, product fan sites) and highlighted positive product reviews in its press releases and online.[36]

When a company has designed a new product or brand, it is excited to let people know about it. The more enthusiastically it shares the news, the better the payoff. The same should be true of your job search. *You* are a new brand that is about to go on the market, you know you have unique qualities to offer, and you should be excited to let other people know this about you, too. Sending the news to potential employers at your target companies is a good way to start. If you take advantage of this tool, in combination with five other power-packed tools for getting the word out, you will be surprised by the positive results you see.

Power-Packed Tool #1: Professional Social Networking

You learned about the power of networking, and especially professional social networking, in Chapter 3. More and more companies are turning to professional social networks such as LinkedIn to identify potential candidates for jobs. But it's not enough to simply create a profile on LinkedIn. To be noticed on a massive professional networking site, just as in the real world, you have to stand out. That means completing your profile, adding content, participating in discussions, and linking to other content, such as your blog. Also, share your content by joining groups on LinkedIn, such as *The Power of Selling* (a group of selling professionals to support you in this class and beyond), Sales and Marketing Executives, and Salesblogcast.com, or other groups in your area of interest. These groups include thousands of professionals with whom you can connect and network. And ask people such as supervisors from your job, internship, or volunteer organization; professors; or other professionals to speak on your behalf by posting a recommendation about you.

Power-Packed Tool #2: Direct Mail

Direct mail is a powerful but often overlooked source you have for getting your cover letter and résumé to people who are making hiring decisions. Now that you've done your research and identified your twenty-five target companies and key decision makers at each one, it's time to put that information to work.

You might think that sending letters to companies that don't currently have open jobs posted might be a waste of time. The fact is that hiring managers don't like to post jobs, as it takes time and energy to come up with the job description, clear it through all the proper channels, sort through résumés and cover letters, and interview potential employees. This means that a number of your contacts may have open positions they haven't yet publicized, and they would be delighted if a qualified candidate like you could save them the hassle of a drawn out hiring process. And if you've done everything correctly (e.g., addressed your cover letter individually to key hiring managers, not just human resources), but your letter doesn't end up in the right person's hands, your contact at the company may very well pass your résumé on to someone else who would be a better fit. ("Hey Dave, is your department still looking for a marketing assistant?") If you want your letter to stand out even more, consider sending it to some top prospective employers with a return receipt requested or via FedEx. It's a good way to ensure that the recipient received your cover letter and résumé and there's a good chance your letter will get opened quickly.

FIGURE 8.9

Sending your résumé and cover letter via direct mail helps you stand out and get the word out about your brand.

© 2010 Jupiterimages Corporation

Sending your cover letter and résumé to several people at your twenty-five target companies will set you apart from your competitors because very few people send information by mail these days. Think about the number of e-mails you get in your in-box daily. A letter stands out, and the best part about sending direct mail to your target companies is that it's easy to do. You can use the spreadsheet you created in Chapter 7 to easily personalize cover letters and envelopes to the people at your target companies by using the **mail merge feature**.[37] Watch the video below to see how it's done. Keep in mind that hiring managers are busy people, and sometimes letters get lost or forgotten. If you don't get the response you were hoping for, send your letter to the same people in your mail merge again in three to four weeks.[38]

Video Clip

How to Do a Mail Merge
You can personalize hundreds of cover letters in just minutes using the Mail Merge feature in Word (Microsoft or Mac). Watch this video to see how easy it is to do.

View the video online at: http://www.youtube.com/embed/uCN4VCU5igE

Power-Packed Tool #3: Company Web Sites

During the preapproach to a sales call, a good salesperson spends time at her prospective company's Web site, researching the organization and its key people in greater depth so that she can go into the meeting knowledgeable about basic company facts and informed of any recent developments. This is also an important technique when researching prospective employers—and it's a task that requires minimal effort on your part. If one of your target companies contacts you for an interview, the knowledge you gained from this Web site research will prove useful.

The online job boards for your twenty-five target companies are another avenue for getting the word out about your brand. It doesn't hurt to apply for published positions, particularly if you take steps (using techniques described here and in other chapters) to set yourself apart from the majority of other applicants. If the Web site gives you the option, sign up for e-mail alerts that will let you know when new positions open up. Company Web sites are excellent resources for finding advertised positions because the job descriptions posted there are often more detailed than the descriptions you might be able to find through general online job boards.[39] Moreover, many companies post open positions only on their Web sites to avoid the cost of posting on other job boards.

Power-Packed Tool #4: Online Job Boards

The benefit of online job boards like Monster.com, CareerBuilder.com, and Yahoo! HotJobs is that they make it a snap to perform searches by industry and keyword, and they often return a wealth of results. In fact, Internet job boards have recently become one of the fastest growing online categories.[40] These sites can be an excellent avenue for learning about career opportunities in your target industry, and they should be an ongoing part of your efforts to find the right employer.[41] These sites might help you find job opportunities through companies that you wouldn't have otherwise considered working for, and they will certainly keep you informed about the kinds of positions for which people are currently hiring in your industry and the particular qualifications for which many employers are searching.

Most sites will allow you to set up e-mail alerts (customized by your chosen keywords) so that new job postings come to your in-box regularly. It's best to enter as many keywords as you can think of that are relevant to your interests and experiences so that you don't miss anything. For instance, if you want a job in advertising, you would choose *advertising* as a keyword, but you could also list words like *promotions*, *account executive*, *account manager*, *account coordinator*, *customer services*, *brand manager*, *advertising agency*, and *social media*.[42] You might also consider creating a separate e-mail account to keep track of your job-related e-mails, particularly if you have subscribed to alerts through several job search Web sites. In fact, it's a good idea to go through a number of Web sites so that you can stay informed about as many opportunities as possible. You can go through general job boards like Vault.com or CareerBuilder.com, industry-specific job boards like MarketingSherpa.com, location-specific job boards like SeattleRecruiter.com, or a combination of these options.

TABLE 8.2 Online Job Boards

General	
CollegeGrad.com http://collegegrad.com	Career information and job board directed at college students
Vault.com http://vault.com/wps/portal/usa	Job board, internship opportunities, and information on career planning
Experience http://www.experience.com	Job board, articles, and career planning advice
CareerBuilder.com http://careerbuilder.com/	One of the largest job boards on the Internet; includes career planning articles
Craigslist http://www.craigslist.org/about/sites	Location-specific job boards
Industry Specific	
Association Job Boards http://www.associationjobboards.org/find.cfm	Includes links to Web sites of professional associations and job boards
SMEI http://smei.associationcareernetwork.com/Common/HomePage.aspx	Job board for sales and marketing executives
Accounting.com http://www.accounting.com	Job board for *accounting* positions
Sologig.com http://www.sologig.com	Job board for *freelancing*, *contracting*, *consulting*, and *temporary* work
TalentZoo.com http://www.talentzoo.com	Job board for *marketing*, *advertising*, and *PR*
Stylecareers.com http://www.stylecareers.com	Job board for *fashion*, *apparel*, and *retail*
Mediabistro.com http://www.mediabistro.com	Job board for *marketing*

Source: Adapted from Kim Richmond, Brand You, 3rd ed. (Upper Saddle River, NJ: Pearson Prentice Hall, 2008), 221–23.

Although it's important to use direct mail when submitting a cold-contact application, when you apply for positions you find on online job boards, you should apply through the Web site using the format they prescribe. Just make sure you include a cover letter when you submit your résumé. Hiring managers are likely to throw away résumés that come in without cover letters because a cover letter is what allows you to personalize your application, sending the message that you care enough to make an effort in your job search. Finally, keep in mind that while many job seekers rely entirely on online job boards for their searches, and while these sites can be a good avenue for learning about opportunities, they are not an end-all method. They are strongest when used in combination with your direct-mail campaign and the other power-packed tools mentioned in this chapter.

Power-Packed Tool #5: Get Out There

Finally, when you want to let people know you are on the market and have unique skills to offer, consider integrating a number of methods discussed in other chapters of this book to let people see your face. Phone calls, letters, and online communications are critical to your job search, but nothing creates an impression and establishes personal connections like face-to-face interaction.

- **Informational interviews**. (See the *Selling U* section in Chapter 5.) Develop a list of contacts that work in your field of interest and get in touch with several of them to ask about setting up an informational interview: "You do what I would like to do. Could I come in and learn about how you got into the industry?" People naturally love sharing their knowledge and expertise, so most of your contacts will be more than willing to help.[43] Informational interviews are excellent resources for establishing connections and generating job leads.

- **Mentors**. You are never too young nor too old to have a mentor. Mentors can help you develop your knowledge and skills, build your network, and learn inside information about working in your chosen field.[44] Mentors are your allies: the people who most want to see you succeed—and the ones who often have the resources to help you do so.

- **Networking**. (See the *Selling U* section in Chapter 3.) It's impossible to overstate the importance of building your network. Online tools like LinkedIn are powerful resources, but face-to-face networking with personal and professional connections alike can generate surprising results. Who knows, your stylist might tell you, "Oh yeah, my brother-in-law is in sales. You might want to talk to him about a job. I'm not sure if he has any jobs open, but I'll give you his number so you can touch base with him."

- **Internships and professional organizations**. (See the *Selling U* section in Chapter 14.) Internships are an excellent way to network, learn more about working in your chosen field, gain valuable experience, and sometimes get your foot in the door at a company. Another way to get exposure in any industry is by joining and getting involved in professional organizations. In Chapter 14, you will learn more about the value of applying for internships and joining professional organizations.

Power-Packed Tool #6: Follow-Up

Following up helps you maximize your efforts after networking, applying for an online job, sending direct mail, contacting someone via networking (online or offline), and visiting a job fair. You will leave a good impression, help your contacts to remember you, and set yourself apart from other applicants. Follow-up can sometimes have surprising benefits, so even when a door seems closed, make the effort to send a personal note or thank-you. Consider a college graduate who integrated follow-up into her job search. Shortly after applying for a public relations position at one of her target companies, she received a letter saying the position had been filled. Anika followed up on this letter with a note, thanking the interviewer for her time and mentioning how much she had enjoyed their meeting and her visit to the company. A week later, she got the position—the candidate the company originally hired had changed her mind. Because she was the only applicant who had followed up, she stood out, and the company hired her as a replacement.

Consider these techniques that will allow you to make the most of your follow-up efforts:

- **Send thank-you notes**. Send a personal thank-you note to everyone in your online network who gives you a referral and to anyone with whom you have an informational interview.[45] Also, send a thank-you note or e-mail to contacts you meet at career fairs. It's best to send a thank-you e-mail the same day, then follow up with a handwritten note. When you write your handwritten note and mail it the day of your meeting or interview, your contact will usually receive it the next day. And do it in a timely manner. Don't let weeks go by—send your notes within a day so that they arrive while you are still fresh in your contact's mind.

- **Call**. Call your twenty-five target companies one week after you mail out your cover letter and résumé. If you are sending your direct mailings to at least two contacts at each company, it won't be realistic to follow up with *everyone*. Pick the key contact at your target company—usually the hiring manager in your targeted department—with whom you want to follow up and make sure you actually get her on the phone when you call. If the call goes to voice mail, you can leave a message, but try back again until you reach her.

It's also important to keep thorough records of your communications with your target companies and contacts. Use the Excel spreadsheet you created for your mailing list to record the date you mailed your cover letters and résumés, the date you followed up, the result of your follow-up, and any future actions you need to take (e.g., call back in one week). You can use a similar system when you follow up with your online job board applications. Postings listed on online job boards don't always provide the contact info for individuals at the company, but whenever they do, make sure you follow up with this person by phone one week after you have submitted your résumé and cover letter.[46]

Follow-up is an opportunity to take advantage of the research you've been doing and any information you've gathered from tracking a company's RSS feeds or Google News Alerts. For instance, say you want to work in the entertainment industry and you're following up with a hiring manager at Epic Records. You've found out through the company's RSS feed that they've recently released an online collection of bonus tracks, live recordings, and previously unreleased songs by the group Incubus,[47] so you mention this to the hiring manager when you follow up about your application. This lets the hiring manager know that you've done your research and are genuinely interested in the company, which helps establish a rapport.

Key Takeaways

- You will never see the payoff from your potential employer research unless you get the word out. Let people know you are on the market for a job.
- The most important step to ensure your résumé reaches decision makers is direct mailing your cover letter and résumé to contacts at each of your twenty-five target companies—a task you can accomplish easily with a **mail merge**.
- Keep an eye on the Web sites of your twenty-five target companies to find out about new job postings and stay updated on developments at each company.
- Online job boards will let you find out about new advertised positions daily and can help you identify opportunities you might not have otherwise considered.
- Use networking sites like LinkedIn to make new contacts and connect with people in your industry.
- Follow up—after sending a direct mailing, after meeting someone at a career fair, and so on—to strengthen relationships with people that can help you find a job.
- Leverage techniques mentioned in other chapters—informational interviews, mentoring relationships, networking, internships, and professional organization memberships—to help get the word out about your brand.

Exercises

1. Visit the Web sites of five of the companies on your target twenty-five list. Sign up for a job agent and complete a profile, if those are options on each Web site.
2. Visit three online job boards. Sign up for a job agent and complete a profile, if those are options offered on the sites.
3. Identify at least one person with whom you can meet for an informational interview. Contact the person and meet with him to learn about how he got into the business and ask him for additional contacts with whom you can network.
4. Identify at least two professional organizations that may be of interest to you. Visit the Web sites to see their upcoming events and plan to attend a meeting or event for each one. Explore membership information and learn about the benefits and cost of membership. Join each organization's group on LinkedIn, Twitter, and Facebook to keep up-to-date on events and discussions.

8.6 Review and Practice

Power Wrap-Up

Now that you have read this chapter, you should be able to understand the preapproach in selling.

- You can **describe** the role of key and target accounts.
- You can **complete** a precall planning worksheet.
- You can **list** resources to use to conduct preapproach research about prospects.
- You can **identify** needs and opportunities of prospects.
- You can **generate** ideas for your prospects in an effective brainstorming session.
- You **create** general and specific benefit statements.
- You can **determine** SMART precall objectives.
- You can **explore** six different ways to get your cover letter and résumé to the right people.

Test Your Power Knowledge (answers are below)

1. What is the difference between a key account and a target account?
2. Why is a precall planning worksheet completed?
3. Why are customer demographics important in B2B selling?
4. What is the best source of prospects?
5. What is the role of trade journals in researching your prospects?
6. What are some important pieces of information you should learn when you are researching a prospect?
7. List and explain at least three sources of information you would use when researching your prospect.
8. Should you filter your ideas during the brainstorming process? Why or why not?
9. Name two techniques of effective brainstorming.
10. Create a general benefit statement to use if you were selling Starbucks coffee to your friend.
11. What do the letters SMART stand for?
12. Write a SMART objective for your first meeting with a prospect during which you want to learn who is the decision maker.
13. Name at least one thing you should do to prepare for your presentation to a prospect.
14. Name at least three ways to get your cover letter and résumé to the right people.

Power (Role) Play

Now it's time to put what you've learned into practice. Following are two roles that are involved in the same selling situation; one role is that of the sales manager and the other is that of the salesperson. This will give you the opportunity to think about this selling situation from the point of view of both the sales manager and the salesperson.

Read each role carefully along with the discussion questions. Then, be prepared to play either of the roles in class using the concepts covered in this chapter. You may be asked to discuss the roles and role-play in groups or individually.

Green and Bright

Role: Sales Manager for GreenWay Lighting Company

You are the sales manager for GreenWay Lighting. Your product, LED lighting, can save companies up to 30 percent on their lighting bills starting in the first year after purchase. Target customers are industrial companies, such as manufacturers, that have large facilities. One of your sales reps would like to have a brainstorming session with you, the marketing director, product manager, and several other sales reps before approaching a new prospect, JR Papermills. Before the brainstorming session, you meet with the sales rep to discuss the following:

- What information has the sales rep gathered about JR Papermills, and why is the company a good prospect?
- What information has the sales rep gathered about the person with whom he is meeting at JR Papermills?
- What are the SMART objectives that the sales rep has developed for the first sales call?

Role: GreenWay Lighting Sales Rep

Your company markets and sells energy-efficient LED lighting to businesses and other facilities. You have qualified JR Papermills as a prospect due to the size of the facility (500,000 square feet), number of lights (one million), and plans for expansion (new manufacturing plant planned to be operational by the end of next year). You've done your homework about the company, and you learned that they always like to invest in products that give them a return in the first year after purchase. You want to set up a brainstorming session with several people in the company to help develop ideas you can use when you approach this prospect.

- How will you convince your sales manager that JR Papermills is a promising prospect that is worth taking the time for a brainstorming session?
- If you want to gather more information about the prospect, where would you go to learn more about the company? Where would you go to learn more about the person with whom you are going to meet?
- How would you use your preapproach research to structure a brainstorming session?

Put Your Power to Work: *Selling U* Activities

1. Join at least three new groups on LinkedIn (you should have already set up your profile). Then, add at least three additional people to your network every week based on discussions that take place in the groups. Participate in discussions and keep in touch with the new people in your network.
2. Use the list of twenty-five target companies you developed in Chapter 7 and do a test mail merge to see how it works.

Test Your Power Knowledge Answers

1. Target account is a new, qualified prospect. Key account is an existing customer that is or has the potential to be a significant source of sales.
2. It is an organized way to research and learn about your qualified prospect. It is the information gathered here that helps you plan your approach and presentation and the questions you want to explore.
3. B2B selling requires understanding your prospect as well as their customers, which usually include the end user.
4. Existing customers.
5. Trade journals can give you insights about trends in the industry, your prospect's company, and even the prospect himself.
6. About the company: demographics, financial performance, company news; about the company's customers: demographics, size of customer base, what customers are saying about the prospect; about the current buying situation: type of purchase, competitors and current provider, current pricing; about the contact person: title and role in the company, profes-

sional background, personal information, essential problem your contact needs to solve, prospect's motivation for buying,

7. Online databases (e.g., Hoovers), business directories (e.g., Bizjournals.com), trade journals, company Web site, LinkedIn, blogs, social networks, company employees, complementary and competitive salespeople.

8. During brainstorming, it's best not to filter ideas in order to generate as many ideas as possible. Then, the ideas should be prioritized and modified in order to be implemented.

9. Know your problem or opportunity; generate, don't evaluate; push beyond the wall; use strategic stimuli.

10. I have an idea that will refresh your mind and give you a different environment to work in. Does that sound like something you would be interested in?

11. Specific, measurable, actionable (or achievable), realistic, time-bound

12. Learn who is the decision maker and who are influencers for the buying decision at this account by the end of the first sales call.

13. Prioritize the agenda, personalize the presentation, prepare illustrations, and practice.

14. Professional social networking, direct mail, company Web sites, online job boards, follow-up, and getting out there (networking, informational interviews, professional organizations, internships).

Endnotes

1. Neil Rakham, *The SPIN Selling Fieldbook* (New York: McGraw-Hill, 1996), 39.
2. C. J. Ng, "Customers Don't Buy from People They Like, They Buy from Those They Trust," EzineArticles, August 7, 2008, http://ezinearticles.com/?Customers-Dont-Buy-From-People-They-Like,-They-Buy-From-Those-They-Trust&id=1391175 (accessed July 15, 2009).
3. Noel Capon, *Key Account Management and Planning* (New York: The Free Press, 2001), 142.
4. Gerry Tabio, "Creative Solutions," presentation at Greater Media Philadelphia Sales Meeting, Philadelphia, PA, May 14, 2009.
5. "Frontier Airlines Partners with Pepsi," *Breaking Travel News*, January 9, 2003, http://www.breakingtravelnews.com/article.php?story=40005018&query=inflight (accessed July 15, 2009).
6. Marcel Sim, "Leveraging Your CRM System to Expand Your Client Relationships," Get Entrepreneurial, August 12, 2008, http://www.getentrepreneurial.com/customer-service/leveraging_your_crm_system_to_expand_your_client_relationships.html (accessed July 15, 2009).
7. Marcel Sim, "Leveraging Your CRM System to Expand Your Client Relationships," Get Entrepreneurial, August 12, 2008, http://www.getentrepreneurial.com/customer-service/leveraging_your_crm_system_to_expand_your_client_relationships.html (accessed July 15, 2009).
8. Shonan Noronha, "The Joy of Work," *Inc.*, August 1, 2007, http://www.inc.com/sourcebook/prup/20070801.html (accessed July 15, 2009).
9. Paul Cherry, *Questions That Sell: The Powerful Process for Discovering What Your Customer Really Wants* (New York: AMACOM, 2006), 25.
10. Mark Anthony, "The Psychology of Selling," BNET, April 1995, http://findarticles.com/p/articles/mi_qa3629/is_199504/ai_n8730867/?tag=content;col1 (accessed July 15, 2009).
11. Geoffrey James, "Solution Selling Is Dead," BNET, October 29, 2007, http://blogs.bnet.com/salesmachine/?p=158&tag=content;col1 (accessed July 15, 2009).
12. Philip Elmer-DeWitt, "Munster: 500,000 New iPhones This Weekend," *Fortune*, June 18, 2009, http://apple20.blogs.fortune.cnn.com/2009/06/18/munster-500000-new-iphones-this-weekend/ (accessed July 15, 2009).
13. Allison Stein Wellner, "A Perfect Brainstorm," *Inc.*, October 1, 2003, http://www.inc.com/magazine/20031001/strategies.html (accessed July 15, 2009).
14. Allison Stein Wellner, "A Perfect Brainstorm," *Inc.*, October 1, 2003, http://www.inc.com/magazine/20031001/strategies.html (accessed July 15, 2009).
15. Adapted from Gary Kopervas, "More Effective Brainstorming," presentation at Saint Joseph's University, Philadelphia, PA, October 28, 2008.
16. Allison Stein Wellner, "A Perfect Brainstorm," *Inc.*, October 1, 2003, http://www.inc.com/magazine/20031001/strategies.html (accessed July 15, 2009).
17. Donna Fen, "(Re)born to Be Wild," *Inc.*, January 2006, http://www.inc.com/magazine/20060101/reborn.html (accessed July 15, 2009).
18. Linda Tischler, "Seven Secrets to Good Brainstorming," *Fast Company*, December 19, 2007, http://www.fastcompany.com/articles/2001/03/kelley.html (accessed October 31, 2009).
19. Todd Natenberg, "What's in It for the Prospect? Everything—If You Tell Them," SelfGrowth.com, http://www.selfgrowth.com/articles/Natenberg12.html (accessed July 15, 2009).
20. Philip Gerber, "The Sales Professional: Initial Benefit Statement," *Houston Business Review*, April 2005, http://www.houstonbusiness.com/HBReview/contributors/philipgerber/gerberarchive13.html (accessed July 15, 2009).
21. Gary Duncan, "Every Sales Call Requires an Objective and Decision," *Denver Business Journal*, October 13, 2006, http://denver.bizjournals.com/denver/stories/2006/10/16/smallb8.html (accessed July 15, 2009).
22. American Institute of Public Certified Accountants, "Successful Selling Tips: The Sales Objective," http://www.aicpa.org/Professional+Resources/CPA+Marketing+Toolkit/SellingTips6.htm (accessed July 15, 2009).
23. Susan Greco, "The Need for Speed," *Inc.*, April 2007, http://www.inc.com/magazine/20070401/salesmarketing-smart-selling.html (accessed July 15, 2009).
24. Gary Duncan, "Every Sales Call Requires an Objective and Decision," *Denver Business Journal*, October 13, 2006, http://denver.bizjournals.com/denver/stories/2006/10/16/smallb8.html (accessed July 15, 2009).
25. Susan Greco, "The Need for Speed," *Inc.*, April 2007, http://www.inc.com/magazine/20070401/salesmarketing-smart-selling.html (accessed July 15, 2009).
26. Skills Connection, "How to Get Better Results from your Sales Meetings," video, March 3, 2008, http://www.youtube.com/watch?v=1P6bU1efZbl (accessed July 15, 2009).
27. Virtual Strategist, "How to Set SMART Goals," video, M3 Planning, October 17, 2008, http://www.youtube.com/watch?v=uThBb3kGf4k (accessed July 15, 2009).
28. Roy Chitwood, "Every Sales Call Must Have a Clear Objective," *Puget Sound Business Journal*, September 26, 1997, http://www.bizjournals.com/seattle/stories/1997/09/29/smallb3.html?page=2 (accessed July 15, 2009).
29. Stephanie Clifford, "Practice, Practice" *Inc.*, February 2007, http://www.inc.com/magazine/20070201/features-sales-performance-szaky.html (accessed July 15, 2009).
30. Stephanie Clifford, "Practice, Practice" *Inc.*, February 2007, http://www.inc.com/magazine/20070201/features-sales-performance-szaky.html (accessed July 15, 2009).

31. "Approach Every Presentation as If It Were Your First," Selling Power Presentations eNewsletter, February 20, 2006, http://www.sellingpower.com/content/newsletter/issue.php?pc=569 (accessed March 16, 2010).

32. Stephanie Clifford, "Practice, Practice" *Inc.*, February 2007, http://www.inc.com/magazine/20070201/features-sales-performance-szaky.html (accessed July 15, 2009).

33. Lahle Wolfe, "How Do You Practice Your Sales Presentation?" online discussion board, About.com, June 11, 2008, http://sales.about.com/b/2008/06/11/how-do-you-practice-your-sales-presentation.htm#gB3 (accessed July 15, 2009).

34. Stephanie Clifford, "Practice, Practice" *Inc.*, February 2007, http://www.inc.com/magazine/20070201/features-sales-performance-szaky.html (accessed July 15, 2009).

35. Steven Greenhouse, "Bright Spot in Downturn: New Hiring Is Robust," *New York Times*, May 5, 2009, http://www.nytimes.com/2009/05/06/business/economy/06hire.html (accessed July 15, 2009).

36. "Toyota Promotes Prius Buzz with New Forum," Company Car Driver, June 16, 2009, http://www.companycardriver.co.uk/news/article/?art_ID=315742919 (accessed July 15, 2009).

37. Kim Richmond, *Brand You*, 3rd ed. (Upper Saddle River, NJ: Pearson Prentice Hall, 2008), 142.

38. Kim Richmond, "10 Ways to Get the Word Out about Your Brand," presentation in the How to Market Yourself as a Brand to Get the Job You Want Workshop Series, Upper Merion Township Library, King of Prussia, PA, June 1, 2009.

39. LT International, "Job Searching: The Importance of Examining Company Websites," BNET, January 2008, http://jobfunctions.bnet.com/abstract.aspx?docid=915723 (accessed July 15, 2009).

40. Sarah Radwanick, "Job Search Ranks as Fastest Growing U.S. Online Category in 2008," *Reuters*, January 22, 2009, http://www.reuters.com/article/pressRelease/idUS243039+22-Jan-2009+PRN20090122 (accessed July 15, 2009).

41. Kim Richmond, *Brand You*, 3rd ed. (Upper Saddle River, NJ: Pearson Prentice Hall, 2008), 133.

42. Kim Richmond, *Brand You*, 3rd ed. (Upper Saddle River, NJ: Pearson Prentice Hall, 2008), 139.

43. "Informational Interviewing Tutorial: Learn about How an Informational Interview Should Be an Integral Part of Your Networking and Job-Hunting Plan," Quintessential Careers, http://www.quintcareers.com/informational_interviewing.html (accessed July 15, 2009).

44. Kim Richmond, "10 Ways to Get the Word Out about Your Brand," presentation in the How to Market Yourself as a Brand to Get the Job You Want Workshop Series, Upper Merion Township Library, King of Prussia, PA, June 1, 2009.

45. Allison Doyle, "Informational Interview: What Is an Informational Interview and How It Can Help Your Career," About.com, http://jobsearch.about.com/cs/infointerviews/a/infointerview.htm (accessed July 15, 2009).

46. Kim Richmond, *Brand You*, 3rd ed. (Upper Saddle River, NJ: Pearson Prentice Hall, 2008), 145.

47. "Epic Records to Release The Vault—A Comprehensive Look and Listen inside Incubus," *Reuters*, June 2, 2009, http://www.reuters.com/article/pressRelease/idUS154717+02-Jun-2009+BW20090602 (accessed July 15, 2009).

CHAPTER 9
The Approach: The Power of Connecting

9.1 First Impressions Make All the Difference

Learning Objective

1. Understand the role of first impressions and the importance of a strong approach.

When Paul McCartney returned to New York in July 2009 to play a concert at Citi Field, the new stadium built in the place of Shea Stadium where The Beatles first invaded the American music scene in 1965, the atmosphere was electrifying. He started the concert by saying, "Welcome to the new Citi Field Stadium. It's been a long time since I've been here.... I have a feeling we're going to have a little bit of fun tonight."[1] Then he played The Beatles' classic "Drive My Car," and the crowd went wild.[2]

sales approach

The third step in the selling process; the point at which you make contact with the customer.

Paul McCartney didn't need to *talk* to the audience. In fact, people didn't come to hear him speak at all; they came to hear him sing. But Paul McCartney clearly understands the power of a strong approach. His brief welcome, tip to the past, and promise for a great show were all part of his short but effective **sales approach**. While you might not think of Paul McCartney as a salesperson, his concerts, just like those of other rock stars and recording artists, are actually sales presentations for his new songs and albums.

In all types of selling, the approach precedes the sales presentation. In the case of the concert, you probably already know Paul McCartney and what to expect from him. But when you are meeting someone for the first time in sales, your approach won't be successful unless you how you make a good first impression.

First Things First

FIGURE 9.1

Your approach is your first contact with the customer, whether it takes place by phone, in person, or via computer. The six Cs of the sales approach apply in every situation.

© 2010 Jupiterimages Corporation

"You only get one chance to make a first impression." This is a saying you've probably heard many times before. First impressions are quickly formed, difficult to change, and can have a lasting effect.[3] Think of a first date, your first day of high school or college, or any job interview you have gone into. You were probably nervous because you knew the importance of making a good first impression. Similarly, the sales approach is the most intimidating point of the sales process for many salespeople because they know that the decision to buy or not to buy can often start with this initial contact. The approach is your first phone call to your prospect, the moment on the sales floor where you walk over to a new customer and say, "That's our newest model, and it has one terabyte of capacity. Do you record a lot of videos or music?" or your first visit to a target business when you ask to set up a meeting with your prospect. You've done your research, your planning, and your preparation, but the approach is where the rubber meets the road.

The Six Cs of the Sales Approach

While prospecting and the preapproach are entirely under your control, the approach is the first part of the sales process where you actually come in contact with your prospect and you're not quite sure what she will say; this can be a little nerve wracking. However, if you've researched your prospect, and if you go into the sales call prepared, you can have confidence that you will be able to adapt your sales approach to your individual customer. Keep in mind that you aren't selling a product during your approach; you are actually introducing yourself and opening up the way for the opportunity to make your sales presentation later. Consider these six Cs, or things to keep in mind before and during your sales approach. These six points will help you anticipate your customers' responses, adapt, and execute your approach with success.

The Six Cs of Selling

- Confidence
- Credibility
- Contact
- Communication
- Customization
- Collaboration

Confidence

If you know your product inside and out, and you've set your objectives and prepared a general benefit statement, you will be well equipped going into your call, so have confidence. (On the other hand, confidence without preparation is a sure recipe for disappointment, so make sure you actually *have* done your homework first.) Not only will a confident attitude set the tone for the meeting and help you build credibility with your customer, but it will also help you perform your job better. As psychologist William James said, "Attitude at the beginning of a difficult task...more than anything else, will affect its successful outcome."[4]

Of course, feeling and appearing confident in a stressful situation is more easily said than done, but there are some simple psychological tricks that can help. For in-person sales approaches, sales coach Jim Meisenheimer suggests giving yourself an affirmation before heading into the meeting. For instance, tell yourself "This will be one of the most positive sales calls I have ever had with a new prospect."[5] If you believe you will succeed, it is more likely that you *will* succeed. In addition, dressing well for your sales call (discussed in greater detail later in this chapter), will help you feel more confident and professional.

For sales calls that happen over the phone, prepare for your call by organizing your workspace first. Clear off your desk and make sure you have everything you will need within easy reach—calendar, note pad and pen, fact sheets, precall planning worksheet, and anything else that might be helpful during the call.[6] You should also try standing up (because people feel more powerful when they are standing) and smiling while you talk (it will relax you and will help you to use a positive, energized tone of voice).[7]

Credibility

Building credibility is one of the most important challenges you will face early on in the sales call; you want to convince your customer that you are competent, that you offer valuable solutions, and that you are trustworthy.[8] As sales strategist Thomas A. Freese writes, "Without credibility, sellers won't even get a chance to take a swing at the ball."[9] Open the conversation by introducing yourself and your company; if you are meeting your customer in person, make eye contact and offer a firm handshake. Next, briefly explain the purpose of your call (without making your sales presentation). Your customers are busy people, and will appreciate it if you are direct. In addition, an up-front manner like this conveys trustworthiness.

Depending on the type of sales situation you are in, you may be approaching your prospect, or they may be approaching you. In B2B sales, you are generally approaching your prospect, so you have researched them first. While qualifications like a proven track record, satisfied customers, or number of years in sales might help establish your credibility, according to Jeff Thull, CEO of Prime Resource Group, these qualifications are expected, and listing them isn't an effective way to lead off your sales call. Thull says *exceptional* credibility comes when you can demonstrate that you have done your homework. In other words, it's not what you know about your company and your product that will impress your customer; it's what you know about your customer and his situation.[10] Later in this chapter, you will learn about specific ways to do that.

Contact

By now you might be wondering how you should approach your prospect. Do you want to make your first contact in person, on the phone, or over e-mail? The way you make contact will depend on the specific selling situation. Consider whether you are in a situation in which you will initiate the approach, whether your customers will initiate the approach, or whether your selling will include a mixture of both. For instance, maybe you work for a company that specializes in corporate training and personal development services, and your customers include referrals (in which case the prospect is approaching you) as well as prospects you have identified through research (in which case you are contacting them). Even retail selling can include a mixture of both. If you are selling cars or fine jewelry for instance, your customer might come into the showroom or store and ask you for help directly, or he might just start looking around, in which case you would approach him. Of course, because of the environment, in most retail situations the approach happens in person.

While there's not one set way to make an approach, the constant is to make every approach personal. Every situation is different—some approaches may be made at a trade show, while others may be made in an office, or even on the phone—but it's always a good idea to show appreciation. "In every conversation, include at least one appreciative remark," according to Rosalie Maggio, bestselling author of *How to Say It* and *The Art of Talking to Anyone*. Praise the other person's business acumen, charity work, or even her taste in shoes. As long as the appreciation is brief, sincere, and specific, the feeling will be remembered long after the words are forgotten."[11]

On the other hand, in situations where *you* are generally approaching the customer first, it's important to think strategically about the way you want to contact your prospects. E-mail is one of the most efficient and least expensive ways to get in touch with a large number of prospects, but e-mail—like direct mail—is impersonal and has a low response rate: 2 or 3 percent at best.[12] (Just think of all the "junk" e-mails you delete or send through your spam filters on daily basis). E-mail can work as an extension of the qualifying process because only the prospects with genuine interest will be motivated enough to respond. This makes e-mail a useful approach for smaller, less complicated sales that require the seller to deal with a large number of prospects[13] (e.g., insurance or real estate). On the other hand, e-mail is not the most effective way to reach your best prospects, especially not in complicated B2B sales—after all, in relationship selling you want your approach to be as personal as possible.

Face-to-face interaction is definitely the most personal approach you can make, but it is also the most difficult. In large B2B sales, since your contacts are decision makers with high levels of responsibility, they are busy people. You wouldn't just show up at their businesses without an appointment. In these cases, it's best to call first and ask your contact if you can schedule a time to meet with her in person. Of course, you might get sent right to voice mail, especially when you are trying to contact a busy manager. If you've tried a number of times and can't get through, you can leave a message, but make sure you follow up by calling back later in the day or the next day. Be persistent and call back until you can speak to someone. Also keep in mind that there are always exceptions to the rule. You might have the opportunity to make a face-to-face first contact (and secure an appointment for a sales presentation) if you know your B2B prospect will be present at a trade show or industry event you plan to attend.

Communication

Whether you approach your prospect in person or over the phone, you want to build good rapport. After all, wouldn't *you* rather do business with someone you like? Your customer will too. "Most decision makers base their purchasing decisions on who they are buying from, not what they are buying," says Ray Silverstein, sales columnist for *Entrepreneur* online.[14] Rapport building happens at every step of the sales process, but it begins with your first interaction.

For in-person sales approaches, keep in mind the powerful elements of nonverbal communication that were covered in Chapter 5, such as when people communicate face-to-face, only about 20 to 30 percent of that communication is verbal.[15] This means that it is important to focus not only on what you are communicating but also on *how* you communicate it. You can make an instant positive connection simply by remembering to smile. This is critical: people are naturally wired to smile in response to others' smiles, so by smiling you will put your prospect at ease and help create a positive atmosphere.[16] In addition, consider that people are more likely to trust and respond favorably to people who are similar to them.[17] Responding to your prospect's body language and posture with a similar body language and posture, or mirroring, helps to establish rapport. Learn about the power of nonverbal communication and mirroring during a sales approach in this short video.

Video Link

Interview with Larry Pinci, Author of *Sell the Feeling*
Learn how to create rapid trust.

http://blogs.bnet.com/salesmachine/?p=447

And don't forget to bring some business cards with you. You'll want to exchange business cards with the person with whom you are meeting.

On the other hand, when you communicate over the phone, you won't be able to use body language to help put your prospect at ease or establish rapport; your voice (including your pitch, tone, enunciation, and word choice) is the only tool you have.[18] Sales coach Wendy Weiss suggests recording your voice as you practice your sales approach and listening to how you sound. Is your tone convincing and confident? Does your voice have warmth and passion in it? Are you speaking clearly enough to be understood? Listening to your recorded voice will help you hear how you sound to other people.[19] Speech and language professor Daniel R. Boone adds that "the two most common difficulties in telephone conversations are speaking too loudly or speaking too softly," so it's important to pay attention to your volume as well as your tone.[20] Finally, while you can't mirror your customer's body language over the phone, you can subtly reflect his style of speech. If your prospect speaks quickly, try speeding up your speech as well. If the prospect has a drawl, consciously slow your voice down to match his pacing. Pay attention to the way he speaks and also to his word choice and conversational style and adapt your style to match.[21]

You might be thinking, so now I know how to communicate with my prospect, but I still don't know *what* to communicate. The "what" of your sales approach will depend on the specific selling situation and your precall objectives. In some cases, like retail for instance, your approach might be immediately followed by a sales presentation, but in other cases, particularly larger B2B sales, the purpose of the first contact is to set up an appointment for a sales presentation. In the next section of this chapter you will read more about the dos and don'ts of opening lines, or approaches, in different selling environments.

Customization

Tailoring your sales approach to the individual customer is one of the keys to relationship selling. Even in retail situations in which the prospect is approaching you first (so you aren't able to research her beforehand), you would approach different customers differently. Consider the example from Chapter 7 for instance: selling a gym membership to a prospect who walks into your fitness club. If a woman with two young children comes in, you would probably spend time showing her the child care center, and you would discuss any family centered activities your club offered. If she expressed an interest in aerobics or Pilates, you would show her the class schedule and the fitness rooms where the classes are held. Adaptive selling—especially in situations in which you haven't been able to prepare—involves observation, listening, and asking directed questions to uncover what your prospect needs and cares about.

John Brennan, president of Interpersonal Development, suggests using intuition to customize your behaviors and the substance of your communications to your customers' buying style. "If [something in the interaction] does not feel right," he says, "pay attention." Tune in to your customer's responses. If you get the sense that he wants simplicity, don't go into too much detail. On the other hand, if he uses detail in his own responses, use a higher level of complexity when you respond back.[22] Ultimately, the trick is to get inside your customer's head. Ask yourself, "What would I care about and want to know if I was this person? What would I respond well to?" Is your customer an individual consumer? Is he a technical expert? Is he someone working to earn the respect of higher-level managers in his company? Putting yourself in your customer's shoes and adapting accordingly will help you earn his trust.[23]

Power Player: Lessons in Selling from Successful Salespeople

Great Selling Skills Never Go Out of Style
In 1946, when the American Tobacco Company's account was up for grabs, big advertising firms across the country competed to earn its business. Ben Duffy, the president of a small advertising firm in New York City, also decided to take a shot at the account. Duffy made a phone call and successfully secured an appointment with the president of the tobacco company, but he knew he was just a small firm up against advertising giants and that he would have to do something to set himself apart during the sales call. As he thought about what to do, Duffy decided to put himself into his prospect's shoes. "What questions would I have on my mind if I were the president of American Tobacco?" he asked himself. He made a list of fifty questions then narrowed that list down to ten. The next day when he met with his prospect, Duffy said, "I thought you would have some questions about me, my company, what's in the deal for you, and what's in it for me, so I made a list." Surprisingly, the president had also made a list of ten questions, and seven of the ten questions on the two men's lists were the same. By putting himself in his prospect's shoes, Duffy established quick rapport and walked out of the office that day with a $15 million advertising account.[24]

Collaboration

You've learned how relationship selling is about partnering in Chapter 3. Of course all sales have a bottom line (you ultimately want to close the sale), but your customer has something he wants out of the transaction, too. In relationship selling you want to focus on your customer so he gets what he wants; when you do this, your selling becomes a collaborative process. When you practice collaborative selling, both you and your customer get more out of the situation, and you create ideas that would not have been possible for each party working individually.

Consider a recent selling partnership between Pandora, an online streaming radio site, and Whole Foods Market. Doug Sterne, Pandora's director of sales, approached the natural foods retailer about locally targeted advertising spots in the San Francisco Bay Area. He told Whole Foods that one of Pandora's goals is keeping advertising to a minimum, only airing one commercial per hour of radio time, but that selling advertising is necessary to Pandora's continued success. Meanwhile he learned from Whole Foods that one of their goals was "for listeners to see Whole Foods as a place where they could get complete meals." By sharing their objectives this way, the two companies were able to build an advertising campaign that included fifteen-second audio spots targeting listeners within a certain distance of various Whole Foods locations as well as time-specific promotional ads: one in the morning promoting a lunch special and one promoting a fish special closer to the dinner hour. The collaboration resulted in a successful return on investment for both parties, and Whole Foods is planning to expand their advertising purchases to include the Los Angeles area soon.[25]

Dress the Part

When you meet a customer face-to-face, appearance is an important part of the first impression, so make sure to put careful thought into what you wear to your sales call. A good rule of thumb is to dress a little better than you think your customer will dress.[26] It's hard to go wrong dressing more professionally than you need to, but you *can* go wrong by dressing too casually. What you wear is as much of a communication as what you say or how you use body language; so make sure to dress appropriately and professionally.

At the same time, make sure you know something about your customer and his company culture. As sales coach Dave Kahle says, "You should, *within the context of the customer's world*, look successful, confident, and competent."[27] If you sell agricultural supplies to farmers, or you sell products to maintenance supervisors or people who wear uniforms, for example, dressing too formally will separate you from your customer. However, these cases are the exceptions rather than the rule. When you are selling to managers within a company, dress will be more formal. Find out about the company culture to learn whether dress is business casual or "coat and tie" and dress up a notch.

FIGURE 9.2

It's always best to dress the part when you approach your prospect. While some environments might be more casual, it never hurts to dress professionally.

© 2010 Jupiterimages Corporation

- Customization, tailoring your **sales approach** to the individual customer, is also key in relationship selling.
- A good salesperson works not only to achieve his own objective but also to help his customer achieve her objective. Collaborative selling creates ideas that would not be possible for each party working individually.

Exercises

1. Explain how a salesperson would customize her approach to two customers: a busy, high-powered executive and a friendly, conversational small business owner.

2. You are preparing for a meeting with a manager from a computer gaming company. From your research on company demographics you know that the firm is relatively small, the employees are mostly twenty- and thirty-something males, and the company characterizes itself as creative, fun, and cutting edge. Based on this information, how would you dress for your sales call?

3. Your company specializes in pool cleaning and maintenance services, and you have identified a large health club that has several locations as a prospect and conducted research on the business. You think you have identified some opportunities to help the customer save money. One service option provides biweekly maintenance visits, and the customer pays monthly. Another involves monthly service visits and biannual training sessions at your customer's business so that their staff can learn to perform routine maintenance tasks on their own. You are preparing to approach the health club's manager to set up a sales call. How would you approach the manager? What other type of information would you want to know before you make your approach? What role would each of the six Cs have in your approach?

9.2 How to Start Off on the Right Foot

Learning Objective

1. Understand how to make contact with your prospect.

What is the worst pick-up line you've ever heard? How did the person on the receiving end react? Chances are he or she was not very impressed. During a sales approach there are also certain opening lines to avoid—and others that will be more successful. The following section offers some pointers (and reminders) that will give you the power to start the selling relationship off on the right foot.

During Every Sales Approach

While sales approaches can vary widely depending on the selling situation, there are a few standards that *always* apply.

Always Get the Customer's Name Right

There's nothing more off-putting in a sales approach than a salesperson misspelling or mispronouncing your name. If the salesperson can't be bothered to learn something as basic as your name, it sends the message that he doesn't care about you as a person, and it certainly gets the relationship off to a bad start. In e-mails, double check that the customer's name isn't misspelled or mistyped. For telephone or in-person approaches make sure you've figured out how to pronounce the prospect's name during your preapproach research. Ask contacts who might know (a receptionist, for instance, or your referral source) if you are unsure. And if the prospect has a difficult name, and you can't get a confirmation on pronunciation, avoid using his name in your opening lines.

Always Listen

As sales consultants Andrew Sokol and Ike Krieger say, during a sales call, "Don't be interesting; be interested."[28] In other words, don't try to impress your customer by spending a lot of time talking about your qualifications or how wonderful your company or product is; instead, show your prospect that you are genuinely interested in getting to know him and in understanding his needs. The only way you can do this is to listen. Ask questions and then let your customer do the talking. During in-person sales calls you should engage in active listening, which was discussed in Chapter 5. Show the customer that you are really listening by adopting a listening posture: look the customer in the eye and lean forward or incline your head while she's talking. In any sales approach you should restate the essential points your customer brings up, both to check for accuracy of understanding and to show that you are paying attention.[29]

Video Clip

Listening Power
Listening is called "white magic," and it can help you be a successful salesperson. The best way to listen is to ask good questions and then listen to the answers. The person who is asking the questions has the control. Find out why by watching this video.

View the video online at: http://www.youtube.com/embed/_mzPPdU4AjY

Listening is one of those skills that is easier said than done. While people naturally want to talk, they feel most appreciated when someone else is listening. That's when people open up and share their goals, wants, and needs. Salespeople are often known for their ability to talk, but it is listening that makes the best salespeople.

Video Clip

The 70/30 Rule of Listening
Hear how author and sales trainer Shane Gibson learned about listening...the hard way.

Video:

View the video online at: http://www.youtube.com/embed/qcMDlDZKr-w?rel=0

Listening 2.0

Taking the time to "listen" to the online conversation before you begin broadcasting your message.

You might think about listening as something you do in person or on the telephone, but listening is also a strategy online. Author and sales trainer Shane Gibson has coined the term "**Listening 2.0**" to describe the need to "listen" to the online conversation before you begin broadcasting your message.

Link

Listening 2.0 Podcast

If you think social media are all about getting your message out, it's not that simple. This podcast provides effective ways to listen before you speak online.

http://www.closingbigger.net/2009/10/social-media-listening-strategy

Source: ClosingBigger.net

Be Ready with Your Elevator Pitch

Have you ever heard the term "**elevator pitch**"? It's a concise description of a product or service that should take no longer than an average elevator ride.[30] Every salesperson has an elevator pitch for the product or service he is selling. That way, he can tell people about his product in under sixty seconds, and it's a perfect way to start a conversation or phone call and helps to make a good first impression. In fact, everyone from a CEO to an entrepreneur has an elevator pitch about her company to tell potential investors, shareholders, and other stakeholders. Most listeners don't have the time to hear all the details about a product or service in the first minutes of a conversation so the elevator pitch provides just enough information so the audience knows what he is talking about and wants to know more. In other words, "An elevator pitch is an overview of an idea, product, service, project, person, or other solution and is designed to just get a conversation started."[31]

FIGURE 9.3
Your elevator pitch should take as long as the average elevator ride.

© 2010 Jupiterimages Corporation

elevator pitch

A concise description of a product, service, person, or project that should take no longer than an average elevator ride and is designed to get conversation started.

Video Clip

Elevator Pitch

Here are some tips to develop an effective elevator pitch.

Video:

View the video online at: //www.youtube.com/embed/bZTWx2bftaw?rel=0

Your elevator pitch comes in handy when you are making an approach on the phone or in person. It's the perfect opportunity to tell someone about your company and product or service in less than sixty seconds so that you can engage her in conversation. Remember, an elevator pitch isn't a sales presentation; it's simply a way to begin an interactive conversation and get to your ultimate goal—a meeting with the decision maker.

Approaching by Telephone

FIGURE 9.4
Approaching a prospect by phone requires preparation and skill.

© 2010 Jupiterimages Corporation

Establishing rapport can be a challenging task when you make your approach by phone because you can't read your customer's body language or other visual cues, and she can't read yours. There is also the possibility that you will catch your prospect during a busy or inconvenient time. For telephone approaches, it's best to be brief and direct and to save small talk for your in-person meeting or for a later, scheduled phone call.

Do Give Your Name and the Purpose of Your Call in the First Twenty Seconds[32]

Your prospect will probably decide whether or not he is interested in what you have to say within the first twenty seconds of the call, so it's best to be direct and get this essential information across early on. You might say something like "This is Shamika Lorenz from Selling Solutions, a firm that specializes in helping businesses reduce their selling costs, and I'm calling to let you know about an upcoming seminar for small business owners in your area." Such directness also conveys honesty and lets your prospect know that you won't waste his time.[33]

Do Prepare a Script for Your Opening Statement

Because you want to get your prospect's attention in the first twenty seconds, it's important not to stumble over your words or sound like you are rambling. After you have given your name and the purpose of your call, offer a reference point based on your preapproach research. For example, "I read that your start-up has recently opened a new downtown location." This will personalize your approach and help establish your credibility. Next, lead into a general benefit statement[34] that will address your prospect's "what's in it for me?" question.

Do Ask "Is This a Good Time?"

Keep in mind that asking for permission helps build trust and allows the customer to feel like she is in control of the call.[35] However, it's important to think about the way you phrase your question. It is always easier for people to say yes to a question than to say no, so when you open with something like "Did I catch you at a bad time?" all your customer has to do is agree with you ("Yes, this is a bad time."), and the call is effectively over. On the other hand, if you ask whether this is a *good* time, a yes response will work in your favor.[36] Your customer is only likely to say no if this really is a bad time, and if that happens, you are well positioned to say "I understand. Would Monday at 10:30 be a better time to talk?"[37]

Don't Start Off by Asking, "How Are You Today?"

This common greeting is one you probably use without thinking twice about it. But opening a sales call this way over the phone (when you are contacting a busy stranger who doesn't know why you have called) can be off-putting and will probably come across as insincere.[38]

How to Get through Voice Mail to Get to the Right Person

If you are trying to get to the right person in a company and you are getting the voice mail runaround, use these simple steps:

1. Press "0" during the voice message to try to get to the operator.
2. Visit Gethuman.com to find out the "secret" to getting a human to answer the phone at over 1,200 companies.
3. Be cordial and professional to whoever answers the phone. He has the power to give you valuable information to get you to the person you want to talk to so engage him in conversation and thank him for his help.

Don't Launch into Prolonged Explanations

As sales coach Sharon Drew Morgan says, "Your prospect is obviously not sitting by the phone waiting for a call from you."[39] You want to be personable when you call, but you also want to keep in mind that for busy decision makers, phone calls are interruptions, so the more business oriented the interruption, the better.[40]

Video Clip

The Perfect Telephone Approach
Watch this example of how to make an effective sales approach on the phone.

View the video online at: http://www.youtube.com/embed/HiHaVnBNtl0

Leaving a Voice Mail Message

Sometimes it is difficult to reach the person by phone. Although it's a good idea to call back at different times of the day to see if you can catch the person, it is also a good idea to leave a short voice mail to introduce yourself, your company, a brief reason for your call, and when you will call back.

Learn some tips for doing an effective approach via voice mail.

Video Clip

View the video online at: http://www.youtube.com/embed/ZWc1aoyZz6Q?rel=0

Approaching by E-mail

While an e-mail approach is less personal than an in-person or telephone approach, it might be your best method, depending on the type of sale in which you are engaging. For instance, Internet marketing coach Sean Mize says of his business, "I generate 2,000 subscribers via the Internet every single month, so to try to contact all those individuals by phone, unless I have a huge telemarketing room, would be absolutely impossible."[41] Here are a few things to keep in mind.

Do Write a Number of E-mails in Different Styles and Tones

Online marketing expert Daegan Smith suggests crafting about fifteen different e-mail templates so you can choose between them when you want to get in touch with a prospect.[42] You can think of it a little like building up your wardrobe so that you have different things you can wear on different occasions: you wouldn't wear the same clothes to a baseball game that you would wear to a business meeting. You also wouldn't send the exact same communication to all your prospects. The bottom line is that you want the e-mail to be as personal as possible.

Do Send a Well-Written E-mail

Keep in mind that an e-mailed sales approach is still a first impression, even though the communication doesn't involve any immediate contact. While the e-mail should be personal, it should be more formal than the personal e-mails you send to friends. You want to sound knowledgeable and credible, which means paying close attention to your word choice and style. Give the e-mail the same attention you would give to a business letter. This also means reading the e-mail several times before sending it to check for spelling and grammar mistakes, just as you would with any other business correspondence.[43]

Example of an Effective E-mail Approach

Here is a sample e-mail used to approach prospects to hire the Acme Company to create a logo. This e-mail was reproduced with permission from The Writers For Hire Web site.[44]

FIGURE 9.5

To: Samuel Amed
From: Juan Gerard
Subject Line: A Custom Logo for Your Company

Dear Mr. Amed,

My name is Juan Gerard, and I am the president of Acme Company. I was just browsing your site and was wondering if you had considered a custom logo as part of your marketing campaign.

I know sometimes people don't want to invest in logo design because they think it's not that important or they don't have the funds. But getting a quality, custom logo can be one of the most affordable marketing strategies available. My logo designs start at just $199—one of the most reasonable rates in the industry. It's something almost any business can afford and it's well known that a quality logo can be a lifelong partner to a successful business.

A great logo will not only make your company look more professional (on business cards, Web pages, and stationery), but a great logo is indispensable for marketing and branding. Such a simple symbol can tell your clients worlds about your company.

If you would take the time to review our portfolio, I know you'll be impressed by our work. I hope to hear from you soon.

Sincerely,

Juan Gerard

Do Follow Up Persistently

Don't get discouraged if you don't get a response to the first or second e-mail you send. In B2B sales, it often takes about twelve e-mails before contacts reply, so be persistent.[45] If your prospect doesn't respond right away, it doesn't mean that he isn't interested in what you have to offer—just assume that he is a busy person with plenty of other distractions that come across his desk every day. If you continue to send your e-mails regularly, eventually the message will register on your prospect's "radar screen." Of course, you don't want your e-mails to be an annoyance either, so consider including an "unsubscribe" option somewhere in the body of the message for the prospects who truly aren't interested so that they can request to be removed from your e-mail list.[46]

Don't Send E-mails That Look Like Templates

Again, the goal is to make your e-mails as personal as you can. If you have a number of e-mails drafted, select the one that seems most appropriate to the specific prospect(s) you want to target, and include your prospect's name in the heading and body of the e-mail.[47] This will set your message apart from the average, impersonal "junk" e-mail that people get regularly.

Approaching through Online Social Networks

In some cases you will be able to leverage your online social network to approach a prospect. For instance, if you are a Web site designer and you attend a Webinar on increasing Internet traffic to business's homepages, the other Webinar participants are potential prospects, and you might decide to contact them and ask to be added to their LinkedIn networks. If you are not familiar with using LinkedIn, you might find it helpful to review the videos in Chapter 3.

Video Clip

How to Make Your Approach on a Social Network
Learn how social networking can help you make an effective sales approach.

View the video online at: http://www.youtube.com/embed/IKqsFKLOGqE

Companies are also increasingly using social networks as a budget-friendly way to allow prospects to approach *them*.[48]

Power Selling: Lessons in Selling from Successful Brands

Social Networking Transformation

For PJA Advertising & Marketing, entry into the social networking world has transformed the way the company interacts with customers on every level. Phil Johnson, one of PJA's senior managers, says, "Now our social media activities involve almost everyone who works here and touch almost every aspect of agency life." Early on, the company's vice president of business development used LinkedIn to connect with PJA's prospects and current customers, and today PJA uses LinkedIn in combination with Twitter, Facebook, and links through YouTube and Flickr to approach new customers and direct potential prospects to the company's Web site. The upshot? According to Johnson, it's working. The benefit of using social networks to reach prospects is that you can have greater transparency, he says. PJA might contact a prospect via LinkedIn and direct him to a YouTube video, which might then include a link to the company's Web page or Twitter account, so in the end the prospect gets a view of the agency from a number of sources. "Today, when we walk into a capability meeting, the people we're talking to already have had a lot of exposure to our thinking and our personality," says Johnson.[49]

Do Make a Comment When You Add a Prospect as a New Friend

According to marketing specialist Leslie Hamp, even something as simple as "I noticed we were on the Webinar together, and I'd like to add you as my friend," will work.[50] The point is that you want to give your approach a personal touch. If you just go out and friend all your prospects without making the effort to engage with them, they might not accept your friend request in the first place, and even if they do accept, they may wonder who you are and how you found them. Or worse, they may soon forget about you altogether. You can think of the networking tool as a facilitator, something that gives you the opportunity to connect, but it is still up to you to do the work of socially interacting and leveraging your connections.

Do Aim for Quality over Quantity

There are so many new and interesting social media programs available that it can be tempting to join multiple sites; but if you are a member of more than two or three social networks at one time, you will probably find your efforts spread too thin. You can get the most out of your social networking by focusing on regular contributions to the few networks of which you are a member, rather than by trying to maintain your profile and connections on a number of sites.[51]

Do Contribute to the Community

In social networking situations, just as in face-to-face interactions, you want to build a good rapport by earning the trust and respect of your customers and colleagues. This means considering ways you can participate in and contribute to the online community, rather than simply using the social networking sites to promote yourself or your product. As virtual office administrator Sue Canfield says, "Social networking needs to be about building relationships—not primarily about self-promotion."[52] For instance, if you decide to start participating in a news-related social networking site like Digg.com (where people post links to and comments about news stories), start rating and commenting on other users' postings before you begin bookmarking your content there.[53]

Don't Let Your Language Get Sloppy

As with e-mail approaches, pay attention to your language. Use a higher level of formality when you contact business prospects than you would use when you send social networking messages to your friends; avoid slang (like "u" for "you" or "btw" for "by the way").[54]

Don't Make a Sales Pitch

Even though a social-network approach looks different from an in-person or over-the-phone approach, the purpose is the same—establishing rapport, building trust, and helping your customer discover needs and opportunities—so avoid making your sales pitch during your initial contact. For instance, returning to the example of the Web site design specialist, assume you added ten of your fellow Webinar participants to your social network. Maybe your company has made a short YouTube video that offers advice on incorporating blogging capabilities into business Web sites, so you send a message and link to your ten new contacts: "I thought you might be interested in this video." In the video's description on YouTube, you can post a link to your company Web site or blog where you make a direct sales pitch. This way you are offering your prospects valuable information without coming across as pushy. If a prospect is interested in pursuing your services, he has the resources to follow up on his own.[55]

Approaching Your Prospect through Social Networking: *Dos* and *Don't*s

Use the Following Tips to Make Social Networking More Effective for Your Sales Approach

- **Do** use social networks, especially those that focus on the professional community, as a way to connect with prospects and customers.
- **Do** make a comment when you add a prospect or customer as a friend or connection.
- **Do** focus on quality of connections rather than quantity.
- **Do** contribute to the community.
- **Do** use professional social networking features such as Questions and Answers on LinkedIn.

Avoid the Following When Using Social Networking as a Tool to Make a Sales Approach

- **Don't** let your language get sloppy; always use proper spelling and grammar.
- **Don't** make a sales pitch. Use social networks to get in touch and make connections; you can follow up to set up a meeting or phone call to explore your prospect's needs.
- **Don't** post personal photos, videos, articles, or comments to a professional social networking site such as LinkedIn.
- **Don't** post any inappropriate language, photos, or videos on your personal social networking pages such as Facebook. It's a good idea to remove any inappropriate information as employers, prospects, and customers can see your personal brand 24/7.

Approaching Your B2B Contact in Person

Some managers and buyers are extremely busy, and when you try to reach them by phone, you will only interact with a secretary, so your first contact with your actual customer might be at a trade show or industry event. When John Koss, sales vice president and partial owner of Koss Corp., wants to approach buyers from his megaretail clients, he heads to the Consumer Electronics Show (CES) in Las Vegas. Koss Corp. sells headphones and audio equipment to stores around the country, including big names like Wal-Mart, Target, and Sears. Before heading to CES, Koss schedules appointments with some buyers and hopes that others—like Wal-Mart's buyers, who refuse to make appointments—will stop by his booth. He makes a number of sales approaches at the trade show and then spends the next few months traveling to interested buyers' corporate headquarters, where he gives his sales presentations.[56] Koss's strategy is an example of one typical B2B sales approach situation.

In other situations, if you are selling to smaller businesses at the local level, you might make your approach in person at the customer's place of business. Why make an in-person approach rather than placing a phone call? While visiting in person takes more time and effort, it's more personal: it is often easier to build rapport with your customer during a face-to-face interaction. There are just a few things to keep in mind when making an in-person or telephone approach in B2B sales.

Do Use a Strong, Attention-Grabbing Opener

You want to get your prospect to like you in the first minute of your sales approach, and you want to give him a reason to keep listening to what you have to say. Be up front: introduce yourself and explain the purpose of your call (including the general benefit statement you have prepared) early on. Then, as in any sales call, ask permission to continue.[57] Your opening might sound something like this:

> **You**: *Hello, Aaron. My name is Janeka Jones from iFX, a provider of e-commerce solutions.*
>
> **Aaron**: *Hello.*
>
> **You**: *We met at the South by Southwest conference in Austin last week. You mentioned that an area of growth for your business is personalized apparel. The personalized jerseys you offer on your Web site are really unique. In fact, I ordered one this weekend, which gave me an idea about how we can help you reduce your order processing time. Is this a good time to talk about your business?*
>
> **Aaron**: *I'm running off to a meeting in a few minutes, but I always like talking about my business.*
>
> **Aaron**: *I'm always looking for ways to get the product to my customers faster, but I really can't afford any additional order processing costs.*
>
> **You**: *I can understand that. My idea can actually help you reduce your overall operating costs and improve your processing time. Since you are on your way to a meeting, would it work for you if I stop by on Tuesday morning so we can talk more?*
>
> **Aaron**: *Let's see. Tuesday morning at 10:30 looks like it works for me.*

Do Take Your Lead from the Prospect or Customer

Of course you want to be personable and establish a good relationship with your customer, but buyers often say that it irritates them when salespeople try to engage in too much small talk, especially when it comes across as forced or artificial. When deciding how to balance small talk with business, it's important to take your lead from your customer. In the example where Janeka Jones from iFx approaches a prospect, for instance, it wouldn't be a good idea to make a lot of small talk during your approach because the customer let her know that he was short on time.

Some customers are more people oriented, so getting to know you as a person will be an important part of the sales process for them. Other customers are very task oriented and will prefer to get down to business right away. They may opt for a more formal, businesslike approach and will only be interested in socializing after a transaction or meeting is completed.[58] Start your call with a direct approach, and then pause and give your customer a chance to respond. You can read his reaction to gauge the most appropriate communication style to use. Does he seem anxious to get down to business, or is he open to conversing for a bit first? The bottom line is that you don't want him to feel like you are wasting his time.[59] Susan Greco, writer for *Inc.* magazine, tells the story of a meeting at the Consumer Electronics Show between a salesperson and a buyer for Lowe's home store. The buyer started the meeting off by saying that she didn't have much time and just wanted a quick overview of the company, but the seller, who was naturally chatty and personable, missed these cues. He talked at some length and gave the buyer a thorough tour of all the displays at his product booth. Meanwhile, the buyer looked at her watch (another cue the seller missed) before the seller concluded by saying "We really want your business." The response from the buyer was sarcastic and a little cold: "You *do?*"[60] Instances like this are why it is critical to listen to your customer: both his verbal and nonverbal communications. Your attempts to establish rapport can backfire if you don't pay attention to his signals.

Don't Use Opening Lines That Send the Wrong Message

Avoid insincere openers or openers that convey a lack of confidence in yourself or your product. Here are a few examples of opening lines to avoid:

- "Would you be interested in saving money?"

    An opening line like this immediately puts people on guard. (*Oh no, another phony salesperson trying to get my attention with an obvious ploy.*)

- "You're probably a busy person, so I promise I'm not about to waste your time."

    Of course, buyers don't want you to waste their time, but if you mention time wasting up front, you are suggesting that you are someone who *could* waste your customer's time. This opening conveys a lack of confidence, and it sets a negative tone for the sales call.

- "I just happened to be in the area visiting another customer, so I thought I'd drop by."

    This tells your customer that he isn't a priority—just someone you were able to fit in between other, more important sales visits.

- "I heard that you've been having trouble in your customer service department [or in some other area] lately."

    This opening will also put your customer on guard. (*Who's been talking about our problems? How did she find out?*)[61]

Approaching Your B2B Prospect in Person

Use the Following Tips to Make Your In-Person Sales Approach More Effective
- **Do** use a strong, attention-grabbing opener.
- **Do** take your lead from the prospect or customer.
- **Do** use a personal, sincere approach.

Avoid the Following When Approaching a Prospect in Person
- **Don't** use opening lines that send the wrong message; keep in mind the six Cs of the sales approach.
- **Don't** be insincere.

Approaching a B2C Contact in Person

In B2C sales situations, there is sometimes a greater temptation to focus immediately on selling and to forget about rapport building. In most B2C situations the salesperson hasn't invested time in researching the prospect, and he might figure that this is a one-time sale. However, relationship selling is as valuable in the retail environment as it is in the B2B sales environment. Salespeople who treat their customers as *people* before they treat them as sales prospects are the ones who get good customer referrals and repeat buyers. If you have a restaurant or a coffee shop where you're a regular customer, you might already know how this principle works. Aren't you more inclined to order coffee at a place where people greet you, know your name, and get your drink order right—even if another coffee shop opens up closer to your home or your office? Here are a few dos and don'ts when it comes to earning your customer's trust and building rapport.

Do Talk to Your Customer

Everyone wants to be recognized. Have you ever walked into a retail store, looked around, and left, without an employee ever talking to you? How does an experience like that affect your buying decision? You might agree with sales consultant Donna Seigel who says "Frankly, when [the salespeople ignore me], I'm not inclined to ever go into that store again."[62] Engaging your customer might mean the difference between making or losing a sale. Even if you don't know the person, you can make small talk: compliment the customer (sincerely of course) or discuss the weather, local news or events, or sports.[63]

Do Treat Your Customer Like a Guest

Make your customer feel welcomed and comfortable when she comes into your business. Earl Taylor, longtime employee at Dale Carnegie & Associates, says, "The specific words you say are different, of course, but the motivation and attitude should be that you are truly grateful for the opportunity to interact with this individual and have the opportunity to be of service."[64] Making the customer feel at home means not only interacting with him but also going out of your way to help him. Maybe the customer comes into your computer store looking for printer ink. Rather than leaving him to fend for himself, walk him to the aisle where you keep your printers (don't just point him in the right direction). Once you take him to the aisle, ask if you can help him find the right ink type for his printer.

Don't Ask "Can I Help You?"

"No, thanks. I'm just looking" is the customer's automatic response to this question, so the question itself actually comes across as a polite way of giving your customer the brush off.[65] "I won't bother you, and I don't expect you to bother me." Instead, ask a question that will get your customer talking. An open-ended question like "What brings you into International Jewelers today?" will be a more effective way of engaging someone.

B2C Approach: What's Important to the Customer?

When a customer enters a high-end car dealership, all the elements of the approach should be used to engage the customer, as in the example below:

> **You**: *It is a great car, and it gets over thirty miles per gallon in the city.*
>
> **Customer**: *It is really nice, but I'm not sure a hybrid is what I need. I just came in to learn a little more about it.*
>
> **You**: *That's a good idea. I'll be happy to give you a lesson in hybrids to determine if one is right for you. You should also consider a test drive so you can see exactly how it handles on the road.*

Don't Put Any Pressure on Your Customer

What is the number one fear customers have about talking to salespeople? You might have guessed it: pressure. In fact, some customers will go out of their way to *avoid* salespeople for this reason. Let your customers know that they don't have to worry about pressure when they buy from you. As in *all* selling situations, take your cue from the customer by listening and asking questions to uncover her needs first. *Don't* start the conversation off with a question like "What'll it take to get you into a Lexus today?" That's essentially putting your sales presentation before your approach. Finally, keep in mind that asking your customer's permission will also help take the pressure off: "We have a number of new sports utility vehicles. Can I ask you some questions about the specific characteristics you're looking for?"

Don't Prejudge a Customer

You've probably seen the scene in *Pretty Woman* where Julia Robert's character walks into a high-end clothing boutique on Rodeo Drive and the saleswomen turn up their noses at her because she doesn't fit the right customer image. You probably felt a little triumphant, especially if you've ever been slighted by a salesperson, when her character returns the following day to spend a few thousand dollars at several stores, embarrassing the salespeople who treated her so poorly. The moral of the story for a salesperson? Never make assumptions about a customer based on the way he looks, speaks, or dresses. Treat all your customers with respect and care.[66]

Power Point: Lessons in Selling from the Customer's Point of View

The Approach That Customers Like
Customers can't seem to stop saying good things about WholesaleCars2U in Rocklin, California. The dealership has been recognized for relationship selling and its low-pressure sales approach. As one customer said, "No pressure to buy....They treat you with respect and care. It's refreshing

to know that it wasn't just about the 'bottom line.'" WholesaleCars' customer care wins them repeat business and many referrals. Another customer says, "We will not buy a used car from another dealer again. Trust is something we felt immediately."[67]

Approaching Your B2C Prospect in Person

Use the Following Tips to Make Your In-Person Sales Approach More Effective

- **Do** talk to your customer.
- **Do** treat your customer like a guest.

Avoid the Following When Approaching a B2C Prospect in Person

- **Don't** ask, "Can I help you?"
- **Don't** put pressure on your customer.
- **Don't** prejudge any customers.

Turning a Contact into a Sales Call

You might be thinking at this point, "Fine. Now I know how to establish rapport, but how do I turn the call into a sale?" The transition from the approach into the sales presentation will vary, depending on the selling situation. In a B2B sale, your approach might lead to a face-to-face meeting, which might be an information-gathering session where you learn about the customer's needs in greater detail, and you might not actually make your sales approach for several months. On the other hand, in some B2C sales, the salesperson might be able to launch into her presentation in less than a minute after meeting the customer. There is no formula that applies; the important thing is to understand the environment in which you are working. Sometimes it makes sense to move directly into a sales presentation, and sometimes it doesn't. As salesman and CEO Pat Cavanaugh says, "You don't have to shoot every time you have the ball."[68]

Key Takeaways

- In **all** sales calls, make sure to listen to your customer and ask for her permission before continuing with your approach.
- Use your **elevator pitch** to engage your prospect and secure the opportunity to make the complete sales presentation.
- When making a sales approach over the phone
  - *Do* give your name and the purpose of your call in the first twenty seconds;
  - *Do* remember to ask, "Is this a good time?";
  - *Don't* launch into long explanations. Keep it brief and businesslike.
- When making a sales approach by e-mail
  - *Do* draft a number of e-mail templates from which to choose,
  - *Do* make sure the e-mail is well written and businesslike,
  - *Do* make the e-mail as personal as you can.
- When approaching through online social networks
  - *Do* make sure to comment when you add a prospect to your network,
  - *Do* contribute to the social network of which you are a member,
  - *Do* avoid slang in your communications.

- When approaching a B2B contact in person
  - *Do* use a strong opening line that gets the customer's attention,
  - *Do* follow the customer's lead when it comes to small talk,
  - *Do* be careful that your opening line doesn't send the wrong message.
- When approaching a B2C contact in person
  - *Do* make conversation with your customer;
  - *Don't* just ask, "Can I help you?";
  - *Do* avoid putting any pressure on your customer.

Exercises

1. Take the listening quiz by clicking on the following link: http://www.proprofs.com/quiz-school/story.php?title=test-your-current-listening-skills_1. How did you score? What areas do you feel you need improvement? How will this help you in selling?

2. Review the following video and identify at least three things the salesperson is doing incorrectly on this sales call. What do you recommend he do to change the outcome of the call?

View the video online at: http://www.youtube.com/embed/Ku1t66AETLA

3. Review the following audio to hear a voice mail message that was left for a prospect. Identify at least three things that are wrong with it. What suggestions would you make to change this into an effective voice mail message?

View the video online at: http://www.youtube.com/embed/-Uz9odrFweA

4. Assume you work for a wholesale auto parts distributor whose customers include a mix of smaller, privately owned mechanic's shops and large, national auto repair companies. In the coming week, you plan to approach buyers from two large national chains in addition to ten new prospects at small- to medium-sized companies. Considering that your workweek includes other tasks that require your time and attention as well, outline a plan for how you will approach these contacts.

5. Imagine you are the head of cosmetics purchases for a large department store. Just as you are about to run out the door for a meeting, you get a call: "Hello Mr. Davis. How are you doing today? What if I told you that you could save up to 50 percent on your next big purchase of L'Oreal products? Our company has been selling top name cosmetics at wholesale prices for the past thirty years. Some of our customers include big names like Bloomingdales, Macy's, and Nordstrom." Offer a critique of this salesperson's approach based on the pointers you learned in this section.

6. Assume that you are in sales for a major financial services company. Given the state of the economy and the challenges that baby boomers are facing with retirement, you have new opportunities. What method would you use to approach a fifty-year old prospect that just lost his job and is concerned about his family's retirement nest egg and was referred to you by one of your customers? What would you say (or write) as part of your approach?

9.3 Choosing the Best Approach for the Situation

Learning Objective

1. Describe the different types of sales approaches.

There's more than one way to start a sales approach. The method you use will depend on the specific selling situation, the specific customer, and on *you*. If you want the approach to feel natural, the best way to do this is to be yourself. The following examples offer some approach options, but of course the specific approach you use will be a reflection of your style and may include a combination of these approaches.

The Question Approach

When you are making small talk with an acquaintance and you want to show him that you are interested in getting to know him, what do you do? You ask questions, right? A **question approach** is also an effective way to open a sales call because it shows the prospect that you are interested in listening to him, it begins a dialogue, and it helps you get the information you need to move the sale along.[69] As sales consultant Michel Neray points out, asking questions that reveal something of what you know about the target company can also help establish your credibility. Ask questions that lead, questions that confirm, and questions that will allow you to test your hypothesis about the challenges your customer might be facing. Then, listen to what your customer has to say.[70]

Here's an example.

question approach

Opening a sales call with questions that will engage your prospect in a dialogue.

You: *Hi, my name is James Dotson, and I'm with Infinity Document Reproduction Services. I noticed that your office is currently using the 2004 model of company Techmax copy and fax machines, and I wanted to ask you a few questions about your satisfaction with the machines' performance. Would that be all right?*

Customer: *We don't really have any problems with our current equipment right now, but we're always looking for something better, so sure.*

Notice that the first question simply asks for permission. This is a question you should ask no matter what sales approach you are using. Once you establish permission, you could ask a closed question (one with a yes or no answer) like "Are you happy with your current copy machines?" but then you risk ending the conversation quickly if your prospect says "yes." You could ask an open-ended question like "How well do your copiers work?" but this is broad question, and there's a good chance that you will get a vague answer. Instead, it's better to ask a leading question that demonstrates you know something about the problems your customer might be facing with her current products.

> **You**: *On average, how many paper jams would you say you have to deal with each week?*
>
> **Customer**: *Paper jams, now there's an area we could definitely use some help with. It seems like we have paper jams quite frequently—about two or three a week.*
>
> **You**: *So your copiers are jamming about every other day?*
>
> **Customer**: *At least.*
>
> **You**: *And how long does it take you to get a machine back on line once it jams?*
>
> **Customer**: *It depends on who is at the copy machine. If it's someone like me, I have to call someone to help. But it's usually only a few minutes for someone with experience. Sometimes, if a new employee has tried fixing the machine it can take longer, or we have to wait until the end of the day when we're less busy.*
>
> **You**: *Paper jams are usually a problem, and they cause downtime, not to mention frustration. That's why Infinity just developed a new model called Jam-Free. It's guaranteed to experience fewer paper jams than any other copiers on the market today, and it has been designed with simple interiors that allow you to get them back on line easily in the unlikely event that they do jam, so your new employees should have no trouble using them. Do you think this is something that would help your office run more efficiently?*

A line of questioning like this builds credibility because it demonstrates that you (a) have done your research and understand your customer's problems, (b) are interested in finding a solution specific to your customer's situation, and (c) are competent and won't waste your customer's time.[71]

This line of questioning works well when you have done your research, but what about sales situations where the customer approaches you? In these instances, you won't have specific research to go on, but you can still start the conversation by asking some directed, diagnostic questions to help build credibility.[72] For example, say you work in a store that sells high-end speakers and sound systems.

You: *Welcome to Alpha Audio. Have you been into our store before?*

Customer: *Yes, I was here a couple of months ago but I haven't been back in a while.*

You: *Well, we've just recently redesigned our store to make room for some new product lines. It might take a little while to find your way around and see all the new portable and home audio products. Would you like me to give you a quick overview of the new layout?*

Customer: *Yes, that would be great.*

By asking questions, you are establishing trust by showing your customer that that you are not just some pushy salesperson—and by asking *directed* questions, you are securing permission to follow up and dig more deeply into what your customer is looking for.

You: *All right. First of all, are you looking for speakers that will work in a large space, or will you be using your speakers in a smaller area, like your living room?*

Customer: *I'll be using them in my family room, which is a small area.*

You: *OK. We have a few models that have an excellent sound quality in smaller spaces. I can show you where those are located. Can I ask you another question?*

Customer: *Sure*

You: *What type of amplifier will you be using with your speakers?*

As you begin to ask diagnostic questions, you are building credibility and trust by demonstrating that you are genuinely interested in learning what your customer needs and that you can be a valuable resource in the sale; you are finding out the information you need to know to establish a collaborative selling relationship; and you are opening a dialogue on which to build the relationship.[73]

The Product Approach

product approach

Opening a sales presentation with a product demonstration.

referral approach

Mentioning an existing customer relationship to build credibility and trust at the beginning of your sales call.

When John Koss of Koss Corp. approaches prospects at the Consumer Electronics Show, he has his product booth, complete with visual displays and over forty headphone models, to catch their attention. Koss takes advantage of the noisy, chaotic showroom floor to showcase his noise cancellation headphones: a large banner over his booth announces, "Welcome to the Quiet Zone," and he invites buyers to sit down, try the headphones on, and experience the instant silence.[74] Opening the sales call with a product demonstration can be an effective method of capturing a customer's attention. For instance, a textiles vendor might bring fabric samples to a sales call. After introducing herself and the purpose of her call, she might hand a sample to the buyer and say, "I think you might like this new fabric. It's especially popular for women's scarves this season. Can you tell whether or not it's silk?"[75] The **product approach** is especially appealing to people who are visual or hands-on learners because it allows them to look and touch.

The Referral Approach

You already know that establishing trust is a critical part of relationship selling. What's one way to instantly earn a new customer's trust? Mention someone your prospect already knows with whom you have an existing customer relationship: trust already exists between you and your referral source and between your referral source and your prospect, so the referral allows you to use that mutual relationship as a bridge to build trust with your prospect. As John Carroll, CEO of Unlimited Performance, says, "Tapping into strong, existing relationships" accelerates your ability to build new customer relationships.[76] A **referral approach**[77] might go something like this:

> **You**: My firm recently finished a project for Calloway Industries, and Ms. Calloway suggested that I contact you. She thought your company might be interested in learning about our consulting services. Maybe she already mentioned us to you?
>
> **Customer**: Yes, as a matter of fact, I just spoke with Elaine Calloway. She speaks very highly of you and your company, and she's hard to impress. Based on that, I'd like to hear what you think about what you can bring to my business.

When using the referral approach, just be sure that you *ask* your referral source before mentioning her name to your prospect. Also, it's always a good idea to thank your customer when she gives you a good referral. Send her a personal note to let her know how much you appreciate her support. Chapter 5 includes information about how to write a business thank-you note.

The Customer Benefit Approach

customer benefit approach

Opening the sales call by directing your prospect's attention to a specific benefit of your product or service.

If you are in a sales situation where you have carefully researched your prospect and you already have a good sense of his needs before your first meeting, you might open your sales call with a **customer benefit approach**. The benefit approach goes beyond the general benefit statement to focus on a specific product benefit. This opening is only effective if the benefit you describe is of real interest to your prospect:[78]

> **You**: *Mr. Ling, our awnings can cut your energy costs by at least 20 percent. The savings are often even higher for businesses like yours that get a lot of direct sunlight because of a south-facing storefront.*
>
> **Mr. Ling**: *Yes, sunlight is a problem for us as it fades the merchandise we display in our front window. Do you have something that can really reduce the impact of the sun on our front windows?*

By quickly identifying the benefits of your product, you are letting your customer know what he has to gain from doing business with you. This will not only capture his interest, but it will also establish credibility because it shows that you have taken the trouble to prepare and learn about his specific concerns.

The Survey Approach

The **survey approach** is one that works best in sales that require a complex solution or in sales where the solution is often specifically tailored to customer needs, and the approach ranges in levels of formality depending on the selling situation. For instance, if you go to an upscale spa to have a facial, you might be given a brief, informal survey about your specific skin-care needs before you discuss service packages with the aesthetician. Or if you are in the market for a new home, the real estate agent will most likely ask you questions about your preferences and lifestyle before she even begins to show you listings: "How many bedrooms are you looking for?" "Which neighborhood do you want to live in?" "Is outdoor space important to you?" "How many cars do you have?"

On the other hand, in B2B situations or in otherwise more complex B2C sales, the survey process might be more formalized. If you want to purchase an insurance plan, the agent may guide you through a detailed, computer-based survey to find out about your medical or driving history, your family members, your vehicles, or other details that are very specific to you as an individual customer. In another B2B situation (e.g., your firm needs to purchase an integrated software suite with diverse capabilities like timekeeping, payroll, and benefits), the salesperson might give you a detailed questionnaire that will identify your specific needs and ask you to complete it before scheduling a sales presentation.

The survey approach has the advantage of being a nonthreatening way to establish your initial contact with the prospect, as you are only asking for information and not discussing services or costs. It allows you to gather information and create a sales presentation that will address the customer's specific needs and be prepared with the appropriate information or ask other people in the company to attend the sales call. In addition, the survey helps your customer feel like she is receiving special treatment because you are using the information you gather to tailor-make a solution that matches her needs.[79]

survey approach

Opening a sales call with a survey or questionnaire to better determine customer needs and preferences.

The Agenda Approach

You already know the goals of your sales call and the points you will address before going into a meeting, so why not share this information with your customer? The **agenda approach**, in which you lead off the sales call by giving your customer an overview of your meeting agenda, is particularly appealing to busy executives because it gets straight down to business and lets your customer know you won't be wasting her time. Here is an example of something you might say:

agenda approach

Sales approach in which you open your sales call by giving the customer an overview of your call agenda.

> **You**: *I usually cover three things in my first meeting with a customer. First, I like to find out about the specific event you are planning and what you are looking for in a catering service, next I bring out several products for customers to sample, and finally, if you decide you are interested in our services, I schedule a follow-up meeting where we will go over your customized menu and discuss the service contract. This first meeting should only take fifteen minutes of your time.*
>
> **Customer**: *Great. Let's get started.*

The agenda approach outlines your meeting objectives and lets the customer know how long the meeting will last. If you know your customer is someone who likes to get right down to business, leading off with an agenda approach is often a good idea.

The Premium Approach

premium approach

Offering free products or samples to attract a customer and build goodwill at the opening of a sales call.

Free is always appealing. The **premium approach**, in which you offer your prospects free product samples or other giveaway items, helps build enthusiasm about your brand or products, attracting customers who might not otherwise express interest. Once you've gotten your prospect's attention with the giveaway, he will be more inclined to listen to a sales presentation or at least give you a moment of his time. The premium approach is common in retail situations such as cosmetics, wine retail, or specialty food stores where sampling a product can often influence a customer's decision to buy. In other cases, like trade shows, sales representatives might give out inexpensive promotional items or samples as a way to initiate contact with prospects.

For instance, if you were working at a booksellers' convention, your publishing house might be giving away bookmarks or even free copies of a new best-selling novel. You could use the premium as a way to talk to someone who comes to your booth using the following approach:

> **You**: *Our house publishes some of the best-selling mystery authors on the market. You might be interested in taking this copy of the number one best seller,* One Moment in Time *by Jacque Rolique.*
>
> **Customer**: *I would really like a copy of the book. I've been meaning to read it. Thank you.*
>
> **You**: *I'm Sasha Conti from New World Publishing. What's your name?*
>
> **Customer**: *My name is Ramsey Jackson from Books and Nooks. We have fifty-five stores in the Northeast along with an e-commerce Web site.*
>
> **You**: *It's a pleasure to meet you, Ramsey. Thank you for stopping by our booth. I'm familiar with Books and Nooks, and it's a really special store. Would you also like to see a booklist featuring our newest releases? We have so many new titles that haven't even hit the shelves yet. With this list, you can see what's new and bring the hottest titles to your customers sooner. What kinds of titles are important to your customers?*

The premium approach gives you the opportunity to engage your prospect, learn about her business, and find out how you can help her meet her customers' needs.

The Combination Approach

Effective relationship selling is adaptive. Even if you prepare a script beforehand, you won't follow it word for word; instead, you will modify it based on the feedback you get from the customer during your interaction. Real-world, adaptive selling rarely fits neatly into textbook models. Often, an experienced salesperson will shift fluidly from one type of sales approach to another. For instance, he might start off by offering a product demonstration and mentioning a customer benefit almost simultaneously:

> **Salesperson**: *Here. Try lifting this ultralight graphite bicycle frame. How much would you guess it weighs?*
>
> **Customer**: *Wow! That's amazing. Really light. I'd guess it only weighs about four pounds?*
>
> **Salesperson**: *Close. It's actually even less than that: only 2.9 pounds. Technocycle specializes in engineering cutting-edge bicycle components like that frame you're holding. Our products fit the needs of the serious cyclists like your customers because using Technocycles's components ensures that you will always be offering the best, most competitive technology on the market.*

So what approach should you use in your selling situation? Plan one that best showcases your company or product, that fits your style, and that matches what you know about your prospect. But when you make that first contact with the prospect, let flexibility be your guide. Be prepared to start with a referral and move straight into a question or customer benefit or to scrap your prepared approach altogether in favor of something else.

Key Takeaways

- The **question approach** involves leading off with questions to learn about your prospect and engage him in dialogue.
- In a **product approach**, the salesperson opens the call with a product demonstration or display.
- The **referral approach** is an effective way to quickly establish trust with a prospect because it involves starting the call off by mentioning a mutual connection who has referred you to the prospect and who is willing to vouch for you.
- The **customer benefit approach** requires research beforehand so that you can open your call by mentioning an important, customer-specific benefit of your products or services.
- Sales that involve very specific solutions to customer problems sometimes begin with a **survey approach**.
- The **agenda approach** is a straightforward approach that gets right down to business. It appeals to highly organized people because it involves outlining the meeting agenda at the start of the sales call.
- A **premium approach** is one in which the salesperson offers product samples or giveaway items to attract a prospect and establish goodwill.

Exercises

1. You work for a games and toys manufacturer, and you are preparing to meet with a prospect for whom you have been given a referral by one of your longtime customers. Your referral source has told you that the prospect, a buyer for Toys "R" Us, is very task oriented and time-driven and appreciates working with others who do things efficiently. Given this information, which approach (or combination of approaches) will you use in your sales approach?

2. Write a script for a sales approach that combines the referral and question methods. Assume you are a salesperson from an artisan bakery and you are approaching the manager of an upscale restaurant who may be looking for a new bread supplier. Share your script during a role-play in class.

3. Write a script for a sales approach that uses the product approach. Assume you are a salesperson for an upscale jewelry retailer and you are approaching a couple who is looking for an engagement ring. Share your script during a role-play in class.

4. Identify two situations in which you might use the premium approach. Why would that approach be effective in these situations?

5. Visit a retail store that sells big-ticket products such as electronics, appliances, fine jewelry, or cars. What type of approach did the salesperson use? Was it effective? Why or why not? Which approach, if any, do you think would have been more effective?

9.4 Overcoming Barriers to Success

Learning Objective

1. Identify how to overcome barriers to success in getting an appointment.

When Milton Hershey first opened his candy store in Philadelphia, he had to shut down after six years because he never made enough sales to get the business off the ground. After closing in Philadelphia, he moved to Chicago, then to New Orleans, then to New York, each time failing and starting over again. In fact, it took ten years of rejection and failure before Hershey's business succeeded. You already know how the story ended for Hershey (now a $5 billion company), but now you also know that the Hershey Chocolate Company wasn't an overnight success; the business only took off thanks to one salesman's persistence in the face of failure.[80]

Rejection is a reality that all sales professionals have to deal with occasionally, no matter how experienced or skilled they are; it comes with the territory. Prospects will sometimes hang up on you or refuse to see you, and others will listen to your sales approach and then tell you that they aren't interested in what you have to offer. However, if you approach your sales call with confidence and refuse to take rejection personally, then the possibility of rejection doesn't have to be a barrier to your success. Do you believe in the value of the solution you are selling? Are you doing your best to ensure that your customer gets what he needs and wants? Then you have every reason to be confident.[81] Recognize that it is the *fear* of failure, more than anything else, that creates a barrier between a salesperson and a successful sale.

Overcoming Your Reluctance

Successful selling is all about mastering your attitude, and this is especially true when it comes to facing rejection. Sales coach and author Phil Glosserman puts it this way: "The only person who can reject *you* as a salesperson is yourself."[82] There are all kinds of reasons why a prospect might give you a "no thanks" response, very few of which have to do with you personally. Your prospect might simply be unwilling or unable to make a purchase at the moment, he might be facing pressures at work that prevent him from giving you his full attention, or he might just be having a bad day. Instead of focusing on the way *you* feel ("What if he turns me down?"), Glosserman suggests focusing on the way your prospect feels ("How can I help him get what he wants out of this interaction?"). If you imagine how your customer feels before and during your interaction, you will often find that you forget to feel anxious.[83]

In addition to mastering your attitude, here are a few empowering and practical things you can do to help build confidence (and get a higher rate of yes responses) going into a sales approach:

- Be intentional about the language you use when you approach your prospect; don't use apologetic language or language that conveys uncertainty. For instance, rather than saying "*If* you decide to make an appointment," try a phrasing that conveys greater certainty: "*When* you make an appointment..." or "After we've set up your appointment...."[84]

- Before going in to your sales call, practice with some role-plays. Even if it feels artificial at first, keep at it, and take the task seriously. If you practice various selling scenarios enough times with a role-playing partner, you will learn what a confident approach sounds like, and you will feel more prepared to handle the real situation.[85]

- Don't procrastinate. "The longer you procrastinate about something, the larger it becomes in your mind,"[86] so don't put off a sales call because of nerves. Facing your fears is the best way to overcome them.

- Make difficult calls when you have the most energy. This is usually the start of the business day.[87] Morning sales calls can also be a good time to reach busy prospects before the business day gets into full swing.

- Before going into the call, visualize a successful outcome. Phil Glosserman says to "imagine what you *want* to feel" during the sales call; think of a situation in your life that made you feel that way and put yourself into that frame of mind.[88]

Getting Past the Gatekeepers

So what do you do if you've prepared your opening statement and done your research, but when you make your phone call, it isn't your prospect who picks up the phone; instead, it's her assistant, who wants to know who you are, why you are calling, and why you think your prospect should want to talk to you anyway? This is a likely scenario in B2B sales when your prospects are busy executives who don't have the time to handle every call that comes through their office. If you want to see your prospect, you may have to go through the **gatekeeper** first. His title might be secretary, assistant, administrative assistant, or executive assistant,[89] but his role will be the same: keeping unwanted distractions from interrupting his boss's busy schedule. Salespeople often think of gatekeepers as road blocks—something standing in the way of getting to see the prospect—but if a salesperson treats gatekeepers as obstacles to be overcome, not only is he unlikely to get past them, but he is also missing out on the opportunity to collaborate with people who can be valuable assets to his sale.[90] Gatekeepers are human beings (not obstacles) whose jobs are important to the successful running of their organizations. Think of them as part of the selling relationship and treat them with the courtesy and respect with which you would treat your prospect. Lori Richardson, an experienced salesperson and sales trainer, says, "I like to think of a gatekeeper as someone to get to know—a potential new coach into connecting me with my ultimate contact beyond the virtual *gate*."[91] Gatekeepers are an integral part of the selling relationship for a number of reasons:

- They often have valuable knowledge about the internal workings of an organization, including where the power centers are and how decisions get made.

- They are familiar with their boss's schedule (sometimes even more than their boss is).

gatekeeper

The secretary or assistant whose job it is to screen calls or "guard" the entrance to an executive's office. In B2B sales this is someone you often have to go through first before seeing your prospect.

- They have a significant say in who gets in to see their boss and in how communications get passed on.
- They can determine how outsiders are represented to their boss. They often influence the first impression because they might tell your prospect *about* you before you actually make contact with the prospect.[92]

Put yourself in the gatekeeper's shoes for a minute. You have been answering the phone all day, responding to people who don't often treat you with much respect, and you get another call:

Salesperson:	*Hello, this is Camille Martin. Is Maria Gonzalez in her office right now?*
Assistant:	*Yes, she's here, but she's busy at the moment. Can I ask what you're calling about?*
Salesperson:	*I'd like to schedule a meeting to see her. When would be a good time to call back?*
Assistant:	*I'm sorry, but Ms. Gonzalez doesn't take unsolicited calls.*

Notice that the caller didn't give the name of her organization or the purpose of her call, even when the gatekeeper asked for more information. She was abrupt with the gatekeeper, so the gatekeeper was abrupt in return. When talking to gatekeepers, give them the information they ask for when they want it.[93] Remember that it's the gatekeeper's job to find out whether your call is worth his boss's time, so if you tell him the purpose of your call, you are helping him to see that your call may be valuable.

FIGURE 9.7

It's important to get to know the gatekeeper.

© 2010 Jupiterimages Corporation

Learn the gatekeeper's name and be friendly. Business writer Susan Ward suggests starting off the conversation by asking "I wonder if you could help me?" as a way to show respect and demonstrate that you see the gatekeeper as part of your selling relationship.[94] If you do this, you won't *need* to get past the gatekeeper; he can often tell you everything you need to know—the name of the right person to talk to or the best time to contact your prospect—or even schedule a meeting for you before you ever interact with your prospect. Finally, when the gatekeeper does give you helpful information, remember to thank her. For extra helpful gatekeepers, you might even consider sending a note or small thank-you gift.

Now review the approach shown above using a referral as a way to work with the gatekeeper as an ally, rather than view her as a barrier:

You:	*Good morning. My name is Camille Martin and I'm calling from Preston and Preston; we're a full-service digital photography studio here in Cleveland. I'm following up on a conversation that Jason Kendrick, our company's CEO had with Maria Gonzalez. I understand she is looking for a partner in the digital photography area. May I speak with her?*
Assistant:	*Let me check and see if she is available. Can you give me your name and company again?*
You:	*Thank you. I appreciate your help. I'm Camille Martin from Preston and Preston What's your name?*

Key Takeaways

- Attitude, especially fear of rejection, can be a barrier to success in approaching your prospect.
- Some ways to build confidence and overcome your reluctance include focusing on using language that conveys certainty during the approach, practicing the approach through role-play, making calls at the time of day when you have the most energy, and visualizing a successful outcome.
- In B2B sales you may need to get past **gatekeepers** before you meet your prospect.
- **Gatekeepers** can be your allies if you treat them as part of the selling relationship.

Exercises

1. Think of a time when you succeeded at something you had been reluctant to do. What techniques did you use to help you achieve your goal?
2. Imagine that you are a sales rep for a logistics company and you want to get an appointment with the COO of a hardware manufacturer. You've heard that he can be very difficult to deal with, so you are concerned about calling on him, but he is a large prospect for you. Identify three things that you would do to overcome your reluctance and make the call.
3. Put yourself in the shoes of an executive assistant at a large corporation. It has been a busy morning, and just after lunchtime a salesperson calls and asks to see your boss. Name three things the salesperson could do or say that would make you more willing to help him.
4. Assume you are a sales rep for a firm that sells accounting software that can reduce invoice processing time by 15 percent. You want to get a meeting with the chief financial officer of a prospective company, but you need to go through the secretary to get to the CFO. Which approach would you use with this gatekeeper? Which approach would you use with the CFO? Why would you use each of these approaches?

9.5 *Selling U*: What's Your Elevator Pitch for Your Brand?

Learning Objective

1. Learn how to prepare an elevator pitch for your brand.

Now you know about an elevator pitch and how it can help you in your sales approach. But do you have an elevator pitch for your personal brand? If the answer is no, now is the time to craft it. Just as in selling, your personal elevator pitch should be less than a few minutes and should be a way for you to tell someone who you are, what you've done, and what you're looking for. Your elevator pitch will serve as the approach for your internship and job search in several different ways.

Elevator Pitch 101: Be Prepared

Your elevator pitch is critical because it tells a prospective employer or someone in your network what you have to offer, what makes you different, and what you want to do. You'll use your elevator pitch in many different situations; you may even use it in situations when you least expect it. Chris O'Leary, author of *Elevator Pitch Essentials*, suggests that many people are not prepared to take

advantage of relationships and opportunities that come their way simply because they are not prepared with a compelling statement about who they are and what they are looking for.[95]

Video Clip

See how to craft your personal elevator pitch.

View the video online at: http://www.youtube.com/embed/y1Y02_oZP8U?rel=0

How to Create Your Elevator Pitch

Before you can deliver your elevator pitch, you have to write it first. Start by reviewing your brand
positioning points that you identified in the *Selling U* section in Chapter 1. As you recall, your brand
positioning points are the foundation of your résumé and cover letter and now your elevator pitch.
You can see how you are building a consistent brand story by always focusing on the same key selling points about yourself.

To craft your elevator pitch, keep the following points in mind:

- Who are you?
- What experience and skills do you have?
- What makes you unique?
- What problem can you help your prospective employer solve?
- What are you looking for?[96]

Here's an example of how an elevator pitch comes together from Jobstar.org:

*Hello, my name is Melinda Stevens. I'm a graduating senior from Southton College. I got
your name from the alumni office, where they said you were an alumna from 1983. I understand you're now a CPA and audit manager in Chicago. My minor was in business, and
I'm interested in positions in accounting. I'd like to know how you got where you are today
and what advice you'd have for a college graduate just coming into the job market today.
Do you have a moment right now?[97]*

This is an example of a telephone approach. You can see that it is concise and to the point. If
you are networking, at a job interview, or talking with someone, you might have the time for one or
two more sentences, but not much more. The secret to an effective elevator pitch is to intrigue the
listener so that he wants to hear more. If your elevator pitch is compelling and brief, the listener
will respond by asking a question, and you will get the conversation started.

Video Clip

This video provides some sample elevator pitches and constructive feedback about how the pitches can be improved.

View the video online at: http://www.youtube.com/embed/ZqxmxsZi-2E?rel=0

When to Use Your Elevator Pitch

One of the most common uses for an elevator pitch is networking. For example, if you attend a professional event you'll have the opportunity to meet many new people. And you'll want to tell each one a little bit about yourself. This is a perfect opportunity to use your elevator pitch; it's not too long and gives you the perfect way to start a conversation and give the person to whom you are speaking the chance to ask a question. You might even find something or someone in common as a result of the information in your elevator pitch: "You were an intern at Classic Architects? My brother used to work there. His name is Jeremy Slater. Do you know him?"

Another opportunity to use your elevator pitch is in an interview. Although you will need more preparation than simply your elevator pitch for an informational interview or a job interview, you will have a head start on your preparation with a strong elevator pitch. It's the perfect response to what is commonly the first question that is asked at almost every job interview: "So tell me about yourself." It's important to be ready with a clear, concise, and compelling statement. If you think you can wing it, you will probably start your interview off on the wrong foot. On the other hand, a good elevator pitch allows you to direct the conversation to the things you want to talk about (your brand positioning points).

FIGURE 9.8
Your elevator pitch is the perfect way to start a job interview after introductions and small talk.

© 2010 Jupiterimages Corporation

You've Got the Power: Tips for Your Job Search

Make Your Elevator Pitch Work for You
It might be challenging to think about communicating your brand story in only sixty seconds, but don't forget your objective: you want to get the internship or job. While there's a long way between your elevator pitch and an internship or job, keep your eye on the prize; always have a call to action as part of your elevator pitch. For example, ask for a business card from everyone with whom you speak or meet. That means that whether you are at a networking event or on a job interview, it's always appropriate to ask the person for their business card. (You might want to brush up and review the business card etiquette covered in Chapter 5.)

Then, follow-up is key. After you meet someone, follow up with an e-mail or phone call within twenty-four hours (or on the appropriate date after an interview). Tell the person how much you enjoyed meeting her and mention something specific about your conversation. It's a good idea to include a link to an interesting article or video in your e-mail; that will help you stand out in the person's mind.

Be Yourself

Your elevator pitch is a reflection of you, so when you are creating your elevator pitch, write it down, and then say it out loud in front of a mirror until you are comfortable with it. It's important to rehearse it so that you are comfortable with communicating this brand message in just a few minutes without rambling or stumbling.[98] But you don't want to have your elevator pitch down cold; in other words, you want to deliver it with ease and with a natural tone and pacing, as if you were saying it for the first time. It's hard to get the balance between preparation and spontaneity, which is why it's a good idea to use your elevator pitch frequently. That way you will be able to feel natural saying it and make adjustments based on how it sounds and feels. And don't forget to smile!

Key Takeaways

- An **elevator pitch** is a concise description of a product or service that should take no longer than an average elevator ride and is designed to get conversation started.
- An **elevator pitch** requires preparation, and you should always be prepared because you never know when you might have an opportunity to use it.
- Your **elevator pitch** should be approximately sixty seconds long and should use your brand positioning points as the foundation to answer the following questions:
  - Who are you?
  - What experience and skills do you have?
  - What makes you unique?
  - What problem can you help your prospective employer solve?
  - What are you looking for?
- You can use your **elevator pitch** in many situations including networking and informational or job interviews.
- Write down your **elevator pitch** and rehearse it out loud in front of a mirror. But deliver it naturally, as if it were being said for the first time, and always with a smile.
- Don't forget to make your elevator pitch work for you by asking for a business card and following up with each person individually within twenty-four hours with a thank-you note or follow-up e-mail.

Exercises

1. Write your elevator pitch. Give your pitch to the person next to you and then listen to hers. How long was each elevator pitch? What elements did she include that you didn't? What elements could you include if time permits? What is your call to action (what you want the person to do at the end of your elevator pitch)?
2. Name three situations in which you could use your elevator pitch.

3. Create a short video of your elevator pitch and post it to YouTube (keep in mind that it should not take longer than the average elevator ride).

4. Create your elevator pitch in two PowerPoint slides (use only two slides). Post the "pitch" to Slideshare.net and share it with your class.

9.6 Review and Practice

Power Wrap-Up

Now that you have read this chapter, you should be able to understand how to approach a prospect.

- You **understand** the importance of your first impression.
- You **learned** the elements of making contact.
- You can **describe** the role of an elevator pitch in the approach.
- You can **list** the dos and don'ts of making contact via phone and in person.
- You can **describe** the different types of sales approaches.
- You can **understand** how to create an elevator pitch for your personal brand to use during your approach for networking, interviews, and other contacts.

Test Your Power Knowledge (answers are below)

1. Name the six Cs of the sales approach.
2. Identify one way of demonstrating active listening.
3. What is the 70/30 rule of listening?
4. What is an elevator pitch, and why is it important in a sales approach?
5. Why should you prepare a script for your opening statement for a telephone approach?
6. Describe an effective e-mail approach.
7. Why are social networks an effective way to approach prospects?
8. List two opening lines you should avoid in a sales approach.
9. Describe the customer benefit approach.
10. What is a gatekeeper?
11. What kind of information should be included in the elevator pitch for your personal brand?

Power (Role) Play

Now it's time to put what you've learned into practice. The following are two roles that are involved in the same selling situation—one role is the customer, and the other is the salesperson. This will give you the opportunity to think about this selling situation from the point of view of both the customer and the salesperson.

Read each role carefully along with the discussion questions. Then, be prepared to play either of the roles in class using the concepts covered in this chapter. You may be asked to discuss the roles and do a role-play in groups or individually.

A Good Sport

Role: Operations manager, Trident Office Equipment

You are responsible for all the operations for a major office equipment distributor. Trident counts hundreds of businesses among its B2B customers. As part of building relationships with customers, the company entertains its B2B customers by taking them to professional sporting events, dinner, and other activities. The company is currently a season ticket holder for the local professional football team. However, given the state of the economy, you are reconsidering the company's investment in season tickets. Your time is valuable to you, so you don't want to take the time to meet with a sales rep from each of the teams.

- What will you say when a sales rep from one of the sports teams approaches you?
- What type of approach will you find compelling enough to take the time to meet with a sales rep?

Role: Sales rep for the stadium that hosts the city's minor league baseball team

You have qualified your prospect as someone who is responsible for the decisions for purchases of season tickets to entertain customers. While he has traditionally purchased season tickets for the local professional football team, you believe that you can approach him with an opportunity to save money and have an excellent opportunity to entertain clients and support the local baseball team. The baseball season is longer and offers more opportunities for Trident to entertain its customers, and the cost per game is less for your baseball tickets than what Trident has been paying for football tickets, although the total cost for season tickets is greater. You are preparing your approach to make an appointment on the phone.

- What will you say to approach this prospect?
- What type of approach will you use?
- What is your elevator pitch for the season tickets?

Put Your Power to Work: *Selling U* Activities

1. Ask your professor or another professional to share his elevator pitch with you. Deliver your elevator pitch to him and ask him to critique it.
2. Visit your career center and ask one of the counselors to provide feedback to you on your elevator pitch.
3. Use your elevator pitch in a professional situation such as your internship, class, or interview. What elements do you think work in your elevator pitch? What elements are not as effective? What modifications will you make as a result?

Test Your Power Knowledge Answers

1. Confidence, credibility, contact, communication, customization, and collaboration.
2. Eye contact, lean forward, take notes, and repeat key points to check for understanding.
3. You should be listening 70 percent of the time and asking questions 30 percent of the time to engage the prospect.
4. An elevator pitch is a concise description of a product, service, project, or person that should take no longer than the average elevator ride. It's an important part of the sales approach because it is a good way to give your prospect an overview and get conversation started.
5. You need to get your prospect's attention in the first twenty seconds; you don't want to stumble over your words or sound like you're rambling. A script is a good way to stay focused and communicate effectively.
6. Personalized e-mails that address a prospect's needs can be very effective. An e-mail should be well written and interesting to read and include proper spelling and grammar.
7. You can network, get referrals, and add value to the conversation on social networks.
8. "Would you be interested in saving money?"; "You're probably a busy person, so I promise I'm not about to waste your time"; "I just happened to be in the area visiting another cus-

tomer so I thought I'd drop by"; and "I've heard that you've been having trouble in your customer service department."

9. Opening the sales call by directing your prospect's attention to a specific benefit of your products or services.

10. The secretary or assistant whose job it is to screen calls or "guard" the entrance to an executive's office. It's the person you have to do through first before seeing your prospect.

11. Who are you, what experience and skills do you have, what makes you unique, what problem can you help your prospective employer solve, and what are you looking for?

Endnotes

1. "Paul McCartney's first concert at City Field," video, July 22, 2009, http://www.youtube.com/watch?v=cdHC6OJPShQ (accessed July 26, 2009).

2. "Paul McCartney at Citi Field Opening Song 'Drive My Car,'" video, July 17, 2009, http://www.macca-central.com/news/?id=3070 (accessed July 26, 2009).

3. BNET Health Care Industry, "Social Perception," BNET, March 2001, http://findarticles.com/p/articles/mi_g2699/is_0003/ai_2699000324/?tag=content;col1 (accessed May 16, 2010).

4. Brian Johnson's Philosophers Notes, "Inspirational Quotes: William James," http://philosophersnotes.com/quotes/by_teacher/William%20James (accessed May 16, 2010).

5. Jim Meisenheimer, "7 Things to Do to Prepare for Your First Sales Call," EzineArticles, http://ezinearticles.com/?7-Things-to-Do-to-Prepare-For-Your-First-Sales-Call&id=2409769 (accessed May 16, 2010).

6. Craig Harrison, "Warming Up to Cold Calls," Expressions of Excellence, Fall 2001, http://www.expressionsofexcellence.com/ARTICLES/warmcoldcalls.htm (accessed July 30, 2009).

7. Business Link, "Planning to Sell," http://www.businesslink.gov.uk/bdotg/action/detail?type=RESOURCES&itemId=1081503204 (accessed July 30, 2009).

8. Thomas A. Freese, *Secrets of Question Based Selling* (Naperville, IL: Sourcebooks, Inc., 2003), 113.

9. Thomas A. Freese, *Secrets of Question Based Selling* (Naperville, IL: Sourcebooks, Inc., 2003), 116.

10. Jeff Thull, "How to Establish Sales Credibility: It's Not the Stories You Tell, It's the Questions You Ask," MarketingProfs, February 6, 2007, http://www.marketingprofs.com/7/thull15.asp; Neil Rackham, *The Spin Selling Fieldbook* (New York: McGraw-Hill, 1996), 40.

11. Robert Jones, "How to Make a Powerful First Impression," *Entrepreneur*, November 17, 2008, http://www.entrepreneur.com/startingabusiness/selfassessment/article198622.html (accessed July 30, 2009).

12. Joanna L. Krotz, "5 Steps to Hitting Your Direct Mail Targets," Microsoft Small Business Center, http://www.google.com/search?client=safari&rls=en&q=5+steps+to+hitting+your+direct+mail+targets&ie=UTF-8&oe=UTF-8 (accessed July 30, 2009).

13. Sean Mize, "What's the Most Effective First Contact with a Prospect—Email or Phone?" EzineArticles, http://ezinearticles.com/?id=1206246 (accessed July 30, 2009).

14. Ray Silverstein, "How Do I Build Customer Rapport?" *Entrepreneur*, July 25, 2007, http://www.entrepreneur.com/management/leadership/leadershipcolumnistraysilverstein/article182144.html (accessed August 1, 2009).

15. Katherine Toland Frith and Barbara Mueller, *Advertising and Societies* (New York: Peter Lang Publishing, 2003), 34.

16. Geoffrey James, "Principles of Building Rapport," video, March 9, 2009, BNET, http://blogs.bnet.com/salesmachine/?p=1461&tag=content;col1 (accessed August 1, 2009).

17. Geoffrey James, "How to Build Rapport on the Phone," BNET, September 18, 2007, http://blogs.bnet.com/salesmachine/?p=128&tag=content;col1 (accessed August 1, 2009).

18. Geoffrey James, "How to Build Rapport on the Phone," BNET, September 18, 2007, http://blogs.bnet.com/salesmachine/?p=128&tag=content;col1 (accessed August 1, 2009).

19. Wendy Weiss, "Your Voice Is Your Instrument," Sales Information, 2004, http://www.sales.net63.net/1134.php (accessed July 30, 2009).

20. Daniel R. Boone, "Is Your Voice Selling You on the Phone?" *American Salesman*, August 1, 1993, AllBusiness, http://www.AllBusiness.com/marketing/direct-marketing-telemarketing/393038-1.html (accessed July 30, 2009).

21. Geoffrey James, "To Sell More, Listen to Your Voice," BNET, September 19, 2007, http://blogs.bnet.com/salesmachine/?p=129 (accessed August 1, 2009).

22. John Brennan, "Adapt Your Style to Win over the Customer," EvanCarmichael.com, http://www.evancarmichael.com/Sales/395/Adapt-your-style-to-win-over-the-customer.html (accessed August 1, 2009).

23. John Brennan, "The Art of Adaptation," EvanCarmichael.com, http://www.evancarmichael.com/Sales/395/The-Art-of-Adaptation.html (accessed July 30, 2009).

24. See http://www.bradskiles.com/yahoo_site_admin/assets/docs/Larry_Wilson.24852250.pdf (accessed May 16, 2010).

25. Andrew Hampp, "Pandora Set to Expand Thanks to New Royalty Ruling," *Advertising Age*, July 13, 2009, http://adage.com/mediaworks/article?article_id=137878 (accessed May 16, 2010).

26. Dave Kahle, "What Are Your Views on Dress? Does it Matter?" The Kahle Way, http://www.davekahle.com/qa/dress.htm (accessed May 26, 2010).

27. Dave Kahle "What Are Your Views on Dress? Does it Matter?" The Kahle Way, http://www.davekahle.com/qa/dress.htm (accessed May 16, 2010; emphasis added).

28. Andrew Sokol and Ike Krieger, "What to Say When You Meet a Prospect," video, ArticlesBase, http://www.businesssuccessbuilder.com (accessed August 1, 2009).

29. Edward Delgaizo and Seleste Lunsford, *Secrets of Top Performing Salespeople* (New York: McGraw-Hill, 2003), 54.

30. Aileen Pincus, "The Perfect (Elevator) Pitch," *BusinessWeek*, June 18, 2007, http://www.businessweek.com/careers/content/jun2007/ca20070618_134959.htm (accessed July 26, 2009).

31. Chris O'Leary, "Elevator Pitch 101," January 27, 2009, Elevator Pitch Essentials, http://www.elevatorpitchessentials.com/essays/ElevatorPitch.html (accessed July 26, 2009).

32. "Tips for Successful Cold Calling," AllBusiness, http://www.AllBusiness.com/sales/selling-techniques-telesales/1355-1.html (accessed May 16, 2010).

33. Sharon Drew Morgan, "This is a Sales Call: How to Begin Prospecting Calls with Integrity," EzineArticles, http://ezinearticles.com/?This-is-a-Sales-Call:-How-to-Begin-Prospecting-Calls-with-Integrity&id=34073 (accessed August 2, 2009).

34. Sharon Drew Morgan, "This is a Sales Call: How to Begin Prospecting Calls with Integrity," EzineArticles, http://ezinearticles.com/?This-is-a-Sales-Call:-How-to-Begin-Prospecting-Calls-with-Integrity&id=34073 (accessed August 2, 2009).

35. Sharon Drew Morgan, "This is a Sales Call: How to Begin Prospecting Calls with Integrity," EzineArticles, http://ezinearticles.com/?This-is-a-Sales-Call:-How-to-Begin-Prospecting-Calls-with-Integrity&id=34073 (accessed August 2, 2009).

36. Pieter Petoors, "How to Contact Your Prospect by Phone," Pieter's Blog, March 10, 2009, http://pietpetoors.com/blog/how-to-contact-your-prospect-by-phone (accessed August 2, 2009).

37. Michael McGaulley, "Phone Sales Skills: Your First Contact with the Prospect," Sales Training Source, 2009, http://ezinearticles.com/?Phone-Sales-Skills---Your-First-Contact-With-the-Prospect&id=4068383 (accessed August 2, 2009).

38. Joan Guiducci, "The First 7 Seconds of a Cold Call," AllBusiness, August 1, 1998, http://www.AllBusiness.com/sales/selling-techniques/690353-1.html (accessed May 16, 2010).

39. Sharon Drew Morgan, "This is a Sales Call: How to Begin Prospecting Calls with Integrity," EzineArticles, http://ezinearticles.com/?This-is-a-Sales-Call:-How-to-Begin-Prospecting-Calls-with-Integrity&id=34073 (accessed August 2, 2009).

40. Michael McGaulley, "Phone Sales Skills: Your First Contact with the Prospect," Sales Training Source, 2009, http://www.how-to-sell-your-better-mousetrap.com/phone_sales_skills.html (accessed August 2, 2009).

41. Sean Mize, "What's the Most Effective First Contact with a Prospect—Email or Phone?" EzineArticles, http://ezinearticles.com/?id=1206246 (accessed July 30, 2009).

42. Daegan Smith, "How to Contact Business Prospects, ArticlesBase, April 28, 2008, http://www.articlesbase.com/communication-articles/how-to-contact-business-prospects-398144.html (accessed August 2, 2009).

43. Daegan Smith, "How to Contact Business Prospects," ArticlesBase, April 28, 2008, http://www.articlesbase.com/communication-articles/how-to-contact-business-prospects-398144.html (accessed August 2, 2009).

44. The Writers For Hire, Inc., "Sample Sales Emails: Personal Sales Email," http://www.thewritersforhire.com/personal-sales-email.htm (accessed July 27, 2009).

45. Daegan Smith, "How to Contact Business Prospects," ArticlesBase, April 28, 2008, http://www.articlesbase.com/communication-articles/how-to-contact-business-prospects-398144.html (accessed August 2, 2009).

46. Sean Mize, "What's the Most Effective First Contact with a Prospect—Email or Phone?" EzineArticles, http://ezinearticles.com/?id=1206246 (accessed July 30, 2009).

47. Daegan Smith, "How to Contact Business Prospects," ArticlesBase, April 28, 2008, http://www.articlesbase.com/communication-articles/how-to-contact-business-prospects-398144.html (accessed August 2, 2009).

48. Leslie Hamp, "5 Steps to Effective Business Social Networking," Social Networking News, July 9, 2009, http://socialnetworkingnewstoday.com/ (accessed August 2, 2009).

49. Phil Johnson, "Tweeting Your Way to New Prospects," *Advertising Age*, July 6, 2009, http://adage.com/smallagency/post?article_id=137730 (accessed May 16, 2010).

50. Leslie Hamp, "5 Steps to Effective Business Social Networking," Social Networking News, July 9, 2009, http://socialnetworkingnewstoday.com/ (accessed August 2, 2009).

51. Leslie Hamp, "5 Steps to Effective Business Social Networking," Social Networking News, July 9, 2009, http://socialnetworkingnewstoday.com/ (accessed August 2, 2009).

52. Sue Canfield, "Social Networking Can Work for Your Business," Chief Virtual Officer, May 12, 2009, http://chiefvirtualofficer.com/blog/2009/05/12/social-networking-can-work-for-your-business/ (accessed May 16, 2010).

53. Sudarmaji Lamiran, "How to Quickly and Easily Leverage Social Media to Build a Big List," Social Networking News, July 13, 2009, http://socialnetworkingnewstoday.com/ (accessed August 2, 2009).

54. Leslie Hamp, "5 Steps to Effective Business Social Networking," Social Networking News, July 9, 2009, http://socialnetworkingnewstoday.com/ (accessed August 2, 2009).

55. Leslie Hamp, "5 Steps to Effective Business Social Networking," Social Networking News, July 9, 2009, http://socialnetworkingnewstoday.com/ (accessed August 2, 2009).

56. Susan Greco, "Marketing: Selling the Superstores," *Inc.*, July, 1995, http://www.inc.com/magazine/19950701/2331.html (accessed May 16, 2010).

57. Tom Reilly, *Value-Added Selling: How to Sell More Profitably, Confidently, and Professionally by Competing on Value, Not Price*, 2nd ed. (New York: McGraw-Hill, 2002), 138.

58. Tom Reilly, *Value-Added Selling: How to Sell More Profitably, Confidently, and Professionally by Competing on Value, Not Price*, 2nd ed. (New York: McGraw-Hill, 2002), 140.

59. Edward Delgaizo and Seleste Lunsford, *Secrets of Top Performing Salespeople* (New York: McGraw-Hill, 2003), 51.

60. Susan Greco, "Marketing: Selling the Superstores," *Inc.*, July, 1995, http://www.inc.com/magazine/19950701/2331.html (accessed May 16, 2010).

61. Tom Reilly, *Value-Added Selling: How to Sell More Profitably, Confidently, and Professionally by Competing on Value, Not Price*, 2nd ed. (New York: McGraw-Hill, 2002), 138.

62. Donna Siegel, "Relationship Selling: Getting Your Customers Coming Back for More," SalesMBA, http://www.salesmba.com/articles1/ssrl03.htm (accessed July 30, 2009).

63. Donna Siegel, "Relationship Selling: Getting Your Customers Coming Back for More," SalesMBA, http://www.salesmba.com/articles1/ssrl03.htm (accessed July 30, 2009).

64. Geoffrey James, interview by Earl Taylor, "Building Rapport in Retail," BNET, May 12, 2007, http://blogs.bnet.com/salesmachine/?p=20 (accessed May 16, 2010).

65. Geoffrey James, interview by Earl Taylor, "Building Rapport in Retail," BNET, May 12, 2007, http://blogs.bnet.com/salesmachine/?p=20 (accessed May 16, 2010).

66. Edward Delgaizo and Seleste Lunsford, *Secrets of Top Performing Salespeople* (New York: McGraw-Hill, 2003), 51.

67. WholeSaleCars2U.net, "Testimonials," http://www.wholesalecars2u.net/Testimonials.aspx?wsid=87. (accessed August 2, 2009).

68. Susan Greco, "The Nonstop, 24-7 CEO Salesman," *Inc.*, August 1, 2000, http://www.inc.com/magazine/20000801/19766.html (accessed July 31, 2009).

69. Charles D. Brennan, *Sales Questions That Close the Sale* (New York: AMACOM, 1994), 49.

70. Michel Neray, "How to Establish Credibility," MarketingProfs, February 15, 2005, http://www.marketingprofs.com/5/neray3.asp?part=2 (accessed August 2, 2009).

71. Jeff Thull, "How to Establish Sales Credibility: It's Not the Stories You Tell, It's the Questions You Ask," MarketingProfs, February 6, 2007, http://www.marketingprofs.com/7/thull15.asp (accessed May 16, 2010).

72. Freese, *Secrets of Question Based Selling* (Naperville, IL: Sourcebooks, Inc., 2003), 122

73. Freese, *Secrets of Question Based Selling* (Naperville, IL: Sourcebooks, Inc., 2003), 124–25.

74. Susan Greco, "Marketing: Selling the Superstores," *Inc.*, July, 1995, http://www.inc.com/magazine/19950701/2331.html (accessed May 16, 2010).

75. Barton A. Weitz, Stephen Byron Castleberry, and John F. Tanner, *Selling: Building Partnerships*, 5th ed. (New York: McGraw-Hill, 2003), 245.

76. John Carroll, "Referrals: The Sale's Professional's Best Friend," Unlimited Performance, Inc., 1999, http://www.uperform.com/articles/art-referrals.htm (accessed May 16, 2010).

77. Michael McGaulley, "Sales Hot Buttons for Capturing the Prospect's Attention Early in Your First Phone Contact," How-to-Sell-Your-Better-Mousetrap, 2009, http://ezinearticles.com/?id=4477676 (accessed August 2, 2009).

78. Barton A. Weitz, Stephen Byron Castleberry, and John F. Tanner, *Selling: Building Partnerships*, 5th ed. (New York: McGraw-Hill, 2003), 245.

79. Gerald L. Manning and Barry L. Reece, *Selling Today: Creating Customer Value*, 9th ed. (Upper Saddle River, NJ: Prentice Hall, 2004), 218.

80. Evan Carmichael, "His Secret Recipe: How Hershey Achieved Success," video, EvanCarmichael.com, http://www.evancarmichael.com/Famous-Entrepreneurs/603/His-Secret-Recipe-How-Hershey-Achieved-Success.html (accessed August 1, 2009).

81. Wendy Weiss, "Why Are We All so Afraid?" Sales Information, 2004, http://www.sales.net63.net/1138.php (accessed August 1, 2009).

82. Phil Glosserman, "The Fear of Rejection," video, *Selling Power*, http://www.sellingpower.com/content/video/?date=7/9/2009 (accessed March 16, 2010).

83. Phil Glosserman, "The Fear of Rejection," video, *Selling Power*, http://www.sellingpower.com/content/video/?date=7/9/2009 (accessed March 16, 2010).

84. Laura Laaman, "Assumptions, Sales Practice Help Fight Fear of Rejection," *Pittsburgh Business Times*, February 18, 2005, http://www.bizjournals.com/pittsburgh/stories/2005/02/21/smallb2.html (accessed August 3, 2009).

85. Laura Laaman, "Assumptions, Sales Practice Help Fight Fear of Rejection," *Pittsburgh Business Times*, February 18, 2005, http://www.bizjournals.com/pittsburgh/stories/2005/02/21/smallb2.html (accessed August 3, 2009).

86. BNET Reference Publications, "Facing the Fear of Rejection—Emotional Problem that Can be Devastating to the Success of Sales Representatives," BNET, http://findarticles.com/p/articles/mi_m1272/is_n2623_v125/ai_19313504 (accessed August 3, 2009).

87. "Tips for Successful Cold Calling," AllBusiness, http://www.AllBusiness.com/sales/selling-techniques-telesales/1355-1.html (accessed August 3, 2009).

88. Phil Glosserman, "The Fear of Rejection," video, *Selling Power*, http://www.sellingpower.com/content/video/?date=7/9/2009 (accessed March 16, 2010).

89. Lori Richardson, "Dealing with Gatekeepers," Sales Coach Blog, AllBusiness, April 19, 2005, http://www.AllBusiness.com/sales/selling-techniques/3873127-1.html (accessed August 3, 2009).

90. Michael A. Boylan, *The Power to Get In* (New York: St. Martin's Griffin, 1998), 125.

91. Lori Richardson, "Dealing with Gatekeepers," Sales Coach Blog, AllBusiness, April 19, 2005, http://www.AllBusiness.com/sales/selling-techniques/3873127-1.html (accessed August 3, 2009).

92. Michael A. Boylan, *The Power to Get In* (New York: St. Martin's Griffin, 1998), 124.

93. Michael A. Boylan, *The Power to Get In* (New York: St. Martin's Griffin, 1998), 126.

94. Susan Ward, "Cold Calling Tips," About.com, http://sbinfocanada.about.com/cs/marketing/a/coldcall.htm (accessed May 16, 2010).

95. Chris O'Leary, "Elevator Pitch 101," Elevator Pitch Essentials, January 27, 2009, http://www.elevatorpitchessentials.com/essays/ElevatorPitch.html (accessed July 26, 2009).

96. Michelle Dumas, "How to Create a Compelling Branded Elevator Speech for Your Job Search," EzineArticles, April 23, 2008, http://ezinearticles.com/?id=1128958 (accessed July 26, 2009).

97. Don Asher, "Sample 30 Second Speeches" JobStar, April 14, 2009, http://jobstar.org/hidden/asher2.php (accessed July 26, 2009).

98. Laura Raines, "Making Your Pitch," *The Atlanta Journal-Constitution*, Jobs, http://www.ajc.com/hotjobs/content/hotjobs/careercenter/articles/2007_0225_elevatorsp.html (accessed July 26, 2009).

CHAPTER 10
The Presentation: The Power of Solving Problems

Video Ride-Along with Paul Blake, Vice President of Sales at Greater Media Philadelphia

You met Paul Blake in Chapter 4 when he talked about ethics and doing the right thing. Now hear his tips for making a successful sales presentation. While most salespeople find this step of the selling process to be their favorite, it takes a lot more homework than meets the eye.

Listen to Paul's advice for learning about what makes the customer tick and delivering value "in a big way."

View the video online at: http://www.youtube.com/embed/12O5GV8VAnw

10.1 Preparation: Your Key to Success

Learning Objective

1. Learn how to prepare for a sales presentation.

You've made it! After all your hard work you have reached the point in the selling process where the qualifying, researching, and planning stages pay off. Finally, your story and the customer's story are about to connect in an exciting way. Most salespeople think of the presentation as the best part of the selling process. It's the opportunity to show the prospect that you know your stuff—and the chance to deliver value by putting your problem solving skills to work. So get ready, visualize the best possible outcome to your sales presentation, and take the necessary steps to make this outcome a reality.

Keep Your Eye on the Prize

As excited as you might be about your product, or as eager as you are to demonstrate your solution, keep in mind that your sales presentation is primarily about building a relationship and beginning a partnership, especially in the business-to-business (B2B) arena. When Selena Lo, CEO of Ruckus Wireless, is gearing up for a sales presentation, she focuses her final preparations on making it personal. Lo's company specializes in wireless routers that handle video, voice, and data capabilities for businesses. When she identifies a prospect, Lo's first priority is finding the person she refers to as "the fox": her ally in the prospect company who wants to see technological changes take place in his organization. Lo gives this relationship special attention, often inviting this individual out to dinner before the presentation to win his loyalty and get any additional details about his company.

Several days before the presentation, Lo researches everyone who will be in the meeting. She reads their bios and googles them to find out their employment histories. "You don't want someone to think you checked out their entire past," says Lo, but "you try to strike up more links between you and that person." She prepares the seating arrangement for the sales meeting strategically, making sure that she will be sitting directly across from the highest-ranking person there so that she can make eye contact. On the day of the presentation, she asks a member of her sales team to write down each person's name when they walk in the door—and to make a point of using the names during the presentation.[1] Lo's efforts to give the sales presentation a personal touch are a reminder that in relationship selling, you can never lose sight of the most important thing: your customer. Coach yourself on this on the day of your presentation and keep it in mind in the days leading up to it. What can you do to personalize this presentation and show your customers that it's all about their organization?

Taking a customer-centric approach lies at the heart of delivering value. In these terms, value isn't about offering a good price. It's not just about solving the customer's problems either. As Tom Reilly, author of *Value-Added Selling: How to Sell More Profitably, Confidently, and Professionally by Competing on Value, Not Price*, explains it, delivering value means that you "define value in customer terms, ask questions, listen to customers, and put the spotlight on customer-centric solutions."[2] This might mean that it takes more than one meeting to close your sale; you might need several visits to adequately respond to your customer's needs. According to one study, "Today's presentations typically are conducted over several meetings, with the salesperson often doing more listening than talking."[3] Make it your goal to see that you *and* your prospect get what you want out of the meeting.

It's a good idea to visualize this outcome before going into the meeting. Review your precall objectives. What will it look like to achieve these objectives? What steps will you and your prospect have to take? How will it feel when you both have achieved your goals? This isn't just about calming your nerves; visualizing the outcome you want is actually a powerful tool to help you achieve that outcome. For one thing, it's another form of planning. If you mentally run through a "movie" of the sales presentation, allowing yourself to picture your reactions and the steps you will take to close in on your objective, you will be better prepared when the meeting takes place.[4] Each step of the presentation will come naturally to you because you have already mentally rehearsed, and you will be better positioned to sell adaptively because you have already imagined a number of possible scenarios and customer responses.

mental rehearsal

Running through a scenario (like your sales presentation) step-by-step in your mind before you go into the situation.

For another thing, **mental rehearsal** fools your subconscious mind into believing you have already achieved your goals. Sales trainer and CEO Brian Tracy says, "Your subconscious mind cannot tell the difference between a real experience and one that you vividly imagine," so if you imagine a successful presentation and its outcome several times before your *actual* presentation, you will be as calm and confident as if you had already closed the sale. You will smile more easily, you will speak more slowly and clearly, and you will command attention. In addition, if your subconscious mind believes you have already been in this situation before, it will direct you to say and do the things you need to achieve your objective.[5]

The Power to Adapt

The sales presentation is where adaptive selling makes all the difference. Up until this point, you have researched and prepared and developed a solution that you think will meet your prospect's needs, but walking into the presentation and delivering on that preparation requires a different set of skills. Among other things, it requires flexibility and the ability to think on your feet. The best salespeople adapt their presentations to their prospect's reactions, and they go in knowing they may have to adapt to surprises for which they were unable to prepare (maybe the building has a power outage during the slideshow, for instance, or maybe one of the people from the customer organization decides to send another employee in his place at the last minute). These top-performing salespeople know that keeping a customer-centric focus, visualizing a successful outcome, and mentally rehearsing your presentation before you deliver it will give you the power to adapt with confidence and ease.

Adapting is all about listening. As Paul Blake noted in the video ride-along at the beginning of the chapter, your sales presentation is really a compilation of all the listening you have done to this point. And listening doesn't stop there. It's impossible to adapt if you're not listening. When you are creating your presentation, keep in mind that it is not a one-way communication. Presentations are for listening, adapting, and solving problems.

Video Clip

Listen and Sell
This video highlights the power of listening and tips to listen effectively during your presentation.

View the video online at: http://www.youtube.com/embed/VbuKVirVj60

Logistics Matter

There's nothing worse than putting hours into preparing a killer sales presentation, only to blow your chances because you forgot to bring an important part of your demonstration or because you got lost on your way to the meeting. Don't let disorganization hold you back: take charge of the details so that your only concern on the day of the presentation is the delivery.

The Night Before

The evening before your meeting, read over your precall objectives; practice your presentation a number of times out loud; and walk through your mental rehearsal, visualizing success. You can't practice too many times. The content of your presentation should be second nature by the time you get up in front of your audience so that you can focus your energy on your prospect. Rehearsal is one of the best ways to calm your nerves so that you can focus on delivering your presentation naturally and connecting with your prospect.

Power Player: Lessons in Selling from Successful Salespeople

Rehearse Your Way

Andres Mendes, global CIO of Special Olympics International, says that rehearsing out loud makes him too nervous; he likes to leave room for spontaneity and adaptation. Mendes develops the big themes of the presentation and maps these out into PowerPoint slides that tell the whole story. "I time the slides to move exactly at my pace, so I rehearse the mechanics and make sure those are right," he says.[6]

CIO Magazine columnist Martha Heller, on the other hand, likes to rehearse in the traditional style, delivering the presentation out loud and pacing the room as if she were in front of an audience. She never rehearses the opening though. She likes to adapt her comments to the immediate situation and energy in the room.[7]

The bottom line? While nearly all top-performing salespeople rehearse, not all approach rehearsal in the same way. Find the style of rehearsal that works best for you. Additionally, don't let your rehearsal lock you into delivering a rigidly defined set of remarks. You have to leave room for flexibility and adaptation.

The night before, you should also get together all the materials you'll need for your presentation—handouts, files, product samples, and contracts—and have them ready to go for the following morning. This will save you time tracking down loose supplies at the last minute, when you're trying to get out the door to make it to your meeting. It's also a good idea to set out your clothes the night before for the same reason.

If you are planning to use multimedia equipment in your presentation, make sure in advance that your prospect will have everything you'll need to make it run. If you aren't sure, bring everything (e.g., cables, adapters, remotes) with you. And of course, make sure you know how to use all your equipment. When Keith Waldon, CEO of Earth Preserv, was preparing for a meeting with JCPenney, one of his biggest prospects, he spent hours rehearsing with his multimedia equipment. The technology was a key element of his presentation, and he wanted to make sure everything would work perfectly for the big day. "I had to learn how to use all the remote-control equipment," he says. Waldon also brought a technical assistant with him as backup to safeguard against any glitches.[8]

Getting There

It might surprise you to know how often salespeople show up late to their own presentations because they get lost on the way to the meeting. When you are traveling to an unfamiliar place for your appointment, get directions in advance, and allow extra travel time in case of traffic delays or wrong turns. Make sure you also research the parking situation beforehand. If your prospect is a large corporation with its own complex, are there reserved employee lots and visitor lots? Will you have to walk a considerable distance from your car to the meeting room? If you'll be meeting in an urban area, is street parking available, or will you have to find a parking garage? You don't want to arrive on time only to get delayed because you spent twenty minutes driving around in search of a parking spot. It's a good idea to make a "test" trip in advance of your meeting. That will help avoid surprises with traffic, parking, security, or other areas that might cause a delay. If something unavoidable *does* come up to set you back, make sure you call ahead to let your customer know you will be arriving late.

Besides the extra time you allow for travel, plan to arrive at the meeting a little early. Not only does this convey professionalism, but it also gives you the time to mentally prepare once you arrive and to set up any equipment you'll be using. It's a good idea to allow time to stop in the restroom and take one last look to be sure you're at your best (and it's a good time to use a breath mint). Finally, bring something to read in case you have to wait: a business magazine, a newspaper like the *Wall Street Journal*, or maybe a Kindle.

FIGURE 10.1 Prepresentation Checklist

☐	Assemble supplies such as documents, brochures, product samples, contracts, files, thumb drives, CDs, projector, laptop, cables, remotes, pens, pointers, precall objectives, and client information.
☐	If you plan to use handouts, make sure you have enough copies.
☐	Check your clothes. Does anything need to be ironed? Do you have the right shoes, socks, tie, panty hose, and so forth for the suit?
☐	Make sure you have directions to your meeting. Do you know which building you are meeting in, which entrance to use, and how to find the meeting room?
☐	Research the parking situation.
☐	Write down a contact number or put it in your cell phone to call in case you are unavoidably delayed.
☐	Rehearse your presentation.
☐	Review your precall objectives and visualize success.

Key Takeaways

- When preparing for your sales presentation, stay focused on the essentials: your relationship with the prospect and your precall objectives.
- Practice **mental rehearsal** by visualizing the best possible outcome to the sales presentation.
- Delivering value to the customer means practicing adaptive selling and listening to the customer to understand her needs. Keep this in mind before and during the presentation.
- The night before your presentation, make sure you have all the logistics worked out: your equipment, your wardrobe, directions to the location, and parking information.

Exercises

1. You are preparing for a presentation with three executives to be considered for the internship or job you really want. List the steps you would take to rehearse your sales presentation, making sure to leave room for adaptability.

2. You are preparing a presentation for representatives from a large department store who are considering buying your line of men's shoes. There will be six representatives present, none of whom you have met in person before. You have heard from your original contact at the company that one person in the group is against purchasing your product because he believes he already has something in the line that has the same look. List some things you can do to prepare for this presentation that will address the prospect's concerns.

3. Assume you are a real estate agent and you are selling the dorm room, apartment, or home in which you live. Create a short sales presentation. Rehearse it so that the presentation takes only three minutes. What is the way that works best for you to rehearse?

4. Assume you are sales rep for a major telecommunications company and you are preparing a presentation for a buying group at a national retailer. Identify four sources you would use to personalize the presentation to the people in the room. How would you research each of the appropriate people?

10.2 Dress for Success

Learning Objective

1. Discuss how to dress for success for a sales presentation.

Your appearance communicates volumes about you before you ever open your mouth.

Tom Reilly tells the story of a salesperson that showed up to one of his recent seminars dressed in flip-flops and a T-shirt. "I thought he was there to clean the windows," Reilly says.[9] You want your prospective customers to take you seriously at first glance, so pay careful attention to what you wear on your sales call. Think about it this way, when you are buying a product off the shelf in a store, isn't packaging the first thing that catches your attention? Marketers know that packaging can influence a consumer's decision to buy before she ever even researches the product or reads about its features. In the same way, your prospect will make a judgment about you based on the way you "package" yourself; a professionally dressed salesperson can have a huge influence on a prospect's perception of him, his company, and the product he represents.[10] Your appearance should convey professionalism, competence, and success. Most important, regardless of the dress code at your prospect's business, be sure your appearance includes a smile. A smile is an instant rapport builder. No one wants to buy from someone who isn't excited about the company or product he's representing. Show your prospect that this isn't just a job; it's a passion.

Business Casual or Business?

When you are making a sales presentation at a company, remember the advice from Chapter 9 and dress one step above what you would wear if you worked at the organization.[11] If you are ever unsure about a company's standard dress code, *always* dress up. It's easier to take off a jacket and tie than to put them on at the last minute.[12] However, if your prospect tells you the dress code beforehand, here are some general guidelines to follow.

Business Attire

For most of your business-to-business (B2B) sales situations, business attire will be the norm. For a while in the '90s there was a trend toward more casual clothing in the workplace, but that trend is mostly on the way out. "I see a return to more traditional business wear," says Gary Brody, president of the Marcraft Apparel Group.[13] For that matter, even if your customer says business casual is the standard in his workplace, if you are aiming to dress a notch up from that standard, you might decide that business attire is the way to go. As Mark-Evan Blackman of the Fashion Institute of Technology says, suits "universally project an air of authority."[14]

FIGURE 10.2
Whether the situation calls for business or business casual attire, always be professional.

© 2010 Jupiterimages Corporation

For men, business attire means a suit (matching pants and jacket), a necktie, a long-sleeved shirt, and lace-up shoes.[15] Go for conservative, dark colors such as gray, black, or dark blue for the suit; white or light blue for the shirt. For women, business means a suit (skirt or pants and matching jacket), shoes with moderate heels in a basic pump style (closed-toe), a blouse, and tan or light pantyhose.

Business Casual

Business casual can sometimes be tricky because it's less clearly defined than business attire. According to Monster.com, business casual "means dressing professionally, looking relaxed, yet neat and pulled together."[16] For men, a bare minimum approach to business casual means dress pants and a collared shirt. Women can wear skirts or pants, but skirts should be a conservative length, and pants should be well tailored: not too tight or too loose. On the top, a blouse or a tailored knit sweater are good choices, and for footwear, make sure to wear closed-toe shoes.[17] Business casual for men or women does *not* include workout clothes or shoes, wrinkled clothing, worn blue jeans, shorts, miniskirts, athletic socks, or overly revealing clothing.[18]

Video Clip

Best-Dressed Men
This video provides tips for men to dress in business casual.

View the video online at: http://www.youtube.com/embed/6BXcsWCrz0Y

Video Clip

These videos include tips for what not to wear to work.

View the video online at: http://www.youtube.com/embed/R3FaOzC7eJg?rel=0

Details Matter

Getting the clothes right but missing the mark on the details will create a poor impression just as much as underdressing for the occasion can, so make sure everything from your nails to your hair and choice of accessories conveys professionalism.

- All clothes should be cleaned and pressed. Wrinkled or stained clothing looks very unprofessional. Take the time to review your wardrobe days before your presentation to be sure everything is cleaned and pressed. A trip to the dry cleaner is money well spent.
- If the garment has belt loops, wear a belt. Belts should be dark leather.
- Make sure your briefcase or handbag is professional, not casual.[19]
- Men should avoid sports watches, and women should wear conservative jewelry—nothing flashy.
- Make sure your hair looks professional and well groomed.[20]
- Carry a good quality portfolio or notebook and a nice pen.
- Women should wear hosiery if they are wearing a skirt. Avoid wearing perfume or cologne.[21]

And don't forget good grooming. Body odor, bad breath, poorly manicured fingernails, and messy hair can be a deal breaker.

Video Clip

This video provides some good advice on how to dress for interviews and in the office.

View the video online at: http://www.youtube.com/embed/n0DFwGy8wUg?rel=0

The Image Your Customer Wants

When employees whose businesses rent space in the Coca-Cola building on New York's Fifth Avenue want to bring a canned or bottled beverage to work, they have a list of drinks to choose from. Vermont Pure Water is OK, but Evian is definitely out. Food and drink orders coming into the building are scanned, and anything with non-Coca-Cola brand products gets sent away.[22] While this rule is on the extreme side, it's true that even the products you use reflect an image, and when you're doing business with a potential customer, you want that image to be the right one. This is something worth researching before you go into your sales call. If you know who your prospect's customers are, use those company's products. Does the prospect do advertising for Apple? Don't listen to your Zune while you're waiting for the appointment. If your prospect is a publishing house, read some of their books before you go to your meeting. If they have a radio station or record label, listen to it. Knowing the prospect's products, or their customers' products, is part of your credibility.

Key Takeaways

- When you prepare for a sales presentation, pay careful attention to your appearance because this is an important part of your first impression.
- Always dress more formally than you think your customer will be dressed. When in doubt, dress up.
- Give careful attention to detail, such as accessories and grooming.
- Make sure to convey an image that's in line with your customer's products and values.

Exercises

1. Review the clothes that are currently in your closet. Do you own a suit and accessories that would be appropriate for business attire? Do you have several pieces you could wear at a business casual event? If not, what will you need to purchase to dress for success?
2. Assume you are a salesperson for a financial services company and you are making a presentation to the vice president of operations and her staff about your corporate financial services. What would you wear?

3. Your prospect is sponsoring a team-building happy hour and dinner that is being held at a local restaurant and sports bar on a Thursday evening and has invited you to attend. What would you wear? Would you consider wearing jeans? Why or why not?

4. You have a meeting with your prospect on Friday at his office. The office is very casual, and your client usually wears jeans. What would you wear? Would you wear jeans? Why or why not?

10.3 Making Your Presentation Work

Learning Objective

1. Learn how to deliver your message in a powerful and effective way.

When deciding on the structure of your presentation, there are a number of things to consider. Will you present to a group or to an individual? Where will you be giving your presentation? What tools will you use? Sometimes these options are under your control, but often in business-to-business (B2B) sales, you will have to adapt your presentation to your prospect's needs. In either situation, you can maximize your presentation if you know what to avoid, what to prepare for, and how to make your solution come to life with the tools you have.

Video Clip

Giving presentations worth listening to.

View the video online at: http://www.youtube.com/embed/NUXkThfQx6A?rel=0

The Right Size

A good salesperson can read group dynamics as skillfully as she can read an individual prospect's verbal and nonverbal cues and is comfortable in one-on-one and in group presentation situations. This is critical because as a salesperson sometimes you have control over the kind of presentation you will deliver (group versus individual), but in many situations, the size of the audience to which you will present is determined by the needs and structure of your prospect's organization. In many organizations large purchasing decisions are the responsibility of purchasing committees or of a combination of individual and group decision makers.[23] You might find that you begin with several individual presentations to decision makers in an organization and then are asked to give a follow-up group presentation to a purchasing committee.

Presenting to Individuals

In one-on-one presentations, of course, you only have one person's needs, preferences, and background to research and adapt to, so customization is usually an easy task. You can closely observe your prospect's nonverbal communication and listen to her stated needs and concerns and respond accordingly. Does he look worried when you tell him that your company's integrated marketing plan usually takes four months to develop? You can explain that for preferred prospects you are sometimes able to turn around a faster solution. Does he seem distracted when you begin discussing product features? You can back off and begin asking more questions.

As you learned in Chapter 3 in the discussion about social styles, you will be in a better position to deliver value during your sales presentation if you know something about your buyer's personality before going into the meeting: Is your prospect conversational and people oriented, or is he task oriented and businesslike? Does your prospect care about details and thorough descriptions, or does he prefer to see the "big picture"? Is he competitive? How does he feel about change? Understanding these things about your prospect will help you to favorably position your product and plan your presentation so that you can put emphasis on the things that matter most to the individual. If you know your prospect is highly competitive, for instance, he will probably be interested in learning about the features that set your product apart from others on the market and the ways in which your product can give him or his company a competitive edge.

Writing up a customer trait description before your meeting can be very helpful so that you can use the information as a guideline in preparing your presentation.[24] If you're working with an existing customer or if you've interacted with your prospect prior to the presentation, you can use your observations to write a trait description. If you haven't met the prospect before, try asking other salespeople in your organization, noncompetitive salespeople at other companies, or other contacts you have who might have met your prospect and who can tell you something about her personality.[25] Also, use the company resources including the CRM system to gather as much information as possible about the company and your contact. In addition, it is also a good idea to send a precall questionnaire to your contact to gather information such as the names and titles of the people who will be attending the presentation, how much time has been allotted for you, objectives for the meeting, and any other information that will help you plan the meeting. This information can provide valuable information and help you create an agenda, which is a good idea to send to the prospect before the meeting.

FIGURE 10.3
Learn as much about your prospect as possible before your presentation.

© 2010 Jupiterimages Corporation

In adapting to an individual buyer, it's also important to consider his motivation.[26] What are his responsibilities in the organization? What pressures does he face? Is he on a strict budget? Is he concerned with his status in the company? If you have two buyers who purchase the same product, chances are they'll be doing it for different reasons:[27] one person might buy a car from you because he sees it as a status symbol, while another person might buy the same car because it gets good gas mileage and is well built and reliable. Keep in mind that delivering value isn't *only* about meeting a prospect's needs; it's also about showing him that you understand his specific motivations and concerns. The best salespeople present themselves as advisors their customers can trust.[28] Is a prospect worried about proving herself in a new role in her company? Show him how your product can help him perform her role better, or demonstrate how people in similar positions at other companies have used your product with success.

Video Clip

Sell with Success Stories
Listen to how Rachel Gordon, account manager at WMGK, uses success stories with other customers as a selling tool in her presentations to new prospects.

View the video online at: http://www.youtube.com/embed/ysguVTGkyA4

Presenting to Groups

If customization is that straightforward with an individual buyer, why would you ever choose to sell to a group? Besides the fact that sometimes the nature of the sale demands it, selling to groups is also more efficient than selling to individuals. If you're selling accounting software to a number of departments in an organization, rather than meeting individually with a decision maker from each department, you can save time by giving your sales presentation to a number of decision makers at once. Group presentations can also help you identify the decision makers in an organization if you aren't yet sure who they are. By keeping an eye on group dynamics during the presentation you can usually observe the "pecking order" among members and identify the individuals in the group whose opinions hold the most leverage.

Additionally, group presentations can be a way to win greater support for your sale. If you know one or two people in an organization who are excited about your product, you can allow their enthusiasm to influence others in a group setting.[29] Recall Selena Lo of Ruckus Wireless, who finds the "fox" within each of her target organizations and leverages his support of her product to sway the group buying decision.

If you know what is at stake for each member of the group, you will be able to facilitate the discussion during your presentation much more effectively. This is why it's important to gather information about everyone who will attend your sales meeting. Again, think of Lo's method, where she reads each group member's bio and googles their names before going into a group meeting. Find out the individual's needs within the organization. What is her status? How does she perceive the urgency of the problem you want to solve? Does she have any ego involvement in the product or service?[30] (For instance, an accountant in the organization might feel threatened by new accounting software if it replaces part of her current role.) This will help you understand the most important concerns you will need to address in the presentation, and if certain parts of your presentation apply more directly to certain members of the group, you can direct those parts specifically at those individuals.

Keep in mind that people act differently in group settings than they do when you are interacting with them alone, so finding out about individual members' personalities is less important in group presentations. Instead, adjust your presentation to the dynamics in the room. Watch the group for nonverbal cues; when one member is talking, observe how others react to see whether or not they support what she's saying.[31] If the energy in the room feels low, or if you get the sense that the group is getting restless, consider moving on to the next part of your presentation or changing tactics.

Sometimes you won't know who or how many people you will be presenting to beforehand, so you won't be able to research the individuals. However, it's always a good idea to ask when you call to schedule your meeting. You may be able to find out information that your contact at the organization wouldn't otherwise volunteer.

Video Clip

Group Presentations

Hear about how to use a group presentation to your "unfair" advantage in this video:

View the video online at: http://www.youtube.com/embed/1pilX9TS930

The Right Place

You also might not know *where* your presentation will happen. If you know you'll be presenting to your prospect at his office or in a conference room at his company, you won't have control over the environment. What happens if your prospect has reserved a meeting room and when you arrive there are no empty walls on which you can project the PowerPoint presentation you brought along? When you know you'll be presenting in an unfamiliar environment, make sure to have a contingency plan in place. If slides or other multimedia equipment are central to your presentation, talk to someone at the company to make sure you'll be able to use the equipment. And if this fails, be ready to rely on your handouts, product samples, or the good old whiteboard to carry the presentation through.

Of course, in other situations, you will have control over the environment. In real estate, for instance, the presentation takes place inside the product. In retail, the presentation generally happens at your store. And there are other selling situations in which the prospect will come to your office or a conference room at your company or where you will meet at a "neutral" location like a rented meeting space.[32] Here are a few guidelines to follow, depending on the environment in which you'll be presenting.

Your Place of Business

When the prospect comes to you, treat her like you would treat a guest in your home. Make sure you set up any presentation materials well in advance and have refreshments set out in the conference room or your office. Think about ways you can add personal touches—for instance, a sign with the prospect's name on it ("[Your company name] welcomes [prospect's company name]"), or, for a group presentation, information packets at each person's seat with his or her name on the front. Sales professional John Chapin suggests having small items on hand that you can give to your prospect, such as pens or calculators with your company logo on them.[33] Small, thoughtful details can make an important difference.

A Neutral Location

If you are giving your presentation in a neutral location like a rented conference room you have the freedom to set up and work out any technical bugs well beforehand. When Keith Waldon of Earth Preserv was preparing for the presentation that secured his biggest customer, JCPenney, he rented a boardroom in a building near JCPenney's corporate headquarters. He opted for the rented space so that he could pull out all the stops for the presentation. "I wanted to catch JCPenney by surprise," Waldon says.

When the five executives arrived, Waldon had set up multimedia equipment for video, sound, and slides. He had placed a thick binder of presentation materials (including television storyboards, magazine advertisements, and product comparisons) at each executive's seat with his name and the JCPenney corporate logo embossed on the front. Besides the conference room, Waldon had also rented an empty storefront in the same building, and halfway through the presentation, he took his customers to see the retail window display he had created there to look like one JCPenney might use to display Earth Preserv products in their stores.[34]

Since you will have time to set up beforehand at a rented location, you can treat the presentation the way you would treat a presentation at your home office. Bring refreshments, set up any multimedia equipment well in advance, and arrive early to make sure everything is in working order at the facility. Make sure you know the name of the facility's contact person; you can call her several days ahead of time to find out what equipment she has at on hand and what you will need to bring.[35]

Your Prospect's Place of Business

When you deliver your presentation at your prospect's location, you won't have the luxury of extensive setup time, and you may find that you have to adapt to the space and resources on hand. However, there are a few things you can do to make a good impression and ensure that things go as smoothly as possible:

- Arrive early and set up any technology you plan to use so that you can minimize the chance of something going wrong.
- When it's possible, call ahead to find out about the space in which you will be presenting and the materials that will be available to you.
- Let your prospect know how long you will need to set up—particularly if you are using multimedia equipment.
- When you arrive, the first person you interact with will probably be the receptionist. Introduce yourself and let her know that the customer is expecting you.
- In addition to your presentation items, consider bringing food, coffee, or small giveaway items.
- In B2B sales, if your presentation will be around the lunch hour, it's often customary to offer to take your prospect to lunch before or after the meeting.[36]

Webinars and Video Conferences

So how do you give a sales presentation if your prospect lives across the country, but you have a limited budget for travel? Unless there is a good chance that a prospect will become a key customer, it usually isn't practical for a salesperson to travel long distances to make one presentation. However, thanks to improved technology, it's becoming increasingly common for salespeople to address this problem using Webinars, video conferences, and online meetings. These technologies are allowing companies to reach more prospects in less time and to reach prospects internationally and across long distances.

Video Link

Remote Presentations

Learn more about how and why salespeople are now using the Web to make sales presentations.

http://www.webex.com/overview/index.html

Of course, there are some drawbacks to giving sales presentations through video conferencing rather than in person. For one thing, it's always easier to establish rapport with your prospect if you're able to have a face-to-face interaction. Video conferences offer the benefit of visuals, so you and your prospect can read one another's body language and visual cues, but this is not a complete substitute for sitting in the same room with someone. Additionally, since the presentation relies entirely on technology—both on your end and on the prospect's end—there is a greater chance that a technological malfunction could prevent the presentation from working.

In-person presentations are still the most effective and personal method, so whenever you are able (and when it is practical) to give a face-to-face presentation, this is your best option. However, technology keeps improving, and online meetings and video teleconferences are becoming more successful as an alternative method all the time.[37] Depending on your selling situation, this is something you might consider. As online sales strategist Joanna Lees Castro points out, video conferencing can be *almost* as effective as an in-person meeting in a number of selling situations, and it is certainly a better, more personal approach than e-mail or telephone.[38]

Even though video conferencing feels different from in-person communications, you should essentially treat your online meetings the way you would treat any sales call. Keep in mind that nonverbal communication has a strong influence on interactions—and, especially with good technology, your customer can see you clearly. Pay attention to your body language and facial expressions, and avoid personal gestures (like playing with your hair or scratching an itch).[39] Dress professionally, plan your agenda carefully, and make sure to prepare and get your materials set up ahead of time. If you are conferencing from a location other than your office, arrive early to make sure the technology is set up to run smoothly for your presentation.

It is also important to resist the temptation to multitask during your video conference. Close down any other applications you might have open on your computer, clear off your desk, and make sure you will not be interrupted until the call is over. Mute any cell phones and close the door to the room in which you are presenting. Give your customer your full attention. While this level of focus is a given on your end, unfortunately, you can't always be certain that your prospect will give a video conference meeting *his* full attention by minimizing distractions. For this reason, it is especially important to have a clear agenda that you follow closely. Keep your presentation brief, and be aware that you will have to work harder to hold your prospect's attention. Live interaction from your audience is critical to make sure your participants are engaged.

Besides a greater likelihood of distraction, there are a few other extra considerations to keep in mind in a video conference situation. *Sales and Management* magazine notes that privacy is expected during a video conference, so if you want to record part of your presentation, it is important to ask your prospect for permission.[40] When the presentation is over, Joanna Lees Castro suggests closing the meeting with a clear call to action in which you include a wrap-up and well-defined next steps that you and your prospects should take. At the end of a conventional sales presentation, Lees Castro points out, next-step discussions can happen more organically, as the customer is walking you to the door, but this is obviously impossible in an online situation.[41]

The Right Tools

In the best sales presentations, the product or service comes alive. Try to see the presentation through your prospect's eyes. What is the best way to capture his imagination? How will you tell the story that will make your product or service compelling? In what ways can you delight or surprise your customer? Few people know how to do this better than Dann Ilicic, CEO of Wow Branding. Wow, a small start-up, frequently outperforms big name competitors when vying for a prospect. Ilicic approaches each presentation with the same mind-set: you can't bore your customer into buying from you, so why not dazzle them? One customer said the presentation Ilicic put together for his company couldn't have been better: "Dann unquestionably knocked it out of the park compared with the other firms, and they were really high-end firms with spectacular portfolios."[42]

So how does Wow Branding wow its prospects? Ilicic's approach offers three lessons:

1. **Take customization to a new level**. Ilicic says he and his team spend about fifty hours preparing for a sales presentation. They call low-level employees in the customer company, the company's past customers, and companies that have chosen not to do business with the prospect to learn things the prospects might not even know about themselves. Glumac, an engineering firm in Portland, Oregon, and one of Wow's customers, said Ilicic's technique "was a brilliant move...because he wasn't asking what our imagery should be"; instead, he researched to find out what the image already was.

2. **Never miss an opportunity to delight**. Ilicic likes to surprise his customers with the small things: like stamping green thumbprints throughout a proposal for an agricultural company—or, for a pharmaceutical company, handing out vitamin bottles on which he has replaced the label with a message about Wow. Sometimes he brings in a cake on which he reveals the suggested name for a new company. Because Ilicic's intensive research allows him to understand his customers so well, he is able to perfectly match the wow factor to each prospect and make the product come alive.

3. **Always make the presentation creative and fun**. This technique engages the customer, even when the meeting agenda isn't exciting itself. It also allows Wow to get around difficult or sensitive parts of the presentation. Rather than talking about Wow's successes, Ilicic records customer testimonials about his company and plays these for his prospects. On another occasion, rather than potentially putting a prospect on the defensive by telling the company what their image should be, Ilicic told them that Wow had been assigned a branding project for their biggest competitor. He launched a multimedia presentation to show them their competitor's branding overhaul, and by the end his prospects were asking themselves, "Why didn't we think of that?" After the presentation, Ilicic revealed that he hadn't actually made the campaign for the company's competitor; it was for them.[43]

So what techniques can you use to achieve these goals in your sales presentations? The tools you choose will depend on the situation and your presentation style. As Ilicic demonstrates, the possibilities are almost endless, but whatever tool you use, it is important to carefully consider your choice and how you can maximize its effectiveness.

PowerPoint Presentations

PowerPoint slides provide an easy way to organize your presentation and add helpful visuals. For many salespeople, PowerPoint is one of their go-to presentation tools. It can be an especially helpful tool for salespeople who are starting out and want the security of a clear framework from which to present. An added benefit is that it doesn't take much technological know-how to put together a clean-looking PowerPoint demonstration.

FIGURE 10.4
PowerPoint presentations can be an effective way to get your message across during a presentation.

On the other hand, not all presentation situations lend themselves to PowerPoint (e.g., conference rooms with no wall space on which to project or presentations given in the field), so if you plan to use this tool, make sure that you will be presenting in a space where you can make it work. Additionally, be aware of—and avoid—a number of common mistakes salespeople make when using PowerPoint that can ruin a presentation. As sales coach and author Anne Miller says, "Putting PowerPoint into the hands of some sales reps is like putting matches into the hands of some children."[44] To maximize PowerPoint as a tool to successfully sell your story, use the tips in Figure 10.5.[45]

FIGURE 10.5 Guidelines for PowerPoint Visuals

If you want to...	Then use...
explain trends	line graphs
describe a series of steps	a diagram
compare capabilities	a table
show product/service comparisons	a pie chart or bar graph
explain how your Web site works	the Web site

The following dos and don'ts can also be helpful as you are creating a PowerPoint presentation.

- **Don't** turn down the lights. It takes the focus away from you, and it can put people to sleep.
- **Don't** go overboard with technological gimmicks. Fancy fades and clever add-ons will only distract from you and from the content of your presentation.[46]
- **Don't** hide behind your computer screen when using PowerPoint; make sure you face your audience and make eye contact. This can be a temptation when the computer is set up on a podium close to eye level.
- **Don't** fill your slides with words. Use bullet points, separate each point with white space, and cut out *any* unnecessary words you can.

- **Don't** bore your audience with visual sameness. Slide after slide of bulleted lists gets monotonous; visuals and charts have a stronger impact.[47]

- **Do** make your slides easy to read. Avoid small fonts, visual clutter, and dark text against dark backgrounds.[48]

- **Do** replace descriptive headlines with headlines that sell. No one cares about a headline that describes what's already on the page.[49] For example, rather than writing "Our Statistics" at the top of the page, write "See Significant Savings in the First Year."

- **Do** use the 10/20/30 rule: Make sure you limit your slides to 10 or fewer. Focus on the things you want people to remember, rather than overwhelming them with information. Give yourself 20 minutes to go through your 10 slides. Any more than this and you will reach the limit of your audience's attention span. Finally, use only 30-point or larger font size so that your audience can clearly read what you've written.[50]

Video Clip

10/20/30 Rule
Guy Kawaski, best-selling author, venture capitalist, and entrepreneur, created this rule and describes it in this video.

View the video online at: http://www.youtube.com/embed/liQLdRk0Ziw

- **Do** remember that that PowerPoint is only an *aid*. "You are the star," says communications consultant Ronnie Moore. "The media and visuals support you."[51] Use dynamic speaking strategies, move around, keep your audience involved; don't let your technology take over.

Brochures, Premiums, and Leave-Behinds

It is usually expected that you will have printed material to give your audience during a presentation. In addition to a printed supplement to your PowerPoint presentation (i.e., something that conveys the same information as your slides and on which your audience can take notes), you might decide to bring along brochures with information about your company, products, and services. What are the benefits of brochures? According to sales expert and author Geoffrey James, in some situations you need a brochure to make your firm look serious. However, James lists "I promise to read your brochure" as one of the top ten lies customers tell sales reps. His conclusion: the brochure might gain you credibility, but it probably won't get read.[52] Don't rely completely on brochures because they won't be a focal point of your presentation.

Sometimes a brochure can work as a reminder about you and your company after you've left, but this is assuming your customer doesn't throw the brochure away. When it comes to reminders, a better bet is leaving something functional that your customer will actually use regularly. These reminder objects—calendars, refrigerator magnets, pens, or mouse pads labeled with your company name—are called premium leave-behinds and are a proven method of reminding customers you exist.[53] Almost all salespeople bring some sort of brochure or premium leave-behind on their sales calls.

Samples and Demonstrations

There is almost no better way to make your story come to life for your customer than letting him experience it for himself. Think of television courtroom dramas: when the lawyer is making her final statement to the jury and she wants to pull out all the stops, what does she do? She doesn't just give the jury the facts or tell them the version of the story she wants them to believe—she brings the story to life; she puts the gun in the defendant's hand; she brings out the pictures of the stab wounds. Think about this when you plan your sales presentation. During the presentation, you can bring your story to life by offering product samples for your prospects to try or by running demonstrations that let them see for themselves what your product can do. When winemakers sell their products to large distributors, they don't just bring in descriptions of their wines for the buyers to read; they offer tastings so buyers can experience the product. When caterers want to sell their services to someone who is planning a wedding, they bring in samples from their menus, so the customer can say, "Wow this pasta really is delicious!" Or think of Keith Waldon of Earth Preserv who didn't just tell JCPenney, "We can make displays of our environmentally friendly products for your store windows;" instead, he set up a real shop window display so his prospects could *see* their place in his story.

Power Selling: Lessons in Selling from Successful Brands

Sell to Someone Unexpected

For the founders of Cranium, Inc., maker of the popular Cranium board game, playing is believing. When the company first launched in 1998, they knew that 50 percent of board games failed in their first year. Cranium's strategy? Avoid the traditional board game buyers—toy stores—and sell to someone unexpected. Cranium's founders managed to get an introduction to Howard Schultz, CEO of Starbucks, and they arrived at his office with a game board and challenged him to a match. After playing a few rounds, Schultz decided this was just the game Starbucks had been looking for—something that would support coffeehouse culture—and Cranium, Inc., had its first major sale.

Next on Cranium's list? Barnes & Noble Booksellers. The company's founders scheduled a meeting with Terese Profaci, the bookstore's director of gift merchandising, whose boss told the sales reps on the way in, "I don't know why you're here. We don't sell games." Still, Profaci's boss had her play a round of the game with some employees at corporate headquarters, and in the end, Barnes & Noble was won over.[54]

Besides bringing your story to life, there are a number of other good reasons to use demonstrations:

- **To educate your prospect**. If you are selling a complex product, such as a highly involved software program, the best way to help your customer understand how it works is to show her.

- **To involve your prospect**. Let him find the results for himself. Just as car shoppers get to take the wheel in a test drive—and this often makes the difference between a decision to buy or not to buy—customers who use your products for themselves are more likely to make a personal connection with it. A salesperson selling insulated windows, for instance, might place a piece of glass in front of a heat lamp and ask her customer to put out his hand and feel the heat. Then the salesperson might substitute the sheet of glass for a window sample. "Now put out your hand," she will tell the customer. "Can you feel how this window is going to keep the elements out and save you money on your energy bills?"[55]

- **To prove the performance of your product**.[56] Of course, you can tell your prospect "our air purifiers are quieter than the leading model, and they take up less space in your home." But if you *bring* your air purifier to the presentation and set it next to the leading model, and if you ask your prospect to turn both machines on, he can see for himself that your product is smaller, and he can hear for himself that it makes less noise.

Give Them the Numbers: Cost-Benefit Analysis and ROI

When you present your solution to the customer, especially in B2B sales, closing the sale usually depends on whether the cost of your solution is offset by the value it delivers.[57] If you can quantify your solution using cost-benefit analysis and ROI (return on investment) analysis, you can help your customer determine whether a project or purchase is worth funding.

A **cost-benefit analysis** asks the question "Will this purchase save more money in the long run than it costs?"[58] Imagine you are selling an energy-efficient commercial dishwasher to a pizza kitchen. The dishwasher costs $3,000, but average cost savings per year are $800 in energy bills and $200 in water usage: a total of $1,000.[59] Your dishwashers are guaranteed to last a long time; in fact, you offer a five-year warranty on any purchase. At a savings rate of $1,000 each year, your customer will have saved $5,000 in energy and water expenses by the time his warranty expires. Based on this information, you present this cost-benefit analysis to your prospect:

$$\$3,000 = \text{cost (initial investment)}$$

$$\text{cost savings} - \text{initial investment} = \text{benefit}$$

$$\$5,000 - \$3,000 = \$2,000$$

In this case, the cost savings is $1,000 per year times five years for a total of $5,000, minus the initial investment of $3,000, means that there is a benefit of $2,000.

In other words, the dishwasher has a three-to-two cost-benefit ratio over five years ($3,000 in cost to $2,000 in benefit). You can tell him, "This purchase will save you money in the long run. After you make back what you spent on the dishwasher in cost savings, you will continue to save $1,000 each year." Similarly, you can show your customer a **return on investment (ROI) analysis**. ROI shows the customer the return (profit or cost savings) compared to the investment he will make. In the case of the dishwasher, the ROI would be calculated by dividing the benefit (in this case $2,000) by the cost of the product or initial investment (in this case $3,000), then multiplying the result by 100, which would yield a 66 percent ROI after five years.

$$\$2000 \text{ (savings over five years)} \div \$3,000 \text{ (initial investment)} \times 100 = 66\% \text{ ROI}$$

You can maximize ROI by cutting costs, increasing profits, or accelerating the rate at which profits are made.[60] Some businesses have a minimum ROI that must be met before a purchase can be approved. While you might be able to learn this information in your preapproach, it is more likely that you will have to discuss minimum ROI with your customer during the sales presentation. You might present your solution and find out more about your customer's specific needs (including budget constraints and minimum ROI) during the first sales presentation and then write up a proposal in response to your findings, which you deliver during a second presentation.

cost-benefit analysis

Quantifies the costs of a purchase in relationship to the benefits it provides.

return on investment (ROI) analysis

Shows the return (profit or cost savings) as a percentage of the initial investment.

Key Takeaways

- Presenting to individuals requires a different set of skills and techniques than presenting to groups, so make sure you have a clear strategy for your presentation that takes the size of your audience into account.
- When presenting to an individual, keep your prospect's personality in mind and adapt your approach accordingly. Take his position and responsibilities in the company into account in the way you present your solution.

- Selling to groups can be a more efficient presentation method, and sometimes it is required in your customer organization. When conducting a group presentation, take group dynamics into account, keeping in mind that people act differently in group situations than they do in one-on-one interactions.

- When you are delivering your presentation at your place of business or in a neutral location (like a rented space), treat the customer as you would treat a guest in your home. Set up refreshments and supplies well ahead of time so that you are well prepared when the prospect arrives.

- When you are presenting at your prospect's place of business, try to find out about the presentation venue beforehand—but be prepared to adapt if your prospect doesn't have the equipment or setup you were expecting. Arrive early so that you have time to set up.

- If your presentation is given as a Webinar or video conference, treat the presentation as you would treat an in-person interaction. Dress professionally and set up ahead of time. Make sure to minimize distractions.

- When delivering a PowerPoint presentation, keep your slides brief, uncluttered, and easy to read. Don't let the technology overshadow you, the presenter.

- There is almost no better way to bring your product to life than by using samples or demonstrations to get your prospect involved.

- Your customer will expect you to bring a **cost-benefit analysis** or **ROI analysis** as a way to quantify your solution.

Exercises

1. You are giving a presentation to a busy manager who initially tells you that she can only give you thirty minutes of her time. She seems brisk and businesslike at first, but when you are in her office, you notice a picture of her son in a soccer uniform and mention that your kids are involved in soccer. After this, she relaxes and begins discussing her children at length. Keeping in mind that (a) you have an agenda to get through but (b) establishing a connection is important to you, and you want to take your cue from your prospect, how do you respond, and why?

2. You are giving a presentation to a group and notice that one member of the group is more vocal than others and tends to dominate the conversation. What are some strategies you could use to make sure that other members of the group have a chance to participate and contribute their opinions?

3. Choose a product or service and prepare a short sales presentation that includes a demonstration. What other items do you need besides the product or service to perform the demonstration (e.g., Internet service for software; water for instant coffee; plates, silverware, and napkins for food products)? How is the product demonstration integrated into your presentation? How do you use the demonstration to engage the prospect with the product or service?

4. Assume you are selling environmental design consulting, and an important part of your sales presentation involves using your company Web site to demonstrate previous projects you have completed, interactive customer surveys, and your company's brand image. However, when you arrive at your customer's place of business to set up your presentation, you learn that the Internet has been down all morning and may not be back up until the next day. What could you have done to prepare for this sort of unforeseen problem in advance?

5. Find a PowerPoint presentation you have created for another class—or if this is unavailable, find a PowerPoint presentation online; Slideshare is a good resource: http://www.slideshare.net. Offer a critique of the presentation based on the information you learned in this chapter.

6. Assume you are a sales rep for an Internet advertising company. Your prospect, an online hardware retailer that specializes in compression pumps, is concerned about making the investment for Internet advertising. You want to incorporate the ROI into your presentation. If the prospect spends $90,000 in advertising, it will generate 120,000 clicks to the company Web site. At a 2 percent conversion rate (2 percent of the customers who visit the site make a purchase), that is 2,400 orders. If each order is $230, the sales generated from the online

ad would be $552,000. What is the prospect's ROI (show your math)? How would you incorporate this ROI into your sales presentation?

7. Imagine that you are selling high-end electronic equipment. Your prospect has agreed to purchase a laptop for $800. Now you tell him about the benefits of purchasing the service agreement, which includes free battery replacement and computer cleaning every year for three years for only $120. A replacement battery costs $200, and a computer cleaning costs $85. How much will the customer save if he purchases the service agreement assuming he needs to replace the battery and have the laptop cleaned once a year? How would you incorporate this into your sales presentation?

10.4 How to Use SPIN Selling in Your Sales Call

Learning Objective

1. Understand SPIN and how to use it during the sales presentation.

In 1988, Neil Rackham and his company Huthwaite, Inc., researched more than 35,000 sales calls, observing successful and experienced sales professionals doing what they do best. In the process they disproved a number of popular myths about the selling process, and they developed a sales model of their own, which they called SPIN selling.[61] Today sales professionals around the world incorporate the SPIN selling model into their sales process with great success—and if you learn a few simple principles, you can too. The following section describes SPIN selling in a nutshell.

What Is SPIN Selling?

SPIN selling

A customer centered sales model. SPIN stands for the four kinds of questions successful salespeople ask their customers: **S**ituation, **P**roblem, **I**mplication, and **N**eed-payoff.

SPIN works from the theory that relationship selling is customer-centric. It requires you to adapt your selling process to your customer, and it delivers personal solutions. To make this work, you have to ask your buyer a lot of questions, let him do most of the talking, and give his responses your full attention.

In the SPIN model, there are four components of a sales call: opening, investigating, demonstrating capability, and obtaining commitment. SPIN gets its name from the four kinds of questions that take place during the investigation stage: **S**ituation, **P**roblem, **I**mplication, and **N**eed-payoff.

With smaller sales, these four components of the sale (opening, investigating, demonstrating capability, and obtaining commitment) often happen sequentially and in a short period of time; a customer might walk onto your car lot and commit to buying a car from you an hour later. But often in business-to-business (B2B) sales, especially complex ones, you will incorporate SPIN components into a number of the steps in your selling process. For instance, you will do some investigation during your preapproach, and you might make an early presentation in which you open, investigate, and demonstrate capability. Because larger sales take more time, you won't close the sale at the end of your first presentation, but you might get a commitment from your customer to move the sale forward. SPIN selling is not a rigid, step-by-step model; rather it provides an effective, flexible framework for customer centered selling.[62]

Opening

According to Rackham, the **opening** of the sales call is not the most important part, but it does pave the way for the important steps that come after.[63] At the beginning of every call, you want to set the preliminaries and make any necessary introductions. (In larger B2B sales, you usually won't spend very long on introductions because 95 percent of the time you will be meeting with an existing customer or a prospect you have already met.)[64] If you are following up on an earlier sales call, it's important to recap the conclusions of your last discussion: "The last time we spoke, we talked about pricing and setting a timeline, and you agreed that you would like to move the sale forward if we could put together a proposal that matched your budget and would meet your deadlines." Then, most important, you want to begin the conversation by getting your customer's agreement to let you ask him some questions.[65] This builds rapport and establishes a buyer centered purpose for your call.[66]

Investigation

Investigation—asking questions to uncover your buyer's needs—is at the heart of SPIN selling. This is the stage during which you ask the types of questions that give SPIN its name: situation, problem, implication, and need-payoff. Here's how each of these types of questions works during the sales presentation.

Situation Questions

Situation questions deal with the straightforward facts about the buyer's existing situation and provide a starting place for understanding your buyer's needs.[67] If you ask too many situation questions, you risk boring your prospect and damaging your credibility, so ask situation questions sparingly. If you do careful research before your sales call, you should find out most of the basic information about your customer's current situation before your meeting so that the situation questions you ask are only the ones that will provide information you aren't able to track down elsewhere.[68] For instance, if you are selling Internet connectivity, you might ask your buyer, "Which of your offices are currently using DSL?"

FIGURE 10.6
SPIN selling focuses on asking questions around each of four areas—**S**ituation, **P**roblem, **I**mplication, and **N**eed-payoff—to customize a presentation and learn more about customer needs.

© 2010 Jupiterimages Corporation

opening

The first step in SPIN selling that paves the way for the rest of the sales call.

investigation

The second and most critical step of SPIN selling that involves asking questions to uncover your buyer's needs.

situation questions

In SPIN selling, situation questions deal with facts about the buyer's existing situation.

Customer:	*Our four branch campuses use DSL, but our main offices downtown use a cable service.*
You:	*Oh, they use cable? Who is their provider?*
Customer:	*Ajax Communications. We've been with them for about two years.*
You:	*I understand Ajax sometimes offers their service on a contract basis. Do you currently have a contract with Ajax?*
Customer:	*We had a contract, but that ended a couple of months ago.*

Problem Questions

problem questions

In SPIN selling, problem questions help uncover your prospect's need.

You already know that your prospect will only be motivated to buy if she recognizes she has a need. Asking **problem questions** helps customers understand their needs, and ultimately it paves the way for you to propose a solution that seems beneficial to your customer.[69] Problem questions are the most effective in small sales: "Was limited storage space ever an issue with your last computer? How much has the size and weight of your current laptop affected your ability to carry it with you?" But in B2B sales it is still important to ask a few problem questions so that you and your buyer share an understanding of the problem or need.[70] Sometimes it is tempting to jump right into presenting the benefits of your solution, but keep in mind that your prospect might not always see his problem right away, even if it is already evident to you.[71] Imagine you sell tractors. To understand the difficulties your prospect faces with his current machines, you could ask problem questions like "How much does it cost to maintain your current farm machinery?" "How often do your tractors break down?" and "Who is usually responsible for doing the maintenance work?"

Implication Questions

implication questions

Questions that help uncover the consequences or effects of a prospect's recognized problems.

In larger sales, **implication questions** are closely linked to success because they increase a prospect's motivation to seek change. Implication questions uncover the effects or consequences of a prospect's problems. These questions are especially effective when your prospect is a decision maker whose success depends on understanding the underlying causes of a problem and its potential long-term consequences.[72] Say, for instance, your prospect has offices in five locations, but he only has IT staff at two of the locations. To help him understand the implications of this problem, you might ask questions like this:

You:	If a computer crashes at one of your branch offices, who takes care of the problem?
Prospect:	That depends. Our Bellevue and Redmond offices have their own IT people, but when we have a problem downtown or in North Seattle, we call someone from the east side offices to come fix it.
You:	Wow, that must be a hassle for the IT people! How often do they have to drive out to another location for computer trouble?
Prospect:	Usually not more than three or four times each week. If the problem isn't an urgent one, the IT guys usually make a record of it so that they can fix it during their regular visits.
You:	So your IT people have regularly scheduled maintenance visits that they make in addition to the occasional "emergency" trips?
Prospect:	Yes. Someone from IT visits each of the three locations once a week to run maintenance and fix any issues that have come up since the last visit.
You:	The travel time from Redmond to downtown is about half an hour each way, and it can take an hour during rush hour! Isn't the commute from Redmond to your other locations even longer? In total, how much time and money would you guess your company invests in these maintenance trips each week?

Your buyer might have told you up front that the shortage of IT staff is a problem, but he might not yet realize all the implications of this problem (like higher costs, wasted time, and inefficiency). By asking this set of implication questions you have just asked, you are helping your prospect explicitly state a need (or needs) that you can solve for him.[73]

Need-Payoff Questions

Once you help your prospect uncover his specific needs, you can help him to discover a way out by asking how his problem could be resolved. These questions are called **need-payoff questions**. If you ask your prospect the right need-payoff questions, he will tell *you* how your solutions can help him; you won't even need to spend much time talking about your product's benefits because your prospect will have already convinced himself that your solution will be valuable to him.[74] For example, following the previous conversation about your customer's IT problem you could ask "How would it help if the IT staff could fix at least half of your computer problems remotely?" or "How much time would you save if I could help you find a way to cut down on your IT support calls from the branch offices?"

need-payoff questions

In the SPIN model these questions ask the prospect how your solution could be important or useful to his problem.

Demonstrating Capability

When you present your solution, you can tell your customer about FAB, as discussed in Chapter 6.

- The product *features*, or what the product *has*: "This car has all-wheel drive, and the back seats fold down to expand the trunk."
- Its *advantages*: "The all-wheel drive capability makes for better handling in ice and snow, and the ability to fold down the seats means you get a larger storage capacity than you would with other cars of its kind."
- What the feature *does* and its *benefits*: "The all-wheel drive will give you peace of mind when your daughter drives the car in the winter, and the added storage capacity will be especially helpful for any odds and ends you need to transport during your upcoming move." This

includes what the features *mean*, or the ways in which your solution addresses your prospect's acknowledged needs.[75]

demonstrating capability

In SPIN selling this is the step of the sales call in which you show your prospect that your solution can solve her problems.

All three methods **demonstrate capability**, but which method do you think moves you closer to a sale? If you guessed benefits, you're right. SPIN selling is all about customization; when you are demonstrating capability, you want to show your prospect how your solution applies to the needs he has expressed. Listing a product's advantages demonstrates how that product could be useful to anyone (a generic customer), but you don't want to treat your buyer like a generic customer. OK, so the car you are selling has an excellent sound system that delivers a superior music-listening experience. But what if your prospect only ever listens to talk radio? If you go on at length about the advantages of the sound system, he won't be impressed.

Rackham and his team concluded that salespeople who demonstrate capability by presenting benefits (rather than advantages) don't have to deal with as many objections from their prospects. However, you can only demonstrate benefits successfully if you have asked the right questions to uncover your prospect's specific needs. This is why the investigation stage is so important. Here are examples of some benefits you might share with your prospect:

> *Dr. Hogue, our software gives you the ability to organize large quantities of information (like those complicated medical records you mentioned) visually. If you use this software, it will be easy to identify relationships between patient's medical histories so that you and your staff can save time whenever you have to perform a complicated diagnosis.*

> *Ms. Lewis, you mentioned that you have a long commute to work each day, so I think the podcast versions of our training seminars will be a good solution for you. You can download them onto your iPod and listen to them on your way to work so that you can maximize your time and leave your evenings and weekends open to spend with your family.*

> *Our custom engagement rings will allow you to choose an antique setting in the style you said your fiancée prefers and to pair this setting with a smaller stone that will fit your current budget.*

Obtaining Commitment

obtaining commitment

The stage of the sales call in which you get an agreement to move to the next stage of the sale.

In smaller sales, **obtaining commitment** is fairly straightforward: either your prospect decides to buy, or he tells you that he isn't interested. In complex sales, on the other hand, fewer than 10 percent of calls have one of these two outcomes. It might take several years before your prospect agrees to purchase your solution, so a sales call that ends without a sale is in no way a failure. In between your first sales call and your prospect's decision to buy, you will have a number of calls in which you either decide to move the process forward, terminate the process, or continue the process without an advance. Any time your prospect ends a call by agreeing on an action that moves you closer to the final sale, you have experienced a successful outcome.[76]

In the SPIN model there are three steps to obtaining commitment:

1. Check whether you have addressed key concerns.

2. Summarize the benefits you presented.
3. Propose a commitment that will move the sale forward.[77]

Consider this example:

> **You**: *So what I understand from our discussion is that you are concerned your image has become outdated, and you want your television advertising to appeal to a younger generation?*
>
> **Prospect**: *Yes, that's the biggest issue we're facing right now.*
>
> **You**: *As I mentioned earlier, Rockstar Marketing has successfully overhauled the brand image of a number of well-known retailers, and we think we could do the same for you by creating the youthful image you are looking for.*
>
> **Prospect**: *That sounds like it might be a good fit, but I'd have to get the approval of our marketing committee before I could give you an answer.*
>
> **You**: *Then what I'd like to do, if it's OK with you, would be to write up a more specific proposal. If you could agree to arrange a meeting between our sales team and the members of your marketing committee in about two weeks from today, we could discuss the proposal options at the meeting.*
>
> **Prospect**: *All right, that sounds like a good plan. I'll have my secretary arrange the meeting and give you a call to confirm the day and time.*

The commitment you propose at the end of the call will depend on your precall objectives. According to Rackham and his team, the most effective precall objectives are those that include actions on the part of the customer, such as "get the prospect to agree to call two of your past customers" or "get the prospect's list of vendor selection criteria."[78]

Why Use the SPIN Model?

In relationship selling, the idea of a sales "presentation" can be misleading. To deliver customized value to your prospect, you have to understand his needs and make sure that you are in agreement with him about a solution he could use. This means the sales presentation is a two-way communication. When you make the effort to listen to your prospect this way and when you work to understand his needs, not only will you close more sales, but you will also build stronger, lasting customer relationships. Your prospect will come to trust you and to rely on you as a problem-solving expert.

Key Takeaways

- **SPIN selling** is a four-step model that relies on the theory that successful selling is customer centered and offers customized solutions to your prospect's problems.
- There are four steps to a SPIN sales call: **opening**, **investigation**, **demonstrating capability**, and **obtaining commitment**.
- The **opening** stage builds rapport and establishes a buyer centered purpose for your call.
- The **investigation** stage is at the heart of the SPIN model. The goal of this stage is to ask questions that will uncover your buyer's needs.

- There are four types of investigation questions: **S**ituation, **P**roblem, **I**mplication, and **N**eed-payoff (SPIN).
- In **demonstrating capability**, you explain the benefits of your solution by showing your prospect how your product or service meets his explicit needs.
- In **obtaining commitment**, you get your prospect to agree to advance the sale, continue the sale without advancing, or make a purchase.

Exercises

1. Assume you own a business that rents out retail space in a downtown area. You have found out from your prospect, the owner of a bagel shop, that his current store location is on a side street that doesn't get much foot traffic. List at least one each of the following kinds of questions that may help uncover his unstated needs: situation, problem, implication, and need-payoff. Discuss how these questions would work during the investigation stage of your SPIN selling presentation?

2. Envision a selling situation between a travel agency that offers a variety of discount packages for business prospects and a consulting firm whose employees travel frequently for business. As a salesperson for the travel agency, what specific information would you need to know about your prospect's current situation? How much of this information do you think you could find through research? What specific situation questions would you be likely to ask?

3. Your firm offers state-mandated alcohol handler's training for restaurant employees, and you are making a sales call on a manager who has just opened three large restaurants and will be hiring a staff of over seventy-five servers and bartenders. Your training is more comprehensive than that of your competitors because it includes over five hours of training per employee. Many restaurant companies opt to leave the training up to the individual restaurants, which leads to inconsistency and lack of implementation. Companies may not realize how risky this is; the fine for improper implementation is $10,000 per restaurant. Prepare a presentation that includes the four stages of SPIN selling (opening, investigation, demonstrating capability, and gaining commitment). Include the four types of questions during the investigation stage (situation, problem, implication, and need-payoff).

4. Assume you work for Apple in their B2B division and you are selling iPhones to a major medical supply company for their employees, including their five-hundred-person sales force. They are currently not using smartphones but realize they have a need for them for their employees to stay in touch throughout the day and to access the Internet while they are away from the office. The prospect is also considering other brands of smartphones. Create a short sales presentation for the iPhone using the four stages of SPIN selling (opening, investigation, demonstrating capability, and gaining commitment). Include the four types of questions during the investigation stage (situation, problem, implication, and need-payoff).

10.5 Putting It All Together

Learning Objective

1. Learn the five steps of a successful sales presentation.

As you have probably realized by now, there are many things to keep in mind when planning and executing a sales presentation. It can be enough to overwhelm even the most experienced sales professional.

Video Link

Present Successfully

What are the most important ingredients to a successful presentation? Watch the following video to hear several experienced salespeople share their perspectives.

http://www.inc.com/inctv/2007/07/making-a-sale.html

While there is no one magic formula that will make your presentation come to life, successful presentations generally have a number of elements in common. Thinking of your presentation in terms of the following five steps will help you to plan and execute it with greater ease and success. Before the presentation, it's a good idea to ask your prospect how much time is allotted for your presentation. That will help you tailor your presentation appropriately, keeping in mind your prospect's time. It's also a good idea to start the meeting by setting expectations in terms of time: "Just as a time check, I'll spend thirty minutes on the presentation and allow fifteen minutes for discussion. We'll plan to wrap up by 11 o'clock."

Step 1: Build Rapport

In relationship selling, building rapport with your prospect lays the foundation for a selling partnership that could continue for many years. Especially if the sales presentation will be your first in-person interaction with your prospect, put effort into making a good impression. Offer your prospect a firm handshake and start with some small talk to break the ice. This isn't difficult; you can establish a connection with a complete stranger over something as simple as the weather or a recent sporting event. Experienced salespeople use observation to their advantage, learning about the customer by noticing the environment of the prospect's office. Are their photographs or artwork displayed on the walls? What items does the customer keep on her desk? As Bruce Harris, account manager with UPS, says, "A person's office is a reflection of who they are and serves as an insight into his/her personality."[79] You can make a personal connection and break the ice by questioning your prospect about a family photograph or a trophy he keeps on display. However, make sure not to go overboard on the small talk. Remember that your prospect is busy and has a limited amount of time to meet with you. If you spend too long on chit chat, you will eat up some of the time you need to get through your call objectives. Build rapport and then get down to business.[80] This is also a perfect time to confirm the time that is allocated to you for your presentation. Although you discussed it when you set up the appointment, it's always a good idea to confirm since things change at the last minute. This will help you quickly make adjustments if need be.

In group presentations, it is harder to leave room for small talk because if everyone starts talking, the meeting could lose its focus quickly—and in very large sales presentations, small talk is impossible. Geoffrey James suggests building "group rapport" by opening your presentation with a memorable remark: something challenging or amusing.[81] You could also open with a brief anecdote that establishes a common connection: "When I dropped my son off at school this morning, he told me to make sure not to give a boring presentation today...." A comment like this might get a chuckle out of your audience and will build a connection because others in the audience probably have children as well and may have had common experiences.

Leading your presentation off with situation questions is another way to break the ice and get people talking. In group settings, people are often uncomfortable sharing their opinions right away, but if you ask questions that call for factual observation, rather than opinion (How many departments in your organization would be affected by this decision? What is the average turnaround time once an issue goes to press?), people can answer without feeling threatened.[82] Once you get people talking, you can lead into problem and implication questions that require your audience members to voice an opinion.

Recall from the last section that it's always a good idea to recap the findings of your last meeting in the opening of your call. This is another way to build rapport, remind your customer of your previous discussion, ensure that everyone is on the same page, and transition into your business topic.

Step 2: Make a General Benefit Statement

Keep in mind that to effectively demonstrate capability, you should sell benefits—solutions that address your prospect's specific needs—rather than features or advantages. If your sales call is a follow-up on a previous call, you can make a benefit statement early on that will address issues you discussed in your last meeting:

In our previous discussion, you mentioned that you had a minimum ROI requirement of 20 percent per year, and you said that you would be interested in pursuing this sale further if we could propose a solution that would meet your requirements. I've created an ROI analysis here that shows how outsourcing your back office work through our firm will yield an annual ROI of 25 percent. Other businesses like yours have experienced these results with us and have been very satisfied with the transition. Here's what we envision for your company. (Show a slide with a diagram or chart giving a visual representation of your prospect's cost savings with this solution.) Is this something you would be interested in?

In this general benefit statement, the salesperson has

- recapped the findings of the previous conversation to provide context,
- explained the value in an *idea* that meets the customer's needs, rather than trying to sell a service,
- helped the customer to see himself as part of the story,
- used a closed-ended question to lead into the rest of the presentation.

closed-ended questions

Questions that demand a yes or no response.

open-ended questions

Questions that will help you probe further into the problem your product can solve.

Closed-ended questions—questions that demand a yes or no response—can help to move your presentation forward, keep your customer involved throughout the presentation, and confirm your understanding. Closed-ended questions have a role during your sales presentation, as demonstrated above.

However, closed-ended questions should be balanced with **open-ended questions** that will help you probe further into the problem your product can solve. For instance, you might ask, "What are some of your biggest frustrations with your current back office operations?" It is virtually impossible to learn more from your prospect if you don't use open-ended questions. If you are interested in learning more and engaging your customer in your presentation, be ready with open-ended questions. For example, the situation, problem, implication, and need-payback questions in SPIN selling are all examples of open-ended questions. Open-ended questions start with "who," "what," "when," "where," or "why." Figure 10.7 provides examples of closed-ended and open-ended questions.

FIGURE 10.7 Examples of Closed-Ended and Open-Ended Questions

Closed-Ended Questions	Open-Ended Questions
Do you know who your target customer is?	Who is your target customer?
Are you open on the weekends?	What are your store hours?
Are you planning to launch the new software in the second quarter?	When are you planning to launch the new software?
Is your warehouse in the area?	Where is your warehouse located?
Are you considering a change?	Why are you considering a change?

Asking the right questions is one of the skills required to be a successful salesperson. This is where your ability to ask the right questions really comes into play. It is the open-ended questions that you ask during this portion of the presentation that set the tone for the rest of your presentation. But don't stop here. Ask open-ended questions throughout your presentation to engage the prospect and continue to gain valuable information.

Step 3: Make a Specific Benefit Statement

Once you have investigated to uncover your prospect's needs, deliver a specific benefit statement: one that demonstrates in detail how you are going to solve his unique problem. It's impossible to deliver a specific benefit statement at the opening of your sales call because there is no way you can understand your prospect's needs and expectations without listening to him first.[83] Sometimes, a prospect may ask you to solve a problem that sounds similar to one you just solved for another company or customer, but if you assume you already understand your prospect's situation and treat her just like your old customer, you might lose the sale. Approach each new presentation as if it were your first.

In B2B sales, the specific benefit statement is generally something you prepare before your presentation (recall the discussion of this from Chapter 8). However, before launching into specific benefits, you can investigate to make sure you understand and have all the necessary information: "So let me make sure I understand. What you're saying is that a 5 percent reduction in process time will reduce your costs by 20 percent?" In any selling situation, the information you get from your prospect is usually just the tip of the iceberg, and you won't get an idea of the pressures she is facing unless you can get her talking.

After confirming that you and your prospect are on the same page, you can move forward with your presentation, adapting if you need to based on your prospect's answers to the questions you asked. This is the part of your presentation where the solution really comes to life. Bring your customer into the story with videos, recordings, displays, or anything else that will allow him to experience the product for himself.

> **You:** *So let me just confirm—it sounds like your biggest priorities in purchasing this SUV are gas mileage, safety, and reliability and that you would sacrifice some luxury features if your vehicle met these other conditions?*
>
> **Prospect:** *Yes, those are definitely the most important things. This is really going to be a family car, something I can use to drive the family around and take on camping trips. And our oldest child is going to college soon, so we want a car that will last for a while because we'll need to save money to pay tuition.*
>
> **You:** *OK Cindy, then I think you will be excited about the RAV4 we discussed earlier. It has the best fuel economy of almost any SUV on the market, and Toyotas are known for their reliability, so this car should last you well past the time your daughter graduates from college. You can also feel confident when you drive your kids around in this vehicle because the RAV4 received five stars in National Traffic Safety Administration crash tests.[84] Does that sound like a good option to you?*
>
> **Prospect:** *Yes, that sounds like just the kind of thing we're looking for.*
>
> **You:** *Great! Then why don't we go for a test drive, and you can see for yourself how well this car handles on the road.*

When you demonstrate your product for the prospect, make sure to draw attention to the features, advantages, and benefits that make it a good solution for her particular situation. In the example above, when your prospect takes the car out on the road, you could turn on the climate control settings that allow her to adjust for a different climate zone in the front and back seats and explain that this way she and her family can stay comfortable on long car rides. If she has her kids along, you could turn on the rear DVD player for them. These sort of extra, customer-specific benefits help your customer to make a personal connection to the product and to see her story aligning with your solution.

During this part of the presentation, make sure to ask open-ended questions that will help you learn more about the prospect's needs and her perceptions about the product: "You said that you like to go on family camping trips; how well does your current vehicle meet your family's needs on these trips? It sounds like your current vehicle gets poor gas mileage; how does this affect your frequency of use or the length of your road trips? How would the storage capacity of the RAV4 change the way you use your family vehicle? How important is the car's sound system to you?" Not only will these questions help you to uncover your customer's needs and expectations that are still below the surface, but they will also help you to anticipate potential objections as you transition to the next part of the selling process.

Step 4: Presentation

This is the reason you are here—to present your solution that will solve your prospect's problem. Since you started your presentation by asking questions, your presentation is a perfect way to incorporate the things you just learned from your prospect and incorporate them into your presentation. Yes, this means you have to be quick on your feet. That's another reason preparation is so important. It allows you to be comfortable with your presentation material, yet customize it on the spot to point out specific areas that address your prospect's problem.

You are taking the prospect on a journey so make it interesting, compelling, and relevant. Here are a few tips:

- **Keep your presentation pithy**. A shorter presentation is better. It helps you get to the point more quickly and have more time for dialogue with your prospect.[85]

- **Start with a quick review of the prospect's objectives**. This is a good technique to confirm that you were listening to your prospect throughout the process so far and confirms that you are on the same page. This also provides the ideal platform on which to present your solution and why it will help your prospect reach his objectives.[86]

- **Get a reaction from your prospect throughout your presentation**. Use a combination of open-ended and closed-ended questions to confirm that your prospect is in agreement with the information you are presenting and to gain new insights into how your product or service can help him. "This time savings in your production cycle can help you save at least 10 percent over your current processing. Would you like to see how this would work?" is an example of a closed-ended question that helps keep your prospect engaged. "How do you think your team would like to submit invoices like this?" is an example of an open-ended question that helps the prospect think about the product or service in use in his organization.[87]

- **Use demonstrations whenever possible**. Showing how a product or service will work is far more dramatic and memorable than simply talking about it. If it's possible to demonstrate the product in person, do it. If not, have a demonstration video. Bring samples, mock-ups, or prototypes if the actual product is not yet available.[88]

- **Have fun**. When your passion and enthusiasm come through, it makes a difference to your prospect. A monotone or boring presentation is neither interesting nor compelling. Show your prospect you believe in your product or service with a powerful and personal presentation.[89]

Video Clip

Don't Be Forgettable
Learn why the worst sales presentation is one that is OK.

View the video online at: http://www.youtube.com/embed/_nt7YWymVak

Step 5: Close

If you have successfully delivered value to your prospect in your presentation, it is time to think about closing the sales call. This is where you obtain your customer's commitment, either to buy or to move the sales process forward. Especially if you are expecting your prospect to make a purchase at the end of the sales call, it is a good idea to use a **trial closing** technique to test his buying readiness. How likely is he to make a commitment now? By testing the waters with a trial close (e.g., "On a scale of one to ten, how important would this opportunity be to you?"), you can ask your prospect for an opinion rather than asking him for a commitment, so there is less pressure for both of you. A negative response to a trial close doesn't mean that your prospect won't buy or move forward with the sale; instead, it is a signal to change your strategy.[90] A trial close often leads to objections that you will need to overcome before your prospect feels prepared to make the purchase.[91] Chapter 11 discusses overcoming objections in greater detail.

trial closing

Technique to test a prospect's buying readiness.

If your prospect responds positively to your trial close, it is time to close the sales call by asking for a commitment. There are a variety of closing techniques you might use that will be discussed in greater detail in Chapter 12. Whichever closing technique you choose will depend on the customer, the selling situation, and your goal for the end of the sales call.

Step 5: Recap

According to sales trainer and experienced salesman Tom Hopkins, all successful presentations and demonstrations have three steps: tell your audience what you're going to tell them, tell them what you're there to tell them, and tell them what you've just told them.[92] After making your presentation and successfully closing, recap the important points of your meeting and the direction you and your customer have agreed to take from here: "I'll touch base with you tomorrow once you've checked on that budget detail, and in the meantime, let me look up those part specifications for you." This will reinforce the prospect's decision and pave the way for the next steps, which may include anything from follow-up, to a next meeting, to a formal proposal, depending on the selling situation and the length of the sales cycle.

Video Clip

Sales Presentation Role-Play
See how all the steps come together in this selling role-play. See if you can identify all the selling skills used by the "salesperson."

View the video online at: http://www.youtube.com/embed/6EtltRzL-Qg

Role of the Proposal in the Sales Presentation

proposal

Document that proposes the specific terms of the sale, including pricing, delivery time frame, and the scope of the products or services you are offering.

In many B2B sales and some larger business-to-consumer (B2C) sales, once you have presented your solution, if your prospect is interested, she will ask for a **proposal**—a document that proposes the specific terms of the sale, including pricing, delivery time frame, and the scope of the products or services you are offering. In relationship selling there is no such thing as a standard proposal; the proposal should include the details of a customer-specific solution and should reflect the things your customer values most. Even in retail situations—like car buying—while you might have a basic template you use for your contracts, you will adapt and renegotiate the contract depending on your customer's needs. The key is that the proposal, like your presentation, should be customized to the individual prospect.

Nitty Gritty: The Hows and Whys of a Proposal

While every proposal should be customized, there are a few common elements that good proposals share:

- an introduction
- a definition of the project or need
- a discussion of the solution and its benefits
- the costs associated with the project[93]
- a time frame for completion of the project or project milestones
- a call to action that asks the prospect for a response
- evidence that you are qualified to perform the job.

In addition, a proposal should accomplish three things:

1. **Educate the prospect about the specifics of his need and the pertinence of your solution**. The proposal should showcase the value you are bringing to the individual prospect or organization; help your prospect to see why he can't reach his objectives without the specific solution you offer.

2. **Convince the prospect that you have the competence to deliver what she needs**.[94] Show her how your expertise applies to her situation, by providing relevant information and presenting the proposal in a professional format. This is especially relevant in situations where the proposal will be reviewed by a committee that is unfamiliar with you or your company.[95]

3. **Provide justification for the prospect's investment in clear terms**.[96] The information in the proposal should be practical and should explain the problem and solution in terms that could be understood by someone outside of the industry.[97] In addition, the proposal should include a cost-benefit and ROI analysis (discussed earlier in this chapter). This will give the prospect the financial information as it relates to cost and the expected return on investment.

In some B2B situations, your customer might submit a formal **request for proposal (RFP)**, which sets out very specific guidelines for the format of the proposal and the information it should include. (See Chapter 6.) Organizations usually use RFPs when they are requesting proposals from a number of potential suppliers at once. By providing a proposal structure, RFPs simplify the process of assessing risks and benefits associated with the purchase and can help your prospect make a decision in complex buying situations.[98] If you receive an RFP, make sure that you stick closely to the requested formatting and respond to all the questions in the document. Plenty of qualified salespeople with strong solutions have lost prospects because they failed to respond to everything in an RFP document.[99]

request for proposal (RFP)

A formal request from possible suppliers to provide or create a specific product or service.

Whether or not you are responding to a formal RFP, here are a few things to keep in mind:

- **Do** make sure most of the document discusses your prospect and his objectives and how you and your company will meet them.
- **Do** keep the writing clear and concise. This will make it easy for your prospect to assess the proposal, and it demonstrates a respect for his time on your part. Select the most relevant information and present it in an efficient way.
- **Do** make sure you understand how the proposal will be reviewed, who will be reviewing the proposal, what the primary selection criteria will be, and when you can expect a response.
- **Do** use a straightforward approach to pricing that your customer can easily assess.
- **Do** pay attention to the visual presentation of the proposal. As Kimberly Kayler, president of Constructive Communication, puts it, "Prospective clients facing the task of wading through stacks of proposals filled with thousands of words usually welcome efforts designed to make their lives easier."[100] Graphics can add meaning and make the information more accessible.
- **Do** make it easy for the prospect to accept your services by attaching an agreement he can sign that outlines the terms of the contract.

- **Don't** forget to check grammar and spelling. This is an important part of credibility and professionalism.
- **Don't** overuse "we" or "us." Your language should reflect a customer centered focus.

Figure 10.8 presents a sample of an outline to follow when preparing your proposal.[101]

FIGURE 10.8 Template for Preparing a Strong Proposal

I.	**Introduction**
II.	**Description of Problem/Current Situation**
III.	**Description of Solution/Project**
IV.	**Timelines/Deliverables**
V.	**Costs**
VI.	**Recommendations**
VII.	**Bio Information and Qualifications**
VIII.	**Contract (optional)**

Timing: When to Deliver Your Proposal

Have you ever noticed that when you go into a high-end clothing boutique or a store that sells expensive jewelry and watches, the price tags are hidden? The thing you immediately see is the product itself, beautifully displayed. The goal is a psychological one: to get the buyer to make an emotional connection with the product before he considers the cost. As a buyer, if the cost were one of the first things you saw, you might never make that emotional connection with the product in the first place.

This is something to keep in mind in sales. Never present a proposal—or otherwise mention pricing—early on in the sales presentation, not until your prospect has fallen in love with your product. You want your prospect to pick out the color of the car before she asks about payment; if she picks out the color, she has already imagined herself owning the car, and you have probably made your sale.

Of course, in a situation like car sales, you generally present the proposal in the same day as you present the product. You discuss your prospect's needs, show him the car, let him test drive it, and then tell him, "Let me go talk to my manager to see if we can work out the numbers." The process is a relatively simple one. However, in complex B2B sales, your sales presentation will probably *end* with a request for a proposal, in which case you will agree to a future meeting when you can present your proposal to the customer. B2B proposals are generally more involved, and so they require careful planning and a greater investment of time. If your prospect says, "Just send us the proposal," ask for a face-to-face meeting; you can always send them the proposal ahead of time, but following up with a meeting in-person will help you address objections, answer your prospect's questions, and demonstrate your enthusiasm for the project.

Power Point: Lessons in Selling from the Customer's Point of View

The Art of Bringing the Product to Life

Among the many accolades realtor Susie Stephens of Chico, California, receives for her work is that she knows how to make potential buyers fall in love with a house before they ever discuss offer details with her. As one homeowner put it, "As a seller, you want your house presented and marketed well." According to her customers, Stephens has mastered the art of bringing the product to life: "The videos and photographs [she] produced of the properties we sold were so nice it almost made us want to buy them back from ourselves!" Another customer praised Smith's customization, explaining that she considered "the applicability of the real estate transaction to our personal situation and objectives."[102]

Delivering Value in Your Proposal

Until you understand the areas in which your customer places the greatest value, it is impossible to come up with a proposal. For instance, say your organization offers advertising services, and you find out from your prospect that her company especially values competitive pricing on individual projects. You decide the best way to deliver value is to drop your pricing below the competitor's lowest price and to make up for the lower cost in your **retainer fee**—the fixed fee that your customer will pay in advance to secure your services. This way you can deliver value in the area that is most important to your customer while still generating the profits you need to run your business. In the end, you want a situation where everyone wins—but it takes some work to uncover the key to making this happen.

Sometimes your customer's area of greatest value is determined by business needs, and other times the issues are emotional. For instance, if you are selling a car to a customer that wants a good value on his trade-in, recognize that he might have an emotional connection to his old car (in his mind it has a high value), so offering a low trade-in price, even if it is combined with competitive financing options, might be enough to drive your customer away. In fact, your customer might actually be willing to pay *more* for his new car if you can give him a good price for his trade-in.

retainer fee

Fixed fee that a customer will pay in advance to secure your services.

Key Takeaways

- The most important ingredient of a successful sales presentation is you.
- While there is no single formula for a sales presentation, there are five basic steps: building rapport, making a general benefit statement, making a specific benefit statement, closing, and recapping.
- It's best to ask questions throughout your presentation to learn as much information as possible from your prospect and to keep him engaged.
- **Closed-ended questions** help keep the prospect engaged and should be balanced with **open-ended questions**, which help you probe further into the problem your product can solve.
- The proposal is a written document that includes the specific terms of the sale and is usually prepared after the sales presentation.
- Some prospects submit a **request for proposal (RFP)**, usually when they are evaluating proposals from a number of potential suppliers, which sets out specific guidelines for the format of the proposal and the information it should include.

Exercises

1. Develop two examples each of closed-ended questions and open-ended questions. Ask both questions to at least five of your friends and document the responses. Which type of question was easier to control? Why? Which type of question provided more information? Why? How might you use both types of questions in a sales presentation?

2. Develop a five-minute sales presentation to sell your college to high school seniors using the five steps described in this section. Role-play your presentation. Is it difficult to stay within the time constraint? How should you adjust your selling presentation when you have a limited time frame to present?

3. Assume you are selling biodegradable bags to a major grocery store chain. The bags are 100 percent biodegradable and are priced comparably to nonbiodegradable bags. You are meeting the eight -person buying committee for the first time. Role-play how you would build rapport with the group before you begin your presentation. What questions would you ask to begin your presentation? What general benefit statement would you make?

4. Go to Best Buy or another electronics store and assume you are buying a new computer. What questions does the salesperson ask before he shows you a specific model? Which questions were closed-ended? Which questions were open-ended?

5. Imagine that you are selling children's books to Borders and you arrive at the corporate office to make your presentation and your contact tells you that due to scheduling changes, he can only give you half as much time as he originally planned. How would you adjust your sales presentation?

6. Choose a product or service that can be demonstrated or sampled (e.g., a Web site, software, food, or a beverage). Create a five-minute sales presentation using the concepts in this section and incorporating the demonstration.

7. Assume your prospect is a restaurant on or near campus. Develop a new product or service that your prospect can offer to increase traffic during off-hours. Create a five-minute presentation using the concepts covered in this section.

8. Assume your prospect is one of your classmates. Create a five-minute sales presentation for an iPod Touch using the concepts covered in this section. Include a trial close when you present to your prospect.

9. Watch this scene from the AMC show, *Mad Men*. Evaluate the sales presentation based on the concepts covered in this section. Which elements of the presentation are effective? Why? Which elements are not effective? Why?

View the video online at: http://www.youtube.com/embed/5y4b-DEklps

10.6 *Selling U*: Selling Yourself in an Interview

Learning Objective

1. Understand how to prepare for a successful job interview.

In many ways, gearing up for a job interview is like gearing up for a sales presentation. You can't control the outcome of the interview, but you can control the preparation that goes into the interview. Preparing beforehand, paying attention to logistics, and knowing what to expect will set you apart from your competitors and put you in the best possible position to let your personal brand shine. Here are ten steps that can guide you through preparation for and follow-up after every job interview.

Ten Steps to Successful Interviews

1. Be ready to show and sell.
2. Accept and confirm the interview.
3. Research the company.
4. Rehearse your elevator pitch.
5. Prepare your answers to popular interview questions.
6. Prepare *your* questions and answers.
7. Prepare for the logistics.
8. Prepare your wardrobe.
9. Make a personal connection during the interview.
10. Follow up, follow up, follow up.

Step 1: Be Ready to Show and Sell

In a sales presentation, you want to make your product come to life by showcasing it in a way that gets your audience involved. You want your prospect to "smell the leather in the car." The same is true at a job interview; it's not just about your résumé. Let your interviewer see examples of the work you've done and help her to envision the work you can do for her company. You can start preparing for this now, while you're still a student. Bring your portfolio on every interview. If you need some tips, review the *Selling U* section in Chapter 6.

Step 2: Accept and Confirm the Interview

When one of your target companies calls or e-mails to offer you an interview, don't leave anything to chance. Grab a pencil and paper or your personal digital assistant (PDA) and take down the information you'll need to know on the day of the interview. Do you have the correct day and time written down? Do you know the name, title, and office location of the person with whom you'll be interviewing? Do you have directions to the company's location? Keep in mind that googling the company's address on the day of your interview may not get you where you want to go. Sometimes companies have large campuses with a number of buildings, and Google won't be able to tell you how to find the right entrance to the right building and how to find your contact person's office once you get there. Take care of logistical details like this beforehand, so you won't have anything to slow you down on the big day.

While you have a contact from the company on the phone, take the opportunity to ask whether there is a job description on the company Web site that you can review before the interview. It's also a good idea to ask for the title of the job for which you will be interviewing and the names and titles of the people with whom you will be interviewing. You should also ask for your interviewer's phone number and e-mail, and bring the phone number with you on the day of the interview in case you are unavoidably delayed. E-mail your interviewer several days in advance of the interview to confirm your appointment, or call her the day before. This demonstrates professionalism and ensures that everything will run smoothly.[103]

Step 3: Research the Company and Your Interviewer

Just as you would never go into a sales presentation without carefully researching your prospect's company beforehand, you should never go to a job interview without the same kind of preparation. Begin by reviewing the job description on the company Web site if it's available. Then spend some time on the Web site, researching the company's mission statement and description. If you know which department you might be working in, pay careful attention to any specific details you can learn about this department on the Web site. Some of the basic facts employers will expect you to know include

- How many locations and employees does the company have?
- Does this company deal in B2B or B2C services?
- How long has the company been in business? Have they recently merged or been acquired?
- Is the company expanding globally?
- Does the company have any new products or services?
- Have the CEO or others in the company been recognized for any achievements or publications recently?[104]

Then go beyond Web site research; after all, your interviewer knows what's on his company's Web site, so don't just repeat back the information you find there; show him your motivation and professionalism by coming prepared with your own research. Use the company's product or service and talk to other people who use the product or service. Go online and read what customers have to say about the company. Go through the company's purchasing process so you can understand the workings of the company from a customer's point of view.[105] Read any recent press releases or press coverage about the company.

Don't forget to research your interviewer. Chances are, he has a profile on LinkedIn so you can get some insight about him and even see what he looks like. Also do a Google search as you may learn about his personal hobbies and other pertinent information.

Step 4: Rehearse Your "Elevator Pitch"

Don't be surprised if one of the first questions your interviewer asks is something along the lines of "tell me about yourself." This is a common opening question, designed to put job candidates at ease, but it can be one of the hardest questions to answer. "As part of your job-search arsenal, having a good elevator speech is a critical tool," says Alysin Foster, consultant and managing partner at the Centre for Strategic Management. "Sometimes all you get is 30 seconds to make a good impression."[106]

Review the *Selling U* section in Chapter 5 to be sure your elevator pitch is your strongest starting point. Then, rehearse, rehearse, rehearse so it sounds and feels natural as a response to that dreaded first question, "Tell me about yourself."

Video Clip

Tell Me about Yourself

This video provides insight into what the interviewer means when he says, "Tell me about yourself."

View the video online at: http://www.youtube.com/embed/-ezFNrWMTlc

Step 5: Prepare Your Answers to Popular Interview Questions

"Tell me about yourself" is only one of a number of popular interview questions for which you should prepare before going into the interview. While there's no way to know which questions you'll get for sure, you can be relatively certain that your interviewer will ask at least one or two of the common standbys. Preparing answers to popular interview questions beforehand will empower to respond with clarity and poise. "What traps a lot of people is they think and talk at the same time," says Bill McGowan, founder of Clarity Media Group. "It's better if you know your conversational path."[107] The best way to have a powerful conversation is to review your brand positioning points from the *Selling U* section in Chapter 1 and your FAB in Chapter 6. These can be included in an answer to just about any interview question. Practice telling your stories out loud so they are concise and focused, yet sound natural.

Video Clip

The Best Interview Answers

What's the most important thing to remember when you are answering interview questions? Watch this video to find out.

View the video online at: http://www.youtube.com/embed/IxbRWsYljyE

Some common questions interviewers ask and a few pointers for coming up with a response are shown below.

Common Interview Questions

What Are Some of Your Greatest Strengths?

Most candidates will respond to this question in generalities like "I'm a strong self-starter" or "I'm highly organized." You already have your personal brand positioning points and stories to go with them, so why not use them here? You will set yourself apart if you can illustrate your strengths with the anecdotes you have prepared ahead of time. For example, "My leadership skills are among my greatest strengths. As the shift leader at Olive Garden, I scheduled the wait staff and resolved customer service issues during my shift. The restaurant had the highest customer satisfaction ratings during the two years I worked there."

What Are Some of Your Weaknesses?

The interviewer isn't looking for any deep confessions when she asks you this question. According to CareerBuilder.com, "The secret to answering this question is using your weaknesses to your advantage."[108] For instance, if you say that you have trouble with organization, you can follow this up by saying that because organization doesn't come naturally to you, you make a conscious effort at the beginning of a new project to plan out your goals. It's never a good idea to simply name a weakness and finish off by telling the interviewer it's something you are working on. On the other hand, it's also important to be honest when you respond to the weakness question; don't try to pretend that you are without faults because that won't make you look good either.

This video clip addresses this challenging interview question.

Source: Collegegrad.com

View the video online at: //www.youtube.com/embed/-ezFNrWMTlc

Have You Ever Had a Conflict with a Boss?

This is what is called a behavioral question. The interviewer is looking for how you behaved in a specific situation.

This video clip provides some tips for how to handle this question in an interview.

Source: Collegegrad.com

View the video online at: //www.youtube.com/embed/VeNPpnuKOw4

What Can You Offer This Company, or How Do You See Yourself Fitting in at This Company?

This is one of those questions for which your research beforehand will pay off. This question is as much about your knowledge of the company as it is about your qualifications. Career strategist J. T. O'Donnell says "You can craft a better answer by asking [yourself] what the company wants and why."[109] Then ask yourself how your story and the company's story match up. This is a lot like presenting the customer-specific benefits of your product in a sales presentation. Prepare a story that can illustrate what you have to offer.

Why Do You Want to Work Here?

This question is another opportunity to showcase your company research. Consider what you know about any challenges or issues that the company faces and how your skills and experience will be beneficial.[110] What community service or internship experiences might be relevant? For instance, "I know that your company is about to launch its first e-mail marketing campaign, and I would really like to be involved as this project gets off the ground. Last year I was in charge of writing the e-mail newsletters for the local food bank and expanding their list of subscribers, and I would look forward to putting that experience to work in a professional capacity."

Why Should I Hire You?

This can be a difficult interview question, but not if you are prepared for the answer. Watch this video for some tips.

Source: Collegegrad.com

View the video online at: //www.youtube.com/embed/deuYRMIkG-c

What Is Your Favorite Ad Campaign (or Other Industry Specific Item)?

This is an example of an industry-specific interview question you might hear if you are interviewing for a marketing position. Whatever field you are going into, make sure you have done your research and understand the industry so you can respond to industry-specific questions. For example, if you are interviewing for a job in advertising, be familiar with the major advertising campaigns and be ready to discuss your favorite and why you think it works.

Where Do You See Yourself in Five Years?

Your interviewer won't want to hear that your five-year goal is to be working in a different industry. Talk about your personal goals that relate to the job. This will demonstrate that you understand the company and are motivated to succeed there.[111]

What Are Your Salary Expectations?

This is a problem you should avoid responding to directly if possible. A good response would be to deflect the question: "I would expect compensation that falls in the standard salary range for this industry." It's a good idea to research salary ranges for your industry so that you will be ready to negotiate when the topic of salary does come up, but let your employer put a figure on the table first.[112] If you feel that you have to respond to this question with a direct answer, just be warned that once you name a figure, you shouldn't expect your employer to offer you more than that if you decide to take the job. It's a good idea to do your research before any job interview by researching current salaries for the position for which you are interviewing at Web sites such as Salary.com, or use Web 2.0 techniques and ask an online community such as Salarymap.com.

This video clip provides additional insights for how to answer this interview question.

Source: Collegegrad.com

View the video online at: //www.youtube.com/embed/E7JBQFhgd2Q

How Many Years of Experience Do You Have Using Excel (or Other Software Programs)?

You don't want a question like this to cost you the position, especially considering that many software programs can be learned on the job. Don't give false information, but you can try responding with your own question; try asking how much and what level of experience is required for the job. If you have a more specific idea of the answer the interviewer is looking for, you can provide a more convincing response as to why you should be considered for the job, even if your answer doesn't match exactly what the interviewer is looking for.[113]

What Did You Like Least about Your Last Job?

Interviewers often ask this question to get you to reveal conflicts. Avoid going this route. In job hunting, you should never reveal anything negative about a former employer. Whatever you mention in your response, choose something that isn't directly related to the job for which you are applying. And make sure to end your response on a positive note: "I'm ready for the challenges of my new job."[114]

You might also find it helpful to review this video, which includes some frequently asked interview questions and some ways to answer them.

http://link.brightcove.com/services/player/
bcpid26599544001?bclid=26964187001&bctid=31648299001

Step 6: Prepare *Your* Questions and Answers

Toward the end of the interview, every interviewer will ask you if you have any questions for him. So make sure you have three or four questions in mind. Preparing these ahead of time will show your interviewer that you have thought about the position and the company. Here are a few questions to consider asking:

- What opportunities will there be beyond this position in the company?
- What would the ideal person for this position look like?
- What are some challenges facing the department in the next three months? What role will the person in this position play in tackling these challenges?
- How would you describe your company culture?
- What are the next steps in the hiring process?

After the interviewer responds, be ready to follow up by restating your strengths.[115] For instance, if you ask what qualities the ideal candidate for this job should have, your interviewer might mention something you hadn't thought of mentioning earlier. You can respond by telling a relevant story about a specific time when you overcame an obstacle or helped a colleague solve a problem.

You can ask these questions even if you already know the answer. If you interview with multiple people in the organization, it is OK to ask the same question multiple times. It will help to get a variety of perspectives—and keep in mind that the questions you ask are also a way of showcasing your experience and your knowledge about the company.

You've Got the Power: Tips for Your Job Search

When Do I Ask about Salary?

Finally, even if you have questions about salary and benefits, *don't* ask them now. Always delay a conversation about salary as long as possible. In a sales presentation, you wouldn't pull out a pricing schedule before your customer had expressed a strong interest in buying the product; keep the same idea in mind going into a job interview. It's best to let your interviewer bring up salary—and that might not be until after the second or third interview. Be patient; the longer your prospective employer has to get to know you, the more opportunities you have to point out why you would be a good addition to the company. If you sell yourself well throughout the interview process, you might even receive a higher offer.

This video provides some tips for how to handle the salary question during an interview.

Source: Collegegrad.com

View the video online at: //www.youtube.com/embed/E7JBQFhgd2Q

Step 7: Prepare for the Logistics

Before you interview, take care of the logistics just as you would for any sales presentation. Control the things that are in your power to control so that you can focus on your performance during the interview. Double check that you know where you'll be going (including building, room, and/or suite number) and allow extra time for travel in case you get stuck in traffic. Make sure you know the title of the position for which you will be interviewing. Remember to assemble your materials the night before the interview: have your work samples ready to go in a portfolio and print at least four extra copies of your résumé on twenty-four-pound paper. Bring these extra résumés in your portfolio. Even though your interviewer will have already received your résumé, she may not have it on hand, and you should always be prepared in case you are asked to meet with anyone who was not on the original interview schedule.[116] Arrive early, fix any wardrobe malfunctions, and get ready to give a stellar presentation.

Step 8: Prepare Your Wardrobe

Your wardrobe is part of your personal branding, so make sure you dress like a professional when you go to your interview. This holds true even if you are interviewing in a more casual industry; you can always dress down *after* you get the job.

- Dress conservatively. Go for a suit or dress in dark or neutral colors (black, gray, or navy for the suit). Avoid hypertrendy clothes or clothes that otherwise make a bold statement. Women should avoid dresses with thin straps or low necklines.
- Make sure your suit or dress fits you well. If it needs to be tailored, have it done. You will use the suit in your new job, and a good fit will increase your confidence during the interview.
- Wear appropriate, professional shoes. Both men and women should wear conservative, close-toed shoes in a dark or neutral color to complement their wardrobe. Women should avoid stiletto, open-toe, or platform shoes. Men should avoid athletic shoes and make sure their shoes are polished.
- Wear appropriate accessories. Avoid flashy jewelry or watches. Carry a professional briefcase or handbag—**no backpacks or messenger bags**. Keep in mind that even your accessories are part of your personal brand.
- If you have tattoos or body piercings, make sure they are not visible during the interview. Make-up such as Conceal FX available at Sephora.com will camouflage tattoos. It is acceptable for women to wear conservative earrings—but avoid anything large or distracting.
- Select appropriate hosiery. If you are wearing a suit, your socks should match your pants or shoes. Women wearing skirts and dresses should always wear pantyhose (even if you think you have a great tan).
- Make sure your clothes are ironed. Do this the night before.[117] Lay our your clothes the night before so that you will have one less thing to worry about on the day of the interview. Wrinkled clothing and stains are considered among the biggest grooming red flags for job interviews, according to a recent survey of employers conducted by Gillette Career Advantage.[118]
- Ensure impeccable grooming, including a conservative hairstyle and appropriately manicured fingernails. Don't forget deodorant and a breath mint; body odor or bad breath can be a turn off in an interview. It's a good idea to stop in the restroom right before you go to the interview for one last check in the mirror (it's the perfect time to have a breath mint).

Step 9: Make a Personal Connection during the Interview

Make an effort to connect personally with your interviewer. People want to hire people they like. Smile, make eye contact, and greet him with a strong handshake. Allow yourself to relax and begin the conversation with some small talk. Notice the surroundings in your interviewer's office. Does he have school memorabilia, family photographs, sports paraphernalia, or vacation photos? Try to discover commonalities that will allow you to make a connection. During the interview, remember to smile and maintain eye contact, and when the interview is wrapping up, make sure to close by telling the interviewer you want the job.[119] Most of all, relax, enjoy the conversation, and be yourself.

Step 10: Follow-Up, Follow-Up, Follow-Up

Don't wait to do this! Get in contact while you are still fresh in your interviewer's mind: write a thank-you e-mail the same day. Details on how to write a successful follow-up e-mail are covered in the *Selling U* section in Chapter 11. Besides the e-mail, send a hand-written thank-you note on a plain, white business note card. Mail this the same day, so that your interviewer will receive it the next day or the day after. Very few people send handwritten "thank-you's" anymore, so this extra touch will make you stand out—and it only costs the price of postage, so why not do it?

During your interview you should ask the interviewer for a time frame so that you will know when to expect a response. If you haven't heard back by the appointed date, follow up with a phone call. Asking your interviewer for a time frame is essential to follow-up: if she isn't planning to make her hiring decision for another two weeks, calling her after one week will only be an annoyance. Be persistent, but keep in mind that there is a fine line between persistence and pestering. When you get voice mail, you can leave a message—once—but then keep calling back until you reach your contact. Following up by phone signals that you are still interested in the job and motivated enough to pursue it.[120] Sometimes hiring decisions get delayed because of issues that come up at the company, so not hearing back by the date you were expecting is not necessarily an indication that you weren't selected for the position.

Video Clip

Lisa Peskin, Sales Trainer, Shares Her Insights, Experiences, and Tips for Successful Interviews

Use your selling skills to prepare for and participate in successful interviews

View the video online at: http://www.youtube.com/embed/xMsj3iNusZM

Key Takeaways

- A job interview is like a sales presentation; a successful interview requires a lot of preparation.

- Always be ready for a job interview with a professional portfolio and interview suit including shoes and other accessories.
- When you receive a call for an interview, take the time to write down the date, time, location, title of the position for which you will be interviewing, and the people (names and titles) with whom you will be interviewing.
- Do your homework and thoroughly research the company, its products or services, customers, and competition. The company's Web site is a good place to start, but if possible also use the product or service or call the company's 800 number as though you were a prospective customer.
- Prepare for the most likely questions you will be asked including "tell me about yourself." Review your brand positioning points and stories you want to tell in response to the most commonly asked interview questions.
- Be prepared with questions to ask during the interview.
- Delay the conversation about salary as long as possible; avoid the temptation to bring it up during an interview. It's best to let the interviewer bring up the topic when she is closer to a final decision.
- Smile and be yourself during the interview. The best way to sell yourself is to be yourself.
- Follow up after the interview with a thank-you note.

Exercises

1. Choose one company that is on your target company list, which you created in the *Selling U* section of Chapter 7. Research it thoroughly by visiting the company Web site and that of its competitors, using the product or service, contacting the company by e-mail or phone as a customer, reading about the company and its competitors in the news, and reading blogs and social networking Web sites to see what people are saying about the company and its key competitors. What did you learn about the company that you didn't already know? Based on your findings, list three questions you would ask during an interview.

2. Conduct a role-play with one person acting as the interviewer and one acting as the interviewee using the commonly asked interview questions mentioned in this section.

3. Identify two ways to follow up from an interview and when each should be done.

10.7 Review and Practice

Power Wrap-Up

Now that you have read this chapter, you should be able to understand how to deliver value in a sales presentation.

- You can **plan** the steps you need to take to prepare for a sales presentation.
- You can **describe** how to dress for success at a sales presentation.
- You can **explain** how to deliver the message to your prospect.
- You can **understand** SPIN and how to use it during the sales presentation.
- You can **list** the five steps of a successful presentation.
- You can **understand** how to have a successful job interview.

Test Your Power Knowledge (answers are below)

1. Explain what it means to deliver value to your customer.
2. What is the best rule of thumb for dressing for a sales presentation?
3. List three dos and three don'ts for giving a PowerPoint presentation.
4. Explain the 10/20/30 rule for a PowerPoint presentation.
5. What are the benefits of using samples or demonstrations in your presentation?
6. List the four components of SPIN selling.
7. Give an example of a closed-ended question.
8. Give an example of an open-ended question.
9. What should you always do before making a specific benefit statement?
10. When should you deliver the proposal in a sales presentation and why?

Power (Role) Play

Now it's time to put what you've learned into practice. Following are two roles that are involved in the same selling situation—one role is the customer, and the other is the salesperson. This will give you the opportunity to think about this selling situation from the point of view of both the customer and the salesperson.

Read each role carefully along with the discussion questions. Then, be prepared to play either of the roles in class using the concepts covered in this chapter. You may be asked to discuss the roles and do a role-play in groups or individually.

In the Driver's Seat

Role: Customer at a high-end car dealership

You are considering a new car. You want performance, but you still need some space for passengers. You want the latest and greatest, yet still be comfortable and be able to transport people and things easily. You are willing to pay for what you want, but given the current economic environment, you are concerned about paying too much.

- What type of presentation would you expect to get at the car dealership?
- What questions will you have for the salesperson about the car?
- What questions will you have for the salesperson about the financing for the car?

Role: Salesperson at car dealership

You want to be able to put this customer in the car he wants, but first you need to identify some things. If he has a family and needs space, you have just the car for him. And you have a price reduction for this week only since it's the last week of the month (and you want to make your quota). But you're not sure what is more important to him—luxury appointments, passenger space, gas mileage, status, or price. You want to use SPIN selling to understand exactly what he needs.

- How will you prepare for the presentation?
- How will you start the presentation?
- What questions will you ask in each of the areas of SPIN?
- How will you learn about the prospect's objections (if there are any)?
- How will you trial close?

Put Your Power to Work: *Selling U* Activities

1. Draft a list of the projects you have worked on for which you have samples that could showcase your work. Make a separate folder on your computer where you can save any of these files for use during your interview.

2. Use the list of popular interview questions and guidelines to generate answers that you can deliver during your interview. Write these answers down and save them somewhere where you will be able to review them before going to a job interview.

3. Visit your campus career center and learn about the opportunity to participate in mock interviews. Prepare for the mock interview and dress for success.

Test Your Power Knowledge Answers

1. Delivering value means asking questions, listening to your customer, and defining value in customer terms.

2. Dress one step above what you would wear if you worked at the organization. When in doubt, dress up.

3. Dos include the following:

   - *Do* make your slides easy to read.
   - *Do* replace descriptive headlines with headlines that sell.
   - *Do* use the 10/20/30 rule.
   - *Do* remember that that PowerPoint is only an *aid*.

   Don'ts include the following:

   - *Don't* turn down the lights.
   - *Don't* go overboard with technological gimmicks.
   - *Don't* hide behind your computer screen when using PowerPoint.
   - *Don't* fill your slides with words.
   - *Don't* bore your audience with visual sameness.

4. Make sure you limit your slides to 10 or fewer. Give yourself 20 minutes to go through your 10 slides. And use only 30-point or larger font size so that your audience can clearly read what you've written.

5. Samples and demonstrations bring the product to life and help your prospect to see your solution as part of her story. Samples and demos also educate the prospect, prove the performance of your product, and get the prospect involved.

6. Opening, investigation, demonstrating capability, and obtaining commitment.

7. A closed-ended question requires a yes or no answer, such as "Do you currently use a recycling service?"

8. An open-ended question engages the customer in conversation, such as "How do you currently process invoices?"

9. Check for understanding.

10. Proposals should only come after your prospect has clearly made a connection to your product. Presenting specifics like pricing early on can create objections and prevent your prospect from making an emotional connection to the product.

Endnotes

1. Stephanie Clifford, "Find the Fox," *Inc.*, February 1, 2007, http://www.inc.com/magazine/20070201/features-sales-performance-lo.html (accessed May 16, 2010).

2. Tom Reilly, *Value-Added Selling: How to Sell More Profitably, Confidently, and Professionally by Competing on Value, Not Price*, 2nd ed. (New York: McGraw-Hill, 2002), 23–24.

3. William C. Moncrief and Greg W. Marshall, "The Evolution of the Seven Steps of Selling," *Industrial Marketing Management* 34, no. 1 (2005): 18.

4. Richard White, "Déjà Vu," Pro Excellence, http://www.pro-excellence.com/html/resources.html (accessed May 16, 2010).

5. Brian Tracy, *Advanced Selling Strategies* (New York: Simon & Schuster, 1996), 80.

6. Maryfran Johnson, "Rehearsing Success," *CIO Magazine*, June 10, 2009, http://www.cio.com/article/494729/Why_Even_Successful_Speakers_Need_To_Practice (accessed May 16, 2010).

7. Maryfran Johnson, "Rehearsing Success," *CIO Magazine*, June 10, 2009, http://www.cio.com/article/494729/Why_Even_Successful_Speakers_Need_To_Practice (accessed May 16, 2010).

8. Susan Greco, "Anatomy of a Launch: The Five-Hour Multimedia Sales Presentation," *Inc.*, October 1, 1995, http://www.inc.com/magazine/19951001/2441.html (accessed May 16, 2010).

9. Tom Reilly, "Dress for Success," Tom Reilly Training, 2009, http://www.tomreillytraining.com/Ezine%207-07%20DressforSuccess.htm (accessed May 16, 2010).

10. "Dress for Success," Sales Success Blog, November 29, 2006, http://salessuccess.blogspot.com/2006/11/dress-for-success.html (accessed May 16, 2010).

11. Ross Macpherson, "6 Keys to Making the Right Impression in an Interview," A Career in Sales, 2002, http://www.acareerinsales.com/careerToolsDress4Success.aspx (accessed May 16, 2010).

12. Geoffrey James, "Is 'Dress for Success' Still Mandatory?" BNET, January 22, 2009, http://blogs.bnet.com/salesmachine/?p=732 (accessed May 16, 2010).

13. Paul Burnham Finney, "Redefining Business Casual," *New York Times*, October 23, 2007, http://query.nytimes.com/gst/fullpage.html?res=9405EEDD1F39F930A15753C1A9619C8B63&sec=&spon=&pagewanted=all (accessed May 16, 2010).

14. Paul Burnham Finney, "Redefining Business Casual," *New York Times*, October 23, 2007, http://query.nytimes.com/gst/fullpage.html?res=9405EEDD1F39F930A15753C1A9619C8B63&sec=&spon=&pagewanted=all (accessed May 16, 2010).

15. Andy Gilchrist, "Cracking the Dress Code," Ask Andy about Clothes, http://www.askandyaboutclothes.com/Clothes%20Articles/cracking_the_dress_code.htm (accessed May 16, 2010).

16. Paul Burnham Finney, "Redefining Business Casual," *New York Times*, October 23, 2007, http://query.nytimes.com/gst/fullpage.html?res=9405EEDD1F39F930A15753C1A9619C8B63&sec=&spon=&pagewanted=all (accessed May 16, 2010).

17. Virginia Tech University Career Services, "Business Casual Attire," Virginia Tech University, http://www.career.vt.edu/Jobsearc/BusCasual.htm (accessed May 16, 2010).

18. Paul Burnham Finney, "Redefining Business Casual," *New York Times*, October 23, 2007, http://query.nytimes.com/gst/fullpage.html?res=9405EEDD1F39F930A15753C1A9619C8B63&sec=&spon=&pagewanted=all (accessed May 16, 2010).

19. Gloria Starr, "The New Dress for Success Look," EvanCarmichael.com, http://www.evancarmichael.com/Business-Coach/2445/The-New-Dress-for-Success-Look.html (accessed May 16, 2010).

20. Tom Reilly, "Dress for Success," Tom Reilly Training, 2009, http://www.tomreillytraining.com/Ezine%207-07%20DressforSuccess.htm (accessed May 16, 2010).

21. Ross Macpherson, "6 Keys to Making the Right Impression in an Interview," A Career in Sales, 2002, http://www.acareerinsales.com/careerToolsDress4Success.aspx (accessed May 16, 2010).

22. BNET Advertising Industry, "Adds New Meaning to 'Always Coca-Cola,'" BNET, http://findarticles.com/p/articles/mi_m0BDW/is_12_40/ai_54233838 (accessed May 16, 2010).

23. Gary M. Grikscheit, Harold C. Cash, and Clifford E. Young, *The Handbook of Selling: Psychological, Managerial, and Marketing Dynamics*, 2nd ed. (Hoboken, NJ: Wiley-Blackwell, 1993), 152.

24. Gary M. Grikscheit, Harold C. Cash, and Clifford E. Young, *The Handbook of Selling: Psychological, Managerial, and Marketing Dynamics*, 2nd ed. (Hoboken, NJ: Wiley-Blackwell, 1993), 127.

25. Gary M. Grikscheit, Harold C. Cash, and Clifford E. Young, *The Handbook of Selling: Psychological, Managerial, and Marketing Dynamics*, 2nd ed. (Hoboken, NJ: Wiley-Blackwell, 1993), 136.

26. Gary M. Grikscheit, Harold C. Cash, and Clifford E. Young, *The Handbook of Selling: Psychological, Managerial, and Marketing Dynamics*, 2nd ed. (Hoboken, NJ: Wiley-Blackwell, 1993), 128.

27. Gary M. Grikscheit, Harold C. Cash, and Clifford E. Young, *The Handbook of Selling: Psychological, Managerial, and Marketing Dynamics*, 2nd ed. (Hoboken, NJ: Wiley-Blackwell, 1993), 135.

28. Ian Brodie, "Becoming a Trusted Advisor," Ian Brodie: Business Growth for Professional Service Firms, blog post, July 5, 2008, http://www.ianbrodie.com/blog/becoming-trusted-advisor (accessed May 16, 2010).

29. Gary M. Grikscheit, Harold C. Cash, and Clifford E. Young, *The Handbook of Selling: Psychological, Managerial, and Marketing Dynamics*, 2nd ed. (Hoboken, NJ: Wiley-Blackwell, 1993), 165.

30. Barton A. Weitz, Stephen Byron Castleberry, and John F. Tanner, *Selling: Building Partnerships*, 5th ed. (New York: McGraw-Hill, 2003), 264.

31. Barton A. Weitz, Stephen Byron Castleberry, and John F. Tanner, *Selling: Building Partnerships*, 5th ed. (New York: McGraw-Hill, 2003), 265.

32. John Chapin, "Sales Presentations—How Location Can Affect Your Presentation and What to Do," CompleteSelling.com, blog post, March 14, 2008, http://www.completeselling.com/members/completeselling/blog/VIEW/00000009/00000076/Sales-Presentations---How-Location-can-affect-Your-Sales-Presentation-and-What-to-Do.html (accessed May 16, 2010).

33. John Chapin, "Sales Presentations—How Location Can Affect Your Presentation and What to Do," CompleteSelling.com, blog post, March 14, 2008, http://www.completeselling.com/members/completeselling/blog/VIEW/00000009/00000076/Sales-Presentations---How-Location-can-affect-Your-Sales-Presentation-and-What-to-Do.html (accessed May 16, 2010).

34. Susan Greco, "Anatomy of a Launch: The Five-Hour Multimedia Sales Presentation," *Inc.*, October 1, 1995, http://www.inc.com/magazine/19951001/2441.html (accessed May 16, 2010).

35. John Chapin, "Sales Presentations—How Location Can Affect Your Presentation and What to Do," CompleteSelling.com, blog post, March 14, 2008, http://www.completeselling.com/members/completeselling/blog/VIEW/00000009/00000076/Sales-Presentations---How-Location-can-affect-Your-Sales-Presentation-and-What-to-Do.html (accessed May 16, 2010).

36. John Chapin, "Sales Presentations—How Location Can Affect Your Presentation and What to Do," CompleteSelling.com, blog post, March 14, 2008, http://www.completeselling.com/members/completeselling/blog/VIEW/00000009/00000076/Sales-Presentations---How-Location-can-affect-Your-Sales-Presentation-and-What-to-Do.html (accessed May 16, 2010).

37. "Sales Trends: Electronic Sales Presentations," KnowThis.com, http://www.knowthis.com/principles-of-marketing-tutorials/personal-selling/selling-trends-electronic-sales-presentations (accessed May 16, 2010).

38. Joanna Lees Castro, "Using Video Conferencing to Host an Effective Online Sales Presentation—6 Best Practice Tips," EzineArticles, http://ezinearticles.com/?id=1316495 (accessed May 16, 2010).

39. "Video Conferencing Etiquette Checklist," Manage Smarter, June 8, 2009, http://www.presentations.com/msg/content_display/training/e3i0fe06f39ca140432cc75be4595e2c6e1 (accessed May 16, 2010).

40. "Video Conferencing Etiquette Checklist," Manage Smarter, June 8, 2009, http://www.presentations.com/msg/content_display/training/e3i0fe06f39ca140432cc75be4595e2c6e1 (accessed May 16, 2010).

41. Joanna Lees Castro, "Using Video Conferencing to Host an Effective Online Sales Presentation—6 Best Practice Tips," EzineArticles, http://ezinearticles.com/?id=1316495 (accessed May 16, 2010).

42. Stephanie Clifford, "Fasten Your Seatbelts," *Inc.*, February 1, 2007, http://www.inc.com/magazine/20070201/features-sales-performance-ilicic.html (accessed May 16, 2010).

43. Stephanie Clifford, "Fasten Your Seatbelts," *Inc.*, February 1, 2007, http://www.inc.com/magazine/20070201/features-sales-performance-ilicic.html (accessed May 16, 2010).

44. Anne Miller, "Death by PowerPoint," Sales and Sales Management Blog, February 22, 2008, http://salesandmanagementblog.com/2008/02/22/guest-article-death-by-powerpoint-by-anne-miller (accessed May 16, 2010).

45. Anne Miller, "Death by PowerPoint," Sales and Sales Management Blog, February 22, 2008, http://salesandmanagementblog.com/2008/02/22/guest-article-death-by-powerpoint-by-anne-miller (accessed May 16, 2010).

46. Jim Meisenheimer, "How to Use PowerPoint During Sales Presentations," EvanCarmichael.com, http://www.evancarmichael.com/Sales/407/How-To-Use-PowerPoint-During-Sales-Presentations.html (accessed May 16, 2010).

47. Anne Miller, "Death by PowerPoint," Sales and Sales Management Blog, February 22, 2008, http://salesandmanagementblog.com/2008/02/22/guest-article-death-by-powerpoint-by-anne-miller (accessed May 16, 2010).

48. Jim Meisenheimer, "How to Use PowerPoint During Sales Presentations," EvanCarmichael.com, http://www.evancarmichael.com/Sales/407/How-To-Use-PowerPoint-During-Sales-Presentations.html (accessed May 16, 2010).

49. Anne Miller, "Death by PowerPoint," Sales and Sales Management Blog, February 22, 2008, http://salesandmanagementblog.com/2008/02/22/guest-article-death-by-powerpoint-by-anne-miller (accessed May 16, 2010).

50. Jim Meisenheimer, "How to Use PowerPoint During Sales Presentations," EvanCarmichael.com, http://www.evancarmichael.com/Sales/407/How-To-Use-PowerPoint-During-Sales-Presentations.html (accessed May 16, 2010).

51. Geoff William, "The Perfect Presentation: Technology," *Entrepreneur*, July 13, 2007, http://www.entrepreneur.com/marketing/marketingbasics/article181582.html (accessed May 16, 2010).

52. Geoffrey James, "Top 10 Lies Customers Tell Sales Reps," BNET, April 23, 2009, http://blogs.bnet.com/salesmachine/?p=2323&page=2 (accessed May 16, 2010).

53. Brad Sugars, "Building Repeat Business from Day 1," *Entrepreneur*, May 22, 2007, http://www.entrepreneur.com/startingabusiness/startupbasics/startupbasicscolumnistbradsugars/article178724.html (accessed May 16, 2010).

54. Julie Blick, "Inside the Smartest Little Company in America," *Inc.*, January 1, 2002, http://www.inc.com/magazine/20020101/23798.html (accessed May 16, 2010).

55. EDTM, Inc., "4 Steps to Close More Sales," http://www.solarstop.net/edtm/sales_demonstration.htm (accessed May 16, 2010).

56. EDTM, Inc., "4 Steps to Close More Sales," http://www.solarstop.net/edtm/sales_demonstration.htm (accessed May 16, 2010).

57. Gerald L. Manning and Barry L. Reece, *Selling Today: Creating Customer Value*, 9th ed. (Upper Saddle River, NJ: Prentice Hall, 2004), 256.

58. David H. Miles, *The 30 Second Encyclopedia of Learning and Performance* (New York: AMACOM, 2003), 139–40.

59. Energy Star, "Commercial Dishwashers for Consumers," U.S. Environmental Protection Agency and U.S. Department of Energy, http://www.energystar.gov/index.cfm?c=comm_dishwashers.pr_comm_dishwashers (accessed May 16, 2010).

60. "Cost of Ownership, ROI, and Cost/Benefit Analysis: What's the Difference?" Solution Matrix, http://www.solutionmatrix.com/tco-roi-cba-difference.html (accessed May 16, 2010).

61. Neil Rackham, *The SPIN Selling Fieldbook* (New York: McGraw-Hill, 1996), 8; Greg Woodley, "SPIN Selling Is Good," SellingandPersuasionTechniques.com, http://www.sellingandpersuasiontechniques.com/SPIN-selling.html (accessed May 16, 2010).

62. Neil Rackham, *SPIN Selling Fieldbook* (New York: McGraw-Hill, 1996), 38.

63. Neil Rackham, *SPIN Selling Fieldbook* (New York: McGraw-Hill, 1996), 139.

64. Neil Rackham, *SPIN Selling Fieldbook* (New York: McGraw-Hill, 1996), 40.

65. Neil Rackham, *SPIN Selling Fieldbook* (New York: McGraw-Hill, 1996), 144.

66. "SPIN Selling," review of *SPIN Selling*, ChangingMinds.org, http://changingminds.org/books/book_reviews/spin.htm (accessed May 16, 2010).

67. Greg Woodley, "SPIN Selling Is Good," SellingandPersuasionTechniques.com, http://www.sellingandpersuasiontechniques.com/SPIN-selling.html (accessed May 16, 2010).

68. Neil Rackham, *SPIN Selling Fieldbook* (New York: McGraw-Hill, 1996), 76; Eric Wolfram, "How to Sell—SPIN Selling," Wolfram, http://wolfram.org/writing/howto/sell/spin_selling.html (accessed May 16, 2010).

69. Neil Rackham, *SPIN Selling Fieldbook* (New York: McGraw-Hill, 1996), 90.

70. Neil Rackham, *SPIN Selling Fieldbook* (New York: McGraw-Hill, 1996), 93.

71. "SPIN Selling," review of *SPIN Selling*, Changing Minds Book Reviews, http://changingminds.org/books/book_reviews/spin.htm (accessed May 16, 2010).

72. Neil Rackham, *SPIN Selling Fieldbook* (New York: McGraw-Hill, 1996), 108.

73. "SPIN Selling," review of *SPIN Selling*, Changing Minds Book Reviews, http://changingminds.org/books/book_reviews/spin.htm (accessed May 16, 2010).

74. Neil Rackham, *SPIN Selling Fieldbook* (New York: McGraw-Hill, 1996), 128.

75. Neil Rackham, *SPIN Selling Fieldbook* (New York: McGraw-Hill, 1996), 148.

76. Neil Rackham, *SPIN Selling Fieldbook* (New York: McGraw-Hill, 1996), 42–43.

77. Neil Rackham, *SPIN Selling Fieldbook* (New York: McGraw-Hill, 1996), 44.

78. Neil Rackham, *SPIN Selling Fieldbook* (New York: McGraw-Hill, 1996), 45.

79. Bruce Harris, "The Eyes Have It," *American Salesman* 54, no. 3 (2009): 17

80. Neil Rackham, *SPIN Selling* (New York: McGraw-Hill, 1996), 144.

81. Geoffrey James, "How to Give a Killer Sales Presentation," BNET, May 17, 2009, http://blogs.bnet.com/salesmachine/?p=2940 (accessed May 16, 2010).

82. Gary M. Grikscheit, Harold C. Cash, and Clifford E. Young, *The Handbook of Selling: Psychological, Managerial, and Marketing Dynamics*, 2nd ed. (Hoboken, NJ: Wiley-Blackwell, 1993), 158.

83. Michael T. Bosworth, *Solution Selling: Creating Buyers in Difficult Selling Markets* (New York: McGraw-Hill, 1995), 101.

84. Joshua Rose, "New 2009 Toyota RAV4 Features and Prices," Auto Broker Magic, http://www.auto-broker-magic.com/2009-toyota-rav4.html (accessed May 16, 2010).

85. Kelley Robertson, "How to Create a Powerful Sales Presentation," About.com, http://sbinfocanada.about.com/od/salesselling/a/presentationkr.htm (accessed January 4, 2010).

86. Kevin Davis, "10 Tips for Winning Sales Presentations," Business Know-How, http://www.businessknowhow.com/marketing/winslspres.htm (accessed January 4, 2010).

87. Kevin Davis, "10 Tips for Winning Sales Presentations," Business Know-How, http://www.businessknowhow.com/marketing/winslspres.htm (accessed January 4, 2010).

88. Kelley Robertson, "How to Create a Powerful Sales Presentation," About.com, http://sbinfocanada.about.com/od/salesselling/a/presentationkr.htm (accessed January 4, 2010).

89. Kelley Robertson, "How to Create a Powerful Sales Presentation," About.com, http://sbinfocanada.about.com/od/salesselling/a/presentationkr.htm (accessed January 4, 2010).

90. Doug Dvorak, "How Trial Closing and Closing Techniques Can Save You Time and Help You Make More Sales," EzineArticles, http://ezinearticles.com/?How-Trial-Closing-and-Closing-Techniques-Can-Save-You-Time-and-Help-You-to-Make-More-Sales&id=1019686 (accessed May 16, 2010).

91. Jim Holden, *The Selling Fox* (Hoboken, NJ: John Wiley and Sons, Inc., 2002), 25.

92. Tom Hopkins, "Giving Champion Presentations," *Entrepreneur*, February 7, 2005, http://www.entrepreneur.com/sales/presentations/article75918.html#ixzz0LqUNOCM3 (accessed May 16, 2010).

93. Edward Lowe Foundation, "How to Write a Sales Proposal," eSmallOffice, 2008, http://www.esmalloffice.com/SBR_template.cfm?DocNumber=PL12_4000.htm (accessed May 16, 2010).

94. Edward Lowe Foundation, "How to Write a Sales Proposal," eSmallOffice, 2008, http://www.esmalloffice.com/SBR_template.cfm?DocNumber=PL12_4000.htm (accessed May 16, 2010).

95. Kimberly Kayler, "Send Me a Proposal! Proposals Are Often a Downfall of the Sales Cycle," AllBusiness, August 1, 2005, http://www.AllBusiness.com/manufacturing/nonmetallic-mineral-product-manufacturing/521322-1.html (accessed May 16, 2010).

96. Edward Lowe Foundation, "How to Write a Sales Proposal," eSmallOffice, 2008, http://www.esmalloffice.com/SBR_template.cfm?DocNumber=PL12_4000.htm (accessed May 16, 2010).

97. Kimberly Kayler, "Send Me a Proposal! Proposals Are Often a Downfall of the Sales Cycle," Concrete Construction, August 1, 2005, AllBusiness, http://www.AllBusiness.com/manufacturing/nonmetallic-mineral-product-manufacturing/521322-1.html (accessed May 16, 2010).

98. Glenn Wheaton, "Request for Proposal," Epiq Technologies, November 20, 2008, http://www.epiqtech.com/request-for-proposal-rfp.htm (accessed May 16, 2010).

99. Kimberly Kayler, "Send Me a Proposal! Proposals Are Often a Downfall of the Sales Cycle," Concrete Construction, August 1, 2005, AllBusiness, http://www.AllBusiness.com/manufacturing/nonmetallic-mineral-product-manufacturing/521322-1.html (accessed May 16, 2010).

100. Kimberly Kayler, "Send Me a Proposal! Proposals Are Often a Downfall of the Sales Cycle," Concrete Construction, August 1, 2005, AllBusiness, http://www.AllBusiness.com/manufacturing/nonmetallic-mineral-product-manufacturing/521322-1.html (accessed May 16, 2010).

101. Adapted from Cheryl Smith, "Writing Killer Proposals," Edward Lowe Foundation, "How to Write a Sales Proposal," eSmallOffice, 2008, http://www.esmalloffice.com/SBR_template.cfm?DocNumber=PL12_4000.htm (accessed May 16, 2010).

102. "Testimonials," Chico Real Estate, Inc., http://www.chicorealestate.net/Testimonials.aspx (accessed May 16, 2010).

103. Kim Richmond, "10 Tips for Successful Interviews," presentation in the How to Market Yourself as a Brand to Get the Job You Want Workshop Series, Upper Merion Township Library, King of Prussia, PA, June 1, 2009.

104. Kim Richmond, *Brand You*, 3rd ed. (Upper Saddle River, NJ: Pearson Prentice Hall, 2008), 186.

105. Kim Richmond, "10 Tips for Successful Interviews," presentation in the How to Market Yourself as a Brand to Get the Job You Want Workshop Series, Upper Merion Township Library, King of Prussia, PA, June 1, 2009.

106. Laura Raines, "Making Your Pitch," *The Atlanta Journal-Constitution*, Jobs, 2007, http://www.ajc.com/hotjobs/content/hotjobs/careercenter/articles/2007_0225_elevatorsp.html (accessed May 16, 2010).

107. Sarah E. Needleman, "The New Trouble on the Line," *Wall Street Journal*, June 2, 2009, http://online.wsj.com/article/SB124390348922474789.html (accessed May 16, 2010).

108. CareerBuilder.com, "Answering 6 Common Interview Questions," *CNN.com*, December 9, 2005, http://www.cnn.com/2005/US/Careers/12/09/six.questions/index.html (accessed May 16, 2010).

109. Sarah E. Needleman, "The New Trouble on the Line," *Wall Street Journal*, June 2, 2009, http://online.wsj.com/article/SB124390348922474789.html (accessed May 16, 2010).

110. CareerBuilder.com, "Answering 6 Common Interview Questions," *CNN.com*, December 9, 2005, http://www.cnn.com/2005/US/Careers/12/09/six.questions/index.html (accessed May 16, 2010).

111. CareerBuilder.com, "Answering 6 Common Interview Questions," *CNN.com*, December 9, 2005, http://www.cnn.com/2005/US/Careers/12/09/six.questions/index.html (accessed May 16, 2010).

112. "Common Interview Questions," *USA Today*, Careers and Workplace, January 29, 2001, http://www.usatoday.com/careers/resources/interviewcommon.htm (accessed May 16, 2010).

113. Sarah E. Needleman, "The New Trouble on the Line," *Wall Street Journal*, June 2, 2009, http://online.wsj.com/article/SB124390348922474789.html (accessed May 16, 2010).

114. Kim Richmond, *Brand You*, 3rd ed. (Upper Saddle River, NJ: Pearson Prentice Hall, 2008), 196.

115. Kim Richmond, *Brand You* 3rd ed. (Upper Saddle River, NJ: Pearson Prentice Hall, 2008), 186.

116. Kim Richmond, "10 Tips for Successful Interviews," presentation in the How to Market Yourself as a Brand to Get the Job You Want Workshop Series, Upper Merion Township Library, King of Prussia, PA, June 1, 2009.

117. Kim Richmond, *Brand You*, 3rd ed. (Upper Saddle River, NJ: Pearson Prentice Hall, 2008), 197.

118. "USA Today Snapshots," *USA Today*, Money, December 30, 2009, 1B.

119. Kim Richmond, "10 Tips for Successful Interviews," presentation in the How to Market Yourself as a Brand to Get the Job You Want Workshop Series, Upper Merion Township Library, King of Prussia, PA, June 1, 2009.

120. Kim Richmond, *Brand You*, 3rd ed. (Upper Saddle River, NJ: Pearson Prentice Hall, 2008), 188.

CHAPTER 11
Handling Objections: The Power of Learning from Opportunities

Video Ride-Along with Paul Blake, Vice President of Sales at Greater Media Philadelphia

You heard Paul Blake talk about making a successful presentation in Chapter 10. Now hear his tips about handling objections. While this might sound like the most difficult part of the selling process, Paul shares his advice about how to make this the most productive part of the selling process.

If you think you have to memorize all kinds of responses to objections, you'll be pleased to hear that handling objections is easy...when you use the skills you already learned.

View the video online at: http://www.youtube.com/embed/zo4BFaXhFz0

11.1 Objections Are Opportunities to Build Relationships

Learning Objectives

1. Understand what a sales objection is.
2. Learn how overcoming objections can strengthen a relationship.
3. Understand when and why prospects raise objections.

You've been working really hard at school, and it's paying off. You're doing well this semester with a GPA right where you want it. Spring break is right around the corner, and you and your friends have been talking about going to Mexico. You even had an impromptu "fiesta party" at your place and even do some research about airfares and hotels; there are some great deals out there. You present your case to your parents and end with a strong "close" to seal the deal: "The timing is perfect since it's my senior year. I can book the flights tonight online." You thought you sold them on the trip when they say, "We're worried about you going out of the country without a chaperone." You are deflated, but you won't take no for an answer so you wait for a moment, let it sink in, then deliver your response, just like you planned. You have just experienced the fine art of overcoming objections.

Since you are constantly selling in your everyday life, you have also undoubtedly encountered objections: your friend doesn't want to see the same movie as you, your brother doesn't want to share the car, your parents want you home earlier than you would like. When you attempt to convince someone or "sell" him on your point of view, you are not always successful. But each time you "sell" your idea, you usually have additional information or a fallback position so that you can get what you want while meeting the other person's needs. You are probably more skilled in overcoming objections than you realize.

Occasionally in your sales career, you will encounter a situation in which you are able to close the sale directly after giving your sales presentation. Such a situation, however, is the *exception* not the *rule*. Objections are simply a natural outcome of the sales process. Each potential prospect has his own set of unique needs, and, though you may identify most of them during the preapproach stage of the selling process when you do your research, you will not be able to anticipate all of them. After all, you are not a mind reader. Besides, if all it took to excel in sales was to deliver a perfect script, anyone could do it. But that is not the case. The essence of sales is handling objections and truly understanding how you can help your prospect meet her needs. It is a demonstration of your skills as a salesperson to find the opportunity in these objections, listen to your prospect, and then respond. So an objection is simply a question from a prospect that indicates that she wants more information. If she weren't interested, she wouldn't be asking questions.[1]

The first myth to dispel is the assumption that objections are *bad* or an omen foreshadowing failure. On the contrary, resistance usually portends commitment. If a prospect is asking you questions, you can at least assume that he is interested in your product or service. In fact, in all likelihood, he already knows whether or not he needs or wants to make the purchase. Thus, the reason he is objecting isn't necessarily because your presentation failed to communicate the features, advantages, and benefits of your offering. Rather, he is objecting because he is seeking reassurance; he is on the fence of indecision, and he wants you to provide him with the incentive that justifies an immediate purchase.[2] Supply your prospect with the right information, that is, show him why he wants to buy your product or service.

What Are Objections?

Objections, also called sales objections, are generally defined as prospect questions or hesitancies about either the product or company.[3] While *objection* may sound like *rejection*, you should never assume that when a prospect asks a question or expresses a concern that you have failed to generate interest in your product or service. It is true sometimes that your prospect will object when he truly cannot or does not want to buy. Usually, though, objections mask—intentionally or unintentionally—a request for more information. They simply signal your prospect's level of interest and alert you to what actions need to be taken to bring the sale to a close. If your prospect expresses objections, consider them invitations to continue to sell. Furthermore, leverage these objections into an opportunity to continue to build your relationship with your prospect so that you can continue to create a positive influence on the buyer's decision. The fact is objections help you build your relationship and find the true reason for resistance. Think of objections as opportunities.

How Objections Build Relationships

As an analogy, consider asking someone out on a date for the first time. Even if you have hooked him in with a great pick-up line (approach) and dazzled him with your sparkling personality (presentation), he may still not be convinced that you are serious about him. Naturally, he might respond by playing hard-to-get. How you react will reveal to him your level of commitment. By allowing the relationship to grow slowly and organically, you demonstrate your patience, sensitivity, and sincerity. You establish a foundation of trust that eventually wins him over. On the other hand, if you respond by getting huffy and stomping off, he will probably be glad to see you go.

Objections as Opportunities

You might not keep track of objections in your everyday life (especially as they relate to dating). However, you may find it interesting to know that in sales, a prospect will say no an average of five times before he buys.[4] That means that it's more likely than not that you will experience a prospect who poses at least one objection: asking a question, requesting more information or time, or pushing back due to financial constraints. Without objections, you would have no way of knowing what a prospect is thinking, what concerns she has, or what barriers might be in the way of her saying, "Where do I sign?"

The fact is objections are an important part of the selling process. But thinking about *overcoming* objections might be the wrong frame of reference. The word "overcome" implies that you want to conquer, fight, or win (and, therefore, your prospect loses).[5] Instead, it's best to think about objections as a perfect extension of the selling process. Think back to the steps of the selling process that you have covered so far: prospecting and qualifying, preapproach, approach, and presentation. Throughout each of these steps, your focus is on understanding your prospect's needs and building a relationship based on trust. The same is true for this step: handling objections. This is all about learning more, finding common ground, and providing the solution that is best for your prospect. Objections and conversation help you better understand exactly what your prospect wants and needs. The bottom line is that you don't want to avoid objections; you actually want to encourage objections and ask for them. According to the *Selling Power Sales Management Newsletter*, "Objections are not personal attacks; they're gifts."[6]

Consider Objections before They Occur

If objections are such a positive part of the selling process, you might be wondering how to be prepared for them; how to think about them; how to consider them even before you get them. Here are some strategies for preparing for the objections portion of the selling process that will help you build your relationship.

FIGURE 11.1
Objections are not rejections but are invitations for more information that eventually leads to a yes.

© 2010 Jupiterimages Corporation

objections

Prospect questions or hesitancies about a product or company.

- **Understand your prospect and believe in your partnership**. If you did your homework at every step of the process so far and put together a presentation and proposal that really makes sense for your prospect's business, you should be confident in the fact that you are a true business partner to your prospect. Objections lead to sharing and learning and the ability for you to make adjustments in your proposal that will help your prospect manage her business.[7]

- **Remember WII-FM**. WII-FM (**W**hat's **I**n **I**t **F**or **M**e) is the radio station that everyone listens to. Never lose sight of your prospect's buying motivations. If time is mission-critical to his success, know what you can deliver and by when. If national reach is important to your prospect, be sure you address it in detail in your proposal.

- **Understand risk**. Understand what your prospect considers a risk (e.g., time, money, changing suppliers). When risk outweighs reward in the mind of your prospect, chances are she will find a reason not to buy. Understand her risk factors and address them head on. This will allow you to employ a "risk-removal" strategy, rather than a selling strategy.[8]

- **Anticipate objections**. Think about every possible objection you might get—before you get it. That means making a list of every objection before you even make your presentation and building in the response into the presentation.[9] Your success as a salesperson will largely be determined by your ability to anticipate and handle objections.[10] Write down all the possible objections and go back and incorporate them into your presentation. Then, give your presentation to a friend or colleague and see if they can find any additional objections. Although you can't make your presentation "objection proof," you can anticipate and be prepared for most objections that will be raised.[11] Anticipating objections helps you be responsive, rather than reactive.[12]

- **Raise objections first**. Since you have done so much preparation and you understand and have a good relationship with your prospect, be proactive and be prepared to raise objections first. When you raise an objection, you actually turn it into a discussion point rather than an objection. It shows your prospect that you are thinking about the sale from her perspective and helps you build the relationship.[13]

Objections should not intimidate you or dissuade you from continuing the selling process. Rather, you should consider objections opportunities to learn more about your prospect's needs. The more you understand about your prospect's needs, the greater your ability to determine how your product or service can satisfy them or how your product or service *can be improved* to satisfy them. Remember, selling is about solving problems. The solution that you offer will demonstrate to your prospect whether or not you truly understand his needs and whether or not you have his best interests at heart. By embracing your prospect's objections and handling them effectively, you will inspire his trust, confidence, and most important, loyalty. As a result, both you and the prospect benefit.

Power Selling: Lessons in Selling from Successful Brands

Handling Objections: All in a Day's Work

At iCore Networks, a leading VoIP (voice over Internet protocol) provider, handling objections is an everyday learning experience. Sales reps gather at 8:00 a.m. sharp every day to discuss successes and failures from the previous day and role-play overcoming objections and then put what they learn to work in the field all day. The commitment to coaching and being in front of customers works for the company and its sales force: the average compensation for a first-year sales rep is $92,000.[14]

Learn more about how iCore sells in the following article.

http://www.inc.com/magazine/20090901/a-sales-force-built-around-cold-calling.html

Why Prospects Object

While prospects may voice their objections in different ways, just about every objection comes down to one of four reasons: no or not enough money, no perceived need, no sense of urgency, and no trust.[15] As a selling professional, you have control over each one of these objections. But it's too late if you address it only when the prospect objects. In other words, you are actually handling objections at every step of the selling process. For example, you can avoid the price objection with thorough qualification during your first step of the selling process.[16]

If a prospect does not have a perceived need or high sense of urgency to buy your product or service, your challenge is to understand the drivers of his business. Every business has challenges, and your role from the time you qualify the prospect is to understand your prospect's "pain points," those issues that cause problems for him and his company and present barriers to growth. If you truly understand your prospect's business, it is much easier to present a solution that addresses the perceived need and reasons to buy it now. "There is no reason for buyers to buy today unless we build in that sense of urgency and give them a reason to buy today," says Dana Forest, director of sales at Simons Homes.[17]

Many objections are raised because the relationship between the prospect and the salesperson is not fully developed. business-to-business (B2B) selling is dependent on trust. If the trust is not there, or the relationship is not yet fully developed, it can be difficult for a prospect to make a change or finalize the purchase. If this is the case, prospects will frequently delay or stall before making a decision, which can be an attempt to derail the sale.

When Prospects Object

While you may not be able to predict your prospect's every objection, you can at least predict that *he will object*. Knowing when to expect objections is the first step to handling them: you will eliminate the chance of appearing caught off guard or unprepared to discuss the product or service that you are selling.

Of course, it is possible that the prospect may object at any time during your sales call—from introduction to close. Still, there are specific points in time during the sales process where these objections are more likely to occur: when you are first trying to make contact, when you are making a sales presentation, and when you are attempting to close the sale, or make a trial close. As you learned in Chapter 10, a trial close includes any attempt to close the sale but usually focuses on asking the prospect's opinion: "What do you think about the turnaround time?" A trial close may occur at any point during the selling process. In other words, if the prospect indicates that she may be interested in making the purchase, it is an opportunity to make a trial close.

Objections are likely to occur at several points during the selling process, including the trial close. It's best to be prepared for objections at every step in the selling process, including the qualifying stage. Know your prospect and be ready to incorporate objections into your sales presentation.[18]

Setting Up the Appointment

Imagine that you are in the middle of a cold call and you are attempting to set up an appointment to meet your prospect. You have barely uttered your name when your prospect exasperatedly grunts, "Don't waste your breath. I'm not buying anything you're selling." How do you respond?

This scenario is meant to illustrate the fact that you may meet resistance as soon as you try to establish contact with your qualified prospect. Hopefully, you will have reduced the rate of this problem occurring by properly qualifying your prospect beforehand and preparing for the most common objections. Nonetheless, anticipate resistance from the beginning.

Using the questioning technique is a good way to engage your prospect in conversation and learn more about what can help her run her business.[19]

> **Prospect**: *No thanks, I'm satisfied with my current supplier.*
>
> **You**: *May I ask you who you are currently using?*
>
> **Prospect**: *We work with Advanced, and they have been doing a good job.*
>
> **You**: *Advanced is very good at what they do. Did you know that Symone offers a money-back guarantee? In other words, if you are not completely satisfied with the conversion or the service, we will completely refund your money. It would be worth thirty minutes of your time to learn more about it. How does Tuesday at 8 o'clock look?*

When you are giving a sales presentation, very often the prospect will ask you questions as you go. It is unlikely that your prospect will wait until you have finished your presentation before asking you questions. However, the experienced salesperson will actually encourage questions throughout her presentation since she knows that responding to them supplies her with precious time that she can use to further demonstrate how her offering can solve her prospect's problem. As a rule, you will want to acknowledge objections as they arise. If you feel that the objection will be addressed at a later point during the presentation, you may postpone your response, but you will need to communicate this information to your prospect. For example, you might say something like the following:

> **Prospect**: *I'm a little concerned about the financing.*
>
> **You**: *I'm glad you brought that up. I'm going to address that in the next slide, which I think will provide you with the information you are looking for.*

During the Presentation

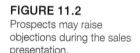

FIGURE 11.2

Prospects may raise objections during the sales presentation.

© 2010 Jupiterimages Corporation

Otherwise, he may think that you are avoiding the question and that you are trying to hide something, are unprepared and do not know how to respond, or are simply not listening—all kinds of impressions that you do not want give.

During the Trial Close

Recall from Chapter 10 that you can test your buyer's readiness after your sales presentation by employing a trial close. If your prospect hasn't expressed any opinions at this point of the selling process, then the trial close is your opportunity to seek them out. If your prospect responds positively to it, then congratulations! This response indicates that you have skillfully executed each step of the selling process: creating rapport, gaining the prospect's trust, listening, identifying his problem, and presenting products and services that will provide him with solutions and value.[20] From this point, you can move to the next step of the process, the close.

If, on the other hand, an objection is raised, then you will use this time to respond to it. Always remember that an unacknowledged concern lessens the opportunity for a sale. Responding means fully listening to your prospect's concerns and objections, asking clarifying questions to determine whether or not you understand them, identifying the types of objections they are, and meeting them. To be clear, "meeting" an objection does not mean saying what you think the prospect wants to hear; you should never make a promise about a product or service that you cannot deliver. How you *meet* an objection will depend on the type of objection you are dealing with. Simply put, meeting the objection means returning to the presentation stage, elaborating on your product's capabilities, and emphasizing in what ways they benefit your prospect. For example, assume you are making a sales presentation for a software product to a B2B client and she presents an objection about the timing of the installation.

Prospect: *This is really an interesting option for us to pursue, but we are planning on launching our service much sooner than your timeline suggests. I'm not sure your implementation timing will work for us.*

You: *When are your planning on launching your new service?*

Prospect: *We want to have everything in place and tested in less than forty-five days.*

You: *So it sounds like the biggest challenge is the installation date. I can talk to our head engineer and see if we can change the installation date. If we can guarantee installation within thirty days, will you commit to the two-year agreement?*

In this example, it's important to note that the objection led to the prospect sharing information that was not previously known: the date of the launch. This is valuable information that the salesperson can use to potentially overcome other objections and provide service that will help the prospect meet his goals.

After you think you have responded to and have overcome all your prospect's objections, you can proceed with another trial close. If you determine that your prospect has new objections, then you will want to repeat the response process. You may have to use a trial close several times before moving to a close. Keep in mind that the sales process is not perfectly linear; rather, it is iterative. Depending on the prospect and the product, it is perfectly appropriate to repeat steps.

FIGURE 11.3

When you have handled your prospect's objections, you have earned the right to ask for the sale.

© 2010 Jupiterimages Corporation

When you are certain that you have addressed all your prospect's objections and that he has no further objections, move to the close. Don't be shy! You have earned this right and, besides, your customer expects you to!

In the same way, you should never allow yourself to become defensive or antagonistic when a prospect makes an objection. Since your goal is to build and sustain an enduring customer relationship, you will want to handle your prospect's objections with as much delicacy as possible. For example, avoid responding to objections with statements beginning with "but": "But our company is better" or "But we offer more value for your money."[21] It's better to respond in a positive way, such as "We are the only company that offers a guarantee on our product. If you're not satisfied for any reason, we'll refund your money. Our goal is for you to be more than satisfied—we want you to be delighted."

Key Takeaways

- **Objections** are a normal part of the selling process and are not a personal reflection on you but rather an opportunity to learn more about how the customer is evaluating the potential purchase.
- **Objections** actually help build relationships because they give you the opportunity to clarify communication and revisit your relationship with the prospect.
- The best way to handle **objections** is to be thorough in every part of the selling process from qualifying through the preapproach, approach, and presentation.
- It's a good idea to anticipate **objections** by reviewing your presentation, writing down every possible objection, and building it into your presentation.
- It's especially important to understand risk from your prospect's perspective so you can create a risk-removal strategy.
- Prospects object for four reasons: money, no perceived need, no sense of urgency, and no trust.
- Prospects may pose **objections** at any time, but especially while setting up the appointment, during the presentation, and during the trial close.

Exercises

1. Go to a local health club and go through the sales presentation as if you were going to join. What objections would you have for the salesperson? Which objections did the salesperson address to your satisfaction? Which objections did the salesperson not address to your satisfaction? Why?

2. Try to sell your professor on conducting class as a study period next week. How would you prepare for the "presentation" to make your case? What are some objections you might receive? How might you handle the objections?

3. Identify the three most common points at which objections occur in a sales presentation. Provide an example of each one in your everyday life.

4. Assume you are selling real estate and you are calling a prospect to set up an appointment. How would you handle an objection that she doesn't have the time to meet with you?

5. Assume you are a financial services salesperson. You have presented an investment strategy to your prospect, and he has objected because he is concerned about the state of the market. How would you handle this objection by making him feel more comfortable with the risk?

6. Contact a salesperson for a local business and ask him how he handles objections. Share your findings with the class.

11.2 Types of Objections and How to Handle Them

Learning Objectives

1. Learn strategies to handle objections.
2. Understand the different types of objections and how to handle them.

Learning how to handle objections is key, especially when many of the same ones occur regularly. There are six strategies that can help you handle virtually any objection.

1. **View the objection as a question**. Many times salespeople hear an objection as a personal attack. Instead, an objection such as "Why are your prices so high?" should be considered a question. That allows a more positive conversation rather than a defensive one.[22]

2. **Respond to the objection with question**. As in every step of the selling process, asking the right questions is critical, and handling objections is no exception. Questions, such as "Can you share you concerns in this area?" or "Is there another way to look at this to make it work for you?" are good ways to engage prospects in dialogue that will help you better solve their problems.[23]

3. **Restate the objection before answering the objection**. It's a good idea to check for understanding and demonstrate that you are listening by restating your prospect's objection. For example, "So what you're saying is you're concerned about the capacity during peak periods" is a good way not only to acknowledge the objection but also to give you time to formulate your response.[24]

4. **Take a pause before responding**. Many times salespeople "oversell" when they are answering an objection. When a prospect raises an objection, stop, listen, and pause for a few seconds. This shows the prospect that you are legitimately listening to her objection, not just trying to sell.[25]

5. **Use testimonials and past experiences**. Don't avoid answering any part of an objection. In fact, objections are the perfect time to share testimonials. For example, "I have another customer who was concerned about the turnaround time. He found that not only were we able to deliver on time, we were slightly under budget."[26]

Testimonials can be very powerful at any point in your sales presentation but especially when a prospect presents an objection.

Prospect: *I'm not sure this is the right database management tool for us. Technology is not our strong suit, and I'm concerned that we would be buying a product that has more horsepower than we need.*

You: *I have several other clients with businesses that are about the size of yours, and they felt that way initially, too. In fact, John Jackson at Premier Services felt the same way, but he said that the product is so easy to use that it took very little time to train his people. He was able to increase his sales by 3 percent and reduce his sales and marketing costs by 5 percent when using our database management tool. Chris Ling at IBS was worried about the same issue. He increased his sales over 5 percent with an 8 percent reduction in selling and marketing costs. Let's take a look at the demo again.*

You can also simply respond to an objection by letting your customers speak for you.[27]

> **Prospect**: *We've tried other cleaning products, but they didn't really work for us.*
>
> **You**: *Here's what my customers say…*

6. **Never argue with the prospect**. "The customer is always right" is always true when it comes to handling objections. It's never a good idea to disagree or argue with the customer, even when he is wrong. Relationships are built on trust, so it's best to use an objection to build the trust, not break it.[28]

*Do*s and *Don't*s of Handling Objections

The following are things you should concentrate on doing when you are handling objections:

- **Do** maintain a positive attitude and be enthusiastic.
- **Do** remember that objections are a natural part of the sales process and should not be considered as a personal affront.
- **Do** maintain good eye contact, even when under fire.
- **Do** listen closely to an objection.
- **Do** acknowledge the objection and then give your point of view.
- **Do** prepare to prove your position with testimonials, references, and documentation.

The following are things you should avoid doing when you are handling objections:

- **Don't** knock the competition. That takes the focus off you and your company, and you never want to do that.
- **Don't** say anything negative about your company.
- **Don't** say anything negative about your product or service.
- **Don't** tell the customer that they are wrong.
- **Don't** tell the customer, "You don't understand."
- **Don't** argue with a customer.
- **Don't** lie to a customer. Long-term relationships are built on trust and honesty. It is far better to say, "I don't know, but I'll find out and get right back to you."
- **Don't** be defensive. That's not a positive approach to an objection.
- **Don't** lose your cool with the customer.
- **Don't** let an objection go by without an answer.

Reprinted with permission from Edward Lowe Peerspectives.[29]

Types of Objections

Prospects may object for any reason, but there are six major categories into which most objections fall. When you are prepared for all these types of objections, you will be able to successfully handle them.

- Product objection
- Source objection
- Price objection
- Money objection

- "I'm already satisfied" objection
- "I have to think about it" objection

Product Objection

Sometimes prospects voice an objection as it relates to the product, called a **product objection**. Comments such as "This isn't as good as your competitor's product" or "I don't want to take that kind of risk" are a reflection of a concern about the performance of the product. For complex purchases, prospects may not fully understand all the functions of the product due to lack of familiarity. Listening is an important skill to use, especially when a prospect voices a product objection. It's a good idea to handle product objections by describing warranties, using testimonials, getting the prospect engaged in a product demonstration, or presenting industry or third-party research to support your claims.[30] For example, consider the following:

> **Prospect**: *I'm not sure your product stacks up to your competition.*
>
> **You**: *So what you're saying is you are not convinced that this product will perform as well as others on the market? I'm glad you brought that up. I have customers who felt the same way when I began talking with them. Now they actually speak for the product themselves. Let's take a look at these three short videos from some of our current customers talking about the product performance and how much better it is than that of the competitors.*

product objection

A concern voiced by the prospect relating directly to the product.

Power Player: Lessons in Selling from Successful Salespeople

The Edge That Works
How do you compete with the big players in a crowded business-to-business (B2B) industry? Bob Ladner, founder and president of a market research firm in Florida, wanted to compete with the big players but couldn't get any prospects to give him a chance. Finally, in the middle of a sales presentation when he was overcoming objection after objection, he asked the prospect, "What do you want? A guarantee?" While it's almost impossible to offer a guarantee in the market research business, Ladner ultimately designed one that works. His successful firm now boasts major clients thanks to the guarantee. "The guarantee is a method of generating confidence," says Ladner.[31]

Source Objection

Some prospects voice objections about the company or about doing business with you as a salesperson. This is called a **source objection**. While this type of objection doesn't happen often, it does happen so it's important to know how to handle it.

Source objections as they relate to the company may be voiced with comments about the stability or financial health of the company or about how the company does business. But this is an opportunity for you to help your prospect understand your company's strengths. Consider the following example:

source objection

A barrier presented by the prospect relating to your company or to you.

> **Prospect**: *Your company hasn't been around for very long. How can I trust that your company will be here in three years to support the warranty?*
>
> **You**: *I'm glad you brought that up. I can see why that might be a concern for you, but let me give you some information about the company that I think will put your mind at ease. Our company is backed by some of the largest investors in the industry. The reason they invested in the company is because they see the vision of how we can bring more solutions to companies like yours. They have made a commitment to support all customer warranties for the next ten years. Talk about putting your money where your mouth is. The bottom line is that we are trying to reduce your risk.*

When a prospect has a source objection as it relates to you as a salesperson, it might not be as obvious to overcome. As with other objections, the best way to handle it is to get it out in the open:[32]

> **Prospect**: *I don't think we would make this purchase from you.*
>
> **You**: *I can respect that. May I ask you why?*

Price Objection

price objection

A concern voiced by the prospect about the perceived value of a product or service.

value

The worth that a product or service provides to a customer.

One of the most common objections is the **price objection**. It is important to ask probing questions to really understand the nature of this objection. Many prospects use the price objection as a negotiating ploy to determine how much flexibility there is in the pricing, while others use it as a way to object due to budget constraints. It's best to always be prepared for the price objection. The bottom line on the price objection is that people buy when they see the **value**. Cost (or price) is what the customer actually pays for the product or service. Value is the benefit that the customer receives from the product or service. It is value that customers assign to a product or service that determines the price. For example, value is what dictates that a shack on the beach in Monterey, California, is worth more than a similar home in Omaha, Nebraska. Or in another example, value is what causes customers to pay more for an iPod than a comparable MP3 player. Customers perceive that the design and function of an iPod delivers more value, even at a higher price, than comparable products made by other manufacturers. This is the essence of value.

"The customer is typically going to throw the price objection out there just out of habit, out of rote," according to sales trainer Chuck Reeves. When salespeople really listen to customers, Reeves says that they actually hear customers saying, "I don't see the value, and if you can convince me there is value, there is return, then I just might pay."[33] Even when budgets are tight, companies make adjustments to purchase the products or services that they find compelling and can help them profitably grow their business. If you think about it, the same is probably true for your personal purchasing; when you want something bad enough, you are able to somehow find the money for it.

Many salespeople believe that price is the barrier standing in the way of making a sale. That is, they think that cutting the price will help them get the sale. Many times salespeople are willing to cut the price or a product or service when a prospect objects because they feel that if the product or service is priced lower, they will get the sale. This situation is sometimes compounded if the salesperson rationalizes cutting the prices because she believes the margins are high enough, or even too high. This "sense of fairness" approach never recognizes the value that the product or service brings to the prospect. If simply reducing the price were the answer, selling would be easy—and probably wouldn't require your skills and intuition.

The truth is that price is not the driving factor in most purchasing decisions. More important, pricing shouldn't be determined based on your product cost. To be successful, you need to understand more about the value your product or service is delivering to the customer. It's the value that should determine the price, not product cost, or even prospect objections.[34]

So be prepared for the price objection. Preparation will make you look at the product or service through the eyes of the prospect and will help you establish the value. The price objection might be handled in the following way:

> **Prospect**: *Your prices are much higher than anyone else I've looked at.*
>
> **You**: *So what you're saying is you think that our prices are higher than others? Certainly, price is part of the equation, but it's also important to look at the value for the price. You mentioned that real-time inventory information was an important strategic issue for your business. Ours is the only product on the market that provides real-time inventory information without any integration costs. Our system is a true plug-and-play application so you can begin getting real-time inventory the day we sign the deal. In fact, one of my customers was concerned about the same thing, and now we provide his entire backend logistics.*

Video Clip

Handling the Price Objection
This video, featuring best-selling author and sales expert Jeffrey Gitomer, discusses how to handle the price objection.

View the video online at: http://www.youtube.com/embed/xrG_SFgcCHc

Timing Is Everything

Timing is everything when it comes to objections. While a prospect may raise an objection at any time during the selling process, it's best to keep the pricing discussion until the end of your sales presentation rather than discussing it early on. (In fact, the same is true about salary when you are on a job interview—always postpone the conversation about salary until an offer is made.) The reason for this is simple: it gives you the opportunity to talk about *value* rather than price.

FIGURE 11.4
It's easier to overcome the price objection when value has already been established in the prospect's mind.

© 2010 Jupiterimages Corporation

Think about the process of buying a new car. First, you go into the showroom and talk to a salesperson, then you go for a test drive and really fall in love with the car—how it handles, the smooth ride, the sound system, the GPS system, the smell of the leather seats. While you probably looked at the sticker price before you got into the car, you don't really start talking about price until after you determined that this car has what you want. At this point, the value has been established, which makes it easier for the salesperson to sell on value than to simply sell on price.[35]

Money Objection

money objection

A concern voiced by the prospect that relates to the budget or financial ability to make the purchase.

An objection that is related to the price objection is the **money objection**, sometimes called the budget objection, which relates to the prospect's financial ability to make the purchase. While some budget objections are true, when the prospect really doesn't have the means to purchase the product or service, it's important to avoid these types of objections with proper qualifying.

Even if you do your homework before you begin the selling process, there is still a good chance that a prospect may present a money objection. In some cases, the prospect's budget may not be large enough to accommodate the cost of your product or service. If this is true, you may determine that this is a prospect for the future when his business is large enough to afford your offering. However, it is worth probing to determine if the objection is price or budget related. Like the price objection, this objection is also related to value. When prospects can't see the value for the price, they object by saying either the price is too high or they can't afford it. The best way to handle it is to anticipate it and be prepared:

Prospect: *I really can't afford this right now.*

You: *You mentioned that you are already paying $5,000 per month on your current plan. This plan even gives you a broader service at a lower cost per transaction cost. If you continue with your current plan, you will actually be paying a higher cost per customer. The fact is you really can't afford not to switch. Let's try this service for thirty days, and I can prove to you that your cost per transaction will be lower.*

In this example, the broader service, which results in a lower cost per transaction, is what establishes the value in this example. It's the value that allows the salesperson to handle the money objection and make a trial close.

Another approach to this objection is to help the prospect see how they can afford your product or service. Consider the following example:

> **Prospect**: *We really can't afford this in our budget right now.*
>
> **You**: *It sounds like this can really help you increase your sales. If I can show you how this product can pay for itself, would you be interested?*

Power Point: Lessons in Selling from the Customer's Point of View

Just Ask

Want to be able to handle objections with ease? Deliver value. When prospects object with price or money objections, differentiate your product with a value-added service. If you want to know which service will make a difference—and help make the sale—just ask your customers. You'll be surprised what you learn when you just ask.[36] This article by Jack Carroll from *Inc.* will help you think differently about handling the price or money objection.

http://www.inc.com/articles/1998/12/14304.html

"I'm Already Satisfied" Objection

Many times prospects will object with what is called the **"I'm already satisfied" objection** (also called the need objection). This can be a more challenging objection than price because it might include a **hidden objection**, an objection that is not openly stated by the prospect but is an obstacle in the way of making the sale. In this situation, a prospect doesn't state his concern about making the purchase. Instead, he might ask trivial questions to avoid the issue or he might not ask any questions at all and simply state that he does not have a need for the product or service.[37] The best way to handle hidden objections is to bring them to the surface. In other words, ask questions to get your prospect to talk openly about her objections. If she says no simply continue to ask questions until you are able to identify the true objection.[38]

Anticipation is best to avoid the "I'm already satisfied" objection. According to sales maven Jeffrey Gitomer, engaging the prospect is key. He preaches that there is a huge difference between customers being satisfied and being ecstatic and profitable. The secret is in engaging the prospect and talking about the value that other customers have received. According to him, when a prospect is satisfied with their current supplier, it's the perfect time to make a sale.

"I'm already satisfied" objection

A barrier presented by the prospect that indicates that there is no need for the product or service.

hidden objection

An objection that is not openly stated by the prospect but is an obstacle in the way of making the sale.

Video Clip

Is Being Satisfied Good Enough?
That's the question to ask prospects if they use the "I'm already satisfied" objection, according to this video featuring Jeffrey Gitomer.

View the video online at: http://www.youtube.com/embed/04KnEx8CsbE

"I Have to Think about It" Objection

"I have to think about it" objection

An objection that is actually a stall.

While the **"I have to think about it" objection** might sound like an objection, it is actually a stall. This "objection" usually occurs when a prospect isn't completely comfortable with you and your product or service. This is the classic stall tactic and is a signal for you to build your relationship. Prospects usually use this objection when they are trying to mask some fear or risk that they have about committing to the sale. Your challenge is to uncover the risk that the prospect sees and build your relationship with him to build a deeper trust.[39] Just as with other objections, asking questions is important to understand why the prospect is stalling and what kind of information will help him feel more comfortable. In reality, this objection is one that is a signal for you to work on improving your relationship with the prospect:

Prospect: *I need some time to think about it.*

You: *I want to give you the time you need to think about it. But let's talk specifically about your reasons for buying now versus later.*

This type of approach will help you engage the prospect in conversation so you can understand more specifically what the barriers are to the sale.

Video Clip

Ultimate Stall

This video, featuring Jeffrey Gitomer, highlights how to deal with the "I have to think about it" objection.

View the video online at: http://www.youtube.com/embed/cCyf8af78A8

Key Takeaways

- There are six strategies that will help you handle any objection: view the objection as a question, respond to the objection with a question, restate the objection before answering the objection, take a pause before responding, use testimonials and past experiences, and never argue with the customer.
- There are six major types of objections: **product**, **source**, **price**, **money**, **need**, and **thinking about it** (which is actually a stall).

Exercises

1. Assume you are a sales rep for an interactive advertising company. Your prospect is learning about how social networking works and has responded to your presentation with the following comment: "I'm not sure this is really for us." What type of objection is this? How would you respond?

2. Imagine that you are a sales rep for a commercial landscaping company. You have just finished a presentation that includes a five-year landscaping plan for your client's property. She responded by saying that she doesn't think there's enough money in the budget for the plan. What kind of objection is this? How would you respond to her?

3. Assume you just presented your ideas to help your prospect increase traffic to his store by adding a sign on the side of the building. The customer was polite and listened to the presentation but said that he's not sure he really needs the additional sign since there is already one in front of the store. What type of objection is this? How would you respond?

4. Choose a type of car that you might like to own. Review the company's Web site along with Edmonds.com to identify the elements that create value for the car. How does the value relate to the price?

5. Assume you work for the school you are attending and are responsible for selling sponsorships of campus events to local companies such as restaurants, gyms, and retail stores. If your prospects say the price is too high, how would you overcome this objection?

6. Visit a retail store that engages in personal selling. Assume you are a customer for the product and present an objection to the salesperson. Record how she responds to it. Is it an

effective handling of your objection? If so, why? If not, what you would suggest to make it more effective?

7. Read the objection outlined in this article: http://blogs.bnet.com/salesmachine/?p=5207&tag=content;col1. Then, take the quiz to identify the correct answer.

11.3 *Selling U*: How to Overcome Objections in a Job Interview

Learning Objectives

1. Learn about common objections you may hear in a job interview and the best way to respond.
2. Understand how follow-up to a job interview can help "overcome objections."

It's exciting to get a call to go on a job interview. During your preparation (described in detail in the *Selling U* section of Chapter 10), you will, of course, research the company and learn everything you can about how it does business. You'll identify some questions that you want to ask because you realize that a job interview is a two-sided exchange—the company wants to learn about you, and you want to learn about the company. You'll plan your wardrobe, transportation, and other details well in advance of the big day. But one thing you may not think about is how to overcome objections during the job interview.

Common Interview "Objections"

Be prepared to answer the most common objections that may be voiced during your interview. Focus on the positive and keep your answers professional. In fact, you should practice your answers to these questions out loud so that your answers are crisp and conversational. When an interviewer presents an objection, take a breath before you answer the question. Restate the objection and then answer it. It's best not to dwell on an objection and talk too much, simply handle them and move on.[40] Here are some common objections and suggested ways to handle them.

Objection 1: You Don't Have Enough Experience

The best way to anticipate and even avoid this objection is to review your portfolio during the interview (see the *Selling U* section of Chapter 6 for more details about preparing your portfolio).[41] A portfolio is a visual way to demonstrate your skills and experience. It's one thing to talk about what you've done, it's quite another to bring it alive to your interviewer. It's especially important to show your work from internships, major class projects, volunteer projects, and other examples of your work.

Objection 2: I'm Not Sure You Will Fit In with the Team

This is another opportunity to refer to your portfolio by talking about projects that you work on with other people. Chances are you've worked on teams for class projects, internships, volunteer projects, and other areas. Be prepared with specific examples about how you have worked in collaboration with a team or taken on the leadership role within a team.[42]

Objection 3: The Position Doesn't Pay as Much as You Are Looking For

Your response to this objection should be something like "Salary is only one part of compensation. I'm looking for the right opportunity, and I'm willing to look at other areas of the total compensation program, including benefits, advancement, exposure, and other elements of my personal and professional growth." It's best not to take this conversation into a salary discussion. Wait to have the salary conversation until the company has extended an offer. It's a good idea to have a salary range in mind *before* you go into an interview. Do your research on Web sites such as Salary.com so that you are prepared if your interviewer asks how much you are expecting as a starting salary.[43]

Objection 4: You're Too Experienced for This Position

When you are starting out, it will be rare to hear that you have too much experience for a particular position. However, if you do hear it, be ready with the right answer. It's always best to seek a job you really want. But starting at a level that might be below your expectations is a good strategy, especially in this economy.

When interviewers say this, they are worried that when the job you want comes along, you will leave. Answer this objection by pointing out that you are willing and excited about learning about the business from the ground up. Based on your research of the company, give your interviewer a specific reason about why you want to work for that particular company. People are more willing to give you a chance if you are really interested in working for the company.

"Hidden Objections" during Job Interviews

Although there are some common objections you may hear in a job interview, chances are you will rarely hear an objection on a job interview. This is one major difference between a sales call and an interview. Most managers and recruiters respond during an interview in a more neutral way so as not to imply that the job is going to one candidate over another.[44] Prospective employers prefer to interview all the candidates and then make their hiring decision. Therefore, their objections are often more like hidden objections, those that are not openly stated during the interview. Unlike the sales call, it is not appropriate to keep probing to identify the objection. The best way to overcome objections, hidden or stated, is to be prepared to sell yourself in the most compelling way possible.

The concept of value, described earlier in this chapter, can be a successful way to overcome objections in a job interview whether the objections are stated or hidden. Prepare for the interview, understand the company's needs, and demonstrate how you can meet the needs. Simple. Effective. Powerful.

Follow Up after Job Interviews: Set Yourself Apart

After you've shaken hands and finished your interview, keep in mind that your ability to stand out is not over. Follow-up is the currency of sales; those who follow up significantly increase their chances of getting the sale (or getting the job). Here are some ways to follow up and make yourself memorable.

Thank-You E-mail after a Job Interview

Prospective employers want people who want to work for the company. A thank-you note can set you apart from other candidates and show your interviewer that you really want the job (it's easy for every candidate to *say* she wants the job, but not every candidate writes a thank-you note).

You have the opportunity to say thank you more than once. It's also a good idea to take advantage of every opportunity to demonstrate your interest and enthusiasm for the company. Start with a thank-you e-mail that you send the day of the interview. It's important to use e-mail to thank your interviewer for his time, and it is also is the perfect way to deliver value. Take a minute and recap some of the topics you discussed with each interviewer (if there was more than one). Jot down a list and go online and look for an article, video, or interesting blog that would be worth sharing. Send a personal thank-you e-mail to everyone with whom you interviewed (no group e-mails here). Also, be sure to send a thank-you e-mail to the recruiter, if you worked with one to get the interview. It's important to remember that a thank-you e-mail should be as formal and professional as a handwritten thank-you note.

Now, it's time to write your thank-you e-mail. There are three major parts to a thank-you e-mail. It can be short, but effective.

- First, thank your interviewer for her time.

- Mention something specific that you discussed. Include the link in the e-mail.

- Close your e-mail with a note about next steps.

See Figure 11.5 for a sample thank you e-mail. Additional sample thank-you e-mail notes can also be found at http://jobsearch.about.com/od/thankyouletters/a/thankyouemail.htm.

FIGURE 11.5 Sample Thank-You E-mail

To: Chris Talbert
From: Lee Lonsky
Re: Thank you

Dear Chris,

Thank you so much for taking the time to meet with me today. I thoroughly enjoyed our conversation about the challenges ahead for Horizons Healthcare. It sounds like your efforts to change the culture are working. I thought you might like this video book brief for *Collaboration* by Morten Hansen from BNET.com. It highlights the points we talked about in our conversation about the culture of Horizons Healthcare and the role teamwork and idea sharing play in the success of an organization.

http://www.bnet.com/2435-13724_23-0.html?tag=width;gums

Again, thanks for your time and insights. I'm looking forward to the next steps in the process.

Sincerely,
Lee Lonsky

Handwritten Thank-You Note

Sending a thank-you e-mail is good etiquette, and it reminds your interviewer that you can deliver value to the organization. But don't stop there. As soon as you send your thank-you e-mail, write a handwritten thank-you note to each person with whom you interviewed. You might think that it is unusual to send two thank-you notes, but it is the perfect way to communicate your interest and value to your interviewer in two ways: the thank-you e-mail demonstrates immediacy and helps you deliver value with a link to a relevant article, video, or blog, and the handwritten thank-you note provides a personal touch that few candidates take the time to do. As with the thank-you e-mail, timing is important for the handwritten note. It's best to write and mail it the same day so your interviewer receives it within a day or two of the interview. It's the perfect way to reinforce the fact that you go the extra mile to make an impression and build a relationship.

FIGURE 11.6
Take the time to send a personal handwritten thank-you note within twenty-four hours to everyone with whom you interviewed.

© 2010 Jupiterimages Corporation

Video Clip

Thank-You Note
This video highlights some key elements of a handwritten thank-you note.

View the video online at: http://www.youtube.com/embed/XhxTYEwpPLI

See Figure 11.7 for a sample handwritten thank-you note. Additional sample thank-you notes can also be found at http://jobsearch.about.com/od/thankyouletters/a/samplethankyou.htm.

FIGURE 11.7 Sample Handwritten Thank-You Note

Dear Chris,
Thank you again for taking the time to meet with me on Wednesday. I enjoyed hearing your perspective about the opportunities at Horizons Healthcare. I appreciate you taking the time to review the organizational structure as well as the expectations for the position. I was especially interested in your comments about the corporate culture. It sounds like all the teamwork and planning is paying off.

Thanks again for your time and insights. I'm looking forward to the next steps.

Sincerely,

Lee Lonsky

You've Got the Power: Tips for Your Job Search

*Do*s and *Don't*s of Thank-You Notes

Here are some tips for writing effective thank-you e-mails and notes:

- **Do** ask for a business card at the end of each interview so that you have the correct spelling and title for each person with whom you interviewed.[45]
- **Do** write individual thank-you notes to each person with whom you interviewed. If a recruiter arranged the interview, send a thank-you e-mail or note to her, too.[46]
- **Do** write a thank-you e-mail or note even if you are not interested in the job. It's always a good idea to say thank you to someone for his time.[47]
- **Do** send a thank-you e-mail or note within twenty-four hours.
- **Do** proof your thank-you e-mail or note before you send it, including the spelling of the person's name.

Here are some things to avoid when sending thank-you e-mails and notes:

- **Don't** stop job hunting even if you had a good interview. The job isn't yours until you get an offer.[48]
- **Don't** bother the employer and follow up in a way that becomes annoying.[49]
- **Don't** follow up sooner than the interviewer or recruiter indicates is appropriate.

What If You Don't Hear Back?

At the end of a job interview, it's a good idea to ask about next steps. Usually interviewers or recruiters will tell you the expected time frame in which they will make a decision. This is valuable information because it will help you determine how and when you should follow up.

If you don't hear back from the employer or recruiter within the specified time frame, it's recommended that you call and follow up. Companies frequently have good intentions of making a decision quickly, but other business issues take priority. Following up with a phone call helps remind your prospective employer that you are interested in the position. While it is appropriate to follow up by e-mail, it is more effective to follow up by phone. It's easier to have a conversation with the interviewer or recruiter and get some insight about the timing as well as reinforcing why you are a good choice for the position. Continue to do research on the company so that when you follow up, you can discuss company news. For example, you might say something like "I noticed that you were recently awarded the ACON business. It sounds like this is an exciting time at the agency and one that will need some motivated salespeople. I wanted to follow up on our conversation last week to see where you stand with filling the position."

Follow-Up Tip

Set up a Google News Alert (http://www.google.com/alerts) using keywords for every company in which you are interested in working. The news alerts will be delivered to your e-mail (or other source you specify), and you will know all the latest news about the company—as it happens. It's a good idea to send an e-mail to your contact about the news as a follow-up and a way to keep in touch.

Follow-Up after Sending Résumés

You can see that follow-up is critical after an interview. It helps overcome objections even after the interview is over. The same principle of follow-up applies to every contact you make during your job search.

When you use the tools described in the *Selling U* sections of Chapter 7 and Chapter 8 to get the word out about your personal brand, follow-up will be especially important. Your list of twenty-five target companies and the appropriate people to contact at each that you created in the *Selling U* section of Chapter 7 should include a phone number and e-mail address for each person on your follow-up list. Within one week of sending a cover letter and résumé, a phone call to each person (or at least the top twenty people) on your mailing list will help reinforce your cover letter and résumé and give you the opportunity to sell yourself on the phone.

Follow-Up after Networking

You learned about the power of networking in Chapter 3. But like other forms of contact, networking requires follow-ups. Make it a point to follow up by e-mail or phone with each person on your networking list every four to six weeks.

It's especially important to follow up quickly with those people with whom you connected about a possible job or contact to someone at a company. It's appropriate to follow up within a week, unless the person told you otherwise.

Key Takeaways

- Unlike a sales call, a job interview usually doesn't include stated objections.
- The secret to overcoming hidden objections such as experience or salary is to be prepared and establish the value you can bring to the company during the interview.
- Follow up after a job interview is a powerful way to make yourself memorable even after the interview is over.
- Thank-you notes (both e-mail and handwritten) should be sent within twenty-four hours of an interview to each person with whom you met. It's also a good idea to send one to the recruiter who arranged the interview.
- Thank-you notes are a reflection of your personal brand. Correct spelling and grammar are required, including each person's name and title.
- Follow-up, which may include a phone call or e-mail, is also important for each stage of your job search.

Exercises

1. Assume you went on an interview for a job you want. Write a thank-you e-mail and handwritten thank-you note to the person with whom you interviewed.
2. Imagine that you are networking with someone who said his company may have an opening and asked you for your résumé. It's been a week since you sent your résumé to him. When would you follow up? How would you follow up?
3. Assume that you are on a job interview and the interviewer says, "You have an interesting background, but I'm not sure you have the experience we need for this position." How would you respond?

11.4 Review and Practice

Power Wrap-Up

Now that you have read this chapter, you should be able to understand how to handle objections.

- You **understand** objections are a normal part of the selling process and are not a personal reflection on you.
- You **learn** that objections are opportunities to build a relationship.
- You **recognize** that anticipating objections is the best way to handle them.
- You **understand** the role that risk plays in your prospect's decision and how to help him minimize the risk.
- You can **list** the six strategies for handling objections.
- You can **discuss** the five types of objections and how to handle them.
- You **learn** how to handle objections in job interviews.
- You **understand** how to use a follow-up, including thank-you notes, to set yourself apart and overcome objections even after the interview.

Test Your Power Knowledge (answers are below)

1. What is an objection?
2. What is the best way to anticipate objections?
3. At what point in the selling process might the prospect or customer object?
4. Name the six strategies to handle an objection.
5. Name the five types of objections.
6. What is value?
7. What is a hidden objection?
8. How can you overcome objections after a job interview?

Power (Role) Play

Now it's time to put what you've learned into practice. Following are two roles that are involved in the same selling situation—one role is the customer, and the other is the salesperson. This will give you the opportunity to think about this selling situation from the point of view of both the customer and the salesperson.

Read each role carefully along with the discussion questions. Then, be prepared to play either of the roles in class using the concepts covered in this chapter. You may be asked to discuss the roles and do a role-play in groups or individually.

Meeting Objection

Role: Meeting planner at Capstone Industries, a distribution company

You are responsible for planning the annual meeting for the company. It is the only time that all five hundred employees are in one place. The three-day conference is usually quite a lavish affair; however, this year the budget is much smaller. Your objective is to book a five-star venue despite the budget reduction. You have just taken a tour of the lavish Premier Hotel, and you are impressed. However, the price you received in the proposal is still too high considering the fact that you would be booking five hundred rooms for three nights and three meals per day plus snacks, not to mention the additional business the lounge will realize from your attendees.

- Now that the salesperson has made his presentation, what will you say to tell her that the price is too high?
- What are the points you want to make in your objection?

Role: Event sales rep, Premier Hotel

You are responsible for booking the events at this spectacular five-star hotel. The convention facilities are state-of-the-art and ideal for large corporate meetings. The accommodations are suites, not rooms, so two people can stay comfortably in each one, which helps reduce the overall cost of rooms. The service is impeccable and has ratings above the Ritz Carlton and Four Seasons. In fact, Premier Hotel has received the J. D. Power and Associates Award for the best service in the hospitality industry.

You have done your presentation along with a pricing proposal and presented it to the prospect. This is an important meeting for the hotel, and it's important that you close the sale. However, first you will need to handle some objections.

- What is the value that Premier Hotel offers to Capstone Industries for this meeting?
- What objections are you most likely to get?
- How you will prepare for each one?
- You are not willing to lower the price, so if you get the price objection, how will you handle it?

Put Your Power to Work: *Selling U* Activities

1. Assume you are on a job interview and the interviewer has indicated that you might be overqualified for the position. How would you prepare for a question like this? How would you respond?
2. Visit your campus career center and meet with a career counselor to discuss common objections that may come up in job interviews. How would you handle each one?
3. Meet with your advisor or one of your professors or other professional. Share your career aspirations with them. Ask each of them about objections he may have if he were interviewing you. How would you handle each objection?

Test Your Power Knowledge Answers

1. Questions or hesitancies on the part of the prospect or customer.
2. Review your presentation with someone, write down all the possible objections, and incorporate them into your presentation.
3. A prospect may object at any time, especially when you are setting up the appointment, during the presentation, and during the trial close.
4. View the objection as a question, respond to the objection with a question, restate the objection before answering the objection, take a pause before responding, use testimonials and past experiences, and never argue with the customer.
5. Product objection, source objection, price objection, money objection, "I'm already satisfied" objection, and "I have to think about it" objection.
6. Value is the worth that a product or service provides to a customer. It is not based on cost but on perceived benefit.
7. An objection that is not openly stated by the prospect but is an obstacle in the way of making the sale.
8. Send a personal thank-you e-mail and handwritten thank-you note within twenty-four hours of the interview.

Endnotes

1. John Boe, "Overcome Objections and Close the Sale," Agency Sales, September 27, 2003, http://www.johnboe.com/articles/close_the_sale.html (accessed May 16, 2010).

2. R. T. Edwards, "Power Selling," *American Salesman* 38, no. 3 (March 1993): 13.

3. William C. Moncrief and Greg W. Marshall, "The Evolution of the Seven Steps of Selling," *Industrial Marketing Management* 34, no. 1 (January 2005): 13–22.

4. John Boe, "Overcome Objections and Close the Sale," Agency Sales, September 2003, http://www.johnboe.com/articles/close_the_sale.html (accessed May 16, 2010).

5. Patty Morgan-Seager, "Handle Objections and Have Fun!" Multifamilypro, http://www.smmonline.com/Articles_handleobj.htm (accessed October 24, 2009).

6. "Hug Your Objections," Selling Power Sales Management Newsletter, August 15, 2007, http://www.sellingpower.com/content/newsletter/issue.php?pc=732 (accessed March 16, 2010).

7. Janaé Rubin, "Overcoming Objections" *Folio*, November 2005, 80–81.

8. Jeffrey Gitomer, *Little Red Book of Selling: 12.5 Principles of Sales Greatness* (Austin, TX: Bard Press, 2005), 153, 157.

9. Paul Karasik and James Benson, *22 Keys to Sales Success* (New York: Bloomberg Press, 2004), 119.

10. Felice Philip Verrecchia, "How to Identify and Overcome Objections," Edward Lowe Peerspectives, August 11, 2004, http://www.bankseta.org.za/downloads/faisll/benefits/objections.pdf (accessed October 24, 2009).

11. Felice Philip Verrecchia, "How to Identify and Overcome Objections," Edward Lowe Peerspectives, August 11, 2004, http://www.bankseta.org.za/downloads/faisll/benefits/objections.pdf (accessed October 24, 2009).

12. Keith Rosen, "Respond to your Prospect's Objections," AllBusiness, http://www.AllBusiness.com/sales/selling-techniques-active-listening/4019422-1.html (accessed May 16, 2010).

13. Janaé Rubin, "Overcoming Objections" *Folio*, November 2005, 80–81.

14. Mike Hofman and April Joyner, "A Salesforce Built around Cold Calling," *Inc.*, September 1, 2009, http://www.inc.com/magazine/20090901/a-sales-force-built-around-cold-calling.html (accessed November 22, 2009).

15. John Boe, "Overcome Objections and Close the Sale," Agency Sales, September 2003, http://www.johnboe.com/articles/close_the_sale.html (accessed May 16, 2010).

16. Joan Leotta, "Overcoming Doubts: The Road to a Sale Is Blocked by the Prospect's Doubts," *Selling Power* 20, no. 2, http://www.sellingpower.com/content/article.php?a=5351 (accessed March 16, 2010).

17. William F. Kendy, "An Uncertain Situation: How to Kick-Start the Hesitant Buyer," *Selling Power* 27, no. 9, http://www.sellingpower.com/content/article.php?a=7658 (accessed March 16, 2010).

18. Jeffrey Gitomer, "Objection Prevention & Objection Cure," video, May 18, 2009, http://www.youtube.com/watch?v=CgfmcuE_06w (accessed October 24, 2009).

19. "Telemarketing Tips about Overcoming Objections," September 25, 2009, http://www.mindtools.com/pages/article/newTMC_88.htm (accessed October 25, 2009).

20. "Telemarketing Tips about Overcoming Objections," September 25, 2009, http://www.articlesbase.com/sales-articles/telemarketing-tips-about-overcoming-objections-457823.html (accessed October 25, 2009).

21. Keith Rosen, "Respond to your Prospect's Objections," AllBusiness, http://www.AllBusiness.com/sales/selling-techniques-active-listening/4019422-1.html (accessed May 16, 2010).

22. Pam Lontos, "10 Strategies for Dealing with Objections," FrogPond, http://www.frogpond.com/articles.cfm?articleid=plontos12 (accessed October 24, 2009).

23. Keith Rosen, "Respond to your Prospect's Objections," AllBusiness, http://www.AllBusiness.com/sales/selling-techniques-active-listening/4019422-1.html (accessed May 16, 2010).

24. Pam Lontos, "10 Strategies for Dealing with Objections," FrogPond, http://www.frogpond.com/articles.cfm?articleid=plontos12 (accessed October 24, 2009).

25. Felice Philip Verrecchia, "How to Identify and Overcome Objections," Edward Lowe Peerspectives, August 11, 2004, http://www.bankseta.org.za/downloads/faisll/benefits/objections.pdf (accessed October 24, 2009).

26. Felice Philip Verrecchia, "How to Identify and Overcome Objections," Edward Lowe Peerspectives, August 11, 2004, http://www.bankseta.org.za/downloads/faisll/benefits/objections.pdf (accessed October 24, 2009).

27. Bob Bly, "Overcoming Objections," http://bly.com/blog/general/overcoming-objections (accessed January 6, 2010).

28. Felice Philip Verrecchia, "How to Identify and Overcome Objections," Edward Lowe Peerspectives, August 11, 2004, http://www.bankseta.org.za/downloads/faisll/benefits/objections.pdf (accessed October 24, 2009).

29. Felice Philip Verrecchia, "How to Identify and Overcome Objections," Edward Lowe Peerspectives, August 11, 2004, http://www.edwardlowe.org/index.elf?page=sserc&storyid=6407&function=story (accessed October 24, 2009).

30. Charles M. Futrell, *Fundamentals of Selling: Customers for Life through Service*, 10th ed. (New York: McGraw-Hill Irwin, 2008), 385.

31. Leslie M. Schultz, "Guaranteed Advantage," *Inc.*, June 1, 1984, http://www.inc.com/magazine/19840601/7042.html (accessed October 24, 2009).

32. Charles M. Futrell, *Fundamentals of Selling: Customers for Life through Service*, 10th ed. (New York: McGraw-Hill Irwin, 2008), 386

33. Rick Weber, "How to Overcome the Price Objection," Trailer/Body Builders, January 1, 2003, http://trailer-bodybuilders.com/mag/trucks_overcome_price_objection (accessed November 7, 2009).

34. Tom Reilly, "What Is a Fair Price?" Tom Reilly Training, http://www.tomreillytraining.com/CPO%20article%205.htm (accessed November 11, 2009).

35. Lance Baird, "Overcoming the Price Objection," B2B Insights Blog, October 1, 2009, http://www.godfrey.com/blog/post/2009/10/01/276 (accessed November 7, 2009).

36. Jack Carroll, "Your Price is too High—Not!" *Inc.*, December 7, 1998, http://www.inc.com/articles/1998/12/14304.html (accessed November 22, 2009).

37. Charles M. Futrell, *Fundamentals of Selling: Customers for Life through Service*, 10th ed. (New York: McGraw-Hill Irwin, 2008), 378.

38. Pam Lontos, "10 Strategies for Dealing with Objections," FrogPond, http://www.frogpond.com/articles.cfm?articleid=plontos12 (accessed October 24, 2009).

39. Jeffrey Gitomer, "I'd Like to Think about It—and Other Sales Stalls," video, June 22, 2009, http://www.youtube.com/watch?v=cCyf8af78A8&feature=related (accessed October 24, 2009).

40. Randall S. Hansen and Katharine Hansen, "Closing the Sale and Overcoming Objections in the Job Interview," Quintessential Careers, http://www.quintcareers.com/printable/interview_objections_closing.html (accessed October 24, 2009).

41. Randall S. Hansen and Katharine Hansen, "Closing the Sale and Overcoming Objections in the Job Interview," Quintessential Careers, http://www.quintcareers.com/printable/interview_objections_closing.html (accessed October 24, 2009).

42. Randall S. Hansen and Katharine Hansen, "Closing the Sale and Overcoming Objections in the Job Interview," Quintessential Careers, http://www.quintcareers.com/printable/interview_objections_closing.html (accessed October 24, 2009).

43. Mary Moss, "Tips for Overcoming Objections during a Job Interview," Associated Content, August 13, 2007, http://www.associatedcontent.com/article/337859/tips_for_overcoming_objections_during.html?singlepage=true&cat=31 (accessed October 24, 2009).

44. Kim Richmond, *Brand You*, 3rd ed. (Upper Saddle River, NJ: Pearson Prentice Hall, 2008), 188.

45. Randall S. Hansen, "Job Interview Follow-Up Do's and Don'ts," Quintessential Careers, http://www.quintcareers.com/interview_follow-up-dos-donts.html (accessed November 8, 2009).

46. Randall S. Hansen, "Job Interview Follow-Up Do's and Don'ts," Quintessential Careers, http://www.quintcareers.com/interview_follow-up-dos-donts.html (accessed November 8, 2009).

47. Alison Doyle, "Writing Thank You Letters," About.com, http://jobsearch.about.com/od/thankyouletters/a/thankyouletters.htm (accessed November 8, 2009).

48. Randall S. Hansen, "Job Interview Follow-Up Do's and Don'ts," Quintessential Careers, http://www.quintcareers.com/interview_follow-up-dos-donts.html (accessed November 8, 2009).

49. Randall S. Hansen, "Job Interview Follow-Up Do's and Don'ts," Quintessential Careers, http://www.quintcareers.com/interview_follow-up-dos-donts.html (accessed November 8, 2009).

CHAPTER 12
Closing the Sale: The Power of Negotiating to Win

12.1 Closing Starts at the Beginning

Learning Objective

1. Discuss how to successfully close a sale.

"Show me the money."

It's this line from the classic 1996 movie *Jerry Maguire* that says it all about negotiating and closing the deal. In the movie, Jerry Maguire (Tom Cruise) is a sports agent who has second thoughts about the way business is conducted, and when he voices his concerns, he loses his job and all his clients except one. Maguire's passionate plea to his sole client, NFL player Rod Tidwell (Cuba Gooding, Jr.), has become a dramatic metaphor for negotiations and deal making ever since.[1]

While the movie is fictional, Maguire's character was based on real-life sports agent Leigh Steinberg, whose firm has negotiated and closed more than one hundred multimillion-dollar deals for high-profile clients in every professional sport. Steinberg's philosophy on negotiations and closing deals is based on the fact that life is filled with negotiations and deals—from deciding where to eat to buying houses and cars—and each should be handled with "a clear focus and principled philosophy."[2] There's nothing better than closing a big deal...the right way.

Whether it's a major professional sports deal, business deal, or a major purchase, it's easy to visualize what the "desired state" is in any kind of deal. You can actually see the athlete in your team's uniform, imagine two companies merging together as one, or see yourself in the car you want to buy. In fact, you negotiate every day. You negotiate with everyone from your roommate about how to arrange the furniture to your siblings about who will use the car. You might even negotiate with your professor about when you can hand in an assignment that is late.

The step in the selling process that moves the conversation to a sale (or the desired resolution) is the **close**. Many people believe that the close takes place at the end of the selling process because that's when the prospect agrees to buy the product or service. But nothing could be farther from the truth. **Closing** the sale, or getting the order, starts at the beginning of the selling process, long before you even come in contact with the prospect.

close

Consummation of the sale when the prospect agrees to the purchase.

closing

Bringing the sale to fruition or getting the sale.

Start Strong

"What it takes to win a championship is to have your preparation meet the opportunities, whether it's out on the racetrack or behind the scenes," according to NASCAR driver Kurt Busch.[3] This is true in sports and in selling. Winning in selling—delivering value to customers and to your company—requires good solid preparation and hard work. Sure, there are some sales that fall into your lap. Those are the ones that make it feel like selling is easy. But most sales don't happen that way. In fact, in many industries closing the sale may take weeks, months, or even years.

Despite the term "close," which implies the end, closing the sale starts with the first step in the selling process—qualifying. Sometimes salespeople want to fill their sales funnel (or pipeline) with lots of leads so they don't take the time or ask the right questions when they are qualifying. While it's true that you want to "go out and get as many *nos* as you can," you'll get a lot more *yeses* when you pitch to the right prospects.[4] In fact, the selling process is analogous to building a house; if the foundation is poured right, everything else will easily come together. The same is true in selling—prospecting is the foundation of the entire process.[5]

FIGURE 12.1

Closing the sale is more than one single event; it is an ongoing series of events that occurs throughout the selling process.

© 2010 Jupiterimages Corporation

Not only does closing start at the first point in the selling process, but it also is far from the end of the selling process. In fact, closing is a lot like graduation—it is actually the beginning, not the end. Just like graduation is not the end of your education but rather the beginning or commencement of the rest of your life, the closing in sales is the beginning of the relationship with the customer, not the end of the selling process.

Closing Time

The close sounds like it might be a definitive part of the selling process. It's actually not a single statement, question, or event. Rather, the close is an ongoing series of events that occurs throughout the selling process, according to Mary Delaney, vice president of sales for CareerBuilder.com.[6] Qualifying is the key; it's virtually impossible to close a sale with the wrong prospect. But the preparation doesn't stop there. The preapproach, approach, presentation, and overcoming objections all play a role in the closing the sale. According to author Ray Silverstein, the close is made in the first thirty seconds of the sales presentation. He says that's when a customer has an emotional response to you and your product or service story. Silverstein points to research that was conducted by William Brooks and Thomas Travisano that concludes that people want to buy from people they like and trust.[7] If this sounds familiar, it should be. The concept of building a relationship based on first impressions was covered in detail in Chapter 3. And understanding the difference between needs, which are rational, and wants, which are emotional, makes a difference in how your prospect perceives you and the message you are delivering.

To demonstrate that the close takes place at virtually every point in the selling process, Daniel Sheridan from Extensis Group LLC, a sales training consultancy, says it best: "If you're waiting for a proposal to close, it's too late." He goes on to say that the most important meeting is the first one because that's when trust and rapport are established.[8]

The close builds on everything that has already taken place throughout the selling process—rapport, trust, information sharing. It's also important to know what the close is not. The close is *not* a high-pressure exchange between seller and buyer. It's *not* a time when the salesperson resorts to trickery, manipulation, or other unsavory tactics just to get a sale.[9] While sales are the ultimate financial goal of the selling process, relationships, trust, and understanding a customer's business and providing cost-effective solutions are driving factors behind making the sale.[10] The same principles that guide the rest of the selling process also guide the close.

If closing is not a specific event that happens during the selling process, you might be wondering how you effectively get the order. You learned about the trial close in Chapter 10. The trial close can take place during any part of the selling process. The trial close gives you the opportunity to get specific feedback from the customer as it relates to her likelihood to make the purchase at any point during the process. While the trial close is most likely to come during the presentation, it could come even earlier in the process depending on the prospect and the product or service being purchased. A trial close asks for an opinion ("What is most important to you about this product or service?"), whereas a closing question asks for a decision ("Shall we complete the paperwork?").[11] The trial close gives you the opportunity to learn what the prospect is thinking and will give you some insight as to when to make the close. In some cases, the trial close may result in a close, but if it doesn't, the prospect's response provides valuable insight. The trial close should be done early and often throughout the selling process. Getting the prospect's opinion at various points throughout the process helps you determine your path and how and when you should make your close.[12]

ABC or ABO?

There is an old adage in selling that says, "Always Be Closing" (ABC). This means that a salesperson should never miss the opportunity to close a sale, no matter where it occurs in the selling process.[13] But in today's collaborative environment, it's better to approach closing more like "Always Be Opening" (ABO).[14] In other words, the best strategy is to always be helping your customer identify and solve his problems, just like you do when you are opening the selling process. Focus on asking the right questions and learning about how you can suggest solutions (in some cases, the solution might not even be your product or service). When you deliver value to your prospect, they will look to you for advice and counsel. "You become much more than a salesperson, you become their marketing expert, a resource, an ally," according to Mario Russo, general sales manager at radio station WBEN-FM in Philadelphia. "That's when you are successful in selling."[15]

It's true that asking for the order is critical for success in selling. But if you close too soon, you might run the risk that the customer thinks that the process is over and mentally moves on to something else.[16] That's why it is a good idea to ask **exploratory questions**: open-ended, nonthreatening questions that encourage your prospect to discuss her business needs. This helps supplement the information you gathered during the preapproach, enabling you to understand what the customer needs and how to meet those needs. For example, if you are selling accounting software, you might ask the following exploratory questions: "What are the top three activities that consume your people's time daily?" "What is the ideal way you would like your people to spend their time?" "What are the types of activities that you think can be automated?"[17] None of these is a hard-sell question. Rather, each question allows you to listen and gather information so that you can identify how you can help the prospect solve his problem.

While you always have your eye on the prize of closing a sale, the focus is to extend your relationship with your prospect beyond selling to servicing and being a business partner. That's what ABO is all about. When you focus your selling efforts in this way, it makes it easier to sell addi-

exploratory questions

Open-ended, nonthreatening questions that encourage your prospect to discuss their business needs.

tional products and services to existing customers because you are constantly learning about ways in which you and your company can add value.

Video Clip

Always Be Opening
This video featuring sales guru, Jeffrey Gitomer, highlights the shift from ABC to ABO.

View the video online at: http://www.youtube.com/embed/XGmKNSj8F64

Ask for the Order

When you focus on delivering value to your prospects and customers, you have earned the right to close or ask for the sale. It might seem obvious, but sometimes salespeople get caught up in the selling process and lose track of the fact that it is a buying process for the prospect. Sometimes, simple questions like "Will delivery on Tuesday work for you?" or "Should we start your service the week of the twenty-first?" help you and the customer focus on moving from the sales presentation to the delivery of the product or service. The specific closing questions will most likely differ based on the product or service you are selling. For example, in pharmaceutical sales, industry sales expert Jane Williams adds, "Never end a successful close without adding the proper patient dosing." She says, "It is very important that your physician prescribe your product properly."[18]

Sometimes salespeople don't feel comfortable asking for the order. Earn the right to ask for the order. Be confident: believe in yourself and your product or service.[19] The trust you establish from the beginning will translate into how you can close the sale. Closing the sale is all about presenting solutions for the biggest problems that your prospect faces. "If you can't help them with their biggest challenge, they won't have time for you," says Mary Delaney from CareerBuilder.[20] Author Barry Farber includes the element of confidence in the closing equation by saying, "The important factor that contributes to your success at closing (or knowing when to move on) is the leverage you have going in and the confidence you have to back it up."[21]

Not every contact results in a sale. Typically, 80 percent of prospects say no to a sales offer, and that percentage may be as high as 90 percent during these challenging economic times.[22] This underscores the fact that it usually takes several closes to actually close the sale. In some cases, it will take at least three tries. In other cases, it can take as many as five or more attempts. It's best to view closing as an ongoing part of the process, not a single event in which a prospect can say no. Confidence and the right mental attitude can make all the difference in being able to take all the *nos* on the way to *yeses*.[23]

When to Close

It's rare that a prospect will say, "I'm ready to close this deal." That step in the process usually belongs to the salesperson to actively close the sale. The best way to know when to close is to listen and watch. There are verbal and nonverbal cues that prospects provide that help you understand when she is ready for you to close. Here are some of the signals that the prospect is ready to buy:

- **When the prospect displays positive body language and interaction**. The prospect is engaged, interested, asks questions, reviews literature, and provides insights about his business.
- **When the prospect asks questions**. It is a good time to close after answering a question. Questions like "How long will delivery take?" or "How would that integrate into our current system?" are good cues that the prospect is close to buying.[24]
- **After you handle an objection**. This can be the perfect time to close, as you have just provided some insight that will help the customer make her decision.

Tips for Closing with a Committee

It's one thing to close a deal with an individual buyer. It's another thing to close with a buying committee. Here are four steps to close with a committee:

1. Have a specific, measurable, actionable, realistic, and time-bound (SMART) objective.
2. Know each committee member's name and role in the decision.
3. Identify your champion on the committee.
4. Leverage your champion to help "sell" the committee for you.[25]

FIGURE 12.2
Closing with a committee has some unique challenges.

© 2010 Jupiterimages Corporation

Types of Closes

There is not a single surefire way to close every sale. You should be prepared with several different types of closes and use them as appropriate for each situation. Some situations may require a combination of closes.

Direct Request Close

Direct request close means that you simply ask for the order. This is the most straightforward approach to a close. The fact is customers expect salespeople to ask for the order. This is a simple but effective way to close the sale.[26]

direct request close

Asks the prospect for the order.

> **You**: *Can I write up the order as we discussed?*
>
> **Prospect**: *I think we have covered everything. Yes, let's wrap it up.*

Benefit Summary Close

benefit summary close

Summarizes the benefits of the product or service as you have discussed them throughout the process.

The **benefit summary close** is a natural extension of the selling process. It simply summarizes the benefits of everything you have discussed throughout the process. This approach is especially effective when you are able to integrate and present benefits from the prospect's point of view that you have discussed over the course of several meetings. This is an opportunity to focus on how you can help her solve the largest problem that she faces.[27]

> **You**: *We've talked about the fact that speed is extremely important to you and your company. We can deliver your complete order to your twenty-seven construction sites within forty-eight hours of your commitment. In addition, you'll never be at risk for product performance because we guarantee the product 100 percent. If you ever have a problem, you just call us, and we'll replace it, no questions asked. Will you be willing to commit to an initial order of fifty?*
>
> **Prospect**: *Yes, we are looking for a partner who will not only provide the highest quality product but also be able to deliver it on time to all our locations. It sounds like you have your bases covered. If you can deliver what you say, we have a deal.*

Assumptive Close

assumptive close

Includes a question that when the prospect replies, he is committing to the sale.

The **assumptive close** asks a question that when the prospect replies, she is committing to the sale.[28] In other words, you are assuming that the customer is going to make the purchase. This close can be effective if you have done your job of developing trust and rapport with your prospect.

> **You**: *Shall we set you up on automatic billing?*
>
> **Prospect**: *Automatic billing definitely works best for us.*

Alternative-Choice Close

The **alternative-choice close** gives the prospect a choice between two options rather than a choice between buying and not buying.[29] This close is related to the assumptive close but gives your prospect the option of which product or service they will buy.[30]

You: *Would you prefer the white or blue?*

Prospect: *White is a more neutral color.*

Video Clip

Types of Closes
Hear Lisa Peskin, sales trainer at Business Development University, discuss the assumptive close and the alternative-choice close.

View the video online at: http://www.youtube.com/embed/a--98uNWob0

Compliment or Vanity Close

The **compliment (or vanity) close** helps you relate the purchase to the person and appeal to his or her sense of identity. You are making a positive connection between the purchase decision and the judgment of the buyer. When you use this approach to closing, you are confirming their role as a subject matter expert. You are, in fact, paying them a compliment.

alternative-choice close

Gives the prospect a choice between two options rather than a choice between buying and not buying.

compliment (or vanity) close

Relates the purchase to the person and appeal to his or her sense of identity by paying a compliment.

You:	One of the reasons I like calling on you is because you and your team really understand your business and your customer. You make it easy for your customer to buy from you and you offer them the product at a fair price. No games, no coupons just good, honest value. I think that our product can expand your offering to your customers with a company that shares your values about putting the customer first. I suggest you start by adding this item to your line and let's gauge the customer response.
Prospect:	I'm glad to hear that you feel that way. We do take our commitment to our customers very seriously and we only like to do business with people who feel the same way. I think it would be a good idea to start out with this one product and get some customer feedback. If they like it, we can talk about expanding to more products.

Combination Close

combination close

Using more than one of the closing approaches together to gain agreement on the sale.

It's best to have several types of closes ready to deliver. In some cases, it's a **combination of closes** that helps you ultimately gain agreement with the prospect. Virtually any of the different closes can be used together.

You:	The horsepower on this model is the highest in the industry. And the model is so efficient that it will lower your cost per unit in all your factories starting on day one. Can we wrap this up?
Prospect:	It looks like this is going to be a good short-term and long-term investment for us. Yes, let's get the paperwork ready.

Keep It Brief

Whatever close you use, it's best to keep it focused and brief. Salespeople have a habit of talking too much, especially when they're ready to close. According to Michelle Nichols, contributor for *BusinessWeek*, author, and sales trainer, "Ask yourself what aspect of your offering would customers want so badly that they would miss lunch or cross a very busy street to get it?"[31] That should be the focus of your close.

What Works?

Closing is part of the selling process. A process is a systematic approach, which, by its very nature, can be measured. You won't be able to be successful closing every sale. After all, even professional baseball players only hit the ball three times out of every ten pitches to be considered above average. While hitting the ball 100 percent of the time would be considered unrealistic, every professional hitter takes batting practice to help increase his batting average. His batting coach gives him tips as to how to stand, swing, and ultimately increase his percentage of hitting the ball. The same can be done in closing. Record the information about your closings—what works and what doesn't.[32]

You don't have to wait until the close to be able to track your progress. Sales veteran and author Barry Farber suggests managing accounts and the sales process with a simple visual tool. Post your prospects in the different stages of the sales cycle on a corkboard. While there are several software programs that perform this function, there's nothing more powerful than seeing it play out on the wall in front of you every day.[33]

Closing Complex Sales

A **complex sale** is a term that usually refers to high-value purchases (usually $100,000 and higher). Products and services such as enterprise systems, health care providers, commercial real estate, manufacturing equipment, logistics services, and other major business-to-business (B2B) purchases are considered complex sales. These types of sales have a long selling cycle because there is a lot at stake for such a major purchase and there are multiple people involved in the decision-making process. In fact, it may take as long as six months to three years to close the sale.[34] The product or service commitment is usually a long-term commitment with a contract as long as three, five, or even ten years or longer.

> **complex sale**
>
> Sale of a high-value product or service (usually over $100,000) that may take years to close.

While the selling skills discussed throughout this book apply to complex sales, there are some differences. According to Jeff Thull, author of *Mastering the Complex Sale*, there are four phases to a complex sale.

1. **Discover**. As with any other sale, research about the prospect and his needs is critical to success. During the discover phase, you set the stage for the ongoing relationship or engagement. This stage includes your detailed research about the company and its current provider including several meetings and phone calls with the prospect. It is at this stage that the prospect determines whether the engagement has potential.

2. **Diagnose**. In a complex sale, the decision is likely to be centered on what should be changed, such as the location of a warehouse, and includes a collaborative effort between the salesperson and the customer to determine if the change is feasible and desirable. This stage also includes extensive financial analysis to determine the impact of the decision on the company. The role of the salesperson is to be a true business partner and help the prospect understand the trade-offs and benefits of making a major change in the operation.

3. **Design**. Complex sales usually involve products and services that are customized for each customer. For example, an ad campaign, software, retail fixtures, or other major purchases are adapted, adjusted, or designed exclusively for that customer. At this stage, the sales rep works closely with key people in the customer's organization to design the best solution to fit the customer's needs.

4. **Deliver**. If the first three phases are implemented correctly, this final stage should logically follow. At this point, the key people at the customer's organization have been involved in the design and financial justification of the product or service so the presentation of the formal proposal should lead to acceptance. Then the efforts are focused on the delivery of the product or service and implementation. For products such as software and other major purchases, there may even be training, troubleshooting, and other transition issues that are handled by the salesperson.[35]

During each of these phases, it's important to identify all the decision makers and their positions in the process. As with every stage in the selling process, this is about asking the right questions. "How will your organization go about making this decision?" and "Who else do I need to talk to?" are good questions to ask during the discover phase so that you can get input and feedback from all involved at the beginning of the process. Once you identify all the people involved in the decision-making process, you'll want to identify the decision makers. Again, the right questions will help you focus your efforts appropriately. Knowing to whom the expense will be charged helps you identify the ultimate authority. The person who controls the budget is most likely different from the person who will be evaluating the technical aspects of the product or service. For example, while the chief information officer may make the budget decision, the systems implementation manager may be evaluating the technical aspects of the software. Finally, you want to identify the "power broker," the person who will ultimately make the final decision. This is usually the person, a subject-matter expert, who is the right hand of the person who controls the budget.[36] In other words, you want to identify with whom you will be negotiating and ultimately closing the sale.

Key Takeaways

- **Closing** is not an event but an ongoing part of the selling process that starts with prospecting and qualifying.
- **Closing** is all about helping the customer solve the single largest challenge he faces.
- Salespeople should always ask for the sale and make it easy for the customer to go from the conversation or sales presentation to the sale.
- The prospect provides verbal and nonverbal cues that make it easier to know when to close.
- There are several different types of **closes**. Each can effectively be used alone or in combination with other **closes**.
- **Complex sales** have a longer selling cycle, have many people involved in the decision making, and require a modified selling process.

Exercises

1. Assume you are selling coffee to a chain of restaurants. The buyer is very concerned about changing the brand of coffee that the restaurant uses because coffee is the last experience that the customer has with the restaurant and she doesn't want to change anything about the current experience. You have sampled your coffee in a blind taste test with her and in several of her restaurants, and all who have tasted it have chosen it as the better-tasting coffee. Now that she is convinced that this change would be a good one, which type of close would you use and why?

2. Assume you are selling paper to a major high-volume printer. Your firm has just introduced a new type of recycled paper that is less expensive than previous options. The buyer is someone whom you know and respect. You have learned a lot of what you know about the industry from him. You feel like you are bringing him a new product that can bring benefit to his company. You are preparing a compliment close. What would you include in the close?

3. Think about a high-ticket product or service that you recently purchased from a salesperson. How did the salesperson approach the close? Which approach to closing did she use? Was it effective? Why or why not?

4. Name the type of close that is used in each of the following examples:
   - "Would you like the pay-as-you-go or the family plan?"
   - "Shall we formalize the deal with your signature?"
   - "I really enjoy working with you and your team, and the way you are growing the company so fast. That's why I'd like to suggest this service plan."
   - "With the extra capacity, you'll be able to expand your service as you need it, yet it won't cost you any additional monthly fees. You can sign right here, and we can start your service on Monday."

5. Create a closing for each of the following situations and identify the type of close you are using:
   - You are a real estate agent, and you just finished showing a house to a newly married couple.
   - You are a fine jewelry salesperson, and you are showing a diamond engagement ring to a young man.
   - You are selling high-end electronics, and you are demonstrating a home theater system to a couple who just bought a new house (and it's the week before the Super Bowl). You are able to have it delivered and installed before Super Bowl Sunday.

- You are selling memberships to a health club, and you just took a couple on a tour. They recently moved to the area and are not familiar with all the competitors.
- You are selling accounting software, and you just finished a demonstration of the product for a group of lawyers in a firm.

12.2 Collaborate to Negotiate

Learning Objective

1. Learn how to negotiate so that all parties win.

Now that you have learned about the role of closing in the selling process and techniques to close the sale, it's time to dig a bit deeper into the process of negotiating. Depending on the product, service, or prospect, some sales might be straightforward like, for example, buying a computer ("I'll take the MacBook Pro with the fifteen-inch screen"). The price is posted and there is no room for negotiation. However in many situations, especially in business-to-business (B2B) selling, the pricing, length of contract, terms, options, delivery dates, services, and other aspects of the sale can all be negotiated. Negotiation, like selling, is a process. Following the process helps improve your chances of getting what you want.

The Art of Negotiation

Simply put, "**negotiating** is the act of discussing an issue between two or more parties with competing interests with the aim of coming to an agreement."[37] While that might sound like an impossible task, it is not as difficult as you might think. Even people with differing positions or points of view share a common interest, which becomes the basis for finding common ground. It's these common interests—security, economic health, personal recognition, control—that motivate people. If you take the time to understand your prospect's interests in a negotiation, you can successfully collaborate and find a solution that supports the interests of all parties.[38]

It is negotiating that provides profit for organizations. The collaboration between parties is what provides companies the opportunity to exchange goods and services for money.

negotiating

The act of discussing an issue between two or more parties with competing interests with the aim of coming to an agreement.

FIGURE 12.3

A successful negotiation ends with all parties agreeing to a compromise that is mutually beneficial.

© 2010 Jupiterimages Corporation

Link

Sales Negotiations
This series provides insights about how to negotiate in B2B selling.

Why negotiate:

http://www.sellingpower.com/content/video/?date=9/7/2007

How to negotiate using value:

http://www.sellingpower.com/content/video/?date=9/10/2007

What makes a good negotiation:

http://www.sellingpower.com/content/video/?date=9/11/2007

It might be helpful to think about a negotiation like an iceberg. Although you can see the tip of the iceberg, it can be deceiving because it does not tell the entire story. The same is true when you are negotiating; your prospect may say something that appears to be obvious but really wants to achieve other things that are hidden below the surface. Using the process of negotiation to learn more about your prospect's motivations and interests, you can understand what is below the tip of the iceberg. It's usually the part of the iceberg that you can't see that is more substantial and has more impact that the portion that is visible. When you come prepared, listen, and probe during the negotiation process, you can learn a lot about what lies below the tip of the iceberg and use this information to collaborate and eventually reach a common ground on the issues. For example, assume you are selling advertising space for a men's magazine to the hottest new beer company. Your contact at the beer company wants to get the word out about this new brand but has a very small budget, so he doesn't want to pay the full published rate for the ads. You don't want to sell at less than the published rate because that will lower the value of your ad space. The tip of the iceberg shows that this is a price negotiation. However, if you ask the right questions and listen more, you will learn that his ultimate objective is to get people to taste the beer because that is the best way to get new customers. If he can get a major sampling opportunity, then he can use it to go to other media partners to get other sampling campaigns. Now you have gotten below the surface of the iceberg and understand his motivations. With this additional information that wasn't readily visible on the surface, you can offer him an advertising package that includes ads in the magazine in addition to sampling opportunities at three upcoming national events that the magazine sponsors. Now the negotiation is focused on all parties winning by getting something they want, rather than simply negotiating on price. Getting below the surface provides valuable information and insights for negotiating.

Definition of Negotiating

Understand that negotiation takes place only *before* you agree to anything: "If you ask for something before a contract is signed, it's called 'negotiating.' If you ask for something after a contract is signed, it's called 'begging.' It's better to be a good negotiator than an expert beggar."[39]

Negotiate to Win-Win-Win

A successful negotiation can be measured by its ability to deliver a mutually beneficial solution to all parties. Some people believe that negotiation is an act that yields a "win" for one side and therefore a "lose" for the other side. The win-lose approach usually ends up in a lose-lose deal that doesn't work for anyone.[40] This philosophy of negotiating is selfish and short term. In addition, this approach implies that negotiation includes some kind of confrontation or manipulation to "trick" one side into doing something that it doesn't want to do. This is an unethical approach to negotiating which doesn't have a place in the business world.[41]

In selling, negotiating and closing go hand-in-hand. Just as closing is not a one-time event, negotiating is a process that has both short-term and long-term impacts.[42] The best negotiations are collaborative in nature and focus on delivering mutual satisfaction. According to Leigh Steinberg, lawyer and sports agent, "The goal is not to destroy the other side. The goal is to find the most profitable way to complete a deal that works for both sides."[43] Effective negotiating is based on respect and is seeded with open communication. Collaborative negotiating is dependent on the following three elements:[44]

1. **Building trust**.[45] You've already learned in Chapter 3 that establishing and building trust is key to relationship building. Negotiating is the ultimate extension of a relationship because you and your customer are agreeing to concede on some points to make the relationship go even farther. If your prospect signs a contract with your company for products or services, you are now even more dependent on each other to make the relationship work. It is the true win-win-win relationship. But if your prospect doesn't trust you, or you don't trust her, it will be difficult to enter

into a negotiation that will work for both of you and both of your companies. Building trust is the precursor to all business transactions, especially negotiating and closing.

The best way to build trust during the negotiation process is to gain trust before the formal negotiation. And then, during the formal negotiation, focus on the ends rather than the means.[46] In other words, instead of focusing on going head to head on each issue to be negotiated, concentrate on keeping the end goal in mind. Take the time to listen and understand exactly what is motivating your prospect so you can deliver what is important to her. "Negotiation is needs based," according to the online *Selling Power Sales Management Newsletter*. Understanding what is important to you and to your prospect drives your negotiation.[47]

Power Player: Lessons in Selling from Successful Salespeople

Honesty: The Best Negotiating Tool
Marty Rodriguez, one of the top real estate brokers worldwide for Century 21, has a simple formula for successful negotiations. She feels strongly that the real estate business isn't just about closing the deal—it's about providing honest information to help customers make the decision that's right for them. She tells prospects everything from the fact that there is structural damage on a property to whether she thinks a deal is out of their price range. "When you treat people that way they're not only happy to give you a commission—they become raving fans," according to Rodriguez.[48]

2. **Gaining commitment**.[49] Part of the process of closing is gaining commitment on every specific element of the sale. To do that effectively, strive to gain commitment long before you begin the formal negotiation. That means using every touch point you have at the company to help you. While you might think it is impossible to enlist others in your prospect's company to help you sell, consider the creativity of Art Fry, the creator of 3M Post-it notes. Fry stumbled upon the semisticky adhesive years before the product was introduced after creating the first version of the product as a way to mark hymns in his hymnal at church, he started giving his new invention to secretaries and coworkers at 3M. Soon secretaries were taking the pilgrimage between buildings on the 3M corporate campus just to get more of the sticky note pads. It was the demand from the people who used the product that ultimately generated interest in marketing the product to consumers. Fry successfully gained commitment from others in the company as a way to "sell" his new invention as a marketable product.[50]

3. **Managing opposition**.[51] It's true that although a negotiation is a collaborative effort, it is inherently a situation that addresses opposing views. The best way to manage this is to be prepared and know what's important to you and your prospect.

Power Selling: Lessons in Selling from Successful Companies

Searching for Common Ground
Microsoft wanted to be more dominant in the Internet search business and saw the acquisition of Yahoo! and the development of a new search engine named Bing as the way to gain market share quickly. Although Microsoft made a bid to buy Yahoo! in early 2008, it wasn't until July 2009 that a deal was closed. The original $45 billion takeover bid was shunned by Yahoo! much to the dismay and dissatisfaction of the shareholders because senior management wanted the company to remain a separate company.[52] Then, newly appointed Yahoo! CEO Carol Bartz saw an opportunity for common ground and negotiated a deal that was a win for everyone. Under the ten-year agreement, Microsoft's Bing will be used to power Yahoo! searches. Yahoo! will receive 88 percent of the revenue from all searches done on Yahoo! Web sites. Customers and advertisers now have a viable alternative to Google. Negotiating a solution that lets everyone win, including the customer, takes creativity and time.[53]

The Three Elements of Negotiation

Every negotiation, whether it is in business, politics, or your personal life, includes three critical elements. Understanding the role of these elements can help make you a better negotiator.

1. **Information**. When you do your homework, research, and ask questions about what is important to your prospect, you may be able to avoid negotiating on price all together. If you have information, and share information at the appropriate time, you can make a negotiation a huge win for everyone.[54]

2. **Power**. According to Herb Cohen, known as the world's best negotiator, power is based on perception. If you perceive you have the power to influence your situation, you do (conversely, if you don't believe you have the power, you don't).[55]

3. **Time**. Time is the great negotiator. Ninety percent of all negotiating occurs during the last 10 percent of the set time frame. Deadlines force decisions to be made and negotiations to come to fruition. Use time to your advantage by never revealing your deadline. Don't negotiate when you're in a hurry; chances are you won't get the result you want.[56]

Everything Is Negotiable

Many salespeople are afraid of negotiating. They are worried that they won't be up to the challenge to persuade someone to do what they want or to pay their price. Confidence and preparation go a long way to achieving a satisfactory result on both sides. Negotiating and closing are ways of gaining agreement. The old saying goes, "Everything is negotiable," and it's true. Your prospect believes the same thing so be prepared to negotiate about virtually every aspect of the sale. For less complex sales, the close might come as a result of a simple question at the end of the presentation. However, for more complex sales, there are various elements of the sale that must be agreed upon to close the sale. Elements such as price, length of contract, service, terms, and options are common points to be negotiated as part of the close.

One for All

Negotiations in B2B selling usually require multiple parties to be involved from both companies. You may find yourself negotiating one-on-one with a prospect or being a member of a negotiating team that works with a prospect team to negotiate a deal. Either way, the same principles of negotiating apply.

Many salespeople are concerned about negotiating price. They think that lowering the price will make the sale. In fact, price is rarely the motivating factor behind any purchase. That's not to say that price isn't important, but customers buy *value*, not price. If price were always the determining factor in purchases, premium brand such as Porsche, Apple, and Neiman Marcus would not exist. If you've ever shopped at Nordstrom, Banana Republic, or Abercrombie & Fitch, you decided that those retailers offered more value than Old Navy, eBay, or Wal-Mart for the item you bought. Price is a part of the value equation but not all of it. According to author Kelley Robertson, "Everything you say and do from the first contact with a prospect affects the value of your product or service in their mind."[57] That means establishing value with your presentation, demonstration, testimonials, follow-up, and everything that comes before the actual negotiation. How is your product or service different? What advantage does it offer? What is the most important problem it will solve for your prospect?[58]

Holding Firm

Forty percent of customers ask for a price concession not because they want it to close the sale but because "they had to ask."

Fifty percent of salespeople give price concessions on the first request.

The best salespeople negotiate on value, not price, and use creative negotiating to find common ground.[59]

If your prospect wants to negotiate on price, use your creative problem solving skills to get to the end that will work for all parties. Use **concessions**, something that you are willing to compromise, to create value during the negotiation. For example, use length of the contract, payment terms, service, delivery date, training, or other elements to demonstrate to your prospect that you are willing to work with him and give him something that has value to him.

concession

A point on which you are willing to compromise.

> **You**: *I'm not able to meet that price, but I can offer you three months of training worth $3,000 at no charge.*
>
> **Prospect**: *How many employees would be included in the training?*

The following is another example:

> **You**: *That pricing is only available if you carry the entire product line. If you add all ten of the products into all your stores, I can meet that pricing.*
>
> **Prospect**: *We can take a look at that.*

The bottom line is that it's best not to make a concession without getting a concession. In these examples, the salesperson always used another part of the deal to give something and get something in return. This win-win-win approach helps reach common ground and close the sale faster.[60]

Steps of the Negotiation Process

While negotiation has some elements of being an art, there are three specific steps that can be followed to help ensure success with each negotiation.

Three Steps of the Negotiation Process

Steps	Activities
1. Prenegotiation	• Get in the right frame of mind; be confident about the value of your product. • Do your homework; know who's sitting on the other side of the table and what's important to him. • Set prenegotiation goals; identify the minimum that you will accept for the deal and be ready to walk away if you can't get it. • Identify an offer that is higher than your prenegotiation goals to allow some room for negotiating.
2. Negotiation	• Make your initial offer and hold firm. • Identify other "currencies" with which to negotiate to reach common ground. • Be specific and identify every element of the deal in detail; put it on paper to avoid surprises later. • If you encounter a deadlock, put the issue aside and come back to it at a later time in the negotiation. • Avoid getting emotionally involved; be ready to walk away if you can't make a deal that is mutually beneficial.
3. Postnegotiation	• Celebrate with all appropriate people; consider dinner, cocktails, or another get-together. • Use the negotiation to build your relationship. • Record what you've learned. • Be ready for the next negotiation.

Step 1: Prenegotiation

Start off in the right frame of mind. Be confident by knowing that you are one of the finalists for your prospect's business. If you are confident that you have the best product and represent the best value for the price, you already have the beginning of a good negotiation. On the other hand, if you're not confident or don't believe in the value of your product, chances are you will not negotiate well.[61]

Once you believe you are presenting the best option with the best value to your prospect, dig below the surface in research and conversation to learn what's really important to your prospect. Ask a lot of questions; negotiators report that they often have to ask five levels of "why" to get to the "root cause" or true motivator of the person with whom they are negotiating.[62]

prenegotiation goals

Objectives that are identified before a negotiation begins and which identify the minimum you are willing to accept to make the deal happen.

Identify your **prenegotiation goal**, the minimum that you will accept during the negotiation. This is critical to your success as a negotiator so that you don't give away more than you want in order to make the deal. Prenegotiation goals should be realistic based on what you want to get out of the negotiation and what your prospect wants or needs to get out of the negotiation. This is where you have the opportunity to explore creative solutions that may address different aspects of the sale. (Are you willing to provide additional services rather than provide a price concession? Will shorter payment terms help your prospect be able to sign on the dotted line?)

It's a good idea to realize that your prenegotiation goals should not be the same offer you put on the table. Always allow some negotiating room as the first offer is rarely, if ever, accepted. Your prospect wants to feel as if she was able to get you to move from your original position. When you identify your prenegotiation goals, you know where you may end up, and also give yourself some room to negotiate.[63]

Step 2: Negotiation

This is where it all comes together—your preparation, prenegotiation goals, strategy, and understanding of your prospect's needs. Although you have done your homework and set your prenegotiation goals, hold firm on your initial offer. This allows you to learn more about what your prospect thinks is important and why. If you give in too early in the process, your prospect will feel like the negotiation was too easy and may have an expectation of getting even more concessions than you are willing to give. The general rule of negotiating is not to accept the first offer. That means you will need to reiterate the value you deliver and hold firm to your initial offer.[64]

As the negotiation progresses, consider offering a concession to move toward common ground. But for every concession you give, get one in return. For example, "I'll be able to look at pricing like this if we were able to be your exclusive distributor in the Northeast." This is an example of using other "currencies" to make the negotiation work. In this case, the currency of exclusivity is used in exchange for a price concession.[65]

Specificity is key in negotiating and closing, because once an issue is negotiated, it will be difficult to revisit it. Define each negotiated point in specific terms such as the number of days until delivery, specific payment terms, options that are clearly spelled out, and any other information that will clearly define your agreement. In most cases, all these elements are included in the contract that is signed as a result of the negotiation. It's always best to clarify each point during the negotiation and put it on paper to avoid misconceptions, bad memories, or surprises down the road. If there is no contract, it's a good idea to follow up the negotiation with a written summary of the agreed upon points.[66]

If you encounter an issue during the negotiation that causes a **deadlock**, or a stop in the discussion, set the issue aside and revisit it after other elements have been negotiated. You may find a way to include the thorny issue in a concession for a different negotiating point. It's not worth getting held up on points during the negotiation; simply set them aside and revisit them at a later point in the negotiation. When you leave the most difficult issues until the end, other issues have already been resolved and both parties are motivated to find a resolution.[67]

> **deadlock**
>
> A point in the negotiation at which discussions stop due to disagreement on an issue.

Negotiator and author Herb Cohen says, "Negotiation is just a game. You care about the outcome, but not that much." You have to avoid getting emotionally involved in the negotiation because the more emotionally attached to the outcome you become, the more you push to get what you want.[68] Getting emotionally involved in a negotiation makes it extremely difficult to walk away from it. That's why many professional people such as actors and actresses, professional athletes, writers, and others have agents negotiate their contracts.[69] It's a good idea to remember that it's not personal, it's business.[70] Not all negotiations end in a deal. Based on your prenegotiation goals, you may need to walk away from a deal if it isn't mutually beneficial. Keep in mind that your ability to negotiate is directly linked to your ability to walk away from the deal. If you don't have any other options, you have given up any power you might have. It's a good idea to always keep your options open.[71]

Video Clip

This video features an excerpt of a speech by Herb Cohen. Cohen is an entertaining and thought-provoking speaker who underscores the concept of "care, but not too much" in negotiating.

View the video online at: http://www.youtube.com/embed/Ov64t4jvGbw?rel=0

Step 3: Postnegotiation

At this point, every element of the deal has been negotiated, agreed to, and documented on paper. It's a good idea to take some time to celebrate a successful negotiation including all appropriate people at dinner, cocktails, or another get-together. This is a good way to recognize everyone's contribution to making the negotiation a success and to look forward to enjoying the benefits of the partnership.[72] There's one thing that's true about every negotiation—it will surely lead to other negotiations in the future.[73]

Key Takeaways

- Many times closing includes **negotiating**, the act of discussing an issue between two or more parties with competing interests with the aim of coming to an agreement.
- A successful **negotiation** is one that focuses on open, honest communication and yields a win-win resolution.
- **Negotiations** require building trust, gaining commitment, and managing opposition.
- Every **negotiation** includes three elements—information, power, and time.
- **Negotiating** starts long before the formal exchange; it begins with your first communication with the prospect and includes every contact you have had with her. Those communications establish the value of your product or service.
- While price is a common **negotiating** point, it is rarely the deal breaker that most salespeople perceive it is.
- Every **negotiation** includes three parts—prenegotiation, negotiation, and postnegotiation.
- Avoid getting emotionally involved in a **negotiation** as it makes it easier to walk away, if need be.

Exercises

1. Assume you are buying a used car from someone. If your prenegotiation goal is $10,000 and he is holding firm at $12,000, how would you find common ground for a successful negotiation?

2. Assume you are buying a house from someone. She has indicated that the chandelier in the dining room has sentimental value. You think that the chandelier makes the dining room, and you want it included in the sale of the house. You are willing to increase your offer to reflect the inclusion of the chandelier. How would you approach this negotiation?

3. Assume you are selling medical supplies to a doctor's office and the doctor says, "I won't pay anything over $3,000 for the machine, take it or leave it." How would you respond?

4. Imagine that you are a sales rep for a paint manufacturer and you are selling to Home Depot. The buyer provided positive responses in all your previous meetings and is ready to narrow down his choices for paint suppliers.

   - Identify three ways you could prepare for your negotiation to make it as productive as possible.
   - How would you go about identifying your prenegotiation goals?

5. You are trying to sell accounting software to a regional grocery store chain, but negotiations have stalled. How can you get back on track?

6. Think about a negotiation in which you have been involved that yielded a win-win-win resolution. How did you get to the win-win-win solution? Think about a negotiation in which you have been involved that didn't result in an agreement. Why do you think the negotiation wasn't successful? What would have made it more successful?

7. How would you handle a situation in which a prospect wanted a guarantee that your company will not raise the price of the product he was buying for the next five years? Would you agree to hold the price to get the sale?

8. Contact a local law firm or company that specializes in negotiating. Invite a person from the firm to come to class and share tips and techniques that she uses in successful negotiations.

12.3 *Selling U*: Negotiating to Win for Your Job Offer

Learning Objective

1. Understand how to negotiate and accept the right job offer.

So you've completed all your interviews and it's the moment of truth...you are on the verge or receiving an internship or job offer. Congratulations!

As difficult as it has been to get to this point, you're not quite there yet. This is the stage of the job searching process that really tests your mettle to get what you want. Just like negotiating and closing (outlined in the previous sections of this chapter), the quality of the job offer starts long before you actually receive the offer.

Know What You're Worth

Before you even begin thinking about looking for an internship or job, your first step should be to determine your value based on the marketplace. As with every step of the selling process, doing your homework is key. If you don't do your research to find out competitive compensation packages for the position and city in which you are seeking an internship or job, you might be disappointed with the job offers you receive.

There are several Web sites—Salary.com, JobStar.com, and SalaryExpert.com are just a few—that include compensation ranges for hundreds of different positions in areas across the country. Visit the sites listed in Table 12.1 to gather compensation information before you go on any interviews.

TABLE 12.1 Web Sites for Researching Compensation

Riley Guide	http://rileyguide.com/salguides.html
Salary.com	http://swz.salary.com
JobStar.com	http://jobstar.org/tools/salary/sal-prof.php
SalaryExpert.com	http://www.salaryexpert.com/index.cfm?fuseaction=Main.Home_Personal
Bureau of Labor Statistics	http://www.bls.gov/NCS

It's a good idea to use these tools as a guide as there are many assumptions that are made when these numbers are prepared. However, this information can be extremely helpful to understand the range of compensation being paid for a specific role in a specific city.[74] You will be able to negotiate more effectively if you walk into every job interview knowing how much you are worth.[75]

Establish Your Value Early

Just as in the selling process, establishing your value begins with your first contact with your prospective employer. Many times you have the opportunity to meet at least one or two people at the company, usually someone in human resources as well as your hiring manager. In some cases, you may meet with several different people with whom you will be working. In some cases, you may also talk with or meet with a recruiter. At any rate, you have the opportunity to establish your value with as many people as you meet. Everything you say and do has an impact on how people perceive you and your value. Are your résumé and cover letter professional? Did you do your research before you contacted the employer? How did you make contact? When you went in for an interview, did you dress appropriately and professionally? Were you prepared for the interview? Did you bring samples of your work to demonstrate your skills? Did you follow up with a thank-you e-mail and handwritten thank-you note within twenty-four hours? All these elements help establish your value long before an offer is extended. When it comes to making an impression on a prospective employer, everything matters.

Just as in the selling process, if you do your homework and establish your value early in the process, you will be more likely to get the offer you want.

Compensation versus Salary

One thing to know before you walk into any interview: compensation is different from salary. **Compensation** is the total amount of money and benefits that you are paid for a particular position. Compensation can include salary, insurance, vacation or sick leave, stock options, signing bonus, car allowance, 401(k), child care or elder care assistance, and any other type of payment received in exchange for your services to the company. **Salary**, a fixed amount of money that is paid regularly in exchange for services provided, is only one element of compensation. When you are considering a job offer, it's best to keep in mind that salary is not the only element of compensation. This will allow you to be creative in your negotiating as there are several elements other than salary that can be included in your total compensation package.

Starting Out at a Start-Up

Working for a start-up company can be exciting and lucrative—with the right compensation agreement. The high-risk environment of a start-up might provide exactly the right place for you to start your career. But enter the business with your eyes wide open. "There's no shortage of start-ups to work for, but most are going to fail," says Greg Carney of Carney-Neuhaus.[76] This article provides insight about how to structure compensation with a start-up company.

http://career-advice.monster.com/salary-benefits/negotiation-tips/negotiating-compensation-startup/article.aspx.

compensation

Money and benefits received in exchange for providing services to a company including elements such as salary, commission, bonus, benefits, and any other elements in payment for providing services.

salary

A regular payment from an employer in exchange for services.

Timing Is Everything

Although you may want to discuss compensation on your first interview, it's a good idea to postpone discussing the topic as long as possible.[77] Just as in the selling process, you want to put focus on establishing your value and learning about what's important to your prospective employer before you begin discussing compensation. A word of caution: you should be prepared to give your desired salary range on an interview as many employers want to understand your salary expectations as soon as possible. If you can avoid the topic, do so until you receive a job offer. Here's an example of how you can deflect the conversation.

> **Interviewer**: *What are your salary expectations?*
>
> **You**: *I'm sure your total compensation package is competitive for the position. What's most important to me is the opportunity to learn and be a part of an organization like yours.*

If you are forced to give a salary range, be sure you can live with the lowest number you give. Once you say a number, it will be extremely difficult to negotiate above that salary.[78]

Receiving the Offer

Most job offers are extended over the phone, although some may be extended in a letter and still others may be presented in person. Since companies usually interview multiple candidates for each position, chances are you won't receive a job offer on an interview. However, you should be prepared to respond to a job offer if one is presented during an interview.

Video Clip

Responding to an Offer in an Interview
The following video provides suggestions about how to handle this situation.

View the video online at: http://www.youtube.com/embed/er2km7Aja1o

When you receive an offer, it will most likely come over the phone. When you get a phone call about an offer, write down every element of the offer (it's OK to ask the person to hold while you get a pencil and paper). Thank the person who made the offer and tell her how pleased you are to receive the offer. Even if you think you want to accept the offer, don't accept it right away.

You:	*I'm very excited about this offer. Thank you so much for extending it to me. It's a very big decision, and I'd like to have a few days to think about it. Can I get back to you on Thursday? What time is good for you to talk?*
Employer:	*I'm glad to hear that you are happy about the offer. We are all very excited about the prospect of you joining our team. I'm happy to answer any questions you might have about the company or the offer. Don't hesitate to give me a call. In fact, let me give you my cell phone number so you can call me at any time. Then let's touch base on Thursday at 10:00 a.m.*
You:	*I just want to repeat the elements of the offer so that I have it correct. The base salary is $45,000 with the opportunity to earn a bonus of 5 percent based on meeting performance objectives. There is a car allowance of $3,000 a month. I'll be eligible for medical insurance after thirty days of employment, and I'll receive one week of vacation after working for twelve months. Is that right?*

It's worth noting the time element of this negotiation. You should take as much time as you need to evaluate the offer, but you should be reasonable and state the time frame you need. Recall from earlier in this chapter that time is one of the elements that is always present in a negotiation. Sometimes a prospective employer or recruiter will try to create a deadline to force you to make a decision by a specific date. Use time to your advantage and negotiate for more time so that you don't feel as if you are under pressure to make this important decision.

Evaluating the Offer

Congratulations on your offer! Although it's a difficult economy, don't feel pressured to take the first offer you get. Take the first offer you get for a job you really want. This is a special moment; it is the time when the power shifts from the prospective employer to you (remember that power is one of the elements that is always present in a negotiation). Your prospective employer has now indicated that you are their choice for the position. You have the opportunity to take the offer, **counteroffer** (your response to the job offer), or walk away. Whatever your choice, you have the power. As soon as you make your choice, the power shifts back to your prospective employer. That's why it's a good idea to take your time and completely evaluate your offer before you respond.

Now that you have all the elements of the offer, you can begin to evaluate it. Just as in a negotiation in selling, identify what is important to you. Consider making a list that includes both elements of compensation as well as other elements such as culture, opportunity, environment, commuting distance, and so on. Figure 12.6 and Figure 12.7 can provide some ideas to help you create your list.[79],[80]

> **counteroffer**
>
> A candidate's response to a job offer.

FIGURE 12.6 Compensation Elements to Consider in a Job Offer

Salary

Bonus

Vacation, sick leave, personal holidays, time off

Health insurance (medical, dental, optical)

Life insurance

Stock options

401(k) or pension plan

Maternity leave

Child care

Tuition reimbursement

Relocation reimbursement

Travel reimbursement

FIGURE 12.7 Other Elements to Consider When Evaluating a Job Offer

Company culture

Work environment

Commuting time

Hours required

Flextime

Opportunity for personal development

Opportunity for advancement within
    the company

Type of work

People with whom you will be working

Performance/salary review timing

Only you can determine if a job offer is right for you. The following are some additional resources that you may want to review to help you evaluate a job offer:

- http://careerplanning.about.com/cs/joboffers/a/evaluate_offer.htm
- http://rileyguide.com/salguides.html
- http://www.ehow.com/how_2068763_evaluate-job-offer.html
- http://career-advice.monster.com/salary-benefits/Negotiation-Tips/Job-Offer-Evaluation-Checklist/article.aspx

Negotiating the Offer

After you have had the time to evaluate the job offer, it's time to identify any gaps that there might be between what you think is important and the offer. If you think the offer is perfect as is, then accept it as is. Keep in mind that many employers expect candidates to negotiate by presenting a counteroffer, a candidate's response to a job offer. Since the economy is challenging, candidates don't have as much bargaining power as when the economy is healthy. However, this is the time you have the most negotiating power with your prospective employer so it's a good idea to take advantage of the opportunity.

Video Clip

Should You Negotiate a Job Offer?
Hear why Tonya Murphy, general sales manager at WBEN-FM, thinks candidates should negotiate a job offer.

View the video online at: http://www.youtube.com/embed/Y80BDVO1BZk

This is the time when you should identify your prenegotiation goals. Remember that your prenegotiation goals are the minimum that you will accept. Your counteroffer will be above your prenegotiation goals to allow room for negotiation. You won't be able to negotiate every element of the offer. Choose one or two key areas and focus your negotiation on those. Keep in mind the things that are important to you and to your prospective employer so that you can easily find common ground. For example, if speed and availability are important to your prospective employer, you may want to use that fact to negotiate a more flexible work arrangement. While it may be difficult to negotiate a higher base salary in this economy, you may be able to negotiate on another area such as getting additional vacation time.[81]

When you have identified the areas you wish to negotiate along with your counteroffer for each, contact the recruiter or prospective employer to begin the negotiation. As with any negotiation, approach it with a confident, collaborative attitude. It's important to note that you should not accept the offer until you negotiate the offer. Once you accept the offer, you have lost your power to negotiate.

You: *I wanted to follow up and thank you again for the offer to join the company. I'm really excited about it. Based on the interviews, I believe I can bring value to your company. I wanted to talk about one area of the offer.*

Employer: *Great. What questions can I answer for you?*

You: *The base salary is lower than I expected. [Important note here: say this point and wait for a response. Many people feel obligated to talk more, but less is more in a negotiation.]*

Employer: *We have made the base salary as high as we could. There's really nothing we can do to make it any higher.*

You: *One of the things that could make the offer more attractive is additional vacation time.*

Employer: *We might be able to take a look at that. Let me touch base with Casey. I can't make you any promises, but I can talk to him and let you know.*

You: *That would be great. I really appreciate it.*

Just as in a selling negotiation, you have to be ready to accept the offer as is or be ready to walk away. That's a lot harder to do when you are negotiating on behalf of yourself since you are emotionally involved with the decision.

Video Clip

Negotiating a Job Offer
The following video outlines these key points about negotiating a job offer.

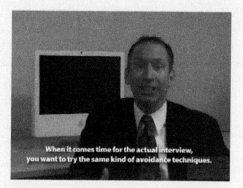

View the video online at: http://www.youtube.com/embed/B9chfMVXCz0

Link

Negotiating Tips

Read about how to negotiate your best compensation package.

http://career-advice.monster.com/salary-benefits/negotiation-tips/salary-negotiation-guide/article.aspx

You've Got the Power: Tips for Your Job Search

Negotiate before You Accept

Use your power when you receive a job offer. Thank the employer for the offer, evaluate it, and negotiate the offer *before* you accept it. Once you accept the offer, you have lost any power to negotiate.

The Offer Letter

Once you agree on the final elements of the offer, you should ask for an **offer letter**, a formal letter from the company (on company letterhead) that outlines the terms of the offer. All companies should provide an offer letter as a matter of course for an internship (paid or unpaid) or a job offer. If you received the original offer in the form of a letter, you already have the offer letter; however, you should request an updated letter to reflect the final offer on which you agreed. If you find any discrepancies in your offer letter, contact the person at the company as soon as possible to have a new offer letter issued.

A offer letter simply reiterates the terms of employment that you have negotiated and may be conditional based on requirements such as a background check or drug test or may make reference to company documents such as the benefits summary or employee handbook. While some information in offer letters may vary depending on the company, some key information should be included in the offer letter:

- Title
- Salary
- Bonus
- All other elements of compensation (e.g., stock options, benefits)
- Start date
- Any conditions of employment

Some companies request that you sign a copy of the offer letter and return it to the company. If this is the case, sign the letter and make a copy for your files before returning it to the company. The offer letter is your documentation of the compensation the company has agreed to give you.[82],[83] See sample offer letters in Figure 12.8 and Figure 12.9.

offer letter

A formal letter from the company (on company letterhead) that outlines the terms of the offer for employment.

FIGURE 12.8 Sample Offer Letter

Arnold Associates
77 Sixth Avenue Evanston, IL 60044
847-664-2345 www.arnoldassociates.com

June 1, 2010

Ms. Lakia Lee
3606 Walnut Creek Road
Chicago, IL 60614

Dear Lakia,

On behalf of Arnold Associates, I am pleased to offer you the position of Financial Analyst. In this important and very visible position you will report to Barry Johnson, Controller. Your start date will be June 8, 2010.

Your compensation package includes the following:
• Annual salary of $37,500 with first performance review in 6 months
• Bonus opportunity of 5% based on achievement of company and individual performance goals
• Two weeks of vacation every year
• All of the benefits as outlined in the Arnold Associates Benefits Handbook

This offer is contingent upon successfully passing a drug screening to be conducted by OMA Labs by June 15.

We are delighted to extend this offer to join the Arnold Associates team. Everyone who met you during the interview process was very impressed with you. We are looking forward to your response. Please don't hesitate to let me know if you have any questions.

Sincerely,

Manuel Santiago

Manuel Santiago
Human Resources Manager

FIGURE 12.9 Sample Offer Letter

Vista Global Pharmaceuticals
5 Wellness Circle
Wilmington, DE 30452

p. 800-999-2020
f. 302-999-2121
www.vista.com

March 1, 2010

Mr. Jason Sebastian
18 Center Street
New Bedford, DE 19095

Dear Jason,

We are pleased to extend an offer to join Vista Global Pharmaceuticals as a Territory Manager responsible for the Philadelphia, Southern New Jersey, and Delaware territory.

The compensation for the position includes $48,000 annual base salary; 5% commission on sales over $300,000; car allowance of $3,000 per month; and auto insurance for your car provided by the company. In addition, you are eligible for company benefits as specified in the Vista Global Pharmaceuticals Handbook.

Your start date is April 1, 2010. You should report to Building D, first floor at the campus at 5 Wellness Circle in Wilmington, DE, at 8:30 a.m. Please ask for Alena Scirnova when you arrive.

This offer is contingent on a successful background check. In addition, you will be required to take a drug screening administered by an outside lab and paid for by the company no later than April 1, 2010.

Please confirm your acceptance of this offer by signing and returning this letter to me by March 8, 2010. Please don't hesitate to let me know if you have any questions.

Welcome to Vista Global Pharmaceuticals.

Sincerely,

Walter G. Kordanina

Walter G. Kordanina
Manager, Human Resources and Talent Recruiting

I agree to the terms and accept this offer of employment.

_____
Name

_____
Signature

_____
Date

Key Takeaways

- Before you begin your job search, do your research and know what you are worth in the marketplace.
- **Salary** is only one element of total **compensation**. Use all elements of compensation to creatively negotiate to get what you want.
- Avoid discussing **compensation** as long as possible; don't bring it up unless the interviewer brings it up. Your goal on every interview is to establish your value so that your offer reflects what you are worth.
- Before you begin **negotiating** a job offer, be sure you understand all the elements of the offer.
- Carefully evaluate an internship or job offer based on what is important to you including the offer as well as other aspects of the job and company.
- Identify one or two elements of a job offer that you want to negotiate. Determine your **prenegotiation goals** for each and approach your prospective employer to discuss each element. Focus on what is important to the company as you negotiate each point.
- The final offer that you accept should be documented in an **offer letter**. Whether you are being offered an internship (paid or unpaid) or a full-time job, the company should provide an offer letter within a few days of your acceptance of the offer.

Exercises

1. Visit Salary.com, or one of the other Web sites mentioned in this section, and determine the total compensation for at least three different positions in which you are interested in pursuing. Is the compensation higher or lower than you expected for each position?
2. Identify three ways that you can establish your value in the eyes of your prospective employer during the interview process.
3. Assume you received a job offer with a base salary of $35,000 and commission of 10 percent. How would you plan to approach your prospective employer to increase your overall compensation?
4. Have you ever received an offer letter? If so, what position was it for? What information did it include?
5. When you are negotiating your job offer, is it ever appropriate to exaggerate your accomplishments a little bit to get an offer that you think you deserve? Why or why not?

12.4 Review and Practice

Power Wrap-Up

Now that you have read this chapter, you should be able to understand how closing and negotiation work in the selling process.

- You **learn** the role of the close in the selling process.
- You **understand** how the close is an opportunity to build a relationship.
- You **recognize** that closing is a natural part of the selling process.
- You can **list** the different types of closes.

- You **understand** how to negotiate so that all parties win.
- You **realize** that a job offer can be negotiated.

Test Your Power Knowledge (answers are below)

1. Explain the statement "The close, or getting the order, starts at the beginning of the selling process, long before you even come in contact with the prospect."
2. What is a trial close?
3. Describe three times during a sales call that are good times to close.
4. Assume you are selling a video game. Give an example of an alternative-choice close.
5. Describe the role that trust plays in negotiating.
6. What are the three elements that are always present in a negotiation?
7. Why do salespeople think they need to lower the price to have a successful negotiation?
8. Describe what a concession is in a negotiation.
9. Name the three steps in the negotiation process.
10. What is a prenegotiation goal?
11. Is the following statement true or false? You can get more as a result of a negotiation in which you are emotionally involved.
12. How do you know if you received a good job offer?
13. What is the difference between compensation and salary? Why is it important to know this when negotiating a job offer?

Power (Role) Play

Now it's time to put what you've learned into practice. The following are two roles that are involved in the same selling situation—one role is the customer, and the other is the salesperson. This will give you the opportunity to think about this selling situation from the point of view of both the customer and the salesperson.

Read each role carefully along with the discussion questions and be prepared to play either of the roles in class using the concepts covered in this chapter. You may be asked to discuss the roles and do a role-play in groups or individually.

Sweet Success

Role: Purchasing manager at ProFood, the food service supplier for campus cafeterias and restaurants

You are responsible for purchasing the products to be offered in college cafeterias and restaurants. You try to include new products that reflect the eating trends of the students. One of the trends is for more natural and organic food choices. The challenge is that, in order to offer new menu options, some of the existing options need to be eliminated. Any new products must be able to generate more revenue than existing items at a lower cost. You are especially interested in increasing sales at the snack bars with impulse items like individually wrapped cookies and cakes. The Organic Delight Desserts option is exactly what you are looking for, but the price is too high, and you're not sure you want all the flavors that come packed together in one case. The price from the sales rep is $20 per case. There are four flavors packed in a case—chocolate, strawberry, lemon, and mocha. At this rate, you might only put this in your top ten schools. If you can get a better price with the option to order individual flavors by the case, you might consider putting the line in all three hundred colleges and universities.

- Are you interested in negotiating to get what you want from the sales rep, or will you just take a pass and wait for another product?

- If you want to negotiate, what are your prenegotiation goals?
- What will you ask for during the negotiation? Is this different from your prenegotiation goals? Why or why not?

Role: Territory manager, Organic Delight Desserts

You are selling a new line of 100 percent organic desserts. These cookies and mini cakes are individually wrapped and are an excellent impulse item, or ideal for cafeterias. Since this is a new product line, it would be ideal to get placement with ProFood because it could lead to distribution at hundreds of schools. You just need to sell the purchasing manager on the line. You have sampled the products, and she likes the taste and thinks the packaging is perfect for her schools. Now you are down to negotiating on price and packaging. You have quoted $20 a case for a case that includes all four flavors—chocolate, strawberry, lemon, and mocha. You might have some flexibility to have a custom cases made up in each flavor so she can order only the flavors she wants. However, it will cost additional handling to do that.

- Are you going to make this a "take it or leave it" proposal?
- If you are going to negotiate, what are your prenegotiation goals?
- How will you find common ground to make this a win-win-win situation?
- What will you ask for during the negotiation? Is this different from your prenegotiation goals? Why or why not?

Put Your Power to Work: *Selling U* Activities

1. Visit the campus career center and ask about salary information that is available for positions that you are interested in pursuing. Compare this information to similar information you have gathered from Web sites mentioned in this section that include salary information. What information is consistent? What information is different? Ask a career counselor to help you understand the differences.

2. Talk to a campus career center counselor, advisor, or other professor or professional (and use this information in this section) and create a list of elements that might be included in a job offer. Identify those elements that are most important to you. What are your prenegotiation goals as it relates to this list?

Test Your Power Knowledge Answers

1. If you do your prospecting and qualifying correctly, you can significantly improve the number of times you are able to close a sale.

2. A trial close is when you ask your prospect their opinion. A close is when you ask for a decision.

3. When the prospect is demonstrating positive body language, when the prospect asks questions, and after you handle an objection.

4. "Would you like to preorder Guitar Hero Van Halen or take Guitar Hero Metallica with you now?"

5. Negotiating is based on trust. If your prospect doesn't trust you, chances are she will be unwilling to compromise and find common ground during the negotiation.

6. Information, power, and time.

7. Forty percent of prospects ask for a lower price. Salespeople should work to get below the surface and understand the prospect's true needs. Prospects are looking for value, not necessarily price. Salespeople should demonstrate the value of their product or service and negotiate on other elements rather than price. Reducing the price decreases profit, commission, and value of the product or service in the mind of the prospect.

8. A concession is something on which you are willing to compromise such as price, service, terms, options, or other elements of the deal. It's best to get a concession when you give a concession.

9. Prenegotiation, negotiation, and postnegotiation.

10. Goals that you identify before the beginning of a negotiation that establish the minimum that you are willing to accept to make the deal happen.

11. False.

12. Do research before beginning your job search by visiting Web sites that include salary information.

13. Salary is only one portion of total compensation, payment for services provided to an employer. There are several elements of compensation, including salary, vacation, insurance, hours, travel, relocation, and others that can be used to increase the total value of your job offer.

Endnotes

1. Jean-Marc Rocher, "Plot Summary for Jerry Maguire," IMDb, http://www.imdb.com/title/tt0116695/plotsummary (accessed November 19, 2009).

2. Alan M. Webber, "How to Get Them to Show You the Money," December 18, 2007, *Fast Company*, http://www.fastcompany.com/magazine/19/showmoney.html (accessed November 19, 2009).

3. Joe Guertin, "When Did 'Closing' Become a Bad Word?" Agency Sales, March 2006, http://www.allbusiness.com/sales/1064380-1.html (accessed March 16, 2010).

4. Joe Guertin, "When Did 'Closing' Become a Bad Word?" Agency Sales, March 2006, http://www.allbusiness.com/sales/1064380-1.html (accessed March 16, 2010).

5. Tim Connor, "The Myth of Closing Sales," Roderick Martin, http://roderickmartin.com/the-myth-of-closing-sales (accessed November 17, 2009).

6. "Closing the Deal," Selling Power Sales Management eNewsletter, May 17, 2004, http://www.sellingpower.com/content/newsletter/issue.php?pc=368 (accessed March 16, 2010).

7. Ray Silverstein, "How to Close a Sale in the First 30 Seconds," *Entrepreneur*, http://www.entrepreneur.com/management/leadership/leadershipcolumnistraysilverstein/article178590.html (accessed November 17, 2009).

8. Simona Covel, "Finding the Right People to Make the Sale," *Wall Street Journal*, May 29, 2008, http://online.wsj.com/article/SB121199448885726503.html (accessed November 17, 2009).

9. Geoffrey James, "Close More Sales: Train Your Sales Team," *Selling Power* 23, no. 8, http://www.sellingpower.com/content/article.php?a=6389 (accessed March 16, 2010).

10. Ram Charan, "What Your Customer Isn't Saying about Your Sales Pitch," *Wall Street Journal*, May 29, 2008, http://online.wsj.com/article/SB121182439378120865.html (accessed November 17, 2009).

11. D. Forbes Ley, "Trial Closing Questions Tell You When to Ask for a Decision," The Bachman Company, http://www.bachmanco.com/pretz/PDF/Trial%20Closing%20Questions.pdf (accessed November 18, 2009).

12. D. Forbes Ley, "Trial Closing Questions Tell You When to Ask for a Decision," The Bachman Company, http://www.bachmanco.com/pretz/PDF/Trial%20Closing%20Questions.pdf (accessed November 18, 2009).

13. Michelle Nichols, "The Two-by-Four Closing Question," *BusinessWeek*, April 19, 2007, http://www.businessweek.com/smallbiz/content/apr2007/sb20070419_586407.htm (accessed November 17, 2009).

14. Joe Takash, "Connect with the Buyer," http://www.joetakash.com/media-resource/wp-content/uploads/2009/03/independent-agent.pdf (accessed May 16, 2010).

15. Mario Russo, Executive Panel in Marketing 2335—Public Relations and Publicity, Saint Joseph's University, Philadelphia, PA, November 18, 2009.

16. Mark Hunter, "Close Too Quick and You Lose Profit," *Fast Company*, November 4, 2009, http://www.fastcompany.com/blog/mark-hunter/sales-hunter/close-too-quick-and-you-lose-profit (accessed November 17, 2009).

17. "Closing the Deal," *Selling Power*, May 17, 2004, http://www.sellingpower.com/content/newsletter/issue.php?pc=368 (accessed November 17, 2009).

18. "Closing Arguments," Selling Power Pharmaceuticals eNewsletter, September 11, 2007, http://www.sellingpower.com/content/newsletter/issue.php?pc=648 (accessed March 16, 2010).

19. Laura Lorber, "Three Tips for Closing a Sale," *Wall Street Journal*, http://online.wsj.com/article/SB121198785761226199.html#printMode (accessed November 17, 2009).

20. "Closing the Deal," Selling Power Sales Management eNewsletter, May 17, 2004, http://www.sellingpower.com/content/newsletter/issue.php?pc=368 (accessed March 16, 2010).

21. Barry Farber, "Wrap It Up," *Entrepreneur*, April 2008, http://www.entrepreneur.com/magazine/entrepreneur/2008/april/191580.html (accessed November 17, 2009).

22. "Sales Closing—Closing Throughout the Sales Cycle Process Using Different Types of Closes," Money Instructor, http://www.moneyinstructor.com/art/saleclose.asp (accessed November 17, 2009).

23. Joe Takash, "Connect with the Buyer," http://www.joetakash.com/media-resource/wp-content/uploads/2009/03/independent-agent.pdf (accessed May 16, 2010).

24. "Tips for Closing a Sale," AllBusiness, http://www.AllBusiness.com/sales/selling-techniques-closing-sales/450-1.html (accessed November 17, 2009).

25. Steve Atlas, "Closing: How to Use the Right Techniques to Close a Committee," *Selling Power* 20, no. 8, http://www.sellingpower.com/content/article.php?a=5547 (accessed March 16, 2010).

26. Gerald L. Manning, Barry L. Reece, and Michael Ahearne, *Selling Today: Creating Customer Value*, 11th ed. (Upper Saddle River, NJ: Pearson Prentice Hall, 2010), 310.

27. Barton A. Weitz, Setphen B. Castleberry, and John F. Tanner, Jr., *Selling: Building Partnerships*, 7th ed. (New York: McGraw-Hill, 2008), 319.

28. Geoffrey James, "Sales Reps' Frequently Asked Questions on Closing," *Selling Power*, http://www.sellingpower.com/content/article.php?a=6389 (accessed November 17, 2009).

29. "Alternative Close," ChangingMinds.org, http://changingminds.org/disciplines/sales/closing/alternative_close.htm (accessed November 18, 2009).

30. Charles M. Futrell, *Fundamentals of Selling: Customers for Life through Service*, 10th ed. (New York: McGraw-Hill Irwin, 2008), 417.

31. Michelle Nichols, "The Two-by-Four Closing Question," *BusinessWeek*, April 19, 2007, http://www.businessweek.com/smallbiz/content/apr2007/sb20070419_586407.htm (accessed November 17, 2009).

32. Raymund Flandez, "Sales Outsourcing First Teaches Workers to Ask A Lot of Questions," *Wall Street Journal*, September 12, 2008, http://online.wsj.com/article/SB121199452139126417.html (accessed November 17, 2009).

33. Barry Farber, "Wrap It Up," *Entrepreneur*, April 2008, http://www.entrepreneur.com/magazine/entrepreneur/2008/april/191580.html (accessed November 17, 2009).

34. Steve Kayser, "Shooting the Donkey in the Complex Sales Process…Hollywood Style," http://scottymiller.wordpress.com/category/tips-on-navigating-the-complex-sale (accessed January 7, 2010).

35. "Winning Strategies to Succeed in Complex Sales," Prime Resource Group, March 2010, http://www.masteringthecomplexsale.com/sales-training-book-press-release.htm (accessed January 7, 2010).

36. "Ten Keys to Winning Complex High Dollar Sales," Best-Coaching-Training.org, May 9, 2009, http://www.best-coaching-training.org/2009/05/29/ten-keys-to-winning-complex-high-dollar-sales (accessed January 7, 2010).

37. "Negotiation," *Entrepreneur*, http://www.entrepreneur.com/encyclopedia/term/82556.html (accessed November 20, 2009).

38. Stephanie Mojica, "The Art of Sale Negotiation Skills," Associated Content, December 26, 2008, http://www.associatedcontent.com/article/1313361/the_art_of_sale_negotiation_skills.html?cat=35 (accessed November 19, 2009).

39. RCM Staff Report, "27 Principles of Negotiating with a Meeting Facility," MeetingsNet, February 1, 2003, http://meetingsnet.com/ar/meetings_principles_negotiating (accessed November 19, 2009).

40. Robert J. McGarvey, "Covering the Bases," *Entrepreneur*, June 1997, http://www.entrepreneur.com/magazine/entrepreneur/1997/june/14260.html (accessed November 20, 2009).

41. Daniel Roach, "5 Simple Rules for Unbeatable Sales Negotiation," Associated Content, September 29, 2008, http://www.associatedcontent.com/article/1047808/5_simple_rules_for_unbeatable_sales.html?cat=3 (accessed November 19, 2009).

42. "Negotiating to Win-Win," Selling Power Sales Management eNewsletter, January 6, 2003, http://www.sellingpower.com/content/newsletter/issue.php?pc=248 (accessed March 16, 2010).

43. Alan M. Webber, "How to Get Them to Show You the Money," *Fast Company*, October 31, 1998, http://www.fastcompany.com/magazine/19/showmoney.html (accessed November 19, 2009).

44. Herb Cohen, *You Can Negotiate Anything* (New York: McGraw-Hill, 1980), 163.

45. Herb Cohen, *You Can Negotiate Anything* (New York: McGraw-Hill, 1980), 163.

46. Herb Cohen, *You Can Negotiate Anything* (New York: McGraw-Hill, 1980), 163.

47. "Negotiating to Win-Win," Selling Power Sales Management eNewsletter, January 6, 2003, http://www.sellingpower.com/content/newsletter/issue.php?pc=248 (accessed March 16, 2010).

48. Polly LaBarre, "Saleswoman for the 21st Century," *Fast Company*, December 18, 2007, http://www.fastcompany.com/node/36271/print (accessed November 18, 2009).

49. Herb Cohen, *You Can Negotiate Anything* (New York: McGraw-Hill, 1980), 163.

50. Greg Beato, "Twenty-Five Years of Post-it Notes," March 24, 2005, http://archives.secretsofthecity.com/magazine/reporting/features/twenty-five-years-post-it-notes-0 (accessed November 20, 2009).

51. Herb Cohen, *You Can Negotiate Anything* (New York: McGraw-Hill, 1980), 183.

52. Peter Burrows and Robert D. Hof, "Yahoo Gives in to Microsoft, Gives Up on Search," *BusinessWeek*, July 29, 2009, http://www.businessweek.com/technology/content/jul2009/tc20090728_826397.htm (accessed January 7, 2010).

53. David Goldman, "Microsoft and Yahoo: Search Partners," *CNNMoney.com*, July 29, 2009, http://money.cnn.com/2009/07/29/technology/microsoft_yahoo/index.htm (accessed January 7, 2010).

54. Herb Cohen, *You Can Negotiate Anything* (New York: McGraw-Hill, 1980), 19.

55. Herb Cohen, *You Can Negotiate Anything* (New York: McGraw-Hill, 1980), 20.

56. RCM Staff Report, "27 Principles of Negotiating with a Meeting Facility," MeetingsNet, February 1, 2003, http://meetingsnet.com/ar/meetings_principles_negotiating (accessed November 19, 2009).

57. Kelley Robertson, "Let's Make a Deal: Negotiating Techniques," The EyesOnSales Blog, January 18, 2008, http://www.eyesonsales.com/content/article/lets_make_a_deal_negotiating_techniques (accessed November 19, 2009).

58. Kelley Robertson, "Let's Make a Deal: Negotiating Techniques," The EyesOnSales Blog, January 18, 2008, http://www.eyesonsales.com/content/article/lets_make_a_deal_negotiating_techniques (accessed November 19, 2009).

59. Colleen Francis, "Negotiation Quick Hits," The EyesOnSales Blog, November 13, 2008, http://www.eyesonsales.com/content/article/negotiation_quick_hits (accessed November 19, 2009).

60. RCM Staff Report, "27 Principles of Negotiating with a Meeting Facility," MeetingsNet, February 1, 2003, http://meetingsnet.com/ar/meetings_principles_negotiating (accessed November 19, 2009).

61. Colleen Francis, "Negotiation Quick Hits," The EyesOnSales Blog, November 13, 2008, http://www.eyesonsales.com/content/article/negotiation_quick_hits (accessed November 19, 2009).

62. John Hoult, "Negotiation 101," *Fast Company*, September 30, 2000, http://www.fastcompany.com/articles/2000/10/act_podziba.html?page=0%2C0 (accessed November 17, 2009).

63. John Hoult, "Negotiation 101," *Fast Company*, September 30, 2000, http://www.fastcompany.com/articles/2000/10/act_podziba.html?page=0%2C0 (accessed November 17, 2009).

64. Anthony Tjan, "Four Rules of Effective Negotiations," *Harvard Business Review*, July 28, 2009, http://blogs.harvardbusiness.org/tjan/2009/07/four-rules-for-effective-negot.html (accessed November 17, 2009).

65. Anthony Tjan, "Four Rules of Effective Negotiations," *Harvard Business Review*, July 28, 2009, http://blogs.harvardbusiness.org/tjan/2009/07/four-rules-for-effective-negot.html (accessed November 17, 2009).

66. "Customers' Negotiating Tactics," Selling Power Sales Management eNewsletter, July 1, 2002, http://www.sellingpower.com/content/newsletter/issue.php?pc=212 (accessed March 16, 2010).

67. RCM Staff Report, "27 Principles of Negotiating with a Meeting Facility," MeetingsNet, February 1, 2003, http://meetingsnet.com/ar/meetings_principles_negotiating (accessed November 19, 2009).

68. Danielle Kennedy, "Let's Make a Deal," *Entrepreneur*, October 1996, http://www.entrepreneur.com/article/printthis/13404.html (accessed November 20, 2009).

69. Christina Novicki, "Secrets of a Superagent," *Fast Company*, October 31, 1996, http://www.fastcompany.com/magazine/05/superagent.html (accessed November 19, 2009).

70. Alan M. Webber, "How to Get Them to Show You the Money," *Fast Company*, October 31, 1998, http://www.fastcompany.com/magazine/19/showmoney.html (accessed November 19, 2009).

71. RCM Staff Report, "27 Principles of Negotiating with a Meeting Facility," MeetingsNet, February 1, 2003, http://meetingsnet.com/ar/meetings_principles_negotiating (accessed November 19, 2009).

72. Alan M. Webber, "How to Get Them to Show You the Money," *Fast Company*, October 31, 1998, http://www.fastcompany.com/magazine/19/showmoney.html (accessed November 19, 2009).

73. Christina Novicki, "Secrets of a Superagent," *Fast Company*, October 31, 1996, http://www.fastcompany.com/magazine/05/superagent.html (accessed November 19, 2009).

74. "Evaluating the Salary Information You've Found," The Riley Guide, http://www.rileyguide.com/saleval.html (accessed November 21, 2009).

75. Kim Richmond, *Brand You*, 3rd ed. (Upper Saddle River, NJ: Pearson Prentice Hall, 2008), 201.

76. Dona DeZube, "Negotiating Compensation for a Job at a Startup," Monster.com, http://career-advice.monster.com/salary-benefits/negotiation-tips/negotiating-compensation-startup/article.aspx (accessed November 22, 2009).

77. Kim Richmond, *Brand You*, 3rd ed. (Upper Saddle River, NJ: Pearson Prentice Hall, 2008), 202.

78. Kim Richmond, *Brand You*, 3rd ed. (Upper Saddle River, NJ: Pearson Prentice Hall, 2008), 202.

79. Adapted from Kim Richmond, *Brand You*, 3rd ed. (Upper Saddle River, NJ: Prentice Hall, 2008), 204; and Paul W. Barada, "Job Offer Evaluation Checklist," Monster.com, http://career-advice.monster.com/salary-benefits/Negotiation-Tips/Job-Offer-Evaluation-Checklist/article.aspx (accessed November 21, 2009).

80. Adapted from Kim Richmond, *Brand You*, 3rd ed. (Upper Saddle River, NJ: Prentice Hall, 2008), 206; and Paul W. Barada, "Job Offer Evaluation Checklist," Monster.com, http://career-advice.monster.com/salary-benefits/Negotiation-Tips/Job-Offer-Evaluation-Checklist/article.aspx (accessed November 21, 2009).

81. Kim Richmond, *Brand You*, 3rd ed. (Upper Saddle River, NJ: Pearson Prentice Hall, 2008), 208.

82. Kim Richmond, *Brand You*, 3rd ed. (Upper Saddle River, NJ: Pearson Prentice Hall, 2008), 212.

83. John Steven Nisnick, "Job Offer Letter Sample," About.com, http://jobsearchtech.about.com/od/jobofferletters/a/jobofferletter.htm (accessed November 21, 2009).

CHAPTER 13

Follow-Up: The Power of Providing Service That Sells

Video Ride-Along with Rachel Gordon, Account Manager at WMGK Radio

You met Rachel Gordon in Chapter 6 when she shared her tips for finding the decision maker. Now she talks about the importance of follow-up and provides some valuable tips about how she follows up with prospects and customers.

Ride along with Rachel and hear about the importance of handwritten thank-you notes and other elements that are important to making the sale again and again.

View the video online at: http://www.youtube.com/embed/AyoIRc_slxA

13.1 Follow-Up: The Lasting Impression

Learning Objectives

1. Understand what follow-up entails and why it is so important.
2. Discuss the ongoing nature of follow-up.

You have spending power, and lots of it. Millennials (or Gen Y, if you prefer) are estimated to have over $1.3 trillion in direct spending for apparel, food, music, entertainment, and other products and services. That number is understated due to the influence you have on parents and other older people who seek your tech-savvy advice on all types of products from computers to cars.[1] You are one of the most sought-after consumer groups around. More sales and marketing efforts are aimed at you than at any other generation. You determine where and when you will spend your money. You have the power.

So what is it that makes you decide to choose Nintendo over Xbox, Mini Cooper over Chrysler, or Apple over Toshiba? Of course, the product has a lot to do with your choice. Price is certainly a consideration, but you don't always buy the lowest-priced product or service. Think about it. It's the ongoing relationship you have with the brand that makes a difference. It's the fact that the company continues to serve up exactly the new products and services you need (how do they do that?). It's how the company keeps in touch on Facebook and other ways that keeps you engaged in the conversation. And it's the fact that you feel appreciated as a customer. When a company makes you feel like they forgot about *you*, it's time to move on and spend your money elsewhere.

What Is Follow-Up?

Follow-up entails everything that takes place after the sale is closed from getting signatures on all contracts and paperwork to scheduling delivery. It also includes your ongoing relationship with your customer. Relationship is the key word here. If you were involved in transactional selling, only focused on making the short-term sale, you would not be worried about follow-up because someone else in your company would take care of it. You would move on to the next customer. In many retail selling environments, this may be the case. You would not expect to receive a thank-you note from the checker at the grocery store or the cashier at a fast-food restaurant. However, you would expect to hear from a real estate agent who sold you a new home, or from a financial services consultant who is managing your money.

It's the attention to detail to be sure that your transaction goes smoothly that you rely on your salesperson to do. Think about how you feel when your salesperson adds value to your new investment with additional information and insights. That makes you feel like a valuable customer. Chances are, when you need something else (another house or more money to invest), the first person you will call will be the salesperson who continues to follow up with you. When one of your friends wants to buy a house or invest some money, you will be very likely to go out of your way to recommend your salesperson.

While the specific follow-up activities may vary from company to company and even customer to customer, Figure 13.1 provides a summary of some of the most common follow-up actions that are expected. Many companies have a checklist or best practices that are used as guidelines to ensure that all details are covered. In the case of complex sales, follow-up may include a transition team with members from both the company and the customer. The transition team may work closely together, including weekly or in some cases daily status calls, to ensure that the transition to the new product or service goes smoothly. For example, the implementation of a new logistics system or software program may require that the old system runs parallel with the new system until all aspects are completely set up and appropriate training is conducted. This is especially true for products or services like these that have a direct impact on the operation of the customer's business.

FIGURE 13.1 Areas That Require Follow-Up

Sign contracts

Schedule delivery and confirm that it was made correctly and on time

Schedule and conduct training

Schedule and ensure that installation is implemented correctly

Conduct credit checks

Add customers to all appropriate company correspondence

Generate invoice

Send welcome package to new customer

Introduce key people to new customer

Schedule status call with customer

Why Follow Up?

No matter what product or service you are selling, the sales process can be challenging. The selling process starts with prospecting and qualifying (that was six chapters ago!). Depending on the complexity and buying cycle of the product or service, it could takes weeks, months, or even years until you close the sale. In fact, 81 percent of all sales happen on or after the fifth sales call, according to study conducted by the Association of Sales Executives.[2] It takes time, energy, and commitment to get to the point where the deal is done. Some salespeople spend all their time and effort to research the prospect, get the appointment, make the presentation, handle objections, and close the sale—and then expect to collect their commission check. They seem to literally disappear after the sale is completed.[3]

Relationship selling doesn't work that way. The relationship really begins with the close of the sale; follow-up is what makes a relationship grow and prosper. Follow-up is how most customers evaluate the performance of the product or service they just bought. As you may recall from Chapter 1, *you* are the brand to the customer. How you proactively handle follow-ups will make all the difference in your relationships and your sales. In other words, the best way to make the sale is by the way you handle things *after* the sale.

Here's the not-so-subtle point here. Even though the sale is closed, you should never assume the sale is closed.[4] This is especially important when there is a gap in time between the closing of the sale and the delivery of the product or service (as in the delivery of a major software package, installation of new equipment, or bringing on board a new product or service vendor). A customer can have second thoughts, sometimes called buyer's remorse or cognitive dissonance (covered in detail in Chapter 6). This is when a customer may think that the decision she made is not the right one. She may be in contact with a competitor, receive additional information, or be concerned that she made the wrong decision, paid too much, or didn't consider some alternatives properly. You can help avoid letting your customers be vulnerable to alternatives.[5],[6] Increase your return on your time investment and your customer's return on her financial investment and put your follow-up plan into place immediately.

Plan Your Follow-Up

Put together your follow-up plan even before you begin your prospecting efforts. While follow-up is the last step in the selling process, it is the step that can have the most impact on your customer.

You worked hard to establish trust with your customer during the selling process. After the sale is the time to put that trust to work and continue to earn it every day. Lip service, saying that you'll do something but not really putting in the effort to do it, doesn't go very far in sales. And just going through the motions will put you farther behind. It may seem more exciting to be working on a new proposal rather than doing follow-up for a sale that has already closed.

Think about your follow-up plan with the following five elements in mind:

FIGURE 13.2
Completing the appropriate paperwork and following up internally are critical to delivering your product or service as promised.

© 2010 Jupiterimages Corporation

1. **Demonstrate your personal commitment and connection to the customer.** Start by saying thank you to your customer for her business. "Customers want to know you care about them, their business, their challenges, and them as individuals," according to author and professional speaker George Hedley. "The number one reason customers stop doing business with a company is an attitude of indifference," he says.[7] How you follow up after the sale is a good indication of how you will respond throughout the relationship.

Start off on the right foot by sending a thank-you letter. Everyone likes to feel appreciated, especially right after they have made a commitment to spend money. Your letter should be professional, yet personal, and sincere. This is the perfect opportunity to reinforce to the customer that she has made a wise decision; this is a perfect opportunity to reiterate the product or service benefits with a focus on the information you learned about the customer's business during the selling process.[8],[9]

Besides demonstrating good business etiquette, a personal thank-you letter also serves some operational objectives. It should include your contact information, phone numbers, e-mail address, Web sites for customer contact (in addition to your contact information), receipt or order confirmation, and a list of next steps.[10]

Don't just say thank you after you close the sale. Be ready to follow up with three to five "selling points" timed after the sale. For example, after a salesperson sells a car, she follows up with an article about a safety award that the brand was awarded. She also sends a birthday card to the customer with a note to indicate the value of the car has increased based on current market conditions.[11]

Most of all show your customers that you appreciate them and their business regularly with a handwritten thank-you note, an unexpected visit, or small gift like a box of candy. Little gestures go a long way; they are like "one-a-day vitamins" for your business.[12]

Video Clip

Follow-Up Letter
Looking for tips about how to write a sales follow-up letter? This video includes some great tips.

View the video online at: http://www.youtube.com/embed/8RxHDK3Hpkc

What If the Answer Is No?

So what if you didn't get the sale? Send a thank-you note anyway. It's a professional way to set yourself apart and keep the door open for future conversations. A personal thank-you note or letter really stands out in today's fast-paced world. You might be surprised where a thank-you note or letter can lead. See a sample thank-you letter.

http://www.bestsampleletters.com/sales-and-marketing/appointment-setting-and-follow-up/post-sale-follow-up/follow-up-letter-to-lost-sale-letter.html

2. **Deliver as promised**. While you are the person on the front line with the customer, you have a team of people who are responsible for delivering the product or service as specified. "Don't just check the box," says executive coach and author Marshall Goldsmith.[13] Take the time to follow up internally to be sure all the i's are dotted and t's are crossed so that your customer's delivery is flawless. That means taking the time to share details and insights about the customer's business and preferences with your entire team (whether your team is large or small). When salespeople just fill out the forms to get things moving internally, there's a high likelihood that some nuances can fall between the cracks. Keep in mind that your customer made the purchase because you can deliver consistently for her, but you can't deliver the product or service alone. There are most likely internal processes for communication and delivery, contracts to be signed, schedules to be communicated, and other operational activities that require the entire team to be working in harmony. Follow the internal processes and go a step farther. Make your coworkers care as much about delivering consistently for the customer as you do; take the time to share information about the customer that goes above and beyond your internal forms. You'll also be surprised to see that everyone involved will add value when each has a connection to the customer. And don't forget to say thank you to your team. You couldn't do it without them; share the positive feedback from your customer with the team.[14]

Call the customer to be sure the delivery was made as promised and everything is to the customer's liking.[15]

3. **Add value to your customer's business**. Follow-up isn't a one-time event. Rather, it is an ongoing process that takes place after the sale is closed. Just like when you researched, asked questions, and listened to your customer to learn as much as possible about you might solve his business challenges before he made the commitment to buy, you want to continue to do the same thing as part of your ongoing follow-up.

Build your credibility by creating a systematic follow-up system so that your customer knows he can count on hearing from you regularly. You might touch base in person or by phone, e-mail, text, or a combination of these contact methods. The key is to communicate regularly in the manner or manners in which your customer prefers. It's a good idea to get into a routine to get and give status updates.[16],[17] Believe it or not, some salespeople actually forget to follow up.[18] They get so busy with making new proposals and putting out fires that they lose track of time and details.

What's important to the customer should be important to you so make yourself easily accessible and respond to his inquiries in a timely manner.[19] Deliver the same energy, enthusiasm, and level of service you did before you closed the sale. And just as you did when you were working to close the business, be honest about timing and resolution of issues. In other words, set expectations and then overdeliver on them.[20]

Adding value goes beyond the typical "I'm just checking in." Every time you contact your customer, offer some insight, news, or expertise to help him and his business. Make yourself the trusted advisor and key collaborator. Provide insights from industry events, forward copies of relevant white papers, make introductions to subject matter experts in your company, and send company (or your own) newsletters. You can complement your personal follow-up with the Internet to provide valuable updates and networking connections through a blog, Twitter updates, LinkedIn discussions, and other social networking tools. All these types of communications help add value to your customer's business so that when she has a problem (any problem), you deliver so much value that she calls you first to help her solve it. This is how you earn your seat at the table as a true business partner, not a salesperson.[21]

4. **Get feedback**. It's not enough to talk to your customers; it's also important to listen.[22] Ask for their input, insight, and ideas about everything from things you can do better to new products and services. Customers, especially those with whom you have good relationships, can provide invaluable guidance to you and your company. One-on-one planning meetings, product development meetings, and other forward-looking events are ideal ways of gaining firsthand feedback and getting buy-in from the start. There's nothing that your customer would rather talk about than his business. Be genuine and ask him about it, then listen and use the information to help his business (and yours) grow.[23]

Customer Feedback Meets Social Networking

FIGURE 13.3
Asking customers to share ideas online is a good way to get feedback.

© 2010 Jupiterimages Corporation

IdeaStorm (http://www.ideastorm.com) is a Web site created by Dell that literally turns customer feedback into a social network. You can post, vote, promote, or demote ideas for Dell. What makes this Web site so unique is that you can actually see the ideas that have been put into action. Talk about showing customers you care about what they think, Dell puts customer feedback to good use.[24]

Starbucks has incorporated MyStarbucksIdea into its Web site as a place for customers to share their ideas, vote on their favorites, discuss the pros and cons, and see the actions that have been taken as a result.[25] Suggest an idea at http://mystarbucksidea.force.com.

5. **Make your customers into fans**. Focusing on your customers' businesses as if they were yours, adding value, and showing your customers that you appreciate their business makes them more than customers—it makes them fans. Fans share stories of their great experiences. Your customers can help you sell with testimonials, referrals, and references. One of the most effective ways to handle objections from prospects is to call on excited and energized customers who are more than satisfied with your product and service. There are no more powerful words to win over a new prospect than those of a more-than-satisfied customer.[26] Use customer testimonials as part of your selling presentation, on your company's Web site, and on your professional Web site and social networking pages. In fact, it's a good idea to ask customers to write a recommendation for you on LinkedIn.

Link

Referrals Build Sales

See how testimonials are used by Atlanta REMAX real estate agent Ellen Crawford on her professional Web site.

http://www.atlantabesthomes.com/testimonials.htm

Reward your best customers with special offers and added value such as additional training, additional advertising space or time, or other additional service.[27] While you may extend a special pricing offer, focus on delivering value and giving your best customers the opportunity to experience the other services you have to offer. This lets your best customers know you appreciate their business and gives you an opportunity to move your relationship to the next level by becoming an even more important business partner to them.

It is these loyal customers who build your business in two ways. First, they buy more from you because they feel that you are bringing them value in more ways than simply selling a product. Second, when they are loyal customers, they become fans or advocates of your product or service, and they tell their friends about you.

FIGURE 13.4

Make your customers into fans, and they will tell their friends about you.

© 2010 Jupiterimages Corporation

Power Point: Lessons in Selling from the Customer's Point of View

The Making of a Fan—Yahoo!-Style

Blogger Michael Eisenberg went from a detractor to a promoter of Yahoo! with one e-mail. Eisenberg made a "not-so-flattering post" about the functionality of what was then the new MyYahoo! in March 2007. Within twenty-four hours he received an e-mail from the manager of Yahoo!'s Front Doors Group that said, "I would love to find out what you would like to see and which features you are most concerned about losing. We want to be sure that our heavy users remain satisfied. If you have a few minutes to e-mail me, I'd very much appreciate it." Eisenberg promptly posted the response from the Yahoo! manager on his blog along with his fanatic endorsement of the company that can be summed up in one word: "Kudos!"[28]

Heroic Recovery: How a Service Failure Can Be a Good Thing

No matter how good you and your company are at taking care of customers, there will be a time when something doesn't go as planned or as your customer expected. When you experience a setback, your mettle is put to the test. "Errors are inevitable, dissatisfied customers are not."[29] It's not about the fact that the problem occurred; it's how you respond that matters. When a salesperson responds quickly to a service failure and delights the customer with the outcome, it is called **heroic recovery**. The salesperson has the opportunity to perform a "heroic" action to save the customer's business. For example, when a food service distributor sales rep personally delivers a case of ground beef that was missing from the truck earlier in the morning to a restaurant before lunch, he goes above and beyond to demonstrate service and help the customer avoid missed lunch sales.

In some cases, heroic recovery can improve a customer's perception of the quality of service provided by a salesperson. Some customers actually rate companies higher when there has been a service failure and it has been corrected quickly than if there was no service failure at all. In addition, service failures can ultimately help identify service issues that are important to the customer. For example, an industrial packing company had an internal service standard of shipping 95 percent of all orders complete. This had a negative impact on the company's ability to make deliveries within seventy-two hours, which is the industry average. After conducting focus groups, the company learned that customers valued complete shipments more than the seventy-two-hour delivery window. The company has since changed its policies and has created a competitive advantage based on service that is important to the customer.[30]

This is not to imply that a constant state of heroic recovery is acceptable to a customer. In fact, providing excellent service begins with understanding what the customer values and then having

heroic recovery

Response to a service failure that delights the customer.

internal operations in place to be able to consistently deliver that level of service. Recall from Chapter 1 that consistency is one of the elements of a brand. If you as a salesperson, or your company, can consistently deliver on a service promise, then heroic recovery is not efficient or effective in servicing the customer or creating a loyal customer.

Part of heroic recovery includes taking care of the customer—whatever it takes to make the impact of the service failure right for the customer. In addition, it includes internal analysis to identify where and why the service failure occurred, what it takes to correct the problem, and how to prevent it from happening again. As a salesperson, you want to be able to recover from a service failure with confidence so that you know the root cause of the problem has been fixed.

Power Player: Lessons in Selling from Successful Salespeople

Inspiration from Air Conditioning

Said Hilal, CEO of Applied Medical Resources, owned one of the early Mercedes S series and was happy with the performance of the car. After one year, Mercedes notified him that the air conditioner was appropriate for Europe but was underpowered for the United States and offered to replace the air conditioner. Hilal was so impressed with how Mercedes proactively handled the issue that he decided to use the same approach to his business. "We ask our customers what they want to see in our future product—what problems they have that we can help resolve," says Hilal. "We consistently remind ourselves to listen to what the customer needs, not what we need."[31]

The bottom line is that companies and salespeople should view heroic recovery efforts as an investment in customer service perceptions, rather than as a cost. If handled properly, service failures can improve a relationship with a customer even more so than excellent service.[32]

Key Takeaways

- Follow-up is what builds a relationship after the sale. You should never assume the sale is closed.
- Follow-up should take place regularly so your customer knows he can count on hearing from you.
- A personal thank-you note or letter is appropriate after the close of the sale. The letter can also include some operational information such as contact information and receipts.
- Follow up to be sure everything is delivered as promised. Do your follow-up inside the company and touch base with the customer to be sure everything is to her satisfaction.
- Add value to your customer's business with industry information, white papers, blogs, and newsletters. These bring value to your customer and keep your name in front of him.
- Feedback is an important part of follow-up.
- Customers can become your best-selling tool with testimonials and referrals.
- **Heroic recovery** can be a way to delight your customer (only if a service failure occurs infrequently and it is handled in a satisfactory manner).

Exercises

1. Identify a company with whom you have a relationship (you purchase its products or services on an ongoing basis). What makes the relationship work? What role does follow-up play in the relationship?

2. Identify a company from which you have purchased products or services that doesn't follow up with you. Why do you continue to purchase the products or services? If another alternative comes along, will you be open to trying the new alternative? Why or why not?

3. Assume you work for a video game manufacturer and you sell video games to bricks-and-mortar and online retailers. Identify three things you would do as part of your follow-up plan after you close the sale to Best Buy.

4. Assume you are selling security systems to businesses, how would you use a news article about recent security issues as part of your follow-up with your customers?

5. Assume you sell landscaping to businesses. Once you have arranged for the landscaping to be installed, are there any other opportunities for follow-up?

   - If so, what would you do to follow up during the spring and summer?
   - What would you do to follow up during the fall and winter?

6. Imagine that you are a sales rep for a major insurance company. How can you gather customer feedback to improve your service? How can you use customer feedback that you receive about products and services for which you are not responsible?

13.2 Customer Satisfaction Isn't Enough

Learning Objective

1. Understand how customer satisfaction relates to customer loyalty.

Customer loyalty and retention are the holy grail in sales—and in all areas of business, for that matter. Loyal customers are how successful businesses are built. Not only is it easier to sell more to existing customers, it is financially prudent to do so. Some companies have increased their profit by as much as 100 percent by focusing on retaining an additional 5 percent of customers. Since it costs about five times more to acquire a new customer than to retain an existing customer, companies are well served to focus on retaining existing customers and making them into advocates for their brand.[33] In other words, "Customer acquisition is an investment, but customer retention delivers profitability."[34]

Follow-Up, Feedback, and Fans

Earlier in this chapter, the five elements of follow-up were discussed including getting feedback from customers. This concept is so important, it's worth drilling a little deeper into it. It is loyal customers who buy more from you in the form of more products and services more often. Companies that focus on creating customer loyalty usually invest in developing an effective **customer feedback loop**, a formal process for gathering, synthesizing, and acting on customer feedback. The most successful customer feedback loops are simple, focus on understanding what is important to customers, and empower **front-line employees** (i.e., those who interact with customers on a day-to-day basis, such as salespeople). For example, Charles Schwab, an online investment services company, has a process whereby managers review customer feedback daily from comments on the company Web site, transactions, and other communications with the company. Managers and sales reps respond personally to negative customer comments. Cheryl Pasquale, a branch manager, says she looks forward to customer calls to follow up on complaints or less-than-positive comments. She feels she has an opportunity to turn "critics into fans."[35]

customer feedback loop

A formal process for gathering, synthesizing, and acting upon customer feedback.

front-line employees

Employees who interact with customers on a day-to-day basis, such as salespeople.

There are several different types of customer feedback loops that companies use such as mystery shopper programs, customer satisfaction surveys, and other measurement tools. Some of these methods are expensive, require elaborate reporting, and take a long time to compile and act on the data.[36] Simply asking customers what they think can defeat the purpose if companies don't act quickly on the feedback. It raises customer expectations that action is going to be taken.[37]

Power Selling: Lessons in Selling from Successful Brands

Follow-Up Is Just a Tweet Away

Personal follow-up meets technology with more than half of *Fortune* 100 companies using Twitter as one of the tools in their arsenal to respond to customer service issues. Comcast is a leader in this area. The company believes that Twitter has provided more transparency and improved communication with customers in multiple channels.[38] Comcast uses Twitter to address follow-up issues such as a service call that didn't happen on time, service that isn't operating properly, and even billing issues. According to Frank Eliason, director of digital care at Comcast, Twitter is not a replacement for phone and e-mail follow-up. However, he says, "It gives immediacy to interactions." He finds that customers are surprised—and pleased—to hear from him so quickly on Twitter.[39] The bottom line is to take care of the customer, no matter what method you use for follow-up.

One Simple Question

Successful companies have found that customers can be more than customers; they can be advocates, supporters, promoters, and fans. It's these passionate fans that not only spend their money with these companies but also tell their friends and ultimately their friends' friends to patronize the company. The mutual admiration of brand and customer starts with the culture of the company. Those companies that not only listen to their customers but also engage them in communities, new product development, and other improvements are the ones that have a maniacal focus on the customer. They get it. For example, watch this video of a Southwest Airlines flight attendant that was posted to YouTube by a passenger. Talk about being a fan of the brand—it's hard not to be after you watch this video.

Video Clip

Southwest Gets It
See how an ordinary activity can create an extraordinary customer experience.

View the video online at: http://www.youtube.com/embed/zT6YMnA2CgU

In another example, it's no surprise that Zappos, the dominant online shoe and apparel retailer, has a maniacal focus on the customer when you listen to CEO Tony Hsieh talk about his philosophy of customer service. Zappos has grown to be a billion-dollar business in just ten years. Although shoes have a notoriously high return rate due to fit problems, Zappos offers free shipping both ways to encourage purchases. Hsieh's vision for the ultimate experience in customer service is clear throughout the company (try calling their 800 number for customer service and experience Zappos' unique telephone greeting).

Video Clip

Zappos Gets It
Hear CEO Tony Hsieh talk about why Zappos is a fan favorite.

View the video online at: http://www.youtube.com/embed/py1iRsBcYMc

Many companies have found that **Net Promoter Score (NPS)** is the ideal customer feedback tool because it is simple, keeps the customer at the forefront, allows frontline employees to act, thereby closing the customer feedback loop.[40] Net Promoter Score is based on asking customers the ultimate question: "How likely are you to recommend this product or company to a colleague or friend?" The response is based on a ten-point scale and categorizes responses as follows:

Net Promoter Score (NPS)

Compiled results of customer responses to the question, "How likely are you to recommend this product or company to a colleague or friend?"

- **Promoters** (customers who answer with a 9 or 10). These are customers who are advocates or loyal fans who will willingly tell their friends to do business with the company.
- **Passives** (customers who answer with a 7 or 8). These are customers who might be categorized as satisfied, but do not enthusiastically support the company. They are vulnerable to competitive offerings.
- **Detractors** (customers who answer with a 0 to 6). These are customers who are not happy and are likely to pass along stories about their bad experiences to their friends via word of mouth or social networking.

A company's Net Promoter Score is determined by taking the percentage of promoters (scores of 9 or 10) and subtracting the percentage of detractors (scores of 0 to 6).[41] For example, assume that Widgets, Inc., received the following ratings:

Promoters (score of 9 or 10) = 60%

Passives (score of 7 or 8) = 30%

Detractors (score of 0 to 6) = 10%

The Net Promoter Score for Widgets, Inc., is calculated as follows:

60% − 10% = 50%

Promoters − Detractors = NPS

FIGURE 13.6 Net Promoter Score Calculation

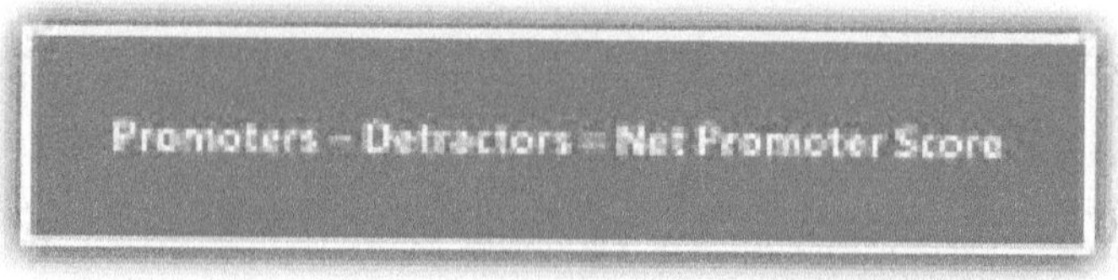

Promoters − Detractors = Net Promoter Score

The premise of Net Promoter Score is simple and elegant. The answer to one question says it all. Customers are then asked why they would be likely or unlikely to recommend the company.[42] If the customer is not a promoter after their experience with the brand, they are at risk either to try another brand or become a detractor of the brand. As you can see from the formula, customers that are passives (scores of 7 to 8), reflect poorly on the brand's NPS. Being satisfied isn't enough; a brand's goal is to have promoters or fans. This process quickly lets front-line managers and employees identify where problems exist and allow them to act quickly to respond and fix them.[43]

Net Promoter Scores vary by industry. The Net Promoter Score Web site includes a comparison by industry here: http://www.netpromoter.com/np/compare.jsp. Some companies that use Net Promoter Score are American Express, Southwest Airlines, FedEx, eBay, Harley-Davidson, and Dell. See additional companies listed on this Web site: http://www.theultimatequestion.com/theultimatequestion/good_profits.asp?groupCode=2.

While Net Promoter Score is a simple concept, it does require a complete operational commitment on the part of every level of management of the company to make it work effectively. Listen to Fred Reichheld, author of *The Ultimate Question: Driving Good Profits and True Growth*, and Brad Smith, CEO of Intuit, Inc., talk about how Net Promoter Score works.

Video Clip

How Net Promoter Score Works
Hear about how Net Promoter Score changes the way companies do business.

View the video online at: http://www.youtube.com/embed/VVv9YngCRQU

Key Takeaways

- Customer loyalty pays. It costs five times more to acquire a new customer than to keep an existing customer.
- A **customer feedback loop** is a formal process for gathering, synthesizing, and acting on customer feedback. Customer feedback loops are most effective when front-line employees have the power to respond to customer feedback to turn "critics into fans."
- **Net Promoter Score (NPS)** is a closed **customer feedback loop** that is based on the theory that a loyal customer is one that will recommend the brand to their friends.
- **NPS** is determined based on a brand's percentage of **promoters** minus the percentage of **detractors**.

Exercises

1. Describe why Net Promoter Score is a closed customer feedback loop.
2. Assume you worked as a financial planner. How would you use Net Promoter Score with your customers? How would you respond to promoters? How would you respond to passives? How would you respond to detractors?
3. Imagine that you are a sales rep for a medical supply company and you have just received your Net Promoter Score for the past month, which is as follows:

    Promoters: 63 percent

    Passives: 28 percent

    Detractors: 9 percent

    Calculate your overall Net Promoter Score. What steps would you take to communicate with the customers in each of the categories?
4. Research one of the companies that use Net Promoter Score and identify at least one way it impacts how the company does business.

5. Research Net Promoter Score online and find some articles that discuss the drawbacks of using it as the customer feedback loop. What do you think? Is Net Promoter Score something you think you might find helpful in sales?

6. Imagine that you are a salesperson for a software company and a portion of your compensation is based on your Net Promoter Score. Is it ethical for you to tell your customers that you need their positive comments to earn your salary? Why or why not?

13.3 *Selling U*: What Happens after You Accept the Offer?

Learning Objectives

1. Learn how to follow up after accepting a job offer.
2. Understand how to adapt to your new job.

So you've got your offer letter, and you're excited about starting your new job in a few weeks. Time to take it easy? Maybe a little. But don't kick back completely. There's follow-up work to be done.

From Classroom to the Corporate World

Just as you should never assume the sale is closed, the same is true about your job. Even though you have your offer, it's really the beginning of proving yourself in your new career. Whether you decide to work for a large corporation, a small company, or start your own business, it all starts right here.

FIGURE 13.7
Classroom challenges are different from corporate challenges.

© 2010 Jupiterimages Corporation

The first thing to realize is that the corporate world is very different from the classroom. For starters, everything will not be mapped out for you in a syllabus with predetermined reading, homework, and final exams. If you think you're busy now while you are in school, wait until you start working! At work, everything is due "yesterday," so it's up to you to prioritize what you need to get done.[44] There are no tests, but you are being tested everyday. You don't get a report card or grades; you get a performance review that provides a platform for feedback and self-improvement as well as a record of your performance for the company.[45] And even if you've had a job while you were in school, there's more expected of you as a full-time employee than as an intern or part-time employee.[46]After all, it's no longer about you; it's about how your performance impacts the company's results.[47] Welcome to the "real world."

Before You Start

Starting strong is important in any job. The first ninety days can make the difference in how well you do at your job, so do your follow-up from your job interviews before you even start working. It will not only give you a head start; it can make the difference about how well you do at the company.[48]

Here are five things you should do before you start your new job.

- **Say thank you**. Drop a handwritten note to your new boss, the human resources person, and any other people with whom you interviewed. Although you already sent thank-you notes to each of these people after your interviews, it's a good idea to send each one a personal note to thank them for their support and tell each how much you are looking forward to working with him. This is a great way to set yourself apart even before you begin your new job.

- **Continue to do your research on the company**. Just because you have a job offer doesn't mean you should stop researching the company. In fact, you should do just the opposite. Visit the company's stores, Web site, talk to customers, read press releases, and talk to current employees. Do everything you can to learn even more about the company you will work for.[49]

- **Dress for success**. Plan what you are going to wear on your first day, even your first week of work. It's best to dress more conservatively during your first days until you can begin to really understand the company culture. Even if the company is very casual, dress up on your first day. According to Alexandra Levit, author of *They Don't Teach Corporate in College: A Twenty-Something's Guide to the Business World*, "You might be overdressed, but I guarantee no one will criticize you for it. Rather, your colleagues will respect that you mean business, and your boss will be proud to introduce you around the company."[50] Try on your clothes, take items to the dry cleaner, or have them tailored as needed. You want to avoid any last-minute fashion emergencies on your first day of work.[51]

- **Plan your route**. Even though you probably know your way to the office, it's a good idea to take a test run during actual conditions during rush hour. You want to avoid being late for any reason so that includes knowing the public transportation schedule, traffic, or parking situation, depending on how you will get to work. Have an alternate route in mind just in case there is a traffic problem on your first day. Allow extra time on your first day. It's better to be early than to be late.[52]

- **Walk in with a smile**. While you will most likely be nervous with anticipation on your first day of work, follow the process similar to what you did for your job interview. Arrive a bit early, use the restroom, take one last look at yourself, use a breath mint, and smile. People will be helpful, so just relax and enjoy your first day on the job. A smile goes a long way on your first day and every day.[53]

> ### You've Got the Power: Tips for Your Job Search
>
> #### Impress Your New Boss
> You already sent your thank-you note to the people with whom you interviewed and have just accepted your offer. What's next? It's a good idea to send a handwritten note to your new boss and tell her how much you are looking forward to working with her. It's the perfect way to make a good first impression before you even start your new job.

After You Start

Your first few weeks on the job will be a whirlwind. You will meet lots of people, and it will be difficult to remember anyone's name, title, or function. It takes a while to adjust and fit in at any company. Remember how it felt when you were a freshman? By the time you became a sophomore, you knew a lot of people, and you knew the ropes. The same thing happens at a job. There's no magic time frame to adjust to a new job; everyone is different. It's good to know that you're not alone and that adjusting to your new job just takes time—and commitment.[54] Here are five tips to help you get your feet on the ground at your new job.

- **Listen, observe, and ask questions**. This is the best way to learn the ropes and the company culture. There is no stupid question, so take advantage of the fact that you are new to ask as many questions as possible. When you watch and listen to other people, it's easier to understand the culture or the unwritten rules of the company.[55]

- **Avoid office gossip**. It might sound obvious, but engaging in office gossip can only hurt you. You never know to whom you are speaking so it's better to heed your mother's words: "If you can't say something nice about someone, don't say anything at all." But do pay attention to the office grapevine. This will help you understand the informal rules, who's who in the office, and how people perceive what's going on in the company.[56] On similar note, it's never appropriate to use company time and resources to check or update your status on social networking sites. Even if other employees do it, avoid the temptation to participate in social networking at work.

- **Find a mentor**. A mentor is someone who has experience in the area you wish to pursue and who exhibits a "generosity of spirit," a natural gift to go out of her way to help others.[57] A mentor is a person with whom you develop a personal relationship: someone whom you trust and are comfortable asking questions to and getting feedback from to take your career to the next level. Some companies offer formal mentoring programs, but at most companies finding a mentor is usually a less formal process. Go out of your way to get to know people whom you think might be a good mentor and take the time to get to know them. You should consider having several mentors throughout your career.

- **Stand out**. Perception is reality so be the person who stands out.[58] Volunteer to work on projects, especially those that others don't want to do, come in early, stay late, and deliver high-quality work on time.[59] Going the extra mile pays off.

- **Fine-tune your writing and speaking skills**. Now that you are working, you have to develop and communicate your ideas and point of view to your boss, your colleagues, and even your clients. Be a good listener and a confident communicator. It will make a difference in how people perceive you and your work.[60]

Now, it's time to relax, enjoy, and start this next chapter in your life.

Key Takeaways

- Even though you receive a job offer, there are still a lot of things you can do to follow up after your interview and before you start your new job.
- The corporate world is different from the classroom with a different environment and expectations. Your performance is no longer just about you; it's about how you help the company achieve its goals.
- It takes time to adapt to a new job.

Exercises

1. Assume you just accepted a job offer to become a sales rep at a national food manufacturer. Write a personal note to your new boss to tell him how you are looking forward to starting your new job. Who are some other people in the company to whom you might also write a note?

2. What is a mentor? Identify someone who is currently a mentor to you. What makes him a good mentor? How might you be able to find additional mentors when you begin working?

3. Identify two resources that would be helpful to fine-tune your writing and speaking skills. How can you use these resources to help prepare you for your career?

13.4 Review and Practice

Power Wrap-Up

Now that you have read this chapter, you should be able to understand the importance of follow-up on your relationships and sales.

- You can **understand** the role of follow-up in the selling process.
- You can **identify** how to plan your follow-up even before you begin prospecting.
- You can **learn** that follow-up is a personal commitment and has a reflection on you as a brand.
- You can **identify** ways to add value to your customers' businesses as part of follow-up.
- You can **describe** how follow-up can build your business with additional sales from your existing customers, testimonials, and referrals.
- You can **define** heroic recovery and the impact it can have on how customers perceive you.
- You can **understand** how the customer feedback loop works.
- You can **describe** how Net Promoter Score works to improve follow-up and customer service.
- You can **list** things you can do after you accept a job offer.

Test Your Power Knowledge (answers are below)

1. How many calls does it take on average to close a sale?
2. True or false: After the sale is closed, the role of the salesperson is finished.
3. What does this statement mean: "Even though the sale is closed, you should never assume the sale is closed"?
4. Name three areas that require follow-up on the part of the salesperson.
5. Identify three ways that you can add value to your customers' businesses during the follow-up process.
6. Name three benefits of having a loyal customer.
7. Describe how heroic recovery can have a positive impact on your relationship with your customer.
8. What is a customer feedback loop?
9. Describe Net Promoter Score?

10. What is the formula to calculate NPS?

11. Identify at least one thing you can do after you receive your job offer but before you start your job.

Power (Role) Play

Now it's time to put what you've learned into practice. The following are two roles that are involved in the same selling situation—one role is the customer, and the other is the salesperson. This will give you the opportunity to think about this selling situation from the point of view of both the customer and the salesperson.

Read each role carefully along with the discussion questions. Be prepared to play either of the roles in class using the concepts covered in this chapter. You may be asked to discuss the roles and do a role-play in groups or individually.

Let It Snow

Role: Facilities manager at the Tri-County Office Complex

You are responsible for the overall maintenance at the largest office complex in the area. There are ten office buildings in the complex, which provides office space for thirty companies. You oversee the exterior maintenance, which includes everything from trash and snow removal to lawn care and window washing. You have just signed a contract with All Weather Maintenance Co., two days ago. It's 5:00 a.m., and a major snowstorm just hit, so you are on your way to inspect the property to be sure that the walkways are shoveled and parking lot is plowed.

- What role do you expect the salesperson to play now that the contract has been signed?
- Who will you call if the snow removal is not completed to your satisfaction?
- How will this experience impact your expectations of All Weather Maintenance Co., for other snowstorms and situations that require maintenance, especially time-sensitive maintenance?

Role: Sales rep, All Weather Maintenance Co.

You recently signed your largest client, Tri-County Office Complex. You have a very good relationship with the facilities manager based on the selling process. You have communicated the maintenance requirements to your company's operations department. Now the job is up to them to conduct year-round maintenance. Your normal hours are 8:00 a.m. to 5:00 p.m., but you were concerned about the weather report last night, so you set your alarm early. You wake up at 5:00 a.m. to see a blanket of snow and ice and immediately wonder if the maintenance crew made it to the Tri-County Office Complex.

- What action, if any, do you take?
- What kind of follow-up will you do with the customer?
- When will you do follow-up?
- What will you say to the customer?
- What will you do to ensure that time-sensitive maintenance is completed as expected?

Put Your Power to Work: *Selling U* Activities

1. Visit your career center and ask them for information about mentors. Learn how you can get a mentor even before you start your job.

2. Identify someone who already works at the company from which you received an offer. Set up a meeting with her before you start your new job to learn more about the company, company culture, and other things that will be important to know for your new job.

Test Your Power Knowledge Answers

1. Five.
2. False.
3. Good salespeople help avoid buyer's remorse by following up quickly after the sale is closed and reinforcing the fact that the buyer made a good decision.
4. Contracts to be signed, delivery to be scheduled, customer shipping and billing information to be added to CRM system, credit checks, addition of customers to all appropriate correspondence, invoice to be generated, welcome package to be sent to customer, introductions to be make to all appropriate internal people on the team, and status calls to be scheduled.
5. Phone and in-person regular status updates, newsletters, white papers, industry information, networking, asking questions, spending time in the business.
6. Additional sales from the loyal customer, testimonials to be used in presentations for prospects, and referrals to new customers.
7. If a service failure is handled quickly and meets or exceeds the expectations of the customer, it can have an even more positive impact on how the customer perceives the service from the sales rep and the company.
8. A formal process for gathering, synthesizing, and acting upon customer feedback.
9. NPS is a closed loop customer feedback system that relies on the answer from customers to one key question: "How likely would you be to recommend this product or service to your friends or colleagues?"
10. NPS = Promoters – Detractors.
11. Say thank you with a personal note to your new boss, continue to do research on the company, dress for success, plan your route, and walk in with a smile.

Endnotes

1. Sarah Littman, "Welcome to the New Millenials," *Response Magazine*, May 1, 2008, http://www.responsemagazine.com/response-magazine/welcome-new-millenials-1192 (accessed November 25, 2009).
2. David Frey, "Follow-up Marketing: How to Win More Sales with Less Effort," Marketing Best Practices, http://www.marketingbestpractices.com/Articles/FollowUpMarketing.htm (accessed November 22, 2009).
3. Jeff Schmitt, "The Personal Touch: Make the Sale...after the Sale," Sales & Marketing Management, September 9, 2009, http://www.salesandmarketing.com/article/personal-touch-making-salex2026after-sale (accessed November 23, 2009).
4. Jeff Schmitt, "The Personal Touch: Make the Sale...after the Sale," Sales & Marketing Management, September 9, 2009, http://www.salesandmarketing.com/article/personal-touch-making-salex2026after-sale (accessed November 23, 2009).
5. Jeff Schmitt, "The Personal Touch: Make the Sale...after the Sale," Sales & Marketing Management, September 9, 2009, http://www.salesandmarketing.com/article/personal-touch-making-salex2026after-sale (accessed November 23, 2009).
6. Joan Leotta, "When Buyers Change, Grin and Sell It," *Selling Power* 21, no. 5, http://www.sellingpower.com/content/article.php?a=5769 (accessed March 16, 2010).
7. George Hedley, "Customer Care = Cash," *American Salesman*, March 2009, http://www.hardhatpresentations.com/CustomerCareCash.htm (accessed March 16, 2010).
8. Dana Ray, "Phenomenal Follow-up," *Selling Power* 19, no. 6, http://www.sellingpower.com/content/article.php?a=5081 (accessed March 16, 2010).
9. Joan Leotta, "When Buyers Change, Grin and Sell It," *Selling Power* 21, no. 5, http://www.sellingpower.com/content/article.php?a=5769 (accessed March 16, 2010).
10. Joan Leotta, "When Buyers Change, Grin and Sell It," *Selling Power* 21, no. 5, http://www.sellingpower.com/content/article.php?a=5769 (accessed March 16, 2010).
11. Sean McPheat, "Post Sales Follow Up," Master of the Sales Force Blog, http://www.mtdsalestraining.com/mtdblog/post-sales-follow-up.html (accessed November 23, 2009).
12. George Hedley, "Customer Care = Cash," *American Salesman*, March 2009, http://www.hardhatpresentations.com/CustomerCareCash.htm (accessed March 16, 2010).
13. Marshall Goldsmith, "Don't Just Check the Box," *Fast Company*, February 1, 2005, http://www.fastcompany.com/magazine/91/mgoldsmith.html (accessed November 23, 2009).
14. Jeff Schmitt, "The Personal Touch: Make the Sale...after the Sale," Sales & Marketing Management, September 9, 2009, http://www.salesandmarketing.com/article/personal-touch-making-salex2026after-sale (accessed November 23, 2009).
15. Kelley Robertson, "The Power of Follow Up," About.com, http://entrepreneurs.about.com/od/salesmarketing/a/poweroffollowup.htm (accessed November 23, 2009).
16. Dana Ray, "Phenomenal Follow-up," *Selling Power* 19, no. 6, http://www.sellingpower.com/content/article.php?a=5081 (accessed March 16, 2010).
17. Jeff Schmitt, "The Personal Touch: Make the Sale...after the Sale," Sales & Marketing Management, September 9, 2009, http://www.salesandmarketing.com/article/personal-touch-making-salex2026after-sale (accessed November 23, 2009).
18. Kelley Robertson, "The Power of Follow Up," About.com, http://entrepreneurs.about.com/od/salesmarketing/a/poweroffollowup.htm (accessed November 23, 2009).
19. Dana Ray, "Phenomenal Follow-up," *Selling Power* 19, no. 6, http://www.sellingpower.com/content/article.php?a=5081 (accessed March 16, 2010).
20. Jeff Schmitt, "The Personal Touch: Make the Sale...after the Sale," Sales & Marketing Management, September 9, 2009, http://www.salesandmarketing.com/article/personal-touch-making-salex2026after-sale (accessed November 23, 2009).

21. Jeff Schmitt, "The Personal Touch: Make the Sale...after the Sale," Sales & Marketing Management, September 9, 2009, http://www.salesandmarketing.com/article/personal-touch-making-salex2026after-sale (accessed November 23, 2009).

22. Tamara Monosoff, "Focus on Core Customers," Entrepreneur, October 21, 2009, http://www.entrepreneur.com/article/printthis/203774.html (accessed November 23, 2009).

23. George Hedley, "Customer Care = Cash," American Salesman, March 2009, http://www.hardhatpresentations.com/CustomerCareCash.htm (accessed March 16, 2010).

24. Alister Cameron, "Dell IdeaStorm—Ultimate Customer Feedback Example," WebProNews, February 27, 2007, http://www.webpronews.com/blogtalk/2007/02/27/dell-ideastorm-the-ultimate-customer-feedback-example (accessed November 23, 2009).

25. Starbucks, http://mystarbucksidea.force.com (accessed November 24, 2009).

26. Jeffrey Gitomer, "Objection Prevention & Objection Cure," video, May 18, 2009, http://www.youtube.com/watch?v=CgfmcuE_06w (accessed November 24, 2009).

27. Jeff Schmitt, "The Personal Touch: Make the Sale...after the Sale," Sales & Marketing Management, September 9, 2009, http://www.salesandmarketing.com/article/personal-touch-making-salex2026after-sale (accessed November 23, 2009).

28. Michael Eisenberg, "Yahoo!—Great Customer Feedback Loop," March 13, 2007, http://sixkidsandafulltimejob.blogspot.com/2007/03/yahoo-great-customer-feedback-loop.html (accessed November 19, 2009).

29. Chia-Chi Chang, "When Service Fails: The Role of the Salesperson and the Customer," Psychology & Marketing 23, no. 3 (March 2006): 204.

30. Gabriel R. Gonzalez, K. Douglas Hoffman, and Thomas N. Ingram, "Improving Relationship Selling Through Failure Analysis and Recovery Efforts: A Framework and Call to Action," Journal of Personal Selling & Sales Management 25, no. 1 (Winter 2005): 58.

31. Ilan Mochari, "What You Learn on the Other Side," Inc., November 1, 2002, http://www.inc.com/magazine/20021101/24833.html (accessed November 23, 2009).

32. Gabriel R. Gonzalez, K. Douglas Hoffman, and Thomas N. Ingram, "Improving Relationship Selling through Failure Analysis and Recovery Efforts: A Framework and Call to Action," Journal of Personal Selling & Sales Management 25, no. 1 (Winter 2005): 58.

33. Chia-Chi Chang, "When Service Fails: The Role of the Salesperson and the Customer," Psychology & Marketing 23, no. 3 (March 2006): 204.

34. Guy Maser, "How to Earn Your Customers' Loyalty," CRMBuyer.com, July 16, 2009, http://www.crmbuyer.com/story/67608.html (accessed November 23, 2009).

35. Rob Markey, Fred Reichheld, and Andreas Dullweber, "Closing the Customer Feedback Loop," Harvard Business Review, http://hbr.harvardbusiness.org/2009/12/closing-the-customer-feedback-loop/ar/pr (accessed November 23, 2009).

36. Rob Markey, Fred Reichheld, and Andreas Dullweber, "Closing the Customer Feedback Loop," Harvard Business Review, http://hbr.harvardbusiness.org/2009/12/closing-the-customer-feedback-loop/ar/pr (accessed November 23, 2009).

37. Dr. Laura Brooks, "Closing the Loop on Customer Feedback,"Sales & Marketing Management, April 23, 2009, http://www.salesandmarketing.com/article/closing-loop-customer-feedback (accessed November 23, 2009).

38. Jon Swartz, "Twitter Helps Customer Service," USA Today, November 18, 2009, 3B.

39. Rebecca Resisner, "Comcast's Twitter Man," BusinessWeek, January 13, 2009, http://www.businessweek.com/managing/content/jan2009/ca20090113_373506.htm (accessed January 8, 2010).

40. Rob Markey, Fred Reichheld, and Andreas Dullweber, "Closing the Customer Feedback Loop," Harvard Business Review, http://hbr.harvardbusiness.org/2009/12/closing-the-customer-feedback-loop/ar/pr (accessed November 23, 2009).

41. Net Promoter, "How to Calculate Your Score," http://www.netpromoter.com/np/calculate.jsp (accessed November 25, 2009).

42. Rob Markey, Fred Reichheld, and Andreas Dullweber, "Closing the Customer Feedback Loop," Harvard Business Review, http://hbr.harvardbusiness.org/2009/12/closing-the-customer-feedback-loop/ar/pr (accessed November 23, 2009).

43. Net Promoter, "How to Calculate Your Score," http://www.netpromoter.com/np/calculate.jsp (accessed November 25, 2009).

44. Alexandra Levit, The Don't Teach Corporate in College: A Twenty-Something's Guide to the Business World (Franklin Lakes, NJ: Career Press, 2009), 134.

45. Dawn Rosenberg McKay, "From College Campus to Corporate Climate: How to Make the Transition to Your First Job after College Graduation," About.com, http://careerplanning.about.com/cs/firstjob/a/post_grad.htm (accessed November 23, 2009).

46. Dawn Rosenberg McKay, "Your First Job: Making a Good Impression," About.com, http://careerplanning.about.com/cs/firstjob/a/first_job.htm (accessed November 24, 2009).

47. Dawn Rosenberg McKay, "From College Campus to Corporate Climate: How to Make the Transition to Your First Job after College Graduation," About.com, http://careerplanning.about.com/cs/firstjob/a/post_grad.htm (accessed November 23, 2009).

48. Andy Wang, "The First 90 Days," Forbes, September 7, 2006, http://www.forbes.com/2006/09/06/leadership-pink-careers-cx_ag_0906ninetydays.html (accessed November 25, 2009).

49. "Brave New World: What to Do before You Start a New Job," Workplace911, February 22, 2008, http://careerplanning.about.com/cs/firstjob/a/new_job.htm (accessed November 25, 2009).

50. Alexandra Levit, They Don't Teach Corporate in College: A Twenty-Something's Guide to the Business World (Franklin Lakes, NJ: Career Press, 2009), 51.

51. Dawn Rosenberg McKay, "Starting a New Job: What You Can Do before Your First Day," About.com, http://careerplanning.about.com/cs/firstjob/a/new_job.htm (accessed November 24, 2009).

52. Dawn Rosenberg McKay, "Starting a New Job: What You Can Do before Your First Day," About.com, http://careerplanning.about.com/cs/firstjob/a/new_job.htm (accessed November 24, 2009).

53. Dawn Rosenberg McKay, "Starting a New Job: Fitting In," About.com, http://careerplanning.about.com/od/newjobfirstjob/New_Job_First_Job.htm (accessed November 24, 2009).

54. Dawn Rosenberg McKay, "Starting a New Job: Fitting In," About.com, http://careerplanning.about.com/od/newjobfirstjob/New_Job_First_Job.htm (accessed November 24, 2009).

55. Dawn Rosenberg McKay, "Your First Job: Making a Good Impression," About.com, http://careerplanning.about.com/cs/firstjob/a/first_job.htm (accessed November 24, 2009).

56. Dawn Rosenberg McKay, "Your First Job: Etiquette and Gossip," About.com, http://careerplanning.about.com/cs/firstjob/a/first_job_2.htm (accessed November 24, 2009).

57. Alexandra Levit, They Don't Teach Corporate in College: A Twenty-Something's Guide to the Business World (Franklin Lakes, NJ: Career Press, 2009), 106.

58. Alexandra Levit, They Don't Teach Corporate in College: A Twenty-Something's Guide to the Business World (Franklin Lakes, NJ: Career Press, 2009), 75.

59. Dawn Rosenberg McKay, "Starting a New Job: Fitting In," About.com, http://careerplanning.about.com/od/newjobfirstjob/New_Job_First_Job.htm (accessed November 24, 2009).

60. Alexandra Levit, They Don't Teach Corporate in College: A Twenty-Something's Guide to the Business World (Franklin Lakes, NJ: Career Press, 2009), 161.

CHAPTER 14
The Power of Learning the Ropes

Video Ride-Along with Priya Masih, Sales Representative at Lupin Pharmaceuticals

Meet Priya Masih. Priya has been in sales for five years with experience in the telecommunications, insurance, and pharmaceutical industries. She is currently a sales representative at Lupin Pharmaceuticals. She has learned how to manage herself, her time, and her results for a successful career in sales. But it's not always easy. One of the biggest challenges of being successful in sales is to stay motivated, even when you don't make the sale.

Priya shares how she stays motivated to achieve new heights every day.

View the video online at: http://www.youtube.com/embed/w0y1EKbE1q0

14.1 Managing Yourself, Your Income, and Your Results

Learning Objectives

1. Understand how to manage yourself as a selling professional.
2. Learn the keys to managing your time.
3. Identify the elements that drive your results and income.

So imagine that you landed your dream job in sales, you've been to the corporate office for training and orientation, you've set up your home office, and you've picked up your company car—now what?

Sales is a challenging, exhilarating, demanding, and rewarding profession. You want to be successful and enjoy what you do, but you really haven't had a chance to focus on the actual job between graduation and job interviews. Here's your chance to look ahead to how you learn the day-to-day activities that go on in the profession of selling, identify the resources to help you be a partner to your customers, and bring success to yourself and your company. It sounds like a tall order, but it's easy when you have people to guide and support you.

Be an A-Player

FIGURE 14.1
Just like professional athletes, the best salespeople are A-Players.

© 2010 Jupiterimages Corporation

No matter what job you have or what company you sell for, you can and should be an "A-Player." That means being the best at what you do. You don't have to be a celebrity or a person who went to Harvard, according to blogger Auren Hoffman in her April 2009 post "The A-Player Janitor": "An 'A-Player' by definition is incredibly productive and smart and has that 'it,' that rockstar-esque factor that makes everyone want to work with her."[1] Her point is that hiring managers want to hire the best person for every job. So you don't have to be an A-Player in everything, just be an A-Player in the *one* thing you do best.[2] Find your sweet spot and focus on it. In sales, being an A-Player means connecting with customers. You might be surprised to learn what makes someone an A-Player in sales according to this video.

Video Link

What Makes an A-Player?

http://www.sellingpower.com/content/video/?date=8/29/2009

Managing Yourself: Making the Most of Your Resources

"The best part of a career in sales is that it is undefined," according to Ann Devine in a recent article on The Black Collegian Online.[3] Every day is completely different; some days you will be researching leads, and other days you might be making a presentation to a prospective customer. This exciting, unstructured, and sometimes unpredictable environment rarely gets boring. But it's this lack of structure that can present a challenge in choosing priorities and accomplishing goals. Those who are successful realize how to manage themselves and their time and use the resources that are available to them from their company, their colleagues, and their community.

You might be wondering what managing yourself means. When you are in sales, one of the most important jobs you have is being sure that you have clear direction about what you want to accomplish and what you need to do to get there. Even though you are used to managing yourself and your time at school, it can be a daunting task to be responsible for calling on customers and generating sales, especially if you are based in a location remote from the company office such as your home office. So first things first—identify your resources. Even though you're traveling solo, you are not alone.

Manage Yourself for Success

A great salesperson starts with great habits. Here are a few tips from Richard E. Goldman, author of *Luck by Design: Certain Success in an Uncertain World*.

- **Learn by doing**. Take the initiative to seek out information and teach yourself how to do things; the power of learning is by doing.
- **Make your own choices**. You might not have all the information you need at the time, but the best decision is the one you make. Don't let someone else make your decisions for you.
- **Believe in yourself**. You got this job because you are smart and talented. Don't ever believe you can't succeed.[4]

Ride-Alongs

One of the best ways to learn the ropes and get the inside track is to go on ride-alongs (also referred to as shadowing) with colleagues, traveling with an experienced sales rep or sales manager to make sales calls. The video ride-alongs at the start of each chapter are a virtual way for you to get some powerful insights from experienced sales professionals. Sometimes a ride-along is included in the interviewing process; it's an opportunity for you to experience firsthand exactly what the job entails and for the company to see how you react in the selling environment before you get a job offer. Other times a ride-along is an training opportunity that takes place after you've been hired. Either way, always take advantage of as many opportunities as you can to ride-along with experienced salespeople. There are some tips that will help maximize your ride-along experience.

- **Always be professional**. It is likely that you will be traveling with a salesperson or sales manager at least for a day and sometimes for a week or longer. Even though you will get to know each other, always remember your role on the ride-along.
- **Avoid highly personal or inappropriate topics**. While it's always appropriate to tell the truth, it's best to avoid controversial topics, especially as they relate to the company.
- **Mind your manners and avoid alcohol if you go out to lunch or dinner**. Since you will ultimately be in the role of entertaining clients, the person with whom you are riding will undoubtedly be watching your social behavior.
- **Above all, be yourself**. You won't be able to learn if your focus is on acting in a way that isn't natural.[5]

Use Your Sales Manager

Many salespeople don't realize that their **sales manager** (i.e., the person to whom they report) is ultimately responsible for delivering the company's sales goals. As such, the sales manager wants to do everything he can to help his salespeople be successful. Even before you start your job, it's a good idea to touch base with your sales manager. Chances are you interviewed with him, so you probably have his contact information. A good way to get off to a great start is to send him a handwritten thank-you note after you've accepted the position. What better way to start a new relationship than with a personal note.

Your sales manager can be your most important source of company information as well as customer insights. He had a lot of experience selling before he became a sales manager, and he would likely share his insights to help you be successful. Not only can he make your job (and your life) easier, he can teach you a lot about selling. It's always a good idea to keep your sales manager updated with the status of your customers and prospects. He will appreciate your proactive and regular updates about the standing of each lead and customer in addition to your regular one-on-one meetings, staff meetings, or conference calls.

Sometimes new salespeople are nervous about asking questions of their sales managers, which is natural. It's best to remember that your sales manager doesn't expect you to know everything. Your questions show him that you are interested in learning more about the business from him and help him identify what areas would be most beneficial for coaching. Your sales manager can be a part of your success story. Ask questions, ask his opinion, keep him in the loop, help make him look good, and you will have a relationship that works and grows.

sales manager

Person to whom a salesperson reports and who is accountable for delivering on sales goals.

span of control

The number of people that
report to one manager.

territory management

Organizational strategy
whereby salespeople are
responsible for a
designated geographic
area such as a city or
cites, state, or region.

territory manager

Salesperson that is
reponsible for the
customers in a designated
geographic area.

Just as communication is important with customers, it is critical to building your relationship with your sales manager. He probably has a **span of control**, or the number of people reporting to him, ranging from a two to twenty or more people. It's important to understand the organizational structure of a sales department. While each company is different, the basic structure of a selling organization is shown in Figure 14.2. In some companies, salespeople may be responsible for a city or cities, region, or other geographic area. This is called **territory management**. In this case, salespeople, usually called **territory managers**, are responsible for the customers in their specific geographic area. This organizational strategy helps minimize the amount of travel time between customers.

FIGURE 14.2 Sales Department Organization Chart

In other companies, salespeople may be responsible for specific brands, products, or product categories. In the case of food manufacturers, these categories might be noncarbonated beverages, prepared meals, or dairy products. In the professional services arena, the organization might be vertical, such as retail sales, financial services, or health care. This product or category approach may require salespeople to travel to customers in various parts of the country based on the needs of the customers. It requires the salesperson to develop expertise in a specific product or discipline. These sales positions may have titles such as account manager, product manager, or sales rep. The different types of sales positions are discussed in more detail in Chapter 2.

Resources and Resourcefulness

onboarding

Employee orientation
process or method for a
new employee to learn
about company practices,
policies, and procedures.

The company you work for, whether it is large or small, has resources. A laptop, the customer relationship management (CRM) system, your expense account, the company owner, the human resources department, accounts receivable department, and others are all resources that can help you do your job. Take the time to explore all the resources when you start with the company. In larger companies, you will most likely participate in an orientation session or process frequently referred to as **onboarding** to learn about how the company operates and how your can take advantage of resources to help you do your job. In a small company, the process is less formal and requires you to be more proactive about understanding what's available. Either way, it's your responsibility to explore and understand your resources. Remember that all the skills you use when you are communicating with customers are the same when you are communicating inside your company: build lasting relationships that are mutually beneficial. While every company is different, here are some internal resources that are available in most companies.

- **Human resources department**. Whether you work for a large company or a start-up, it's a good idea to know the key people in HR. Chances are, you interviewed with someone in the department, but don't stop there. Continue your relationship by learning who handles employee relations (for questions about the company policies or an ethical dilemma) and who handles benefits (for questions about medical, dental, other insurance, 401(k) plan, and other company benefits).

- **Finance department**. You'll want to get to know the people who handle accounts receivable. Since most salespeople are responsible for collections, you will most likely be working closely with people in finance, accounting, or accounts payable. They can provide helpful information about company processes and policies for payment of invoices. You're not the first person to be challenged by customer payment issues, so take advantage of their knowledge and experience.

- **Procurement or product development department**. Whether you are selling a product or a service, you will want to know those who make the decisions about exactly what will be available for sale. Customers may have specific questions about the performance of the product or service that you may need some additional information to answer. In addition, building a relationship with people in this department will help give you insight into what will be available in the future. More important, it will help you provide input and feedback based on the customer's perspective.

- **Marketing department**. The people who are responsible for getting the word out about your company's brand are important to know. You can get insights about advertising, promotions, and other communication activities. You can also get important information about future plans and help shape the marketing plan for the future based on your experience with customers.

- **Information technology department**. Everything from your laptop to your reports is supported in the IT department. It's especially important to get to know the people who man the help desk. Chances are, you will have a technology emergency at some point in time so it's best to build a strong relationship from the start.

- **Other salespeople**. Create relationships with the best-performing salespeople so you can learn the best practices. Go on ride-alongs and learn what makes them successful.

- **Other resources**. Explore the CRM system and company intranet, especially the online communities. This is an excellent way to learn about how sales were won, see examples of successful proposals, and learn about best practices of the top performers.

Power Selling: Lessons in Selling from Successful Brands

School of Hard Rocks

Imagine going to employee orientation and getting the employee handbook that looks more like a comic book than a manual. That's how Hard Rock Café onboards its mostly millennial sales force of wait staff and other support roles during its one-day orientation. Jim Knight, senior director of training and development, completely revamped the company's School of Hard Rocks corporate university. Knight used comic books as his inspiration and got employees involved in telling the Hard Rock Café story; all the illustrations and photos in the handbook were done by Hard Rock employees. The results are impressive: employee turnover rate is now fifty-five points lower than that of the industry.

Besides using company resources, it's also important for you to stay on top of changes in technology, not only to be effective but also to redefine practices. In fact, Helen Hast, a professor at the Harvard Graduate School of Business, has identified managing technological change as of the five core competencies for the twenty-first century. According to a recent article on BNET, she said, "When we have a new tool, we first use it for what we are already doing, just doing it a bit better. But gradually, the new tool changes the way we do things."[6]

While resources are important for you to be effective in sales, it's resourcefulness that will make you successful.[7] Think about it: Evan Williams, Biz Stone, and Jack Dorsey figured out a way to make Twitter—the microblogging site they founded in March 2006—one of the most popular Web sites in the world without the use of traditional advertising to spread the word.[8]

It would be hard to argue that Williams, Stone, and Dorsey had all the resources they needed to launch this hugely successful Web site; they had no money for advertising, or anything else for that matter. But they were resourceful about getting people to try their new service, use it, and engage with it. While you might not invent the next Twitter, you can certainly sell the next big idea by using your resources and being resourceful.

Managing Your Time: Organizing and Prioritizing

Depending on the type of business you are in and the company you work for, you might have as few as one customer and as many as a hundred or more. You might be wondering how you determine which customers to call on each day, how much time should be spent on prospecting versus calling on existing customers, how much time should be devoted to nonselling activities such as travel, paperwork, and internal meetings. While there is no hard-and-fast answer to these questions, your goal should be to spend as much time as possible with customers or prospects. It's impossible to sell if you are not in front of a customer.

Consider this: Salespeople spend approximately fourteen hours a week engaged in face-to-face selling. That means that 70 percent of the time, in an average forty-six-hour workweek, salespeople are doing something other than face-to-face selling.[9] See Figure 14.3 for a complete breakdown of activities.

FIGURE 14.3 Activities of Salespeople in an Average Workweek[10]

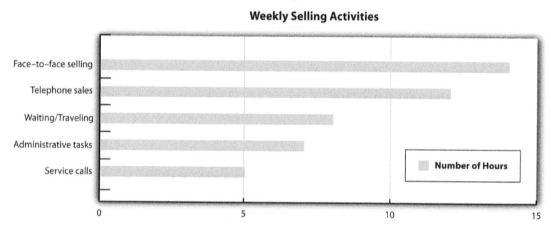

Since your objective is to spend as much time as possible with customers, you'll need to balance where you physically spend your time and with which customers you spend it. This is where territory management strategies come into play. Based on the **call cycle**, the frequency at which you call on each of your customers, and where each is located, you'll develop a plan to call on your existing customers and allow time for prospecting. In other words, you will need to have a plan to invest your time wisely to meet your goals.

To plan your sales calls, you'll need a map (Google maps or MapQuest) and sales and potential sales information by customer (your company CRM system should include some, if not all, of this information), and your call cycle. Identify the location of each of your customers with a red dot or push pin. Then, divide your territory into sections by geography (designated as one, two, three, etc.), this can become the basis of your territory management plan. Review your customer data, including current sales and potential sales, to organize and prioritize your customers and calls. Figure 14.4 includes an example of a territory management worksheet.

call cycle

The frequency at which you call on each of your customers (e.g., once every twenty days).

FIGURE 14.4 Territory Management Worksheet

Customer	Current Sales	Potential Sales	Territory Section	# of Calls per Month (call cycle)
A	$3,000	$10,000	1	2
B	$2,000	$3,000	1	Once every other month
C	$10,000	$10,000	1	2
D	$1,000	$6,000	2	1
E	$3,000	$12,000	2	2
F	$2,500	$3,000	2	1

Based on this, you would plan your route so that you are making calls in one section of your territory on a given day, then covering another section on another day. This will ensure that you regularly visit your best customers and those with the most potential for growth, minimizing your travel time. While this might seem like a lot of work to do, it will save you time in the long run and help you increase your sales...and your income.

Time Management

I am definitely going to take a course on time management...just as soon as I can work it into my schedule.
— *Louis E. Boone*

If you've ever felt this way, it's time to focus on **time management**. Salespeople get paid on results, not on the number of hours worked. As a salesperson, there are so many demands on your time: client needs, internal meetings, follow-ups, proposals, phone calls, e-mails, text messages, and the emergency du jour. All these can be time thieves, or activities that literally steal your time away from selling. You can easily fill your days with demanding tasks like these that really do not bring value to customers or ultimately close sales. Keep in mind that according to renowned sales consultant and motivational speaker Zig Ziglar, "Nothing happens until someone sells something."[11] To understand how to avoid getting caught up in the daily sea of details, it's a good idea to realize why these interruptions and administrative demands consume your day. Here are three key reasons that time can get away from you:

- **Poor planning**. Avoid getting caught up in the moment and make a plan every day of selling activities—not time-fillers—that you want to accomplish. True selling activities include things like identifying six new prospects, setting up three appointments for the coming week, or closing at least one sale. "Write your top three outcomes at the top of your plan" is good advice.[12]

- **Procrastination**. Fear of rejection causes many salespeople to stay involved in meaningless tasks. It's hard to get an appointment with a customer, as they don't always have time to give to salespeople. Customers want true solutions, not a sales pitch. It takes time, research, and creativity to really understand a customers' business.[13]

- **Making tasks too big**. Thinking about how long it takes to go from identifying a prospect to actually closing a sale can sometimes make the job seem overwhelming. Sales success comes from a series of wins, not one home run. It's best to set short-term goals to make steady progress toward the larger, longer-term goal.[14]

time management

The practice of organizing and prioritizing your activities to ensure that you can achieve your goals.

FIGURE 14.5

Time management skills can help prevent you from feeling overwhelmed.

© 2010 Jupiterimages Corporation

Mastering Time Management

While there are many theories on the best way to manage yourself and your time, one of the best resources is *The Seven Habits of Highly Effective People* by best-selling author and management expert Stephen R. Covey. The book is based on seven principles that appear to be simple, but provide a framework to make you more efficient, effective, and successful.

- **Habit 1: Be proactive**. Take ownership and control your environment.
- **Habit 2: Begin with the end in mind**. Develop personal leadership that helps you stay focused on your goals.
- **Habit 3: Put first things first**. Avoid distractions and time wasters with personal management; this is the essence of time management.
- **Habit 4: Think win-win**. Build success through cooperation with others, not on a win-lose attitude.
- **Habit 5: Seek first to understand, then to be understood**. Develop strong relationships by listening and understanding.
- **Habit 6: Synergize**. See and appreciate what others have to contribute.
- **Habit 7: Sharpen the saw**. Focus on self-renewal in four areas: spiritual, mental, physical, and social/emotional.[15]

Covey's philosophy has been embraced by so many that his consulting firm, FranklinCovey, advises thousands of people and companies around the world. His time management and personal planning tools are very popular with a loyal following. You can learn more about Stephen Covey and his philosophy at http://www.franklincovey.com/tc.

Video Clip

Choosing Success
Hear Stephen Covey talk about choosing success.

View the video online at: http://www.youtube.com/embed/U8LM4C1I70U

Power Point: Lessons in Selling from the Customer's Point of View

Don't Waste My Time

If you think your time is valuable, think about how valuable your customer's time is. When your customer thinks that doing business with you helps her save time, it can be a reason she won't do business with anyone else. Ask Marcia F. Borello, who sings the praises of BankAtlantic in Tampa, Florida: "I do my banking exclusively at BankAtlantic because I save so much time. At so many other banks, I waste my precious free time in my lunch hour waiting in long lines hurrying to make my banking transactions before the bank closes at 4 pm. BankAtlantic's long hours and seven day service make it convenient for me to do my banking when I choose to."[16]

The moral of the story is that when you save time and save your customer's time, you get more business.

Top Three Time-Wasters for Salespeople

Selling is all about making things happen. According to Ray Silverstein, "When you're selling, time is your most valuable asset."[17] But sometimes salespeople can get sidetracked doing tasks that don't really generate sales. Here are the top three time-wasters:

1. **Focusing on the urgent**. E-mails, phone calls, paperwork, and even meetings can be unnecessary tasks that appear to be urgent but take time and focus away from selling.
2. **Being too comfortable**. Habit, routine, and being comfortable can be barriers to breaking through to sell the next big idea.
3. **Lacking trust in other people**. Salespeople can miss a huge opportunity for teamwork and sharing the workload when they think that no one else can do it as well as they can.[18]

Work Smarter, Not Harder

Being successful in sales doesn't require working longer hours; it requires taking control.[19] Time management is all about taking control of your time, your life, and your results. Here are six road-tested tips for effective time management that you can use for school and in sales:

1. **Get organized**.[20] Get all the right tools to do your work efficiently and effectively. Be sure your work space is adequate with appropriate light, get file folders for each subject, organize your electronic files by folder, and choose a naming convention (e.g., customer name_topic_date) so it will be easier to find files that may have been saved to the wrong folder.[21]

Consider using a time management product to help you stay organized. Franklin Covey offers a world-renowned planning system at http://shopping.franklinplanner.com/shopping/index.jsp?. Day-Timer also offers paper and electronic options (including iPhone apps) for planning at http://www.daytimer.com. In addition, Microsoft Outlook and other e-mail programs offer excellent tools to help you organize and plan your time.

2. **Set goals for the day, week, month, and year**. If you don't know what you expect to accomplish, you'll never know if you get there. Write down the goals you want to accomplish every day in a to-do list; it's a good idea to write down your goals at the end of the day for the next day.[22] Invest fifteen minutes at the end of every day to plan for the next day.[23] Take the time to write down your goals for the coming week, Sunday night is a good time to do this. Be clear and realistic about what you want to accomplish and by when.

Video Clip

Time Is Money
Hear how Andrew Sykes, pharmaceutical sales specialist whom you met in the video ride-along in Chapter 5, manages his time.

View the video online at: http://www.youtube.com/embed/V45K01SntKs

3. **Prioritize your activities**. Now that you have created your action plan, or to-do list, review it and reorder it to put the most important things first. Focus your time on the most important activities.[24] Lee Iacocca, the former CEO of Chrysler, said it best: "If you want to make good use of your time, you've got to know what's most important and then give it all you've got.[25] In other words, do important and challenging things first.

Sometimes people think it's best to do a lot of small things first so that you can scratch them off your list. But it's best to take on more challenging things when you are fresh and leave the smaller things for later or when you have a few minutes in your day.

4. **Create a schedule**. Using your to-do list as a guide, put times to your activities so that you can identify the amount of time it will take to accomplish each one. Also, during the day this schedule will serve as a guide and help keep you on track. And "manage minutes" effectively; use travel time, waiting time, and other downtime to return phone calls and e-mails or to think about solutions for customer problems.[26] Include addresses, phone numbers, and e-mail addresses for each person you need to contact if they are not already in your address book. This will help save time and prevent distractions.[27]

5. **Delegate work to others**. Although you might be working independently, chances are there are other people in the company that can help with certain activities. Clerical and administrative tasks should be delegated to your assistant or other support person. Always thank someone (subordinate, colleague, family member) who helps you get your work done.[28] Delegation is the true secret to success: a survey conducted by Watson Wyatt shows that high-performing salespeople spend 30 percent less time on administrative tasks than the low performers.[29]

6. **Maximize selling time**. Your objective should be to spend as much time as possible in front of customers; it's practically impossible to sell anything if you're not talking to and learning about your customers.[30] That means that you will have to manage interruptions.

Video Clip

See how all these time management tips come together to maximize selling time in this video featuring George Ludwig speaking about the "sales traffic school."

View the video online at: http://www.youtube.com/embed/sUL7XsuOC2A?rel=0

Link

How Good Are Your Time Management Skills?

Take the quiz by clicking on the link and learn about the areas of your time management that might need some focus.

http://www.mindtools.com/pages/article/newHTE_88.htm

Managing Your Results: Set Goals and Determine Your Income

Patricia Schneider, a former beauty queen, aspiring actress, and law firm clerk, started selling Mary Kay Cosmetics because she heard that the company awards a pink Cadillac for meeting certain goals. With 150,000 miles on her Toyota Celica, she decided that she could sell makeup. She got her first pink Cadillac in 2003; in 2009 she earned her fourth one.[31] Patricia learned that if you want to earn cars and money, go into sales.

salary

A regular payment from an employer in exchange for services.

pay period

The interval of time for which an employee is paid.

commission

Income that is based on the percentage of sales (or gross profit) generated.

straight commission

Compensation method that includes only a percentage of what is sold with no guarantee of salary.

gross profit

The difference between sales generated and the cost of the product or service.

compensation

Money and benefits received in exchange for providing services to a company including elements such as salary, commission, bonus, benefits, and any other elements in payment for providing services.

- **salary**. This is a regular payment from your employer in exchange for your services. Salary is a set amount and is usually the same amount for every **pay period**, or interval of time for which you are paid. A pay period may be weekly, biweekly, monthly, or quarterly depending on the company and the position. Most companies have biweekly pay periods. In most sales positions, if salary is included as one of the components of the compensation plan, it is usually a small portion of the compensation. This allows the company to provide incentive to the salespeople with a greater opportunity to earn more money based on the amount of sales (or gross profit) generated but still provides some regular guaranteed income to the salesperson. In other words, salary doesn't necessarily provide incentive for a salesperson to sell more since it is paid no matter what sales are generated.[32] If a company pays salary, the salary usually makes up 15 percent to 40 percent of total compensation.[33] The percentage of salary will be higher for new salespeople; whereas more experienced salespeople will earn a higher percentage of their compensation from commissions. For example, if total compensation is $50,000, salary might be $20,000 for a new salesperson (approximately 40 percent of total compensation); whereas an experienced salesperson might earn $24,000 in salary but earn a total of $120,000 including commission (20 percent of total compensation).

- **commission**. This is income that is based on the percentage of sales or gross profit generated. Commission is usually the largest portion of salesperson compensation. It is designed to be an incentive to the salesperson to sell more. This is one of the ways that salespeople have virtually unlimited income. Most sales jobs include some kind of commission element; others pay **straight commission**, which means that the salesperson makes only a percentage of what she sells without any guaranteed salary.[34] Depending on the company, commission might be paid on sales dollars, on **gross profit** dollars, or as a percentage. Gross profit is the difference between sales generated and the cost of the product or service. Gross profit may be expressed as dollars or a percentage. Gross profit dollars are calculated by multiplying the gross profit percentage times the sales.[35] When salespeople have control over pricing, commission plans are usually based on gross profit to ensure that the company makes a profit on each sale.[36] For example, if a 15 percent commission is paid on sales of $1 million, the income for the salesperson is $150,000 ($1,000,000 × 0.15 = $150,000). If a 25 percent commission is paid on gross profit (the difference between the selling price and the profit) based on a 35 percent gross profit and $1 million in sales, the commission would be $87,500 ($1,000,000 × 0.35) × 0.25 = $87,500. This calculation is also shown in Figure 14.6.

While most sales positions include commission, some positions pay a combination of salary plus commission. This helps provide some steady income for a salesperson, especially during businesses that have peaks and valleys.

Do you want to earn enough money to drive a pink Cadillac, a BMW, or Mercedes? Or is your goal to buy a condo? Maybe you want to be able to travel to the islands during the winter or experience exotic locations around the globe. All these can be possible in sales because how much money you earn every year is usually up to you. It's not too good to be true; it's the reality of sales. The lifeblood of every company is its sales force, those people who connect to customers and generate sales for the company. That's why most selling jobs provide at least some portion of **compensation**—money and benefits received in exchange for providing services to a company that is based on performance. Compensation may include one element such as salary or several components including salary, commission, bonus, benefits, and more. To understand how compensation works in sales, it's important to know the terms.

Generally, it takes time for a new person to build up a customer base and begin earning higher commissions. For more detail about how commissions are calculated, follow this link:

http://compforce.typepad.com/compensation_force/2009/01/sales-commission-calculation-basics.html

FIGURE 14.6 Commission Calculations

Commission based on sales

Sales: $1,000,000
Commission rate: 15%
Commission: $150,000 ($1,000,000 × .15)

Commission based on gross profit

Sales: $1,000,000
Gross profit: 35%
Gross profit dollars: $350,000
Commission rate: 25%
Commission: $87,500 ($1,000,000 × .35 × .25)

- **draw**. This is an advance against future commissions or bonuses. Earning a draw provides steady income to the salesperson, especially if commissions are paid on a monthly or quarterly basis.[37] For example, a salesperson might be guaranteed a draw of $2,000 per month; if the salesperson earns more than $2,000 in commissions she makes whatever she earns. If she earns $1,500, she is paid $2,000 for the month. In some cases, the $500 shortfall would be deducted from future commission earnings; this is called **recoverable draw**. On the other hand, a **nonrecoverable draw** means that a shortfall in commissions earned would not be owed to the company. Generally, a draw is designed to provide an income to a salesperson while he is building his customer base.[38]

- **bonus**. This is an incentive paid to sell a particular product or service or to reach a specific sales goal. Bonuses are paid in addition to salary and commission. They are usually paid quarterly but may be paid monthly.[39] Bonuses can be a significant portion of total compensation, depending on the industry and company. For example, in primary care pharmaceutical sales, a bonus can be between $20,000 and $25,000 and as high as $50,000.[40]

draw

An advance against future commissions or bonuses.

recoverable draw

A shortfall in commission earnings that must be repaid to the company from future commission earnings.

nonrecoverable draw

Shortfall in commission earnings that is not repaid to the company.

bonus

An incentive paid to sell a particular product or service or to reach a specific sales goal.

Plan to Earn

Now you can see why managing yourself, managing your time, and understanding compensation plans are so important to success in sales. All these elements are linked to the company's goals, which ultimately determine your sales goals. For example, if the company is planning a 6 percent sales increase for the year, each salesperson is responsible for delivering a certain portion of that increase. Since some salespeople are new, their goals will undoubtedly be less than those salespeople who have been at the company long enough to develop customer relationships and steady income streams.

The most important aspect of sales is to understand your sales goals: exactly what is expected and by when. Most companies establish annual sales goals or quotas, expectations of sales for a specific time frame, by salesperson, and then break down the goals by month and sometimes by week. Establishing specific, measurable, actionable, realistic, and time-bound (SMART) sales goals (covered in Chapter 8) provides a clear set of expectations for the salesperson and the company. For example, a SMART sales goal is "to increase dollar sales of accounting software with current customers by 8 percent by December 31, 2011."

When this goal is broken down by month and by week, it provides a way to measure progress regularly. More important, the SMART goal provides a method by which to have a regular conversation with your sales manager to discuss how to remove barriers or gain access to additional resources to achieve the goal. SMART goals become the basis of sales quotas.

Since many business-to-business (B2B) sales have a long sales cycle, many companies use **key performance indicators (KPIs)** to help gauge the productivity of each salesperson. KPIs might be compared to miles per gallon; they are a measure of efficiency and effectiveness. So while sales or gross profit might be included in a SMART goal, KPIs provide insights into performance; they can act as a way to diagnose problems in the selling process. KPIs are used to evaluate performance and compensation. Results are how salespeople are evaluated and paid. If a salesperson is not generating the desired results, chances are he won't last long in his position at that company.

KPIs may be organized by type of goal—performance KPIs or conversion KPIs. **Performance KPIs** are those that include outcomes such as sales, new accounts, units sold, or gross profit percent. **Conversion KPIs** are used as a measure of a salesperson's productivity or efficiency but do not have outcomes. Examples of conversion KPIs are sales per customer or closing ratio.[41] The following are some performance KPIs and conversion KPIs that are commonly used to measure the effectiveness of salespeople.

Performance KPIs

- **Sales quota (sales goal)**. Expected sales volume to be generated in a specific time frame; salespeople are usually given quotas by day, week, month, quarter, and year, which may be used as the basis for compensation and sales incentives.
- **Sales versus quota**. Sales generated compared to the sales goal or quota by the salesperson during the designated time frame; when a salesperson falls short of his sales goal, it is an opportunity for improvement.
- **Gross profit**. Difference between the cost of the product and the selling price.
- **Number of new accounts**. Number of customers who were not doing business with the company during the prior period.

---

key performance indicators (KPIs)

Measures of productivity that relate to achieving goals.

performance KPIs

Measures of productivity that include outcomes, such as sales, new accounts, units sold, or gross profit percent.

conversion KPIs

Measure of a salesperson's productivity or efficiency that do not have outcomes, such as sales per customer or closing ratio.

sales quota (sales goal)

Minimum sales volume to be generated in a specific time frame; salespeople are usually given quotas by day, week, month, quarter, and year upon which their commission is based.

sales versus quota

Sales generated compared to the sales quota by the salesperson during the designated time frame.

Conversion KPIs

- **Sales per customer**. Total sales generated by the salesperson divided by the number of customers; high sales per customer indicates sales rep productivity.
- **Sales per employee**. Total sales generated divided by the number of employees at the company; high sales per employee indicate a productive sales force.
- **Customer penetration**. The percentage of a customer's business (in total dollars and across product lines) that is being done with the salesperson; high penetration usually indicates a productive salesperson (and usually a good relationship with the customer).
- **Cost per sale**. The cost of generating the sale (cost of sales rep compensation, travel and entertainment, marketing materials, promotional discounts, and other expenses); low cost per sale usually indicates a productive salesperson who is able to close the sale quickly and at a higher gross profit (and, therefore, lower cost).
- **First appointment-to-proposal ratio**. The number of days it takes after a first appointment with a prospect until a proposal is made; a low number of days usually indicates a salesperson who moves quickly on an opportunity.
- **Closing ratio**. The percentage of times that a salesperson coverts a prospect to a customer by making a sale; a high closing ratio usually indicates a productive salesperson.[42]
- **Call cycle**. The frequency at which a salesperson calls on a customer (e.g., once every twenty days); call cycle will vary depending on the size and potential of the customer; a shorter call cycle indicates that there is more contact with the customer.
- **Call-to-sale ratio**. The percentage of calls that result in a sale; a low call-to-sale ratio usually indicates a productive salesperson.

Your sales manager will undoubtedly set quotas for you for many KPIs based on the goals of the company. Sales goals or quotas are used by companies "to align sales force performance to the business plan."[43] In many instances, sales quotas are used as the basis of incentives, such as additional commission, cash, and other incentives. You can use KPIs to set your goals for your annual income and see what it will take to make your earnings goal a reality. See Table 14.1 for this example.

Assume you wanted to make $45,000 in a year and you are paid a $500 commission on every sale. What will it take to earn your target income? Do the math below.[44]

sales per customer

Total sales generated by the salesperson divided by the number of customers.

sales per employee

Total sales generated divided by the number of employees at the company.

customer penetration

Percentage of a customer's business that is being done with the salesperson.

cost per sale

Cost of generating the sale (cost of sales rep compensation, marketing materials, and other expenses).

first appointment-to-proposal ratio

Number of days it takes after a first appointment with a prospect until a proposal is made.

closing ratio

Percentage of times a salesperson converts a prospect to a customer by making a sale.

call-to-sale ratio

Percentage of calls that result in a sale.

TABLE 14.1 Goal Setting

KPI Name	Calculation	KPI Goal
Annual earnings	$45,000	
Commission per sale		
Number of sales	Earnings ÷ commission per sale *$45,000 ÷ $800*	57
Closing ratio		10%
Number of prospects	Sales × number of prospects per sale *50 × 10*	570
Number of prospect calls	Number of prospects × number of calls per prospect *570 × 2.5*	1,425
Average number of sales calls per month	Number of prospect calls divided by 12 *1,425 ÷ 12*	119
Average number of sales calls per week	Number of monthly prospect calls divided by 4 *119 ÷ 4*	30
Average number of sales calls per day	Number of weekly prospect calls divided by 5 *30 ÷ 5*	6

Set Your Goals

It might seem a little overwhelming to think about achieving a specific sales goal. But it's easier than you think when you use these tips of the trade to help you plan:

- **Write down your goals**. Believe it or not, you actually increase your chances for success when you put your goals in writing. Whether you are setting goals for your career, for the year, or for the day ahead, write them down and prioritize them.

Video Clip

What Can You Do in Twenty-Four Hours?
Listen to author and selling expert Brian Tracy talk about what you can accomplish when you write down your goals and commit to achieving them.

View the video online at: http://www.youtube.com/embed/2iDbs3vh6KM

- **Understand what it takes to achieve your goal**. If your goal is to generate a 10 percent increase in sales over last month's sales, do the math and determine what that means in dollar sales, then determine how many sales calls you will have to make to achieve your goal. See Table 14.1 for an example.

Video Clip

It's All in the Numbers
Watch this video to see why life is a numbers game.

View the video online at: http://www.youtube.com/embed/oE1yi32gRIM

- **Schedule success**. Once you determine how many sales calls you will need to make to achieve your goal, plan your schedule so you plan the time it takes.
- **Track your progress**. Track your daily progress against your goal and make adjustments where necessary.
- **Stay focused**. It's easy to lose focus, especially if things aren't going according to plan. Review your plan and see where you have opportunities and start each day with determination to reach your goal.[45]

Video Link

How Measuring and Metrics Drive Success

Learn more about how metrics and measurements can help you achieve your goals in this video.

http://www.sellingpower.com/content/video/?date=7/30/2009

Key Takeaways

- Companies want to hire A-players for their sales positions, people who can connect with the customer and help the company achieve its goals.
- Resources such as **ride-alongs**, your **sales manager**, CRM, and other technology tools can help you learn more about the company, especially during the **onboarding** period.
- **Territory management** is the practice of managing your customers in a geographic area or territory; you determine whom you call on and when you call on them to minimize your travel time and maximize your selling time.
- **Time management** is the practice of organizing and prioritizing your activities to ensure that you can achieve your goals. This is especially important in sales because your goals can only be achieved by maximizing your selling time.
- **Compensation** can include many elements such as **salary, commission, draw, bonus**, and more. Commission is designed to provide incentive to the salesperson to increase her income by achieving and exceeding the sales goal.
- **Key performance indicators (KPIs)** provide a roadmap to improve performance and achieve sales goals.

Exercises

1. Identify three resources that are available to you through your school. How do these resources help you succeed? Do you use these resources? Why or why not?

2. Think about a situation in which you have gone through an onboarding process. What information or resources were available to you to help you become familiar with your new environment? How did you learn about these resources? Did you use these resources after you learned your way around?

3. Visit your campus Student Services Center (or similar office) and ask about the availability of a time management seminar (most schools offer them to students at various times of the year at no cost). Attend the seminar and identify at least two new habits that you will implement into your personal time management process.

4. Using the concept of the "Sales Traffic School" discussed in the video clip in Section 1.5, which of the following activities would you classify as "red," "yellow," or "green"? Indicate your choices in the chart below.

Activity	Color (Red, Yellow, Green)
Prospecting	
Responding to customer e-mails	
Attending internal meetings	
Customer follow-up	
Writing a proposal	
Meeting a friend for lunch	
Precall research	

5. Assume you are a financial advisor and you want to earn $7,000 a month. Based on earning $1,000 per sale in commission and having a 10 percent closing ratio and an average of 2.5 calls per prospect, use the following form to determine how many sales, prospects, and calls you will need to make each month to meet your goal. Why did you choose the priority of each of your activities?

KPI Name	Calculation	KPI Goal
Monthly earnings		
Commission per sale		
Number of sales		
Closing ratio		
Number of prospects		
Number of prospect calls		
Average number of sales calls per month		
Average number of sales calls per day		

6. Assume you are a salesperson earning 10 percent commission and you have sold $540,000 in products this year. What are your commission earnings for the year (show your math). Based on this, if you were on a draw of $50,000, would you earn your draw or commission?

7. Assume you are territory manager for a health care insurance company. The activities listed in the table below need to be completed tomorrow. The time it takes to complete each activity is also included. Using the "Day Planner" below, plan your day by entering the activity in the time of day that you would use to get that activity completed. You may not have enough time to complete all activities so you will need to decide what activities will not get done (don't forget to allow time for lunch).

Activity	Comments	Time to complete activity
Travel to and from sales call	Prospect sales call	1 hour
Return call to boss	Boss sent an e-mail and asked you to call him as soon as possible	15 minutes
Check e-mails and voice mails and respond as needed	Check at least three times daily	15 minutes each time
Travel to and from customer call	Key customer call	1 hour and 15 minutes
Travel to and from customer call	Customer with low sales but high potential	1 hour
Paperwork	Complete once daily	30 minutes
Customer follow-up	Complete at least twice daily	15 minutes each
Urgent phone call	Call comes in at 10:15 a.m.	30 minutes
Internal follow-up and meetings	One meeting during the day	1 hour
Prospecting and qualifying	Allow time at least once during the day	1 hour
Precall preparation for upcoming prospect call	Prospect call is in one day	30 minutes
Write a proposal	Proposal is due in two days	1 hour
Finish up proposal	Proposal can go out as soon as it is finished	15 minutes

Day Planner			
Time of day	**Activity**	**Time of day**	**Activity**
8:00–8:15		12:00–12:15	
8:15–8:30		12:15–12:30	
8:30–8:45		12:30–12:45	
8:45–9:00		12:45–1:00	
9:00–9:15		1:00–1:15	
9:15–9:30		1:15–1:30	
9:30–9:45		1:30–1:45	
9:45–10:00		1:45–2:00	
10:00–10:15		2:00–2:15	
10:15–10:30		2:15–3:00	
10:30–10:45		3:00–3:15	
10:45–11:00		3:15–3:45	
11:00–11:15		3:45–4:00	
11:15–11:30		4:00–4:15	
11:30–11:45		4:15–4:30	
11:45–12:00		4:30–4:45	
		4:45–5:00	

14.2 Motivation, Learning, Enjoyment, Success

Learning Objectives

1. Learn how to stay motivated and expand your knowledge every day.
2. Discuss how to stay positive with a healthy mind and body.

Never Give Up

It was Super Bowl Sunday in 2005, and the New England Patriots were playing the Philadelphia Eagles. Everything was perfect for New England Patriots linebacker Tedy Bruschi as he waited with excited anticipation before the game, visualizing its outcome. Talk about pressure—the Patriots had a chance to win their third Super Bowl. He played with his young sons, both under the age of five at the time, on the field hours before game time; it was great that his wife Heidi came to the Alltel Stadium with the boys early so that he had some time with them before the game. He was motivated by more than simply winning this historic game; he wanted to show his sons that you can do anything you set out to do.

The game, like the day, could not have been more perfect for Bruschi. He had a sack, seven tackles, and an interception. He was only one story in a team filled with winners. The final score was 24–21, Patriots. They had done it!

It was almost impossible to go to sleep that night. In fact, Bruschi didn't get to bed until 4:00 a.m. and then was up at the crack of dawn (literally) to appear on *Good Morning America*. The next few days were nonstop celebrations, interviews, and photographs. Life was indescribably good.

On February 16, 2005, just ten days later, Bruschi awoke at 4:00 a.m. with a headache and numbness in his body that was so severe that he had to crawl to the bathroom. Seven hours later things went from bad to worse when his vision blurred and he could no longer move his arm or leg. At the hospital he learned that he had had a stroke.[46]

After an agonizing recovery, eight months later Bruschi returned to the game he loved. He battled back to the field and played for four more seasons before retiring in August 2009. His teammate Larry Izzo said of Bruschi, "To come back from his stroke in '05 and play four more seasons at such a high level, was nothing less than amazing. When I think of Tedy Bruschi, I think of his toughness, his courage, the passion and desire he played with, and his production. He made plays. He was a true warrior. The heart and soul of our team."[47]

What motivated Bruschi? It would have been enough just to survive a stroke, but to come back and play football at a professional level is almost unthinkable. Most players don't ever make the cut to play in the NFL, but Bruschi survived a life-threatening stroke and came back to play at the top of his game. His passion, drive, and will to survive and win outpaced even his physical challenges.

Video Clip

Be a Rock Star
Are you a rock star…or a top-performer wannabe? Listen to what it takes to be a rock star in this video featuring sales guru and best-selling author, Jeffrey Gitomer.

View the video online at: http://www.youtube.com/embed/jVnua5BY5OM

You Can Do It!

"Don't Stop Believin'," the number one hit from the rock band Journey in 1981, became the anthem for the Chicago White Sox throughout the 2005 season in which the team won the their first World Series championship after eighty-eight years.[48] The song was more than background music for the team; it became the promise to their fans…and themselves throughout the season.

Is being successful in sales as easy as having a great song or a catchy slogan? Not really. In fact, the White Sox were far from being the favorites at the beginning of the season. After all, eighty-eight years is a long time to go without a championship. No one really believed they could do it. But even when others might not see your vision, you have to believe in yourself even when things don't go your way. Successful sales professionals will tell you that's what it takes to make it in sales: an unwavering belief in yourself that you can achieve the goals you set. Hard work? Absolutely. Setbacks? Just about every day. Believing in yourself? As they say, priceless.[49]

Motivation is especially important in sales because you will hear *no* more than you will hear *yes*. Your motivation, goals, and drive to succeed will make you successful.

Video Clip

Believe and Achieve
Listen to Lisa Peskin, sales trainer at Business Development University, talk about the need to believe in yourself, stay focused, and stay motivated in sales.

View the video online at: http://www.youtube.com/embed/nf-JKUWjAl8

You *can* do it, but only if you believe you can. What is the difference between the salesperson who makes $1 million a year and one that makes $50,000? It is the belief in himself that he can achieve her goals. It starts with a positive mental attitude every day. That means making the most of every day and taking control of your plan to accomplish your goals. "Motivation is an inside job. It's up to you," according to sales expert and author Jim Meisenheimer.[50] Here are a few of his tips from his article "25 Ways to Get Motivated to Start Selling More":

- Take pictures of your top ten customers and top ten prospects. Put the pictures in clear view (your computer wallpaper, on your cell phone, on your refrigerator) along with your SMART goal for each one. This visual reminder will help you stay focused.

- Tell your family how you are going to celebrate together when you become the number one salesperson at your company. You will make your goal real by telling someone close to you, and you will have their support to get through the challenging days.

- Invest fifteen minutes every day to read articles, books, blogs, listen to podcasts, or view videos about your industry or the selling profession. Sellingpower.com, Salesandmarketing. com, bnet.com, SalesHQ.com, and SalesVantage.com are all excellent sources of information about selling.

- Before the year ends, write yourself a check for December 31 of the next year for the amount you want to earn. Make three copies and have each laminated. Put one in your brief case, one on your car console, and one in your office. When you look at it every day, ask yourself, "What can I do today to get closer to this goal?"[51]

Link

Twenty-Five Ways to Get Motivated to Start Selling More
You can read the entire article by clicking on the following link:

http://www.evancarmichael.com/Sales/407/25-Ways-To-Get-Motivated-To-Start-Selling-More. html

Act Like You Run the Place

David C. Novak, chairman, CEO, and president of Yum Brands, whose chains include KFC, Pizza Hut, Taco Bell, and Long John Silver's shares his advice for young people: "I tell people that once you get a job you should act like you run the place. Not in terms of ego, but in how you think about the business."[52] In other words, if you think about your sales territory or product line as if it is your own business, you'll make decisions that will be in the best interest of growth.

Fail...to Succeed

It may seem counterintuitive, but the best way to succeed is to fail. The fact is, failures can be a positive experience because they can help you avoid repeating mistakes.[53] Since failures are much more painful than the sweet taste of success, we tend to remember our failures more vividly.[54] But as important as the actual failure is what you do as a result of the experience. "You don't have control over what happens to you in life," says Lisa Peskin, sales trainer at Business Development University, "but you absolutely have control over how you choose to handle it."[55] Peskin has over twenty years of experience in business-to-business (B2B) selling. To overcome the feeling of failure especially on daily sales calls, she suggests the "rocking chair test": will you remember that someone said no to you today when you are sitting in a rocking chair fifty years from now? "Don't get upset over the small stuff" is her advice to salespeople. "If you want something you never had, you must do something you've never done, and that may result in some failures, but a lot of successes."[56]

It might be hard to imagine that successful people ever had failures. But Shantanu Narayen, CEO of software maker Adobe Systems, says, "You know, there is no such thing as failure. You're always learning." He goes on to share his personal experiences: "I have looked back at aspects of my career where somebody might look at it and say, you know, that start-up was not successful, and I look at it and I say, 'I learned how to build a team, how to raise money, how to sell a vision, how to create a product.' It was a great steppingstone for me."[57]

personal responsibility

Acknowledging and accepting that you are accountable for your choices.

Failure is a fact of life. Although the White Sox were eventually named World Champions again in 2005, each member of the team missed more balls than they hit. In baseball, a 0.333 batting average is considered outstanding (Ty Cobb's average, the highest in baseball is 0.366), which means that the batter misses almost seven times out of every ten at bats. Similarly, an average of 70 percent of people who walk into a retail store don't buy anything, and 99 percent of people who visit a company's Web site don't make a purchase.[58],[59],[60] So, it is inevitable that you will have to fail in order to succeed. But that doesn't mean that failure should become a way of life. With failure comes **personal responsibility**, acknowledging and accepting that you are accountable for the choices you make with your prospects and customers, in your career, and in life. Someone who is personally responsible doesn't rationalize why a failure occurs, doesn't blame others, and doesn't feel sorry for himself. Here are four simple steps that can help you turn failure into growth:

1. Objectively analyze your role in the failure. What did you do that may have caused an outcome other than the one your preferred?

2. Imagine if you had done something different. What impact would it have had on the outcome?

3. Determine what prompted you to take the actions you took.

4. Decide that when the situation occurs again, you will do something differently.[61]

Failure is about learning and taking personal responsibility, which can be the key to your personal success. "The price of greatness is responsibility," said Winston Churchill.[62]

Link

Rate Your Personal Responsibility

You can rate yourself on a personal responsibility scale to identify if you have areas in which you need to develop personal responsibility.[63]

http://www.livestrong.com/article/14698-accepting-personal-responsibility

Unfortunately, you are going to hear *no* more often in sales than you hear *yes*. In fact, *no* is part of the game of sales. But don't take it personally. "Don't get dejected when you've been rejected—just get your skills perfected," is advice from selling expert and author Harvey Mackay.[64] *No* is what helps you hear *yes*. Of course, you wouldn't expect every prospect you contact to buy your product or service. Think about it: do you buy everything that is pitched to you? So it is hearing *no* that helps you fine-tune your sales presentation to ultimately hear *yes*.[65] There should be no fear in *no*.

Video Clip

Positive Reinforcement

Want to stay motivated to keep going even when you hear *no*? Watch this video about being positive and being creative featuring sales guru Jeffrey Gitomer:

View the video online at: http://www.youtube.com/embed/Bh9oO5gKc-g

Power Player: Lessons in Selling from Successful Salespeople

The Eyes Have It

"Sell with your eyes" is the advice that Jessica Sciarabba, AT&T retail sales consultant, gives to all sales reps. "The best piece of advice about how to have a successful career in sales came from my first boss. He taught me how to make a personal connection with customers by looking at them and showing my interest in them with my eyes. It makes a difference and it really works."[66]

Positive Energy from a Healthy Mind and Body

It's virtually impossible to be successful in sales and in life if you don't take care of yourself. Conflicting priorities; lack of time; demands of work, family, and friends; the negativity of some people; and even the state of the economy can take a toll on you. Stress is a real part of everyday life; unfortunately there is no magic formula to avoid it. But you can learn to balance work and your personal life for a better balance and potentially less stress.

Video Clip

Make Time for Yourself
Listen to how Rachel Gordon, account manager at WMGK, balances work and her personal life to be a better salesperson.

View the video online at: http://www.youtube.com/embed/xV8q_N4g1GU

Take Good Care of Yourself

Have you ever been on an airplane and listened to the directions from the flight attendant about safety? She says that in case of an emergency, put on your oxygen mask first and then help those around you to put theirs on. The theory is that you can't really help anyone else until you are taken care of. That same theory applies to mental, emotional, and physical health. You won't be able to provide support and ideas to your customers unless you are healthy in mind and body. To start off every day with the energy and enthusiasm to conquer the world, take the time to take care of yourself with the following tips:

- **Get a good night's sleep**. Avoid caffeine in the late afternoon and evening, and go to sleep early. It's best not to assume that your current sleep time is enough; experiment with what is your optimum night's sleep.[67]
- **Eat a healthy breakfast**. You might think you don't have time, but it's best to make time to eat breakfast. It provides fuel to start your day. A healthy breakfast can be fast and easy, especially if you plan it the night before. Oatmeal with almonds, cold cereal with fruit, a smoothie with fruit, low-fat yogurt and wheat germ, and even cold veggie pizza can be a healthy breakfast. You owe it to yourself to start right. Use some tips from this article from the Mayo Clinic for some healthy options: http://www.mayoclinic.com/health/food-and-nutrition/NU00197.[68]
- **Exercise**. It's a good idea to do some kind of regular physical exercise such as working out or walking. This helps reduce stress and helps you manage weight.
- **Don't procrastinate; get right into your day**. Jump in with both feet and start your day off right. If you stop to watch television, text your friends, or do other activities, your morning will be half over before you know it with nothing to show for it.[69]
- **Start your day with the most important task**. Use your prioritized to-do list and conquer the most important item first; leave everything else for later. You might be tempted to do the small things first so you can scratch them off you list. But when you take on the more important and biggest challenge first, you have the most amount of energy and drive. And you will have a huge sense of accomplishment with time to spare for your smaller to-dos.[70]
- **Smile and enjoy your day**. Your attitude sets the tone for your customers. Always wear a warm, genuine smile; people like to do business with people who enjoy what they do. A smile can break tension in a meeting and put everyone at ease.[71]

- **Don't worry about what you can't control**. Worry causes stress, and stress breeds doubt. It's a good idea to make a list of all the things that are causing stress in your life. Review them and identify which ones you have control over and develop an action plan to take control over that element. For those over which you don't have control, don't stress. It's simply a waste of time to worry about things you can't control.[72]

- **Take time for yourself**. Chances are you have multiple responsibilities and demands including work, family, school, community, and others. Even though you want to do it all, it's a good idea to schedule some time for yourself regularly. Do something that you enjoy whether it is reading a book, going to the mall, or taking a bike ride. This "me time" can go a long way to rejuvenate yourself and refresh you to take on the next big challenge.

Video Clip

Be Inspired
The bottom line is you *can* be successful in your career. It's up to you. This video will inspire you.

View the video online at: http://www.youtube.com/embed/vsRw6-w53FU

Key Takeaways

- You have to believe in yourself so that others will believe in you.
- Expand your knowledge every day by reading an article, part of a book, or blog about selling or the industry you are selling in.
- Failure can be one of the best ways to succeed; it teaches you how to avoid the same mistakes twice.
- **Personal responsibility** is a key element in success.
- You can create positive energy by taking care of yourself in mind and body.

Exercises

1. Think about a situation in your life that seemed almost impossible. What did you do to overcome it? How did you determine your course of action? How long did it take? How did you stay motivated?
2. Identify at least one goal that you would like to accomplish in your life. How will you achieve it? What are the steps you plan to take?

3. Assume you are a designer and you want to sell your new designs for home furnishings called "The Ultimate Dorm Room" to Target. You met with the buyer once, and she made some suggestions and said she would consider it again in six months. What would you do to continue to stay motivated until you meet with her again?

4. Identify at least three resources for information about the selling profession (hint: several are mentioned in the chapter). Read, watch, or participate in them at least once a week for the next three weeks. What did you learn? Will you continue to use these as resources? Why or why not?

5. Contact a B2B salesperson and ask him what he does to stay motivated. Which pointers might you find helpful? Why? Which pointers don't you find helpful? Why not?

6. Discuss a group situation in which you were involved and someone did not take personal responsibility. What impact did the lack of personal responsibility have on the team in achieving its goal? What might the outcome had been if the person had taken personal responsibility?

7. Watch this video and discuss three things that can make a failure into a learning experience: http://www.sellingpower.com/content/video/index.php?mid=309.

14.3 *Selling U*: It's Your Career—Own It!

Learning Objective

1. Understand how to leverage internships and professional organizations to get the job you want.

When Jay Leno was young, he saw a Mercedes/Rolls-Royce dealership in his hometown in Boston and thought it would be a great place to work given his passion for cars. When he applied for a job the manager responded with the usual: "We're not hiring right now." Leno was undaunted; the next Monday morning he returned and went to the car wash bay. He told them he was the new guy and started washing cars. A few days later, the manager saw him and said, "What's he doing here?" The head of the car wash team said he was a hard worker; Leno said that he figured he would work there until he got hired. Needless to say, he got the job.[73]

This same "can-do" positive attitude and willingness to work can help you get the job you want. Even in this difficult economy, there are opportunities to demonstrate your passion and skills and set yourself apart, just like Jay Leno did. Finding the right job requires focus, time management, and motivation...and sometimes even working for free. You have to keep a positive mental attitude throughout your search and manage your time to gain experience while you are going to school. Here are two key things that you can do every day to help you get the job you want: internships and professional organizations.

Build Your Résumé with Internships

internship

An educational arrangement that provides experience in a work situation.

"One hundred percent of the students I hire have had **internships**," says Michelle Goza, a campus recruiter for Gap. "It's foolish not to pursue the opportunity."[74] Paid or unpaid, internships can make a difference in whether you are considered for another internship or the job you want.

An internship, or more than one internship over the course of your academic career, can provide insight into an industry or a specific company or position. What better way to learn about something you might want to do during your career...or not want to do. (Some internships teach you what you don't want to do during your career, which is as valuable as learning what you want to do.) Internships are almost the norm today, and many employers expect to hire recent grads for entry-level positions who have had some kind of internship. "There is no such thing as too much experience, just not enough," says Craig Bollig, a journalism major at the University of Wisconsin, Oshkosh.[75]

Internships aren't just for undergraduates any more. Due to the challenging economy, recent graduates are finding internships to be an excellent way to build their experience while they continue to look for the full-time job of their dreams. "The need for experience is always growing and one internship may not cut it like it did before," adds Bollig.[76]

Video Clip

Get Experience
Andrew Sykes, pharmaceutical sales specialist at AstraZeneca, shares his advice on getting experience.

View the video online at: http://www.youtube.com/embed/qfVGdv8bTYI

If internships are so important to building your résumé and your experience, you might be wondering how you go about getting the right internship. First, stop by your campus career center. The people there are skilled at helping you understand the options that are available and can provide insight as to how to find the right internship to help you meet your career objectives. And most campuses include internship postings on the campus Web site. It's a good idea to take the time to learn all about your internship options.

Consider an internship the same way you would consider a job: Is this the right fit for my experience and skills? Are the company values in line with my personal values? What will I be doing? Who will I report to? Will I be paid for the internship? If so, how much? How will I be evaluated during the internship? What is the possibility of getting a full-time position after graduation? While the interview process is usually more abbreviated for an internship than for a full-time job, take the time to ask questions so you understand the expectations of the role.

You've Got the Power: Tips for Your Job Search

Internship Offer Letter
Before accepting any internship (or full-time job), it's best to get an offer letter.[77] Even if you are accepting an unpaid internship, an offer letter outlines your areas of responsibility, dates of employment, and other specific information that you should agree upon with your employer before you begin. See the *Selling U* section of Chapter 12 for more specifics about offer letters.

The Right Internship for You

Internships come in all shapes and sizes; some are formal, structured programs while others are created by the student. Either way, here are some considerations when you are pursuing an internship:

Paid versus unpaid. Some, but not all, internships include a paycheck. Many large corporations have structured internship programs that include paid internships. However, many industries such as advertising, entertainment, and public relations offer unpaid internships as a way for you to gain experience. So you want to make some money and gain some experience in the field of your choice? You might be able to do both since approximately half of all internships are paid. But in today's challenging job market, you might find it worth your while to accept an unpaid internship. While that might be a tough pill to swallow, consider Lindsey Roberts's point of view after she graduated with an MBA from a top business school, "I could either sit at home all day and drive myself nuts going from company websites, to Indeed.com and back to Gmail and Facebook, or I could get out there, put my education and experience to work while I continued my job search."[78] It's not only graduate students who are accepting unpaid internships. According to the *Wall Street Journal*, the recession has tightened the internship market; experienced workers who have been laid off are now successfully participating in unpaid internships for the same reasons students do: to build their résumés and increase their chances for full-time work.[79] So you might think twice about holding out for a paid internship. Before you make a decision about a paid versus an unpaid internship, put your internship consideration to the test. The right internship, paid or unpaid, allows you the opportunity to get experience, a chance to network, and the opportunity to test drive a job to see if it's something you like to do.[80] Those three things can be well worth temporarily foregoing a paycheck.

Credit versus noncredit. In many cases, you may be able to earn credit hours for your internship. Begin by visiting your faculty advisor and learn about the requirements to earn credit for internships. Internships usually require a faculty mentor or other university liaison. Besides working the specified number of hours each week, students are usually required to write a paper. In addition, an employer evaluation is usually included in the grade. It's best to understand the requirements for credit long before the internship is finished so that you can be sure that all the details are in order between your employer and the school. Be sure to fill out all the appropriate paperwork before the beginning of the internship. Just a note, although the internship does not usually require a textbook or classroom learning, most schools include the standard course fee for a credit internship.

It doesn't matter if your internship is paid or unpaid, for credit or noncredit, the payoff can be significant. Internships are like an extended job interview; the company gets to know you and your work, which could result in a full-time job offer after graduation. "Internships are so powerful," affirms Wendy Washington, a senior vice president at Universal Records, whose assistant is a former intern for the company. "We get our employees from our intern pool. They know the system. They know how things work, and you can't get a better character reference. Interns who work for our company have a better shot of becoming employed here than someone who just sends in an application."[81] That's why it's especially important to stand out in everything you do. And don't forget to keep copies of the projects you work on; they are excellent examples of your work to include in your portfolio and serve as a demonstration of your on-the-job experience.[82]

Video Clip

Internship "How To"
This video provides an overview of how to get an internship.

View the video online at: http://www.youtube.com/embed/12eAN_2YEns

The Best Places to Look for an Internship

Your campus career center and faculy advisor can be the best resources for getting an internship. In addition, there are several Web sites that can give you access to internships by industry or by geography. Table 14.2 provides some places for you to start your search.

TABLE 14.2 Recommended Web Sites for Internships

Web Site	Comments
GoAbroad.com http://www.internabroad.com/search.cfm	International internships
InternWeb.com http://www.internweb.com	Internships and entry-level jobs in technology industries
InternSHARE http://internshare.com	Internship listings with ratings and reviews
Vault http://www.vault.com/intership-programs	Internship listings
TheFreeLibrary.com http://www.thefreelibrary.com/ Getting+the+big+break:+with+the+right+internship,+you+can+beat+the. ..-a094672526	
Summerinternships.com http://www.summerinternships.com	Internship listings
Internzoo.com http://www.internzoo.com	Internship listings

Link

Companies That Hire the Most Interns

Don't forget to apply directly to companies for internship opportunities. Enterprise Rent-A-Car, Walgreens, and General Electric are among companies on the *Forbes* list of "U.S. Companies That Hire the Most Interns."[83] This is an excellent source of possible internships in addition to local companies.

http://www.forbes.com/2009/07/07/biggest-intern-companies-leadership-careers-jobs_slide_9.html?thisSpeed=15000

Professional Organizations: Your Key to Growth

professional organization

A nonprofit business group that is dedicated to supporting and improving the industry.

collegiate chapter

An arm of a professional organization based on a college campus.

student membership

Reduced fees offered to students as an incentive to join the professional organization.

You're probably really pressed for time this semester. A full course load, your job, your community service work, family, friends—it seems like you can't possibly fit in another thing to do. You already have twenty-eight hours for every twenty-four-hour day. Just when it seems like you can't do another thing, there is one thing you should consider: it's worth making time to join a **professional organization** while you're in school, then continue as a member after you graduate. It can build your experience and enhance your résumé.

There are most likely several professional organizations on your college campus. organizations such as the American Marketing Association, American Association of Advertising Agencies, American Society of Women Accountants, Sales & Marketing Executives International are just a few that may have a chapter on your campus called a **collegiate chapter**. If you're not sure about what professional organizations are available on campus, you might consider visiting your campus student services center or career center. The people who work there will likely have information about the purpose of each group; date, time, and place of the next meeting; and more. In addition, many professional organizations may not have a collegiate chapter, but they offer **student membership** into their organization at reduced rates. It depends on the organization whether they offer a collegiate chapter or a student membership. Collegiate chapters are usually extensions of national organizations such as the American Marketing Association, and usually have student members on campus and hold regular events and activities on campus while leveraging and participating in national conferences, competitions, and best practices. Professional organizations that do not have a collegiate chapter but offer a student membership rate usually have events and activities with professionals in the local area but not on campus.

Being a member of a professional organization in school helps build your professional network, and hone your skills. It's also a great résumé-builder because it signals to your prospective employer that you are willing to take the time to get involved in a business function during your spare time (of which you probably have none). Participation in a professional organization can help make you stand out as a candidate or help you meet the right people. In fact, some professional organizations, such as the Philly Ad Club, offer a formal mentoring program. This is an excellent way to meet an executive in the industry of your choice.[84] The networking aspects of professional organizations are well documented and are covered in Chapter 3. The reason for the existence of most professional organizations is to promote the health and advancement of the industry and bring people together for networking purposes. In addition, most professional organizations offer a newsletter that includes information about the industry and companies that can be very helpful for job leads and interviewing research.[85]

You might think that simply joining a professional organization is enough. However, what will help you stand out within the organization is to get involved. Keep in mind that all professional organizations are volunteer organizations, so it is easy to get onto one of the committees or even take on a leadership role of a committee. This allows you to demonstrate your skills, work ethic, and commitment to people who are usually more senior than you are (in the case of a campus professional organization, you stand out to your professors, which is a good strategy). It's a great way to build your leadership, teamwork, and networking skills.

There are several professional organizations off campus that invite students to join, usually at a reduced rate. For example, the PRSA (Public Relations Society of America) costs $290 for an annual membership while the fee for a student in the PRSSA (Public Relations Student Society of America) is $50.[86],[87] It's a good idea to talk to your faculty advisor, as she will most likely know what local organizations have a student rate. These off-campus professional organizations are excellent for networking to find the right people to whom you should be speaking to get the job you want. Professional organizations will serve you well throughout your career. Even after you graduate, you will be a student of the business. Professional organizations provide a platform for ongoing learning about industry trends, case studies, and best practices. Successful people stay involved in one or more professional organizations even after they have established careers.

There are professional organizations for virtually every profession and industry. Table 14.3 includes a list that can help you see some of what's available.

TABLE 14.3 Professional Organizations

Professional Organization Information and Web Site	Comments
Sales & Marketing Executives International http://www.smei.org	Web site of SMEI
Wikipedia http://en.wikipedia.org/wiki/List_of_professional_organizations	List of professional organizations
American Marketing Association http://www.marketingpower.com/Pages/default.aspx	Web site of the American Marketing Association
PRSSA (Public Relations Student Society of America) http://www.prssa.org/about/join.aspx	Web site of PRSSA
10 Top Professional Networks for Women in Finance http://www.theglasshammer.com/news/2009/07/23/top-10-professional-networks-for-women-in-finance	Professional organizations for women in finance
Women's Career Networking and Professional Organizations http://www.quintcareers.com/womens_networking_organizations.html	Women's networking organizations

Key Takeaways

- The best way to get the job you want when you graduate is to work on it right now with **internships** and by joining **professional organizations**. Both are expected by prospective employers of new hires for entry-level jobs.
- **Internships** provide an opportunity to gain experience, test drive a job, and network; many result in full-time job offers.
- Some **internships** are paid while others are unpaid; some **internships** qualify for college credit while others do not. It's best to consult your faculty advisor before you accept an **internship**.
- Professional organizations provide exposure to executives, industry news, and best practices and enhance your résumé. The best way to take advantage of your professional organization membership is to get involved one of the organization's committees.

Exercises

1. Visit your campus career center and meet with one of the counselors. Learn about internships that are offered and how to apply for them. Discuss three things that you learned during this meeting.
2. Identify a student who has had an internship in your target industry. Set up a meeting to discuss how she landed her internship and what advice she can give you about finding the right internship.
3. Review your campus Web site and identify at least two professional organizations that may be of interest to you. Attend at least one of their meetings and determine which might be the right organization for you to join.

14.4 Review and Practice

Power Wrap-Up

Now that you have read this chapter, you should be able to understand the key elements of how to manage your time and resources to be successful in sales.

- You **understand** that although you might be working alone, you have resources available to help you be successful every day.
- You can **discuss** how to manage your time to accomplish your goals.
- You can **recognize** all the key elements of compensation and how you can leverage each to earn the income you want.
- You can **describe** how to set SMART goals and use key performance indicators to help measure progress.
- You can **appreciate** how important believing in yourself is to being successful in sales and in life.
- You can **understand** that failure is a part of selling, but how you react to failure is what can make you successful.
- You can **recognize** that having a healthy mind and body contributes to your chances of success.
- You can **understand** that you can prepare now for the full-time job you want by having internships and getting involved in professional organizations.

Test Your Power Knowledge (answers are below)

1. What is a ride-along?
2. If you are going through the onboarding process, what are you doing?
3. Name three reasons time can get away from you.
4. List three things you can do to improve your time management.
5. What is the difference between a commission and a draw?
6. If you are earning 12 percent of sales as a commission, how much would you earn on annual sales of $1,100,000?
7. Is it possible for an employer to offer a salary plus commission plus bonus as part of a compensation plan?
8. What is a KPI, and how is it used in sales?

9. Name three ways to get motivated to sell more.

10. How does personal responsibility relate to failure?

11. Name three things you can do to ensure you have a healthy mind and body?

12. Why is it important to have at least one internship?

13. Why is it important to join a professional organization?

Power (Role) Play

Now it's time to put what you've learned into practice. The following are two roles that are involved in the same selling situation—one role is the customer, and the other is the salesperson. This will give you the opportunity to think about this selling situation from the point of view of both the customer and the salesperson.

Read each role carefully along with the discussion questions. Be prepared to play either of the roles in class using the concepts covered in this chapter. You may be asked to discuss the roles and do a role-play in groups or individually.

Time Is on My Side: Managing Customers and Your Time

Role: Food and beverage manager at a major luxury hotel chain

You are a significant customer, one that all your liquor distributors want to have because you have a four-star brand name. All the sales reps want to add your hotel chain to their client list. That's why you split the business between several reps. You feel like that provides your business the best service and keeps all the reps on their toes.

You like it when sales reps spend time talking with you and demonstrate that they care about the business. In fact, you are always impressed when one goes out of her way to personally deliver a case of something that didn't get delivered on the truck (it seems like that happens often). When a rep doesn't respond quickly to a delivery error, you take away some of the business from them.

- You believe that when sales reps spend more time at your account, they care more about your business. How do you tell the sales rep that you expect more face time?

- When something is missing on a delivery, you expect the sales rep to bring the missing part of the shipment to the hotel that day. Do you think that is unreasonable?

- You call the sales rep often to see if he will do special things for the hotel, including tastings and other events. You want the sales rep to host a sampling event for a convention next week. You realize it's not very much advance notice, but you want to ask anyway. What will you say to the sales rep?

Role: Liquor distributor sales rep

You have a very small part of this luxury hotel's business; you really want to get more because the hotel has the potential to be your largest customer. However, the food and beverage manager is very demanding, and it takes a lot of your time; in fact, too much time. It seems that a sales call always takes at least two hours. It also seems that you are regularly doing hand deliveries because the food and beverage manager forgets to order things and expects a delivery within a few hours of his call. This account has been a time management challenge. You have to determine if you can get a commitment for more of the hotel's business and reduce the amount of time you spend servicing the account.

- Although this customer has the potential to give you more business, he hasn't yet. He asks for a lot of your time with in-person meetings, personal follow-up on missed deliveries and short notice for special tastings and other events. Should you always say yes to his requests in hopes of getting more business?

- If the customer is always right, what is the best way to balance your time and get additional business to offset your time investment?

- You are extremely busy with another customer on the date that this customer has requested a sampling at his convention, and you have a personal commitment that night. What will you say to this customer about his request?

Put Your Power to Work: *Selling U* Activities

1. Use your professional social networking skills by going to LinkedIn (see the *Selling U* section in Chapter 3) and join your school's alumni group. Use the Q & A feature to identify people who are in your target industry. Ask for their advice about what to look for when choosing an internship. If you haven't already done so, join *The Power of Selling* group on LinkedIn and start a discussion or use the questions and answers feature to get input about what to look for when choosing an internship. This group is there to help you.

2. Visit your campus career center and review the Web sites mentioned in the *Selling U* section in this chapter. Identify at least two professional organizations in which you might be interested. Visit their Web sites and review the mission, events, news, membership benefits, and cost. Attend one meeting for each of the organizations to help determine if one might be a good organization to join.

Test Your Power Knowledge Answers

1. Traveling with an experienced sales rep or sales manager to make sales calls.

2. Being exposed to an employee orientation process or method for a new employee to learn about company practices, policies, and procedures.

3. Poor planning, procrastination, and making tasks too big.

4. Get organized, set goals, prioritize activities, create a schedule, delegate work to others, and maximize selling time.

5. Commission is the income that is based on the percentage of sales (or gross profit) generated; a draw is an advance against future commissions or bonuses.

6. $1,100,000 \times 0.12 = $144,000.

7. Yes. Compensation may include as many elements as the employer chooses to offer. Usually commissions and bonuses are higher than salary to provide incentive for salespeople to sell more.

8. KPI stands for key performance indicator: a measure of productivity that relates to achieving goals. KPIs are used to measure progress against SMART goals and are often used to determine compensation and incentives for salespeople.

9. Take pictures of your top ten customers and top ten prospects; tell your family how you are going to celebrate when you achieve your goal; invest at least fifteen minutes every day to read articles, books, or blogs about your industry or profession; and write yourself a check for the amount you want to earn and keep copies with you.

10. Although failure is a part of selling (and of life), personal responsibility means acknowledging and accepting that you are accountable for your choices, learning from failures, and not making the same mistake again.

11. Get a good night's sleep, eat a healthy breakfast, exercise, get right into your day, start your day with an important task, smile, don't worry about what you can't control, and take time for yourself.

12. An internship provides practical work experience and gives you insight about what you might want to do (or not want to do) after graduation. Also, it's a great way to network. In addition, many internships result in full-time job offers.

13. Professional organizations offer students and professionals unique opportunities to network and learn about trends and best practices in the industry; they also provide a chance to stand out and be noticed by getting involved in a committee.

Endnotes

1. Valeria Maltoni, "How Do You Become an A-Player?" Social Media Today, April 17, 2009, http://www.socialmediatoday.com/SMC/85675 (accessed September 4, 2009).

2. Auren Hoffman, "The A-Player Janitor," Summation Blog, April 9, 2009, http://blog.summation.net/2009/04/the-aplayer-janitor.html (accessed September 4, 2009).

3. Ann Devine, "Is a Career in Sales Right for You?" The Black Collegian, http://www.black-collegian.com/career/career-reports/sales-grad05.shtml (accessed August 19, 2009).

4. Richard E. Goldman, "Managing Yourself First," Focus, July 8, 2009, http://www.cuckleburr.com/book-excerpt-managing-yourself-first-from-luck-by-design (accessed August 18, 2009).

5. "What Do I Do on a Ride Along?" PharmBoard.com, http://pharmboard.com/what-do-i-do-on-a-ride-along (accessed August 29, 2009).

6. Sean Silverthorne, "5 Personal Core Competencies for the 21st Century," BNET, August 13, 2009, http://blogs.bnet.com/harvard/?p=3332&tag=nl.e713 (accessed August 19, 2009).

7. Tony Robbins, "Tony Robbins: Why We Do What We Do and How We Can Do It Better," video, January 16, 2007, http://www.youtube.com/watch?v=Cpc-t-Uwv1I (accessed September 5, 2009).

8. Ashton Kutcher, "The Twitter Guys: The 2009 Time 100," *Time*, http://www.time.com/time/specials/packages/article/0,28804,1894410_1893837_1894156,00.html (accessed September 5, 2009).

9. Gerald L. Manning, Barry L. Reece, and Michael Ahearne, *Selling Today: Creating Customer Value* (Upper Saddle River, NJ: Pearson Prentice Hall, 2010), 31.

10. Data from Gerald L. Manning, Barry L. Reece, and Michael Ahearne, *Selling Today: Creating Customer Value* (Upper Saddle River, NJ: Pearson Prentice Hall, 2010), 31.

11. Ann Devine, "Is a Career in Sales Right for You?" The Black Collegian, http://www.black-collegian.com/career/career-reports/sales-grad05.shtml (accessed August 19, 2009).

12. John Hacking, "Time Management for Sales People," Buzzle.com, October 15, 2007, http://www.buzzle.com/articles/time-management-for-sales-people.html (accessed September 5, 2009).

13. "Procrastination Costing Your Sales Team," ArticlesBase, April 29, 2009, http://www.articlesbase.com/education-articles/procrastination-costing-your-sales-team-893170.html (accessed September 5, 2009).

14. John Hacking, "Time Management for Sales People," Buzzle.com, October 15, 2007, http://www.buzzle.com/articles/time-management-for-sales-people.html (accessed September 5, 2009).

15. "The Seven Habits of Highly Effective People," Businessballs.com, http://www.businessballs.com/sevenhabitsstevencovey.htm (accessed January 2, 2010).

16. Marcia F. Borello comment, Bank Atlantic, https://www.bankatlantic.com/Customerfeedback/default.html (accessed September 13, 2009).

17. Ray Silverstein, "Time Management for Sales Pros," *Entrepreneur*, March 20, 2007, http://www.entrepreneur.com/management/leadership/leadershipcolumnistraysilverstein/article176034.html (accessed September 5, 2009).

18. Dave Kahle, "Biggest Time Wasters for Sales People," Business Know-How, http://www.businessknowhow.com/growth/timewast.htm (accessed September 5, 2009).

19. Tom Metcalf, "3 Steps to Better Time Management for Sales Reps," Sales Reps, Increase Your Productivity! Blog, January 3, 2007, http://telenotes.blogspot.com/2007/01/3-steps-to-better-time-management-for.html (accessed May 16, 2010).

20. Doug Dvorak, "How to Use Time Management to Become a More Successful Sales Professional!" EzineArticles, http://ezinearticles.com/?How-to-Use-Time-Management-to-Become-a-More-Successful-Sales-Professional&id=1081316 (accessed September 6, 2009).

21. Margot Carmichael Lester, "5 Ways to Get and Stay Organized" SalesHQ.com, http://www.saleshq.com/training/articles/1353-5-ways-to-get-and-stay-organized (accessed September 6, 2009).

22. Doug Dvorak, "How to Use Time Management to Become a More Successful Sales Professional!" EzineArticles, http://ezinearticles.com/?How-to-Use-Time-Management-to-Become-a-More-Successful-Sales-Professional&id=1081316 (accessed September 6, 2009).

23. Jim Meisenheimer, "25 Ways to Get Motivated to Start Selling More," EvanCarmichael.com, http://www.evancarmichael.com/Sales/407/25-Ways-To-Get-Motivated-To-Start-Selling-More.html (accessed August 19, 2009).

24. "How Good Is Your Time Management?" Mind Tools, http://www.mindtools.com/pages/article/newHTE_88.htm (accessed September 6, 2009).

25. Donald Latumhahina, "Time Quotes: 66 Best Time Management Quotes," Life Optimizer Blog, March 8, 2007, http://www.lifeoptimizer.org/2007/03/08/66-best-quotes-on-time-management (accessed August 19, 2009).

26. Margot Carmichael Lester, "5 Ways to Get and Stay Organized" SalesHQ.com, http://www.saleshq.com/training/articles/1353-5-ways-to-get-and-stay-organized (accessed September 6, 2009).

27. Jim Meisenheimer, "25 Ways to Get Motivated to Start Selling More," EvanCarmichael.com, http://www.evancarmichael.com/Sales/407/25-Ways-To-Get-Motivated-To-Start-Selling-More.html (accessed August 19, 2009).

28. Doug Dvorak, "How to Use Time Management to Become a More Successful Sales Professional!" EzineArticles, http://ezinearticles.com/?How-to-Use-Time-Management-to-Become-a-More-Successful-Sales-Professional&id=1081316 (accessed September 6, 2009).

29. Doug Dvorak, "How to Use Time Management to Become a More Successful Sales Professional!" EzineArticles, http://ezinearticles.com/?How-to-Use-Time-Management-to-Become-a-More-Successful-Sales-Professional&id=1081316 (accessed September 6, 2009).

30. Shane Gibson, "How to Operationalize Your Selling Strategy," SalesHQ, http://www.saleshq.com/training/articles/1990-how-to-operationalize-your-selling-strategy (accessed September 6, 2009).

31. Lori Basheda, "May Kay Consultant Scores Fourth Pink Cadillac," *Orange County Register*, August 18, 2009, http://www.bta.org/ (accessed September 6, 2009).

32. Jim Kahrs, "Sales Compensation: Creating a Plan that Works for Your Dealership," Prosperity Plus Management Consulting Inc., http://www.prosperityplus.biz/ArticleSalesComp.html (accessed May 16, 2010).

33. "Sales Compensation Plan Components," Online Business Advisor, http://www.onlinebusadv.com/?PAGE=178 (accessed August 19, 2009).

34. "Sales Compensation Plan Components," Online Business Advisor, http://www.onlinebusadv.com/?PAGE=178 (accessed August 19, 2009).

35. Jim Kahrs, "Sales Compensation: Creating a Plan that Works for Your Dealership," Prosperity Plus Management Consulting Inc., http://www.prosperityplus.biz/ArticleSalesComp.html (accessed May 16, 2010).

36. "Sales Compensation Plan Components," Online Business Advisor, http://www.onlinebusadv.com/?PAGE=178 (accessed August 19, 2009).

37. Jim Kahrs, "Sales Compensation: Creating a Plan that Works for Your Dealership," Prosperity Plus Management Consulting Inc., http://www.prosperityplus.biz/ArticleSalesComp.html (accessed May 16, 2010).

38. "Sales Compensation Plan Components," Online Business Advisor, http://www.onlinebusadv.com/?PAGE=178 (accessed August 19, 2009).

39. "Sales Compensation Plan Components," Online Business Advisor, http://www.onlinebusadv.com/?PAGE=178 (accessed August 19, 2009).

40. Cory Nahman, "Frequently Asked Questions Regarding the Profession of Pharmaceutical Sales Representative," http://www.coreynahman.com/how_many_products.html (accessed August 19, 2009).

41. Baron A. Weitz, Stephen B. Castleberry, and John F. Tanner, *Selling: Building Partnerships*, 5th ed. (New York: McGraw-Hill, 2003), 397.

42. Jeff Hardesty, "Setting and Exceeding Sales Goals through Key Performance Indicators (KPIs)," UnArchived Articles, June 14, 2006, http://articles.webraydian.com/article312-Setting_and_Exceeding_Sales_Goals_through_Key_Performance_Indicators_KPI.html (accessed August 19, 2009).

43. Renee Houston Zemanski, "Tough Truth about Quotas," *Selling Power* 22, no. 6, http://www.sellingpower.com/content/article.php?a=5998 (accessed March 16, 2010).

44. Baron A. Weitz, Stephen B. Castleberry, and John F. Tanner, *Selling: Building Partnerships*, 5th ed. (New York: McGraw-Hill, 2003), 397.

45. "How to Exceed Monthly Sales Targets," eHow, http://www.ehow.com/how_2252974_exceed-monthly-sales-targets.html (accessed August 19, 2009).

46. Tedy Bruschi with Michael Holley, *Never Give Up: My Stroke, My Recovery & My Return to the NFL* (Hoboken, NJ: Wiley & Sons, Inc., 2007).

47. Karen Guregian, "Tedy Bruschi a Role Model to Pats, Fans," *Boston Herald*, September 1, 2009, http://www.bostonherald.com/sports/football/patriots/view/20090901tedy_bruschi_a_role_model_to_pats_fans (accessed September 7, 2009).

48. Mark Newman, "Soxabration: Reliving 2005," White Sox, March 27, 2006, http://chicago.whitesox.mlb.com/cws/history/championship05.jsp (accessed January 3, 2010).

49. Priceless.com, http://www.priceless.com/us/personal/en/index.html (accessed September 7, 2009).

50. Jim Meisenheimer, "25 Ways to Get Motivated to Start Selling More," EvanCarmichael.com, http://www.evancarmichael.com/Sales/407/25-Ways-To-Get-Motivated-To-Start-Selling-More.html (accessed August 19, 2009).

51. Jim Meisenheimer, "25 Ways to Get Motivated to Start Selling More," EvanCarmichael.com, http://www.evancarmichael.com/Sales/407/25-Ways-To-Get-Motivated-To-Start-Selling-More.html (accessed August 19, 2009).

52. Adam Bryant, "You Win a Floppy Chicken," *New York Times*, July 12, 2009, business, 2.

53. Stacy Blackman, "Want to Succeed? Learn How to Fail," BNET, July 21, 2009, http://blogs.bnet.com/mba/?p=962 (accessed September 7, 2009).

54. Dave Kahle, "Learning from Failure," *American Salesman*, February 2009, http://www.davekahle.com/article/learningfromfailure.html (accessed May 16, 2010).

55. Lisa Peskin, "Top 10 Secrets of Selling in a Recession" *Philadelphia Business Journal* Workshop, Philadelphia, PA, July 29, 2009.

56. Lisa Peskin, "Top 10 Secrets of Selling in a Recession," *Philadelphia Business Journal* Workshop, Philadelphia, PA, July 29, 2009.

57. Adam Bryant, "Connecting the Dots Isn't Enough," *New York Times*, July 19, 2009, business, 2.

58. Baseball Almanac, "Career Leaders for Batting Average," http://www.baseball-almanac.com/hitting/hibavg1.shtml (accessed September 7, 2009).

59. Amanda Ferrante, "Retailers Counting on Conversion to Drive Store Metrics," Retail Store Ops Blog, March 17, 2008, http://retailstoreops.blogspot.com/2008/03/retailers-counting-on-conversion.html (accessed September 7, 2009).

60. The Conversion Chronicles, http://www.conversionchronicles.com/, September 7, 2009 (accessed May 16, 2010).

61. Dave Kahle, "Learning from Failure," *American Salesman*, February 2009, http://www.davekahle.com/article/learningfromfailure.html (accessed May 16, 2010).

62. Wayne Mansfield, "Seven Tips for Handling Stress in Challenging Times," Article Dashboard, http://www.articledashboard.com/Article/7-Tips-for-Handling-Stress-in-Challenging-Times/612133 (accessed September 8, 2009).

63. James Messina, "Accepting Personal Responsibility," LIVESTRONG.COM, November 18, 2009, http://www.livestrong.com/article/14698-accepting-personal-responsibility (accessed September 9, 2009).

64. Harvey Mackay, "8 Tips for Handling Rejection," WMAR-ABC2, July 5, 2009, http://www.abc2news.com/content/financialsurvival/yourjob/story/8-tips-for-handling-rejection/dM-Sg9DHiEaJcrnqMgDp44w.cspx (accessed September 9, 2009).

65. Hal Becker, "Become a Pro at Dealing with Rejection, and You'll Win More often at the Sales Game," *Kansas City Business Journal*, March 4, 2005, http://kansascity.bizjournals.com/kansascity/stories/2005/03/07/smallb6.html (accessed May 16, 2010).

66. Conversation with Jessica Sciarabba at AT&T store in King of Prussia, PA, August 26, 2009.

67. Donald Latumahina, "How to Get Your Morning Off to a Great Start," Life Optimizer Blog, July 28, 2009, http://www.lifeoptimizer.org/2009/07/28/how-to-get-your-morning-off-to-a-great-start (accessed August 19, 2009).

68. Mayo Clinic Staff, "Healthy Breakfast: Quick, Flexible Options to Grab at Home," MayoClinic.com, http://www.mayoclinic.com/health/food-and-nutrition/NU00197 (accessed September 8, 2009).

69. Donald Latumahina, "How to Get Your Morning Off to a Great Start," Life Optimizer Blog, July 28, 2009, http://www.lifeoptimizer.org/2009/07/28/how-to-get-your-morning-off-to-a-great-start (accessed August 19, 2009).

70. Jonathan Figaro, "A Simple Tip to Be More Productive," Life Optimizer Blog, July 25, 2009, http://www.lifeoptimizer.org/2009/07/18/be-more-productive (accessed August 19, 2009).

71. Diane Gray, "Some Sales Tips from the Best Salespersons," Associated Content, March 14, 2007, http://www.associatedcontent.com/article/166636/some_sales_tips_from_the_best_salespersons.html?cat=35 (accessed August 19, 2009).

72. Tim W. Knox, "Can You Handle the Stress of Running a Business?" *Entrepreneur*, October 6, 2003, http://www.entrepreneur.com/startingabusiness/startupbasics/askourideasandinspirationexpert/article64824.html (accessed September 8, 2009).

73. Jay Leno, "Jay Leno Says: Persistence Pays Off," *Parade*, September 6, 2009, http://www.parade.com/celebrity/2009/09/jay-leno-persistance-pays-off.html (accessed May 16, 2010).

74. "Make the Most of Your Internship," WetFeet, http://www.wetfeet.com/Undergrad/Internships/Articles/Make-the-Most-of-Your-Internship.aspx (accessed September 8, 2009).

75. Anya Kamenetz, "Take This Internship and Shove It," *New York Times*, May 30, 2006, http://www.nytimes.com/2006/05/30/opinion/30kamenetz.html (accessed September 11, 2009).

76. Craig Bollig, "Maybe One Is Not Enough," Internships for Dummies Newsletter, Spring 2009, http://www.uwosh.edu/journalism/docs/LowRes09.pdf (accessed September 8, 2009).

77. Kim Richmond, *Brand You*, 3rd ed. (Upper Saddle River, NJ: Pearson Prentice Hall, 2008), 210.

78. Lindsey Roberts, "A Millennial's View on Cost/Benefits of an Unpaid Internship Post-MBA," Millennial Marketing, August 10, 2009, http://millennialmarketing.com/2009/08/a-millennial's-view-on-costbenefits-of-an-unpaid-internship-post-mba (accessed September 11, 2009).

79. Sarah H. Needleman, "Starting Fresh with an Unpaid Internship," *Wall Street Journal*, July 16, 2009, http://online.wsj.com/article/SB10001424052970203577304574280201046918712.html (accessed September 11, 2009).

80. Rich DeMatteo, "3 Reasons to Take an Unpaid Internship," Corn on the Job Blog, July 23, 2009, http://cornonthejob.com/2009/07/23/3-reasons-to-take-an-unpaid-internship (accessed September 11, 2009).

81. "Getting the Big Break with the Right Internship: You Can Beat the Odds and Become a Success in the Entertainment Industry," TheFreeLibrary.com, http://www.thefreelibrary.com/Getting+the+big+break:+with+the+right+internship,+you+can+beat+the...-a094672526 (accessed September 11, 2009).

82. "Make the Most of Your Internship," WetFeet, http://www.wetfeet.com/Undergrad/Internships/Articles/Make-the-Most-of-Your-Internship.aspx (accessed September 8, 2009).

83. Joyce Lee, "U.S. Companies that Hire the Most Interns," *Forbes*, July 7, 2009, http://www.forbes.com/2009/07/07/biggest-intern-companies-leadership-careers-jobs.html (accessed September 11, 2009).

84. Philly Ad Club, "Philly Ad Club Mentor Program," May 5, 2009, http://www.phillyadclub.com/news_article.php?id=1973 (accessed September 12, 2009).

85. Sally Kearsley, "It Pays to Join a Professional Association," http://www.jobscareers.com/articles/developingyourcareer.html (accessed September 12, 2009).

86. Public Relation Society of America (PRSA), "Receive a Free PRSA Chapter Membership," http://www.prsa.org/membership/documents/PRSA%20Individual%20Membership%20Application%20with%20Chapter%20Pricing.pdf (accessed September 12, 2009).

87. Public Relations Student Society of America (PRSSA), "Join PRSSA," http://www.prssa.org/about/join.aspx (accessed September 12, 2009).

CHAPTER 15

Entrepreneurial Selling: The Power of Running Your Own Business

Video Ride-Along with David Fox, Founder and CEO of Brave Spirits

Meet David Fox. He is an entrepreneur who founded Brave Spirits, a company that makes vodka, gin, whiskey, and rum. What makes Brave Spirits different from other spirits makers is that $2 of every bottle sold is donated to charities that support the men and women of America's military, fire departments, and police departments. The company is dedicated to celebrating the bravery of those who serve our country.

Ride along with David and learn about the role selling plays in being an entrepreneur.

View the video online at: http://www.youtube.com/embed/dfFeoRsVAio

15.1 The Power of Entrepreneurship

Learning Objectives

1. Understand the entrepreneurial spirit and what it takes to be an entrepreneur.
2. Discuss the role of entrepreneurial businesses in the economy.

Her owners couldn't imagine putting their beloved Zoe, a seventeen-year-old Jack Russell terrier, in the dark belly of the cargo hold of a jetliner when they moved from California's Bay Area to Delray Beach, Florida, in 2005. Although most commercial airlines have been working on policies and procedures to make pets more comfortable when traveling, and give their owners more peace of mind, husband-and-wife team Alysa Binder and Dan Wiesel just didn't feel that options like Delta's Pet First and Continental's PetSafe really filled the bill. So on July 14, 2009, they launched Pet Airways, the first airline dedicated exclusively to transporting animals in a safe and comfortable environment. The airline includes nineteen turboprop Beech 1900 planes that have been converted to comfortably carry up to fifty live animal crates and one certified pet attendant. Pet "passengers" can fly one way for $149 and round trip for $250 to or from any of five major airport locations.[1] Who else but entrepreneurs would conceive a business idea like this?

It All Starts with an Idea

entrepreneur

A person who has an idea and takes on the risk of bringing the concept to market.

Entrepreneurs have started all different kinds of businesses from overnight shipping to electronics, music, skin-care products, to retail stores, because each saw an unmet need in the market. Fred Smith started FedEx in 1971 based on a paper he wrote for a Yale University economics class and used his $4 million to start the company.[2] Sam Walton founded Wal-Mart in 1962 because he was convinced that Americans wanted a new type of store, a discount store, so he and his wife put up 95 percent of the money to build the first Wal-Mart store in Rodgers, Arizona.[3] In 1930, Colonel Harland Sanders started cooking for weary travelers who stopped by his gas station; they ate at his own dining table because he didn't have a restaurant.[4] William Hewlett and David Packard decided to start a business and "make a run for it themselves" in 1939; their first product was an audio oscillator, an electronic instrument used to test sound equipment. They decided the name of their company on the toss of a coin.[5] Jay-Z saw hip-hop music as a way to get out of the projects in Brooklyn and parlayed his passion and business prowess into a net worth of over $350 million. He is CEO of Def Jam Recordings and Roc-a-Fella Records, part-owner of the New Jersey Nets, and co-owner of the 40/40 Club, among other things.[6] Estée Lauder started selling creams that were created by her uncle and founded Estée Lauder in 1946 "with four products and the belief that every woman can be beautiful."[7],[8] Walt Disney, a cartoonist, saw the opportunity to entertain as his driving force when he founded Walt Disney Company in 1923.[9] His passion for his craft led to the creation of the company when he said, "I am interested in entertaining people, in bringing pleasure, particularly laughter, to others, rather than being concerned with 'expressing' myself with obscure creative impressions."[10]

entrepreneurship

Starting a new concept as a result of an idea that fills a need and taking the risk to bring the idea to market.

Entrepreneurship is about helping people see the benefit of a new way of doing things; it's about having an idea and having the passion and perseverance to make it come alive. What sets an entrepreneur apart from any other businessperson is that fact that she is willing to assume risk to make a profit.[11] An entrepreneur is not only open to new ways of thinking and of doing things, but he also has the vision, drive, energy, and optimism to bring an idea from concept to reality. Generally, an entrepreneur is someone who says, "There's a better way, and I will find it." Entrepreneurs are willing to take risks to make things better.[12]

Video Clip

Why Become an Entrepreneur?
David Fox, founder and CEO of Brave Spirits, talks about why someone should consider being an entrepreneur. It might surprise you to hear what he says about being your own boss.

View the video online at: http://www.youtube.com/embed/wnJ5FRrFXYE

Guy Kawasaki, famous entrepreneur, venture capitalist, speaker, and author of several books on entrepreneurialism including *The Art of the Start: The Time-Tested, Battle-Hardened Guide for Anyone Starting Anything*, provides a holistic way of viewing entrepreneurship.

Video Clip

Making Meaning
The idea of starting, restarting, or growing something—whether a business or a nonprofit organization—is grounded in "making meaning," which is the cornerstone of Guy Kawasaki's concept of entrepreneurship as shown in this video.[13]

View the video online at: http://www.youtube.com/embed/L3xaeVXTSBg

Entrepreneurialism and the Economy

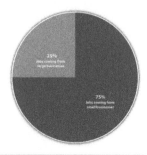

patent

The right of exclusivity to
make and market a
specific product or service
granted by the United
States government.

free market system

An economy in which an
individual's success is
dictated by demand on the
part of the consumer, not
by the government.

Imagine that in 1899, the director of the United States Patent Office made the proclamation that everything that could be invented had already been invented. He certainly underestimated the power of the American entrepreneur. Everything from airplanes to telephones, computers to the Internet, not to mention the iPod and even skateboards, have all been products developed and marketed by entrepreneurs over the past 110 years.[15]

Today, entrepreneurs literally power the country. There are twenty-seven million businesses in the United States; 99.7 percent of them are considered small businesses, according to David C. Dickson, district director for the Small Business Administration. That means that only 80,000 businesses are considered large businesses; the other 26.9 million are small businesses.[16] Small businesses provide approximately 75 percent of the new jobs added to the American economy every year.

Besides providing jobs, entrepreneurial businesses are more likely to provide specialty and custom goods and services to consumers and businesses. In fact, small businesses produce nearly thirteen times more **patents** (rights of exclusivity to make and market the product or service granted by the United States government) per employee than large firms.[17],[18] Small businesses represent one-third of all companies that have fifteen or more patents.[19]

Entrepreneurialism is critical not only for the growth of the economy in the United States but also globally. The Kauffman Foundation, in conjunction with researchers from Babson College and the London School of Business, found that the disparity in entrepreneurial activity in some countries is contributing to a gap in economic growth. "The Global Entrepreneurship Monitor (GEM) report provides conclusive evidence that promoting entrepreneurship and enhancing the entrepreneurial dynamic of a country should be an integral element of any government's commitment to boosting economic well-being," according to Paul Reynolds, GEM project coordinator at both Babson College and the London Business School.[20] According to the study, Canada, Israel, and the United States are those countries that are experiencing the highest level of activity, while Denmark, Finland, France, Germany, and Japan have the lowest levels of activity. The GEM constructed a framework for countries to work within to encourage entrepreneurial activity that includes raising the participation level to those outside the core age group of twenty-five to forty-four and increasing the participation of women in the entrepreneurial process.[21]

Entrepreneurship is rewarded in the United States because the economy is based on a **free market system**—one in which an individual's success is dictated by demand on the part of the consumer, not by the government.[22] Because entrepreneurial businesses are so important to the economy, free market governments not only support them, but they often encourage entrepreneurial business ventures. According to Harvard Business School professor Josh Lerner, the United States government played a key role in the early development of Silicon Valley. The government has also provided support for the growth of innovation in places such as Tel Aviv and Singapore.[23]

While statistics are no guarantee of success for the future, especially in today's tough economy, you might find it interesting to know that small businesses employ a little more than half of all private sector workers, pay 44 percent of all private sector payroll, and have generated 64 percent of new jobs over the past fifteen years. In 2008, approximately 530,000 new businesses were created every month, which was a slight increase over 2007.[24]

These facts reflect the importance of creativity, ideas, passion, drive, independence, and risk taking in the economy. Entrepreneurialism isn't limited to a specific type of organization or business; it's a state of mind, a way of thinking and behaving, a way of pushing for something better than the status quo. Entrepreneurs can be found in large multinational corporations as well as non-profit organizations, and new business start-ups. Every large business or organization had to start small but think differently.

Getting Started

Being an entrepreneur can be exciting and invigorating. Having the vision to create products and services that can meet and exceed customers' needs and imaginations and the passion to bring them to market can be exhilarating. Imagine having a hobby in college that turns into a multibillion-dollar business. That's how Mark Zuckerberg created Facebook and Michael Dell created Dell. Both had a unique idea and vision and were willing to take the risk to make it a reality.

Where does it all start? The entrepreneurial drive starts early for most who have it. Think about when you were young. If you were the one in the neighborhood who set up a lemonade stand, went door-to-door selling products, or set up a lawn-mowing service in the neighborhood (and hired your friends), you may have the makings of an entrepreneur. While you and many of your friends (and perhaps your siblings) participated in activities like this when you were young, not everyone will grow up to be an entrepreneur. A recent study, which focused on the behaviors of identical twins, has found evidence that entrepreneurialism may be based on genetics, not environment.[26] In fact, the study found that a connection between different genes causing someone to be extroverted is important to salesmanship, which is also a strong trait in many entrepreneurs.[27]

Genetics or not, the current state of the economy has forced many who are out of work to consider owning their own business. "These are people that two years ago did not aspire to own a business, but circumstances have dictated that they look at freelance opportunities," says Ken Yancey, CEO of nonprofit entrepreneur-mentoring group Service Corps of Retired Executives (SCORE). In fact, Internal Revenue Service (IRS) data confirm that the number of nonemployer firms (those that have paid employees) is up 8.1 percent from 2007 to 2008.[28] These "accidental entrepreneurs" have come of age due to a variety of circumstances. Some, like Maureen Rothman, president of Rothman Associates, started her business when her employer went out of business. Although she had over fifteen years of selling and sales management experience, when people encouraged her to start her own business her first thought was, "I'm not an entrepreneur." After developing a business plan and getting input and direction from resources such as SCORE, she said that everyone told her to "just do it." "On 09.06.05 [September 6, 2005]," as she likes to say, "I did it!"

and launched Rothman Associates, a manufacturers' representative for hospitality seating products.[29]

Entrepreneurial at Any Age

Whether it's the challenging economy or the idea of controlling your destiny, entrepreneurs begin their journey at different ages.

Tech-savvy teenagers are starting online businesses since the Internet has lowered the barriers to entry and provided anonymity from their age. Challenges in finding part-time work also drive teens to start traditional businesses such as yard work, party planning, and tutoring.[30]

At the other end of the spectrum, many baby boomers who are reaching retirement age are now asking themselves if retirement is "when you stop working completely or retire from one job and begin another." Independence, passion, flexibility, and additional income are significant motivators to "mid-life entrepreneurs." In fact, boomers compose nearly half of the nation's self-employed workers.[31]

Leaving corporate life behind for a chance to build a business and chase a dream is a trend that is occurring across the country in industries of all kinds from technology to personal services. Ali Galgano recently traded in her high-powered job as corporate recruiter doing work for firms such as Goldman Sachs for her own jewelry company, Charm & Chain. Brent Bouchez, David Page, and Nancy McNally gave up their glitzy, perk-filled jobs at an advertising agency on Madison Avenue in New York to start their own marketing firm named Five-0, which is focused on marketing to baby boomers. Kelly Elvin gave up a lucrative career as a lawyer to become a dog trainer. All have learned that life as an entrepreneur is very different from life in the corporate world. The thrill of running your own show and making your dream come alive is a learning process. There are no bosses, no corporate initiatives, no departmental deadlines, and no performance reviews. Everything is all you, all the time. Skills such as time management, understanding financial statements, building a good support system, and overcoming the isolation of working alone are all challenges in the entrepreneurial world. "Entrepreneurs have to be willing to listen and learn and make judgments and be adaptive," according to Monica Doss, director of the Kauffman Foundation's FastTrac entrepreneur training programs.[32] As for the issue of timing, some ideas might not work in the current economic environment. Entrepreneurs have to understand when it's no longer feasible to keep a business running.[33]

Who's the Boss?

Check out the Web site for Ali's company at http://www.charmandchain.com.

What Does It Take?

Entrepreneurialism is based on dreams and risk. Not every idea is commercially viable or economically feasible, and not every dream comes true. But there are some common ingredients that are part of being an entrepreneur.

What's the Big Idea?

Every business starts with an idea—that unique product or service that will serve customers better than any other. "Entrepreneurs are often so passionate about their ideas, they can lose objectivity," according to Nancy A. Shenker, president of theONswitch LLC. "Rather than taking the time to thoroughly plan and research, they sometimes plow ahead with execution, only to spend valuable dollars on unfocused or untargeted activities," she adds.[34] That's why it's important to research the viability of a business idea starting with the size of the market and if the idea will be compelling enough to meet an unmet need in the marketplace. Checking out the competition can be extremely educational. You might be surprised about what you learn by visiting your competitors and asking questions to their customers.[35] The bottom line is that there has to be some recognition by the customer that there is a need for the product or service you want to bring to market. Without demand, it will be virtually impossible to have a successful business.

You might be wondering if there's more to being an entrepreneur than simply selling a product or service for a profit. **Social entrepreneurialism** uses the concepts of entrepreneurship to bring about social change. While some social entrepreneurial efforts are nonprofit organizations, others are for-profit companies that focus on adding value to society. For example, City Year is a nonprofit organization that provides full-time year of service for young people from the United States and South Africa with the objective that they will go on to use their skills to better the world. Social entrepreneurialism is recognized and supported by several mainstream organizations.

social entrepreneurialism

Using the concepts of entrepreneurialism to bring about social change.

Link

Best Social Entrepreneurs

View a list of the most successful social entrepreneurs"[36]

http://www.investopedia.com/articles/investing/092515/10-most-successful-social-entrepreneurs.asp

The Difference Is in the Questions

No one plans to bring a mediocre product or service to market, but the best way to avoid that fate (and ultimately failure) is to ask yourself the right questions before you start your business. For example, can you really answer the question "What sets your product or service apart from what the competitors offer?" A claim like "the best burger in Seattle" doesn't offer any real point of difference to the customer. Asking the right questions helps identify important opportunities or explain the lack of them.[37] A good start is to ask yourself these three questions:

1. What are you selling?
2. To whom are you selling it?
3. Why would they buy it from you?

If answered honestly and specifically, these questions help identify the validity of a new business idea.[38]

Hard Work, Long Hours

You might consider the concept of being your own boss to be a good deal. After all, you can do what you want, when you want, and work as hard as you want on what you want do to because you're the boss. Well, that's not really completely true. The challenge of bringing an idea to life is hard work and there's no guarantee of success. According to the U.S. Census Bureau, only 48.8 percent of the new businesses that were started in 1977 were still around in 2000.[39] Being an entrepreneur is hard work. Think about Melissa Carter, the owner of San Diego's first CiCi's Pizza. She works about seventy hours a week and put in even more hours before the grand opening in August 2009.[40] Dan Sanker, president and founder of CaseStack, a logistics outsourcing company, admits that he really doesn't take any time off, despite his good intentions. Sanker strongly encourages people to follow their dreams and do something entrepreneurial as he has done. But he also reminds the aspiring entrepreneur to keep in mind that business ownership does not provide complete freedom and flexibility because you will ultimately "be beholden to investors, clients, and employees."[41]

Vinny Lingham, founder of do-it-yourself Web site building company Yola, who recently secured $20 million in investor funding and was featured on the cover of the July 2009 issue of *Entrepreneur* magazine, says, "Success may look like it happened overnight but that's rarely the case in reality. You have to be prepared to put in long hours, take risks, and make personal sacrifices." But he goes on to say, "And ideally the best time to make them is when you're young, which is why I encourage young entrepreneurs to go for it."[42]

Video Clip

The Best and the Worst
Listen to David Fox, founder and CEO of Brave Spirits, share his thoughts about the best and the worst of being an entrepreneur.

View the video online at: http://www.youtube.com/embed/lxnSvOUZvDk

Get Rich Quick? Probably Not

franchise

A form of business organization in which a person, or franchisee, pays a company to use its name and market its products.

franchisee

A person or organization that pays to use a company's name and market its products.

Entrepreneurs are motivated by discovery, creativity, and innovation. While almost three-quarters of current business owners surveyed by the Kauffman Foundation said that "building wealth" is the reason they became an entrepreneur, it may take a long time to realize the financial benefit of entrepreneurship.[43] For example, a **franchise**, a form of business organization in which a person, or **franchisee**, pays a company to use its name and market its products, can cost hundreds of thousands of dollars in up-front fees.[44] A Subway franchise can cost as much as $250,000, not including any royalty fees, rent, product, or labor costs.[45],[46] Meanwhile, businesses that require inventory, such as retail stores or restaurants, require an investment in inventory, real estate, or even technology before the doors even open. But if the franchise or business idea is right, and the business is well run, the payback can be significant financially and personally.

Interestingly, it's more than money that motivates many entrepreneurs. It's more than "riches" according to Scott Laughlin, director of the University of Maryland's Tech Entrepreneurship Program. Entrepreneurs are more interested in "wealth"; he points to two of the most famous entrepreneurs, Bill Gates from Microsoft and Warren Buffet from Berkshire Hathaway, who have pooled their resources into the $60 billion philanthropy called the Bill & Melinda Gates Foundation. "Wealth is broader, encompassing less tangible rewards such as respect and independence," says Laughlin.[47]

Top Ten Franchise Opportunities

View Entrepreneur magazine's Franchise 500 List

https://www.entrepreneur.com/franchises/500/2015/

Key Takeaways

- **Entrepreneurship** is the practice of selling ideas and having the passion and perseverance to make it become a reality. **Entrepreneurs** are willing to take risks to bring a product or service to market.
- Some of the world's largest companies were started by **entrepreneurs**.
- **Entrepreneurs** have a significant impact on the economy of the United States and the world.
- **Entrepreneurs** protect their ideas by applying for a **patent** from the United States government.
- **Entrepreneurs** flourish in a **free market system**, one in which an individual's success is dictated by demand on the part of the consumer, not the government.
- Being an **entrepreneur** requires a unique idea, passion, and hard work to bring it to fruition.
- **Social entrepreneurship** includes nonprofit organizations as well as for-profit companies that focus on impacting society in a positive way.
- An **entrepreneur** may start a business based on a new idea or expand an existing brand by buying a **franchise**.

Exercises

1. Review the list of *Entrepreneur* magazine's fastest-growing franchises: https://www.entrepreneur.com/franchises/500/2015/. Visit the Web sites of at least three of the franchises and answer these three key questions about their business: What do they sell? To whom do they sell it? Why do people want to buy it from them?
2. Visit the Web site of *Entrepreneur* magazine: http://www.entrepreneur.com. Read a current article about an entrepreneur and discuss his or her unique idea.

15.2 Selling Yourself and Your Idea

Learning Objective

1. Understand how entrepreneurs sell themselves and their business ideas to secure funding to grow their businesses.

So you have a unique idea, the passion and perseverance to bring it to market, and the willingness to take the risk. Now what?

Being an entrepreneur in some ways is like being a student: you have to do your homework. In the business setting, that means creating a **business plan**: a road map of the who, what, when, where, why, and how of your business. A business plan is a document that details everything about the business from the product position in the marketplace to the financial information for the next three years. But a business plan is not simply like a term paper—a project that's completed and then put on the shelf. A business plan is a dynamic document and should serve four purposes:

business plan

A document that details everything about the business from the product position in the marketplace to the financial information for the next three years.

1. **Sell you on the business**. While this might sound like a no-brainer, the business plan development process includes rigorous research that can be a good eye-opener about the feasibility of your idea. Ideally, your business plan helps put your idea and its potential into perspective and gives you the details you need to move from concept to reality. However, even if you determine

that your idea doesn't have as much potential as you thought or might cost more than you anticipated, the process of creating a business plan helped you reach that conclusion.

2. **Sell others on the business**. In many cases, a business needs some kind of support—financial, consultative, or other resources. In this case, the business plan plays the role of the selling and marketing materials for your idea. How you make your idea come alive and support it with the necessary research and financial data can be the difference between someone becoming a stakeholder in your new venture or taking a pass.

3. **Give you confidence**. Having a great idea is one thing, doing the research to understand exactly what it will take to make the idea real is quite another. Having a better understanding of what it takes to launch and manage the business puts you in control to solicit investors and other supporters and start your journey.

4. **Improve your chances of success**. A business plan is a lot of planning and work, but it's worth it. According to a study conducted by AT&T, 42 percent of entrepreneurs who had written a business plan rated themselves as more successful than the 58 percent who hadn't written one.[48]

Writing Your Business Plan

Every business or organization is different, but a business plan is a common method of planning the launch and management of the business.[49] While there is no single business plan format, the elements of a business plan are standard. The following business plan outline serves as a guide to developing a business plan. Keep in mind that the order in which you write your business plan should not necessarily follow the order in which you present your plan.

Business Plan Outline

1. **Table of contents**. Page numbers for each section.
2. **Executive summary**. Write this section after the plan is completed; this should be a compelling summary of the plan and how it will work.
3. **General company description**. A high-level description of the product, service, or organization and the unmet need it meets.
4. **Products and services**. A detailed description of the product, service, or organization; how it works; manufacturing costs; and so on.
5. **Marketing plan**. A detailed description of the current state of the market, including competition, your positioning, target audience, and how customers will learn about your product, service, or organization and the cost to get the word out.
6. **Operational plan**. A detailed description of how you will run the day-to-day operations, including product costs, real estate, inventory levels, labor, credit, and so on.
7. **Management and organization**. A detailed description of the principals of the company, including bios, board of directors, advisory board, banker, attorney, insurance agent, mentors, and so on.
8. **Personal financial statement**. A personal financial statement for each partner in the business. This is important as business owners often provide capital to start up or support the business; investors want to see the financial standing of the principal individuals.
9. **Start-up expenses and capitalization**. Accurate accounting of the expenses that are required to get the business started.
10. **Financial plan**. A twelve-month profit and loss statement, three-year financial projection, projected cash flow, and opening day balance sheet.
11. **Appendices**. Supporting information such as brochures and advertising, blueprints, leases, equipment, list of assets available, letters of recommendation, and any information that will help support your plan.

Link

Business Plan Template
A complete template with detailed descriptions for each section is available at the SCORE Web site.

http://www.score.org/resources/score-business-plan-template

Presenting Your Business Plan

Once you have identified your breakthrough idea (think iPod as the standard for a breakthrough idea), conducted your research, and written your business plan, it's time to put everything to use. Whether you plan to fund the business yourself or find an investor to provide some capital (money), you will need your business plan to secure resources from your bank, insurance company, lawyer, attorney, and other support areas. Your business plan is the universal document for discussions with each of these people. In fact, you should first present your business plan to family, friends, and mentors to get some feedback before you take it out "on the road."

Types of Investors

When it comes to **investors**, people who are willing to invest financial support based on the potential for the success of your business, there are several different types. Here is a summary of the types of investors:

- **Banks**. Banks are a common source of lending, and most offer several different types of business loans, including **Small Business Administration (SBA)** guaranteed loans. (The SBA does not actually provide loans; they simply guarantee them to banks that make the loans.) Banks are the most regulated form of lending; ratios must meet their requirements, and all paperwork must be in order.[50]

- **Private investors (or angel investors)**. These are people who are willing to invest money or resources to seed the business or get it up and running. Private investors can include anyone from your uncle who invests $5,000 to a friend of the family who lets you use their second home for office space. Private investors may want to have a say in major business decisions.[51] Each deal is negotiated separately; be sure to agree to terms with a contract. This is the least regulated area so it's best to be informed about your angel's background.[52]

- **Venture capital firms** (also referred to as **VCs**). VCs usually specialize in investments of $1 million and above, although there are no hard-and-fast rules. They are looking for a fast return on their investment, especially with the opportunity for an **initial public offering (IPO)** to take the company public. VCs look for a strong management team and an idea with market potential. Most want a return within three to five years and want to have a say in major decisions that impact the company.[53]

- **Equipment leasing companies**. If you business requires equipment, leasing can be an option that frees up cash and provides an option to buy at the end of the lease.[54]

- **Government programs**. There are many programs at the local, state, and national level designed to support the growth of small businesses. The SBA is only one of the many programs available. Many programs offer opportunities for minorities, business loans, tax incentives, and grants, just to name a few. Research is key to find the program that can potentially support your business; they are not all listed in one place.[55]

A complete summary of types of investors is available at http://www.businessplanmaster.com/small-business-loan-sources.html.

investors
People or firms who are willing to invest financial support based on the potential for the success of the business.

Small Business Administration (SBA)
Independent agency of the federal government that supports and protects small businesses.

private investors (or angel investors)
People or firms who are willing to invest money or resources to seed the business or get it up and running.

venture capital firms
Firms that usually specialize in investments of $1 million and above.

initial public offering (IPO)
When a company issues common stock for the first time.

Selling Your Business Plan—and Yourself

When you present your business plan to anyone—a banker, a lawyer, an accountant, you are asking her to make a commitment to support your business idea. While the contents and details of your business plan are critical to gaining support, you are selling more than your business idea—you are selling yourself. How you communicate your vision and supporting details in a clear, concise, and confident manner can make the difference between getting financial or other support or walking away empty handed.

All the concepts that you have learned in the *Selling U* section of each chapter apply when you are selling your business plan. Thinking about yourself and your business idea as a brand is where it all starts. Remember from Chapter 1 that a brand is unique, consistent, and relevant and has an emotional connection with its customers. Your personal brand and your business brand need to accomplish the same goal. *Fast Company* magazine identifies personal marketing as one of the first steps for Gen Y entrepreneurs to start their own business: "One of the most important requirements of entrepreneurship is the ability to sell yourself and your ideas."[56]

Video Clip

Evolution of a Business Plan
Listen to David Fox, founder and CEO of Brave Spirits, discuss the role and evolution of his company's business plan.

View the video online at: http://www.youtube.com/embed/4cgfnozhQOA

Just as you use your résumé to tell "stories" about your three brand positioning points for your personal brand, your business plan pitch should be equally concise and powerful. Although you have worked for hours (probably months, if not years) on your business plan, your presentation or pitch should focus on the key points and demonstrate not only that it is a potentially profitable business idea (or nonprofit organization that can achieve its goals) but also that you are the right person to make the concept come alive.

Gen Y Entrepreneurs: Get Ready to Sell…Yourself

Fast Company magazine suggests Gen Yers start marketing themselves as a brand even before they start their business. Here are some things you can do now:

- Join professional organizations and become visible, especially to high-profile people in the industry.

- Volunteer at a nonprofit organization that is related to the business you want to start. Demonstrate the quality of your work by working on a committee or major project that is important to moving the organization forward.
- Get a mentor who will give you personal guidance and advice on your career, business idea, and resources.
- Write a blog, post entries to Twitter, share your observations and theories, and get feedback.
- Read everything you can about the industry you want to enter.[57]

Key Takeaways

- A **business plan** is a road map for your business and a tool to present your business idea to potential resources and investors.
- A **business plan** has certain key elements, including a statement of purpose and marketing, operational, and financial plans.
- An **investor** is a person or organization that provides financial or other support to your business.
- Types of **investors** include banks, **private investors**, **venture capitalists**, equipment-leasing companies, and government programs.
- When you present your **business plan** to prospective **investors**, you are selling more than your idea; you are selling yourself.

Exercises

1. Assume you are starting an online business called FitMePerfect.com, a Web site where customers can order jeans made to their exact body measurements. What kind of information would you include in the marketing plan section of your business plan?
2. Contact a local bank and talk to the commercial lending officer to find out the process for applying for a business loan.
3. Discuss three things you can do now to prepare for a career as an entrepreneur.

15.3 *Selling U*: Inspiration, Resources, and Assistance for Your Entrepreneurial Journey

Learning Objectives

1. Meet some experienced entrepreneurs and learn from their successes and failures.
2. Understand the resources available to help you pursue your entrepreneurial dream.

Entrepreneurial Resources

No matter what stage you are in your entrepreneurial journey, there are resources to help you get to the next step. Table 15.1 includes some of the best places to begin your research.

TABLE 15.1 Entrepreneurial Resources

Resource Name and Web Site	Description
Government Resources	
Small Business Development Centers http://americassbdc.org	1,100 branch offices of the Small Business Administration; provide free one-on-one counseling and other resources
SCORE https://www.score.org	SBA partner; counselors to America's small businesses; free one-on-one counseling and other resources
Small Business Administration http://www.sba.gov/	Free tools and resources for small businesses including online Start-up Assessment Tool
United States Chamber of Commerce https://www.uschamber.com/members/small-business	Arm of the United States Chamber of Commerce; comprehensive free resources for small businesses
Trade Journals	
Inc. magazine http://www.inc.com	Online articles and hard copy magazine with news, tips, and insights for and about entrepreneurs
Entrepreneur magazine http://www.entrepreneur.com/	Online articles and hard copy magazine with news, tips, and insights for and about entrepreneurs
Organizations and Networks	
Entrepreneur's Organization (EO) http://www.eonetwork.org/Pages/default.aspx	Online network and chapters throughout the United States
Collegiate Entrepreneurs' Organization (CEO) http://www.c-e-o.org	Online network and chapters throughout the United States
Women Entrepreneurs in Science and Technology (WEST) http://www.westorg.org	Nonprofit organization dedicated to supporting women entrepreneurs in science and technology
International Organizations	
The Indus Entrepreneurs (TIE) http://www.tie.org	International nonprofit for the advancement of entrepreneurialism
Research and Resources	
Kauffman Foundation http://www.kauffman.org	Organization to connect entrepreneurs and provide resources
Global Entrepreneurship Monitor http://www.gemconsortium.org	Organization to connect entrepreneurs and provide resources
A Few Blogs and Twitter Posts Worth Reading	
Guy Kawasaki http://holykaw.alltop.com/ http://twitter.com/GuyKawasaki	Blog and microblog on entrepreneurial issues, tips, new technology, and more
Seth Godin http://sethgodin.typepad.com/	Entrepreneurial thoughts of the day
Michael Simmons http://twitter.com/michaeldsimmons http://www.facebook.com/michaeldsimmons#/michaeldsimmons?v=wall	Part motivation, part entrepreneurial insights

Resource Name and Web Site	Description
Mark Cuban http://blogmaverick.com/	Entrepreneurial insights from the owner of the Dallas Mavericks
Books	
Guy Kawasaki's books http://www.guykawasaki.com/books/index.shtml	
Seth Godin's books http://www.amazon.com/s/ref=nb_ss?url=search-alias=aps&field-keywords=seth+godin&x=0&y=0	
Jeffrey Gitomer's books http://www.amazon.com/s/ref=nb_ss?url=search-alias=aps&field-keywords=jeffrey+gitomer&x=0&y=0	
Free and Low-Cost Business Tools and Software	
10 Free or Cheap Tools for Start-ups http://www.inc.com/ss/10-free-or-cheap-tools-start-ups?nav=mostpopular#0	
Great No-Cost Software http://www.inc.com/magazine/20090901/great-no-cost-software.html?nav=mostpopular	
Miscellaneous (worth checking out)	
E-commerce Starter Kit http://www.inc.com/guides/sales/20696.html	
American Express Open http://www.openforum.com	Articles, videos, and forum for and about entrepreneurs

Don't stop here! Look up local entrepreneurial organizations and get involved. Meet people, learn the ropes, and share your passion. If you have the entrepreneurial spirit, go for it and enjoy the journey!

15.4 Review and Practice

Power Wrap-Up

Now that you have read this chapter, you should be able to understand the opportunities and resources available to pursue a career as an entrepreneur.

- You **understand** that entrepreneurs have a dream and are willing to take the risk to change the way things are done and the way people think.
- You can **describe** the impact that entrepreneurs have on the economy.
- You can **discuss** the free market system in which entrepreneurs can thrive.
- You can **identify** reasons and motivations for being an entrepreneur.
- You can **recognize** opportunities for social entrepreneurialism.

- You can **describe** the elements of a business plan.
- You can **list** the different types of investors.
- You can **appreciate** the lessons learned from experienced entrepreneurs.
- You can **understand** what resources are available to help you realize your dream and start your business.

Test Your Power Knowledge (answers are below)

1. What is entrepreneurship?
2. Name the government agency that oversees all policies and protects the interests of small businesses.
3. Why is a free market system a good environment for entrepreneurs?
4. Describe social entrepreneurialism.
5. Describe a business plan.
6. Name five different types of investors.
7. Identify at least one entrepreneur who inspires you.
8. List three resources that can help you to start your entrepreneurial journey.

Power (Role) Play

Now it's time to put what you've learned into practice. The following are two roles that are involved in the same selling situation; one role is that of the investor and the other is that of the entrepreneur. This will give you the opportunity to think about this selling situation from the point of view of both the investor and the entrepreneur.

Read each role carefully along with the discussion questions. Then, be prepared to play either of the roles in class using the concepts covered in this chapter. You may be asked to discuss the roles and do a role-play in groups or individually.

Pitch Your Plan

Role: Potential investor from Gateway Investment Partners

You have invested in several entrepreneurial start-ups over the years, and you are looking for the next great business idea. You've been talking to young entrepreneurs, but you haven't seen a business that you think is compelling. You're looking for a great idea and a smart, passionate entrepreneur who knows what it takes to build a business.

- What are the characteristics you are looking for in an aspiring entrepreneur?
- Is the idea a viable one? Does it have the potential to be profitable? Has the entrepreneur clearly communicated the opportunity in the business plan?
- Why would you be willing (or not willing) to invest in this business idea?

Role: Entrepreneur

You have an idea for a new business called FILL. It is a store that sells eco-friendly household cleaning products in bulk; customers buy a container or bring their own and fill each with products. Customers may also recycle any containers at the store. The products are sold by the ounce. Your philosophy is to make it easy for customers to save the planet. You have an opportunity to get some seed money to start your business if you successfully pitch your business idea to the potential investor from Gateway Investment Partners.

- How would you sell yourself and your idea to a potential investor?
- How do you make your passion for the idea come alive?

- What are the key points in your business plan?
- How do you use your selling skills to secure funding from this investor for your new business idea?

Put Your Power to Work: *Selling U* Activities

1. Identify at least one local entrepreneur. Make an appointment to meet her and learn about how she started her business.
2. Watch the video book brief for Guy Kawasaki's book *Reality Check: An Irreverent Guide to Outsmarting, Outmanaging, and Outmarketing Your Competition* at http://www.bnet.com/ 2422-13724_23-243321.html. Describe the concept of "frame or be framed."

Test Your Power Knowledge Answers

1. Starting a new concept as a result of an idea that fills a need and taking the risk to bring the idea to market.
2. Small Business Administration (SBA).
3. Free market system is an economy in which an individual's success is dictated by demand on the part of the consumer, not by the government, so it encourages entrepreneurialism.
4. Social entrepreneurialism: using the concepts of entrepreneurialism to bring about social change.
5. A business plan is a road map that includes the who, what, when, where, why, and how about the business or organization.
6. Bank, private investor (also called angel investor), venture capitalist, equipment leasing company, and government program.
7. Describe one of the entrepreneurs discussed in the chapter who inspires you.
8. Identify at least one resource from Table 15.1.

Endnotes

1. Dan Reed, "For Passengers of New Airline, When the Fur Flies, It's in Style," *USA Today*, June 19, 2009, B1.
2. Funding Universe, http://www.fundinguniverse.com/company-histories/FedEx-Corporation-Company-History.html (accessed September 21, 2009).
3. Wal-Mart Stores, Inc., About Us, http://walmartstores.com/AboutUs/297.aspx (accessed September 21, 2009).
4. "Colonel Harland Sanders: From Young Cook to KFC's Famous Colonel," KFC.com, http://www.kfc.com/about/colonel.asp (accessed January 3, 2010).
5. HP, "HP Timeline—1930s," http://www.hp.com/hpinfo/abouthp/histnfacts/timeline/hist_30s.html (accessed September 21, 2009).
6. Black Entrepreneur Profile, "Shawn 'Jay Z' Carter," http://www.blackentrepreneurprofile.com/profile-full/article/shawn-jay-z-carter/ (accessed September 21, 2009).
7. "Famous Women Entrepreneurs," About.com, http://entrepreneurs.about.com/ (accessed September 21, 2009).
8. Estée Lauder, "About Estée Lauder," http://www.esteelauder.com/about/index.tmpl (accessed September 21, 2009).
9. The Walt Disney Company, "Corporate Information," http://corporate.disney.go.com/corporate/overview.html (accessed September 21, 2009).
10. "Quotes," JustDisney.com, http://www.justdisney.com/walt_disney/quotes/quotes01.html (accessed September 21, 2009).
11. "What Is an Entrepreneur?" ZeroMillion.com, http://www.zeromillion.com/business/starting/entrepreneur.html (accessed September 21, 2009).
12. Federal Reserve Bank of Dallas, "Everyday Economics," http://www.dallasfed.org/educate/everyday/ev3.html (accessed September 19, 2009).
13. Guy Kawasaki, "The Art of the Start," video, April 29, 2006, http://www.youtube.com/watch?v=L3xaeVXTSBg (accessed September 28, 2009).
14. U.S. Department of State's Bureau of International Information Programs, "Entrepreneurship Aids the Economy: Most Economists Agree that Entrepreneurship Is Essential to Any Economy," May 12, 2008, http://www.america.gov/st/business-english/2008/May/20080603233010eaifas0.8230554.html (accessed September 19, 2009).
15. Guy Kawasaki, "The Art of the Start," video, April 29, 2006, http://www.youtube.com/watch?v=L3xaeVXTSBg (accessed September 28, 2009).
16. District Director David C. Dickson, Philadelphia, Small Business Association, SCORE Open House, September 22, 2009, Valley Forge, PA.
17. United States Patent and Trademark Office, "What Is a Patent?" http://www.uspto.gov/go/pac/doc/general/#patent (accessed September 28, 2009).
18. U.S. Department of State's Bureau of International Information Programs, "Entrepreneurship Aids the Economy: Most Economists Agree that Entrepreneurship Is Essential to Any Economy," May 12, 2008, http://www.america.gov/st/business-english/2008/May/20080603233010eaifas0.8230554.html (accessed September 19, 2009).
19. U.S. Department of State's Bureau of International Information Programs, "Entrepreneurship Aids the Economy: Most Economists Agree that Entrepreneurship Is Essential to Any Economy," May 12, 2008, http://www.america.gov/st/business-english/2008/May/20080603233010eaifas0.8230554.html (accessed September 19, 2009).

20. Small Business, "Entrepreneurs Add Vitality to the Economy," http://www.smallbusinessnotes.com/aboutsb/vitality.html (accessed September 19, 2009).

21. Small Business, "Entrepreneurs Add Vitality to the Economy," http://www.smallbusinessnotes.com/aboutsb/vitality.html (accessed September 19, 2009).

22. Federal Reserve Bank of Dallas, "Everyday Economics," http://www.dallasfed.org/educate/everyday/ev3.html (accessed September 19, 2009).

23. Sean Silverthorne, "Government's Positive Role in Kick-Starting Entrepreneurship," HBS Working Knowledge, December 7, 2009, http://hbswk.hbs.edu/item/6318.html (accessed January 3, 2010).

24. Laura Petrecca, "Tough Times Drive Start-Ups," USA Today, September 14, 2009, B2.

25. Theresa Howard, "Investors Seek Pot of Gold on TV," USA Today, June 25, 2009, B1, 2.

26. Nicos Nicolaou, Scott Shane, Lyn Cherkas, Janice Hunkin, and Tim D. Spector, "Is the Tendency to Engage in Entrepreneurship Genetic?" Management Science 54, no. 1 (January 2008): 167–79, http://mansci.journal.informs.org/cgi/content/abstract/54/1/167 (accessed September 21, 2009).

27. Jim Hopkins, "Starting a Business: What It Takes," USA Today, October 25, 2006, http://www.usatoday.com/money/smAllBusiness/2006-07-30-starting-your-business_x.htm (accessed September 19, 2009).

28. Laura Petrecca, "Tough Times Drive Start-Ups," USA Today, September 14, 2009, B1.

29. Maureen Rothman, SCORE Open House, September 22, 2009, Valley Forge, PA.

30. Eilene Zimmerman, "Teenagers Are Building Their Own Job Engine," New York Times, June 28, 2009, B10.

31. Susan L. Reid, "Take Control of Your Retirement: Become a Midlife Entrepreneur," American Express, August 25, 2009, http://www.openforum.com/idea-hub/topics/innovation/article/take-control-of-your-retirement-become-a-midlife-entrepreneur-susan-l-reid (accessed September 28, 2009).

32. Laura Petrecca, "From Corporation to Start-up: Who Is Going to Fix the Printer?" USA Today, September 21, 2009, http://www.usatoday.com/money/smallbusiness/startup/week2-corporation-to-startup.htm (accessed September 21, 2009).

33. Laura Petrecca, "Leaving Corporate Life Behind," USA Today, September 21, 2009, B1, 2.

34. Karen E. Spaeder, "How to Research Your Business Idea," Entrepreneur, http://www.entrepreneur.com/article/printthis/70518.html (accessed September 19, 2009).

35. Karen E. Spaeder, "How to Research Your Business Idea" Entrepreneur, http://www.entrepreneur.com/article/printthis/70518.html (accessed September 19, 2009).

36. Ilya Bodner, "Social Entrepreneurship," Fast Company, June 2, 2009, http://www.fastcompany.com/blog/ilya-bodner/true-business-credit-card/social-entrepreneurship (accessed September 21, 2009).

37. Max Chafkin, "The Wexley Way: How to Think Creatively in 8 Easy Steps," Inc., February 19, 2009, http://www.inc.com/articles/2009/02/wexley.html (accessed September 19, 2009).

38. Ridgely Evers, "The Three Toughest Questions," Inc., April 1, 2008, http://www.inc.com/resources/startup/articles/20080401/revers.html (accessed September 19, 2009).

39. Scott A. Shane, "Failure Is a Constant in Entrepreneurship," New York Times, July 17, 2009, http://boss.blogs.nytimes.com/2009/07/15/failure-is-a-constant-in-entrepreneurship (accessed January 3, 2010).

40. Laura Petrecca, "Leaving Corporate Life Behind," USA Today, September 21, 2009, B1, 2.

41. "Interview with an Entrepreneur—Dan Sanker of CaseStack," E-Shadow.com, http://www.e-shadow.com/interview-with-an-entrepreneur-dan-sanker-of-casestack (accessed September 19, 2009).

42. Juliette Pitman, "Persistence Pays: Vinny Lingham," Entrepreneur, July 2009, http://www.entrepreneurmag.co.za/article/h/?a=1516&z=161&title=Persistence+Pays:+Vinny+Lingham (accessed May 16, 2010).

43. Laura Petrecca, "Leaving Corporate Life Behind," USA Today, September 21, 2009, B2.

44. "Franchise," InvestorWords.com, http://www.investorwords.com/2078/franchise.html (accessed September 28, 2009).

45. "Subway Franchise for Sale," Docstoc, http://www.docstoc.com/docs/2418199/Subway-Franchise-for-Sale (accessed September 28, 2009).

46. "2009 Franchise 500 Rankings," Entepreneur, http://www.entrepreneur.com/franchises/rankings/franchise500-115608/2009,.html (accessed September 28, 2009).

47. Jim Hopkins, "Starting a Business: What It Takes," USA Today, October 25, 2006, http://www.usatoday.com/money/smAllBusiness/2006-07-30-starting-your-business_x.htm (accessed September 19, 2009).

48. David E. Gumpert, "The Basics of Business Plans: Sell, Sell, Sell," Inc., October 24, 2000, http://www.inc.com/articles/2000/10/14871.html (accessed September 19, 2009).

49. SCORE, "Business Plan for a Startup Business," http://www.score.org/resources/business-plan-startup-business (accessed September 29, 2009).

50. "Small Business Loan Sources, Take Aim," Business Plan Master, http://www.businessplanmaster.com/small-business-loan-sources.html (accessed September 28, 2009).

51. "How to Get Funding from Angel Investors," Wall Street Journal, http://guides.wsj.com/small-business/funding/how-to-get-funding-from-angel-investors (accessed September 19, 2009).

52. "Small Business Loan Sources, Take Aim," Business Plan Master, http://www.businessplanmaster.com/small-business-loan-sources.html (accessed September 28, 2009).

53. "Small Business Loan Sources, Take Aim," Business Plan Master, http://www.businessplanmaster.com/small-business-loan-sources.html (accessed September 28, 2009).

54. "Small Business Loan Sources, Take Aim," Business Plan Master, http://www.businessplanmaster.com/small-business-loan-sources.html (accessed September 28, 2009).

55. "Small Business Loan Sources, Take Aim," Business Plan Master, http://www.businessplanmaster.com/small-business-loan-sources.html (accessed September 28, 2009).

56. Lindsey Pollak, "Gen Y Entrepreneurs: Here Are the First Steps to Starting Your Own Business," Fast Company, March 15, 2009, http://www.fastcompany.com/blog/lindsey-pollak/next-generation-career-advice/are-you-gen-y-considering-entrepreneurship-first-s (accessed September 28, 2009).

57. Lindsey Pollak, "Gen Y Entrepreneurs: Here Are the First Steps to Starting Your Own Business," Fast Company, March 15, 2009, http://www.fastcompany.com/blog/lindsey-pollak/next-generation-career-advice/are-you-gen-y-considering-entrepreneurship-first-s (accessed September 28, 2009).

Epilogue: You've Got the Power

What a Journey!

Hear some parting thoughts from the author, Kim Richmond.

Kim Richmond
Author, The Power of Selling

View the video online at: http://www.youtube.com/embed/ilUYBquXTiY

You've met sales professionals and learned the importance of ethics, communication, and relationships. You've practiced the seven steps of the selling process and participated in role-plays to hone your skills. You've even learned how to market yourself as a brand and sell yourself to get the internship or job you want.

This is it. This is where it all comes together...the real world. Whether you are graduating or getting ready for your next semester, you'll be able to use your selling skills to get what you want in life. And don't forget the tips you learned in *Selling U* about selling the most important product of all: yourself.

In addition to all the things you learned in this book, here's the one thing you should remember every day: *believe*.

Believe in the products and services you sell, believe in your company, believe in your customers. But most of all, believe in yourself. You can do anything you want to do in life with your newfound selling skills and a true belief that you can do it. The fact is you have the skills and the knowledge and now you have the power to achieve. Even on those days when the wind is at your face, remember that *you* are the most important product you will ever sell. Customers and prospective employers buy you before they buy your products, services, or even your skills. They want to believe in you, and that's why it's so important that you believe in yourself.

Put your selling skills to work every day and remember...you've got the power!

Index

Notes

Notes